W9-BHP-430

Mrs. Paul Clewell
20 So. 16th St
Easton, Pa.

THE COMPLETE HOME ENCYCLOPEDIA

BY DOROTHY PACE

THE COMPLETE HOME ENCYCLOPEDIA

CAXTON HOUSE · PUBLISHERS · NEW YORK

COPYRIGHT 1947 CAXTON HOUSE, INC.

CONTENTS

CONTENTS

ILLUSTRATIONS

PHOTOGRAPHS

PHOTOGRAPHS

DRAWINGS

CHAPTER III

DRAWINGS

DRAWINGS

ACKNOWLEDGMENTS

MANY of the photographs reproduced in this volume were supplied through the courtesy of manufacturers, retailers, institutions, and other sources. Gratitude for the use of these photographs and the source of each is hereby acknowledged.

Frontispiece—arrangements for photographing made through the courtesy of B. Altman & Co., New York.

Westinghouse Electric Corp., p. 2; Macy's Department Store, New York, p. 4; General Electric Co., p. 5; (*top*) Westinghouse Electric Corp., (*bottom*) Estate Stove Co., p. 6; (*top*) American Stove Co., (*bottom*) Estate Stove Co., p. 7; (*top*) General Electric Co., (*bottom*) American Stove Co., p. 8; General Electric Co., p. 9; Westinghouse Electric Corp., p. 10; (*top, left*) Reynolds Metals Co., (*top, right*) Revere Copper & Brass Co., (*bottom, left*) Corning Glass Works, (*bottom, right*) Enameled Utensil Manufacturers Council, p. 11; (*top*) Westinghouse Electric Corp., (*bottom*) Revere Copper & Brass Co., p. 14; (*top and bottom*) General Electric Co., (*center*) National Pressure Cooker Co., p. 15; (*top*) Electrolux Corp., (*bottom*) The Hoover Co., p. 16; International Silver Co., p. 18; H. Simmons Mattress Co., p. 20; United States Rubber Co., p. 21; James McCutcheon & Co., New York, p. 22; Westinghouse Electric Corp., p. 24; James McCutcheon & Co., New York, p. 25; International Silver Co., p. 27, p. 28, p. 29.

Macy's Department Store, New York, p. 52; Metropolitan Museum of Art, New York, p. 57, p. 58; (*left and top*) Metropolitan Museum of Art, New York, (*bottom*) New York Historical Society, p. 59; (*top and bottom*) Metropolitan Museum of Art, New York, (*center*) New York Historical Society, p. 60; Metropolitan Museum of Art, New York, p. 61, p. 62; Westinghouse Electric Corp., p. 63; Gimbel Bros., Inc., New York, p. 64; City Gardens Club, New York, p. 65; United States Plywood Corp., p. 68; Macy's Department Store, New York, p. 73, p. 74; Gimbel Bros., Inc., New York, p. 76.

Photographs taken at the Flea Market, New York, p. 80, p. 98; Sherwin-Williams Co., p. 104; Metropolitan Museum of Art, New York, p. 106; Frederic Lewis, New York, p. 108.

Modernage Furniture Corp., New York, p. 122; (*top and bottom*) Lightolier Co., (*center*) Georg Jensen, Inc., New York, p. 129; (*top and bottom*) Lightolier Co., (*top, right*) Georg Jensen, Inc., New York, (*bottom, right*) United States Plywood Corp., p. 130; Lightolier Co., p. 132; (*top and bottom, right*) Georg Jensen, Inc., New York, (*bottom, left*) Macy's Department Store, New York, p. 133; New York Botanical Gardens, p. 134, p. 139, p. 141, p. 143, p. 146; City Gardens Club, New York, p. 147.

Barret Textile Corp., p. 148; Waverly Fabrics, p. 153, p. 155; Lord & Taylor, New York, p. 158; Waverly Fabrics, p. 165, p. 167, p. 168; Stern Brothers, New York, p. 170; Waverly Fabrics, p. 177; Singer Mfg. Co., p. 179; Macy's Department Store, New York, p. 181; Lord & Taylor, New York, p. 184; Macy's Department Store, New York, p. 188, p. 189; Lord & Taylor, New York, p. 191; Macy's Department Store, New York, p. 193; Gimbel Bros., Inc., New York, p. 194; New York Historical Society, p. 196, p. 198, p. 205.

Macy's Department Store, New York, p. 208; Katzenbach & Warren, Inc., p. 210; Macy's Department Store, New York, p. 215; Gimbel Bros., Inc., New York, p. 219; United States Plywood Corp., p. 226, p. 228; S. C. Johnson & Son, Inc., p. 230; Interchemical Corp., p. 237; Bigelow-Sanford Carpet Co., Inc., p. 238, p. 240; Armstrong Cork Co., Inc., p. 242; Bigelow-Sanford Carpet Co., Inc., p. 244, p. 245; Lord & Taylor, New York, p. 247; Metropolitan Museum of Art, New York, p. 250, p. 253; Worcester Museum of Art, Worcester, Mass., p. 254; Lord & Taylor, New York, p. 256; Metropolitan Museum of Art, p. 257.

J. P. Sloane & Co., New York, p. 260, p. 267, p. 268; Westinghouse Electric Corp., p. 270, p. 276, p. 278; Anthracite Institute, p. 289; Delco Appliance Division of General Motors Corp., p. 290; Armstrong Cork Co., Inc., p. 292; Devoe & Raynolds Co., Inc., p. 305, p. 306, p. 309, p. 310; Interchemical Corp., p. 312.

Westinghouse Electric Corp., p. 326, p. 329; Macy's Department Store, New York, p. 332; (*top*) The Silex Co., (*bottom*) Westinghouse Electric Corp., p. 337; Thor Electric Washing Machine Co., p. 339; ©Warner Bros. Pictures, Inc., p. 342, p. 350, p. 352, p. 353, p. 354, p. 355, p. 356, p. 357.

PREFACE

We have addressed this volume primarily to the American housewife because she is the one who normally assumes the major responsibilities of running the home, selecting its furnishings, caring for its equipment—doing the countless things necessary to keep it bright and new looking. However, we hope that other members of the family will also find information of interest to them in these pages. To this end, we have included fairly comprehensive chapters not only on such feminine pursuits as quilting and laundering, but also on such jobs as plumbing and wiring, which are ordinarily taken care of by the man of the house.

Since pictures can often illustrate a process more clearly than any number of words, graphic aids have been included wherever visual explanation seemed indicated.

Every effort has been made to keep explanations as simple and as basic as possible. We have not presupposed that the reader possesses even an elementary technical knowledge of the subject matter of this book. Such an assumption would have put the beginner at a disadvantage, for the person who embarks upon any work for the first time needs to have basic steps explained fully. And even the experienced worker who has advanced beyond the fundamentals likes to review them occasionally. It should be remembered, however, that two workers may not always proceed in exactly the same manner, and yet the outcome is often satisfactory to both. The reason, of course, is that there are often more ways than one to do a thing, and it does not necessarily follow that one way is better than another. The best way is whatever way the worker finds easiest and quickest. The ways given here are those that we know have accomplished results—and in the end, it is the result that counts, in household projects as in other matters. We have attempted to explain fully how to care for the home, how to improve its appearance, and how to do both at a minimum of expense.

No doubt home is where the heart is, and a home to be a real home demands more than tasteful furnishings and efficient equipment. Yet even the most happily coordinated families want to improve a house which doesn't quite measure up to their ideal (and how many of us are ever completely satisfied with our material surroundings?). The dream house cannot be conjured up by rubbing a lamp, but an existing structure can often be improved by the magic of a few changes. Of course, one way to change the appearance of a house is to call in a professional decorator, order new furniture, drapes, and carpets, hire a painter or paperer to redecorate, and contract for other services. But few of us can afford the expense of remodeling our homes in this fashion. We also want our homes to function smoothly, but the cost of calling in a repairman every time a minor friction develops can be prohibitive. Yet a principal item in the bill for most of these services is time and labor, rather than materials. The majority of house repairs and improvements requires more time and patience than skill, and they are not difficult to master. Some jobs, of course, do require special skills, and in instances of this sort the reader has been advised to seek professional aid.

Don't be dismayed at the thought of being your own decorator, repairman, or upholsterer just because you have never hammered a nail or repaired a leaking faucet or explored the interior of a loveseat. Any person in good health, of normal intelligence, and possessed of the ability to follow instructions can learn to do them. They require no extraordinary talents. However, they do take time, patience, and effort. These will be the chief expenditures in any of the undertakings described. But you will find that the results are well worth the price. Not only will you have distinctively furnished rooms that are pleasant to live in and a house that operates efficiently, but also yours will be the not inconsiderable pride and satisfaction that comes of creating and doing things yourself.

But before ambition prods you into trying everything at once, it might be well to formulate a plan so that first things come first. Budget not only your money, but also your time and energy. By undertaking multiple projects, by attempting more than could be accomplished, many a promising beginner has become discouraged. It is normally better and wiser to start on a smaller scale; because even a minor success—something concrete achieved—breeds enthusiasm and confidence. Unless you begin a job with the determination to stick with it until it is completed, your homemaking endeavors will satisfy no one—yourself, least of all.

The methods described for making slipcovers, draperies, curtains, quilts, and for reupholstering, restyling, and refinishing furniture, for using tools, for arranging furniture and using color and pattern, and for nearly all the minor repair work about the house, are, in most cases, based upon the author's own experience or knowledge. Reliable sources have been consulted for much of the other information. Innumerable manufacturers, institutions, and individuals have generously contributed of their knowledge and time to make this book possible. Among the many that the author is particularly indebted to are: American Gas Association, Anthracite Institute, Armstrong Cork Co., Inc., Bigelow-Sanford Carpet Co., Fueloil & Oil Heat magazine, Gas Appliance Manufacturers Association, Interchemical Corporation, Metropolitan Life Insurance Company (for information on some antidotes), National Adequate Wiring Bureau, National Safety Council, New York Botanical Gardens, United States Plywood Corporation, Westinghouse Electric Corporation, and the staff members of various government bureaus. Both the author and the publisher are also grateful to many other manufacturers, retailers, and institutions for contributing many of the photographs which illustrate these pages.

The author also wishes to thank Arthur Zeiger for his tireless work in editing the manuscript.

DOROTHY PACE

New York, N. Y.

THE COMPLETE HOME ENCYCLOPEDIA

I

HOUSEHOLD EQUIPMENT

CHAPTER I

KITCHEN & CLEANING EQUIPMENT

ONCE upon a time they made jokes about the bride who thought she had fully equipped her kitchen when she bought a can opener and a saucepan. Now, with complete, pre-cooked frosted meals needing only to be slipped into an oven for warming, some may well wonder whether or not even the can opener and the saucepan are any longer necessary. Lest such gloomy thoughts give us dyspepsia, perhaps we had better assume that the fine art of cooking will not disappear from our kitchens, and that the tempting odors of stews, roasts, and steaks, and the fragrant aromas of cinnamon apples, pumpkin pies, and gingerbread will still waft about in the future to whet our appetites. And since good cooking requires good equipment, we still need more than a mere saucepan and a can opener.

WORKING LAYOUTS AND LARGE EQUIPMENT

PROBABLY no room in the house has undergone so many transformations in the past thirty years as the kitchen. New "dream kitchens" come from the drafting boards of the architects and industrial designers every day with the result that the kitchen has become one of the most interesting rooms in the house Occasionally, we see designs which depart so radically from those we had thought were already completely up-to-date, that we may sometimes wonder whether our kitchens will become obsolete before they are even built. No doubt further thought and planning will bring us kitchens in the future better than anything yet built. But until a fixture has become sufficiently standardized in design to be mass produced, its cost of production and installation is likely to be beyond the means of the average person. Therefore, in planning a kitchen, we must expect to utilize the standard types of equipment already available in the market.

Layouts. One of the most workable layouts is the kitchen with the main equipment grouped in a U-shaped arrangement with the sink in the center, the range on one side, and the refrigerator on the other. In between the range, refrigerator, and sink are work counters. Above are cabinets and beneath, both drawers and cabinets. Another good layout is the L-shaped arrangement, with the sink located about halfway between the range and the refrigerator. Less convenient is the linear arrangement with all equipment lined up against one wall, but some kitchens will not easily adapt themselves to any other plan. Even so, the sink should still hold center place if possible. In any plan, the three main working centers — cooking, preparation and clean-up, and refrigeration—should not be

The peninsular arrangement of this kitchen brings the sink and range within a few steps of the refrigerator. A double sink helps to speed up the task of washing dishes by hand. Dishes can be transferred immediately from suds to rinse water.

too widely separated. Instead, they should be as close together as possible without crowding, and still allowing ample counter space — a very important feature in any kitchen. Existing floor plans may not always permit a perfect layout to remodel an old kitchen. The placement of the work areas may have to be determined by the location of windows, pipe lines, and other features. A room may be too large to place the various items of equipment as near to each other as they should be for convenience. In that case, perhaps an "island" or "peninsular" arrangement of some of the equipment may be the solution. The center work table was a feature of the old-fashioned kitchen, and it wasn't such a bad idea. The same principle can be adapted to an island working area with a counter top for food preparation and drawers and cabinets underneath. A peninsular arrangement may help to create a separate eating area or a snack bar. If possible, both sink and range should be located near a window. If the kitchen has only one window, then the sink should be located in front of it.

Cabinets and Counters. Nearly any type of kitchen layout can be achieved with the standardized cabinets and counters now manufactured in units of various widths which can be combined in a number of ways. The choice of stainless metal. linoleum, enamel, or tile for counter tops is largely a matter of preference and the amount which can be spent. All give satisfactory service. Metal cabinets are sturdier, of course, than wooden ones, but the difference in price may make the selection of wood cabinets much more desirable. Cabinets with counter tops are now generally uniform in height to correspond with the range and sink.

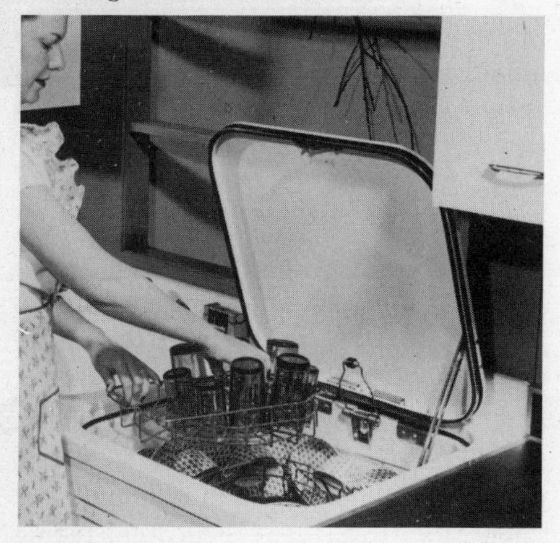

The tiresome chore of dishwashing is eliminated with an electric dishwasher which automatically washes and rinses all tableware and cooking utensils. Heat of water dries dishes.

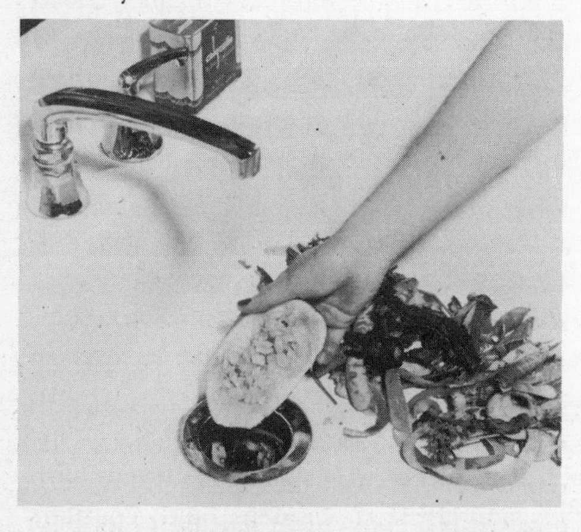

A sink with an automatic garbage disposal unit does away with garbage can.

The Range. The choice between a gas or electric range depends largely on which is cheaper to operate in your communlty. Both give excellent results. A gas oven heats slightly quicker than an electric one, and the same holds true for some of the top burners as well; but in some models the difference, if any, is negligible. However, the inquisitive fingers of little children have been known to open the jets on gas stoves with unhappy results. If the stove has an automatic pilot light, such a danger is minimized, of course. Sometimes the controls are located at the back, out of reach of little hands.

Here are some points to consider when selecting a range:

1. Burner Arrangement. Nearly all the newer ranges have a work surface — sometimes this is located at one side or the other of the burners, or it may be in the center with the burners on each side. At least one model has the burners located at the rear with the work surface in the front. All these arrangements are convenient, but the center work surface with burners on each end makes it possible for two people to use the stove at the same time without getting in each other's way too much. Electric ranges usually have burners in two or more sizes or else merely a section of the burner need be turned on. The heating element may be enclosed or open. Sometimes the burners are slightly raised above the surface of the stove to prevent large pans from touching the enameled surface and damaging it when they are hot. Electric units should lift up or slip out for easy cleaning. Some have small drip pans underneath which can be washed as easily as a utensil. The heating element itself is not damaged from spilled food. If you are choosing a gas range, select one which has burner openings on the side of the unit so that they will not clog when

The electric range above has four burners located on the right side. The work surface at the left provides space for serving dishes, utensils, or electrical equipment.

The built-in griddle in the gas range below supplies a large, evenly heated cooking area for frying and grilling. A divided arrangement of the burners permits two cooks to work at once without spoiling the broth.

food is accidently spilled on them. Grids on new ranges are designed to hold even a very small utensil without danger of tipping. A range should have a minimum of three surface burners, and for very large families or people who entertain a great deal, there are models which have six. At least one range is made in units, so that burners may be located in one place, and the oven in another.

Deep-well cookers are appearing in both gas and electric ranges. They use a very minimum amount of fuel, and perform an amazing number of cooking chores from stewing to steaming.

2. Ovens and Broilers. Some ranges have one oven for roasting and another for baking. Others have ovens big enough to accommodate both processes at once. An oven should certainly be large enough to take care of a good-sized turkey plus a number of other "fixins" for a Thanksgiving dinner. Racks should slide smoothly, remain level when they are out, and have safety stops to prevent them from falling if they are jerked out too quickly. If this should happen, a guard rail at the rear will also prevent pans from slipping backward. Some gas ranges have a separate steam oven, to steam pressure—cook foods. It helps to retain the color and flavor of vegetables, and is also useful for defrosting foods. There are also models with small surface ovens for special purposes. Many ranges now have electric lights which turn on when the oven door is opened and off when it is shut. Some ranges have peepholes on the outside—a good feature if you are worried about whether the cake is browning properly and fear to open the door to find out lest the batter should fall. An adjustable oven rack for even browning of meat is a convenient feature to look for, and so is a warming oven or a rack for warming plates. Some ranges have storage space for pots, pans, and so on, which may or may not be important to your needs. The broiler, if separate, may be designed to swing out, or slide out like a drawer. The separate broiler is usually more convenient for the cook to reach, but the broiler-oven combination saves space. The new ceramic broiler racks prevent fat from overheating.

All the better new ranges have ovens and broilers which are thoroughly insulated and designed for completely even distribution of heat.

3. Heat Control. All the good ranges now have thermostatically controlled ovens. Some will time the cooking period, either in the oven or on top of the stove. Some gas ranges have indicators for regulating the flame without having to push the kettle aside for further examination. Electric ranges should have at least four heats; most have five, and some have even six or seven.

4. Other features to check for are electric outlets for plugging in the mixer or the coffee maker; an electric clock—some will turn equipment on or off and do other tricks; a top light, which most ranges have; a towel drying rack; timing charts for cooking various foods; a built-in griddle plate.

Of course, not every feature is available in any one range, so when you decide to buy a new one, the thing to do is to check the features which are most important to *your* needs.

For homes without gas or electricity, or which have no gas but where electric rates prohibit the installation of an electric range, there are ranges which can be operated on "bottled" gas, or liquified petroleum. Such ranges operate like gas ranges, and are perfectly safe. Most of the better ones have a number of the same features as the new gas and electric ranges.

A swing-out broiler helps to protect the cook from hot, spattering grease. Space beneath a broiler rack can be used as a warming oven.

A large broiler oven can be used for roasting meats as well as broiling, while the regular oven takes care of the baking. An oven light permits the cook to check the entire contents at a glance.

Deep-well cookers can be used for many purposes from stewing to steaming; however, the addition of a deep-well cooker usually means one less burner.

Care and Cleaning of the Range. The fine porcelain enamel used on good ranges will give years of service and retain an unblemished surface if it is properly treated. Wipe up spilled acid foods (such as fruit juice, milk, tomatoes, and so on) immediately, or they will scar or pit the enamel. Don't allow cold liquids to come in contact with the enamel while it is hot or it will craze. If burners are level with the enamel, do not use pans larger than the unit, or the enamel may become overheated. A damp cloth is usually all that is needed to keep the enamel sparkling clean. But never wipe the stove while it is hot with a wet cloth. A non-scratching cleansing powder may be used to remove congealed foods. A gritty powder may damage the surface. Remove the broiler grill immediately after using, and clean it thoroughly every time it is used. If the oven is wiped out frequently with a paper towel, it will not need a thorough scrubbing quite so often. Oven doors on good ranges are very sturdy, but even so the hinges may become weakened if the door is used to support a too-heavy kettle or other utensil. Wipe burners clean after every using, and lift gas burners out for a scrubbing at least twice a month. Never scrub the heating element of the electric burner. If food is spilled on it, turn the heat on low until the food is burned off. Manufacturers supply detailed instructions on the care of their ranges, and these should be kept in a convenient place for easy reference.

The Refrigerator. Like ranges, refrigerators may operate either on gas or electricity, and again, the choice may be partly determined by which is the cheaper in your locality. However, a refrigerator uses so much less fuel than a range, that this consideration may not be quite so important. The perfect refrigerator, embodying every feature housewives crave, has apparently not yet been designed; but so many excellent features are offered in standard models that at least most of the more important demands have been met.

Don't worry about whether milk containers will fit, or whether the space between the shelves is large enough to accommodate a can of peaches for chilling—industrial designers have seen to matters of this kind on all models.

Peek ovens let the cook watch the pie-crust brown without opening the oven door. Modern timing devices, though, make oven watching unnecessary.

Foods stay fresh longer in refrigerators designed to provide the degree of cold and humidity best suited to the keeping needs of each kind of food.

Special compartment in this refrigerator has separate temperature control which keeps butter cool but soft enough to spread easily.

Size is an important consideration — most women want bigger, not smaller refrigerators. But remember that a small one costs less to operate than one you can practically stand in. On the other hand, real savings in both time and money can often be had if the refrigerator is large enough to accommodate a supply of food for several days or even a week. Many of the newer refrigerators have compartments for storing frozen foods. One model features shallow shelves on the door for storing bottles, cans, or packages.

Formerly, one of the chief drawbacks of automatic refrigerators was the fact that food dried out in them unless everything was kept tightly covered. Some manufacturers have now eliminated this difficulty in various ways. The refrigerator may have special compartments where moist foods may be stored uncovered. Another solution is the refrigerator with cooling mechanism in the walls so that it never comes in contact with the food and cannot dry it out. Or the refrigerator may have compartments each of which is humidified and cooled to the degrees best suited to preserve certain kinds of food. Vegetables which need cool, moist air to be crisp and fresh are kept in one compartment. Others which need less cold are kept in another compartment.

Care of the Refrigerator. Probably everyone knows that the principle rule for refrigerator care is to defrost regularly, and yet, if the refrigerator has no automatic defrosting device, how often we forget to do so! The frost should never be allowed to build up more than ¼ of an inch. Otherwise, it forms an insulating blanket which makes the motor run too often and may even cause the temperature inside to rise so high that food spoils. In order to speed defrosting time so that foods do not remain unrefrigerated any longer than necessary, place an electric fan before the cooling mechanism. If this is not convenient, remove the ice trays, fill them with boiling water, and put them back. Within a minute or so, the frost will loosen and fall off. Then refill with cold water.

If the motor runs too much, it may be that the condenser needs cleaning. The condenser consists of a set of coiled tubes with metal fins attached to catch dust. It may be located underneath the refrigerator

A number of refrigerators now feature large storage compartments for frozen foods, as well as other compartments with different degrees of cold and humidity.

or at the rear near the bottom. A front panel may have to be removed to reach it, or it may be at the side. On some older models, the condenser is on top. When too much dirt collects in the condenser, air cannot circulate freely. The motor becomes overheated and works too hard. Therefore, it is necessary to clean the condenser out at regular intervals (about once a month). This may be done with a long handled brush or with the narrow attachment of the vacuum cleaner. Always pull the refrigerator plug from the outlet first.

If the motor still runs too often in spite of regular defrosting and cleaning of the condenser, perhaps the door is not properly sealed when it is closed. To check the seal, close the door on a narrow slip of paper. If you can pull the paper out, the seal is not tight enough. Either the rubber gasket on the inside of the door is worn out and needs to be replaced or the hinges or latch need to be tightened. For this work, call the repair service department of the manufacturer or the dealer from whom you bought the refrigerator. The rubber gasket deteriorates more readily if it is allowed to come in contact with acids, oils, or perspiration.

Treat the fine porcelain or enameled finish of a refrigerator with the same care as that given to your range. The inside must be washed out thoroughly at regular intervals (if possible, do this after each defrosting) to keep it clean and sweet-smelling. Never wash it with soap. Instead, use soda and hot water or one of the soapless commercial cleaning compounds. And don't forget to wash off the cooling unit, too, as food odors tend to collect there.

If the mechanism in the refrigerator is sealed, it is self-oiling. If it is an open, belt-driven mechanism it will have to be oiled occasionally. Check the manufacturer's di rections for the amount and kind of oil to use, where to use it, and how often.

COOKING UTENSILS

EACH cook will undoubtedly have her own ideas as to what utensils are essential for a properly equipped kitchen. Perhaps one woman does little or no baking, and therefore may not want cake pans, muffin tins, a pastry bag, and so on. If so, such equipment would be useless to her, and merely take up space. The woman who cooks for two people will want to buy smaller saucepans and frying pans than one who must prepare meals for a family of twelve. But for the cook who must prepare meals for the family regularly, and who wants to provide varied and interesting meals, the following list of equipment should be adequate. Not all of these things will be used constantly, and some may not be essential to every kitchen, but each one is important for the preparation of some recipe.

Containers for individual servings are estimated for a family of six. More or less may be needed according to the size of the family or the number of guests entertained.

3 saucepans of assorted sizes, with covers
1 double boiler
1 pressure cooker saucepan
1 soup kettle (about six-quart size)
1 deep frying pan, with cover (good for stews because meat can be browned and stewed in same pan)
3 frying pans (4 inch, 8 inch, and 10 inch sizes are useful)
1 griddle
3 to 5 mixing bowls (nested ones take up less space but require the extra operation of removing the whole stack to separate one bowl)
1 or 2 casseroles, with covers, or 6 individual casseroles (or both)
6 custard cups
1 coffee maker (drip, vacuum, or percolator, as preferred), either electric or top-of-stove type.
1 tea pot
1 deep-fat frying kettle and basket
1 medium roasting pan (about 8 x 12 inches) with rack
1 large roasting pan (not necessary if oven has rack for holding roasts)
1 trivet
2 loaf pans
2 muffin pans (large and small cups)
2 pie plates
3 layer-cake pans
1 square cake pan (about 7 inches)
1 oblong cake pan (about 6 x 9 inches)
1 tube cake pan
1 cake cooler
2 cookie sheets

The flat tops and recessed knobs on the covers of these aluminum utensils make it possible to stack the pans.

Copper bottoms help to distribute heat evenly on stainless steel cooking utensils and make them heat faster.

Glass baking dishes save extra work when they are used for both cooking and serving. Rim on pie plate holds in juices.

Enameled ware is made in many colors and can be selected to match or contrast with kitchen color schemes.

1 oven-proof platter
Storage jars for cereals, coffee, tea, flour, rice, and so on (unless kitchen has other provisions for storing staples)
1 bread box
1 cake box
1 tea kettle (optional)
1 bread board
1 meat board
1 wooden meat mallet
2 asbestos mats
2 or more pot holders
1 set refrigerator dishes
1 colander
2 strainers (small and medium sizes)
1 ricer
1 food chooper
1 blade chopper
1 or 2 wooden chopping bowls
1 grater (select one with exposed surfaces for easy cleaning)
1 floating blade peeler
1 carving knife
1 carving fork
1 or 2 paring knives
1 bread knife
2 case knives
2 case forks
1 boning knife (optional)
1 fruit knife (optional
1 knife sharpener
1 knife rack
1 pair scissors
1 pair tongs
2 flexible spatulas (large and small)
1 pancake turner
1 long-handled ladle
1 long-handled fork
1 strainer ladle
3 wooden spoons (different sizes)
6 tablespoons
6 teaspoons
1 large mixing spoon
1 set measuring spoons
2 measuring cups (1- and 2-cup sizes—flameproof glass cups can be read easily and also used to melt foods without breaking). Some cooks prefer set of measuring cups in fraction sizes.
2 sccops
1 whisk
1 apple corer
1 can opener (swing-out, wall type probably most efficient)
1 egg beater (rotary)
1 flour sifter (a fitted sifter and measuring cup saves work, avoids spilled flour)
1 pastry blender
1 rubber bowl scraper
1 pastry bag and tubes (or aluminum cylinder-and-plunger type)
1 pastry brush
1 pastry jagger
1 set of cookie cutters in various shapes
1 doughnut cutter (can be used for biscuits if center section is removable)
1 rolling pin with revolving handles (for flakier pastry, select type in which ice cubes can be inserted)
1 pastry cloth (and pastry board, if desired)
1 set of shakers for salt, pepper, flour, sugar (and for paprika, cinnamon, and nutmeg, if desired)
1 set of thermometers for deep-fat frying, candy making, and meat roasting (if oven of range has no thermometer, an oven thermometer is necessary)
1 cork screw
1 jar and bottle opener
1 funnel
1 fruit juice extractor (not essential if you have electric mixer with juicer attachment)
1 scrubbing brush for vegetables
1 set of stainless steel skewers
1 potato masher
6 individual gelatin molds or 1 large mold (optional)

1 nut cracker
2 utility trays
1 clock (unless part of range)

The choice of material from which the utensils are made is more or less a matter of personal preference. Some women prefer aluminum because it heats very quickly. The bottom of an aluminum utensil should be fairly thick; otherwise the food may be scorched rather easily. However, aluminum will become pitted from certain acids, and it darkens when foods with an alkali content are cooked in it, and must be frequently cleaned with steel wool to be kept bright. Enameled cooking ware heats less quickly, but it resists stains and is easy to keep clean. It must be handled rather carefully, however, as the enamel is a vitreous substance which may chip if it is knocked about or crack if the utensil is plunged into cold water while hot. Chipped utensils are unsanitary and should be discarded. Stainless steel resists nearly all stains, as its name implies, and is easy to clean. It tends to heat unevenly, and may develop "hot spots" that scorch food. To overcome this difficulty, the bottom may be coated with copper which distributes the heat evenly. However, copper-bottomed stainless steel ware is more expensive than other types. Some women prefer heat-resistant glassware for baking because the containers are often attractive enough to be brought to the table for serving. Flameproof glassware for use on top of the stove permits the cook to see what's cooking. It cannot be heated to as high a temperature as other types of cooking utensils, however. All glass cooking utensils must be handled with care. Like enamel, they should never be plunged into cold water while hot or put into a hot oven immediately after being taken from a cold refrigerator. Nor should they be cleaned with steel wool or harsh abrasives. If food has become baked on, the containers should be soaked until it can be removed easily.

Gadgets. In addition to the above equipment, there are a whole medley of gadgets on the market which few women can resist. Melon ball cutters, potato curlers, knives for making roses out of radishes, butter molds, egg slicers, nut choppers, and so on may not be essential, but if they add fun to the chores of cooking, then you may want to put them on the list, too. However, many gadgets are of little practical value and merely clutter up shelves and drawers. So before succumbing to their temptations, it might be well to stop and ask whether they are worth bringing home.

CLEANUP EQUIPMENT

NEAR the sink should be grouped the various utensils and equipment for washing dishes and performing other cleanup chores. The following list gives some of the items most commonly used:

1 dish pan (unless sink is designed for dishwashing)
1 dish drainer
1 sink strainer
1 sink stopper (unless drain closes)
3 dish cloths
1 dish mop (optional)
1 rubber dish scraper
2 dozen dish towels
Towel rack
1 set of brushes for cleaning bottles, counters, and so on
Paper towels
Steel wool pads or stainless metal pads
Soap dish and soap
Wax paper
1 covered garbage pail (unless sink has garbage-disposal unit)
1 metal waste basket
Cheesecloth
Cleaning powders and polishing compounds

Electric ovens are convenient and especially useful in kitchenettes too small for a range.

ELECTRICAL EQUIPMENT

LUCKY is the woman with electrical servants to take the labor out of many kitchen tasks. Electrical equipment is not essential, of course, but how we want it if we can afford it! Here are a few of the most-wanted items:

1 mixer and beater (with grater, fruit juice extractor, coffee grinder, food chopper, and slicer)
1 toaster
1 coffee maker
1 grill
1 waffle iron

Care. If you have electric appliances, here are a few tips on how to care for them. Never plug more of them into one outlet than it can carry. Otherwise, you will overload the wire and burn out a fuse. Many appliances need oiling at regular intervals. Therefore, be sure to save the manufacturer's instructions as to where the oil should be applied and how often. Toasters usually have crumb trays which must be removed and cleaned regularly. Chromium plated fixtures generally need only to be wiped with a damp cloth (but not while hot) and polished with a soft, dry one to be kept gleaming. Never touch the heating units with anything damp while an electrical appliance is plugged into an outlet. Never detach a plug from an outlet by yanking on the cord, as this weakens it. Instead, grasp the plug and pull. When buying appliances with movable parts, such as a mixer, be sure it has sufficient weight to remain in one spot. Otherwise, the vibrations of the motor might cause it to "walk" off the counter or table.

MISCELLANEOUS KITCHEN EQUIPMENT

IN ADDITION to cooking and cleanup equipment, various miscellaneous items which may be found useful are: twine, wrapping paper, scotch tape, toothpicks,

Pressure-cooker saucepans are now made in many styles. Pressure cooking cuts down cooking time and helps to retain food values and flavors.

paper napkins, cook-book holder, index box for recipes, memo pad, pencils, calendar, rubber bands, thumb tacks, pins, a comfortable stool and a step stool.

CLEANING EQUIPMENT

THE right cleaning tool for every job will help to eliminate much of the drudgery so often associated with house cleaning. If possible, cleaning equipment should be kept in its own closet, with each item in place on shelf, hook, or whatever is the most convenient way of storing. Above all, every single tool should be completely accessible. It should be easy to reach and remove without having to disturb any other item. Cleaning tasks will be much easier if the equipment is kept in order and replaced where it belongs after each using.

The Vacuum Cleaner. Undoubtedly the most helpful single piece of cleaning equipment you can invest in is a good vacuum cleaner with a motor powerful enough to create real suction. It is even better if you can afford two cleaners—especially if you have many rugs or carpets. For these, the floor type of cleaner with an agitator brush is more thorough. For bare floors, upholstery, and dusting of everything from lamps to Venetian blinds, the tank type of cleaner with attachments is recommended. Too often these attachments are not put to work as they should be, partly because of the nuisance of carrying them about and changing from one to another as needed. Yet this bother can easily be eliminated by wearing an apron with pockets of the right size to hold each attachment.

Care of the Vacuum Cleaner The most important step in caring for the vacuum is to empty the bag after each using. The porous material of which the bag is made cannot function properly when it is choked or clogged with dirt. After the bag has

New automatic coffee makers will brew coffee when you want it, turn themselves off, and then keep coffee warm without any attention.

A good-sized pressure cooker is useful for canning as well as for cooking complete meals for a large family. Divider sections keep food flavors separate.

Electric grills can be brought to the table so the hostess can cook, serve, and eat without getting up. Some grills have waffle grid inserts.

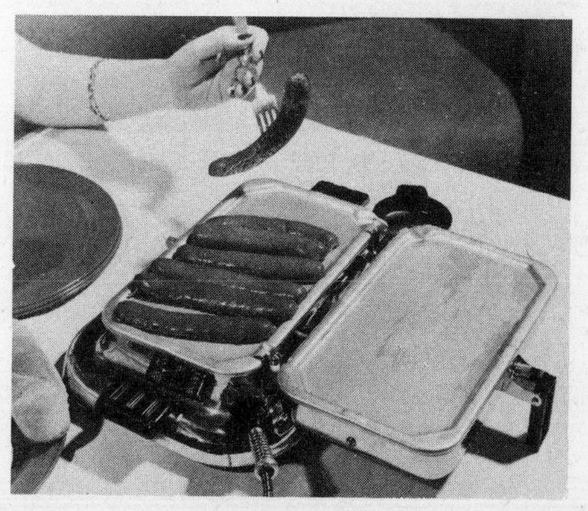

For thorough cleaning of carpets, a vacuum cleaner with an agitator brush is usually preferred.

The tank type of vacuum cleaner with attachments will perform many types of cleaning chores.

been emptied, the inside should be brushed with a whisk broom. Never wash the bag. If a hole appears, the bag will have to be replaced. Therefore, be careful not to let the vacuum pick up sharp objects such as needles, bits of broken glass, or anything else which might cut or puncture the material.

Some models need to have the belt replaced about once a year. Some need new dust filters every six months or once a year, depending on how much the vacuum is used. Most vacuums are self-oiling, but some of the older models will have to have three drops of oil about once a month, or oftener if it is used a great deal. Sometimes hairpins or other objects collect in the fan of some cleaners and have to be removed.

Keep all brush attachments clean, and clean the agitator brush since it may collect threads which hamper its action. The bristles of an agitator brush should be about ⅛ of an inch above the surface of the carpet when in use, and the distance should be checked occasionally unless you have a model in which the brush adjusts its position automatically to accommodate itself to the depth of the pile. When any brush has become too worn to operate efficiently, it should be replaced.

Other Cleaning Equipment. For quick cleanup between vacuumings, spot removal, scrubbing, and other tasks, the following list of equipment should be adequate:

1 carpet sweeper
1 broom (either corn broom or push broom, as preferred)
1 dustpan
1 long-handled dust mop
1 long-handled floor mop (and mop bucket with wringer attachment, or else self-wringing mop)
1 electric polisher (if you have floors polished with hard wax. Some vacuum cleaners have waxer attachment) or 1 floor waxer
1 pair of lamb's wool dusting mitts
Cleaning cloths (soft, clean old rags or cheesecloth)
1 whisk broom
1 scrubbing brush
1 pail
1 or 2 sponges
1 or 2 pans
1 chamois
1 long-handled brush for cleaning toilet
1 rubber squeegee for cleaning windows
Various cleaning and polishing compounds (the market offers a wide variety, and the housekeeper will probably find that certain ones fit her needs better than others. Useful items include: soap; non-scratching scouring powder for porcelain or enamel; soapless chemical cleaner; silver polish and metal cleaner; wallpaper cleaner; drain solvent; toilet-bowl cleaner; leather cleaner; rust remover; dry-cleaning fluid; liquid wax; hard wax or furniture polish; borax or other water softener; bleaching fluid; disinfectant)
1 or 2 pairs of rubber gloves
1 pair of canvas household gloves
1 box with handle and compartments to hold cleaning supplies

Plan your cleaning tasks so that waste motions are eliminated. Wherever possible, use both hands to do a job. Difficult jobs should be scheduled on a staggered basis so that hard work is not left to be taken care of all at once. Time yourself to see how long it takes to complete any task. Then study the method you have used and see if there are any wasted motions which could be eliminated.

CHAPTER II

LINENS BEDDING & TABLEWARE

BREATHES there a housewife with soul so dead whose eyes will not gleam with joy at the sight of beautiful household linens neatly stacked, or lovely polished silver, or sparkling glassware, or fine china? For many centuries, no self-respecting bride would have dreamed of starting her married life without a dower chest filled with enough household linens to last a lifetime. And she usually had to spin the flax and weave it herself until the industrial revolution transferred these tasks from the home to the factory. Naturally, so much work took a long, long time, so she had to start as soon as she was old enough to hold a spindle. In fact, the term *spinster,* which now means an old maid, originally referred to a young, unmarried female who was supposed to be spinning the linens for her dower chest. (In England, until the time of Queen Elizabeth, *spinster* was a title given to young, unmarried gentlewomen.)

Nowadays, few young women want to tuck their linens away in a dower chest to turn yellow through the years. A lucky bride sometimes manages to start housekeeping with all her linens bestowed upon her by her friends at showers. Many another doesn't even begin to think about sheets and pillowcases until she's ready to say, "I do." Then she rushes in a flurry to the nearest store, only to discover that she has no idea about size, quality, grade, or amount. "How long should a sheet be?" she wonders, and then remembers that she doesn't have a mattress yet to put it on. So let's begin with the mattress, springs, and pillows.

MATTRESSES, SPRINGS, AND PILLOWS

Mattresses. Bed, where we hate to go at night and even more to leave in the morning, is yet a wonderful place—or at least it ought to be, since we spend approximately one-third of our lives there. We may choose to have the headboard upholstered in leather just because it tickles our fancy; but when we select a mattress, the primary consideration is comfort. Yet the mattress which you find comfortable may be a positive thing of torture to another. Some want a mattress they can sink down into, while others crave a rock-like firmness. It's the person who is to sleep on it who should do the testing. And by testing, we don't mean a gentle prod here and there with the fist. We mean that the person should lie down on it—stretch out full length, and roll around a bit. But alas, the majority of people would feel too silly if they did this in full view of other customers in a store. Knowing this fact, a few (very few) stores have provided rooms where customers may bounce around in privacy to their heart's content without diminishing their dignity one whit.

Construction. The second most important consideration is quality. A mattress of good quality will retain a firm, level surface (hard or soft) for many, many years, while one of poor quality will soon develop "sleepless hollows." And where does quality count? In the construction.

The three main types of construction are innerspring, solid pad, and foam rubber. Innerspring and pad mattresses may vary widely in quality. Foam rubber is still fairly uniform in quality.

The coils in an innerspring mattress may be open or closed. The number of coils per mattress is one indication of quality. In the open-coil type, the number may vary from 180 to 400 for a mattress to fit a double bed. Fewer coils than 180 indicate substandard construction. As a rule, the greater the number of coils, the better the quality, although other factors, such as the kind and amount of wire used in the coils, the way in which they are joined, and the padding, also determine quality. In closed-coil mattresses, each coil is encased in a muslin pocket and responds to pressure independently of every other coil. More coils must be used in this type of construction—no less than 500 for a double bed. One make has as many as 850. Naturally, the cost is greater.

Coils must be well insulated and padded. Otherwise, they will soon begin to jab you in the back. If you can feel the coils when you lean on the mattress, you may be sure that it's not sufficiently well padded.

Coils can be individually depressed in mattresses of closed-coil construction.

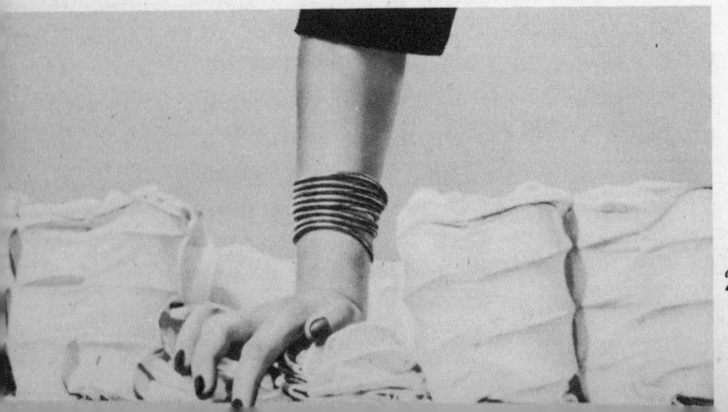

Mattress padding may be of hair, cotton, or kapok. Hair is usually confined to solid-pad construction. The best quality of hair comes from the horse's mane, and the second best from his tail. The poorest quality comes from the back of the hog. Hog hair tends to mat into a hard lump with usage. The best quality horse hair mattresses are resilient and yet have a firmness which some people prefer to the yielding softness of an innerspring. But a good horsehair mattress is not cheap. Sometimes horsehair and hog hair are combined to lower the cost. If the percentage of hog hair is less than horse hair, the mattress will probably give satisfactory service.

Cotton may be packed into layers, spun, or fluffed. Layered cotton usually holds its shape well without lumping or shifting. Spun cotton, found in solid-pad cotton mattresses of good quality, is ginned by a special process which straightens the fibers into a vertical position. Mattresses filled with spun cotton will billow up with shaking. Fluffed cotton, used in mattresses of the cheapest type, does not give satisfactory service because it soon becomes hard and lumpy. When it is combined with layered cotton, the results are better. Mattresses thus filled might be suitable for a summer home or camp where long wear is not the primary consideration.

Kapok-filled mattresses are far less popular than the cotton-filled kinds. Yet kapok has the virtue of resisting dampness and is recommended for some allergy cases. Kapok is softer than cotton, but does not wear as long.

Foam-rubber mattresses are made by whipping air into rubber while it is in a liquid state. A mattress made of foam rubber weighs considerably less than an ordinary one; it is also insect proof and sag proof. Unlike an innerspring mattress, a foam-rubber one is not injured if you bend it double or even roll it up, and it can be washed like a rubber sponge. The millions of tiny air cells make the mattress self-ventilating. It doesn't squeak; it never needs rebuilding; and it's supposed to last a lifetime. However, foam-rubber mattresses are still on the costly side.

Tickings. The mattress ticking may be tufted, quilted, or smooth. Many like to have the ticking smooth, but that is a matter of preference. However, it is important that the ticking fabric be stout, whether it is a handsome damask or simply a plain woven stripe. A thin, loosely woven ticking will soon split. Hair mattresses require the heaviest ticking — weighing about half a pound to the yard—to keep the hair from working out. Be sure to protect the ticking with a mattress cover. Quilted cotton pads are made for this purpose; but you may use an old, clean blanket.

Care of the Mattress. Turn the mattress over regularly (about once a week)—from side to side one time and from top to bottom another, so that weight is evenly distributed. No mattress except the foam rubber type should be folded when it is turned, as folding is apt to strain the springs and the ticking. If the mattress is too heavy to keep straight while turning, get someone to help you with it. Air the mattress regularly—it's a good idea to throw the bedclothes back in the morning upon arising and let the bed air near an open window. A weekly cleaning with the upholstery attachment of the vacuum also helps to keep the mattress fresh.

Sizes. The standard length for a mattress is 74 inches. The double-bed size is 54 inches wide and the twin bed, 39 inches. Occasionally, one can find a double-bed mattress 60 inches wide, and some manufacturers make mattresses which are 80 inches long for those very tall people who can't stretch out in the average bed. Custom-built mattresses can be made in special sizes—or shapes, too. One company made a round mattress for a woman who wanted to be sure she would never get out of bed on the wrong side. Any mattress other than a standard size will probably require a custom-built bedstead, too. Of course, custom-built means custom price. However, the difference relative to foam-rubber mattresses may not be prohibitive, since the foam rubber can easily be cut to specification, whereas an innerspring must be built to specification.

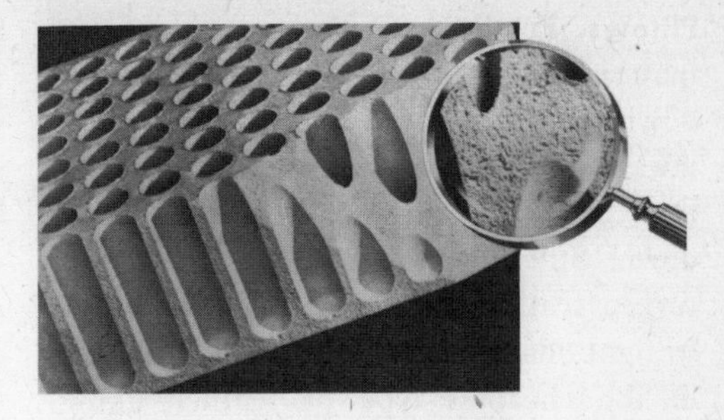

Cross-section view of foam rubber mattress.

Springs. More sleeping comfort is assured if the mattress rests on good springs. Closed box springs are protected from dust, but usually cost more than open springs. By screwing six legs onto the wooden frame of a box spring, the need for a bedstead can be eliminated. An innerspring mattress is usually paired with a platform-top coil spring, which has steel bands across the top of the coils for better mattress support. Open-top coil springs are more flexible and therefore more comfortable with a solid-pad mattress. The double-deck type is more resilient than the single-deck. In addition to coil springs, one can also find various types of flat springs to use with a solid-pad mattress. They are not as comfortable as coil springs, but they cost less.

Pillows. Feathers are the common filling material for pillows. The best grade is down, which makes a very soft, light pillow. Goose or duck feathers are the next best. Sometimes they are combined with down. Still less expensive are chicken or turkey feathers. Since these feathers are straight shafted, they must be curled, or, in the cheapest type of feather filling, simply chopped. Occasionally, chicken and turkey feathers have an odor. For people who are allergic to feathers, kapok is often recommended as a pillow filling. Foam rubber is also coming into use for pillows. Pillows are made in all sizes, but the most common size is 22 inches by 38 inches.

Pillow tickings should be closely woven and featherproof, and the pillow should be plumply filled. When selecting a pillow, shake or pound it to test its resiliency. When you air your pillows, hang them in the shade as the sun may destroy the natural oil in the feathers and cause them to dry out and lose their resiliency.

BLANKETS AND QUILTS

DURING sleep, body temperature drops slightly, and adequate conservation or reinforcement of body heat is very important whenever the room temperature goes below 75° F. The best body insulating material is wool. Wool is "warm," not because it provides any heat itself, but because good quality wool, more than any other fiber, has the power to retard the flow of heat from the body.

Woolen Blankets. Blankets are made of woolen yarns. The best quality woolen is that which comes straight from the sheep's back and is called *virgin,* or *pure* wool. However, there are various grades of virgin wool, and that's why it comes in a wide range of prices. Lower in quality are the blankets made of reprocessed or reused wool (*see the section on Wool in the chapter on Fabrics*). When you buy a blanket, examine the label which tells you the fiber content. Also examine the nap, which should be deep and springy. It is the quality of the wool and the fleeciness of the nap that make a blanket warm, not its weight. The lightest blankets weigh approximately 1¾ pounds and the heaviest about 4. A pair of medium-weight blankets and one light-weight are usually adequate for each bed except in the coldest winter weather. The number of blankets on the bed can be varied to suit changing weather conditions.

Woolen blankets should have deep, springy naps.

Blankets of Rayon, Cotton, and Mixed Fibers. While the insulating properties of rayon are not as great as those of wool, they are still very good. Rayon fibers are lustrous and take dye well. The nap may mat after repeated washings, thus lessening the blanket's insulating qualities, but this tendency depends upon the quality of the rayon and the way it is washed. Cotton blankets provide less insulation than either wool or rayon, and for this reason they are often preferred for use in summer.

Sometimes blankets are made of a mixture of fibers. Such blankets do not have the warmth-retaining property of a good all-wool blanket, but they cost less. Better insulation is provided if the nap is largely of wool.

Blanket Sizes. For a standard-size double bed, blankets should be at least 72 inches by 90 inches, although some people prefer to have them 80 inches wide. The 72-inch width can be used on twin beds as well, although the usual width for a twin bed is 66 inches. Most mixed-fiber blankets in twin-bed size are only 84 inches long, which allows only 10 inches for tucking under the mattress on a standard 74-inch long bed—not really enough. Of course, baby blankets come in smaller sizes to fit cribs. Be sure to have blankets large enough for the bed on which they are to be used.

Blanket Bindings. Fine wool blankets are usually bound in rayon taffeta or satin, which is more luxurious but less durable than sateen. The binding on a good wool blanket will wear out and probably have to be replaced several times before the blanket itself wears out. Ready-made bindings in a variety of colors are sold for this purpose at notion counters. To replace a worn binding, rip it off, being careful not to injure the blanket, and baste the new binding in place over the edge of the blanket. Turn the edges at the ends to the inside and baste together. Then stitch the binding on the machine with thread to match. If you have no machine, the binding may be stitched by hand, but a double set of stitches is suggested for greater durability.

Blanket Care. Handle blankets gently. When you make the bed, avoid hard twisting or pulling on the blanket. Do not jerk or tug on a tucked-in blanket to remove it from the bed. Lift the mattress and pull the blanket out gently. Be careful not to soil blanket edges by letting them drag on the floor. For sleeping comfort, arrange the blanket on the bed so that the shoulders will be well covered. Turn the top sheet back over the edge of the blanket to help keep the binding clean. Don't pile sheets or other items on top of blankets placed on shelves or in drawers or the nap will be crushed. Protect blankets from moth damage when you store them during the summer months. Launder carefully to prevent shrinkage—some blankets are now treated with resin to resist shrinkage (*see the chapter on Laundering Equipment and Methods for information on laundering blankets*). With proper care, a really fine blanket may last fifteen or twenty years.

Quilts. Some women like both blankets and quilts for bedclothes. Quilts filled with down or wool batting are very retentive of warmth. Down also has the advantage of being extremely light weight. Cotton-filled quilts offer a rather small amount of insulation compared to their weight. While the primary purpose of a quilt is to provide insulation, it is usually selected for the attractiveness of its cover. Rayon taffeta or satin covers add a note of luxury to the bedroom, and for that reason may be preferred to a sturdier but less pretentious cotton cover. Many housewives keep a quilt folded at the foot of the bed to provide extra warmth when it is needed. However, the slippery surface of a satin- or taffeta-covered quilt tends to make it slide off the bed rather easily if the sleeper is restless.

Whether the filling is of down, wool batting, or cotton batting, it should be securely anchored either with quilting or tufting. Quilts, of course, should not be washed, and when the cover has become soiled, the quilt must be sent to the dry cleaner. The filling of a quilt may last as long as a blanket, but the cover may wear out and have to be replaced or re-covered. Fine, handmade quilts are often handsome enough to serve as bedspreads (*see the Chapter on Quilt Making*).

Electric Blankets and Quilts. Probably the most revolutionary thing in bedclothes since man first learned to keep himself warm with woven fabrics instead of animal skins is the blanket or quilt which actually warms the body instead of merely preventing the escape of body heat. Electric blankets and quilts look exactly like ordinary ones, but inside they contain a network of small wires which give off heat when the

Electric blankets and quilts are thermostatically controlled to provide even heat regardless of outside temperature.

blanket is turned on. The amount of heat is controlled by a thermostat. All one needs to do is to set the dial for the temperature preferred for sleeping. Let's say you like to sleep at a temperature of 70° F. First, turn the blanket on to warm the bed before you crawl in. Chill, wintry air may quickly lower the room temperature, yet *you* sleep in a toasty temperature of 70° all night whether the room temperature becomes higher or lower. For those who share a double bed but do not like to sleep at the same temperature, one manufacturer provides an electric blanket with separately controlled heating units on each side. Only one blanket is needed except in the most drastic climates. And the average weight of an electric blanket—around 5 pounds—is only slightly more than that of an ordinary blanket. Various types are made, but all have safety controls. The wires inside the blanket are thoroughly insulated so that it can be washed like an ordinary one.

HOUSEHOLD LINENS

WHAT we refer to as "household linens" are now more often than not actually "household cottons" and sometimes rayons as well. Fabrics of linen for household use have been largely replaced by those of cotton, which is durable, just as satisfactory for most uses, and considerably cheaper.

Sheets and Pillowcases can be either of muslin or percale. Percale is finer, lighter, and smoother than muslin, and, grade for grade, slightly higher in cost. The difference in wearing qualities between the two depends upon grade. A fine grade of percale may outwear a poor or medium grade of muslin. But a fine grade of muslin usually outwears even a fine grade of percale. However, for those who send their laundry out at pound rates, percale may prove to be more economical than muslin in the long run because of its lighter weight. Several plans have been worked out to set grade standards based on thread count, yarn staple, and so on, for both muslin and percale sheets, and some sheets do carry labels bearing such information. However, no uniform method of grading has as yet been accepted by all manufacturers. But, generally speaking, good percale must be made of long-staple cotton and have at least 180 threads to the inch (some very fine percales may have as many as 300). A muslin sheet may have a smaller thread count and still be closely woven because the yarns are heavier. The weave should be close, in both muslin and percale, for long wear.

Sheets vary a good deal in size. For the standard length bed of 74 inches, the best sheet length is 108 inches. Anything shorter is not adequate for turning back and tucking in. A few manufacturers make sheets which are slightly longer. The width for a twin bed should be at least 72 inches. For a double bed, the width may be 81 or 90 inches — preferably 90, although the 81-inch width can do double duty for twin beds. Sheet measurements are based on torn, not hemmed, sizes. Sheets of special size can be made from sheeting which is sold in various widths by the yard. Pillow cases vary in size, too, but for the average-sized bed pillow, the pillow case should be about 25 by 40 inches.

With care, good sheets will give years of service. Do not tug or pull on them sharply to remove them from the bed. If you launder them at home, vary the position of the fold from time to time to lessen the strain on the fibers. Hemstitched sheets will wear out more quickly along the line of hemstitching than sheets with plain stitched hems.

What is an adequate supply of sheets? The minimum number is six for each bed —two on the bed, two in the laundry, and two on the shelf. Additional sheets or replacements can be bought as needed. The same rule applies to pillow cases—one for each pillow, one in the laundry, and one on the shelf.

Towels. The turkish toweling fabric used for bath towels has a raised pile made of small loops — usually on both sides, but sometimes only on one. The cost of the towel is determined by the depth and thickness of the pile. The greater the depth and thickness, the longer the towel will wear and the more it will cost. If the pile is thin and sparsely looped, the yarns of which it is formed tend to snag and pull out more readily, thus weakening the fabric. The minimum number of bath towels needed is from three to six for each person, depending on how often they are changed, which is usually once or twice a week.

Sizes and colors are matters of personal preference. White is always a safe choice if you live in rented quarters, because towel colors may not always harmonize with bathroom colors when you move into a new home.

Hand towels are usually of huck (short for *huckaback*), either of linen or cotton or a mixture of both. Linen generally absorbs moisture more readily than cotton, and is therefore a good choice for hand towels. However, cotton huck towels give very satisfactory service at considerably less expense. Whether of cotton or linen, the fabric should be firm and closely woven for long wear. Towel sizes vary, of course. A popular size is 16 inches by 28 inches. Some housewives take great pride in fancy guest towels of fine, plain-weave linen adorned with handwork. But when these are of postage-stamp size, men almost invariably spurn them. As with bath towels, the minimum number of hand towels needed per person depends on how often they are changed. If changed twice weekly, the number is six. If changed daily, approximately twenty are needed.

Kitchen towels can be of cotton, linen, a mixture of linen and cotton, or either cotton or linen or both mixed with rayon. Rayon helps to make towels lintless — an important feature for polishing china and glassware. Linen towels also shed little lint. Cotton generally sheds more, but the amount may not be great if the cotton is long stapled. A supply of at least two or three dozen towels is required.

Table Linens and Their Substitutes. The fine, white linen damask tablecloths which were once considered essential for any properly equipped dining table have now been largely superseded by the more easily laundered, less expensive place mats. That is not to imply that linen damask is no longer fashionable—anything lovely never goes out of fashion — and many women treasure such cloths, bringing them out

Monograms add decorative personal touch to towels and other linens. In this set, hand towels are of turkish toweling to match bath towels.

only for holiday feasts. Then the damask is carefully washed and ironed by hand until it's polished to a satiny gleam. Lace and embroidered cloths of linen and other fine fabrics are also prized and sometimes handed on as heirlooms, since lovely table linens are among the housewife's most cherished possessions, and she usually has very definite ideas about them.

For everyday use, most women prefer something more practical which can be washed or wiped clean with little effort. Place mats are the most practical answer to this need—and they are made of numerous materials. In addition to almost every type of cotton, rayon, and linen fabrics, mats are also made of straw, plastics, cork, lace, crochet work, and other materials.

Those who dislike place mats can choose from a wide assortment of inexpensive table cloths of cotton, rayon, linen, or a mixture of fibers, either in white or colors as well as in prints. Plastic fabrics which need only to be cleaned by wiping with a damp cloth can also be used. Tablecloths of woven spun glass are still something of a novelty and still fairly expensive. However, they are impervious to stains. Other woven textiles are sometimes treated with thin, nearly invisible coatings of plastic to render them stain resistant.

Napkins can either match or contrast with the cloth or mats. Size is a matter of preference, although a napkin ought to be large enough to serve the purpose for which it is intended. Dinner napkins are often larger than luncheon napkins, but this is an arbitrary matter.

No rules can be given for the minimum number of table linens needed for an adequate supply. It depends on whether tablecloths are supplemented with place mats or used only occasionally, and on how quickly a cloth becomes soiled. Certainly no meal is appetizing if it is served on a soiled cloth, and the housewife who prefers cloths to mats ought to have a supply large enough to permit a fresh cloth for every meal, in case the cloths must be changed that often. The same thing applies to napkins, although napkins are often used for more than one meal when each member of the family tags his or hers with a napkin ring. Napkin rings would not appear on a formal dinner table, of course, but their use seems justified in family surroundings.

CHINA, GLASSWARE, AND SILVERWARE

CHINA is selected primarily for shape and decoration. Traditional patterns, such as Wedgewood, Lowestoft, or Staffordshire need not be confined to their own period settings, as they have a timelessness in their decorative effect which makes them adaptable to many styles or periods. Brightly painted or colored potteries are gay for informal settings — both indoors and outdoors. There are no rules to follow—simply let good taste and imagination guide you, and then select whatever style of china or pottery pleases you the most.

What we call "china" is sometimes a translucent type of porcelain, occasionally designated as a soft-paste porcelain to distinguish it from the true, or hard-paste porcelain, which is made from a special clay (kaolin) fused with quartz and feldspar.

Another type of china is the sem-vitreous ware which is not translucent. This ware in a good grade does not break or chip readily if it is handled with care. Low-priced china is often of poor quality and tends to chip and break rather easily.

One designer has brought out a new type of chinaware which has much of the beauty of real porcelain but not its fragility. This new ware is said to have thermo-shock-resistant properties much higher than any other kind of china or pottery, and it can be subjected to high heat and considerable rough usage without breaking.

Although china is a kind of pottery, the term "pottery" is often used in the trade to mean a type of glazed or unglazed ware made from a non-white clay. Such potteries come in many brilliant colors as well as subtle pastels, or they may be painted with gay and splashy decorations. This type of ware adds color to a table setting, and while it gives satisfactory service, much of it tends to chip or break more readily than the best grades of china.

Since all types of china and pottery are breakable, it is wise to select them from open-stock patterns. Some open-stock patterns are carried year after year and replacements can be made long after the original set was purchased. Others are offered only for a limited length of time — three years, five years, and so on. The longer a pattern is available, the more assurance you have that your set can be kept complete with replacements as they are needed.

In former days, most housewives selected two sets of china if they could afford to do so. One set was for everyday use, and another, the "best" china, for use when company was entertained or on festive occasions. Many women now prefer to have two or more sets, not restricted to use on any particular occasion, but to vary the appearance of their table settings. Since interesting table settings help to avoid montonous meals, two medium-priced sets, each in a different color or pattern, may be better than one of the best quality.

Individual pieces in a set no longer need to match each other completely as long as the pieces in any one size or shape are the same so that place settings are uniform. Two colors are often combined in a set for contrast. For example, dinner plates may

Place mats are easier to launder than large table cloths and may be of fine lace and linen or materials which can be cleaned with a damp cloth.

be of one color, salad plates of another, soup bowls or cups of the first color, and so on. Or decorated dishes may be combined with ones of solid color to match a dominant tone in the decoration. Individual place settings can even be of different colors if the pieces match in design. Serving pieces, such as meat platter and vegetables dishes, can match the rest of the set or not, as preferred.

What is the minimum amount of china to buy for a simple service? A bride could begin housekeeping with place settings for two, of course, but soon she would want enough china to be able to entertain a couple of guests. Therefore, a "starter" set for a small family probably ought to consist of at least:

4 dinner plates
4 cups
4 saucers

4 cereal dishes (can also be used for soup)
1 platter
1 vegetable dish

The next step is to increase the number of pieces in the service and to enlarge it to six settings. To do this, add to the above list 2 each of the dinner plates, cups, saucers, and cereal dishes, as well as the following:

6 bread-and-butter plates
6 dessert plates
6 soup cups
6 13-inch plates

Eventually, the following pieces can be added:

6 soup plates
1 sugar bowl with cover
1 creamer
1 sauce boat
1 large bowl

Further enlargements of the service can be made by two's of all the pieces which are in the individual place settings.

Care of China. China should be washed and rinsed with water that is hot but not boiling, as boiling water may craze or crack the vitreous glaze. The same thing may happen if china is placed in a too-hot oven to warm. The dishes may be scratched if they are carelessly rubbed together. Decorated china should not be rubbed too vigorously even with a dish cloth or dish mop. While it is true that the decorations are fired on, too much rubbing can wear them off in time. Besides being easy on the hands, mild suds are also best for china. China or pottery which is cracked or chipped is unsanitary and should be discarded.

A modern setting for a buffet supper.

Glassware. The fine glassware called "crystal" is a flint glass containing lead. Such glass is hard, brilliant, and rings with a musical sound when tapped. Crystal can be made quite thin and it will still retain more strength than ordinary glassware. For fine dinner table service, the traditional choice is crystal ware. Stemmed or footed glasses are usually preferred for formal service. They may be plain, etched, or cut. "Correct" service calls for glasses of specific sizes and shapes for each kind of wine or other beverage. But since only the most elaborate households are equipped to serve dinners of many courses, each accompanied by a different wine served in its own special glass, the average homemaker will find one set of wine glasses and one set of water goblets adequate. If only one set of wine glasses is used, a good choice might be the 4-ounce burgundy or sauterne glass. With a set of 10-ounce water goblets, this service will be sufficient for all but very formal dinners. Other glasses, such as sherry, cocktail and liqueur glasses, can be added as needed or wanted. As with chinaware, it is advisable to buy glassware from open-stock patterns.

Inexpensive glassware may be preferable to crystal for everyday use, because, while it is readily breakable, the cost of replacement is negligible. Newer types of glassware which tend to resist breakage even when dropped have also appeared. Nicked glassware should always be dis-

Fine silverware adapts itself to both traditional and modern settings.

carded. Colored glassware in itself can be quite handsome, but it can often make liquids served in it look unappetizing. For example, a rose-colored wine looks gray in a green glass. If the color of the glass does not conflict with that of the liquid, the effect may not be objectionable. But, to be safe, it is better to confine the use of colored glass to water or other clear liquids.

Silverware. Every housewife yearns for a set of fine sterling silver flatware. It has become almost a symbol of gracious living — no matter how much more practical stainless steel might be, we shall probably go right on polishing the cherished silver.

Sterling silver flatware is a major investment—one to last a lifetime and then be handed on as an heirloom. According to government specifications, sterling must be 925/1000 pure silver. Those for whom sterling is a "must" can select from open-stock pattern and add to it through the years. A good way to do this is to buy individual place settings at a time. An adequately complete place setting usually consists of 1 knife, 1 fork, 1 teaspoon, 1 cream-soup spoon, 1 salad fork, and 1 butter spreader. Other pieces are a matter of choice, but novelty pieces seldom serve any real purpose. Knives and forks can be either dinner or luncheon size and either kind can serve for both meals. Stainless steel is often preferred for knife blades so that they may have a better cutting edge. Knife handles, if thick, are usually hollow, not only to lessen the cost but also to lighten the weight.

In appearance, silver plate offers most of the advantages of sterling at only a fraction of the cost. While no silver plate lasts as long as sterling, a good silver plate will last for many, many years. Plating should be heavy, and each piece should have extra inlays of silver at points of greatest wear. Medium-weight plating is still cheaper and usually has extra reinforcements of silver at points of wear. Of course, medium-weight plating cannot be expected to give unlimited service, but it may be economical as a "fill-in" until one can afford a better grade of silver. Light-weight plating does not give satisfactory service—stainless steel would be a better investment.

Silver patterns need not be selected to match any style or period of decoration. If the pattern is well designed in itself, it will harmonize with any type of interior.

When not in use, silverware should be kept in a chest or in cloth cases especially treated to resist tarnish. Silverware tarnishes less when it is used regularly and washed with soap and hot water than when it is left unused and exposed to the air. All tarnished silver should be cleaned before using. For this purpose, use one of the silver polishing pastes or else one of the special cloths treated to remove tarnish. Black tissue paper will retard tarnishing.

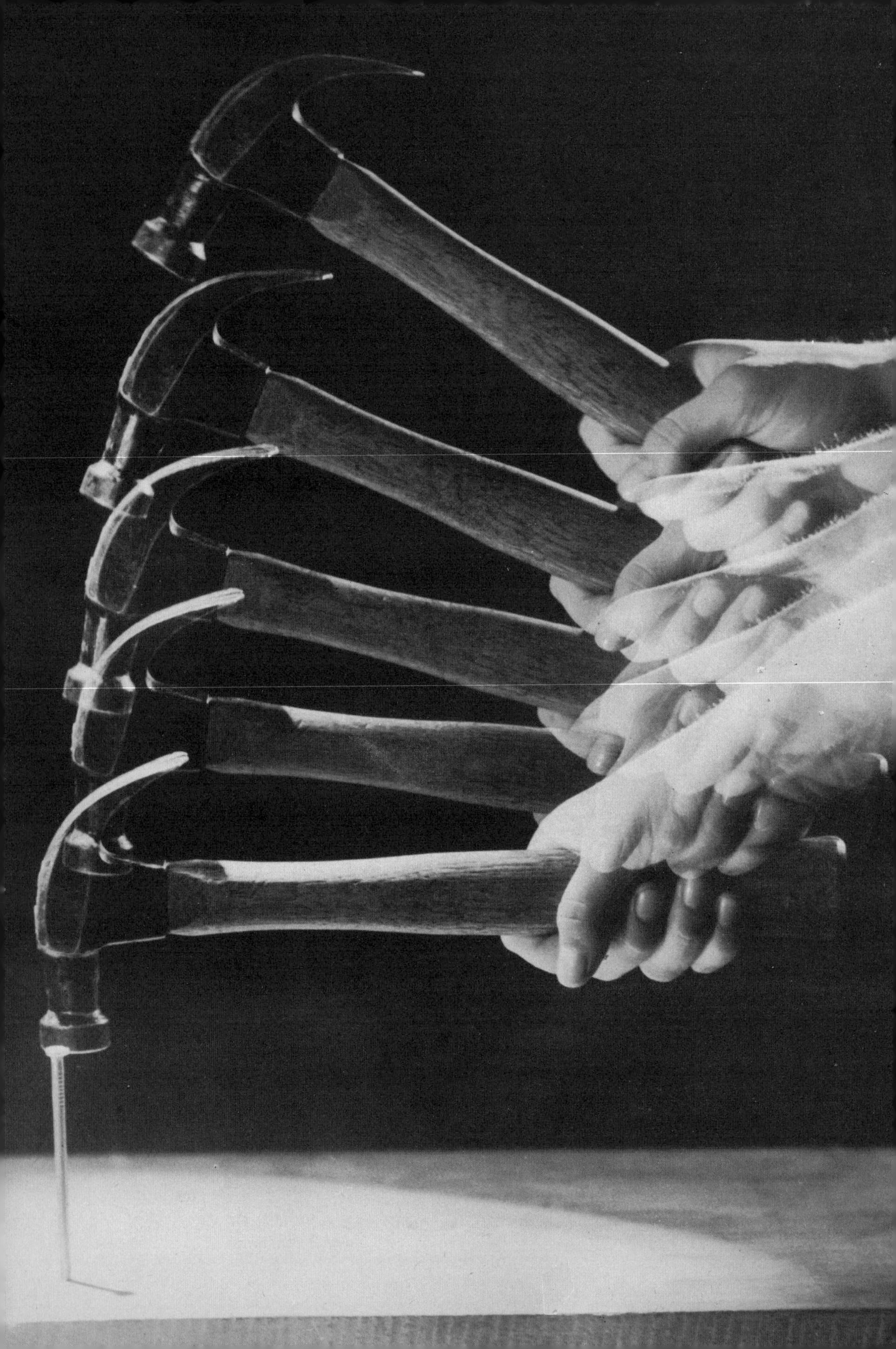

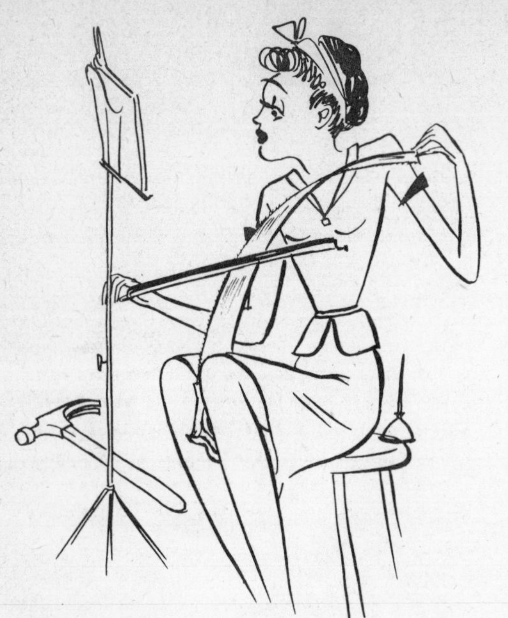

CHAPTER III

TOOLS AND HOW TO USE THEM

ACCORDING to rumor, a clever woman can fix anything with a single "tool" — a hairpin. We cannot verify this as a fact, since we have no hairpins handy. But we do have saws, hammers, screwdrivers, and so on, and they work just fine.

The question of which tools we think you ought to buy is something we cannot answer without quite a few "ifs." If you plan to do such-and-such a job, then you will need such-and-such tools. About all we can do is to tell you the names of tools, what each one will do, and how you should use it. It seems a bit foolhardy to set down any "minimum" list of tools for the home workshop, because as anyone who has ever developed a love of working with tools knows, there never is a "minimum." He (or she) always yearns for just one more chisel or another drill. After every known hand tool has been acquired, the home craftsman then begins to hanker after power tools. And so it goes.

But it does seem reasonable to assume that even the most unhandy home owner will at some time need a hammer and some nails, a screwdriver, and a pair of pliers. And, unlike the beaver, he cannot cut even a simple block of wood with his teeth—he needs a saw for that. Of course, *which* kind of saw depends upon *how* he wants to cut the wood.

Quality. It pays to buy good tools. We are mistaken when we think that cheap tools are an economy because we intend to use them for only one or two jobs. If that's all we expect to do with them, it would be cheaper in the long run to have the work done by a carpenter. Good tools will work for you; cheap tools frequently will not. And good tools will last; cheap ones undoubtedly will not. Therefore, buy the best tools you can find. Make a friend of your hardware dealer, and ask his advice about the quality of the tools you intend buying. If you order by mail, a careful study of the catalog will provide you with considerable information as to quality.

TOOLS AND THEIR USES

The following tools are listed and described in alphabetical order for easy reference, and not in the order of their importance.

Awl. Any of several types of small, sharp-pointed tools for piercing. The *brad* awl is often used to make holes for small nails and screws.

Brace and Bits. A brace is a revolving tool for holding *bits,* which are tools in various

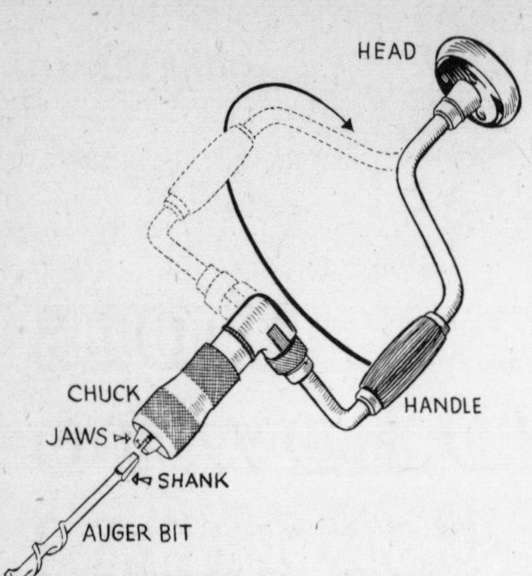

FIG. 1. A brace and bit. To place a bit in the brace, hold the chuck in one hand and turn the handle to the left with the other to open the jaws. Insert the shank end of the bit in the jaws and turn the handle to the right until the jaws grasp the shank firmly.

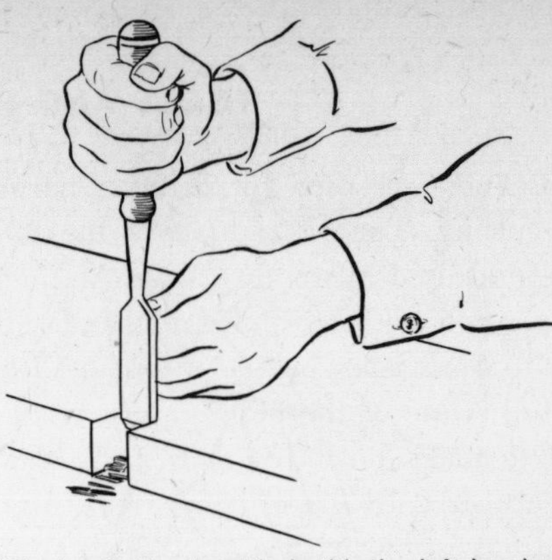

FIG. 4. Guide the chisel with the left hand and apply pressure with the right. Keep both hands back of the blade or above the cutting edge at all times. Hold the chisel vertically or at an angle, according to the direction of the cut. Always push the blade away from you as you cut.

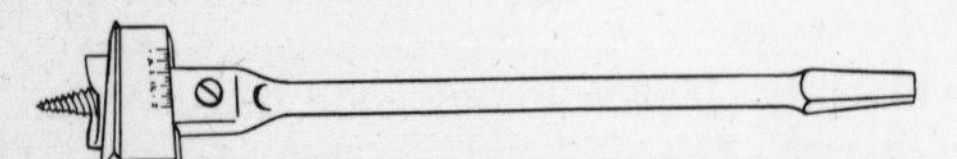

FIG. 2. A twist bit (top) is used to drill holes for nails and screws and can be had in various sizes. An expanding bit (bottom) can be adjusted to cut holes of various sizes. Although it is comparatively expensive, it may actually be an economical buy because it takes the place of a number of large bits.

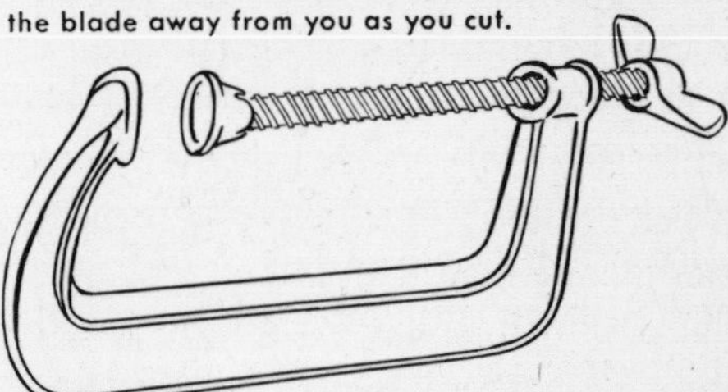

FIG. 5. Clamps are made in many styles and sizes. The C-clamp (above) serves many purposes. Both large and small C-clamps are useful for holding furniture parts together when joints are reglued, although a tourniquet made from heavy cord and a stick can often serve the same purpose. Triangular corner clamps are necessary for gluing right-angle joints (such as those on a picture frame) together.

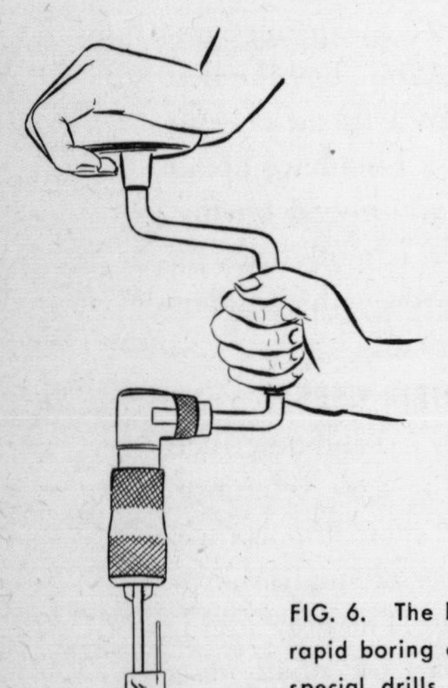

FIG. 3. Hold the brace perpendicular to the surface being drilled and rotate the handle by turning to the right. In this picture, a depth gauge is attached to the bit to regulate depth of hole. When drilling on thin pieces of wood, start the hole on one side and finish on the other to prevent splintering.

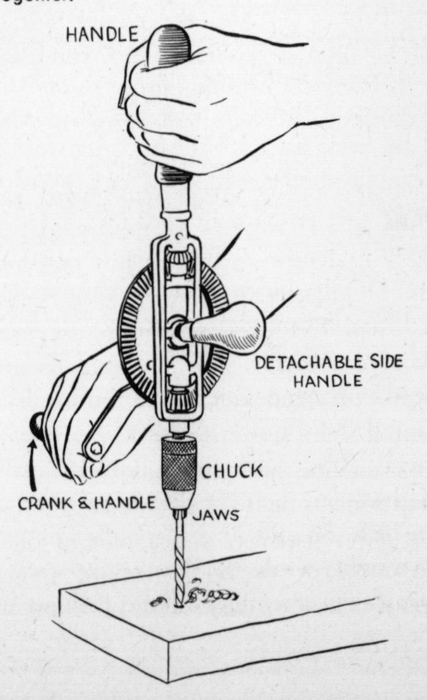

FIG. 6. The hand drill (right) is useful for rapid boring of small holes in wood. With special drills, it can bore holes in metal. Hold the handle in the left hand and press down steadily. Turn the crank handle with the right hand.

forms and sizes used for drilling, boring, and cutting. The *auger* brace is the common kind used in woodworking. An auger brace fitted with a ratchet makes it possible to bore holes in places too small for the full swing of the brace. *Twist* bits are used to make holes for nails and screws, and are sized by 32nds of an inch. *Auger* bits are twist bits with spurred feed screws, and are sized by 16ths of an inch. *Foerstner* bits are spurless bits used for boring holes in thin wood, or on end grain where other bits might split the wood. They are sized by 16ths of an inch. An *expanding* bit can be adjusted to cut holes of various sizes. *Countersunk* bits are used to widen screw holes so screws may be sunk below surface of the wood. Depth of holes can be regulated with an adjustable bit gauge. Buy bits in various sizes as they are needed. Few craftsmen need an unlimited assortment. (*Note:* Many home craftsmen prefer a hand drill to a brace and bits for average drilling jobs.)

Chisels. Woodworking chisels are sharp, narrow-bladed knives for paring, beveling, notching, carving, and similar cutting jobs. Made in various sizes. Craftsmen may want to start with a ¾-inch chisel and later add ¼-, ½-, and 1-inch sizes. Chisels must be kept sharp with oilstone. No chisel should ever be used as a substitute for a screwdriver can opener, or other tool.

Clamps are used for holding two sections of wood together while glue hardens in joints. Obtainable in various shapes and sizes. "C" clamps have many uses.

Drills. *Hand* drills, which operate somewhat like an egg beater, are useful for drilling small holes quickly, either in wood or in metal. Removable drill points are sized by 64ths of an inch ranging from 1/16 to ½ of an inch. Shanks of drill points are usually straight, while bit shanks are square. A *breast* drill resembles a hand drill except

FIG. 7. Files come in many shapes and sizes. They are especially useful for trimming edges or surfaces that cannot be reached with a plane, spokeshave, or scraper, and for smoothing metal edges.

FIG. 8. Gouges are chisels with curved blades for cutting rounded grooves. They are used for woodturning with a power lathe, but are not essential for the workshop without power tools.

FIG. 9. To drive a nail into wood, grasp the end of the hammer handle; rest the face of the hammer head on the nail; hold the nail in position with the left hand; start the nail with a light tap of the hammer; remove the left hand, and drive the nail in with sharp, quick blows of the hammer.

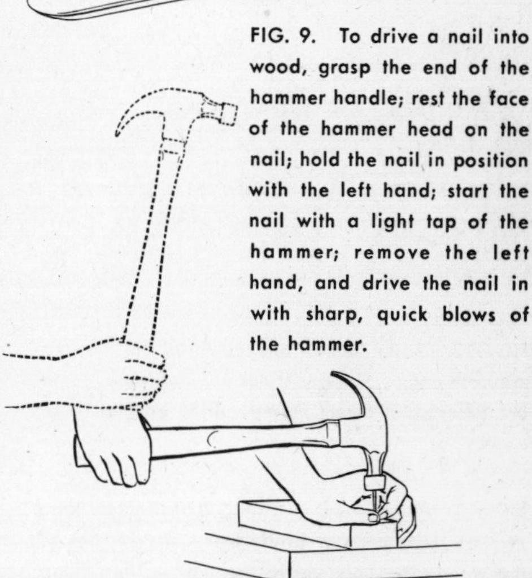

FIG. 10. If a nail bends, remove it with the claw of the hammer. A piece of wood slipped under the head of the hammer will act as a lever and prevent the hammer from marring the surface of the wood being worked on. Bent nails are best avoided by keeping the eye on the nail head and not on your thumb, which should be out of range of the hammer.

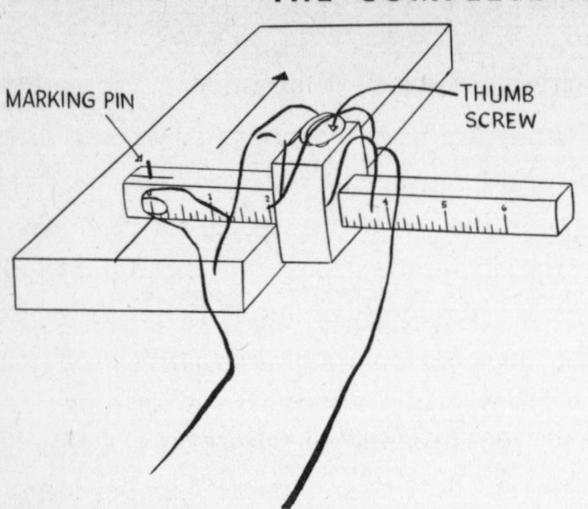

FIG. 11. With the marking gauge, lines can be measured and marked in one operation. Simply adjust the head of the gauge to the proper measurement; place the head against the edge of the wood; hold the head and push it forward, using the thumb to guide the marking pin.

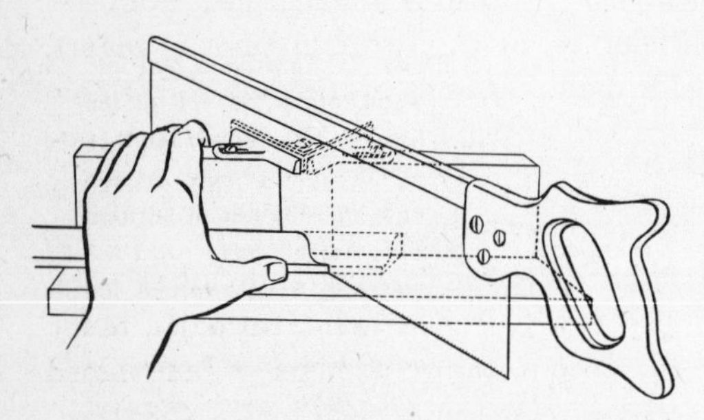

FIG. 12. Miter boxes are essential for cutting accurate angles. Various styles are available. Some are adjustable; others permit cutting only at fixed angles.

FIG. 13. The nail set is a small tool used to hammer finishing nails or brads below the surface of the wood. The hole above the nail is then filled with putty or plastic wood.

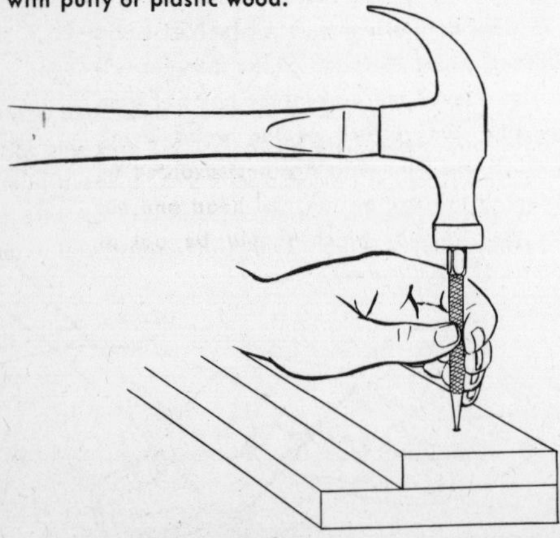

that it has a breast plate so that drill may be steadied with the body. *Push* drills are simpler and less expensive; they are satisfactory for occasional small drilling jobs in wood. A set of assorted drill points to fit usually comes with the push drill.

Files are made in a great variety of shapes, sizes, and degrees of coarseness and fineness. Few home craftsmen will need more than one or two.

Gouges are chisels with curved blades and come in various sizes. Useful for cutting channels in wood.

Grindstone. A small, hand-driven carborundum wheel grindstone is useful for sharpening hatchets, axes, chisels, and knives. Someone will have to turn it for you, though.

Hammers come in many shapes, sizes and weights. For all general work, a *claw* hammer is most useful. Frequently used weights are 10 ounces, 13 ounces, and 16 ounces. Select the weight which feels right to you. The claw end is used to extract nails. A light weight hammer is good for driving tacks. A *magnetized* tack hammer is needed

FIG. 14. The parts of a plane and how they fit together. After the lever cap is slipped under the lever cap screw, press down the cam. Loosen the lever cap screw a bit if the cam does not snap into place readily. The cutting edge of the plane iron should project no more than a hairbreadth through the blade opening.

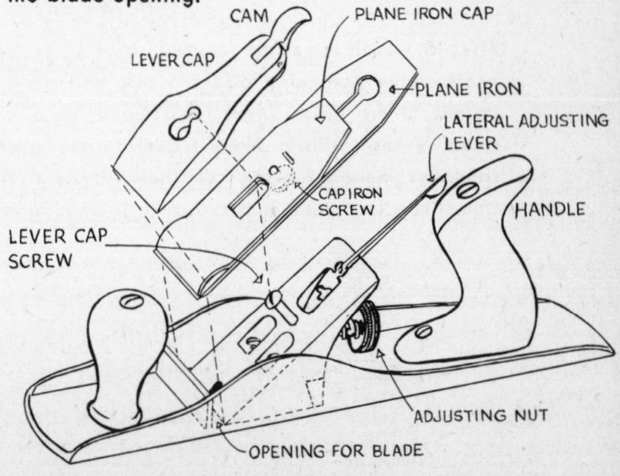

for upholstery work; also serves many other purposes.

Hatchet can be used to cut plugs and wedges quickly as well as to chop kindling; not essential for woodworking.

Level. As the name implies, this instrument indicates whether or not a surface is level. While it is essential for carpentry and cabinet making, it may not be of great importance to the average home workshop.

Marking Gauge. This is a handy device for marking straight lines on wood quickly and accurately. Usual size adjusts to mark line anywhere up to 6 inches from edge.

Miter Box is used to guide saw while cutting wood at an angle. Various forms available. Box with swivel arm which locks at any angle between 45 and 90 degrees is most versatile. Mitered corners of picture frames, moldings, and other articles are difficult to cut accurately without a miter box.

Nail Set is small, punch-like tool used (with hammer) to sink finishing nails below surface of wood. Comes in several sizes; 1/16 of an ich is size frequently used.

Oilstone and **Oil Can.** The oilstone is used to sharpen chisels, gouges, plane irons, and knives. Used in combination with machine or neat's-foot oil (kept in oil can).

Pincers. A small pair of pincers may be found useful for levering out nails, especially if they are too deep-set to be removed with the claw of a hammer.

Planes are used to smooth or whittle down a wood surface. *Bench* planes, used for smoothing with the grain of the wood, come in four sizes: (1) the *smooth,* or *smoothing* plane, about 8 inches long; (2) the *jack* plane, about 14 inches long; (3) the *fore* plane, about 18 inches long; and (4) the *jointer* plane, about 22 or 24 inches long. A *block* plane, about 7 inches long, is used for smoothing across the grain of the wood and for the ends of boards. A *rabbet* plane is an opensided plane which is used for smoothing or cutting grooves or sharp corners. A *combination* plane is an expensive tool with interchangeable irons for doing the work of several kinds of planes. Of these, the home workskhop will seldom need to be equipped with more than one or two, and a good choice would probably be the smoothing plane.

Pliers serve for bending and cutting wire, gripping, and many other purposes. Made in various forms and sizes. Long-nosed pliers are useful for tight places. Combination pliers act as wrench as well as pliers.

Putty Knife. A flexible, dull-bladed knife for mixing and applying putty, plaster, and so on.

Rules. At least one accurate rule of some kind is needed in every home workshop. Many craftsmen prefer to have several. A six-foot folding rule is helpful. So, too, is a

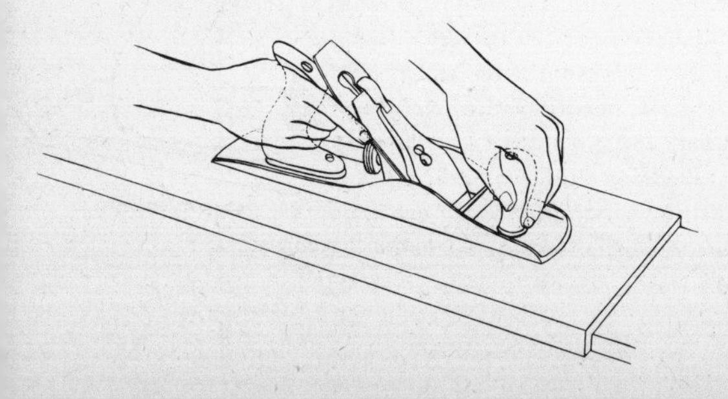

FIG. 15. Push the plane forward, pressing on the knob at the beginning of the stroke and on the handle at the finish. Move with the grain of the wood (except with a block plane). If the grain roughens, move the plane from the opposite direction. Keep the plane iron sharp for a smooth cut.

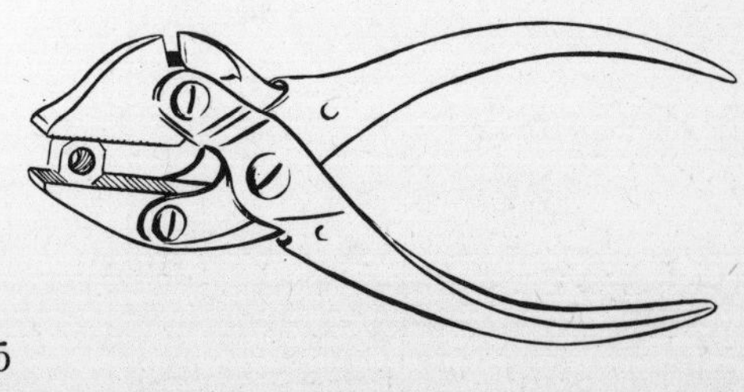

FIG. 16. Pliers come in many styles and sizes. The pair shown here has adjustable jaws and wire cutter. For tight places, a pair of long-nosed pliers is useful. Pliers are used to bend and cut wire or small metal rods, hold or pick up objects, and so on.

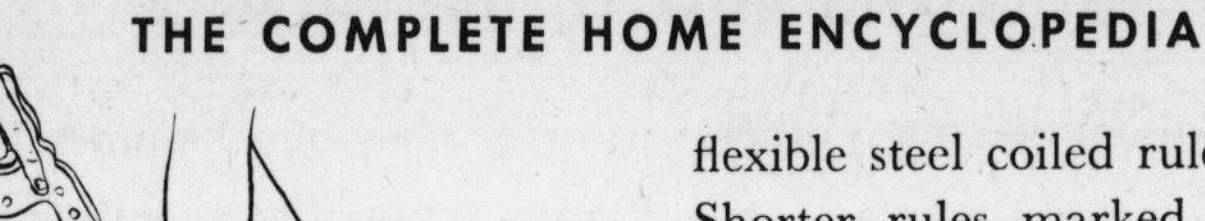

flexible steel coiled rule in a rewind case. Shorter rules marked at intervals of at least 1⁄16 of an inch are useful for small jobs.

Saws. Of the many kinds of saws made, the *handsaw* will probably be most useful for all general purposes. Handsaws are of two kinds: (1) the *crosscut* saw, for sawing against the grain of the wood, and (2) the *ripsaw,* for sawing with the grain of the wood. The principal difference between the two is the number of teeth to the inch. A ripsaw usually averages about 5½ to 6 teeth to the inch; a handsaw, about 7 or 8. Handsaws with 10 teeth to the inch make a smoother, more accurate cut, but are slower to work with. A handsaw can be used to cut with the grain of the wood, if necessary, but only with a good deal of work. If one must choose only a single saw, a crosscut saw with 8 teeth to the inch is probably a good selection. Lengths vary; 24- and 26-inch sizes are in general use.

Other saws include: (1) the *coping* saw, a U-shaped saw with a handle and a narrow, detachable blade; used for cutting sharp angles, curves, and scrolls; (2) the *compass* or *keyhole,* a short, narrow-bladed saw useful for starting cuts in a flat surface, or cutting out irregularly shaped holes; (3) the *backsaw* or *tenon* saw is a small crosscut saw with fine teeth (usually about 14 to the inch) and a reinforced back; useful for fine cabinet work; may be pre-

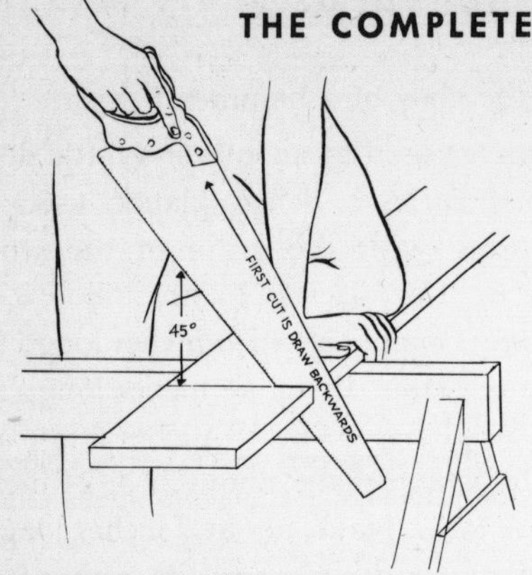

FIG. 17. The crosscut saw is held at an angle of about 45° from the surface of the work. To start the cut, draw the saw backward, steadying the blade with the thumb of the left hand. Keep the width of the blade vertical to the work surface. Old boxes make satisfactory substitutes for trestles.

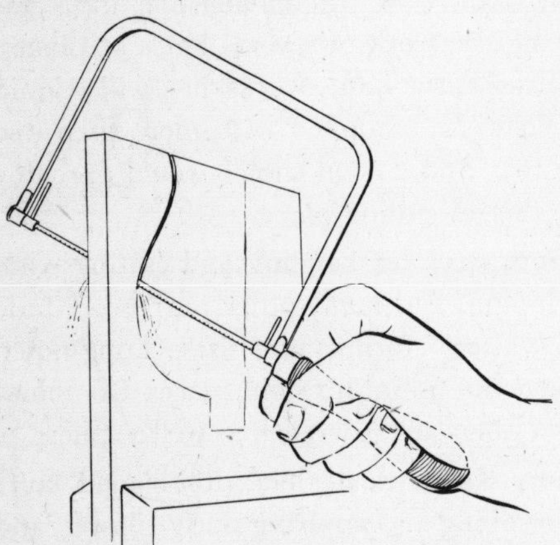

FIG. 18. The coping saw is used to cut curves, scrolls, and other irregular shapes, usually in thin wood. Blades are detachable and can be changed from coarse to fine to suit the type of work.

FIG. 19. The compass or keyhole saw is used to cut holes of various shapes. To start the cut, first drill a hole with a brace and bit or a hand drill. When working on a small piece of wood, clamp it in a vise.

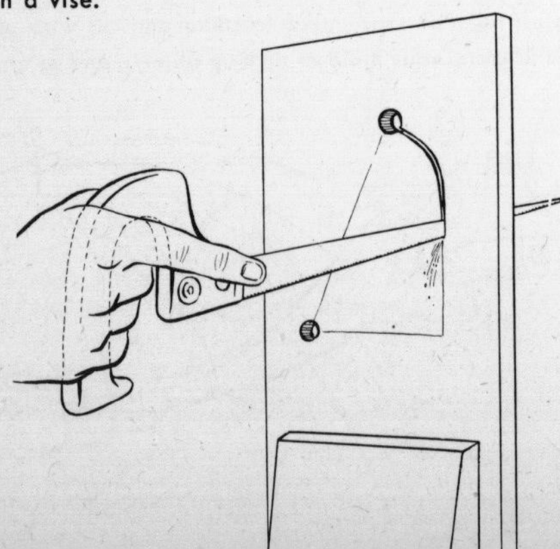

FIG. 20. To screw two pieces of wood together, first bore holes in each slightly smaller in diameter than the diameter of the screw. Use a screwdriver to fit the head of the screw. If the tip is too wide, the wood will be marred. A tip which is too small will slip out of the screw head. Hold the handle of the screwdriver firmly and press down with the palm of the hand as shown. If the screw is difficult to turn, remove it and soap the threads or enlarge the hole.

ferred to regular crosscut saw for remodeling furniture; (4) the *web* or *turning* saw consists of a thin, narrow, detachable blade secured by a frame; used for exterior curves or interior curves fairly close to the edge; (5) the *hacksaw* has narrow detachable blades; used for cutting metal.

Scraper, a wide-bladed tool, preferably with a handle, for removing paint, varnish, wallpaper, and so on.

Screwdrivers. At least three sizes are usually needed to fit various kinds of screws. In addition to the ordinary screwdrivers, there are automatic ones which turn by pressing on the handle.

Spokeshave, a small,double-handled blade for smoothing convex or concave curves in wood.

T-Bevel, an instrument with a blade and an adjustable arm for laying off or testing mitered corners or beveled edges.

Trowel, any of variously shaped tools for applying, spreading, and smoothing plastic materials. A plasterer's trowel may be useful for patching walls.

Try-Square, a tool with a blade secured to a handle at a right angle; used for testing squareness of wood blocks, joints, angles, and so on. Usual length of blade is 6 or 8 inches; should be marked off at intervals of ⅛ of an inch at least.

Vise, any of variously shaped devices with adjustable jaws for clamping wood (or

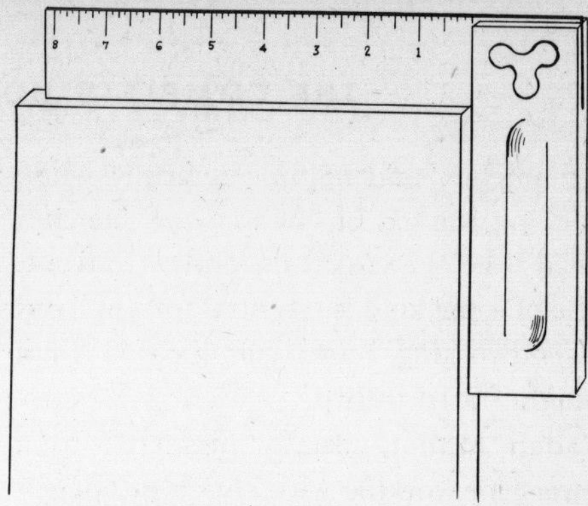

FIG. 21. The try-square is used to test the squareness of lumber, joints, and so on. To test the accuracy of a square, draw a line along one edge, turn the square over, and draw another line along the same edge. The lines will be paralleled if the square is true.

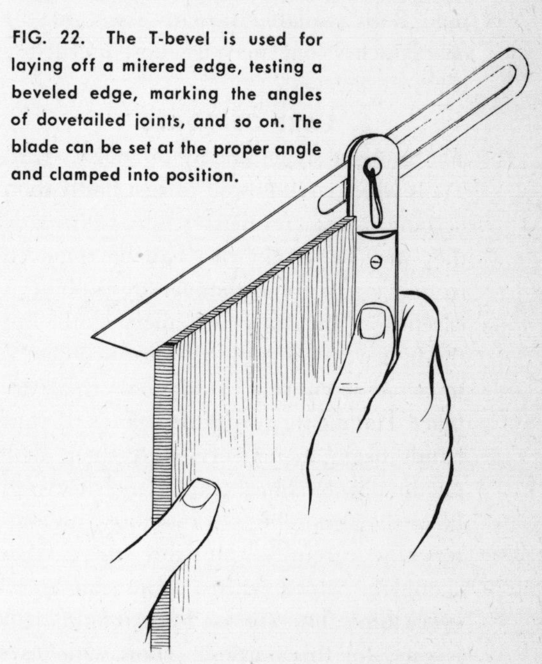

FIG. 22. The T-bevel is used for laying off a mitered edge, testing a beveled edge, marking the angles of dovetailed joints, and so on. The blade can be set at the proper angle and clamped into position.

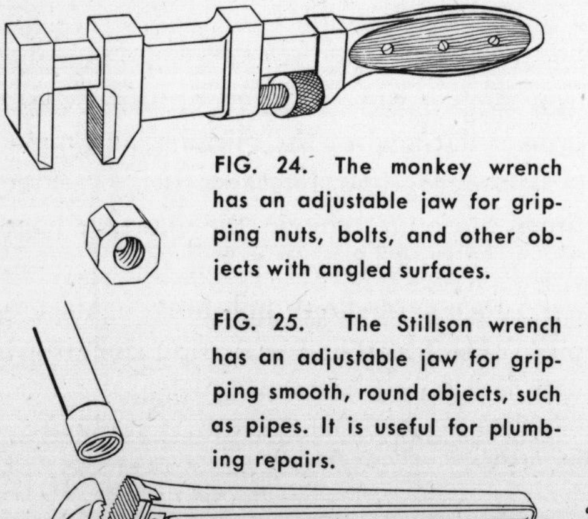

FIG. 24. The monkey wrench has an adjustable jaw for gripping nuts, bolts, and other objects with angled surfaces.

FIG. 25. The Stillson wrench has an adjustable jaw for gripping smooth, round objects, such as pipes. It is useful for plumbing repairs.

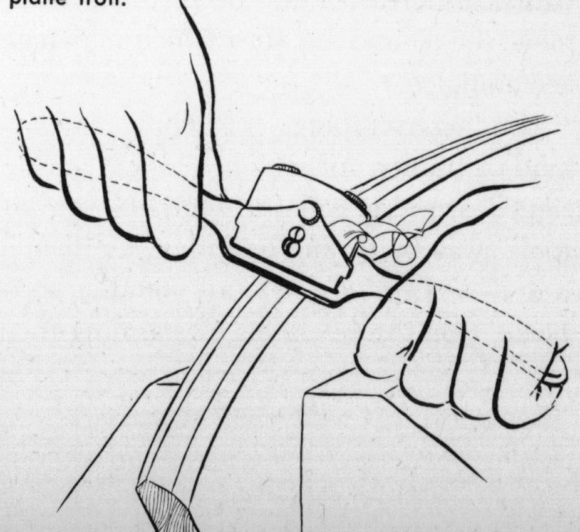

FIG. 23. The spokeshave is a kind of plane for smoothing concave or convex curved edges. Hold the spokeshave as illustrated and push the blade away from you. The blade is sharpened like a plane iron.

other objects) and holding it firmly while it is being worked on. Most work benches have at least one vise at the end or in front. A vise of some kind is essential for any kind of woodworking more complicated than sawing a board in two.

Wooden Mallet, usually preferred to a hammer for working with chisels or gouges.

Wrenches. An adjustable *monkey* wrench is a useful tool to have in every home workshop for changing washers in faucets, removing bolts, and other purposes. A *Stillson* wrench adjusts to fit and grip a round pipe. Both available in many sizes; one 10 or 12 inches long may be most useful for general purposes.

CARE OF TOOLS

The greatest single enemy of tools is rust. Tools which are allowed to rust badly soon become useless, no matter how well made they may be. Slight rust can be removed from a tool without damage by rubbing it carefully with a piece of emery cloth. But the best way to handle the rust problem is to avoid it entirely. Store tools in a dry place. Handle them with dry hands. If your hands begin to perspire, dust them with talcum powder. Since enough moisture may be in the atmosphere to rust tools, no matter how carefully you store them, they should be wiped with a light coat of oil every time they are used. Petroleum jelly is good for this purpose. Tools which are not used for any length of time should be taken out and oiled occasionally. Before using an oiled tool, wipe it off carefully with a little turpentine or kerosene to remove the oil and any dust which may have accumulated.

Bending, scraping, scratching, or any kind of friction for which a tool is not designed are also bad for tools. Never put tools away by tossing one upon another in a drawer. Don't leave a saw standing in its blade. Don't store chisels by standing them on their blades. Turn planes on their sides when they are not in use to help keep the blade sharp. Learn to use your tools efficiently and use each tool for the purpose for which it was designed. For example, if you attempt to cut a piece of metal with an ordinary crosscut saw, you will ruin the saw.

To prevent wooden handles from shrinking or warping, wipe them with linseed oil; or, if the atmosphere is very humid, *soak* them in the linseed oil.

SHARPENING TOOLS

All cutting tools must be kept sharp for efficient use. Saws are usually quite difficult for the average crafteman to sharpen at home, and therefore it is better to take them to an expert. But chisels and plane irons are not too troublesome to sharpen if a little care is exercised. Since these tools need to be sharpened fairly often as a rule, it is worth while to learn how to do it well.

To sharpen a plane iron, loosen the lever cap screw and the cam and slip out the iron. Separate the cap from the cutting iron. Pour a few drops of neat's-foot or machine oil on the oilstone. Draw the beveled cutting edge of the iron over the oilstone, holding the iron with the right hand and steadying it with the left so that the iron tilts at an angle of about 35 degrees. The edge of the iron should be diagonal to the edge of the oilstone. Move the iron backwards and forwards, always keeping it tilted at the same angle. When the iron appears to be sharpened, turn it over, press it flat against the oilstone, and move it backwards and forwards two or three times more to remove the hairline edge that may be bent over during the sharpening process. A final polishing against a piece of soft leather (or an old razor strop) will develop a keen cutting edge.

Chisels and gouges are also sharpened on

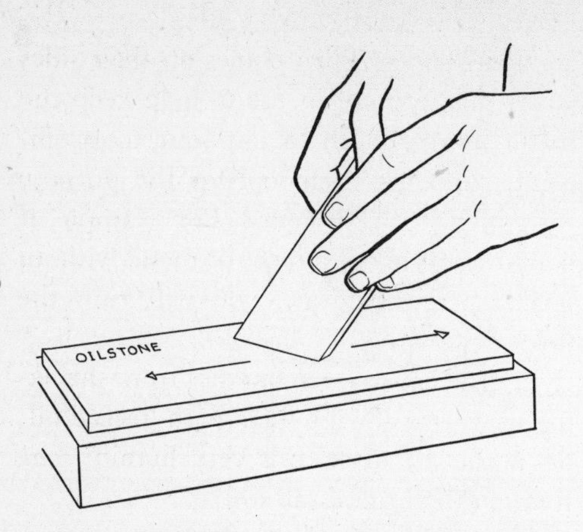

FIG. 26. To sharpen a plane iron, hold it in the position illustrated, and move it backwards and forwards, keeping the blade diagonal to the edges of the oilstone. Lubricate the oilstone with a few drops of neat's-foot or machine oil.

FIG. 27. After the iron has been sharpened, turn it over and press it flat against the oilstone. Move the iron back and forth once or twice to remove the hairline edge. A few finishing strokes on soft leather will produce a razor-sharp edge.

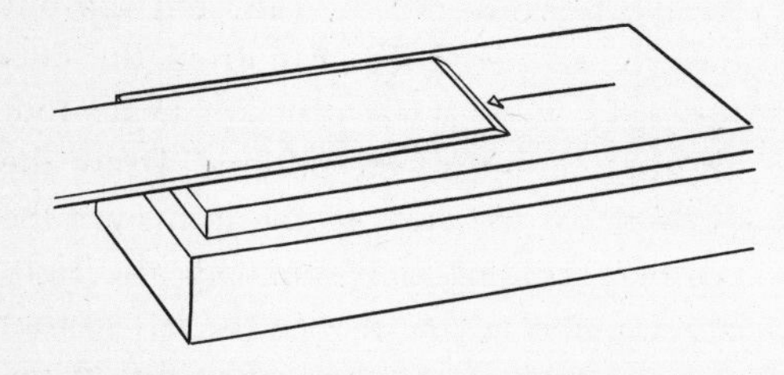

the oilstone by much the same method. A gouge, however, being rounded, must be rolled from side to side while it is being moved backwards and forwards.

The oilstone should be wiped after using and occasionally cleaned with a little kerosene.

TOOL STORAGE

Each craftsman has his own ideas as to what is the most convenient way of storing tools. A few general points should be kept in mind, however. Keep those tools which are used most often within easy reach. The wall above a work table is one of the most accessible places. Hooks, racks, fitted slots, or any other type of holder may be used to support the tools, so long as the support is firm. It should also yield the tool easily when it is needed.

A work bench or work table is greatly to be desired if the space for it can possibly be found. In fact, a good craftsman deserves a room to himself (or herself) where work can be carried on without disturbance to the rest of the family (or to the worker). A simple, ready-made work bench is not expensive, and nearly every kind of old kitchen or library table, kitchen cabinet. or even a desk can be easily converted into a work table or made to do duty as one.

If space is simply not a available for a work table, tools may be stored in a tool kit. Well designed tool kits can be bought for a small amount of money. Or a drawer or two can be set aside to keep tools in. Drawers used for this purpose should be sectioned off so that each tool has its own compartment and is in no danger of sliding on top of another when the drawer is pushed shut. Slotted pieces of wood may be fastened to the bottom of the drawer to keep small tools in place.

Shallow drawers or trays divided into small sections are useful for storing nails, screws, and other small items of hardware. Another method of storage is to place such articles in small, screw-topped glass jars. The contents of the jars are easily visible when they are lined up on shallow shelves.

Drills, bits and other small tools should be kept in cases wherever possible. Cases to fit drills and bits of various sizes are not expensive.

A good light above the work table is of the utmost importance. A light on a traveling crane, adjustable to various heights, is a good arrangement.

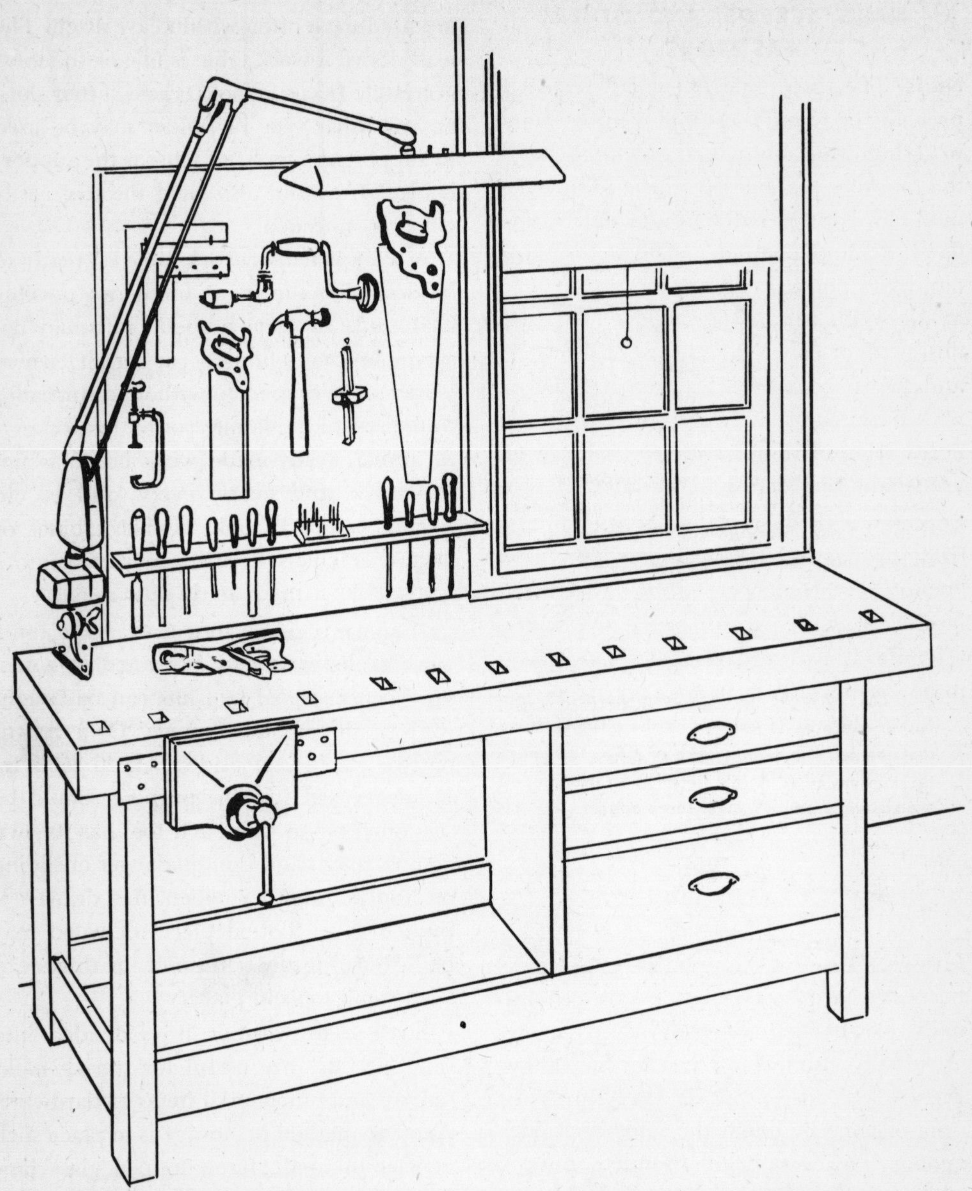

FIG. 28. A good work bench makes any home craftsman more efficient. Each tool should be kept in its own place, and adequate storage space in the form of drawers or shelves should be provided for nails, screws, tacks, miscellaneous hardware, and other supplies. Good lighting is essential. The work bench shown here is equipped with a fluorescent lamp on an adjustable arm which can be moved into any position over the bench. If one does not care to invest in a ready-made work bench, any solidly built table or a cabinet of the right height will serve as an adequate substitute. If space cannot be spared for any kind of a work bench, store the tools in a tool chest, closet, or drawers where they cannot scratch each other.

NAILS, SCREWS, AND OTHER FASTENERS

Nails. The three types of nails which will probably be found most useful in the home workshop are known as the *common* nail, the *finishing* nail, and the *brad*. The common nail is the familiar round nail with a flat head and pointed end. The finishing nail has a pointed end but almost no head at all. With a nail set, it may be driven flush with or below the surface of the wood and the space above can then be filled in with putty or plastic wood so that little or no marring of the surface is visible. Brads are simply small finishing nails.

Common and finishing nails vary in size from twopenny to fortypenny. The term "penny" is frequently abbreviated "d" (for the English sign for pence or pennies, after the Latin word, *denarius*). Approximate lengths of various sizes are:

2d	1 inch	9d	2¾ inches
3d	1¼ inches	10d	3 "
4d	1½ "	12d	3¼ "
5d	1¾ "	16d	3½ "
6d	2 "	20d	4 "
7d	2¼ "	30d	4½ "
8d	2½ "	40d	5 "

Screws. Where greater holding power is necessary, screws may often be preferred to nails. Flat-headed and oval-headed screws are usually countersunk, and the hole above the screw head is then filled with putty or

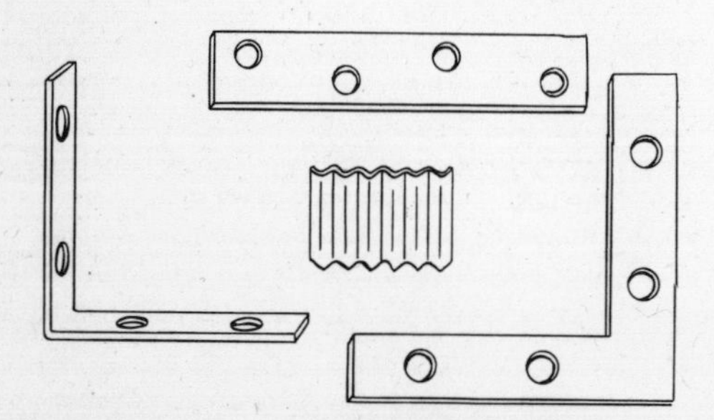

FIG. 32. A supply of angle irons, corner irons, mending plates, and corrugated fasteners in various sizes will serve many purposes.

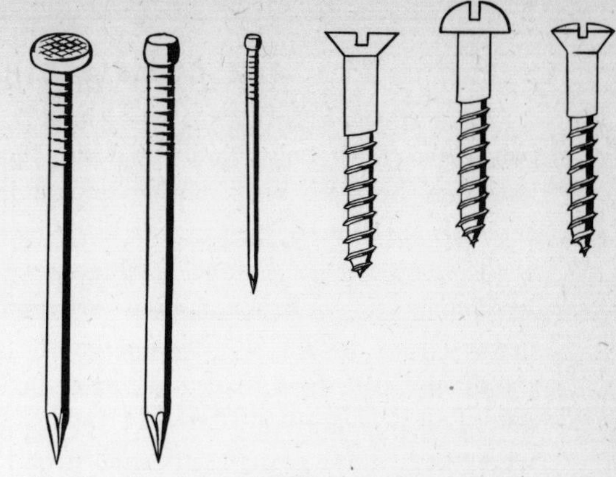

FIG. 29. (from left to right) A common nail, a finishing nail, a brad, a flat-headed screw, a round-headed screw, and an oval-headed screw.

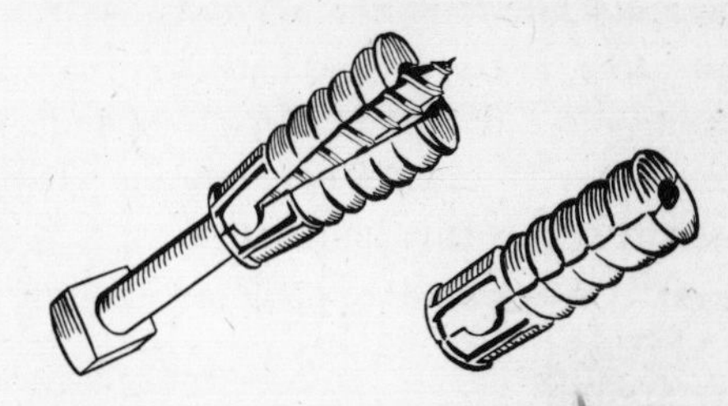

FIG. 30. A toggle bolt is useful for attaching heavy objects to solid brick or masonry walls. Drill a hole in the wall to fit the diameter of the bolt. Insert the bolt until the head is flush with the wall. As the head is turned, the toggle wings expand and hold the bolt fast.

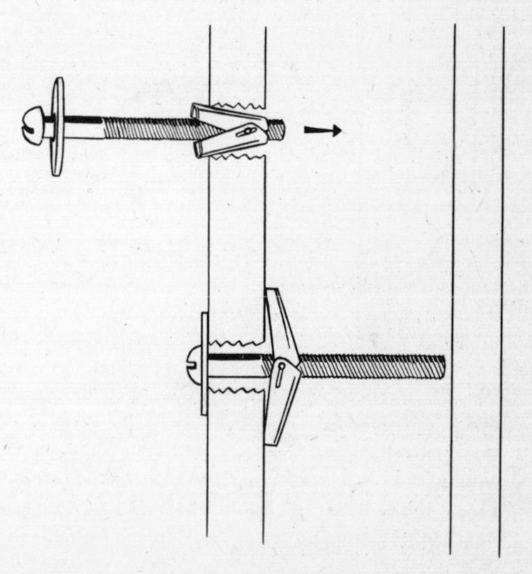

FIG. 31. A split-wing toggle screw can be used to attach heavy objects to a plaster wall. Drill a hole in the wall to fit the screw and insert it. The toggle wings expand, move up the screw threads, and lock against the back of the lath.

plastic wood. In fine cabinet making, the hole may be filled with a plug of wood, carefully cut and selected to match the rest of the wood surface. Round-headed screws are not counter-sunk. When screws are used in hardwood, a hole slightly smaller than the diameter of the threads must be drilled first. This procedure must also be followed when large screws are used in softwood. Select screws of the proper size for the job at hand. In order to hold securely, the screw should be long enough so that at least half of its length will be imbedded in the joining piece of wood. Special expanding screws may be used in plaster walls where a secure grip is essential.

Tacks. Various kinds of tacks are useful for many purposes about the house. A supply of No. 4 carpet tacks and thumb tacks should be kept on hand. Brass-headed upholstery tacks are used for many reupholstery jobs.

Other Fasteners. Angle irons, corner irons, and mending plates are used in conjunction with nails or screws to reinforce as well as to fasten. They come in various sizes for every purpose.

Corrugated cleats are useful for fastening butt joints and sometimes for reinforcing other types of joints.

For hanging pictures, there are small nails with a reinforcing piece which enables the nail to withstand much greater weight than it could otherwise hold.

II

DECORATING YOUR ROOMS

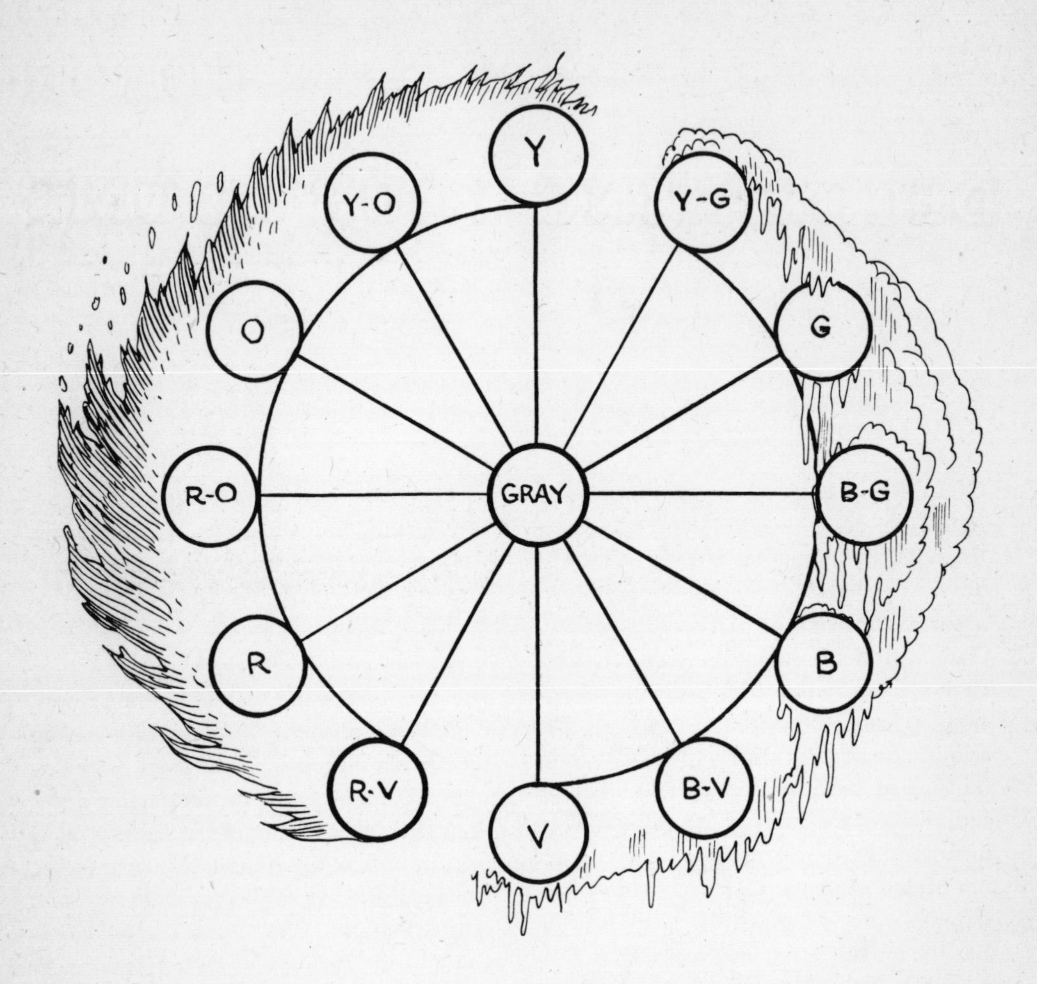

FIG. 1. Colors are classified as being either warm or cool. The blues and greens are the coolest of the cool colors, and the reds and oranges are the warmest of the warm. Warm and cool colors lend contrast to one another.

CHAPTER IV

COLOR AND PATTERN

COLORS have the power to stimulate the mind, to relax, or even to depress it. Sometimes colors may affect us in a pleasant or adverse manner because they remind us of a particular event or place which we associate with some happy or unhappy experience. Even without such special associations, science shows that we are all, consciously or unconsciously, affected by color. This is so because visible light — or the light which the human eye is capable of distinguishing — is composed of all the colors of the rainbow, and each has its own definite wave length. Red, for example, has the longest wave length of all. It is the warmest of the "warm" colors, and hence the most stimulating. It is not by accident that red stands for danger.

Since color does have such an important psychological effect, the color schemes of our homes ought to receive the most careful consideration. But we don't have to be experts in the science of color for this. And remember, personal taste is one of the best guides as to whether a color scheme is "right" or "wrong." If you like a color scheme and instinctively feel at home with it, then it's "right" for you. However, all too often we visualize some color scheme in our mind, and then when we have actually applied it to a room, we do not like it at all. Gradually it begins to get on our nerves, and we do not know quite why. Perhaps, then, it might be worth while to learn a few facts about color.

The Color Wheel. Color, in its purest form, is seen only in light, when it is broken up by a prism into its separate parts, or colors, to form the spectrum. In nature, tiny drops of water in the atmosphere can act as a prism to break up sunlight — and then we see the rainbow. Objects about us look red, yellow, blue, or any other color because of the presence of certain substances called pigments, which have the power to absorb some parts of light and to repel others. When pigments are mixed, the new combination admits other parts. If pigments could be obtained which would absorb nothing but true red, yellow, and blue, they could be mixed to produce every other color of the spectrum. Actually, however, such pigments do not exist. But for all practical purposes the colors we see in pigments are pure red, yellow, or blue, and therefore, they are known as *primary* colors.

Theoretically, the primary colors can be mixed to form other colors in various ways.

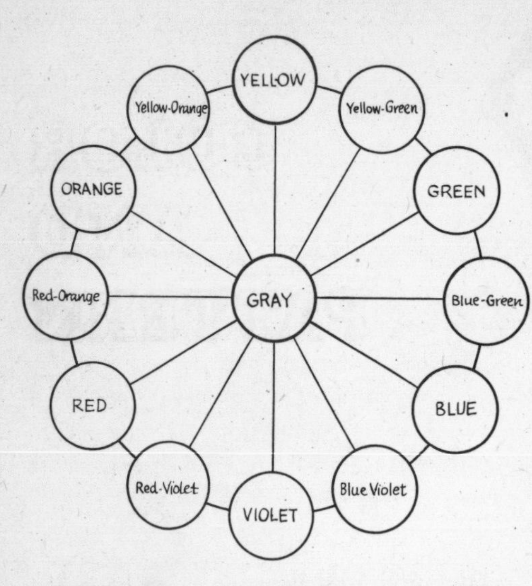

FIG. 2. The color wheel, showing primary, secondary, and intermediate hues. Colors lying opposite each other are complementary. Those lying side by side are analogous. Complementary colors gray each other when mixed.

When blue is mixed with yellow, green is formed. Green, therefore, is called a *secondary* color. Other secondary colors are orange (a mixture of red and yellow), and violet (a mixture of blue and red). On the color wheel, these primary and secondary colors are arranged as illustrated because they have a definite relationship to each other. For example, red is opposite green, because when these two colors are combined they gray each other. Therefore, they equalize, or complement, each other, and so are called *complementary* colors. In the same way, yellow is the complement of violet and blue is the complement of orange. In pure form, the mixture of all these colors would produce black, which has the power to absorb all the colors of the spectrum. Pure white, on the other hand, absorbs none of them. These facts are important because they mean that certain colors absorb more light, and consequently more heat, than do others. White, therefore, actually absorbs less heat than black, and the choice of light colors for summer clothes is based on a sound reason.

Pure colors, meaning colors which are not grayed, lightened, or darkened, are called *hues.* All colors of pure value lying intermediate between the primary and secondary colors are also hues, and each has its complement. Thus, yellow-green is the complement of red-violet, while red-orange is the complement of blue-green, and so on. The secondary colors on each side of any primary color are said to be *analogous* to it. For example, yellow is analogous to both green and orange. Any intermediate hues are also analogous — red-orange to red, blue-green to blue.

Now, let us visualize the color wheel as having a cone at either side (as illustrated in Fig. 3). To end of one cone represents white, and the end of the other, black. All the different colors which result when black is mixed in various degrees with any hue are called *shades.* But when white is mixed with any hue, the resulting colors are called *tints.* Besides being mixed with black and white, hues can also be mixed in every possible combination with each other to form a practically limitless variety of hues, tints, and shades.

The colors lying on the blue side of the color wheel are called *cool* colors. They include, besides blue, blue-violet, blue-green, and green, and any hues in between. The warm colors are those on the red side of the color wheel, such as red-violet, red-orange, orange, and yellow-orange. Most yellows are classed as warm colors, but yellow-greens are on the cool side. Tones of violet in which pink or red predominate are warm colors, while those with more blue are cool.

Complementary Color Schemes. Two complementary colors placed side by side will intensify each other. When both the colors are hues, the degree of intensification is generally too great to be pleasing, if the colors are used in large areas or where they constantly meet the eye. But if one or both of the hues is reduced to a shade or a tint or is grayed by its complement, the effect is much more satisfactory. For example, let us imagine that we are planning a complementary color scheme for a living room, and that the colors we have chosen are red and green. Can you visualize the effect that would be produced if we painted the walls a brilliant emerald hue and covered the floor with the brightest Turkey red carpet? Almost anyone would be jarred by such a combination. Both the walls and the floor are large areas. Therefore, if we use a hue on either one it may be too stimulating in a room which is used a great deal (although hues are sometimes employed on floors in modern treatments). We can use tints or shades of either color, or we can introduce a third tint or shade. Now let us imagine that we have selected a soft shade of gray-green for the walls and a slightly deeper shade of gray-green for the carpet. In order to prevent such large areas of green from becoming monotonous, we decide to introduce generous amounts of white, which always adds sparkle to a color scheme, and some bright yellow-green for further contrast. We select a bold fabric for drapes which has a white background printed with brilliant red flowers, green leaves, and just a hint of yellow-green. We repeat this fabric in the slipcover of a chair and the sofa, and emphasize the red in the print with a bright red cushion at each end. We can repeat any of these colors in a plain fabric to cover another chair. Further accents are supplied by white Venetian blinds, a white scatter rug before the fireplace, brilliant red lamp bases with white shades, smaller accessory decorations in white and yellow-green, pictures which accent the colors of the room, and green plants.

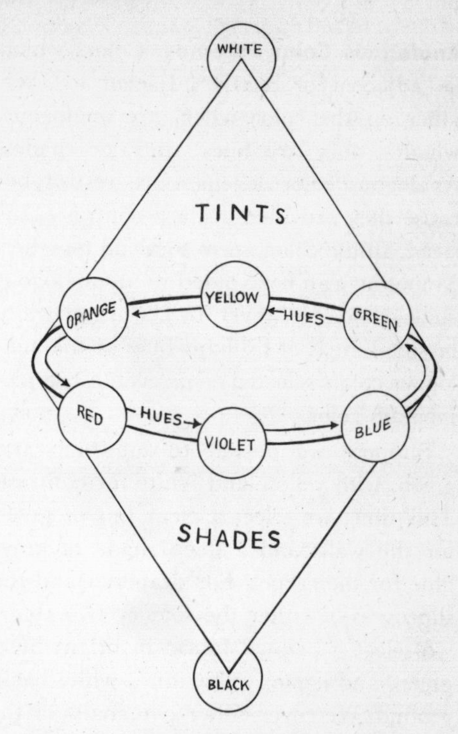

FIG. 3. The color cone indicates the value of a color. Pure colors of full intensity are called hues. A hue mixed with white becomes a tint, while hues mixed with black are shades. Tints or shades may be of any degree of intensity.

The possible ways in which such a color scheme could be developed are almost endless. As another variation, we could for example, begin again with a soft shade of gray-green for the walls. But this time we select a rug in a soft shade of reddish brown for the floor. We use a slightly deeper more brilliant green for two chair covers. For the sofa and the drapes we select a fabric with a green background to match the walls, but printed in white, beige, deeper green, and clear red, slightly on the yellowish side. For other chair covers we use a beige (which, in this case, really happens to be a tint of the same color as that which appears in the carpet). Accessories provide bright-colored accents.

Analogous Color Schemes. Colors which lie adjacent or nearly adjacent to each other on the color wheel are analogous, whether they are hues, tints, or shades. Analogous color schemes are restful because they provide no sharp contrasts. Instead, all the colors seem to blend together. Monotony can be avoided in an analogous color scheme, however, by accents of white or small areas of brilliant hues of the analogous colors selected — or even a complementary color.

Suppose we decide to use blue and green, with yellow and white for contrast. This time, we select a clear tint of green for the walls and a deep shade of gray-blue for the carpet. For draperies and the slipcovers of either the sofa or two chairs we select a printed fabric in bright blue, green, and lemon yellow on a white background. We cover either two chairs or the sofa in a deep, bright shade of blue. Sparkle is provided in accessory furnishings and pictures in brilliant hues of green, yellow, and perhaps a bit of blue.

Sometimes analogous color schemes are much more closely related than this, and might even be said to verge on monotone schemes. For example, such a scheme might include brown, beige, white, and yellow; or brown, beige, white and pink (which is a tint of red). Since brown is a mixture of both red and yellow (as well as blue), such color schemes are very closely related.

How to Use Patterns. Patterns add interest to a decorating scheme. They break the monotony of large, plain areas. They may be bold and vivid or so indefinite as to amount to little more than textured effects. Some patterns can also do tricks because of dominant lines which divert the eye. But, oh my, how awful patterns can be when they are wrongly used!

Pattern, of course, can be used almost anywhere you choose to put it. *But* — too much pattern in too many places, or too many different patterns, and the result is confusion. In other words, a little pattern sometimes goes much further than you think.

A great deal of skill is required to combine a number of patterns in one room and keep them all under control. Therefore, it might be well to use just one or two patterns — or at the most three, depending on how definite they are. A bold, definite pattern may be so dominant that a second pattern cannot be introduced without causing a clash.

Let's begin with the floor. If we cover it with a fairly bold patterned carpet, then we should keep the slipcover or upholstery fabrics plain. A small monochromatic print might be used in the drapes or they could be trimmed in some way to add interest above the floor level. On the other hand, if bold patterned wallpaper is used, the floor covering should be plain and so should the drapes. But a small indefinite stripe might appear in some of the slipcover or upholstery fabrics. If a bold print is used for draperies and repeated in some slipcovers or upholstery, then the walls and floor covering should be plain. On the other hand, both drapes and wallpaper *could* have pattern if both were not too definite, and preferably if one were a monotone print. The same would be true if pattern were used in both carpet and drapes.

If one is not quite sure about pattern, then these might be good rules to follow: (1) if you select a very bold, splashy pattern, do not use it in too large an area, and do not use any other patterns with it; (2) if you are using a definite but not too bold pattern, you can use a second pattern in the same room, if the second pattern is fairly indefinite and repeats some colors in the first pattern; (3) if the principal pattern is fairly indefinite, it might be combined with two even more indefinite patterns, providing all three bear some color relationship. You would not, however, select them only for upholstery. Instead, they would appear on walls or floors and perhaps on some of the upholstery or drapes as well.

Fabric, wallpaper, or rug patterns can also set the keynote for the color scheme of your entire room. Select one in a print you like and from it choose your two major plain colors and a minor accent color. The plain colors need not match the colors in the print exactly. They may be either slightly lighter or darker, as long as they blend harmoniously. An indefinite monotone print can often be treated as a plain color.

Scale should play an important part in choice of patterns. Small rooms call for small scaled patterns. Only large rooms can accommodate large repeat motifs. Definite patterns on the wall make the walls appear to advance. Light neutral colors or tints make the walls appear to recede.

Light Affects Color. Colors change their values according to the amount or kind of light under which they appear. Reds and blue-greens are particularly subject to change. A reddish violet may look quite different under artificial light than it does under daylight. It is well, therefore, to examine samples of fabrics, wallpapers, and rugs under both artificial light and daylight before making any final selections. Examine all the materials to be used in a room in combination.

The exposure of the room determines the quality of daylight it receives. Rooms with southern or southwestern exposures receive sunny, warm light which has a great deal of yellow in it. Windows facing north or northeast admit the cool, clear, steady north light. According to decorating rules, rooms receiving cold north or northeastern light should be decorated in warm colors in light tones, while rooms with southern or southwestern exposures should have cool colors, which may, if you prefer, be in darker tones. This theory is based on the fact that warm light tends to equalize cool colors and vice versa. A cool or very neutral color becomes even cooler or more neutral under cold light. And slate grays become almost menacing. However, while it's a good thing to keep these facts in mind, it's no decorating crime to toss the "rules" away if it suits your purpose to do so. You may love green but feel quite liverish if you have to look at yellows or pinks. And yet your apartment faces north. Must you, then, give up green? Of course not! In fact, some people find the cool, luminous quality which gray-green assumes under north light to be restful and quite lovely. On the other hand, warm light on warm colors may be exhilarating.

Color and Proportion. Cool colors appear to recede and warm ones to advance. Dark colors also seem to advance more than light colors. Therefore, a too-high ceiling can be made to appear lower by painting it in a darker tone than the wall color. A color lighter than that used on the walls will make the ceiling appear higher. Dark walls will make a small room appear smaller.

A narrow room can be made to appear wider by painting one end wall in a darker color than that used on the side walls. The same trick will make a square room seem longer than it is wide.

Color can be used to minimize architectural defects. If the woodwork is badly designed or chops the room into irregular wall areas, paint the walls and the woodwork in the same color. Unlovely objects become much less noticeable when they assume the color of their background. For example, a radiator or a badly proportioned piece of furniture which is painted to match the wall seems to melt into the background.

Vertical patterns appear to add height and horizontal patterns to add width. Wallpaper with vertical stripes will make the walls seem higher. The horizontal lines of a Venetian blind will make a narrow window appear wider. In a small room with high ceilings use as many horizontal lines as possible. The horizontal lines of bookshelves help.

Matching Colors. When you have decided upon the color scheme for a room and worked it out in detail, collect color samples in fabrics or papers. Take these with you whenever you shop. Select samples of all fabrics, carpeting, wallpaper, or paint colors, and compare them together critically before making any final choice. Color matching can sometimes be a very tedious task. A plain green fabric which appears to match the green in a print during daylight may develop a bluish cast under artificial light. Prints which look gay against one background may seem quite drab and characterless against another.

Sometimes retailers have groups of fabrics dyed and printed to order so that they will all blend or match harmoniously. One of the most far-reaching schemes to assure perfect matching or harmonizing is that called the Basic Home Furnishings Color Co-ordination Plan. Under this plan, more than 270 manufacturers of carpets, upholstery and slipcover fabrics, paints, wallpaper, and other home furnishing materials supply their merchandise in various tones of nine standard colors. These colors have all been given names, which are Alamo Tan, Grand Canyon Rose, Adirondack Burgundy, Great Lakes Blue, Great Smoky Gray, Prairie Mauve, Cape Cod Beige, Santa Fe Cedar, and Shennandoah Green. Each color comes in eight tones which range in value from dark to light. These may be combined in a great variety of ways, and a blending color scheme is almost guaranteed to result. Merchandise which comes in any of these colors bears a label to that effect so that one can be sure of a perfect match or blend. In making use of such a plan, one need not be limited to the colors selected by the manufacturers. With careful planning, they can be combined with other colors too. But any one who has trudged wearily from shop to shop, clutching a handful of color swatches and trying to match them in vain, will certainly welcome any plan calculated to make shopping less of an effort.

SUGGESTED COLOR SCHEMES

Type of Room	Exposure	Floors	Walls and Woodwork	Ceiling	Draperies or Curtains	Slipcover, Upholstery, or Other Fabrics	Furniture	Accessories
Informal living room; no definite period	North and east	Polished dark wood and large braided rugs in beige and brown with red and yellow	Soft shade of yellow	Same as walls, but lighter in tone	Ruffled tie-back drapes of glazed chintz in all-over print of yellow, rose-red, white, and green on brown	Same fabric as draperies; also rose-red fabric printed with tiny flower sprigs in cream and yellow fabric	Several periods combined; or French provincial or simple modern	Brilliant red accents in lamp bases, ash trays; natural parchment shades; bright flower prints matted on soft brown; green plants
Early American living room	Southwest	Hooked rugs in floral or small geometric patterns on dark polished wood floor	Scenic wallpaper with indistinct print in tones of green and yellow on cream background; woodwork painted cream	Cream	Sheer, ruffled cream-colored tie-back curtains edged in rust color	Soft shade of green with yellow cording; light rust printed in tiny, pale yellow, geometric design	Maple; early American	Flower prints; bright green or yellow accents in lamps, ashtrays
Formal eighteenth-century living room	North and west	All-over carpeting in deep gold tone	Wallpaper printed in gold, gray blue, and white on pale beige background; woodwork painted to match background	White	Overdraperies of beige satin damask trimmed in blue; sheer white glass curtains	Gold and beige striped satin; gray-blue damask or velvet	Mahogany; eighteenth century	Gilded wall brackets; gold-framed mirrors and pictures; brilliant blue porcelain lamp bases with beige silk shades.
Modern living room	South and east	Gunmetal gray all-over carpeting; white contour rug	Walls painted gunmetal gray, slightly lighter than carpet; white woodwork	White	Glazed chintz in brilliant, bold pattern of chartreuse and green on white	Chartreuse; bright geranium pink; drapery fabric may be repeated	Bleached; modern	Plants; large pictures in which geranium pink is repeated; mirrors; brilliant green accents
Dining room; no definite period	Northeast	Warm, medium brown all-over carpeting	Gay floral print in red, yellow, green, and brown, on cream background	Cream	Glazed chintz in light brown; valance edged in red and yellow	Ruby red on chair seats	Walnut	Yellow or red may be repeated in table setting
Young girl's bedroom	Southeast	Light gray carpeting	Walls, light gray-blue; woodwork, white	White	Sheer, white, glass curtains; overdrapes with floral print of rose, blue, green, and tan, on white background	Gray-blue, white trim; bedspread same fabric as drapes; white dressing-table skirt with rose-red bows	Mahogany or walnut	Rose-red, bright blue, and white in lamps, pictures, ornaments
Modern bedroom	East	Light brown all-over carpeting	Paneled in bleached oak, or covered with wallpaper printed to simulate bleached oak	Same as walls	Dusty pink with bold, modern scroll print in white and mauve-pink; white glass curtains	Dusty pink, banded with drapery fabric	Bleached oak	Brown lamp bases, white shades; green plants, emerald green and bright pink in pictures, ornaments
Neo-Victorian living room or bedroom	North and west	All-over carpeting in floral pattern; dominant tones: plum, raspberry, and pink	Wallpaper printed in pink and mauve shadow stripes	Pale pink	Plum satin damask trimmed in raspberry; embroidered white net or lace glass curtains	Plum satin damask trimmed in mauve; raspberry satin trimmed with pink taffeta swags	Mahogany; bleached mahogany and rosewood; marble-topped tables	Gilt or crystal wall brackets; artificial flowers under glass bells; pink shells; brilliant blue- or red-violet accents in lamp bases, ornaments

CHAPTER V

FURNITURE

FURNITURE, as everyone knows, is a major investment. And like any other major investment, it should be carefully studied before buying. Too often the selection is based primarily on style and price. Both are considered important, and rightly so, but function and quality should demand just as much attention. Of course, we would all like to possess the finest furniture that can be made. But few of us can afford to do so. Yet cheap, low-grade furniture is seldom worth in wear, comfort, or style even its correspondingly smaller cost. What to do? Admittedly, some compromise must be made on some point, but which one is something that each homemaker must solve personally. Some people prefer to buy one or two very good pieces at a time and add to them whenever the budget permits. In the meantime, they "fill in" with less expensive items. This is a good idea if too much money isn't invested in the "fill in" furniture, and if the contrast between the good pieces and the cheaper ones isn't so great as to appear distinctly inharmonious. Others prefer to buy second-hand furniture and then to replace an entire roomful of such pieces from time to time. Very often well made but badly designed furniture can be bought very cheaply and either restyled at home or disguised with paint. But one who expects to live in a city for only a short while may have no time either to hunt for second-hand furniture or to restyle it. In that case, he will probably do better to buy medium or even low-grade furniture, if suitable furnished accommodations are unavailable.

But first, let's study a few facts about furniture construction. Too few people know what to expect for their money's worth in this respect.

CONSTRUCTION

Woods. For long and satisfactory service, furniture should be made of solid hardwood, plywood, or veneer. Solid soft woods are easily dented and often subject to warping or swelling. Hardwoods include not only the expensive kinds such as mahogany, walnut, and oak, but also the less expensive gumwood or maple. Furniture made entirely of wood (as opposed to upholstered pieces) are called in the trade *case goods.*

Much fine furniture is made of solid hardwood and is priced accordingly. But more often thin sheets of hardwood are welded to a less expensive hardwood or even a soft wood. This process of combining woods is called *veneering.* When several layers of wood (usually anywhere from three to seven) are welded together, the product is called *plywood.* Plywood can be molded into various shapes.

Originally, the purpose of veneering one wood to another was to produce furniture which simulated in appearance that made of costly solid hardwood. Veneer still serves this purpose, but it is also used to give strength. Formerly, the methods of gluing did not always produce perfect adhesion, and the thin top layer of wood often warped or curled from its base. As a result, veneer acquired the reputation of being only a cheap imitation. But thanks to modern methods of manufacture, any unfavorable attitude towards veneer has now largely disappeared. Actually, good veneer is stronger than solid wood and less apt to warp. Also, a veneer surface usually presents a finer pattern in the wood than the poorer qualities of solid hardwoods. For large surfaces, such as table tops, veneer is usually preferable to solid wood. (*Note: A table listing the principal kinds of woods used in furniture will be found at the end of this chapter.*)

Joints and Other Details. In well made furniture, the parts are fitted together with mortise and tenant, doweling, or dovetailed joints. (*See chapter on Repair and Restyling of Furniture.*) The joints should be carefully constructed to fit together perfectly. They are glued for strength, and, in the case of a mortise and tenon or dowel, sometimes reinforced with screws as well. Chair seats are reinforced with corner blocks. In cheap, poorly constructed furniture, the parts are merely joined with nails, screws, or glue. Furniture made in this way is no stronger than its joints. Be sure to examine joint construction when you buy furniture. You will not be able to see doweling or a mortise and tenon, but if all parts fit together smoothly without any evidence of nails, glue, or screws on the surface, and if the wood is of good quality and well finished, you may be reasonably sure that the piece is not jerry built. If the piece has drawers, pull them out. Are the bottom and sides of the drawer smooth and well finished? Sometimes they are now made in one piece with molded plywood so that corners are rounded for easy cleaning. The front panel should be joined to the sides with dovetailing. The drawer should slide easily on smooth tracks, and when shut, no openings should show. Take the drawers out. Are there wood panels between drawer spaces to protect from dust? These almost always found in really well built pieces. Ask the dealer questions. A reliable dealer will not misrepresent facts about construction, and most such dealers are even anxious to explain them. It is only the merchant of questionable standards who does not want to have his wares examined too closely.

Finish. All fine furniture is finished to a smooth, lustrous glow on exposed surfaces. The finish may be shellac, varnish, or oil, well rubbed to a soft, satiny sheen. Cheaply finished furniture has a too-bright glare. As a general rule, fine woods are left in their natural colors, although they may also be either bleached or stained. If stained, it is only to deepen the natural color slightly. Avoid less expensive hardwoods that are stained to resemble more expensive ones. For example, gumwood is sometimes stained to look like mahogany. If you have doubts, examine the grain closely. Mahogany has an open grain (but not quite so open as oak), while the grain of gumwood cannot be seen without a magnifying glass. This does not mean that gumwood is unsatisfactory for use in furniture. On the contrary, it gives excellent service if it is well seasoned. But it has peculiar color markings which some (but by no means all) people find rather unsightly. For this reason, it is often used in unexposed parts. And in good furniture, all unexposed parts are also smoothly finished. Examine the sides and interior surfaces of drawers, the undersides of chair panels, and so on. If they are rough, you may be sure that the piece is of inferior quality.

Cheaper woods are used for painted furniture, since color and graining are unimportant. It should, however, be priced accordingly. Furniture with shadings or stenciled decoration are often garish and less to be desired than plain painted pieces.

Decoration. Any carving should be of good design and cleanly and sharply cut from solid wood. Veneer, of course, cannot be satisfactorily carved, but in cheap furniture, separate carving or molded wood decorations are sometimes glued on. These can rarely fool even the inexperienced. Avoid them like the plague. Not only are they apt to fall off, but they are in poor taste.

Another form of decorating is to inlay the surface of one wood with small pieces of other woods of various colors to form a pattern. This process is called *marquetry* (or sometimes *parquetry,* although this term is usually applied to floors of inlaid woods). Good marquetry in any design more elaborate than a narrow, straight border is work which calls for the highest skill. Thus, furniture with such decoration is usually quite costly. Marquetry is seldom used in modern furniture.

Painting is a very old method of decorating furniture — in fact, the ancient Egyptians practiced the art. It does, however, require more or less artistic skill (depending on the style of the decoration) to be effective. Hence, it is a hand process whereby each piece receives individual treatment. Pieces with good painted decoration are apt to be rather expensive. Don't confuse hand-painted decoration with stenciled designs, which seldom show any artistic qualities.

Metal mountings usually serve a utilitarian purpose (drawer pulls, for example), but they may also be purely decorative (such as ormolu). Again, they should be well designed and smoothly finished. Cheap metal mountings are sometimes simply stamped out on a die press and have rough edges which may cut the fingers.

Upholstery. The process of manufacturing an upholstered piece of furniture begins with a wood frame. It should be of hardwood (usually fine hardwood for the exposed parts and structural hardwood for the concealed parts) and the joints and methods of finishing are the same as those used in case goods. Strips of strong jute webbing material are then laced across the back, seat, and arms (wooden slats are occasionally used, but then the chair is less resilient). Next comes a covering of burlap, and then the springs, which should be close enough together to support the weight of the body evenly but not so close as to snag each other. In most well made chairs, this means from nine to twelve springs in one seat. Stout twine is used to tie the springs vertically, horizontally, and diagonally in both directions. Since each spring is tied on both sides by each twine, it is held securely in place by knots at eight points. The springs are then covered with burlap which is tacked to the frame. On top of this burlap goes the stuffing. The best stuffing is long, curled horsehair, but in medium-grade furniture it may be combined with moss. In furniture of poor quality, the stuffing may be excelsior, kapok, cocoa fiber, straw, cotton, or even sawdust or old rags. In good construction, the stuffing is covered with burlap, stitched together with the first layer of burlap, and then another layer of stuffing is added.

All curves and edges are padded with layers or rolls of cotton felt so that the finished chair will hold its shape. Next comes a covering of muslin, carefully fitted, and the covering for the underside of the chair to hide the webbing. The final covering of upholstery fabric goes on top of the muslin, and should be sleekly fitted, well seamed, evenly placed, and of good quality. (*For information on upholstery fabrics, see the chapter on Fabrics.*)

And how can you know whether the springs are properly tied and whether a chair is stuffed with horsehair or excelsior? The answer is, you can't (unless your state has a law requiring a contents label). Fancy carvings (usually of poor design and workmanship) and deceptively rich-looking fabrics (which may actually be of poor quality) are often used to distract the eye from poor construction. Some indication can be gained by observation and comparison of pieces in different price brackets. But the best way is to ask details of the merchant, and to buy from stores of known reputation. Of course, well made upholstered pieces cost more than those of inferior quality, but the difference in the long run may actually prove to be a saving. The stuffing in poorly made pieces is not anchored to the burlap (or no burlap at all is used). The chair soon loses its shape. The muslin undercover may be omitted, in which case the stuffing pops out as soon as the upholstery fabric becomes threadbare. The springs are not properly tied and soon work loose.

Quite different in construction is upholstered furniture made from foam rubber. This rubber takes the place of both springs and stuffing and is long wearing and has a lasting resiliency.

Above all, a chair should be comfortable. By all means sit in the chair before you buy it to find out if the arms and the seat are of the right height and whether the back is comfortable. And don't forget that if a chair is to be especially used by any member of the family, he or she should be the one to do the testing. Big chairs are not necessarily the most comfortable ones.

Design is important, too, but it may not always be an indication of quality since badly designed pieces are sometimes of the best construction.

QUALITY

Manufacturers class furniture as low grade, medium grade, and standard grade. Standard grade is the finest, and much of it is custom made. Only the best quality of materials are used. Design and workmanship are also of the best. But furniture of this type is usually in the luxury class for most families.

Medium-grade furniture may be of good design, or a good reproduction of a well designed original. The construction and workmanship are good, and the woods are hardwoods (though not of the finest quality, as a rule).

Occasionally, low grade furniture is not badly designed and may even appear to be a satisfactory substitute for something better — for awhile. But construction is generally inferior, and fabrics, finishes, and decorations are often garish and of poor quality. Such furniture does not wear well, and, unless nothing else is obtainable at a comparable cost, is usually not worth buying.

STYLE

Furniture styles ought to harmonize with architectural styles. A house which is pure Georgian in style on the outside but furnished in sleek, modern, functional style on the inside is something of an anachronsm. But a great many variations or possibilities may lie within this limitation — enough at least to satisfy all but the most exacting tastes.

The trend is either towards complete modern or else a judicious combination of styles of various periods. Modern furniture is extremely adaptable to present-day living conditions. But really good modern is still quite costly—often more so than good reproductions of period styles. It is therefore small wonder that more period style furniture is sold than modern.

Only museums or very wealthy persons have the means to furnish rooms in authentic period styles. Indeed, slavish copying of past styles is entirely out of keeping with present day living. Instead, decorators select the best designs from what the past has to offer and combine them with modern fabrics, rugs, and accessories in new arrangements to give an entirely fresh and contemporary interpretation.

Authentic period pieces are usually too costly for the average pocketbook. But good reproductions are usually available, and sometimes these are scaled down in size to adapt them to the proportions of modern rooms, which are often smaller in size than those of the manor house of the past for which the original pieces may have been designed. But to be good, reproductions should be fairly faithful copies of the originals. Only a master designer can borrow ideas from past styles and reinterpret them in an entirely new, original, and beautiful way. Therefore, it is a good thing to study original pieces in order to know what to look for in reproductions.

The most popular period styles of furniture are the eighteenth-century English, Early American, Colonial American (which closely followed eighteenth-century English styles), and Federal American. French Provincial is also popular, and a limited amount of interest is shown in styles of other periods, especially the Victorian, which has had a weak revival. In the 1920's, Spanish and Italian Renaissance designs became a fashion which has waned.

Any of the eighteenth-century English, Colonial American, and Federal American styles can be combined. French Provincial blends well with Early American. But there are no hard and fast rules for combining styles — it's the total effect that matters.

Chippendale armchair with pierced splat and delicately carved arms and legs (English, about 1760).

Chippendale fall front desk with cabinet top (English, 1770-1790).

Eighteenth-Century English Styles. The furniture styles of eighteenth-century England are usually divided into two periods — Early Georgian and Late Georgian. The Early Georgian includes the furniture style known as Chippendale; the Late Georgian, those known as Adam, Hepplewhite, and Sheraton.

The designs of Thomas Chippendale, one of the greatest of the great English cabinetmakers, show considerable variety. Much of his early work is a refined treatment of the Queen Anne style. Some of his later work can scarcely be distinguished from that of Robert Adam. Chippendale's most characteristic work appears in his chairs. Many of the early ones display the ball-and-claw foot and the curved form of leg known as cabriole. Chair backs varied, too. Those of "Chinese" Chippendale, one of the more familiar styles, are of lattice work design, and are combined with straight legs. The ladder back is another typical style, as is the pierced or interlaced splat. Chippendale also made cabinets, tables, settees, bookcases, four-poster beds, and other pieces. Cabinets are often crowned with pediments, either broken or curved. Mahogany was used almost exclusively.

Chippendale tilt-top table with claw feet (English, about 1750-1765).

"Chinese" Chippendale chest (English, about 1750).

The Adam brothers, Robert and James, were contemporaries of Chippendale. They were architects, but they exercised considerable influence on furniture design because they planned interior furnishings as well as the house itself. Their designs were carried out by the great cabinetmakers of the period. Robert Adams was the better known. He was a student of classic architecture, and his furniture design shows the classic influence. It combines delicacy and austere simplicity. Straight lines were favored, and appear in chair legs and backs, although some backs were rounded. Decorative detail is beautiful but restrained. Adam sideboards are especially noteworthy. The center consists of a serving table and the ends are cellarettes. The Adams used a great deal of mahogany, but also some of the lighter woods, such as satinwood and harewood. Much of their furniture is painted.

The designs of George Hepplewhite are graceful and delicate. He is credited with introducing the shield-back design for chairs. Other curved chair-back designs include interlacing hearts and ovals. Most of the chair seats are upholstered. Arms are very short and the front legs are straight and slightly tapered. The winged upholstered chair may have been introduced by Hepplewhite. Sideboards have serpentine fronts. Bookcases are tall, often with leaded glass doors. Mahogany was the favorite wood — often inlaid with satinwood, rosewood, and other decorative hardwoods. (Inlay is a characteristic decoration of Hepplewhite furniture.) He was also fond of painted decoration.

The earlier designs of Thomas Sheraton are among the finest of the eighteenth-Century English cabinetmakers, and the best of this work brought the period to a close. His later designs are influenced by French Empire style, and tend to be heavy and slightly ungainly.

Sheraton was influenced by Hepplewhite and the Adams, but his better pieces bear the impress of his own originality. The typical Sheraton chair has a square back, often with a broken top rail and a high center panel. He also designed chairs with oval and "broken shield" backs. The arms are high in back and curve forward. Chair backs and sometimes seats are often caned instead of upholstered. Legs are round or occasionally square, delicately tapered, and with reeded decoration. Sideboards have curved fronts, but the central part of the curve is concave — just the opposite of Hepplewhite's sideboards. Tables are round or oval in shape. Bookcases are crowned with broken pediments.

Detail showing shield back of Hepplewhite style armchair (English, 18th century).

Both Sheraton and Hepplewhite were fond of designing odd, ingenious pieces of furniture, such as revolving bookcases, sewing cabinets, and desks with secret drawers and panels. Sheraton also favored inlay work, especially delicate strips of holly or boxwood. He also used fine veneers of rare woods. Other decorative details include painting and carving. Sheraton preferred mahogany for his work, as did the other designers of the period. Almost none of his original pieces remain, but his works are known from his drawing book on furniture designs.

Hepplewhite side table with reeded legs and wood inlay decoration (English, 18th century).

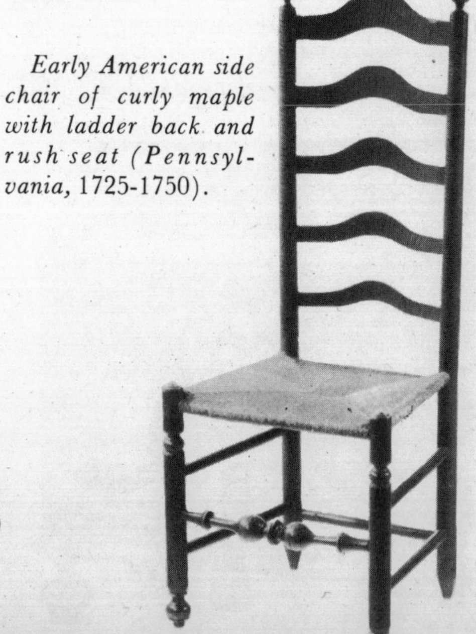

Early American side chair of curly maple with ladder back and rush seat (Pennsylvania, 1725-1750).

Early American highboy of pine (1690-1700)

Early American sawbuck table (1700-1750).

Early American Furniture. The early colonists brought or imported some of their furniture from England—those who could afford to do so. But they also began to make their own pieces very early from the most available native woods—maple, pine, oak, walnut, and the fruit woods, such as cherry and apple. All furniture was carefully treasured, for it was difficult to come by. Each piece was made to order to fit the needs of the individual householder, and therefore no two pieces are ever quite alike. Designs were based on the furniture known in England, but modified and simplified by local cabinetmakers. Much of the work shows the influence of the Jacobean style of England — but the process of simplification produced the sturdy, homely style which has come to be known as Early American. It is still one of the most popular styles in America today.

Typical pieces include gateleg tables, butterfly tables, stretcher tables, trestle tables; windsor chairs, ladder-back chairs, and a variety of chairs with rush seats; secretaries, chests, dressers, and four-poster beds. Good reproductions are available, sometimes slightly modified to fit present-day needs, and occasionally original pieces can be found which are not too costly.

Early American chest of drawers made from walnut (late 18th century).

Early American slant-top desk (18th century).

Early American gate-leg table (1675-1700).

Federal American sofa table with drop leaves. Sheraton style influence (early 19th century).

Colonial Period. As wealth increased in the colonies, many families of means began to import fine furniture from England. Local cabinetmakers copied the designs, and while they sometimes modified them slightly, much of the work produced in America during the eighteenth century faithfully duplicates the English furniture of the period. For this reason, the so-called "Colonial Style" differs little from the Georgian style of England.

Federal American. After the Revolution, furniture styles were largely borrowed from France (although French influence had made some headway before that). The dictates of Napoleon extended to all forms of arts and crafts. The first effects on furniture appeared in the transitory style called Directoire, which soon gave way to the full-fledged Empire style. This style of furniture is entirely different from that made for the French kings. It is heavy, massive, and often highly ornamented with gilt or bronze ormolu mounts. The favorite wood was mahogany.

American cabinetmakers based most of their designs on those of the French, but they were also influenced by the English Regency style, a refined interpretation of the Empire style in England. In the United

Colonial American chest-on-chest (New England, about 1750).

Federal American roll-top desk. Sheraton style influence (1805-1810).

Duncan Phyfe sofa (Federal American, about 1805).

Windsor armchair (American, 18th century).

States, the result was less ornate than the French prototype. Leading cabinetmaker of the period was Duncan Phyfe. His earliest work was largely influenced by that of Thomas Sheraton, and his last work is in the Victorian style. His work in the Empire style is better known but less fine than those of his Sheraton-period.

A typical Duncan Phyfe work is the lyre-backed side chair with concave-curving legs and convex-curving back. The lyre motif also appears in table bases. Earlier Duncan Phyfe sofas have straight legs and often caned backs and seats. Later sofas are well padded and have curved legs. He worked mostly in mahogany until he began to turn out massive Victorian pieces, after which he used a great deal of rosewood.

Victorian. The preference of overstuffed, over-elaborate interiors in England during the time of Queen Victoria was reflected in the United States, where, if possible, the style was even more appalling than in the land of its origin. Perhaps the principal reason why Victorian interiors appear so tasteless to us now is that pattern, ornament, and decoration appeared almost everywhere. Floral carpets, huge motifs on wallpaper, fringe, heavy, carved and stuffed furniture of rosewood or black walnut, gilt, draperies and an endless array of curios produced an almost suffocating effect. However, individual pieces sometimes have great charm, and if they are used in harmonious settings with controlled amounts of pattern, they may be very pleasing. The dark woods are often given a modern interpretation by bleaching.

French Provincial. Just as the early settlers in America simplified English design, so too did the people of the French provinces simplify and modify the elaborate designs of the French court. The result is the delightful style known as French Provincial. The principal wood used was beech, which has a soft, grayish yellow color. French Provincial is full of gentle, graceful curves, but is restrained, solid, and well proportioned and easily adapted to modern interiors. Good reproductions are available.

Federal American lyre-back chair. Influenced by Directoire style of France (1800-1810).

Wall cabinet and shelves at right are made of interchangeable units. Any number of arrangements are thus possible with this flexibly designed modern furniture.

Modern Furniture. What we call modern design is perhaps not yet a definitely formulated style. The most distinctive characteristic of this furniture is its functionalism. Furniture and architecture are often planned as a unit, with the result that walls and furniture are sometimes an inseparable part of each other. Not all so-called modern design is good. Too much of the cheap or medium grade modern is merely "moderne"—heavy and dull—one reason why more people have failed to appreciate the virtues which good modern has to offer. But the finest modern furniture has a beauty as clean cut and well defined as that of an airplane. All kinds of materials are being used. In addition to the traditional woods (often bleached), one finds furniture of molded plywood, metal, glass, and plastics, and in many new and striking combinations.

Some modern furniture is made in units which are designed to be interchangeable so that any number of combinations can be produced.

SECOND-HAND FURNITURE

The points to look for in second-hand furniture are the same as those in new furniture. A few tips may be helpful, however. Wobbly pieces sometimes have nothing wrong with them except loose joints. If the structure of the joint is undamaged, it may be repaired. Such a piece can sometimes be picked up quite cheaply, and if otherwise good, a real bargain may result with a little effort. If the joint is broken, don't bother to bring the bargain home, because it cannot be repaired.

One should have a very sound knowledge of values when shopping for second-

This lovely retreat for a summer afternoon offers wide chairs and folding chairs as well as plants and flowers.

hand furniture — otherwise it is easy to end up by spending as much or more than if new furniture were bought. The excitement of bidding at an auction may tempt one to pay a ridiculous sum just because someone else wants the same thing. Unreliable second-hand dealers sometimes try to charge whatever the traffic will bear, so that bargaining ability may be helpful. Perhaps furniture is advertised for sale at bargain rates by an "owner who is leaving town." If such is really the case, it *may* be a bargain. Sometimes, however, the "owner" never leaves town at all, but simply sells a new roomful of furniture every day or so at outrageous prices to unwary bargain hunters. This racket has popped up now and again in the larger cities, but has never been permitted to flourish.

Second-hand furniture, to be a bargain, should cost considerably less than a new piece of comparable quality. But when does a second-hand piece become an antique, which if good, will be more expensive than new furniture? That is difficult to say. According to the customs authorities, a piece becomes an antique if it is more than one hundred years old, but this definition is no guide for the collector to follow. Anything Victorian is now labeled antique. Thirty years ago, one could pick up a Victorian piece almost for the cost of carting it home. Today, well-made Victorian brings fancy prices. Bargains can still be found among the fumed oak and golden oak pieces so popular during the early 1900's. Most of the furniture of this era is of such bad design (it has no style) that it is doubtful if it will ever have any value as antiques. Yet some of it is sturdy and well made, and can occasionally be redesigned to follow more modern lines. If bargains are essential, don't overlook the possibilities to be found here.

Matching pairs bring higher prices than units. A pair of loveseats will cost more together than both would cost if sold singly. The price of a chair is less when sold singly than when it is part of a set.

An upholstered piece may have its coverings in shreds, but if the frame is sound and the springs are intact, it may be rejuvenated with a little money and much labor. Sometimes it is even worth while to replace missing springs.

SUMMER FURNITURE

Summer furniture occupies a class by itself. More attention has been paid to it with the increasing trend towards outdoor living, and some manufacturers have offered really fine designs. They are totally unrelated in feeling to traditional designs, partly because such furniture must be made from weather resistant materials.

Typical pieces include chairs and sofas (sometimes on wheels for easier moving), gliders, tables (often with umbrellas), serving tables on wheels, and so on. They may be of willow, cane, bamboo, rattan, reed, fiber, painted wood, wrought iron, chromium, or other materials. Upholstery or cushion covers are of moistureproof fabrics.

Willow is good for summer furniture because of its strength and lightness. The word *cane* is applied to various grasslike plants, and even to rattan, which is really a species of climbing palm. The cane used for woven chair seats is brittle and apt to disintegrate when wet. The reed used in furniture comes from a South Sea Island vine, and is less durable than willow. Rattan is the same, tough, woody stem used for Malacca walking canes. Bamboo makes sturdy and attractive summer furniture. Fiber is actually twisted paper coated with synthetic resinous substance, but if well made is just as durable as any of the other materials. None of them should be exposed to drenching rain, however.

PRINCIPAL WOODS USED IN FURNITURE

Name	Description	Color	Uses
Ash (white)	Tough, fairly hard, with coarse grain	Sapwood almost white; corewood light brown with dark rings	Occasionally for furniture
Basswood	Soft	White, light yellow	Cheap, unpainted furniture
Beech	Strong, hard	Varies from white to brown	Furniture, especially French Provincial pieces
Birch	Fine grained, hard, and strong	Corewood, reddish brown; sapwood, light yellow	Red birch used as substitute for mahogany; white, for oak or walnut; curly birch (cut from crotch) used as veneer.
Cherry	Hard, close grained	Reddish brown to light yellowish brown	Early American furniture; now fairly scarce
Chestnut	Rather soft; open grained	Tan to light brown	Veneers, some cabinet work
Ebony	Very heavy hardwood	Black	Inlay; sometimes veneer; too rare for use in large pieces
Gumwood (red)	Fine grained hardwood; distinct markings; has tendency to warp	Reddish brown, often with grayish yellow markings	As substitute for walnut or mahogany in cheaper furniture; veneer
Holly	Hard, heavy	Pure white or grayish white	Mostly inlay; scarce
Mahogany	Strong, hard, and very durable; open pores; darkens under exposure to light	Reddish brown	Fine furniture; veneer
Maple (sugar)	Very hard, durable; close pores	Light yellow to light brown, sometimes tinged with red	Early American reproductions and modern furniture
Oak (white)	Hard, heavy, durable; close grained; open pores	Light tannish brown	Fine, sturdy furniture
Oak (red)	Hard, but softer than white oak; coarser grain	Brown to reddish brown	Same as white oak
Pine (white)	Soft, but fairly durable	Creamy white	Cheap, unpainted furniture
Prima vera	Similar in grain to mahogany; sometimes called "white mahogany"	Pale yellow	Inlay; veneer
Redwood	Soft, coarse grained, rather light weight	Dull, grayish red	Summer furniture
Rosewood	Heavy hardwood; has faint odor of roses	Reddish brown, often with straight black brown	Victorian furniture; inlay
Satinwood	Hardwood with irregular figure, satiny luster	Yellowish or golden brown	Fine cabinet work; inlay
Teak	Very heavy hardwood; resists warping	Golden brown; almost no figure markings	Oriental chests, stands; inlay
Walnut	Heavy hardwood; American walnut has small pores and good figure markings; more expensive Circassian walnut is ribbon figured	American: deep reddish to dark brown; Circassian: light brown with dark markings	Fine furniture, veneer

CHAPTER VI

FURNITURE ARRANGEMENT

FURNITURE may be of the finest quality and beautifully designed, but if the pieces do not go well with each other, or are badly grouped and wrongly placed, the room will not be attractive.

Good furniture arrangement depends upon a number of factors. The size of the room, its use, the number and placement of doors, windows, and other architectural features should all be considered when planning a furniture arrangement.

Rearranging the furniture is supposed to be a favorite occupation with women. They are believed to be impelled to do so by sudden whims — usually to the distress of other members of the family, especially the male members, who find themselves pressed into service. So, before we start to shove that sofa across the room to find out how it will look against the other wall, it might be worth while to do some less strenuous planning on paper. Let us make a floor plan of the room on paper and in scale. To do this, we will need a folding ruler, although a yardstick will do. Measure the length and breadth of the room and jot these down. Any ells, nooks, bay windows, or projections such as fireplaces must be measured also. In order to locate doors, windows, and other architectural features on our scale drawing, we must measure the distances between them and the ends of the wall.

Making a Floor Plan. With this information at hand, we make a floor plan of the room. It may be in any scale you wish, but unless you have a very large sheet of paper, it might be well not to have the scale too large. You will probably find that a scale in which ½ inch represents 1 foot will be a convenient one to work with. Then you can easily translate the actual measurements of your room into scale measurement if you remember that 10 feet will be represented on paper by 5 inches, or 18½ feet by 9¼ inches, and so on. Or use graph paper, which is already ruled into squares of whatever size you may need.

To make the diagram, you will need a pencil, a ruler, a sheet of paper, and you will also find it very helpful to have a small device called a triangle, in order to draw the corners of the room at true right angles. Triangles are made of metal or plastic, and may be bought for a small sum at the dime store or at any store which sells art or drafting materials. You use the triangle by laying one side forming its square, or right angle, along a ruled line. Draw along the other side forming the right angle to represent the corner of a floor plan.

After the lines are drawn to represent the outer edges all around the floor, indicate the doors and windows by short in-

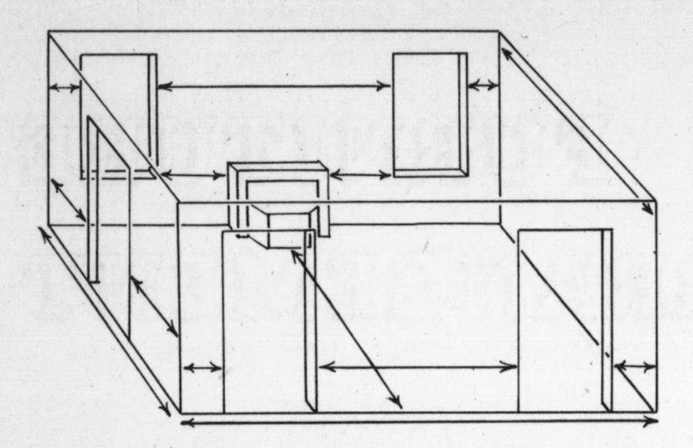

FIG. 1. To make scale drawing of floor plan, first measure length and width of room. Then measure all distances from wall ends to doors or windows and distances between doors and windows. If room has nooks or any projections, such as fireplace, these must be measured, too.

tersecting lines. Or do as architects do, and use a thick black line for the solid wall, thin double lines for windows, and blank spaces for door openings. Be sure to locate doors and windows in the proper places and in scale, according to the actual measurements you have taken. If the room has a fireplace, indicate its projection into the room in proper scale.

Now measure the breadth and length of each piece of furniture. On another sheet of paper, measure and draw quadrangles (or circles for circular tables) to represent each piece, using the same scale as you used for the floor plan. It is a good idea to draw these on paper of a different color from that used for the floor plan, so that the furniture pieces can be easily distinguished and visualized. Label each piece, such as sofa, chair, desk, and so on, and cut them out. Don't attempt to indicate fussy details; it's only the size of each piece and its relation to the room and other pieces that we are trying to find. Make scale pieces for the rugs, too, using a paper of still another color. Now we are ready to move the furniture around as much as we please — and with no backaches!

Perhaps this seems like a good deal of bother. Actually, in the long run, it isn't. It provides you with an easy way of trying out every possible grouping of furniture, and then studying the results critically to find the best effect. And don't forget that moving actual pieces of heavy furniture around to test every possible grouping can be very hard on the floors *and* the furniture, as well as on you. A floor plan diagram will also be a great help when you intend to buy new furniture. By measuring the new piece before you purchase it, and by testing it out in scale, you can avoid getting something that's in the wrong scale for the rest of the furniture or for the size of the room. Be sure to mark the room measurements on the plan, including the length of each wall, window, and door area. It might be helpful to make a note of height and width measurements of windows on the plan, too, for use in estimating curtains or drapery materials. In fact, if you keep a scrapbook of floor plans for each room in the house, with all measurements indicated in ink, it can serve as a permanent reference, not only for room measurements but also for furniture measurements. And don't forget to mark the electrical outlets, radiators, and the direction in which the doors swing open.

If you expect to move, you can save yourself endless time and effort by making

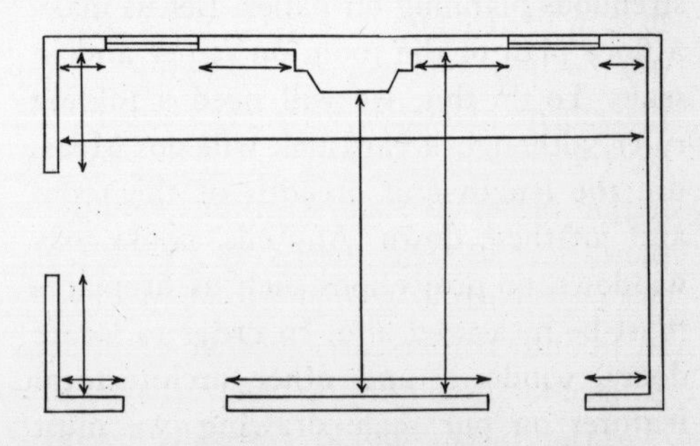

FIG. 2. Translate all measurements into scale on paper, indicating doors and windows, as shown.

scale diagrams for each room in your new home. Number the pieces of furniture on the diagram. Then tie tags with corresponding numbers on the actual furniture pieces. Give the diagrams to the movers — and sit down and relax!

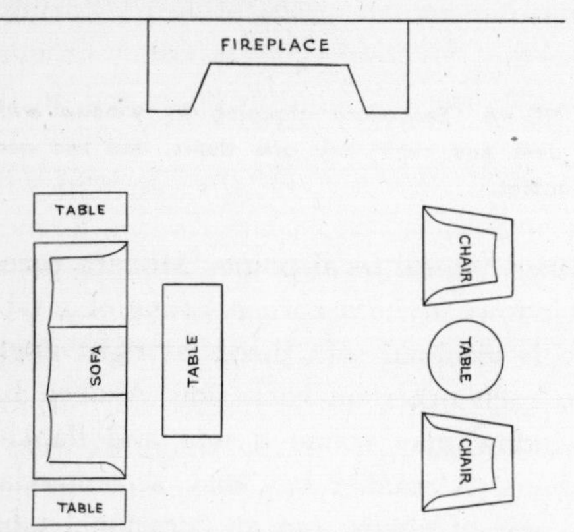

FIG. 3. Center-of-interest grouping beside fireplace in large living room, using sofa, two chairs, end tables, coffee table, and lamp table.

The paper cutouts representing the furniture pieces can be held in place temporarily or permanently with a drop of paper cement. But before we decide upon a final arrangement of the furniture, we ought to consider a few points.

Balance and Proportion. In general, the big tall pieces of furniture, such as highboys, secretaries, breakfronts, and so forth, should be placed against the wall. Sofas should be placed either parallel with the wall or at right angles to it. Never place the sofa in a position which is diagonal to a wall. In fact, diagonal placement is usually best avoided. An exception is the placement of chairs to form a group for convenience of conversation. Even so, the major pieces in such a group should be parallel or at right angles to a wall. Corner cupboards or triangular cabinets *made* to fit into corners are another exception. Rugs, too, should not be placed diagonally.

Major pieces should generally be centered against a wall area, unless the wall is very long and therefore able to accommodate more than one big piece without appearing to be overcrowded. However, we must consider both the area of the entire wall and the separate areas between doors and windows. In some treatments,

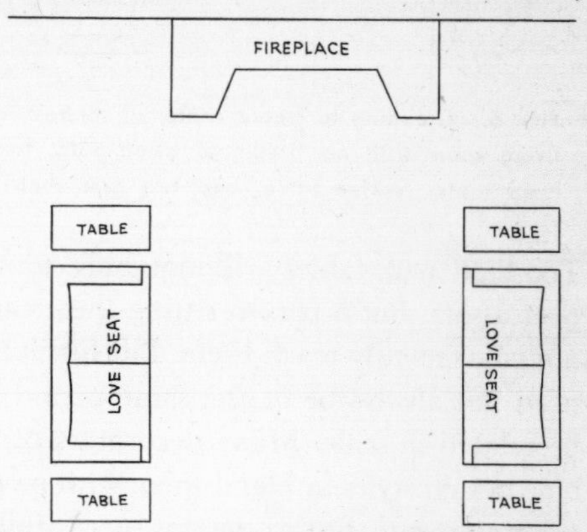

FIG. 4. Very symmetrical grouping beside fireplace in medium sized living room, with matching loveseats and end tables.

the windows, doors, and fireplace may be considered as the central points of a grouping. A mass on one side of a door, window, or fireplace, generally needs to be balanced by a mass of proportionate size on the other side.

If the bulky pieces of furniture are confined to only one end of the room, it looks unbalanced. A large piece of furniture against one wall usually needs to be balanced by something of related size against the opposite wall. It need not always be a piece of furniture. Doors, windows, or a fireplace may serve as balancing features. Or picture groupings above a piece may lend the increased proportions necessary to balance.

The furniture pieces themselves should be in the same scale and should also be proportioned to the size of the room. For example, a spindly little coffee table would look lost in front of a massive sofa. A giant four-poster bed would produce a feeling of suffocation in a tiny bedroom.

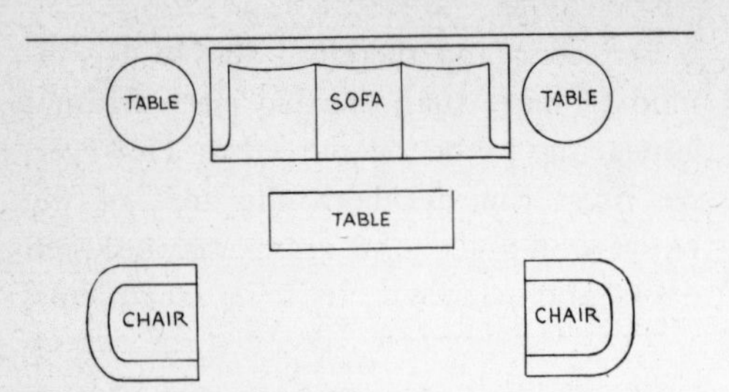

FIG. 5. Grouping to create center of interest in living room with no fireplace, using sofa, two lamp tables, coffee table, and two arm chairs.

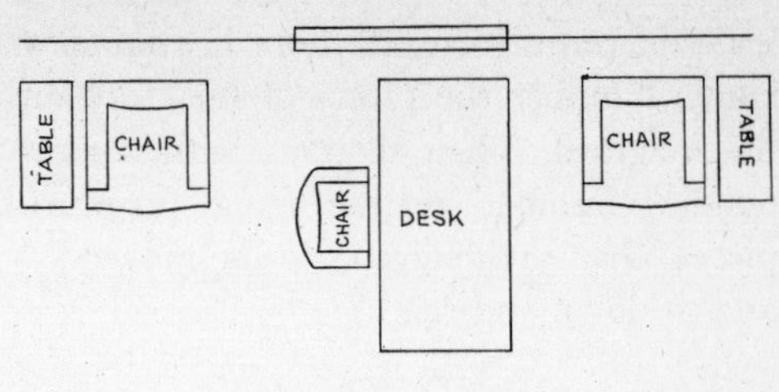

FIG. 6. Secondary grouping by window with desk and chair, two arm chairs, and two end tables.

Too-high end tables will not only tower over a sofa, but a person sitting there cannot conveniently reach them. But furniture need not always be of the same period to be related in scale. Many decorators combine period styles or blend them with modern treatments. But to do this successfully, scale is of utmost importance.

One way to help achieve a feeling of balance is to buy certain pieces of furniture in pairs. For example, end tables, occasional chairs, arm chair, love seats, consoles, and bookcases can all be better utilized in furniture arrangements if you have them in pairs.

Focal Points. Every room needs at least one major focal point, and large rooms need more than one. A focal point is a center of interest — one that naturally attracts attention. Sometimes the architecture of the room will provide a natural focal point — a fireplace, for example. A bay window or a unit of several windows may serve as a focal point. Furniture groupings gravitate naturally to such areas. If your room has a natural focal point, make the most of it. Don't allow a fireplace to stand in lonesome isolation, ignored by every chair and sofa. Instead, flank it with a pair of loveseats or chairs, or place a sofa on one side, a pair of chairs on the other. Of course, a very small room may not permit such groupings.

Corner windows and bay windows are other natural focal points. Modern corner windows invite a corner setting of a table with sectional sofa pieces at right angles to each other on each side. A deep bay window may frame a sofa and flanking chairs. A smaller bay may accommodate a pair of chairs and an occasional table. Or it may serve as a cheerful spot for games with a bridge or backgammon table and chairs.

However, if you have no fireplace, no bay windows, no corner windows, don't be discouraged. A plain wall can be made into a focal point by arranging the furniture next to it in an inviting conversation group. Utilize the space between two windows in the same way. If the room is narrow, with a single end window, use it as a backdrop for the sofa, and make it dramatic with drapes which extend from each side of the window to the ends of the wall.

Recessed wall spaces make wonderful focal points, especially when they are treated with a color or pattern which contrasts with the rest of the room. Such spaces can be created by framing them with built-in closets or cupboards extending from floor to ceiling. A dressing table set into such a recess is charming. A recessed wall covered with mirror not only looks luxurious, but is brightened with reflected light. Of course, a plate glass mirror large enough for any sizable wall space is an

item of no small expense. However, dime store mirrors in a tiled arrangement will produce an effect almost as interesting and at considerably less expense. An image in such an arrangement will be choppily reflected, but the glitter will be there.

Minor focal points can be considered after the major ones are taken care of. A minor focal point might be a console table flanked by a pair of chairs, a chest of drawers, or a piano and chairs. Most rooms need several minor focal points.

Traffic Lanes and Entrances. Rooms are meant to be *lived* in, and that includes walking around in them. Don't place any pipiece of furniture in a position where it's sure to be tripped over every time an unwary person passes. Does your furniture arrangement allow you to bring a large tray of hors d'oeuvres from the kitchen to the living room without weaving in and out between the furniture like a football player training on an obstacle course? One should be able to go in a direct line from any door to any principal point in the room. And, of course, never allow any piece of furniture to jut out beyond a door or window frame.

How does your room appear as you enter it? Is it friendly and inviting? It won't be if your sofa, for example, presents its back to the entrance. But a sofa can face the fireplace in a large room and still not look uninviting if it is backed by other pieces facing the door. For example, you might section off the sofa with bookcases, and place in front of them a pair of chairs and a small table.

Convenience and Suitability. Choose furniture that suits the particular needs of your family and reflects their interests. Furniture above all should be functional. Each piece should serve a purpose. You want it to be as handsome as possible, too. But think twice about giving space to some piece which no one ever uses.

Have tables which are of the right height for their purpose. End tables should

Formal living room with harmonious combination of eighteenth-century and contemporary styles of furniture. Note symmetrical arrangement of gilt framed mirrors, lamps, and tables, and the feeling of balance between the mass of the breakfront and that of the fireplace.

be the same height as the arm of the chair or the sofa. Sofas need tables at both ends. Such tables usually match, but they do not necessarily always have to. However, unmatched tables should be related in size, and they look better if they are both of the same kind of wood. Convenience calls for a table beside or near every armchair. And have a generous sized ashtray on each table within easy reach. Don't overcrowd the tables with miscellaneous objects. A too-small table on which is placed, for example, a tall, narrow vase full of flowers, a group of magazines, a figurine, a lamp, and an ashtray, is not only cluttered and confusing, but it also makes the person sitting beside it uncomfortable. He has to watch carefully every time he reaches out his arm lest he knock something over.

Coffee tables or cocktail tables should be of a height which is easy for the person seated nearby to reach. A height which is level with the sofa seat is a convenient one. The coffee or cocktail table should be placed approximately one foot away from the sofa. If it is closer, it must be pushed aside in order to sit down, and if it is much farther away, the sitter must stretch or get up to reach it. Do you eye your guests nervously for fear they will forget to set their glasses on their coasters and thus mar the beautiful wood finish of your table? If so, it would be much better to have a table topped with glass, tile, or other material impervious to stains.

And remember, the family's needs are more important than following any "decorator" scheme. Perhaps you love fragile rococo chairs, delicate porcelains, and satin upholstery. But if you have several lively youngsters, they would either need to have their normal activities restrained in such a room or else they would soon ruin it. How much better to have sturdy fabrics, floor coverings, and furniture which can take a little "rough house" now and then and be none the worse for it!

Does the family like to read? Then be sure to have comfortable chairs with bookstands nearby and plenty of good light available—daylight and artificial light.

If the family likes to play games, and you have no game room, you might reserve a closet where games, card tables, and other play equipment can be stored.

Unity. Whatever style of decoration you prefer, it is generally advisable to carry it out consistently throughout all rooms in the house or apartment which are shared by the family. To go from an Early American living room into an ultra modern dining room can be a bit jolting to one's sense of harmony. Variety can be achieved through the use of color, but a conglomeration of styles under one roof usually creates a feeling of disunity. Only a house which is so large that one section is more or less independent of another can afford to have more than one style of decoration. However, play rooms and bedrooms can be exceptions to this rule.

FIG. 7. Secondary grouping between two windows with two armchairs and large occasional table.

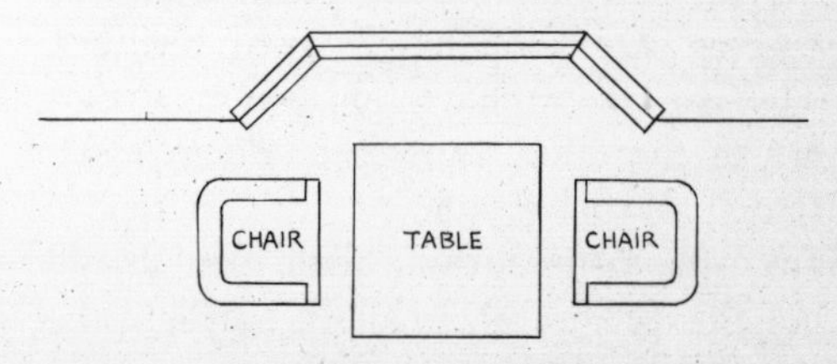

FIG. 8. Focal point beside small bay window with game table and two armchairs.

A charming minor focal point created with chest of drawers, mirror, two side chairs, and candlesticks of Early American design against pine-paneled wall. Balanced arrangement produces feeling of restful stability.

Unity does not mean that furniture of various periods cannot be used together. They can, as we have said before, if they are in the same scale. But it does mean that if you have adhered fairly closely to any period style in one room you should not change abruptly to another style in the next room.

Nor does unity mean that you should strive to "match" your furniture too closely. Nearly all woods go together, and if you have a fine mahogany chest of drawers, don't feel that you should not use it in the same room with a walnut table. Suites of living room furniture, all carefully matched, are something else to avoid. Dining room and bedroom suites are still in favor, but they are far from being considered the essentials they once were.

And unity does not mean monotony.

Don't fill a room with nothing but overstuffed chairs, or only wooden arm chairs, or upholstered pieces which all have button tufting, or anything else which is too much of a sameness. Variety is just as important to interesting decorating as to anything else in life — but it ought to be variety which is harmonious.

AROUND THE HOUSE

The Hall is the introduction to the rest of the house. It should offer the visitor a cheerful welcome and set the mood for the other rooms. No matter how tiny it is, give it a point of interest — a narrow table topped by a beautiful mirror might be one way. There should be a chair or two if the hall is large enough for them without looking overcrowded. Gay wallpaper adds a cheerful note, and plants or flowers always give a fresh, alive quality which is especially attractive in the hall.

The Living Room. Most of the points about furniture arrangement which have already been discussed apply to any room, but particularly to the living room. However, there are a few special considerations which ought be kept in mind. The living room is a room which all the members of the family and their friends share, and therefore its style, color scheme, and arrangement ought to please the entire family. If there are young people in the family who have the privilege of using the living room on certain evenings to entertain their friends, then a rug which can be rolled aside for dancing is more suitable than wall-to-wall carpeting. And, of course, they will need a cabinet for records and a radio or phonograph. Naturally, if the adults in the family want a formal, sedate living room and the young people want one which can be used for games and dancing, the best thing is to have a formal living room and a separate game room, if possible.

A piano grouping ought to be somewhat apart from any other major furniture grouping in the living room. For the sake of the piano, it is usually better to place it near an inside, rather than an outside wall, unless the house is very well insulated. Piano strings and keys are very sensitive to dampness and are sometimes more apt to be subject to it if placed near a window or an outside wall. However, for those who practice at the piano for hours at a time, continued use of artificial light may prove tiring to the eyes. If that is the case, it would be more sensible to have the piano by the window, since eyes are more precious than piano strings.

The Dining Room. A gloomy dining room is no aid to digestion. Here is one place where color and imagination can be put to work. Since most dining rooms are used only during mealtimes, they can afford to be gay in their style without being tiring. Be sure to have a clear route between the dining room and kitchen, and leave plenty of space in which to pass around the table after everyone is seated.

Living-Dining Room. Since the dining room is used so seldom, more and more house plans leave it out altogether. Instead, the living room expands and one end of it is used for dining. The customary dining room table, chairs, and sideboard look out of place in such a setting. What is needed is a table more in the style and in the scale of the living room furniture. Dishes, linens, and silverware might be stored in shallow, built-in cupboards and drawers instead of in a sideboard.

The Bedroom offers a wonderful opportunity to express the individual preferences of the occupant. If a young daughter likes feminine frills and ruffles and a son wants his room as trim as a ship, let them express these tastes in their own bedrooms. But a few general rules apply to any bedroom. The beds should be placed so that they are easy to make. If possible, the bed should not face a window, as the direct light may be annoying to the sleeper. Double-decker bunks may be space saving, but it's quite a feat to turn the mattress, for example, on the upper bunk. If a bedroom must be shared by more than one person — usually necessary in a large family — the arrangement is generally more satisfactory if each person has his or her own articles of furnishing. For example, a bedroom for girls can be quite charming with twin beds, twin dressing table, chairs, and desks. Bedrooms for younger children should be easy to keep clean, and woods, fabrics, and floor coverings should be durable and able to withstand much active usage.

Bed-sitting rooms should be decorated more as sitting rooms than as bedrooms, since they usually serve primarily as a place where one can entertain guests and secondarily as a bedroom. Skirted dressing tables do not belong in such a room, nor does the usual bed with its flounced spread. Instead, sleeping accommodations can be provided for with a studio couch, a sofa bed, or a day bed. The type of dressing table with a hinged top which opens up to reveal a mirror is very suitable for the bed-sitting room. Closed, such a table is thoroughly suitable for a living room. The bed-sitting room may do double duty as a library, a study, a guest room or as a second living room for parents when young people are entertaining in the main living room.

Lighting may be direct or indirect and either general or local. General lighting is usually more pleasing if it is indirect, but lamps for reading ordinarily supply direct lighting. Indirect lighting is lighting which is not directed at any special object or towards any particular part of the room. Instead, it is either directed toward the ceiling and then diffused by reflection, or it may be recessed behind a cornice or hidden from view by some other means. Modern furniture sometimes has indirect lighting built right into it.

Lamps for reading should be high enough to cast sufficient illumination for a person to read by while seated comfortably in his chair. He should not have to lean over in order to get enough light to see his book or paper. Since end tables should be of the same height as the arm arm of the chair or sofa, this means that lamps should be big and high enough to be useful.

Indirect lighting not only provides general illumination but it can also serve as a most dramatic kind of modern decoration. Fluorescent lighting is frequently employed for such effects.

III

RESTYLING FURNITURE

CHAPTER VII

RESTYLING AND REPAIRING FURNITURE

A STORY pops up now and then about some lucky woman who found an antique secretary in such a decrepit state it seemed almost beyond repair. But when she examined it carefully she discovered a little, carefully concealed button. She pressed it. A panel slid away and revealed—a secret drawer. Inside she found a diamond-studded gold brooch (or, perhaps, a letter from George Washington). The old secretary turned out to be a treasure trove after all. But that's not the way we recommend that you go hunting for treasure in furniture. Treasures there are: but the treasures are the money you can save by turning out-of-date, unattractive old furniture into good-as-new, useful, and smart pieces. All it takes is some courage, a little imagination, and quite a bit of hard work. So, let's mix a metaphor and find the gold in them thar white elephants.

RESTYLING

To be worth restyling, any piece of furniture must be soundly constructed and of good wood (*see the Chapter on Furniture for construction details*). Joints must be intact, for broken joints cannot be mended. Occasionally, small parts, such as a chair rung, with broken joints can be replaced if the piece itself is worth it. Loose joints are a different matter — the pieces can be taken apart, glued, and reassembled.

Perhaps you have furniture now—nothing much wrong with it except that it's dated and unlovely. Perhaps you want to furnish a home or apartment and find that the cost of new furniture would wreck the budget. Then why not buy second-hand furniture and restyle it yourself? Look for such furniture in the second-hand furniture stores, the junk shops, the Salvation Army thrift stores, and the auction houses. Storage warehouses often sell or auction off unclaimed furniture. Watch the want-ads for furniture offered for sale directly by the owner. Acquaint yourself with the prices of new furniture in order to be able to judge better whether or not a second-hand piece is a bargain. White elephants must be bargains or they are not worth the time and work it takes to restyle them. The furniture that's most apt to be a bargain is the kind made from approximately 1890 to 1930. During that period, there appeared the heavy fumed or golden oak pieces, the dressers with huge, standup, tilting mirrors attached, the lop-sided secretaries, the glass-fronted china cabinets, the elephant-leg tables, and the bulbous-footed chests. In the 1920's, furniture factories turned out their version of "period" pieces which some wag described as "African Renaissance." Among all such examples, one can often find pieces which are soundly constructed of good, solid hardwood or fine veneers. Many of them can be given simpler lines to bring them more up-to-date.

General Points to Consider. Before buying any piece, study it carefully. First examine the construction and the wood. If these are sound, then try to visualize the piece as it would appear if certain parts were altered. Projecting tops on chests can often be cut down to give the uncluttered, simple, flush lines of modern pieces. Too-long or too-thick legs can sometimes be cut down to more graceful proportions. Glued-on carving can be removed. Odd compartments, stand-up pieces at the back of chests, and ornamental bric-a-brac can be taken off. Glass-fronted cabinets can be modernized by replacing the glass with wire mesh or netting. Simple, modern knobs or drawer pulls can be substituted for old-fashioned hardware. In fact, nearly anything superfluous can be stripped off, so long as the structural elements of a piece remain. The structural elements of a table are the top and the legs and sometimes a stretcher; of a chest, the top, the sides (with or without legs), and the supporting front and back panels (although the purpose of the chest's structural elements is to support drawers, the drawers are a separate part, and sometimes it is desirable to remove one or more of them to improve the lines of a piece). It is easy to determine the structural elements of other pieces just by studying each part to see which ones are joining or supporting elements. These must be preserved or replaced, although they can be trimmed down if necessary. Not all pieces can be restyled, though. Some are too complex to be worth the undertaking.

Dark-colored woods can be bleached for a modern finish—golden oak, no longer fashionable, bleaches to a beautiful, pale blonde color. Flamboyantly grained veneers can be covered up with a coat of paint. Not every color of paint looks well on furniture. The best colors are white, black, dark Venetian red, leaf green, bottle green, and, in the proper setting, eggplant or dark olive green. A deep shade of gray-blue is sometimes effective when it is decorated with designs in white and bright colors and placed against a white background. Pastels, tans, and grays look wishy-washy. Browns look dull. Another objection to the use of brown is that it may appear to be a tasteless intention to imitate a natural wood color. Brilliant hues often tend to look garish, although Chinese red is sometimes effective if it is confined to a limited area. (*For refinishing methods, see the Chapter on Refinishing Furniture*).

Now, let's talk about some typical examples of old furniture pieces and what was done to revive them.

A Dining-Room Set. Mrs. J. found a dining room set at a second-hand store. The set consisted of a table, six chairs, and a buffet. The legs of the buffet and the table were cut in an ungainly scrolling shape, and the corners of the table were cut off at an angle (Fig. 1). The massive size of the table made it unsuitable for use in the average small, modern dining room (including Mrs. J.'s), and so she

FIG. 1. This oversize and badly proportioned dining-room table was part of a suite.

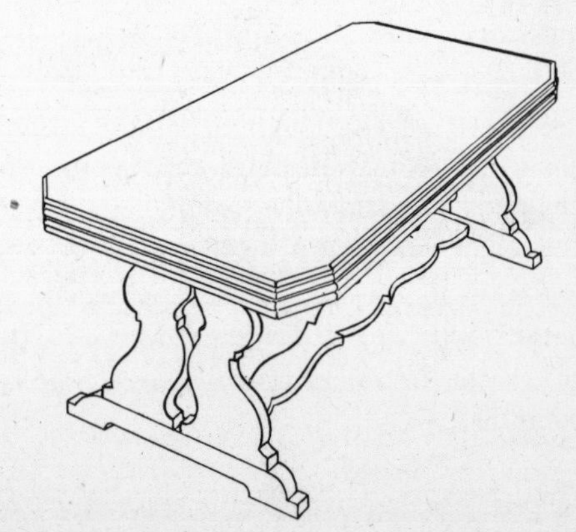

was able to buy the whole set for a ridiculously small sum. The wood itself was solid oak, but fumed to a dirty, dark brown. All the pieces were well made and the joints were sound.

Mrs. J. decided to cut down the legs of the table and the buffet in order to change the scrolling shape to straight simple lines. To do this, she first unbolted and unscrewed the legs from the table top. The legs were fastened to bases with mortise-and-tenon joints. The glue no longer held firmly, and Mrs. J was able to separate the base from the leg by moving it back and forth a little, very carefully, so as not to damage the joint. Then she measured and marked straight lines on the sides of the legs as cutting guides. With a rip saw (the cuts were with the grain of the wood), she sawed off the scrolls and narrowed the legs to the straight proportions shown in Fig. 2. The stretcher joining the two bases was removed, and the fancy scrollwork was sawed off to correspond to the new lines of the legs. The protruding feet of the bases were sawed off with a crosscut saw.

Next, the dropped edge fastened to the table top with screws was removed. In order to scale the table down to fit the size of the room and to eliminate the outmoded angled corners, 6 inches of the table top were sawed off at each side. This left the side edges straight, while the edges at each end were beveled. So 1 inch of the top was sawed off at each end. All cuts were planed and sanded smooth.

Mrs. J. then cleared off all the old glue from the mortise-and-tenon joints, applied new glue, and reassembled the legs and the bases. She had no clamps large enough to hold the pieces together firmly while the glue dried, so she made a tourniquet of heavy twine and a stick. She wrapped a double strand of twine under the base, and carried the twine up over the top of the leg and down, and knotted the two ends together. With the short stick, she twisted the twine until it was taut as she could make it. Then she tested the legs with the try-square to be sure their position was absolutely vertical. The stretcher and bases were also fitted together with mortise-and-tenon joints. These she reglued and reassembled. With a long, double strand of twine and a stick, she made another tourniquet to hold the two bases and the stretchers together firmly. Then she left the pieces alone for forty-eight hours to allow the glue to dry.

Two days later, after the glue had dried, she rebolted and rescrewed the table top to the legs. The cuts on the table had exposed the natural color of the white oak in sharp contrast to the dated fumed finish that had been given to the table. Mrs. J. wanted a bleached oak finish, so she removed the wax from the wood and applied one of the commercial bleaches. The bleach lightened the color of the wood considerably, but the contrast between the cut surfaces and the bleached surfaces was still too great. When another application of bleach failed to restore the fumed oak to its natural color, she decided to paint the pieces. The bleach had raised the grain of the wood slightly,

FIG. 2. The same dining-room table as it appeared after the legs had been cut down, the sides and dropped edge cut off, and the top covered with linoleum.

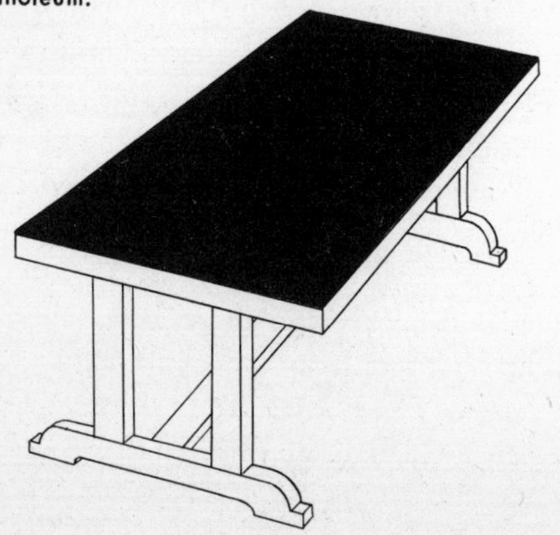

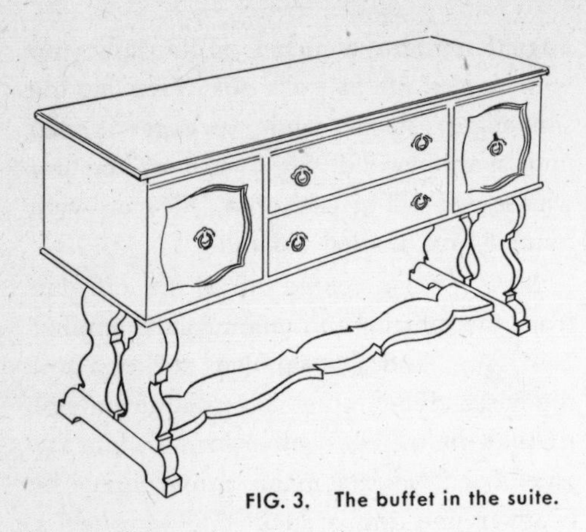

FIG. 3. The buffet in the suite.

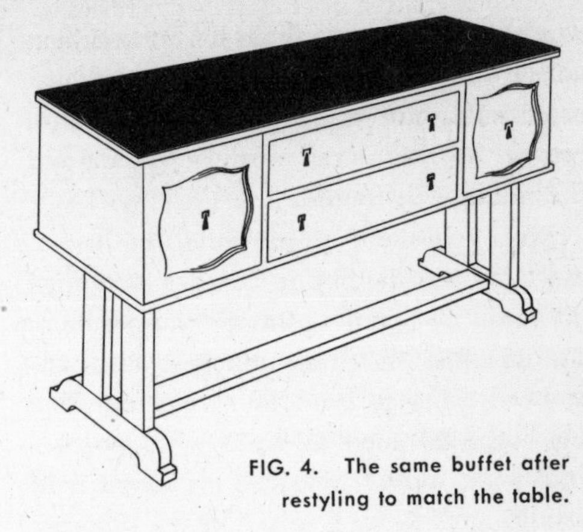

FIG. 4. The same buffet after restyling to match the table.

so she had to sand the wood smooth before painting. She selected white paint to harmonize with the blue-and-white wallpaper of her dining room. But since a white-painted top is none too practical for a dining-room table, she hit upon the idea of using linoleum for a cover. She bought a strip of linoleum in a deep, bright blue. She cut the linoleum with a linoleum knife so that it would fit the table top exactly. Then she applied linoleum cement to the table top to make the linoleum adhere firmly. She piled the table top with books to weight the linoleum down, and left them until the cement had dried.

In the meantime, she tackled the buffet (Fig. 3). She removed the legs and the stretcher and cut them to correspond in shape to the stretcher and legs of the table. Before removing the stretcher and legs, she took the drawers out of the buffet to lighten its weight so that she could lift the top and set it on the floor without too much effort. (Two pairs of hands are often needed to lift the heavy pieces.) After the legs and stretcher had been cut, she reglued the joints and reassembled the pieces, securing them with tourniquets in the same manner as the table. After the glue had dried, she rebolted and rescrewed the legs to the top of the buffet. Next, she removed the old-fashioned brass pulls on the drawers and the brass rings on the cupboard doors. She replaced these old hardware pieces with plain wooden knobs.

No time was wasted on the buffet by trying to bleach it. Instead, Mrs. J. simply removed the wax and applied the white paint. The top of the buffet was also covered with the blue linoleum. The remodeled buffet is shown in Fig. 4.

The knobs and curves on top of the chairs (Fig. 5) were cut off to make the top of the chair backs level. The front legs curved forward slightly, but since the curve could not be eliminated except by replacing the legs, Mrs. J. decided to leave them as they were. Also, the shape of the chair legs was not nearly so objectionable as that of the table and buffet legs. The seats of the chairs were upholstered in a dingy green and brown imitation tapestry. She turned the chairs upside down and removed the screws holding the chair seats in place. The upholstered seats could then be lifted right out of their frames. Next, she removed the wax finish on the chairs and painted them white. She removed the green and brown upholstery material from the chair seats and replaced it with a twilled cotton fabric in cherry red. The old padding material on the chair seats was still in good condition. Over it she stretched the new twilled fabric, bringing the edges over to the underside of the chair seat. She tacked the fabric in place. Then the chair seats were returned to their frames and screwed in place.

The shape of the splats in the chair back bore a resemblance to those of the buffet and table legs as they had been originally, but could not be eliminated by any structural change. So Mrs. J. covered the chair backs with slipcovers of the cherry-red cotton. The back and front of each slipcover were smartly fitted together with narrow boxed sections. The restyled chair appears in Fig. 6. At the cost of only a few dollars and her own efforts, Mrs. J. had furnished her dining room with a set of furniture which appeared more modern.

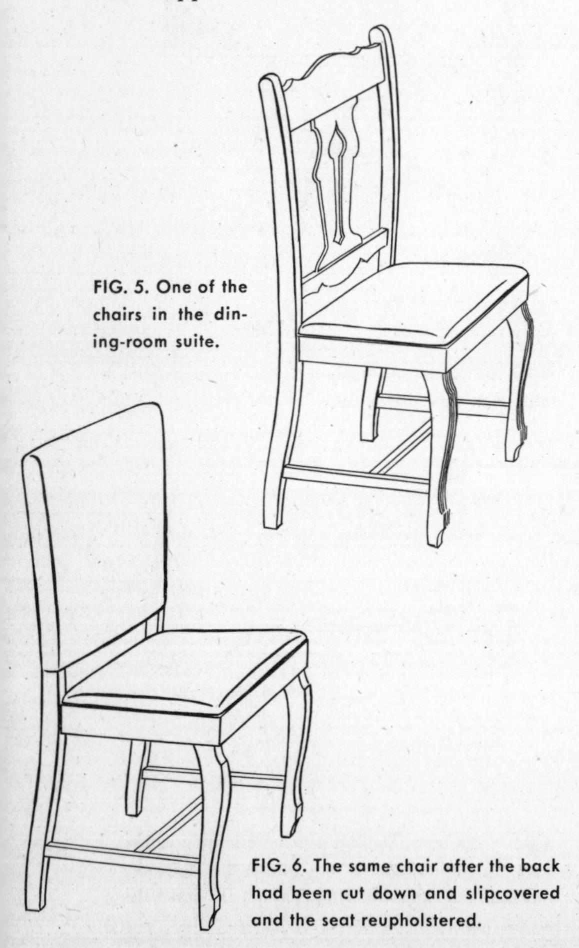

FIG. 5. One of the chairs in the dining-room suite.

FIG. 6. The same chair after the back had been cut down and slipcovered and the seat reupholstered.

FIG. 7. An old-fashioned, round dining-room table on a pedestal.

A Round Dining-Room Table on a Pedestal. Mrs. M. owned a large, round golden-oak dining-room table (Fig. 7) which had originally belonged to her mother. It rested on an octagonal pedestal supported by spreader feet. The table took up too much room in Mrs. M.'s small dining room, so she decided to make a drop-leaf table from it. First, she detached the top of the table by removing the bolts and screws holding it in place. Then she turned it upside down and laid it on the floor. The dropped edge fastened to the underside of the table top was unscrewed and removed. The table top was of the extension type which opened up in the middle for the insertion of extra leaves. Mrs. M. did not want to destroy this feature, so she sawed each side of the table top off along the ends of the extension structure.

At the hardware store she bought two sliding braces which she screwed to each side of the center section as supports for the drop leaves. Next, she returned the two sawed-off side sections to their original positions and fastened them to the center section with four hinges, two on each side (Fig. 8).

When she put the table top back in place on the pedestal, she found that the spreader feet jutted out beyond the top when the drop leaf hung down. So she removed the top again. Next, she unbolted

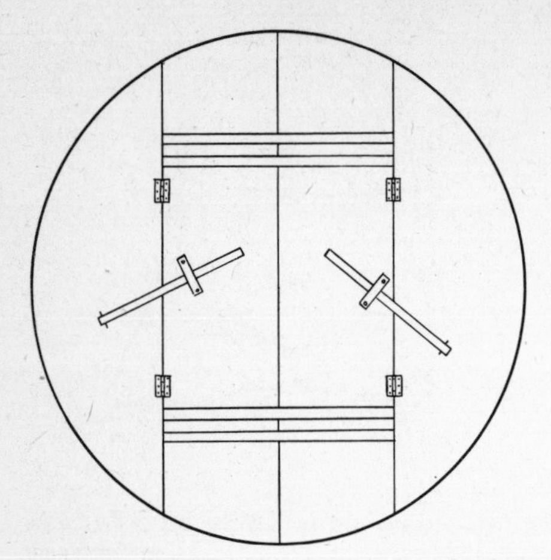

FIG. 8. The table top removed from the pedestal and turned upside down. The dropped edge was cut off and two sections were cut from the top and fastened back in place with hinges and braces.

FIG. 9. The table becomes a drop-leaf after the top is replaced. The pedestal was turned so the feet would not project.

the pedestal from the spreader feet, turned it around one-eighth of its distance from its former position, and bolted it back in place. When the table top was again replaced, the spreader feet were now at a 45° angle to the top and no longer a tripping hazard (Fig. 9).

After the old varnish had been removed, Mrs. M. bleached the golden oak color to a modern wheat tone. Now she has a handsome drop-leaf extension table at practically no cost except that for the hardware and the bleach.

A Marble-Topped Victorian Occasional Table. Letitia L., a young secretary who lived at home with her parents, wanted to change her bedroom into a bed-sitting room. She needed a coffee table to place in front of the new studio couch, but found that the budget could not be stretched to cover the cost of a new one. After rumaging through the attic, she found a tall old Victorian occasional table with a white marble top (Fig. 10). The ornately carved and curving legs were braced near the bot-

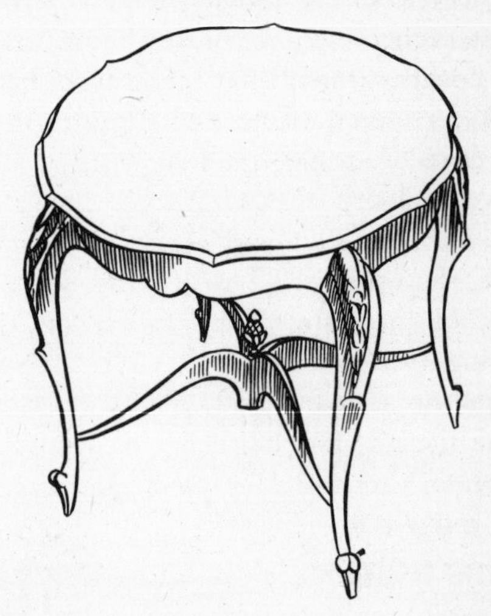

FIG. 10. A marble-topped Victorian occasional table with carved stretchers.

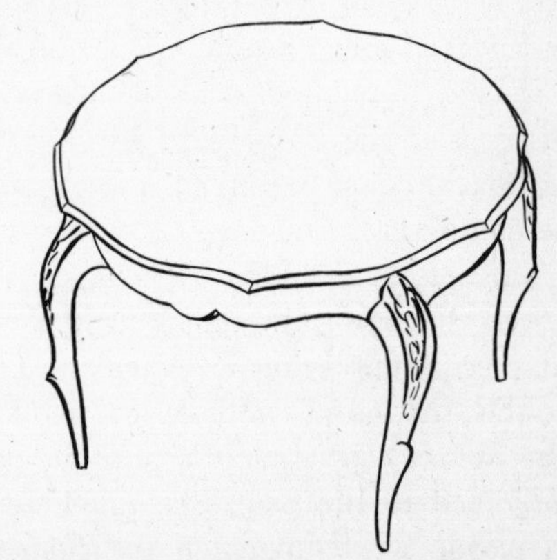

FIG. 11. The occasional table is turned into a coffee table by cutting off the legs above the stretchers and painting them an antique white to match the marble top.

tom with four stretchers surmounted at their central joining point by a dome-like ornament in the shape of a pineapple. In order to bring the table down to the right height, Letitia sawed the legs off above the stretchers. (The stretchers were not needed to brace the shortened legs.) While the table was of walnut, the graining of the wood had no particular distinction. Therefore, she decided to paint the legs an antique white to blend with the marble top. For this purpose she purchased some flat-white enamel and mixed a very small amount of burnt umber with it. At the same time, she bought a small can of wiping stain made for use on a bone-white finish. After two coats of enamel had been applied and allowed to dry, the stain was wiped on. As soon as the stain had reached the sticky stage, she wiped it off with a rag, leaving a bit of the stain in the hollows of the carvings. After the stain had dried overnight, she sealed it with a coat of clear white shellac. The finished table added a decorator's touch to the room at a cost of only a few cents (Fig. 11).

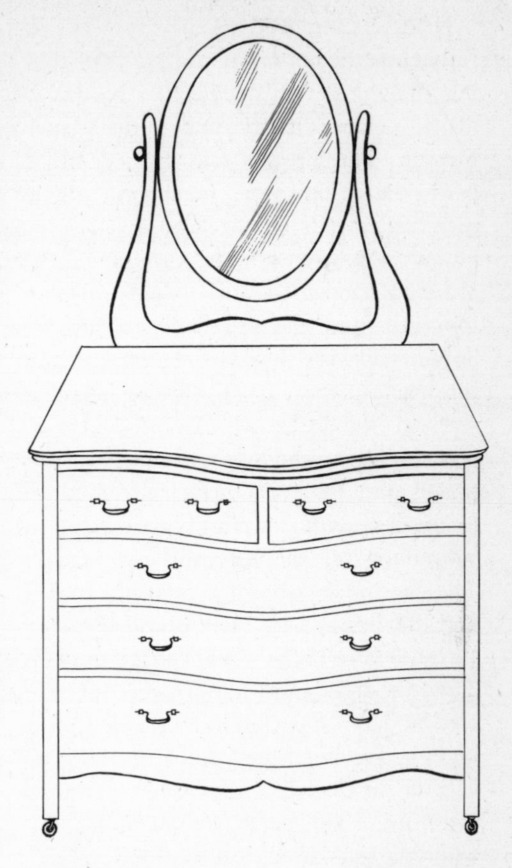

FIG. 12. An old dresser with an attached swinging mirror.

An Old Dresser Becomes a Console. Mrs. C. found an old dresser with a serpentine front and an attached, stand-up swinging mirror (Fig. 12) in a junk shop. The dresser was of solid walnut, and beautifully constructed throughout, but too dated to be used as it was. However, Mrs. C. decided that it could be turned into a handsome console by removing the mirror and the two bottom drawers. First of all, she removed the mirror by unbolting the upright pieces supporting it. After she had done this, she found two holes at the back of the dresser top where the uprights had been joined to the base. She filled them with plastic wood to match the color of the walnut—but not until she had completed the structural changes and removed the old varnish.

FIG. 13. The dresser is turned into a console by removing the mirror and the two bottom drawers. The old drawer pulls are replaced with new fixtures.

Next, she removed all the drawers. The rail across the bottom had a graceful curving design, so she decided to retain the piece, moving it up under the second drawer. The dresser was turned on its back, the casters were taken off, and an inch and a half of the legs sawed off to lower the height to better proportions. In order to remove the dust panels, the bottom rail, and the rail between the two bottom drawers. it was necessary to take the whole dresser apart. The top was unscrewed and lifted off. The dresser back was also unscrewed and removed. The dust panels and the rails (which were joined to the legs with doweling) were removed by pulling off the legs and side panels. The legs were separated and the panels and the dresser back were sawed in two to correspond to the new level of the drawers. Then the sides and the rails were reassembled and the doweling was reglued. New holes had to be drilled on the inside of the legs for the dowels of the bottom rail to be fitted into. The parts were held together while the glue dried with tourniquets made of double strands of heavy twine and a stick. The dowel holes in the legs into which the dowels of the bottom and second-from-the-bottom rails had been fitted were filled with plastic wood to match the color of the walnut after the old varnish had been removed. When the glue was dry, the top was screwed back into place.

Next, Mrs. C. removed the old drawer pulls. Then she stripped off the shiny old varnish down to the bare wood. She refinished the walnut with oil and wax, rubbing the piece until it glowed with a soft, satiny luster. Then she replaced the old drawer pulls with handsome reproductions of eighteenth-century hardware. The wood filler in the holes on the legs was not noticeable because it was below eye-level, but the filler on the top of the console was slightly visible. However, Mrs. C. covered both spots with a fine, old pair of Chinese ginger jars. Their resting place was a worthy setting for these old heirlooms, for Mrs. C.'s ungainly dresser had now become a lovely console (Fig. 13), with lines very similar to those of a fine, eighteenth-century English piece. Her only cost, besides her labor, was the few dollars she spent for the dresser, another few dollars for the new hardware, and a very small sum for the varnish remover, oil, and wax. Later, the framed mirror from the dresser was hung above a dressing table.

FIG. 14. This outsize and overdecorated sideboard was too large to fit into the average small dining room of today.

A Pair of Cabinet End Tables from a Sideboard. Mrs. A. needed a pair of end tables to flank the sofa in her living room. But the sofa itself, which she had just bought, had cost more than she had intended to pay, and so she decided that the end tables would have to wait. Then one day she spotted an old, bulky sideboard (Fig. 14) in a thrift shop. The piece consisted of two cabinet-like sections at each end and a curving center section fitted with drawers. Cabinet doors were decorated with gaudy, glued-on carving, as was the back panel on top. The piece was finished in several kinds of wood veneer in various dizzy grainings. The old sideboard had obviously once been part of a dining-room set, and now, because it stood in forlorn isolation and was too large and too ugly to adapt itself to any modern setting, Mrs. A. found that it could be obtained practically for the cost of having it carted home. Mrs. A. has a flair for seeing the possibilities which can be developed from monstrosities such as this sideboard, and after she had examined it, she found that each of the cabinet-like sections very nearly formed a complete unit, and the sections could, with some carpentry, be turned into a pair of cabinets to serve as end tables next to her sofa. So she bought the sideboard and had it carried home.

The first thing Mrs. A. did was to chisel off the ornate carved decorations from the cabinet sections in order to gain a clearer impression of the basic lines of the piece. Then she removed the fancy brass door pulls. After that, she took off the back panel from the top of the sideboard. When she had removed the drawers and unscrewed the top panel, she found that the cabinet sections could easily be separated by cutting through the front drawer rails, the stretcher, and the back panel. The detached cabinets, however, now had but three legs each. Since the bulbous front legs would still look awkward even after they were cut down, Mrs. A. decided to saw off all three legs and add new, short tapered ones to give the cabinet a modern appearance. She bought eight short, rounded and tapered legs, complete with dowels, and six large, square wooden knobs from a lumber dealer. Then she upended the cabinets, and, at the end of each stile, drilled a hole into which the dowel of the leg was to be fitted. Mrs. A. had only one clamp long enough to extend from the top of a stile to the end of a leg, so only one leg could be glued and dried at a time—a job which took over two weeks to finish. However, while she was waiting for the glue to dry on the second cabinet, the first one was, by that time, ready for further work.

Two end sections were cut from the long top panel of the sideboard to fit the tops of the cabinets. The sections were screwed to the cabinet tops, using the original screws and holes. The ends and front of this panel were finished with grooved beveling which Mrs. A. could not very well duplicate on the newly cut edges, not only because she lacked the necessary woodworking skill to do so, but also because the veneered wood permitted no such treatment. However, the inner sides of the cabinet would not be visible when they were placed against the ends of the couch. So all she did was to sandpaper the cut edges smooth.

FIG. 15. The end sections of the sideboard were removed and turned into cabinet end tables by adding new legs, removing the carving and hardware, and attaching three square knobs to each door. Shelves were installed in one cabinet to hold records.

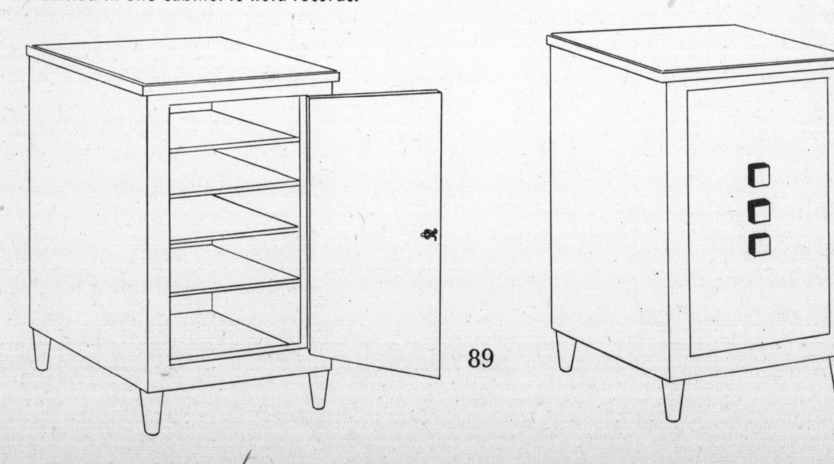

Each cabinet was already fitted with one shelf, but Mrs. A. wanted to add more shelves to one of the cabinets so that it could be used to hold the family's record albums. From the plywood dust panels under the drawers in the center section of the sideboard she cut four new shelves to fit inside one of the cabinets. She supported these shelves with angle irons screwed to the edges of the stiles on the inside of the cabinet (the screws would have punctured the side panels). The shelves were attached to the angle irons by drilling holes through the plywood and fastening it to the irons with short, blunt screws and small nuts.

The cabinets were now ready to be finished. Since Mrs. A.'s sofa was slipcovered in a glazed chintz with a striking floral pattern of eggplant, blue-violet, magenta, and green on a white ground, she decided to paint the cabinets an eggplant shade. First, she sandpapered all the rough spots where the glued ornaments had been. She applied three coats of flat paint, sanding each coat smooth after it had dried before applying the next. The final coat was rubbed to a soft gleam with fine sandpaper and pumice.

The square knobs were painted a vivid magenta color, also with flat paint. When they were dried and also smoothed with sandpaper and pumice, three were attached to each cabinet door. One was fastened to the place where the old metal fixture had been, one above, and one below, so that they formed a vertical row. The knobs were held with screws driven through the back of the cabinet doors. After a light waxing and polishing, Mrs. A. had a pair of modern cabinet end tables (Fig. 15) that would have cost a tidy sum to duplicate in the workshop of an interior decorator.

An Old Buffet Becomes a Chest Combined with Shelves. The dowdy looking buffet shown in Fig. 16 was a relic which Mrs. S. had inherited when she was a bride and had relegated to the basement years ago as a chest to hold fruit jars. But the buffet had a stout heart—neglect and

FIG. 16. This old buffet was a relic of another day.

FIG. 17. With restyling and a topping of bookshelves, the buffet becomes a handsome piece of furniture.

battering had not injured its sturdy frame.

Mrs. S. wanted a tall piece of furniture as a focal joint for a wall area between two doorways in her living room. She had visualized a handsome breakfront standing there, but all the ones she looked at cost hundreds of dollars. A friend suggested that open shelves atop a chest of drawers might be a good-looking and far less expensive substitute, and even described such an arrangement that another woman had made from an old dresser and a new, unpainted bookcase.

Mrs. S. remembered the buffet in the basement and went down to examine its possibilities. She decided that its basic lines were simple enough, and that all it needed were a few alterations and some paint, plus a topping of shelves.

First, she unbolted and removed the mirrored back panel with its shelf and curved supports. Then she planed the overhanging top edge until it was flush all-around with the front, back, and sides. To do this, she had to lay the buffet on the floor and turn it first on one side and then on another. Next, the front legs were cut off at the point where the S-curve began, and the back legs at a corresponding level. The superfluous curved ornament on the front between the doors was pried off.

Mrs. S. could not find a ready-made bookcase of the right size to fit the top of the newly reconstructed chest, so she had a woodworking shop make one from white maple. In the meantime, she refinished the chest. First, she sandpapered all the old blistered varnish smooth, and the edges of the top as well. Then she painted the piece with a flat paint in a deep shade of olive green as a foil for the slightly grayed yellow-green walls of her living room. The inner surfaces of the cupboards, doors, and drawers were painted chartreuse. After the bookcase arrived, that, too, was painted

FIG. 18. After the glass pane in the door of this china cabinet was broken, the cost of replacing the glass made the cabinet as good as useless—so the owner thought.

FIG. 19. A few alterations turned the cabinet into a useful bookcase after all.

olive green on the outside and chartreuse inside. As a final touch, Mrs. S. added the Pennsylvania Dutch decorations to the cupboard doors and drawer, but gave the design a modern interpretation with an original color combination — gray green, chartreuse, white, sharp red, and yellow. She admires her finished chest-shelf combination (Fig. 17) more than any breakfront she could have bought.

China Cabinet into Bookcase. The china cabinet shown in Fig. 18 had served for many years in Mrs. T.'s dining room, but when the glass pane in the door was broken, she hesitated to pay for the cost of a replacement because the piece had become so outmoded. She did, however, need another bookcase for the library, and realized that the china cabinet could be made into a very fine bookcase with little effort. The cabinet was of solid walnut and well made, and therefore definitely worth salvaging.

The paneless door was taken off simply by removing the hinges. The fancy pierced carving over the panes in the side panels was pried out and the glass panes were removed. Then the door and panel frames were taken off and the legs were cut down to within 2 inches of the bottom shelf. Next, Mrs. T. decided to pry off the decorative molding across the bottom and the carved panel across the top at the back. The only curves now left on the piece to mar the otherwise straight lines were on the inside of the sawed-off legs. She disposed of these curves by cutting them out with a chisel and sandpapering the edges smooth. Then she planed off the overhanging top edge to make it flush with the top front panel and the sides. The holes left by the nails which fastened the door and panel frames were filled with plastic wood. The newly evolved bookcase now needed only to be refinished. Mrs. T. removed the old varnish on all inside and outside surfaces with varnish remover, sanded the bare wood smooth, and then rubbed the bookcase to a satiny glow with raw linseed oil followed by wax. With relatively little effort and almost no expense, the old china cabinet was turned into a smart, modern bookcase (Fig. 19) to grace Mrs. T.'s library.

An Outsize Desk from a Pair of Old Chests. Mr. F. was a draftsman, who, in his spare time, was studying to be an architect. He wanted a desk with a very large working surface and plenty of drawers to hold his drafting supplies and drawings. He designed the type of desk he had in mind, but when he took the plans to a cabinet maker, he found that the cost of having such a desk made to order was greater than he could afford. Mr. F. could do simple woodworking, but he hesitated to tackle a job which called for cabinetmaking skill. When Mrs. F. looked at his drawings, she remarked that the side sections with drawers might be made from a pair of twin oak chests (one of which is shown in Fig. 20) that her sister was planning to discard. The drawers in the chest were not as shallow or as numerous as those in Mr. F.'s drawing, but he thought that deeper drawers might serve his needs well enough. With a little carpentry and

FIG. 20. One of a pair of twin chests which were about to be discarded.

FIG. 21. The chests after they were cut down and made into a large desk by adding a plywood top.

the addition of a plywood top, Mr. F. decided that he could turn the chests into a desk which would serve his needs satisfactorily. So, with the consent of Mrs. F.'s sister, they asked a truckman to pick the chests up and deliver them.

The desk height which Mr. F. wanted was 32 inches. The four bottom drawers of the chests measured 32 inches exactly, not counting the base or legs. The legs could be removed, but not the base, and that would add an extra 2 inches to the height of the desk. With the addition of the plywood top, his desk would be 35 inches high if he used all four of the bottom drawers—much too high! On the other hand, if he used only three of the bottom drawers, it would be approximately 27 inches high—much too low! Mrs. F. suggested that perhaps the shallow top drawer, which was 4½ inches deep, could be shifted into the position of the drawer beneath it — and presto! there would be the right combination of drawers to give approximately the right height without having to cut down any of the drawers themselves.

First, Mr. F. unscrewed the tops of the chests. Then he took out the second drawer from the top of one chest and replaced this drawer with the top drawer. He marked the position of the top edge of the drawer on the side panels of the chest, removed all drawers, turned the chest over, and cut down the side panels and back about 1/16 of an inch above the mark he had made. Then he cut the legs off flush with the base. He repeated these steps with the other chest. Next, he placed the two chests side by side with enough space between them to allow for adequate knee room, and measured the distance between the outer ends.

Mr. F. bought a ¾-inch-thick, oak-finished plywood panel in the nearest size to correspond to the over-all top measurement of his desk. When the plywood arrived, he cut it to fit across the tops of the chests, leaving edges flush all around. He attached the plywood panel with angle irons on the inner sides of the chest and with finishing nails on the outside top edges. The edges of the plywood panel showed a cross-section view of the construction, and had to be covered with a flat, ¾-inch wide molding to match. The molding was nailed on with tiny, nearly invisible brads. The old glass knobs on the chest were replaced with simple wooden ones bought from the hardware store. The chests, which were in good condition, needed no refinishing. So Mr. F. applied a light oak oil stain to the plywood to match the color of the chests. By careful application and testing of color depth, he was able to duplicate the tone of the chests very closely. He sealed the stain with a coat of shellac and then waxed both the plywood top and the chests. Both Mr. and Mrs. F. are pleased with the finished desk (Fig. 21) which now stands in their living room. The desk not only gives Mr. F. adequate working and storage space, but it also serves as a buffet table when the F.'s entertain a number of guests at supper: Mrs. F. simply covers the desk with a long pad and cloth.

FURNITURE REPAIRS

Furniture need not always be discarded because of a split leg, loose joints, and other ailments. A simple repair job will often cure the trouble.

Broken Legs. Careless treatment can sometimes cause a leg on a chair, cabinet, or other piece of furniture to split. The split usually occurs along the grain of the wood. To mend the leg, the split piece should be fitted into place on the leg and held there firmly with a C-clamp. In order to prevent the clamp from marring the wood, it

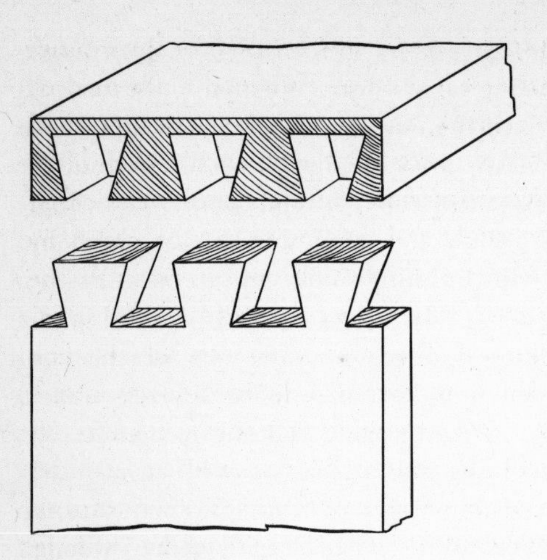

FIG. 22. A dovetailed joint. Drawer sections are usually joined in this way.

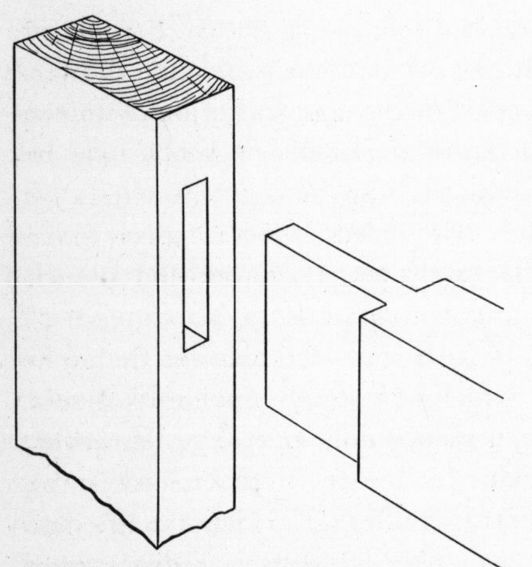

FIG. 23. A mortise-and-tenon joint.

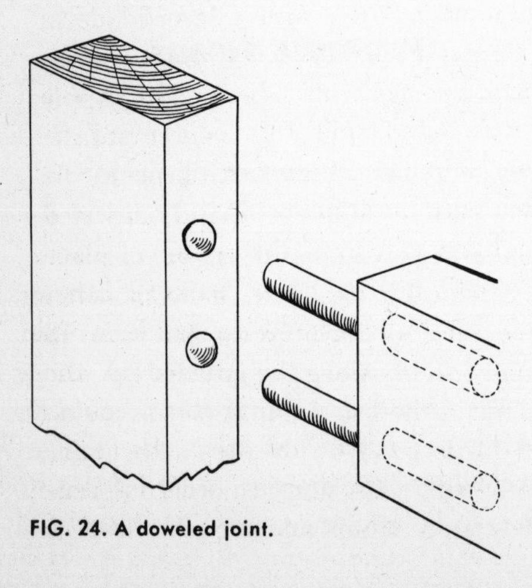

FIG. 24. A doweled joint.

should be protected with small pieces of cardboard where the clamp comes in contact with the surface. With a dowel-bit and a brace or a hand drill, a hole is then drilled through the split piece and on into the leg. A dowel stick of the right diameter to fit the hole is then cut a little longer than the hole is deep (dowel sticks can be bought in various diameters). The dowel stick should fit snugly, but if it is a trifle too thick to be wedged into the hole, a little sandpapering will thin it to the proper size.

Remove the clamp and separate the split piece from the leg. With a small brush, apply glue inside the holes in both parts and also to the split surface of each section. Fit the pieces together again and hold them securely with two C-clamps. Then, with a hammer, drive the dowel stick into the hole. Leave the clamps on the leg for 48 hours while the glue has an opportunity to dry. Then sand the end of the dowel stick until it is flush with the surface of the leg. If the surface of the leg has not been marred, all that needs to be done is to touch up the end of the dowel stick with a shellac stick in a color to match the wood. If the leg has been marred, it may have to be entirely refinished.

Loose Joints. Dampness causes wood to swell, while heat and dryness cause it to shrink. Shrinking and swelling loosen the glue in joints, and when this happens, chairs, tables, and other pieces begin to wobble, creak, and sometimes to fall apart. The three principal types of joints used in furniture construction are mortise-and-tenon, doweled, and dovetailed (*see illustrations*). The procedure for mending any of these joints is simple. Separate the joined parts completely. Scrape away all old glue from both parts of the joint and smooth the part which fits into the hollow part with sandpaper. New glue is then applied to both parts of the joint, after which they are fitted together. The parts must be held together firmly while the glue dries. A vise, clamps, or a tourniquet (such as that made of cord and a stick, described earlier in this chapter under the heading *A Dining Room Set*) can be used for this purpose. At least 48 hours should be allowed for the glue to dry.

If the tenon of a mortise-and-tenon joint has been broken off, it cannot be repaired. Broken dovetailing cannot be repaired either, if the damage is extensive. The hole left by a missing section or two can be filled with plastic wood, but if a strip of the dovetailing has been broken off, it cannot be repaired except by replacing the damaged part with a new one.

If the part of a joint which fits into the other part has shrunk so much it no longer fits snugly, it can be tightened by inserting thin metal wedges which are made for this purpose. Curved metal wedges are obtainable for use on rounded chair rung joints.

Loose Knobs and Handles. Most loose knobs or handles can be fixed merely by tightening the screw or nut on the inside of the drawer or door. If the nut cannot be turned sufficiently for this, take it off, insert a metal washer or small doughnut-shaped piece of cardboard over the end of the screw, and replace the nut. Screws which penetrate a knob sometimes become loose because the hole in the knob has become too enlarged to hold the screw. Remove the knob and fill the hole with plastic wood. Rescrew the knob in place before the plastic wood has hardened completely.

Sticking Drawers. In good grades of furniture, all parts of the drawers are made of hardwoods, which shrink or swell very little. Such drawers seldom give any trouble. But in less expensive grades of furniture, softwood may be used for the interior parts of a drawer. Softwood tends to swell or shrink as the weather changes, and drawer parts made of such wood often stick, especially during damp weather. If the sticking is slight, it can be cured by rubbing the side and bottom edges of the drawer with soap or paraffin, or by sandpapering the edges. Drawers which stick badly may have to be planed down on one or more edges. If the drawer sticks so badly it cannot be removed at all, the swollen wood can sometimes be shrunk enough to get the drawer out by rubbing it with a medium hot iron on the inside—providing, of course, that the iron can be admitted. It not, it is better to wait for warm, dry weather to shrink the drawer. If you try to pull the drawer out with too much force, the joints or knobs may be loosened or broken.

Peeled or Blistered Veneer. Properly made veneers rarely peel or blister. But if such a condition occurs on a valuable piece of furniture, it is not advisable for the amateur to attempt a repair—such work should be done by a skilled craftsman. However, successful results are often obtained by the home craftsman, so if you want to attempt the repair with the realization that it may not be satisfactory, here is how to proceed. First, slit the blister with a razor blade in the direction of the wood grain. Then soften the veneer with a damp cloth. Apply glue to the underside of the veneer and the surface of the furniture piece beneath the veneer with a knife or spatula inserted through the slit. Press the veneer in place and weight it with heavy books or other objects until the glue dries (at least 48 hours). Peeled veneer is treated in the same way except that it probably needs no slit. After the veneer has dried, the entire surface where the damage occurred usually has to be refinished.

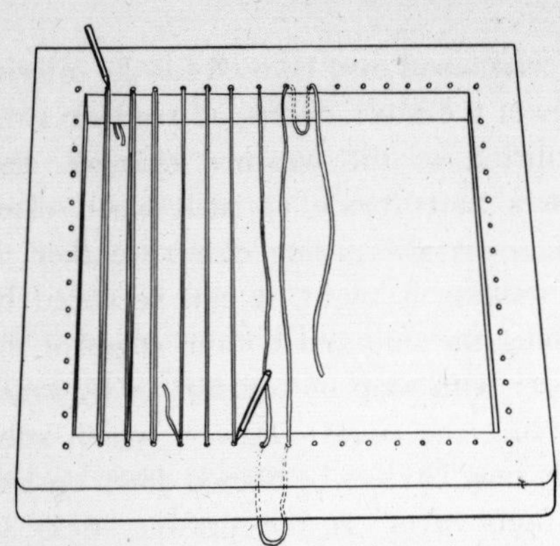

FIG. 25. The first steps in recaning a chair seat.

Recaning. With care, the seat or back of a chair or other piece can be recaned by the amateur for very little money. The cane for such work comes in various sizes in hanks of 1,000 feet. Measure the holes and the space between the holes in the chair seat, or whatever is to be recaned, and buy the size needed as follows:

Size of Hole	Distance Between Holes	Size of Cane to Use
3/16 inch	3/8 inch	Superfine
3/16 inch	1/2 inch	Fine-fine
3/16 inch	5/8 inch	Fine
1/4 inch	3/4 inch	Medium
5/16 inch	7/8 inch	Common

Approximately one hank of medium cane is needed to recane three small or two large chair seats.

The first step is to remove all old cane and to clean out the holes. Then, to make the new cane pliable, soak it in tepid water for a few minutes. The cane should be kept moist while you work with it. A sponge and a bowl of warm water can be used for this purpose. Cut the cane in lengths which are easy to work with. For an average-sized seat, the pieces of cane should be about three times the distance across the chair seat, plus another foot or so for splicing and crossing from one hole to the next hole on the same side.

In working with the cane, remember to keep the glossy side up and always to carry

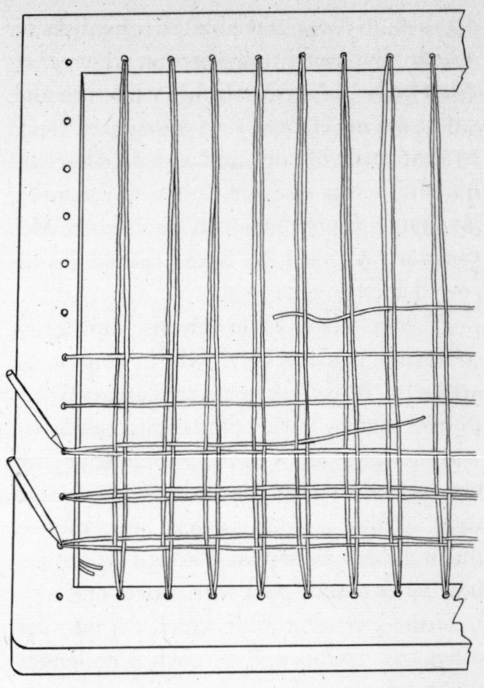

FIG. 26. After the vertical strands of cane are in place, the next step is to weave the horizontal strands.

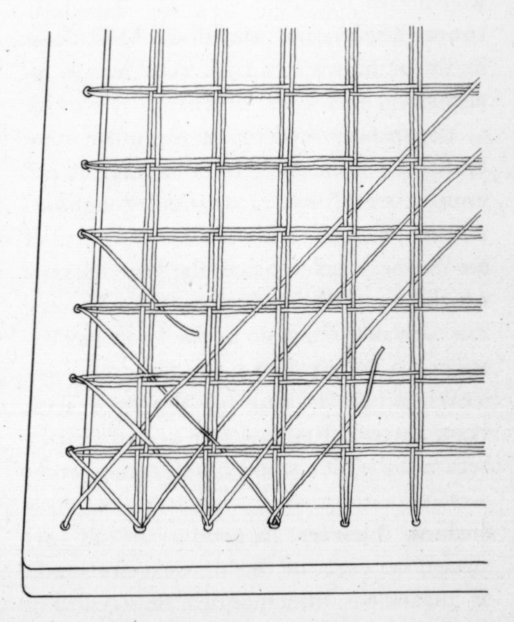

FIG. 27. Diagonal strands woven from each side complete the job.

the strand from the hole on one side to the hole directly opposite on the other side. Begin at any hole next to a corner hole, but do *not* start at the corner hole. (To distinguish strands, we shall describe the first set as vertical.) Push the cane through the hole from the underside, and draw it up to within three inches of the end. Hold the cane end in place with a peg or a pencil and bring the strand straight across the seat to the hole directly opposite. Push the end through the hole to the underside. Stretch the cane taut and bring the free end up from the underside through the next hole on the same side, across the chair seat, and down through the hole directly opposite (the hole next to the hole where you started). Continue from hole to hole until the strand is used up. The end is brought through the hole to the underside and held in place with a peg or pencil. As the cane dries, moisten it with the sponge.

After you have worked the cane all the way across the chair seat, another set of strands are drawn through the same holes in the same way to form a double set of strands in each hole.

You can now begin to splice the loose ends. Splicing is done by twisting the loose ends several times around the stretched strand where it is carried from one hole to the next hole at the right or left and on the underside of the seat. Pegs or pencils are not removed until you begin to splice.

When two sets of vertical strands have been carried from hole to hole across the seat of the chair, they are ready to be woven with another set of horizontal strands. The first horizontal strands are passed between the double vertical strands. It makes no difference whether you pass the horizontal strand over and under or under and over the double vertical strands, but whichever way you do it, it should be done the same all the way across. Remember to keep the glossy side of the cane right side up at all times. Be careful not to skip holes.

Another set of horizontal strands are now drawn through the same set of holes as the first horizontal strands. However, the second horizontal strands are crossed under the vertical strand wherever the first horizontal strand was crossed over, and vice versa. After the second set of horizontal strands are woven, the cane is moistened with the sponge, and the strands are forced together to make them straight and the spaces between them even.

The next step is to weave the diagonal strands. Begin at any corner hole. Weave the cane under the horizontal strands and over the vertical strands, until the corner hole diagonally opposite is reached. Bring the cane down through this corner hole and up through the hole next to it (either on the vertical or horizontal side). If the cane is difficult to push through the hole by this time, force it through with the aid of an awl. After the cane is woven from all holes in one diagonal direction, it is again woven from the same holes in the opposite diagonal direction, but this time, the strands are woven under all vertical strands, and over all horizontal strands (*see illustration*). Of course, loose ends are spliced after each set is completed.

For a professional finish, bind the edges of the caning by laying a strand of cane over the holes. Splice the end to fasten it. This strand is then laced with another strand which is brought up through the holes, over the first strand, and down through the same hole. However, this binding is not essential and can be eliminated if preferred, since it is very tedious to force the cane through the already well-filled holes.

CHAPTER VIII

REFINISHING FURNITURE

NOW AND AGAIN one hears about the ardent collector who spotted the Duncan Phyfe table in an old secondhand store and bought it for a song. The reason was that no one, unless he had the trained eye of our ardent collector, would have recognized it as such because it was disguised under many layers of old paint. But our A.C. carted it home, and after much loving labor, he removed the paint and restored the rich mahogany wood to its original lustrous finish. Now it stands forth resplendently — a treasure to gloat over.

That always happens to the A.C., but never to us. All *we* ever find beneath old paint is something that should have been left hidden. Yet many a gem of purest walnut or mahogany has been uncovered this way. And though the chance that it might turn out to be a Duncan Phyfe table is probably one in a million, it might be a good reproduction. On the other hand, perhaps you have some monstrosity that has to be disguised with paint to match its background so that it won't stick out like a sore thumb. Or if a preference for blondes extends to woods, then you'll want to bleach — the wood, that is. But first, let's get down to the bare wood, because that step is so often necessary in a complete job of refinishing.

Removing Old Finishes. Paint, varnish, shellac, and stain can be removed with a paint and varnish removing compound. Besides this, you will need a brush about 2 or 3 inches wide (an old brush can be used for this purpose); a putty knife or scraper; steel wool, both medium and fine; plenty of sandpaper in grades 0000 to 1½ and a block of wood around which to wrap the sheets; turpentine; cheesecloth or clean, soft rags; and for protection, an old smock or overalls, rubber or cotton gloves, and a generous supply of newspapers.

Spread a thick layer of newspapers out on the floor. and on them place the piece of furniture which is to be refinished. Apply the paint and varnish remover with the brush, and let it stand for about five minutes or so until the old finish softens. Then scrape it off with the putty knife. Steel wool will have to be used to get the stuff off around curved surfaces, carved areas, or small projections. A second application is usually required, but repeat as many times as necessary until every bit of the old finish has been removed. Then clean the wood with turpentine, washed on freely and wiped up with the cheesecloth or rags. After the piece is thoroughly dry, sand it smooth. Always work with the grain of the wood, whether scraping or sanding.

The necessity for this treatment depends upon what kind of a finish you want to apply. It is not necessary if you want to paint. Nor is it required for furniture which is finished only with wax or oil, unless you want to bleach it. Wax or oil must be removed, of course, before paint, stain, shellac or varnish can be applied. But a generous application of turpentine is usually all that is necessary. Rub the turpentine in thoroughly and wipe it up as you proceed.

Wood Fillers. Porous woods often need an application of wood filler. This is used after the old finish is removed and before the new one is applied, unless the wood is to be stained, in which case the stain is applied before the filler. Fillers usually come in paste form, and must be applied or thinned according to the manufacturer's directions. Select the filler in a color to match the wood. Open-grained woods which require filling are oak, walnut, and mahogany. Close-grained woods, such as maple, gum, pine, poplar, fir, cedar, and basswood need no filler.

The consistency of the fillers should depend upon the degree of porousness of the wood. Oak requires a thicker filler than walnut. Apply the filler with a fairly stiff brush, working with the grain of the wood and packing it in well. As soon as it begins to lose its glossy appearance, take a rag and rub *across* the grain. Then use another clean rag, and finish by wiping *with* the grain. After the filler is completely dry (which usually takes from 12 to 48 hours), sand lightly with a fine grade of sandpaper.

Small holes can be filled with one of the plastic wood mixtures, some of which come in colors to match various woods, or with a shellac stick. Shellac sticks also come in different colors, and are used by heating one end slightly over a flame and pressing it into the hole. The plastic wood compounds are mostly pastes which are simply pressed into the hole. The excess shellac or paste is removed with a putty knife before it has set. When the filled area is dry, sand the surface lightly.

FIG. 1. Wood filler should be brushed on with the grain of the wood, then rubbed with a cloth across the grain to pack filler in firmly. A final rubbing with clean cloth is given with the grain to remove all excess filler.

FINISHES

The choice of a new finish should be primarily governed by the type of wood you are working with. Fine woods need only a finish which will enhance and bring out their natural, beautiful lusters and colors to best advantage. They should never be hidden under paint. Bleaching, does not destroy the texture of the grain, and often results in very interesting tones which are especially suited to modern interiors.

The principal methods of finishing furniture are: (1) oiling; (2) waxing; (3)

staining, shellacking, and waxing; (4) shellacking and waxing; and (5) varnishing. Of these, oil or wax (either alone or in combination) are recommended for fine woods, although some people prefer shellac and wax. Paints and lacquers will also be discussed here, although they are really coatings.

Oil or Wax. Opinions differ on how to oil furniture almost as much perhaps as on mixing mint juleps. Some like the oil hot, and some like it cold. But all agree that the chief ingredient for a beautiful luster is elbow grease — the real secret lies in rubbing, and lots of it.

Various kinds of rubbing oils are sold, some under trade names, and many of them produce good results. But the time-honored preference is for raw linseed oil. This brings out the rich color of the wood. The oil must penetrate the wood deeply and evenly and the surface must be smoothed to a dry, satiny finish. In order to make the oil penetrate better, some people heat it. Others thin it by mixing with turpentine — about half and half. The first coat is usually quite generous. It may be allowed to soak in and dry before rubbing. But we prefer to apply it hot and to begin the rubbing process with fine pumice before the oil has soaked in completely. The finest grade of pumice is used, and it is rubbed with felt or soft cloth. Keep the cloth free from lumps of pumice, and work with the grain. Each surface is rubbed for at least fifteen to twenty minutes, and then wiped very clean with a soft rag. This process should be repeated three or four times, allowing an interval of at least two or three days between rubbings. Only a scant amount of oil is used for these subsequent application. Then the piece should be rubbed with oil and rottenstone once or twice. Anywhere from one to five additional coats of oil should then be applied about a week apart, with vigorous rubbing after each coat. By this time a rich, lustrous glow is almost certain. Wood finished in this way needs no other treatment. It resists scratching, heat, and moisture, and afterwards needs only to be rubbed with oil about once a year. Needless to say, only the finest solid hardwoods are worth all this effort, but if you possess a treasure made of such wood, it certainly deserves this treatment.

Waxing produces a good luster with less effort, but it does not bring out the color as well as oil. The color of all woods, however, deepens with age. Colored waxes are also available which combine the qualities of both a stain and a wax. Although waxing alone is sometimes used as a finish, more often it is applied as a final finish on top of something else, such as shellac, varnish, or paint. The wax helps to protect the surface against dirt as well as lend a pleasing sheen. Wax, however, is not a particularly durable finish and must be renewed at frequent intervals. Also, it tends to watermark.

Waxes may be bought in natural lump form and prepared at home if one wishes, but the result undoubtedly would be inferior to the best quality of ready mixed waxes. These consist principally of beeswax, although other waxes are also used

FIG. 2. For smoother finish, brush around small cylindrical surfaces, such as that of a table leg or chair leg.

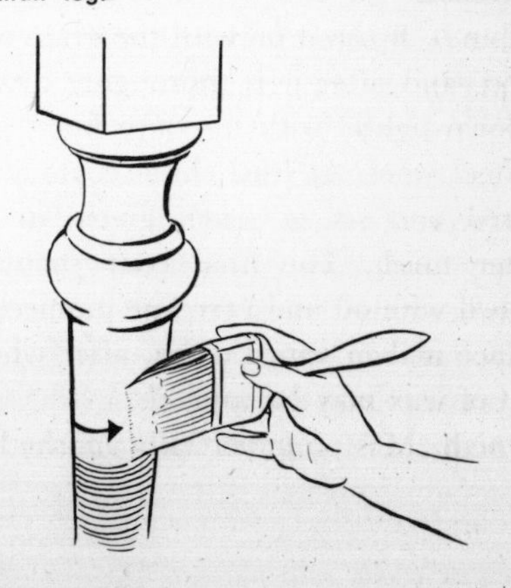

in varying proportions. Most commercial waxes contain some carnauba, an extremely hard wax obtained from a species of palm tree. The cheaper waxes usually contain a high percentage of paraffine, which is too soft to produce a good lustrous finish. They are poor economy even though they cost less. The liquid self-polishing waxes are not recommended for use on furniture.

For best results, apply only the thinnest possible film of wax, using a clean, soft cloth for this purpose. Let the wax dry for about ten minutes before polishing. Hard waxes produce the best luster but it can be brought out only with hard, vigorous rubbing — always with the grain of the wood. Apply several coats, and allow each coat to dry for at least two hours before applying the next.

Shellac. A fine, lustrous, heat- and water-resistant finish can be obtained with shellac and wax with considerably less effort than oiling. It does not, however, bring out the natural deep wood tones. To overcome this difficulty, one can use colored shellac or stain followed by shellac. The color obtained may or may not be as pleasing as the natural tone. Shellac may be applied on unfinished wood or over stain, paint, or varnish, but never over wax or oil. Colorless shellac is also used as a protective coat on top of wallpaper when it is used to decorate furniture.

It is better to apply the shellac in very thin coats — if it is too thick, use alcohol to thin it. Brush it on with the grain of the wood, and after it is thoroughly dry, rub it down lightly with the very finest grade of steel wool. At least three coats are required and six or seven given an even better finish. The final coat should be rubbed with oil and very fine pumice. The surface is then wiped clean, after which a coat of wax may be applied.

Varnish. Most commercially finished furniture is varnished — sometimes with a gloss which is so bright that it is objectionable. There are many different kinds of varnish — some produce a very hard, durable finish which resists stains, scratches, heat, and water. But for successful results, the varnish must be applied under carefully controlled conditions, and for this reason, some other type of finish may be preferable.

First, the varnish must be warm. If it is cold, it should be heated by placing the can in a pan of warm water until the varnish reaches a temperature of at least 70 but no more than 90 degrees. Do not stir the varnish, as this causes air bubbles to form which may remain after drying. The room in which the work is done should be as dust free as possible — in fact, it is a good idea to sprinkle the floor (or newspapers on the floor) with water before starting.

Next, brush the surface of the wood with a soft brush to remove the dust which is bound to be present to some extent. Not all of it can be removed by brushing, however, and the remaining particles should be picked up with a rag which has been first dipped in warm water, wrung out, sprinkled with turpentine, and then with about two teaspoonsful of varnish. Fold and twist the rag until it is nearly dry but still sticky. Then wipe the piece carefully with the rag to remove the last traces of dust.

Do not use the varnish directly from the can, as dust may be transferred from the brush to the varnish in the can. Instead, pour a small amount into another container, such as an old tin cup. To apply the varnish to a flat surface, work with the grain of the wood. Finish the coat off by running the tip of the brush from one edge to the other over the entire surface. Curved legs should be brushed round and round.

Specks of dust inevitably settle on the varnish as it dries and must be removed with a small sliver of wood before the varnish is too hard. The lightest touch with the wood sliver is all that is necessary to remove the specks.

Two coats of varnish give a good finish, but three or four are better The first coat should be thinned slightly with a little turpentine in the proportions of one part turpentine to six of varnish. Allow each coat to dry thoroughly before applying the next. Rub with very fine sandpaper between coats. Drying usually requires at least 48 hours, but may take several days if the weather is damp. After the final coat is dry, rub first with fine pumice and oil and then with rottenstone and oil, and after cleaning, varnish-polish or a film of wax may be applied.

Lacquer. True lacquer is made from a substance called *lac,* but it is doubtful if you will find any lacquer of this kind. The products called lacquer are now made from nitrocellulose or synthetic resins. Many different kinds are produced, and among them are finishes far superior to anything ever made from materials found in nature. Not all of these can be applied at home — some must be sprayed on or baked. Some dry almost on contact. For home use, slower drying brushing lacquers should be selected. These usually dry in about two hours and give a very hard, durable finish. The difficulties of applying lacquer successfully, however, are much the same as those with varnish. Best results are obtained by spraying, but sometimes a smooth finish can be produced with a brush. Spraying requires special equipment and should not be attempted with the sprayer attachment of a vacuum cleaner.

Clean the piece to be lacquered according to the method described in the paragraph above under Varnish. The method of applying the lacquer is also the same as that for varnish. The first coat may be thinned with lacquer thinner, but this is not essential. At least three coats are usually necessary on unfinished wood, although additional coats give a more durable finish. Allow each coat to dry thoroughly before applying the next. Specks or ridges should be removed with medium sandpaper after each coat is dry. After the final coat has dried for about 48 hours, it should be rubbed first with fine sandpaper and linseed oil, and then with a lacquer rubbing-compound followed by lacquer-polish.

Stain. Stains are often used to darken the natural tones of woods. They come in all natural wood colors and quite a few unnatural ones as well. All stain can do is to change the color of a wood, but the choice of color should be appropriate for the type of wood. Pine will not look like mahogany by the mere application of mahogany stain. On the other hand, a darker maple stain is quite appropriate for a maple which is considered too light.

Stains are of several types, but may be classed here as penetrating and non-penetrating, and with either an oil or a water base. Hard woods require a penetrating stain. Water stains penetrate deeply and are non-fading but their use raises the grain of the wood, necessitating much sanding to level the surface. The penetrating stains should not be used on soft wood as an unpleasant color usually results. Oil stains are either penetrating or pigmented. The pigment stains are more like thin paints and obscure the grain of the wood slightly. All stains must be applied directly to the wood, and all existing finishes must first be removed.

To apply water stains, first brush or mop the surface of the wood with water to raise the grain. (Since the stain will raise it anyhow, it is better to do this first

A coat of shellac being given to a chest of drawers to preserve the hand-painted decorations.

and sand the wood before staining so that the color will not be spotty from sanding later.) After an hour or so, sand smooth, beginning with medium coarse sandpaper and finishing with fine. Then apply the stain with a brush. Stroke it on rapidly and freely. One coat is usually all that is necessary, but if a darker color is desired, a second coat may be applied. After the stain has been allowed to dry for 12 to 14 hours, a light sanding should follow.

Oil stains are brushed on without any previous wetting of the wood. After the stain has been allowed to stand for about ten minutes, or until the color is of the required depth, the excess stain is wiped off with a cloth. The wiping must be done before the stain has dried in order to insure even distribution of the color.

Both water and oil stains must be sealed with shellac. In the case of oil stain, it should be allowed to dry for three or four days before the shellac is applied. One coat of shellac is usually sufficient to seal, but several coats give a better finish (*see paragraph on Shellac*). Finish with a coat of wax.

Bleaching. All solid woods can be bleached, and some veneers which are thick enough can be bleached successfully. However, the outcome when bleaching veneers is always doubtful, and therefore the process is recommended only for solid woods.

The ready-mixed commercial bleaches do an excellent job, but a satisfactory and less expensive homemade bleach can be mixed by dissolving one ounce of oxalic acid crystals in a pint of hot water. This solution is not quite as powerful as the commercial bleaches but it is effective unless one wants to change dark woods to a very light tone.

Before the bleach can be applied, the wood must be cleaned of all previous finishes. The bleach is powerful stuff, and one should wear rubber gloves while working with it. Protect the clothing as well and cover the floor with a thick layer of newspapers. Apply the bleach with a brush or a rubber sponge. The oxalic acid solution usually has to remain on overnight, after which it must be washed off with borax dissolved in one quart of warm water. A second coat of bleach may be applied before washing if a lighter color is wanted.

Commercial bleaches are of two types. One type consists of two separate solutions, applied one after the other. The other type is a single solution. As a rule, neither type must be washed off after using, but the manufacturer's directions should be followed in this respect. The bleach must be allowed to dry thoroughly before any finishing coat is applied.

After bleaching and drying, the wood should be sanded smooth as the bleaching process raises the grain somewhat. If by chance the color obtained is lighter than you want, it can be easily darkened with a light application of an oil stain in a light color. If possible, try the stain first on some part which does not show to be sure that the effect is right. If stain is used, it must be sealed with a coat of shellac.

Wood which has been bleached is usually finished with either shellac or wax. A "pickled" finish is obtained by brushing on a thin coat of white paint and wiping it off before it has dried. This is done before waxing or shellacking.

Paint and Enamel. Inexpensive unfinished furniture made of soft wood, such as pine, is more satisfactory when painted or enameled. But hardwoods may also be finished in this way. Badly proportioned furniture can be effectively disguised by painting it to match the color of the background. Paints are somewhat easier to work with than enamels, but enamel gives a harder and more durable finish. The same procedure is followed for applying either one, so we shall speak only of paint.

Select a paint which is specifically intended for use on furniture. Paint may be applied on top of old paint, varnish, or shellac. All that is necessary is to sand the old finish lightly to remove any gloss. Wax and oil finishes must first be removed with turpentine. Stained finishes require a priming coat of aluminum paint to prevent the old color from bleeding through. New wood should be dampened to raise the grain and then sanded smooth. A coat of commercial primer may then be applied, or the paint itself may be mixed with about 25 per cent of turpentine as a primer. Allow this coat to dry for several days and rub smooth with fine sandpaper. Then apply the paint as it comes from the can. After this coat is thoroughly dry, again sand lightly, and apply the second coat. A third coat may be added for greater durability, but two are usually sufficient. Paint may be coated with clear shellac or wax for added protection if one wishes. A liquid wax may also be used on paint.

Care of Brushes. To produce good work, one needs good brushes, and since these are not cheap, they deserve good care. The methods of caring for brushes is discussed in the chapter on Walls, Ceilings, and Woodwork, and so need not be repeated here.

DECORATION

Decorations, if skilfully applied, can sometimes be quite effective on furniture. Painted designs are most popular, but stenciling, decalcomanias, and wallpaper cutouts are also used.

Painted Designs. The person witn artistic ability can work out original designs which may have great charm. Most of us, however, need something to copy or adapt. Pictures of painted furniture often give interesting suggestions, and the delightfully naive designs on Pennsylvania Dutch furni-

Charming designs on Pennsylvania Dutch furniture, such as those on this dower chest dated 1788, offer delightful possibilities for painted decoration if skillfully adapted.

ture are often adapted. Nearly everyone possesses some drawing ability — enough at least to copy or adapt a simple design. Work it out on paper first, and then transfer it to the furniture. To do this, first rub the back of the paper with the side of a soft lead pencil. Then place the paper, right side up, in position on the piece to be decorated and trace the outline of the design.

Use artists' oil paints for decorations, and not ordinary paint. Keep colors clear and fresh and the design simple. Don't attempt fussy details. The charm of painted decorations lies in their simplicity.

Stencils and Decalcomanias. Those who want to decorate furniture but feel that they cannot manage even the simplest freehand drawings can, if they prefer, apply designs with stencils or decalcomanias. The effect, however, generally lacks any spontaneous artistry, and most of the designs available show no imagination. The process of stenciling is very simple. The stencil is placed against the surface to be decorated and the paint is applied through the stencil openings with a small stiff stencil brush with a flat bristle surface. Don't paint with the brush, but press the end of it against the design. Ordinary paints should not be used for this purpose. Instead, use stencil paint or artists' oil paint.

Decalcomanias are merely dampened and laid in place. The design remains and the backing is lifted off.

Wallpaper. If you like, you may cover an entire piece of furniture with wallpaper to match or contrast with a background, or simply cut out part of the wallpaper design and apply it. To cover an entire piece with wallpaper, first remove all wax or oil. Sand any glossy finish, and then apply a coat of wallpaper size. The paper must be trimmed to fit exactly — the most tedious part of the process. If a surface has a projecting edge, cut the paper large enough to fit around the edge. Careful notching and trimming are necessary to sure a close fit. After the paper is fitted, apply wallpaper paste to the back and smooth the paper in place with a wallpaper brush (*see section on Wallpaper in Chapter on Walls, Ceilings, and Woodwork*). When the wallpaper is dry, it should be given a coat or two of clear shellac.

CARING FOR FURNITURE

Oil and wax finishes need to be renewed from time to time. Varnish finishes may be waxed or rubbed down with a good grade of furniture polish. Furniture polish should not be used on shellac. Furniture which has become actually dirty with fingermarks or grime should be washed with a solution of warm water, linseed oil, and turpentine. Add 3 tablespoons of linseed oil and 1 tablespoon of turpentine to a quart of warm water. Then renew the oil, wax, or polish.

White marks on furniture can usually be removed with a quick application of ammonia or alcohol, followed immediately with a rubbing of oil or polish.

Dents, if they are not deep, can sometimes be removed by placing a dampened blotter over the spot and applying a warm (not hot) iron on top of the blotter. Repeat until the dent disappears.

Light scratches will sometimes become less conspicuous if rubbed with the meat of a black walnut or by brushing with an oil stain of the right color. Use a small, fine brush for this purpose. If the scratch is deep a complete refinishing job will probably be necessary.

Handle furniture with care. Careless tugging and pulling may loosen joints. Dampness causes wood to swell, and a too-dry atmosphere may shrink and loosen the joints.

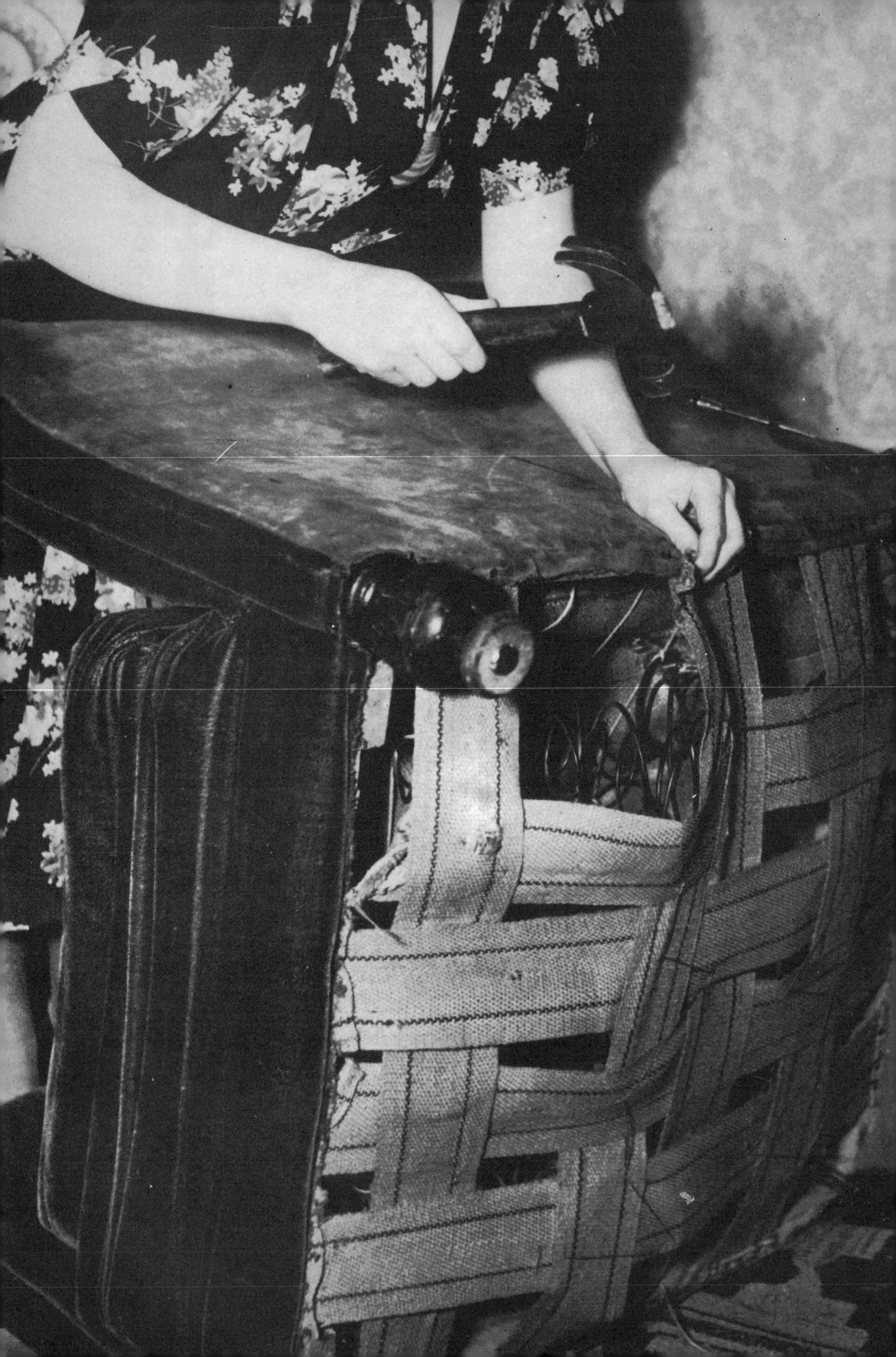

CHAPTER IX

REUPHOLSTERING FURNITURE

IF YOU have ever had a chair or a sofa reupholstered, you realize that such work is far from inexpensive. Yet, like the cost of so many other things, the major part of what you pay goes for labor charges and not for materials or equipment. If you are willing to do the work yourself, you can turn a shabby old chair or some overstuffed horror into a trim, modern piece of furniture you will be proud of and which will give many more years of useful service. The steps involved are not beyond the skill of the average homemaker if she has the patience to follow instructions and to master each step as she goes along. Reupholstery does take time and work — a good deal of both in many cases. The beginner is advised to start on something simple, such as a footstool or a small straight chair. When she has reupholstered a piece of this kind successfully, she will have confidence enough to attempt something a little more complicated. Some pieces may need a complete reupholstery job, while others may involve only a job of rewebbing, recovering, or retying of springs.

What to Reupholster. Any piece can be worth reupholstering if the frame is of good wood, the joints are sound (by "sound," we mean unbroken; if they are merely loose, they can be reglued), and the springs are more or less intact (if the piece has spring construction). A missing spring or two can sometimes be replaced with new ones to match the others, but as a general rule, it is better to stick to pieces which still have a complete set of springs in good condition. The filling may be usable as it is, and if so, the cost of the work will obviously be less than if the filling has to be completely or partially replaced.

TOOLS AND SUPPLIES

Many a person has started an upholstery job and soon become discouraged because he or she lacked the tools to do it properly. The ordinary pins and needles you have in your sewing box are not the kind that can be used for reupholstering. You will need special pins and needles made for the purpose as well as other tools and supplies. Here is a list of what you should have and what each item is for:

A Bench or Trestle of some kind is needed to support the furniture piece. You don't have to have a regular upholsterer's bench, but one with similar dimensions is useful. These dimensions are 36 inches long, 30 inches high, and 8 inches across the top board (which, incidentally, has a cushion top to prevent marring of wood frames).

Tack Hammer. An upholsterer's tack hammer has a head with a face about 5/16 of an inch in diameter. A magnetized tack hammer is a great help for getting into difficult corners.

Ripping Tool for removing tacks from old upholstery. Some people use a screwdriver for this purpose, but that doesn't do the screwdriver any good.

Webbing Stretcher. This is used to stretch the webbing taut across the frame of the furniture. A block of wood about 7 inches long, 3 inches wide, and ¾ of an inch thick will serve the purpose almost as well.

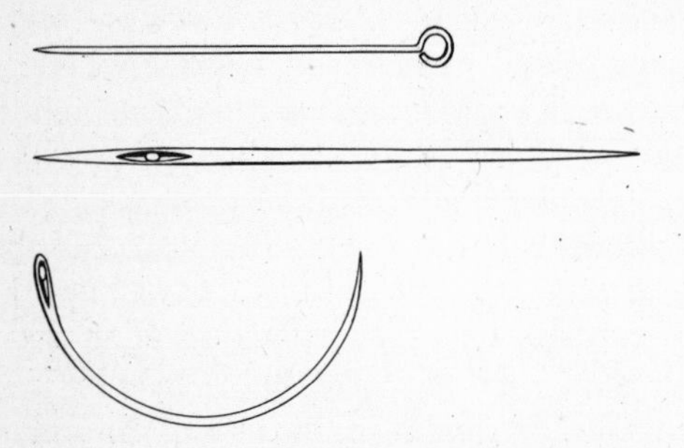

FIG. 1. An upholsterer's pin or skewer for holding muslin or upholstery fabric in place temporarily before sewing or tacking; a long, double-pointed upholsterer's needle; an upholsterer's curved needle.

Upholsterer's Straight Needle. This is a long, double-pointed needle used for sewing padding to burlap, springs to webbing, and so on. The double point makes it possible to sew up and down through the materials without turning the needle around. Such needles are available in lengths of about 6 to 20 inches. A 10- or 12-inch length will take care of most jobs.

Upholsterer's Curved Needle is used to sew burlap to springs and for sewing on flat surfaces where the underside cannot be reached. Curved needles come in sizes from about 3 to 10 inches. A 3- or 4-inch size should be adequate for most jobs.

Upholsterer's Pins, which are about 3 inches long, are used to fit covers in place before sewing or tacking. Several dozens may be needed, depending on the job.

Regulator. This is a sharp-pointed tool, from 6 to 10 inches in length, which is used to even up the padding. An ice pick, sharpened to a needle point, can be used as a substitute.

Scissors. A good pair of large, sharp scissors is essential for cutting heavy burlap, twine, and so on.

Tacks. Both small and large upholsterer's tacks (such as No. 3 and No. 10) are useful. They are sold in boxes and by weight. Quantity needed depends on the size of job. If you are one of those devil-may-care people who uses her mouth as a receptacle for holding tacks, be sure to buy the sterilized kind. Small webbing nails are sometimes used in place of upholsterer's tacks for attaching jute webbing to the frame. Sometimes fancy-headed tacks are used as a finishing detail. Various kinds are available, including brass- and gilt-headed tacks, as well as tacks with heads which simulate leather for use on leather or artificial-leather uphostery. For upholstery trimmed with gimp (ornamental tape-like trimming), gimp tacks are needed. They come in various sizes—Nos. 2½ and 3 are good sizes for most jobs.

Jute Webbing. This is a heavy webbing material which looks like wide tape. It is used to weave a foundatoin on which to support the springs and padding. The usual width is 3½ inches. The webbing is sold by the yard.

Burlap is a coarse cloth of jute, used in upholstery for covering springs. It is sold by the yard and the usual width is 40 inches. Grades and weights vary. For upholstery purposes a medium (10-ounce) or heavy (12-ounce) weight is generally used.

Twine. For tying springs, a heavy twine is needed. A special twine about ⅛ of an inch in diameter is made for this purpose. It is usually sold in 1-pound balls. Linen twine (also called flax and mattress twine) is needed for sewing springs to webbing and burlap and for stitching edges. It usually comes in ½-pound balls.

Padding and Stuffing. A number of materials are used as upholstery padding and stuffing. Among them are hair, moss, cotton, excelsior, kapok, and down. Of these, hair and down are the most expensive. Curled horse hair, the finest and longest-lasting filling material, is very resilient. Goose down is very light and soft, but difficult to work with. Kapok resists moisture, but is also difficult to work with. Excelsior is cheap but soon mats down into a hard, lumpy mass. Therefore, for home upholstery jobs, the best choice of filling materials is probably moss or cotton. Layered cotton is the kind generally used for upholstery work. It comes in various grades and can be had in rolls. The moss used in upholstery work is the kind that grows on trees in the southern states, chiefly Louisiana. The moss must be dried, cured, and ginned. Thoroughly cured moss has a black color. The best grade is sometimes ginned as many as four times to remove all sticks, dirt, and so on, and is labeled XXXX.

Muslin. A well-made piece of upholstered furniture has a muslin cover underneath the top upholstery cover. The muslin holds the padding in shape and thus relieves the upholstery fabric of strain. The muslin also prevents the padding from working through the upholstery fabric. A good, firmly woven grade of muslin should be selected. It may be bleached or unbleached. The usual choice is unbleached because it is cheaper.

Cambric is a slightly stiff, smooth fabric used in upholstery work to cover the webbing on the bottom of the chair, sofa, or other piece. The cover protects the chair from dust. Any firmly woven fabric can be used for this purpose.

Upholstery Fabrics. Almost any type of firm fabric can be used for upholstery covers, but since reupholstering involves a considerable amount of work, it is advisable to select a fabric which will wear well enough to make the labor worth while. However, the beginner probably ought to choose one of the less expensive fabrics. If a mistake is made in cutting, the result will then not be quite so costly. Popular upholstery fabrics include chintz, denim, rep, corduroy, damask, velvet, brocade, mohair, needlepoint (both machine- and hand-made), and many novelty weaves. Satins and taffetas are used for their luxurious effect, but do not wear as well as some of the sturdier fabrics. Leather makes a handsome and durable upholstery material, but it expensive and demands skilled workmanship. Artificial leather, or leather cloth, gives excellent service, and is available in many different textures and colors. Another fabric sometimes used is felt, and it gives satisfactory service if it is of good quality. Newer materials are appearing—glass cloth and plastic fabrics which are stain repellent and easily cleaned.

HOW TO REUPHOLSTER

Now we are ready to begin the actual work of reupholstering. It may not be necessary to perform each of the processes described, but we shall explain all the steps for a complete job from the time a piece is stripped to the bare frame until the final cover is in place. Perhaps you won't have to do anything but replace the covering material. Perhaps the webbing is in good condition but the springs need retying, or maybe the piece needs to be plumped up with a little extra padding. Even the lines of a piece can be altered to make it more up to date, but that is a job which usually involves carpentry and will be discussed later on.

The first step is to remove the old cover. It is probably attached with both stitching and tacks. Snip the stitches with the scissors and pry out the tacks with the ripping tool. Remove the cover carefully as it can serve as a pattern for cutting the new cover if you are not changing the lines of the piece. As a working example, let's assume that you are going to do a complete reupholstery job on a typical chair with a separate cushion. We'll forget about the cushion until the chair is finished. After you have removed the outer cover, strip off the muslin, which is probably fastened only by tacks, snip the stitches holding the padding, remove it, and set it aside (it's a good idea to keep it wrapped up in newspapers until you are ready to replace it). Then snip the twine stitches holding the burlap to the springs and remove the burlap. The next step is to cut the twine on the springs and remove them (the springs may be separate or fastened together in a construction set). Now turn the chair upside down and, with the ripping tool, pry out the tacks holding the webbing in place. Then turn the chair on its arm fronts to remove the webbing from the back. Examine the wood of the frame and the joints to be sure they are sound. If the joints are loose, they will have to be reglued (*see Chapter on Restyling and Repairing Furniture*).

Stretching and Tacking Webbing. The amount of webbing needed depends on the size of the frame and the number of springs.

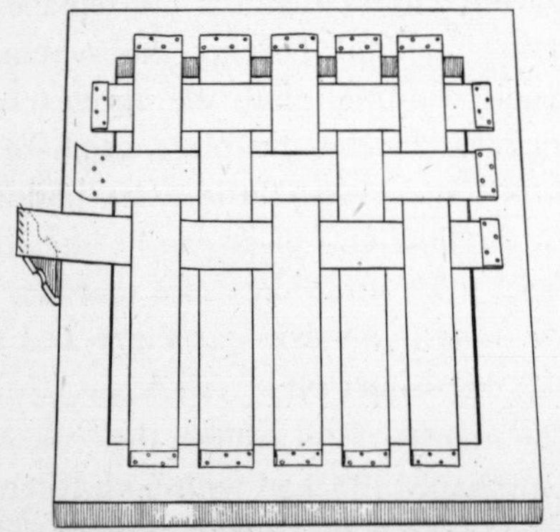

FIG. 2. Method of stretching, tacking, and weaving the webbing on the frame of the furniture piece.

A chair seat with nine springs will require three strips of webbing each way, so that each spring will stand where two strips of webbing cross. To estimate the amount of webbing needed, measure across the frame from one side to another and from front to back, multiply the total measure by the number of strips needed and add an extra 3 inches to each strip for turning under at the ends. If the back has to be rewebbed as well as the seat, estimate the amount of webbing needed for the back, too.

The new webbing strips should be placed as the old ones were. First, tack a strip of webbing to the front of the frame, as illustrated. The end of the tape is turned over and the position of the tacks is staggered so as not to split the wood. Stretch the webbing strip across the frame opening with the webbing stretcher. To do this, stick the teeth of the stretcher into the webbing and stretch it by using the other end as a lever against the side of the frame (*see illustration*). If you have no webbing stretcher, wrap the webbing around a block of wood and use it as a lever. Tack the other end of the webbing in place on the other side of the frame (a magnetized tack hammer will permit you to pick up tacks and hammer with one hand while the other hand is holding the webbing taut with the stretcher). The webbing should be tightly stretched, but not to the breaking point; it should have just enough elasticity to give slightly under the pressure of a person's weight. The webbing must be in a straight line across the frame. Cut the webbing off about 1½ inches from the tacks, fold it over, and tack again through both thicknesses (use the large tacks on the webbing).

When all the front-to-back strips are in place, attach the crosswise strips, weaving them in and out with the first set. Then turn the chair over on its feet.

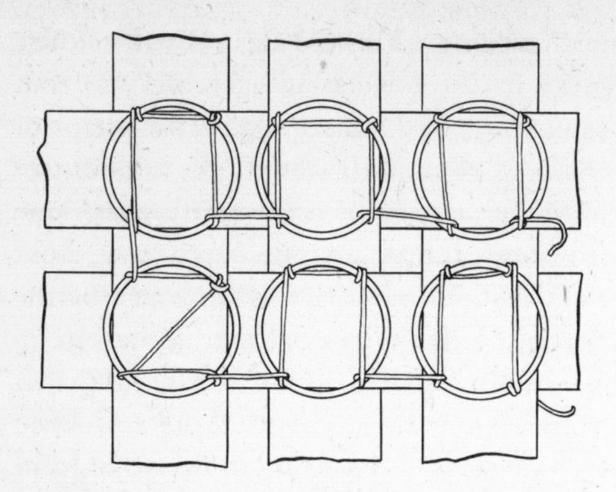

FIG. 3. Springs are stitched in four places to the webbing strips directly over the points of intersection.

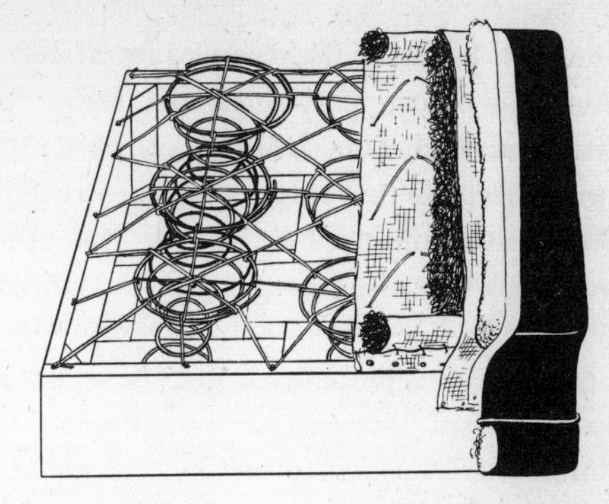

FIG. 4. Cross-section view showing tied springs, burlap cover over springs, rolled edge, moss stuffing, burlap cover over moss, cotton padding, muslin undercover, and outer covering material.

Fastening the Springs. Sometimes the springs are fastened directly to the webbing and sometimes a burlap lining is placed first on top of the webbing. The only advantage of a burlap lining is that it will help to catch any stuffing that might work through the burlap on top of the springs. However, it is easier to sew the springs directly to the webbing, and no great harm is done if the burlap lining over the webbing is eliminated providing the underside of the webbing is covered with a closely woven fabric after the rest of the upholstery work is completed.

Distribute the springs evenly so that each one rests in the center of the crossing place of the webbing strips. Springs must not rub against each other or against the frame. The end of the spring with the tip bent toward the center should be at the top. Sew the springs to the webbing with the stitching twine and the long, double-pointed needle. Stitch each spring at least four times. Knot the twine before going on to the next spring. The knot will keep the twine from coming out of all the springs if it breaks in one place.

In some chairs, the springs are not separate but are held together in a construction unit with metal bands. In other chairs, a solid wood bottom takes the place of webbing. Springs can be attached to a wood bottom with small pieces of webbing or canvas and tacks. A strip of webbing should also be placed across the bottom coil of the spring and tacked to the wood to prevent the spring from rattling when it strikes the wood.

Tying the Springs. The tops of the springs must be tied to the frame with the heavy spring twine. Measure and cut the twine in pieces to correspond to the width and length of the frame, plus an additional length for knots. About 1½ feet of twine should be allowed for knots on a row of three springs. Each row must be tied with a lengthwise, a crosswise, and two diagonal twines. This means that a chair seat with nine springs (in rows three deep) will require 16 pieces of twine.

Hammer a large tack part way into the frame edge in line with each row of springs. Tie a piece of spring twine around the tack and drive it down into the wood.

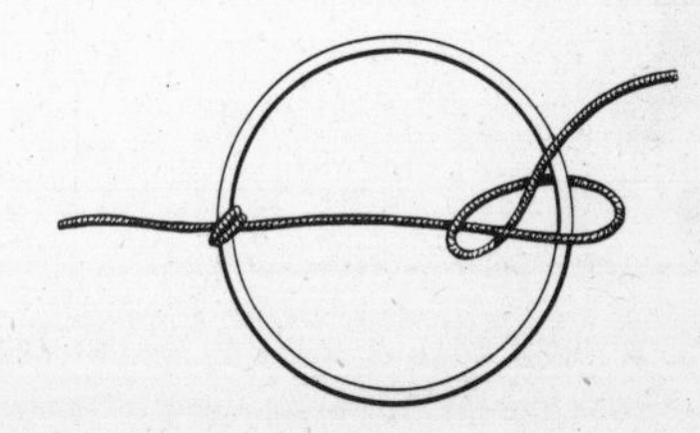

FIG. 5. Method of knotting cord on top coil of spring.

Tie and tack all the twine pieces along one edge before starting to tie. Loop the twine over the top outside coil of the spring and tie the twine in a clove hitch. The springs must all be tied to the same height and kept in an upright position. As a rule, the springs must be compressed somewhat to give the proper contour to the seat, but if they are compressed too much they lose their resiliency and the twine and burlap will soon tear away. Ordinarily, the springs should not be compressed lower than 3 inches above the frame.

Carry the twine across the spring and tie it on the opposite edge. Continue tying all the springs in the row with the same piece of twine. Then fasten the twine around a tack on the frame opposite from where you started and hammer the tack into the wood. Do the same with the other rows of springs. Then tie each row crosswise and finally diagonally, first in one direction and then in another. Each spring will now be tied in eight places as well as in the middle where the strings cross each other (*see Fig. 4*).

In some types of construction, there is a wire edge, bent to the shape of the frame, and the springs must also be tied to this wire edge. The edge helps to prevent sagging. These ties must be very secure as the edge is subject to considerable strain. Use the smaller twine and interlace it over and around the top outer coil of the outside springs and around the wire edge ten or twelve times and then back around over the interlaced twine. Fasten the twine ends with triple knots.

Burlap Cover. The entire surface of the springs is now covered with a piece of burlap cut to fit. Tack the burlap to the edge of the frame. Then, with the curved needle and the stitching twine, sew the burlap to the tops of the springs. Sew each spring in three places. The burlap serves as a foundation for the stuffing and padding, which would otherwise soon fall down into the springs and interfere with their resiliency.

Making an Edge. An edging of some kind is necessary to keep the stuffing on the edge of the frame. If no edge were used, the stuffing would soon work away from the frame and the bare wood would wear a hole in the cover.

A rolled edge is made by blind tacking a strip of burlap around the outer edge of the frame. (Blind tacking is done by tacking on the inside of the burlap and then folding it back over the tacked edge.) The width of the burlap depends on the size of the roll needed, which, in turn, depends upon the size of the frame. If the frame

FIG. 6. A rolled edge is made by blind-tacking a strip of burlap to the frame, bringing the strip over a roll of padding, and tacking the strip to the other edge of the frame.

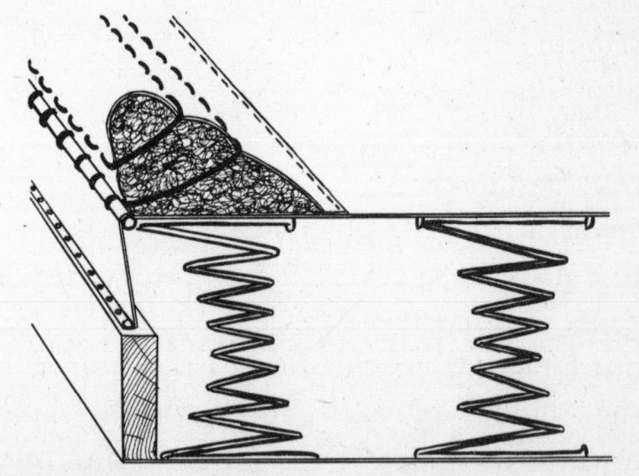

FIG. 7. Method of making a stitched edge in a seat frame with a wire-edge construction.

curves, pleat the burlap strip slightly around the curved portions. Now make a roll of stuffing to fill the burlap edge. Bring the burlap over the stuffing, and tack the burlap to the other side of the frame. The stuffing should be of a uniform amount all around the frame so that the roll will be perfectly even and rounded.

A stitched edge is made by sewing a strip of burlap to the burlap covering the springs. Use the curved needle for this. Stuff the burlap strip and tack the other edge to the frame. If the piece has a wire edge, sew the burlap to the wire.

Stuffing and Padding. The first layer of stuffing material is usually hair or moss. The amount to use depends entirely on the effect you want. The stuffing must be evenly distributed to avoid holes or lumps.

On top of this first layer of stuffing goes another burlap cover. With the curved needle and stitching twine, sew through the top burlap, the stuffing, and the bottom burlap, but do not pull the stitches too tight or the contour will be spoiled. The stitches are merely to hold the stuffing in place. If you can feel any lumps or holes in the stuffing after sewing, even-up the stuffing with the regulator or an ice pick—simply push it through the burlap and draw the stuffing material into the place where you want it.

A second layer of padding, usually of cotton, now goes on top of the burlap. Distribute this layer evenly and carefully, also. The chair is now ready for its muslin cover.

Muslin Cover. If the chair had a muslin cover in the first place, use it as a pattern to cut the new cover. If not, use the outer cover as a pattern. Tack the edges of the muslin cover to the frame, beginning in the middle of each edge and working toward the ends. Draw the muslin into the shape and firmness wanted. After the muslin is in place, it may be necessary to distribute the second layer of filling with the stuffing regulator to eliminate any lumps or hollows.

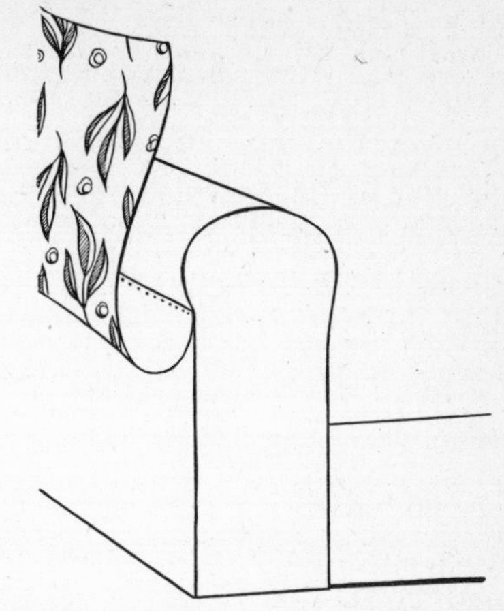

FIG. 8. Blind-tacking the outer fabric covering to the arm of the chair. The fabric will next be smoothed over the arm of the chair towards the seat. Seams in covers are often stitched first.

The Outer Cover. The outer covering fabric can be attached to the frame with fancy-headed upholsterer's tacks or it can be blind tacked. The old outer cover is used as a pattern to cut the cover from the new fabric, unless the lines of the chair have been altered. In that case, you will have to make a paper pattern on the chair. The lines of the chair will dictate the shape of each piece of fabric and the placing of the seams. Seams are made and stitched in much the same way as the seams for a slipcover (*see the Chapter on Slipcovers*). Cord welting or other trimming can be used in the seams if desired. Do not sew up all the side seams on the cover as it must be lifted to blind tack the seams to the frame along the chair arms and the top. The cover is also attached to the foundation materials where the arms join the seat by stitching right through the outer fabric, muslin, padding, burlap, and webbing with the long, double-pointed needle. If the cover is to be fitted around a splat or leg, make miter cuts in the fabric so that it can be folded back and fitted around the wood.

On chairs with exposed frames, the outer cover is tacked down with fancy-headed tacks or tacked and finished with gimp. The gimp is attached with small gimp nails or brads. "Liquid thread" is also used for this purpose, although it is a less durable fastener than a nail. If the frame is not exposed, the outer cover is brought down over the edge of the lower frame and tacked to the bottom edge.

FIG. 9. Building a chair cushion in a box made from corrugated board. Springs are here enclosed in muslin pockets. Some seat springs are in construction sets.

One edge of the unstitched side seams is tacked to the frame. Then the other edge of the seam is folded over and stitched by hand with the curved needle (a small one is good for this purpose) to the tacked edge of the seam along the line of the frame. Use blindstitching and thread to match the color of the cover.

If the cover is to be finished with a pleated or ruffled flounce, it is stitched to the lower edge of the cover. Then the lower edge is blind tacked to the frame.

Cushions. If the chair has a separate cushion, it may or may not have to be rebuilt. If it does, the first step is to make a new foundation cover of muslin. The cover is made in the same way as a slipcover for a cushion is made except that one end is left open completely. Upholsterers use a metal box as a form in which the cushion is built up, but a cardboard box will serve the same purpose. Such a box can be made from heavy corrugated board, as illustrated. A layer of padding is put in and evenly distributed. Then the springs are placed on top of the padding. Seat springs are usually made in a unit. If the springs are separate, they must be tied together, top and bottom. Sometimes each spring is encased in a separate muslin pocket. On top of the springs goes another layer of padding. Then the top pieces of the corrugated board are brought over the filling material. The filling is compressed into shape and the top pieces of the board are fastened together with gummed paper. The muslin cover is slipped over the board, and after the cover is in place, the board is slipped out. The seams at the end of the muslin cover are then stitched by hand. Next the muslin is covered with the upholstery material. Sometimes the filling is put into the outer cover without using a muslin undercover, but such construction is possible only when the outer covering fabric is so firmly woven that none of the filling material can work through.

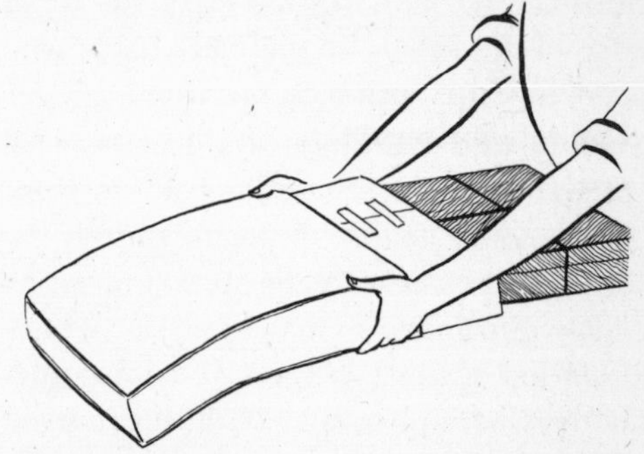

FIG. 10. Top sections of cardboard box are pasted together; muslin cover is slipped over end of box, and the contents of the box are pushed into muslin cover. Another box can serve as a "pusher."

The Dust Cover. The final step is to turn the chair upside down again and cover the webbing with a dust cover. Black cambric is generally used for this purpose, but, as stated before, any firmly woven fabric will serve. The fabric is cut in a size to fit the bottom of the frame, plus enough extra to allow for turning under the edges. Begin at the center of one side and tack the folded cambric edge to the bottom edge of the frame. Stretch the cambric tight across the frame and tack it to the opposite side. Then tack the cambric to the centers of the other two sides in the same way. Work from all centers toward the corners until the cover is stretched and tacked firmly in place.

Springless Construction. The general procedure for upholstering a piece without springs is the same except that the stuffing and padding material are placed on a burlap lining directly over the webbing, or, in some cases, on the wood bottom. If the padding is very shallow, no rolled or stitched edge is necessary. Thick padding usually calls for a rolled or stitched edge.

Mending a Sagging Chair Bottom. Sometimes a chair bottom begins to sag before the upholstery cover itself has worn out and needs to be replaced. To remedy this condition, it is not necessary to strip off all the upholstery. Instead, turn the chair upside down, resting the arms on a bench or table. Remove the dust cover and the old webbing. The released springs will now be exposed. Tack new webbing strips to the frame in the manner described earlier in this chapter. Each row of springs is pressed back into place under the webbing as it it stretched across the frame. Sew the bottom of the springs to the webbing, and finish the job by tacking on a new dust cover.

Upholstering a Headboard on a Bed. Upholstered headboards have become quite a fashion, and if the covering fabric is easy to clean, they are not as impractical as they might seem. Nearly any type of headboard can be upholstered—even a metal one.

Some kind of foundation is needed to hold the padding material in place. On a wooden headboard, burlap can be stretched and tacked as a foundation to tack the padding to it with the curved needle. This work is easier to do if the headboard is unbolted from the bedstead and laid flat. The actual work of upholstering is the same as for any springless surface. Metal headboards usually require a foundation of plywood cut to shape. Two plywood panels are needed—one for the front and one for the back of the headboard. The two pieces of plywood are fastened together with bolts. The back panel of plywood can be upholstered, or if it stands against a wall, left as it is. A foundation on a slatted wooden headboard can be made from webbing.

Headboards are usually upholstered to match the color or fabric of the spread or its trimmings.

RESTYLING UPHOLSTERED FURNITURE

A dated or badly proportioned upholstered piece can often be restyled to give it a more modern appearance. Sometimes work of this kind calls for actual alterations in the frame and elementary carpentry skill.

FIG. 11. An old chair which was cut down and reupholstered on more modern lines.

A great deal of work is usually involved and such a job should be undertaken only when the frame is in excellent condition and the cost of materials is not excessive.

A word of warning about second-hand upholstered furniture: sometimes it is infested with insects or it may even be a source of dangerous disease germs. To be safe, it's advisable to have any second-hand upholstered piece sterilized by a firm which specializes in such work. At least the piece should be thoroughly sprayed with an effective insecticide before being brought into the house.

An Old Chair. Let's use the chair in Fig. 11 as an example of one of the tasteless, badly proportioned upholstered pieces which can sometimes be found in the junk stores and second-hand shops for a small sum and see what can be done with such a horror. Mrs. G. found a chair of this kind and turned it into a handsome addition to her bedroom.

First she stripped off all the old upholstery because the springs were beginning to wear through the seat and obviously needed retying, and the webbing was worn on the bottom. To her surprise, the filling turned out to be curled hair and cotton, both of which she reused, together with some new cotton padding.

After the chair was stripped to its frame, she cut the top of the back frame off about 6 inches, and the knobs near the back of the arms as well. She cut a new section from a piece of 1 x 2 lumber to fit across the top. To do this, she drilled holes in the cut ends of the frame and in the ends of the new section and fitted the pieces together with dowel pins (cut from dowel sticks), glue, and mending plates. All pieces were held together with clamps until the glue dried (about 48 hours).

FIG. 12. The same chair after alterations.

FIG. 13. An ornate mohair sofa of a bygone day.

Then she cut the ugly, protruding feet back about 1½ inches (their thickness was great enough to permit such treatment).

Next came a complete reupholstery job with new webbing, new burlap, and new muslin cover. The old padding was reinforced with several pounds of new cotton padding to round out the arms and back. The old cushion, which had no springs, was discarded, and the seat of the chair was built up with extra padding.

Mrs. G. selected cotton twill in a subdued shade of blue-violet for the outer covering material. For a contrast, she trimmed it with pink, corded welting, and buttons covered with the same pink fabric as the welting. She added a straight, tailored flounce with pleats at the corners to hide the carving across the front of the chair frame and the legs which had been cut back. The completed chair is shown in Fig. 12.

An Outmoded Sofa. Many years ago, when Mrs. R. bought the ornate mohair-

FIG. 14. The sofa after it was stripped to its frame. The front panel was removed and replaced and a new frame was superimposed on the back frame.

covered sofa shown in Fig. 13, it was considered as the height of fashion. The sofa was part of a suite, which also consisted of two matching chairs. The suite was so well made that, like Alice's blue gown, it wore and it wore and it wore, until finally the mohair was no more. But the frames, the springs, and the stuffing were still in good shape.

Mrs. R. wanted a Lawson type of sofa with straight lines instead of the giddy curves of the old mohair. So she stripped the sofa to its frame. Then she sawed off part of the arm tops and sides to make them a narrower width. To hide the curves across the back top, she made a frame of 1 x 3 lumber, and nailed this frame right over the old one. The frame was fastened together with doweling, glue, and angle irons (Fig. 14). The entire front of the frame was then removed. (An operation of this kind can sometimes be quite difficult, as the released tension may cause the wood to curl. If that happens, the wood will have to be braced and clamped into position—a task which may be beyond the strength of the average woman.)

FIG. 15. After alterations and reupholstering, the finished sofa resembles a Lawson-type of sofa.

The front legs were removed and set back into the frame. A 1 x 6 board was nailed across the front of the sofa to take the place of the old curved section. Then the frame was reupholstered with new webbing and burlap and new cotton padding as well as the old padding and stuffing. The carved arm fronts were covered with plywood cut to shape and covered with cotton padding, muslin, and the outer fabric. These plywood sections were attached with finishing nails driven right through the fabrics, padding, and plywood. After the nails were in, the threads in the fabric were pushed together again with a pin, so that no trace of the nails was visible. A pleated flounce was added to the outer cover to hide the legs. The sofa as it looked when it was finished is shown in Fig. 15.

CLEANING UPHOLSTERY FABRICS

Plain-surfaced upholstery fabrics can be cleaned with soap lather or one of the commercial soapless foams made for the purpose if the fabric is colorfast. Test for colorfastness in some inconspicuous spot if you are in doubt (*see the Chapter on Laundering Methods and Equipment for test method*). The only piled fabric that should be cleaned in this way is mohair.

First, remove all surface dust with the vacuum cleaner and the attachment made for this purpose. Then apply the lather with a soft brush, rubbing with a circular motion. If you intend to use a soap lather, make it by dissolving ¼ cup of neutral soap flakes in 1 pint of boiling water. When this solution cools, it forms a jelly which can be whipped into a stiff foam with a rotary egg beater. The lather must be dry—no liquid should actually penetrate the fabric. If you prefer to use one of the soapless chemical preparations, follow the manufacturer's directions.

As the lather becomes dirty, scrape it off with a knife. Then wipe the fabric with a cellulose sponge dipped in clear water and squeezed until nearly dry. Work on a small area at a time and finish it before going on to another section. Work as rapidly as possible, and do not stop until the entire chair is finished. Then dry it in the sun or in front of an electric fan or radiator.

A complete shampooing may not be necessary if the fabric merely has a stain or two but is otherwise clean. Sometimes the stain can be removed with a solvent or absorbent (*see the section on Stain Removal in the Chapter on Laundering Equipment and Methods*).

The procedure for shampooing piled mohair is the same as that for a plain-surfaced fabric, except that the pile should be brushed against the direction of the nap while it is damp, than with the nap after the fabric is dry. Crushed pile can be raised merely by dampening the fabric ever so little with a cloth wrung out of hot water and placed over the surface of the material. The pile is then brushed against the nap, and, after drying, with the nap.

IV

ACCESSORIES

CHAPTER X

PICTURES, LAMPS, AND ORNAMENTS

IT'S the "little things" that make a house look lived in—the books, the lamps and plants, the pictures and mirrors, ashtrays, figurines, vases, and all the other knick-knacks and ornaments. Nothing reveals personal tastes quite so tellingly as the selection and arrangement of its accessory furnishings. Grandmother would have thought her parlor naked if it did not contain a what-not cabinet, a mantel crowded with family photographs, and all the souvenirs from every fair and exposition she and grandfather ever attended.

But decorators of today tend to use only a few ornaments, and to have those few good—to emphasize their importance by dramatizing their setting or using them as color accents. Does that mean we have to throw out all our cherished bibelots just because we are changing the over-all decoration of our rooms? That's a question which each homemaker has to answer for herself. Certainly, if something gives us pleasure because of the happy memories associated with it, that seems reason enough for keeping it, no matter what its shape or color. But perhaps it could be fitted into some appropriate place to enhance rather than detract from its background.

On the other hand, too often we let our homes become catchalls for every sort of gewgaw bestowed on us by well meaning friends and relatives until the result is simply cluttered confusion. We may not even be aware of it, just because we have lived with the objects so long we take them for granted, like the weather. Probably three-fourths of them could be cleared out to good advantage and our everlasting relief, if we only had the courage to do so. Or, if the objects are good in themselves, why not rotate them? Bring out a few at a time, and, after tiring of them, put them away for a while and replace them with other things.

PICTURES

Pictures can be one of the most important accessories to the decorative scheme of a room. The pictorial interest of the subject matter is (or should be) the picture's primary attraction, of course, but aside from this, pictures can lend design interest to a wall and relieve its barrenness when they are grouped in a pleasing arrangement which forms their shapes and sizes into a pattern.

What Kinds of Pictures to Choose? Few of us can hope ever to own original works by great artists, but that does not mean that we have to be content with mediocre art work on our walls. Excellent reproductions of fine paintings are available for modest sums. Look for such reproductions in your local art store or museum or consult one of the catalogues of the Associated American Artists or the New York Graphic Society. Occasionally, in secondhand bookstores, one can find old botanical books with beautiful lithographed prints of fruits and flowers. Original etchings by top-ranking contemporary artists can be obtained for a cost well within the means of the average person. Some photographs make interesting wall pictures, particularly in modern settings. And don't overlook the possibilities of the better Christmas cards, some of which are miniature works of art bearing the names of the best contemporary American artists. The subject matter of many of these fine cards does not stamp them as Christmas-y at all.

Photographic portraits are a touchy subject. They may be cherished because they are tangible reminders of kith and kin, but they seldom hold any interest for the visitor who sees them hanging on the wall or scattered about on the mantel or the tables in our living room. A personal writing desk or a bedside table would seem to be a more appropriate place to keep someone's photograph we want to look at often. Another arrangement for a large collection of family photographs might be to frame and mat them as a group and hang them together in an upstairs hallway. There the entire family may enjoy them, and yet they will not be thrust upon the disinterested eyes of every visitor.

As stated before, the most important thing about a picture is its subject matter. But very little advice on this problem can be offered here since it involves the whole field of esthetics. Certainly, we ought to like the pictures we live with, and no sincere person would choose a reproduction of a painting she did not like just because the critics called it art. However, good taste is not something we are born with, and our tastes often change with education. Our museums and some of our magazines have done much to educate public taste in art, and more and more people have discovered that art is something they can *enjoy*.

In general, however, the colors of pictures should harmonize with the color scheme of the room. That does not mean that a picture should be selected primarily for its colors, as a sort of afterthought. On the contrary, the picture might come first and serve as inspiration for the color scheme of the room. And while a number of great artists have used gloomy or morbid subject matter in some of their paintings, remember that reproductions of such works bring no cheer to our homes.

Picture Frames. Picture frames and mats merely form a background to set off and enhance the picture itself. Over-elaborate frames distract our interest from the picture and detract from its value, but a simple frame will always accent the picture. The colors of the frame and the mat can take their cue from the picture or from the background. Large mats lend importance to a picture.

How to Frame a Picture. Pictures can be framed in a number of ways. One of the simplest ways is to bind the glass, border, picture, and cardboard backing together with passe-partout strips pasted over the edges.

Many varieties of ready-made picture-frame mouldings are sold. Such molding can be bought by the foot, and the molding can easily be made into rectangular frames if the corners are carefully cut at 45° angles. A miter box is almost essential for cutting angles accurately, but if you have no miter box, the store from which you buy the molding will sometimes cut it

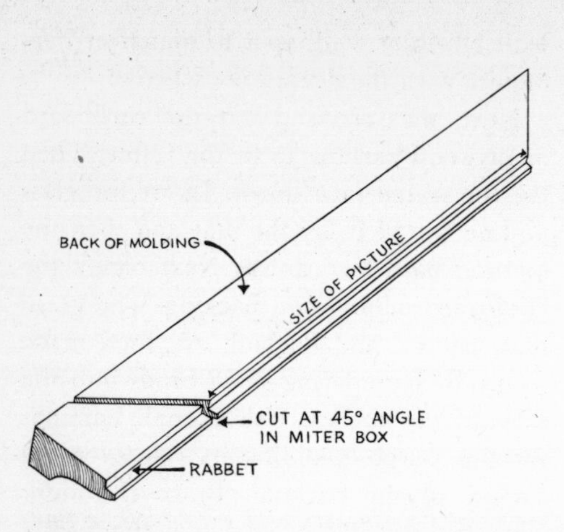

FIG. 1. Picture molding is cut in miter box as indicated.

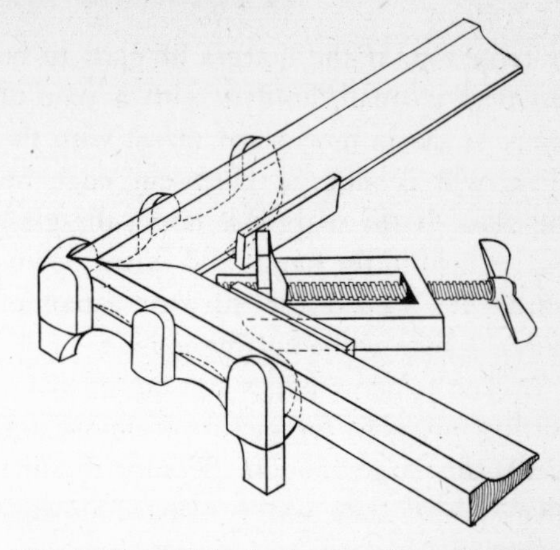

FIG. 2. Mitered joint is glued together and held in place with corner clamp while glue dries. Small brads are then driven into sides of frame through mitered joint.

to the proper size and angle. Other stores will not do so unless they are given the job of framing as well.

If you plan to frame a number of pictures, it will pay you to invest in a miter box, four corner clamps, glass sheets, a glass cutter, heavy cardboard or thin plywood for backing, brown paper, brads, tacks, eye screws, wire, and glue. Molding and matting board can be bought as needed. A sharp knife or razor blade must be used to cut the matting board.

To make the frame, measure the inner edge of the molding to fit the mat. The molding is cut from these measurements at an angle of 45° toward the outside edge. A tenon or back saw is good to use for this purpose. Cut from the back of the molding toward the front. Trim the cuts with a plane or sand them smooth with sandpaper. Assemble the sides of the frame into a rectangle and test the corners with a try-square. The corners must be absolutely square or the frame will be askew. If they are square, fasten the mitered edges together with glue and hold them with corner clamps until the glue has dried. If you have no corner clamps, the frame can be held with wood blocks pushed against each side and held in place with nails or screws driven into a bench top.

After the glue has dried (usually in 48 hours), the corners should be reinforced with small brads driven in through the miters from the sides near the ends. To start the brads, make holes in the frame with a small brad awl. Then drive the brads in with a tack hammer. Brace the opposite side of the frame against something solid so the glue in the joints will not be broken.

The back of the frame molding has a recessed edge, called a *rabbet,* and the glass, mat, picture, and cardboard must be measured and cut to fit upon this edge. To cut a sheet of glass, measure the glass with a try-square or steel ruler. Then move the try-square about 1/16 of an inch, or slightly less, from the line of the cut. Hold the glass cutter nearly vertical and draw it toward you in one steady, even stroke, using the edge of the try-square as a guide. Do not press down too hard on the glass cutter and do not draw it more than once across the line of the cut. The glass must be on a flat surface while you work. Next, move the glass so that the line of the cut rests directly along the edge of a board or table top. If the margin of glass to be removed is small, hold it with a pair of pliers. A sharp, downward thrust with the pliers will produce a clean-cut edge on the glass. If the margin is large, the glass can be held in the hands and thrust downwards. It's a good idea to wear a pair of canvas gloves while cutting glass.

Broken window panes can be saved for cutting into glass for picture frames if the pieces are large enough. Be sure to store them where they won't menace unwary fingers.

Art stores sell a variety of boards suitable for matting pictures. The matting is cut to fit the frame and the center is cut out in any size or shape to fit the picture. According to standard proportions, the bottom margin of the mat is the widest; the top margin, next widest; and the side margins, narrowest. Cut the inner edges of the margins on a bevel slanting outward. Use a sharp knife or razor to cut with. Draw the knife or razor away from you as you cut, and keep the left hand behind the blade. Mats are sometimes covered with fabric or wallpaper to match or harmonize with the decorative scheme.

FIG. 3. Method of driving small brads into rabbeted edge on back of frame to hold glass, mat, picture and backing in place.

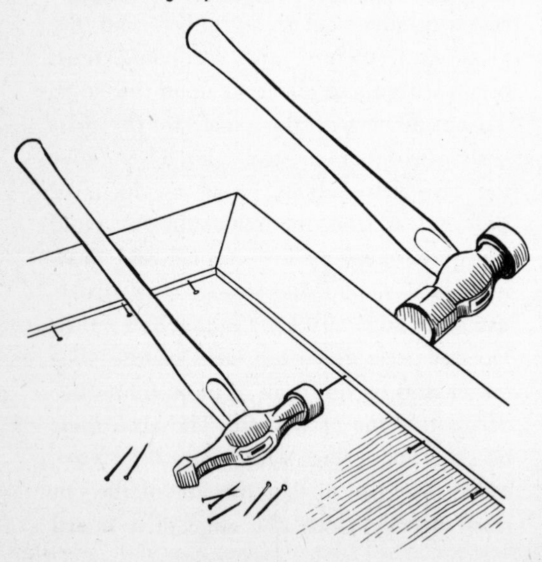

Next, measure and cut the cardboard or plywood backing to fit the frame. Then lay the frame face down. Insert the glass and on top of it lay the mat and then the picture, both face down. Next comes the cardboard or plywood backing. The glass, mat, pcture, and backing are then made secure by hammering small brads into the sides of the rabbet. Use a small hammer for this purpose, sliding its side over the surface of the backing. Brace the outer edge of the frame against something solid to take up the force of the blows.

Cut a piece of brown paper to fit the back of the frame from edge to edge. Glue the edges of the paper to the edges of the frame. Dampen the middle of the paper; as it dries, it becomes taut. Screw small eyes into the side edges of the frame about one-third of the way down from the top. Make a hole in the frame with an awl to start the screws. Thread a wire through the screw eyes from one side to the other. Keep the wire short enough so that it does not show above the top of the frame. Very heavy frames should be hung from chains made for the purpose.

Old frames can often be brightened up with paint, or by bleaching, waxing, or other refinishing methods (*those described in the Chapter on Refinishing Furniture can also be applied to frames*).

Grouping Picture and Other Ornaments on Walls. The barrenness of a wall is seldom relieved by a single picture in lonely isolation, unless the picture is very large and impressive. The secret of banishing that bare look from a wall lies in grouping several pictures or pictures and ornaments together. A symmetrical arrangement is safest, since an assymetrical one must be handled with great skill or it is apt to look merely lopsided.

FIG. 4. A symmetrical arrangement of pictures over a sofa.

A grouping takes on more interest when pictures or ornaments of more than one size or shape are combined. For example, you might place a large picture above a sofa. Then, across the top and down each side, hang a row of smaller pictures, all of the same size and shape. Or a large picture could have two small pictures, one above the other, on each side. Another interesting treatment consists of diagonal rows of pictures or ornaments branching out from each side of a larger central picture. Whatever arrangements you use, plan the entire grouping as a single shape.

Horizontal rows of pictures can help to make a too-high wall appear lower. Vertical rows of pictures carry the eye upwards and help to make a low wall appear higher. A group of closely related pictures look well in closely spaced rows, one above another, to form a block grouping.

Wall ornaments need not be limited to pictures. Very effective wall decorations can also be arranged with plates, tiles, candelabra, clocks, wallpaper cutouts, etc.

The most effective decorating trick to make a room appear wider or longer is to use large sheets of mirror on a wall, but this is an illusion which can often be quite

FIG. 5. A suggested grouping of brackets and a lamp over a console.

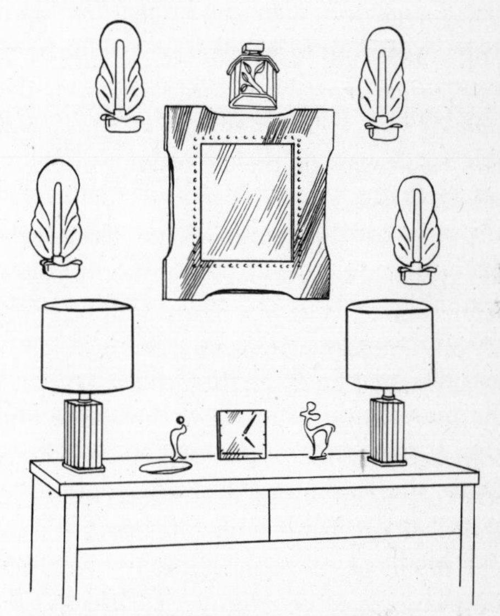

FIG. 6. A trio of pictures above a side chair.

expensive. However, if we cannot afford to cover a wall with mirror, we can still use smaller mirrors to lend sparkle to a room and brighten up dark corners.

LAMPS

Lamps, too, are among the most important decorative accessories of a room. The decorative trend now is to use tall, impressive-looking lamps with large shades and to place these lamps on low tables. This arrangement is much more effective than tiny lamps on high tables. A big lamp looks important, but it must be well designed and well proportioned or it will not be worthy of the attention which its size demands.

Lamps of simple shape and design are always in good taste. The more ornate lamps belong in rooms decorated in period styles. The proportions of a lamp are very important. The base should always have at least as much height as the shade and sometimes more. Tiny shades on large bases look pin headed. Large shades on thin, spindly bases look top heavy.

Remember that the primary function of a lamp is to give light—if it doesn't do a good job of shedding light in the right place, it's not much good as a lamp, no matter how decorative it might be.

Apparently, there are very few things that people won't make into lamps if they have the opportunity to do so. Some things which never started out as lamp bases lend themselves surprisingly well to such treatment. For example, one of the handsomest pair of lamp bases we have ever seen began as copper-covered cylinders used for printing wallpaper. And you would never guess the humble origin of one lamp base made from a tall, cylindrical metal wastebasket of small diameter. The basket was turned upside down and fitted into a groove cut in a square block of wood which served as the base. The top (or shall we say bottom) of the wastebasket was equipped with an electrical fixture and a large square, straight-sided shade. Wastebasket and wooden base were painted to match the shade.

Another pair of lamp bases were made from an old wooden Doric column that once graced a Victorian mantel. The column was cut in two; each half was mounted on a disk of wood slightly larger in diameter, and then equipped with the necessary electrical fixture. Both column and base were painted a flat white and topped with a large white shade, also white and fluted to match the flutings in the column. And, of course, everyone knows that vases and bottles can easily be converted into lamp bases.

It's possible to drill a hole with silicon carbide in a glass or pottery object and equip it at home as a lamp base with a socket, cap, and cord, but it's better to have the work done by an electrician. The cost is not great, and if the job is done by a skilled workman, you can be fairly sure to have a fixture which won't blow out a fuse the first time you turn on the lamp. If you are having an object of any value converted, be sure to take it to an expert. Rewiring a lamp socket is a fairly simple job which one can undertake without being an electrician (*see the Chapter on Wiring and Electrical Repairs*).

Restyling Old Lamps. Many of us have lamps which still function perfectly, but are such ugly ducklings they would look out of place anywhere except in a junk shop. The shade is usually the worst villain — who doesn't remember or hasn't seen the opaque, mottled glass shades, the pleated chiffon shades trimmed with silk flowers and gaudy gold braid, the shades which look like upturned tulips edged with dripping bead fringe? All are of bygone eras. If the lamp base itself is well pro-

Lamp with pottery base in striated texture and shade of handwoven fabric (right).

Base is covered with hand-stitched leather and shade is of woven straw in this lamp (below).

Shade is covered with hand-woven tweed to blend with the pottery base (right).

Lamp with base of crystal globes to reflect light.

Thin plywood mounted on aluminum backing makes the shade and spiral around base on this lamp (below).

A copper lamp which provides both direct and indirect lighting. Container in base holds plants (above).

Silver-finished floor lamp in reeded design with attached tray (below).

FIG. 7. A battered old lamp which was reclaimed with some work and a few inexpensive materials.

FIG. 8. The same lamp as it appeared after re-styling.

portioned, all that may be necessary to bring the lamp more nearly up to date is to add a new shade.

But very often the lamp base is just as dated as the shade. Sometimes badly designed lamp bases can be improved at little cost. For example, the dowdy lamp shown in Fig. 7 was made over into the simple, pleasing lamp shown in Fig. 8 with a little effort and a few inexpensive materials. The shade was removed and the top finial was knocked off. Next, a cardboard mailing tube (obtainable at a stationery store) was slipped over the spindly, ornate shaft. Then a few cents' worth of white casting plaster (sold at art goods stores) was mixed into a paste with water. The empty spaces inside the tube were filled with plaster and the bulging curves on the base were obliterated with plaster molded into a simple, curved shape. A thin coating of plaster was also applied to the mailing tube.

After the plaster was completely dry, base and shaft were coated with shellac and then painted. (The shaft could also be covered with wallpaper or with twine wound around and around from top to bottom.)

The old wire frame of the shade had its curves hammered into a simple, circular shape. Then the shade was re-covered in glazed white chintz and trimmed with moss fringe to match the color of the base.

ORNAMENTS

Some people will have nothing to do with ornamental bibelots, while others dote on them. The interest may even take root and develop into a passion for collecting. The true collector never collects indiscriminately: she usually hankers for a particular type of object—sandwich glass, chased brass, miniature figurines, Delft china, Majolica ware, or what have you. If the collection is good, it deserves a setting worthy of its importance. Perhaps the objects can be displayed on shelves or as wall decorations. Tiny objects look well only in settings scaled to their size. Miniature figurines, for example, might be displayed in a small shadow box with shallow shelves or under a glass top on a recessed shelf of a coffee table.

Those of us who are not collectors but

who still like a few ornaments usually have definite ideas about them. In general, though, the ornaments ought to harmonize both with the decorating and color schemes. Modern rooms call for ornaments of simple form in pottery, wood, or metal. Period examples of crystal, pottery, silverware, or gilt belong in the eigtheenth-century room. Chinese porcelain is also at home in rooms of this period. Early American rooms ask for pewter, pressed glass, copper, and wrought iron.

Cleaning and Polishing Metal. Various kinds of metal cleaners and metal polishing cloths are on the market and some of them do a much better job than any home-made mixtures. However, there are simple methods of cleaning metals with ordinary products usually found in most households.

Brass and copper can be cleaned with a solution made of vinegar and as much salt as the vinegar can dissolve. A paste can be made of this solution by adding flour. After cleaning, rinse the brass or copper well in hot water. To prevent tarnish, coat the article with a clear lacquer made for the purpose.

Wrought iron which has rusted can be cleaned by first soaking in kerosene and then rubbing with fine steel wool or emery cloth. After cleaning, wipe with turpentine or benzine. To prevent rust, apply a coating a beeswax, paint, or lacquer. Steel and tin can be treated in the same way.

Silver which has tarnished should be cleaned and polished with a commercial silver-cleaning compound. To prevent tarnish, keep flatware in a tarnish-resistant chest or bag or in black tissue paper. Keep silver away from salt and rubber, both of which will corrode silver. Egg stains will also corrode it.

Mending Broken Pottery. All types of pottery objects which are broken but not shattered can be mended to look almost as good as new even though they must henceforth be handled with a little more care. Select a dry, sunny day for the work. First, scrub all the broken pieces in warm water and neutral suds and rinse in hot, not boiling, water. Wipe the pieces dry and cover the broken edges with real white lead. Press the pieces together and hold them in place with rubber bands or adhesive tape. Carefully scrape off any surplus lead with a dull knife. Leave the pieces undisturbed for at least two weeks until the lead is thoroughly dry. To hold a broken handle securely while it is mending, bury it in sand, broken ends up. Join the broken edges of the handle and body together, resting the body of the object on the surface of the sand. Fasten a strip of cloth across the object and weight the ends of the cloth.

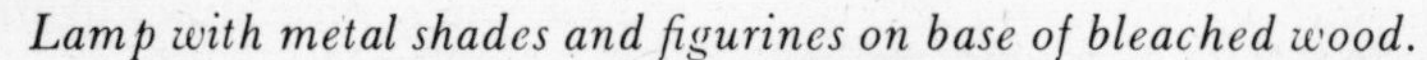

Lamp with metal shades and figurines on base of bleached wood.

Copper plant container and plate, brass candlesticks, and pottery figurines.

"Pictures" made of thin strips of plywood backed by paper in brilliant hues.

Modern crystal vase etched with design of a pearl diver.

CHAPTER XI

HOUSE PLANTS

THE FRESH GREEN of growing plants brings life to a room like magic. Everyone admires plants, but some people hesitate to do a bit of indoor gardening because they have the notion that plants won't thrive except for those who have a "green thumb." Don't believe it. Plants will flourish if their environment is suited to their individual needs. If you like plants, but don't want to spend too much time fussing with them, then choose some of the hardy varieties which need very little care. But once you've started, you will probably become so fascinated watching each new leaf unfold that before you realize what has happened, you will be a confirmed windowsill gardener. And you won't have to spend much money to achieve a very handsome display of foliage, either—although, of course, you *can* order the finest full-grown specimens from the florist if you want a full-fledged display without waiting. But before you rush off to make a selection, make a note of the environment, and then select plants which will thrive in it.

Light. The most important thing to consider when selecting plants is the light they will receive. Certain plants must have sun, and plenty of it. Others will do well without sun, providing they receive ample light. And a very few will grow if they are exposed to light for only a few hours a day. Windows facing north receive little or no direct sunshine during much of the year. Only foliage plants, such as ivy, Chinese Evergreen, philodendron, sansevieria, and so on will grow well there. Practically all the flowering plants require a sunny south window or at least an eastern or western window which receives some sunlight during part of the day.

Insufficient sunlight or daylight can be supplemented with artificial light to which most plants respond amazingly well. For best results, the light should be fairly strong, but not placed near enough to the plant for the heat from the bulb to burn the leaves. However, don't turn the sunlamp (if you have one) on the plants—they will only curl up and die under it.

Temperature. One reason why plants often fail to thrive is that the rooms in which they are kept are overheated. Most plants prefer an even daytime temperature of around seventy degrees. At night they like to be a little cooler, but if the temperature of the room drops much below fifty-five degrees, they may begin to shiver. Don't leave plants next to icy cold window panes during freezing weather. If the plants cannot be removed, protect them with a thick layer of newspaper. Above all, don't expose plants to sudden drastic changes of temperature. Ventilation and fresh air they must have, but they should not stand in front of an open window with a chilling draft blowing on them. Radiators under windowsills should be covered with asbestos tiles to protect plants from too intense direct heat.

Humidity. During winter months, our rooms are not only usually overheated but also as dry as a desert. Many plants cannot tolerate such an atmosphere for any length of time. Since most houses are not yet air conditioned, moisture must be supplied by some means. We thrive better, too, when the air is properly humidified. Some moisture can be added to the atmosphere by placing water containers behind the radiators, but not enough, as a rule, to raise the humidity very many degrees. But plants which need a high degree of humidity can be sprayed with a fine mist of water once or twice a day. Select a good hand sprayer—one which will cover a limited area with a fine mist so that curtains or upholstery will not be dampened. Be careful not to spray hairy-leaved plants, such as African violets, which rot if their leaves are kept wet.

Potting. Potting soils vary according to the needs of each individual plant, but in general a good potting soil consists of a rich garden earth, one-fourth to one-third fine sand (depending on how sandy the earth itself is) and about one-third humus and peat moss mixed. Some plants like more or less sand, some a rich diet of bone meal, some want an acid soil, and others must have an alkaline one, so consult the list of plants further on in this chapter to find if a plant has special soil needs.

Soil, sand, and humus or peat moss should be thoroughly mixed and just moist enough to hold together when squeezed, but to fall apart at a touch. First place a rounded piece of crock and several smaller pieces over the opening in the pot as well as a handful of pebbles to provide drainage. More drainage material and a little powdered charcoal are required if the pot has no bottom opening. Then fill with enough soil mixture to meet the root ends, if you are repotting or starting newly rooted slips or cuttings. Place the young plant in position and continue adding the soil mixture until the pot is filled to within one-half inch from the top edge. Press the soil down gently but firmly. Do not pack it down hard. Water the plant and place in a shady spot for a day or two.

Plants which have outgrown their containers often have to be repotted in larger

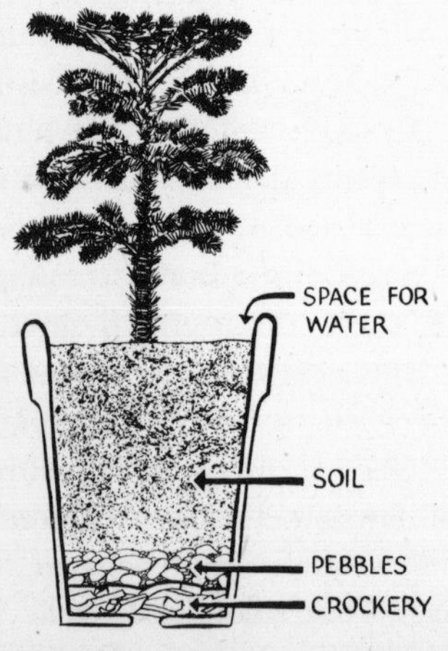

FIG. 1. Method of arranging potting materials to provide adequate drainage.

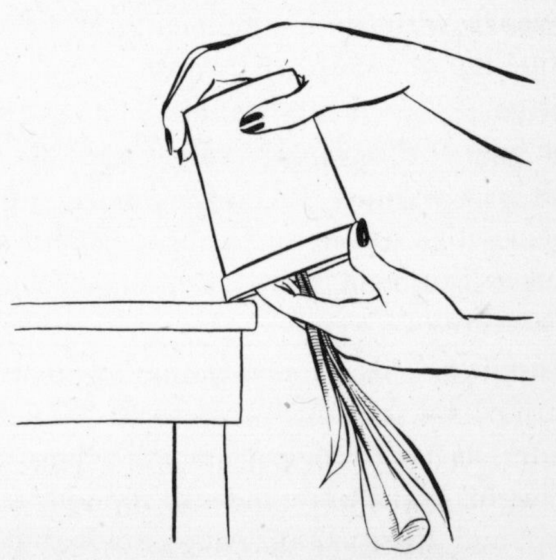

FIG. 2. To remove plant, roots, and soil, turn plant upside down, and tap rim of pot against the edge of a table. Support the leaves and soil with one hand and hold the pot with the other.

ones. To remove the plant, first water it lightly. Then turn the pot upside down and tap the edge sharply. Roots and soil can then usually be lifted out whole. If the roots are badly tangled, some should be carefully cut away. Then repot the plant in a container just one size larger. Plants recover from such treatment more readily if it is done in the early spring.

Fertilizing and Cultivating. The easiest fertilizers to use are the commercial plant foods, especially the liquid ones, which are merely measured and mixed with water according to the manufacturer's directions. Never use more or apply oftener than directed on the theory that if a little is good, more will be better. It isn't. Don't feed plants indiscriminately. Some plants do not want it, and all plants have periods of rest during which time they need less fertilizing than when they are growing.

In order to supply the roots with oxygen, the top soil must be cultivated every few days. Use an old fork or a miniature spade from the dime store for this purpose. Don't dig too deeply lest the roots be injured—half an inch or an inch is deep enough. And don't forget that plants "breathe" through their leaves, so if the leaves are covered with dust, the plants smother. Wipe the smooth-leaved plants with damp cotton, or place cardboard collars around the base of the plant, stand the pots in the tub on newspapers or old rags, and shower them with a rubber hose attachment on the faucet. Brush the hairy-leaved plants with a soft brush.

Watering. More plants are probably harmed by too much water or too little water at too frequent intervals than by drought. Water only when the top soil feels dry, and then apply enough so that the liquid drains through the opening in the bottom of the pot. As soon as drainage is complete, remove all water from the saucer since plants do not like to have their "feet" wet. Plants in glazed pots need watering less often than plants in unglazed pots, from which moisture evaporates more readily. Dormant plants need less water than growing ones. Plants also need more water when they are in bloom. Large plants in tub-sized pots, ferns, and hairy-leaved plants, such as African violets, should be watered by standing the pot in a container of water and allowing the moisture to be drawn up from beneath until the top soil is moist. Never shock a plant with ice water. Instead, apply water at room temperature.

Growth Control. A little persuasion is necessary in order to achieve a neat and pleasing arrangement of foliage. Plants at windows receive light from only one direction, and will therefore grow toward that source. To prevent lopsided growth, turn the plants around every few days. Vines need a trellis or some other support unless they are planted in a hanging container. Sometimes vines which are supposed to hang persist in stretching themselves out. In that case, they can be gently tied down against the pot with a piece of soft string until they learn to grow in the direction intended. Straggly growth should be pruned away, and the best time to do this is in the spring. Miniature trees can be trained to grow in oddly twisted shapes by wiring the stems into position while the plants are very young, or by pulling them into shape with soft string tied around the stems and held in place by the rim of the pot. They should be pulled very slowly—just a fraction of an inch or so every day, and the string should be moved up or down the stem a bit now and then. This process takes time, so don't expect to have your tree on display while it's being "educated."

Propagation. The easiest way to start a window garden is to buy a selection of well-

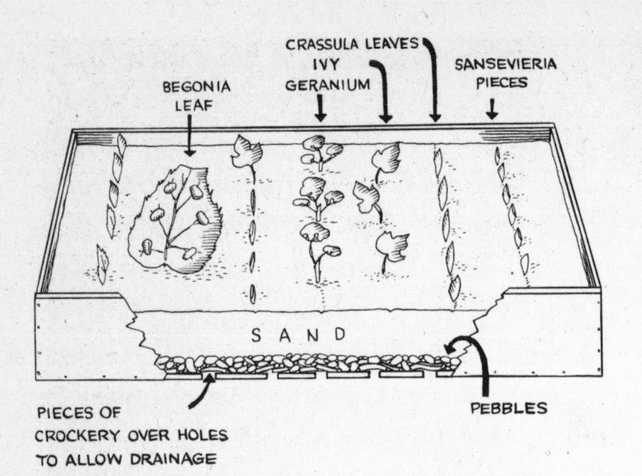

FIG. 3. A box in which to propagate cuttings can be made from a shallow crate. Drill small holes in the bottom to allow for drainage and fill with broken crockery, pebbles, and sterile sand.

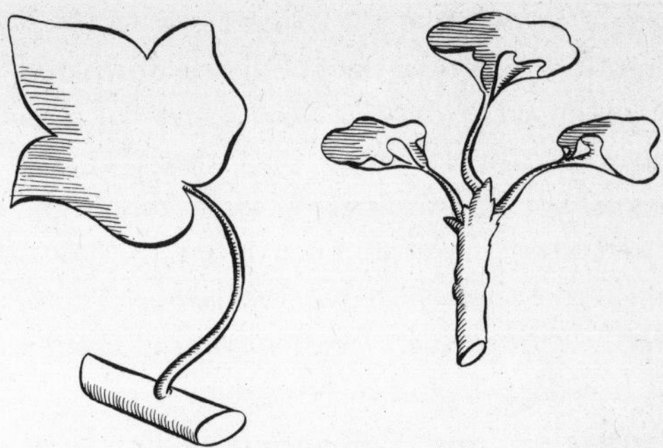

FIG. 4. At the left is a mallet cutting of an ivy leaf ready for propagation. Geranium (right) propagates best from a short stem cutting.

developed plants from the florist or the greenhouse. But this can also be rather expensive. The true plant lover soon wants to experiment with propagation — especially when she finds how easily some plants can be started and at how little expense. Different plants are propagated in a variety of ways—from seeds, from stem, leaf, or root cuttings, and from bulbs. Some plants send up offsets from their roots which can be separated from the parent plant.

Ivy, philodendron, geranium, Wandering Jew, coleus, impatiens, shrimp plant, and some others can be propagated from stem cuttings. The stem to cut should be neither too woody nor too green. Make a clean, downward cut with a sharp razor blade. If the stem has divisions, cut just below one of them. Otherwise, cut just below a joint. Only one or two small leaves should be left on the cutting. Mallet cuttings can be made from the center of the stems on vines such as ivy or philodendron, if preferred. About one inch of stem, with a single leaf on it, is taken for each cutting.

Sansevieria, some begonias, crassula, and African violet, can be grown from leaf cuttings. A sansevieria leaf can be cut into one-inch pieces, and every one will take root. Rex Begonia will root from a single, stemless leaf if the veins are slit and the leaf is held in place against moist sand with small pebbles. A crassula leaf is inserted halfway down into the sand. But only the stem of an African violet should be planted —the leaf should be broken off.

The so-called beefsteak begonia and a number of ferns are propagated best from root cuttings. Cut out inch-long sections of root with a joint, or node, on each section.

The best medium for rooting cuttings is sterile sand, although some will take root in water. To sterilize the sand, bake it in a moderate oven for an hour or two. Wash it well and mix it with a little powdered charcoal. A flat wooden box with holes cut for drainage and covered with pieces of arched

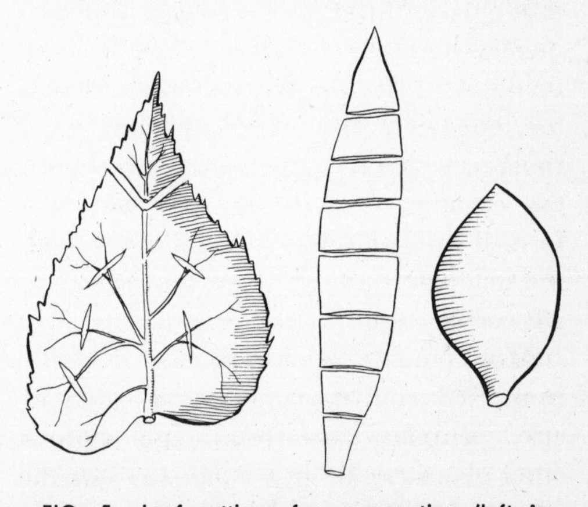

FIG. 5. Leaf cuttings for propagating (left to right) rex begonia, snake plant, and crassula. The begonia leaf is slit across the veins, laid on moist sand, and weighted with pebbles.

Succulents are decorative and easy to grow. Many varieties are available. In the above group (from left to right) are prickly pear (Opuntia), *urbina corderoyi, crassula portulacea, aloe obscura, and agave herida.*

crockery makes a good container for rooting purposes. A large, flat roasting pan can also be used, if a one-inch layer of coarse pebbles is placed in the bottom for drainage. A layer of sand no more than two or three inches deep is needed, and after the cuttings are in place, it should be well soaked. The container is then placed in a warm, shady place for a few days. Cuttings root quicker if treated with one of the commercial hormone mixtures, which must be used exactly as directed. Bottom heat helps, too, but don't place the container over a radiator which becomes hot enough to cook the cuttings. As soon as roots are well formed and new leaves begin to appear, the tiny plants are ready for transplanting. All cuttings root better in the spring.

More patience is needed to start plants from seeds, but morning glories, mignonette, petunia, nasturtiums, and various other plants can be grown this way without too much difficulty. Sow them in rows in shallow beds of sterile sand, or start them in pots. Even small trees can be grown from grapefruit, orange, and avocado seeds. Orange or grapefruit seeds should be dried out for a week or two and then placed about one-half inch deep in sterile sand to root, after which they can be transplanted like a cutting. Avocado seeds should be suspended halfway deep in water by supporting them with toothpicks driven in on four sides. Keep in a dark place until roots begin to form and a stem appears (this may take from six weeks to two months). Then pot in soil. Avocados will also grow in water, but tend to become leggy. After the stem is about three inches high, pinch the top off completely to force branching. Wonderful vines can be grown from sweet potatoes set in water. Only the lower end of the potato should be covered with water. The upper end should be supported by toothpicks resting on the edge of the container—or choose a container with a mouth to fit the potato. A small piece of charcoal in the bottom will keep the water sweet. Replenish water every few days as it evaporates.

Plants can also be propagated with excellent results and no soil at all by using one of the chemical plant foods diluted in water. The plants may be grown in the water mixture alone if supported by some kind of wire netting or in sand. The manufacturer's directions for dilution should be followed exactly.

Insects. It's a rare plant that appeals to no insect, so the indoor gardener may just as well be resigned to a struggle with pests. Watch plants carefully, and at the first sign of unwanted guests, start eviction proceedings before they have an opportunity to set up housekeeping and start breeding families—which they do with startling rapidity.

Scale insects are tiny, sucking creatures, which often look like minute brown, black, or white lumps. They are very fond of ivy and Boston fern, but also attack other plants. Left alone, the leaves soon begin to curl and turn brown. Other sucking insects are red spider, mealy bugs, and aphids. Mealy bugs are white and their young grow in what appears to be small lumps of white cotton. Aphids are tiny green, black, or white insects. The males of some species have wings and can fly. These are the most common of the pests which attack house plants. What to do about them? There are many remedies. But perhaps the simplest way for the householder who doesn't want to fuss or bother with messy treatments, is to use one of the commercial pest control compounds for plants, spraying it on with a sprayer which has enough force to cover the plant thoroughly. Both top and undersides of leaves should be sprayed as well as stems. Use a weak solution on delicate plants. If mealy bugs appear on African violets (which can't be sprayed), pick them off with a toothpick wrapped in cotton and dipped in rubbing alcohol and warm water, half and half.

Red spider is sometimes difficult to get rid of except by immersing the entire plant —pot, leaves, and all—in a tubful of water heated to 120 degrees for half a minute. The hot water does not injure the plant, but the temperature must be accurately determined with a thermometer before immersion.

SELECTION OF HOUSE PLANTS

As stated earlier in this chapter, the most important point to consider when selecting house plants is the light they are to receive. Next, of course, is the hardiness of the plant itself. Some plants adapt themselves quite amiably to almost any condition, while others are decidedly fussy. The amount of care to be devoted to a plant is not so much a matter of time as a matter of adjusting the heat, humidity, and atmosphere to the needs of the plant. In other words, since the Boston fern doesn't like tobacco smoke, Uncle Henry will have to take his pipe elsewhere (or, if Uncle Henry is more important, then the Boston fern is taken elsewhere).

The amateur gardener will no doubt be happier with a first choice of the easy-to-grow plants. For convenience, these are marked (*). However, among the (*) plants, it should be noted that a few are outstanding in this respect. Sansevieria is all but immortal. And, alas, its virtues have made it so common that it has become almost as scorned as the aspidistra. Yet both plants are decorative, and were they difficult to grow they would undoubtedly be quite prized. Plants which are more exacting are marked (**), while those which are quite fussy in their demands are indicated by (***).

PLANTS FOR A WINDOW WITH NO DIRECT SUNSHINE

Aloe (*). A member of the succulent family, cultivated for decorative, often grotesque shapes. Several species are grown, but *aloe arborescens* is one of the easiest to grow in the house. Leaves grow from a center crown, which must be kept dry. Do not water too often—once a week is usually sufficient.

Aspidistra(*). A coarse-leaved plant grown for its foliage. One variety has green and cream striped leaves which are quite ornamental. Plant endures considerable heat and dryness, but center crown should not be wet.

Baby Tears (*). A mosslike plant with feathery foliage. Should be grown in traylike container. Likes an acid soil and very little fertilizer. About once in ten days or two weeks give a solution of ammonia (one teaspoonful to a quart of water). Pinch back well. Spray with water weekly. Keep moist but not soggy.

Begonia (**) (Rex Begonia). One of the numerous varieties of begonias. Has spotted, hairy leaves, which do not like to be wet, so plant must be watered from bottom. Will grow without sunlight, but does better with an hour or so of sunlight a day. Does not like too dry an atmosphere.

Boston Fern (**). The familiar fern with drooping, spear-shaped fronds. Prefers humid, rather cool atmosphere and peaty soil. Dislikes tobacco smoke. Water from bottom of pot, but do not allow pot to stand in water between waterings. Watch for scale. Shower frequently. Remove all brown or broken leaves. Ferns remain dormant during winter as a rule, and should not be fed during this time.

Chinese Evergreen (*). A handsome foliage plant with large, dark green, pointed leaves growing out one from the other on a center stem. Can be grown in earth or water. When grown in earth, more leaves result and roots often send up offsets which can be separated from parent plant. Resists insects and is very hardy.

Dumb Cane (*) (Dieffenbachia). A fine foliage plant with large, pointed, light or dark green leaves mottled with cream. Will grow in water as well as in earth. Habits similar to Chinese evergreen.

English Ivy (*). May be grown as a trailing vine or trained on a trellis. Besides the plain variety, one may also choose variegated and dwarf types. Grows well in water as well as in earth, which should be of acid content. Ivy is subject to scale and red spider which can be controlled by frequent, hard spraying with water.

Grape Ivy (*). May be grown either as a hanging or a climbing vine. Stems have curly tendrils and leaves in groups of three.

Snake plant (sansevieria) *is one of the easiest plants to grow in the house.*

Nephthytis (**). A trailing vine with thick stems and leaves like arrowheads. Easy to grow if atmosphere is not too dry.

Pandanus (*). A fine, easy-to-grow foliage plant with sword-shaped, spiny leaves of green or green striped with cream growing from a center crown, which must not be wet. Roots project themselves from the soil. Be careful not to over-water, or leaves will rot, but do not allow plant to dry out completely. Wipe leaves with damp cloth only; do not wash.

Philodendron (*). A very popular hardy vine which adapts itself to almost any condition. Leaves are dark green and heart shaped. Can be grown on trellis or as trailing plant. Grows in soil or in water.

Pothos (**). A slow-growing vine with a heart-shaped leaf similar to that of the philodendron, except that it is mottled with cream. Pothos needs a warm, humid atmosphere.

Rubber Plant (*). The old-fashioned rubber plant finds little favor now, but the fiddle-leaved variety (called *ficus pandurata*) is quite ornamental. Keep the leaves clean, water twice a week, and feed when growing.

Sedums (*). Various odd-shaped kinds available, all members of the succulent family. Do not overwater—once a week is usually sufficient.

Snake Plant (*) (Sansevieria). A tall plant with fleshy, green leaves mottled or edged with cream. Will grow under almost any conditions except when drowned in too much water. Will even thrive without direct light. Roots send up offsets, or plant may be propagated from leaf cuttings.

Wandering Jew (*) (Tradescantia). A vigorous, handsome trailing vine with slender pointed leaves, either bright green or variegated. Cuttings root easily in water or moist sand. Nip stems often as plant grows very rapidly.

PLANTS FOR WINDOWS WITH FROM TWO TO THREE HOURS SUN DAILY

(Note: Plants in First Group also included)

African Violet (**). Has low growing clumps of hairy gray-green leaves and lovely flowers of deep or light violet, pink, or white. Tolerates no moisture on leaves, so plant must be watered by immersion once or twice a week. Feed sparingly to produce blooms, and remove stems of withered flowers as well as dead leaves. Does not like hot, dry air or chilly drafts. Watch for mites on underside of leaves. Will bloom at north windows in summer.

Aralia (***). An interesting foliage plant with compound clusters of metallic green leaves. Needs a fairly humid atmosphere and rich soil. Subject to scale.

Asparagus Fern (**). Not really a fern. *Asparagus plumosa* is the familiar, feathery greenery which the florist often adds to the box of roses. *Asparagus sprengeri* has an abundance of needle-like little leaves on trailing stems. Use a rich and well-drained potting mixture with high percentage of peat and sand and feed liberally when growing. Watch for spider and scale.

Begonia (**). Many varieties to choose from. Some have dark green shiny leaves, those of others are hairy or vari-colored. Flowers are both single and multi-petaled and range in color from white through yellow, pink, copper, and red. Good drainage is essential for all begonias. Water sparingly, especially during dark days. Keep the hairy-leaved types in east or northeast windows and never allow leaves to be wet. Begonias prefer a rather humid atmosphere. Feed when blooming.

Billibergia (*). Has long, spiky, dark green leaves growing from a center heart and tiny yellow flowers growing from a stalk with cerise bracts which shoot up in spring. Another variety has blue flowers. Likes plenty of water and sun while blooming but little during the rest of the year. After blooming, divide roots and leaves to form new plants. Pot in well drained soil with sphagnum moss and a bit of powdered charcoal.

Christmas Cactus (**). An ornamental plant with flat, jointed leaves shaped like crab claws and bright red flowers which bloom in December. Water very sparingly, especially when in bloom. Fertilize with bonemeal, hydrated lime, and wood ash (about 1 teaspoon each in quart of water) every week when buds appear instead of feeding with commercial plant food. Likes sun while blooming. Afterwards, transfer to north window.

Crassula (*). A fleshy-leaved member of the succulent family. Water only about once a week, and watch for rot.

Cyclamen (***). One of the handsomest flowering plants, with thick green leaves and large blossoms of red, coral, pink, or white with turned-back petals. Prefers cool, even temperature of around 70 degrees and a great deal of water while blooming—water underneath from saucer about twice a day. Remove all dead leaves and blossoms, or plant will rot. After blooming, remove to north window and water only when dry.

Dracaena (**). Several varieties available. *Dracaena fragans* has deep green leaves similar in shape to a corn stalk; so has *dracaena massangeana,* except that leaves are striped with cream. *Dracaena godseffiana* has branching leaves mottled with cream. Easy to grow if air is not too dry. Water sparingly except when growing.

Flowering Maple (**) (Abutilon). A flowering tree with white, pink, or red blossoms. Must be vigorously pruned between blooming periods. Likes plenty of water, and well drained soil, half of sand and half of garden loam. Subject to white fly, which can be controlled by frequent spraying.

Three interesting plants for indoor culture: Dumb cane (diffenbachia), *at the left grows well even in dry rooms. Dracaena (center) and asparagus fern (right) like a more humid atmosphere.*

Maidenhair Fern (***). One of the loveliest varieties of ferns, with delicate sprays of small green leaves, but very exacting in its demands. Needs a humid, not too warm atmosphere, no sudden changes of temperature, rich soil with plenty of humus, and good drainage. Water by immersion.

Marica (*). A flowering plant with blue or yellow iris-like blossoms on the tips of fan-spreading leaves. Fertilize with bonemeal instead of commercial plant food. Blooms in early spring. Water sparingly during rest of year. Resists insects.

Norfolk Island Pine (**) (Araucaria). A small evergreen tree with symmetrical branches. Thrives well if fed regularly with a complete plant food, except when dormant. Spray for mealy bug. Water thoroughly only when top soil is dry.

Peperomia (**). A foliage plant with thick, heart shaped leaves, either dark green or variegated with lighter green somewhat like the markings on a watermelon. Grows well if atmosphere is humid.

Spider Plant (*) (Anthericum). An interesting, small foliage plant with slender leaves on delicate stems, from the tips of which spring small tufts of leaves similar in appearance to a spider. Has few needs except sufficient water and plant food when growing.

Strawberry Begonia (**). Not a begonia and not a strawberry plant, but its leaves somewhat resemble a cross between the two. Its true name is *saxifraga sarmentosa.* Stems are pink and so are the undersides of the hairy leaves. Water only when dry, and then by immersion, since leaves must not be wet. Looks well in a hanging basket.

Wax Plant (**). A striking vine with large, thick leaves and small, waxy flowers. Likes a peaty soil with some charcoal in a small pot and good drainage. Water sparingly and feed only while blooming. Spray for mealy bug.

PLANTS FOR WINDOWS WITH THREE OR MORE HOURS SUN DAILY

(Note: List also includes Flowering Maple and Wax Plant from Second Group)

Azalea (**). A flowering shrub with large single or double blooms of pink, red, or white. Requires a great deal of water; leaves should be sprayed with water if atmosphere is dry. Feed regularly while plant is in bloom, alternating occasionally with a solution of aluminum sulphate (one teaspoonful to a quart of water). Pick off all blossoms as they die. After blooming, decrease feeding, but water each day. When plant is dormant during the fall, place it in a north window, water only enough to keep it from going dry, and do not feed at all. Return to sunny south window in December.

Cactus (**). Any number of varieties to choose from. Water very sparingly. Some need water only once a week; others twice —preferably from a saucer or container beneath the pot. When dormant, decrease amount of water. Do not fertilize with commercial plant foods. Instead, use a teaspoonful each of hardwood ash, hydrated lime, and bonemeal to a quart of water, and water the plants about once a week with this solution during the growing period. Spray occasionally to remove dust so as to discourage mealy bug, but never allow water to stand on cacti or they will rot. One decorative cactus, called *crown of thorns,* is very fussy about drafts and will die if exposed to sudden changes of temperature. If rot appears, it must be cut away with a sharp knife dipped in boiling water after each cut; otherwise the entire plant will die.

Clivia (**). A bulbous-rooted flowering plant with lily-like blooms. Likes a rich, sandy, well-drained soil. Keep in north window and water sparingly until it begins to grow rapidly — usually about January. Then place in sunny south window, feed weekly and water thoroughly whenever top soil is dry. Roots will tend to work their way up out of the soil.

Coleus (**). A favorite foliage plant because of its beautifully colored leaves, which may be bright pink, deep red, or yellow, edged in green. Do not overwater, and above all, see that plant has perfect drainage and good ventilation. Pinch back growth to prevent straggling and remove tiny flowers so that plant will not go to seed.

Flame Crassula (**) (Kalanchoe coccinea). A thick-leaved succulent with scarlet flowers. Water and feed sparingly except when blooming, at which time it needs full sunlight. After blooming, place in east or northeast window.

Geranium (*). Old-fashioned, but ever charming, and one of the most satisfactory flowering plants to grow indoors. Many varieties available, with blossoms ranging from white through all tones of pink, red, salmon, and dark red. Geraniums will bloom either in winter or summer, but not the year around. In order to produce blooms, the roots should be rather pot bound and the center buds and overambitious branches must be nipped back frequently. As soon as buds appear, feed regularly with a commercial plant food. Water only when top soil is dry. After it blooms, allow the plant to rest in an east or northeast window with just enough water to keep it from drying out and no plant food. Spray for white fly or aphis. Before new buds begin to form next year, repot in container just one size larger. Prune thoroughly, and water lightly until new growth develops, after which place in full sunlight.

Impatiens (**). A more or less continuously blooming plant with red or pink blossoms and pale green leaves. Must have perfect drainage and will benefit from a monthly dose of lime water. Nip back frequently as plant grows quite rapidly. When plant becomes too large, take stem cuttings, root in water and start new growths. Must be watched for red spider.

Morning Glory (**). This well-loved annual vine can be grown indoors from seed at a sunny window. Start the seed in late February, and after vines begin to grow, feed regularly and give them some support to climb on. They will require plenty of room, and therefore are more suitable for a sunroom than a single small window. The variety known as *heavenly blue* is one of the showiest.

Plumbago (**). A fall flowering woody plant. The cerise plumbago produces sprays of pendulous bright flowers if placed in a sunny window but the room must not be too dry or warm. Do not overwater. After blooming, prune thoroughly and let the plant go dormant in a northeast window. Repot in late spring.

Shrimp Plant (**). A fascinating flowering plant with pink bracts shaped somewhat like tiny shrimps. Thrives well if given plenty of sun, water, a rich, sandy loam and regular feedings while in bloom. Grows rapidly, so must be well pruned in spring. Cuttings root easily.

BULBS

Bulbs are somewhat in a class by themselves, because they are grown for one forced period of bloom and then discarded. But if you have a sunny window and observe a few rules, you will find that bulbs are among the easiest things to grow. The first rule for success is to buy bulbs of good quality from a reliable dealer. If you have a cool, dark basement or a cold frame, you can grow nearly any kind of bulb in soil. If not, then there are a number of bulbs which grow well in water and pebbles in an ordinary room which is not kept warmer than 70 degrees.

Bulbs can be grown in the same type of potting soil used for other house plants. Plant the bulbs as early as they can be secured in the fall. Cover them with about half an inch of soil, except the jonquils and daffodils, which like to have their tips out. Then water the bulbs thoroughly and store them in a really cool, dark airy place to form roots, a process which takes anywhere from four to twelve weeks, depending on the variety. If the bulbs are kept in the house, water just often enough to prevent drying out. Anytime after roots have formed, the bulbs can gradually be brought to the light. Keep them at a north window for a week or two in a room where the temperature is between 50 and 60 degrees, until the leaves begin to develop. Then bring the bulbs into a warmer room (but preferably not warmer than

Chinese evergreen is one of the most amiable of house plants. When the roots become too pot bound, the plant will bloom (as above); but the flower is not particularly decorative.

65 or 70 degrees), set them in a sunny window, and let them come into flower, turning the pots every other day for even growth. This forcing period may begin at any time after the roots have developed to provide lovely, scented blossoms from Thanksgiving through Easter. Most bulbs require about four weeks from the time they are brought to the light until the blooms appear. Narcissus usually takes only three weeks or less, and forcing of all bulbs takes a little longer during the winter months than in the spring.

Some of the favorite flowering bulbs are crocus, daffodils, hyacinths (Dutch and Roman French), jonquils, narcissus (paper white), and tulips. In addition, there is the lovely lily-of-the-valley, which can easily be grown indoors if you buy the pips already frozen from the florist in February or March. Plant them in peat moss, soil, or sand in a deep container, leaving the tops of the pips uncovered. Set them in a dark, well ventilated place, no more than 70 degrees in temperature. In about fourteen days the leaves should be three or four inches high. Then set the container in a north or east window in a cool room. In about fifteen days the sprays of scented lilies should appear.

Daffodils, hyacinths, jonquils, and paper-white narcissus can easily be grown in water and pebbles, if you do not try to force the bulbs into flower much earlier than their natural blooming period. Rest the bulbs firmly in the pebbles, being sure that no bulb touches another or the sides of the bowl. Add only enough water to cover the lower part of the bulb and a piece or two of charcoal to keep the water sweet. Except for the hyacinth, the bulbs do not need to be kept in the dark while they root, but they should be kept out of the sun until they are ready to bloom. All bulbs thrive better in a room heated no more than 70 degrees. Drafts and hot radiators are their mortal enemies.

MINIATURE GREENHOUSES

Why not recreate a summer woodland scene in minature—right in your own living room? It's easy to grow even fussy plants under glass. These Wardian case plantings, or terraria, as they are called, can be as tiny or large as you wish, or can afford. Any clear glass container will do—a fish bowl, an aquarian tank, or a bottle large enough to accommodate some kind of a plant. If you prefer, you may buy Wardian cases or have them made to order in any size. The top should be glass covered, too, since the "greenhouse" needs little ventilation—just enough to keep the inside of the glass from looking steamy.

First place a layer of pebbles and broken charcoal in your container for perfect drainage. Then add an inch or so of sand and peat moss mixed, and finally a layer of rich garden soil—depth depends on the size of the container and the size of plants. Soil, sand, and peat moss should be sterilized in a hot oven for an hour before planting. Add a little water to the soil before setting in the plants. If you wish, and have room, you can simulate an outdoor scene by adding rocks, a mirror lake, and

tiny animal figurines. Moss is the best ground cover, and it is well worth while to take a trip into the woods in late autumn to gather it for the terrarium. The low growing plant, baby tears, will look like minature shrubbery in this outdoor scene. Then add ferns, something tall, such as sansieveria, in one corner, perhaps an African violet, and any other small plant. (If the container is rounded, the terrarium must be kept out of the sun; otherwise the glass will act as a burning glass, and cook the plants. Therefore, for a rounded container, choose plants which do not require any direct sunlight.) With a little study, really effective plantings can be achieved. Remember not to "spot" tall plants at random, here and there. Instead, use them as background, preferably off to one side. After your scene is complete, add water very slowly—just enough to wet the roots thoroughly. Put the lid in place—and watch your garden grow. Once a month is often enough to water as a rule. But if the plants begin to droop, water oftener.

With patience, even narrow-necked bottles can be planted. For this purpose, try using a quarter-teaspoon measure, securely wired to a knitting needle. The earth will have to be carefully placed, spoonful by spoonful, inside the bottle, without touching the sides. Plant the bottle sideways or right side up. Choose only the tiniest plants, remove the earth from the roots, and place them in tepid water until they are ready to be set in place. Then form the roots into a strand narrow enough to go through the neck of the bottle. Push them into the soil with a knitting needle, and continue until the bottle is planted. Add water—let it seep in very slowly by tipping the bottle slightly if the bottle is planted on the side. Cork the bottle and keep it in a good light but out of the sun. Remove the cork for a while every other day for ventilation.

Why, look! Your thumb's turned green!

CHAPTER XII

FABRICS

SUCH a bewildering variety of fabrics comes from the textile mills that it is sometimes difficult to know just what to choose. Color, design, suitability, and appearance are the first considerations, of course. Serviceability is important, too. And usually the budget must be consulted. Therefore, the more we know about fabrics, the better prepared we are to choose those which will give us satisfaction.

Firm closely woven fabrics outwear thin or loosely woven ones. Yarns which are "floated" across the surface of the foundation yarns to produce a design in satin effect are apt to wear more quickly than the rest of the fabric, especially if such yarns are of rayon and the foundation yarns are of another fiber. This fact should be remembered when choosing upholstery materials—a brocaded satin may soon have a mass of loose threads on its surface. To wear well, upholstery fabrics should be very firm and smooth, without satin brocading, or else with a dense, short pile, preferably uncut.

FIBER CONTENT

The natural fibers of wool, cotton, linen, and silk are now supplemented by a whole new group of synthetic fibers derived from many sources. Manufacturers may combine several kinds of fibers and produce a textile that grandma never saw the likes of. Fibers are fine filaments which are twisted together to form the yarns from which textiles are woven. Fibers are graded according to their length, quality and condition, or their staple. They can be examined by unraveling and then untwisting the yarns. Examine both warp and weft yarns, as each may have a different fiber content.

Wool. Wool fibers are more or less curly and quite lustrous. Because wool fibers have a high degree of resiliency, fabrics woven from them resist creasing and tend to spring back into shape. Wool fibers burn more slowly than cotton or linen and with an acrid odor, leaving a bubbly black bead at the end. Textiles and yarns made of loosely twisted, short wool fibers are called *woolens*. Woolen fabrics have a soft fuzzy surface, and often the weave is not clearly visible. Because of their highly insulating properties, woolen yarns are used in blankets and in napped fabrics, such as flannel. Textiles and yarns made of long, combed, and highly twisted wool fibers are called *worsteds*. Worsteds have a smooth, hard finish. Serge and gabardine are examples of fabrics made of worsted yarns. Most, but not all, wool comes from sheep. It also comes from camels, goats, llamas, alpacas and vicunas. When such specialty fibers as they are termed, are used in textiles, they are generally identified.

Cotton. Because of their cheapness and durability, the fibers of the cotton plant are of more commercial importance than any other. They are used not only to weave cotton cloth, but also as one of the principal sources of cellulose from which rayon is made. The best cotton is long stapled, and is often classified as *Sea Island* or *Egyptian* cotton. Short stapled cotton, classified as *upland,* produces less durable textiles. Untreated cotton yarns look dull and limp, but if mercerized are quite lustrous (*see section on Finishes and Treatments in this chapter*). Cotton will burn readily, leaving no deposit.

Linen. Linen fabric is made from fibers obtained from the flax plant. They are stiffer and more lustrous than cotton fibers, but the luster is not always uniform. Linen absorbs moisture readily, and for this reason a traditional test for linen fabric is to moisten the finger and place it on the underside of the cloth. If the moisture quickly penetrates to the surface, the textile is said to be linen. Unfortunately, this test is not always reliable because the fabric may be coated with a sizing which prevents rapid penetration of moisture. There are also fine cottons which absorb moisture as readily as linen. A crease test is more satisfactory. If linen is crushed in the hand, it will be found to crease more readily than cotton and to remain creased longer.

Silk. The fibers which the silkworm spins to make his cocoon are so fine that several of them must be unreeled together—otherwise they would be too delicate to handle. Yet when these smooth and highly lustrous fibers are woven, they produce textiles which are durable as well as beautiful—and silk has been highly prized for its great beauty ever since the Chinese first discovered how to cultivate the silkworm long before the time of Christ. The finest silk yarns are made from fibers taken from the cocoons in single, long filaments. *Spun* silk is made from the short fibers of cocoons broken open by moths used for breeding purposes or from cocoons damaged during the unreeling process. *Wild silk* comes from the tussah moth (which is also sometimes cultivated). This silk is coarser than the cultivated variety, brownish in color, and difficult to dye, and so it is usually woven in its natural color. Pongee and shantung are made from tussah silk.

Silk, like wool, is resilient and tends to resist creasing. Pure silk fibers burn with an acrid odor like wool and leave a shiny black bead. Weighted silk burns to an ash which retains the shape of the original yarn or fabric.

Silk no longer holds the place of commercial importance it once had, largely because every type of textile formerly made only of silk is now made of rayon with excellent results and at considerably less expense. But some demand for silk will undoubtedly continue.

Rayon. Rayon fibers are produced by chemical means from cellulose (obtained largely from wood or cotton), and may be classified as *viscose, acetate, cuprammonium,* or *nitrocellulose,* according to the type of manufacturing process. The liquid cellulose is forced through the tiny openings of a spinneret into a chemical solution which hardens it. The fine continuous filaments are then gathered together to form the yarn, which is smooth and may have any degree of luster. The process of manufacturing rayon has now been so well perfected that it is difficult to distinguish some rayons from silk in appearance or in feel. However, they are readily distinguishable by burning. Cellulose rayons burn with a quick flame and leave no deposit, while acetate rayons simply melt into a hard ball. A too-hot iron will cause acetate rayon to become stiff or even to fuse and disintegrate. Acetate rayon will also dissolve in pure acetone. Good rayon fabrics are durable and highly serviceable, but all rayons tend to be weakened when subjected to moisture, and therefore should be handled gently when wet.

Nylon. A synthetic fiber, nylon is produced by chemical means from coal, air and water. It is tough, highly resilient so that it resists creasing, and dries quickly. Nylon, so popular for stockings, has many other uses, and new ones are being found for it all the time. Nylon fabrics launder as easily as nylon stockings.

Glass. While glass is no new product, the process of spinning glass filaments fine enough to be made into yarn which can be woven is another accomplishment of modern science. Fabrics made of glass fibers repel dust, moisture, mildew, and insects, and in addition they will not burn. Glass fabrics resembles a coarse taffeta, and may be dyed a solid color or printed. It is highly lustrous and its virtues make it ideal for hangings or draperies. However, it is still comparatively expensive.

Other Fibers. Many other fibers are also used in making textiles, and science will probably continue to add to the list. The fibers made from the casein of milk are similar to wool. Jute, ramie, and asbestos fibers also have many uses.

Plastic Fabrics. The new plastic fabrics are not woven textiles at all, and therefore cannot be said to have a fiber content. Instead, they are sheets of film in varying degrees of thickness, and may be opaque or translucent and in any color of the rainbow. Some plastic fabrics are so impervious to stains that even ink or iodine may be spilled on them and wiped off without leaving a trace. For this reason, they are very suitable for upholstery which must withstand considerable abuse. In addition, there are plastic fabrics which resist mildew and fire, and are therefore excellent for shower curtains or hangings.

WEAVES AND TEXTURES

A textile is woven by running one set of yarns, called the *weft* or the *woof,* in and out across another set of lengthwise

FIG. 1. Plain weave.

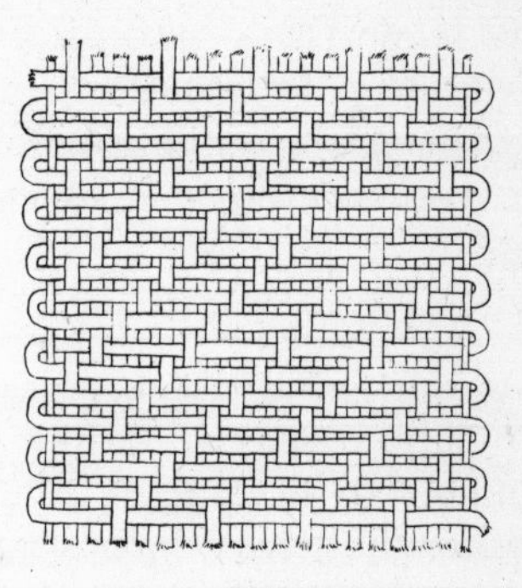

FIG. 2. Twill weave.

FIG. 3. Satin weave.

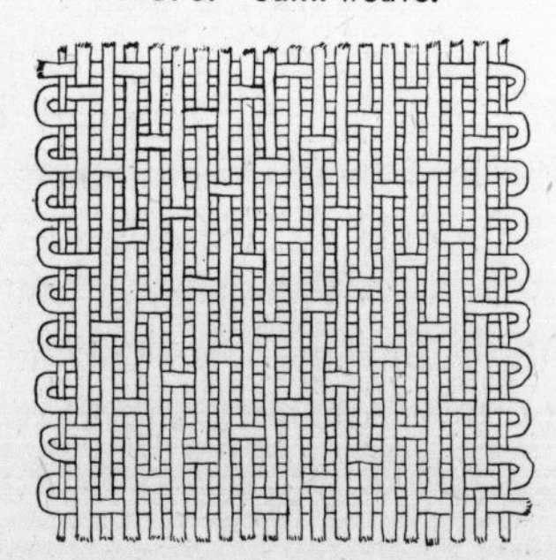

FIG. 4. Leno weave.

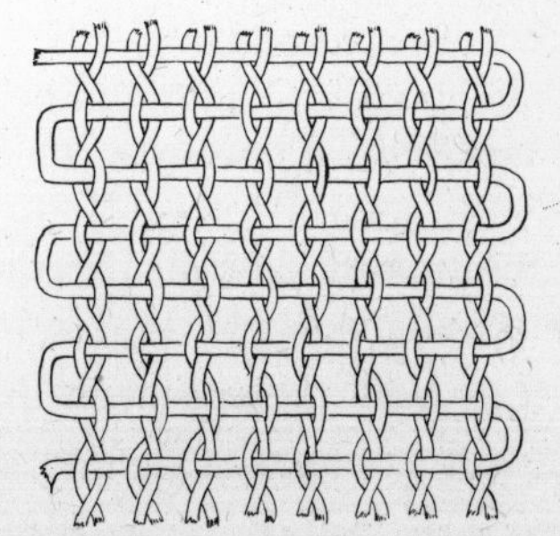

yarns, called the *warp*. Sometimes the warp is called the *back* or *foundation,* and the weft, the *filling*. A fabric with a cotton warp and a wool weft is said to have a cotton back and a wool filling. The edge is called the *selvage,* and is finished to prevent raveling by reversing the weft yarns and bringing them back over the warp. The number of warp yarns determines the width of the textiles, their size and distance apart, the fineness or coarseness of the cloth. There are three basic ways in which the weft yarns may be woven across the warp. These are *plain* weave, *twill* weave, and *satin* weave, and they may be combined in a variety of ways. *Leno* weave is used to make meshed fabrics and nets. Pile fabrics, such as velvet, are woven by lifting an extra set of warp yarns (or rarely, weft yarns) above the foundation weave. Cut-pile velvets are woven double and then cut apart.

Compound textiles are those with more than one set of warp or weft yarns. Elaborate brocades are compound weaves. Machine-made woven designs are produced on the Jacquard loom, a complex device which can reproduce any pattern.

Yarns may be twisted in various ways to produce a number of different textures. A yarn which is alternately thick and thin gives a distinct surface pattern; a knotty yarn produces a nubbed texture. Woven crepe finishes are made from highly twisted yarns doubled back upon each other and again twisted in the opposite direction. Textures which are woven are permanent, but those merely pressed onto the fabric after weaving may not be. Ribbed fabrics are made by alternating the size of the warp yarns. Napped fabrics are made by brushing or teaseling the woven cloth. Textured fabrics are especially popular for modern interiors, but in choosing them, it is well to remember that they gather and hold dust more readily than smooth surfaced fabrics do.

FINISHES AND TREATMENTS

Textiles are subjected to an infinite number of processes to change or improve their appearance or give them special properties. The following are some of the more important of these processes:

Mercerizing consists in treating cotton yarns with a solution of caustic alkali under tension to give them a high luster.

Calendering consists in running the textile between heavy rollers. This process may be used to flatten the threads and impart a high, permanent gloss. A watered, or moire, design is also produced by calendering, but it is not permanent except on acetate rayon.

Glazing. Some textiles, especially chintzes, are often coated with a thin film of resin which is impregnated into the fabric with heat. The resulting finish may have any degree of sheen, from a high gloss to a dull mat surface. The better glazed textiles now have a permanent finish which is not affected by washing.

Sizing. The addition of starch, chalk, or other fillers is called *sizing*. Some sizing is generally added to cotton yarns before weaving in order to strengthen them. Both linen and cotton usually receive some finishing process after weaving, such as a light sizing and then calendering. But excessive sizing may sometimes be used on flimsy materials to give them a deceptively firm appearance, which disappears as soon as the fabric is washed. To determine the amount of size, rub the material briskly between the hands and hold it up to the light. The firmness or flimsiness of the weave can then be easily examined.

Plastic Coatings. Coated fabrics are not new—an example is oilcloth, which has been with us for some time. But the newer plastic coatings are quite different. Some can scarcely be detected, and yet they may render a fabric stain resistant. Other coatings may transform a textile into new products. Some of the leatherettes are examples.

Moisture Repellants. It is sometimes desirable to treat cloth to repel moisture, and this may be done in one of two ways. A durable moisture repellant finish may be applied by the manufacturer and set under heat so that it fuses with the cloth. Fabric treated in this way can be washed without destroying this property if the cloth is rinsed well afterwards, since soap tends to injure the finish. The second type of treatment is only temporary and must be renewed after each washing. Water repellant compounds can be bought which need merely to be added to the final rinsing water.

Permanent Starch Finishes. Organdies, marquisettes, and other fabrics are often treated with chemicals which give them a permanently crisp or "starched" finish because the chemical penetrates the fibers just like a dye. If crispness is desirable for the appearance of the fabric, be sure to select those finished in this way, since they are so much easier to launder.

Fire Retardation. Many a tragedy has been caused when inflammable drapes or hangings caught fire and burned too quickly to be checked. Therefore, it's a wise precaution to have all hangings treated to retard fire. Some drapery materials are so treated by the manufacturer. But they may also be treated at home by soaking them in a solution of sulphate of ammonia or tungstate of soda. A solution of borax will also retard fire, but it tends to weaken the fibers of the cloth. Cloth treated with a fire retarding chemical may ignite if exposed to direct flame, but the flame soon dies out without spreading. The treatment must be renewed after each washing.

Moth and Mildew Prevention. Moth- and mildewproofing compounds are now added to many textiles by the manufacturer. Such compounds, packaged under trade names, can also be bought by the homeowner to treat fabrics at home. When used according to the manufacturer's directions, a number of them give excellent results.

Preshrinking. The linen industry has adopted the ruling that no linen fabric may be labeled *preshrunk, full shrunk, shrunk, shrinkproof, will not shrink, mill shrunk, double shrunk, non-shrinkable,* or similar terms if the cloth still retains any degree of residual shrinkage, however slight. Since even the most thorough shrinking process may not prevent the fabric from shrinking minutely, the use of such terms is now generally qualified by such phrases as "will not shrink more than 1 per cent," or "remaining shrinkage 2 per cent." If a fabric is guaranteed not to shrink more than 1 per cent, for all practical purposes it may be considered as thoroughly preshrunk. This ruling has also been adopted by many cotton manufacturers.

Shrinkage of wool and rayon fabrics can now be controlled by resin finishes. Such finishes are especially desirable for blankets or curtains.

Bleaching, Dyeing, and Printing. Many technical steps are involved in the processes of bleaching, dyeing, and printing cloth. Dyeing, especially, is a highly skilled trade, and is done by various processes according to the type of fiber. The process known as *vat dyeing* does not refer to the type of receptacle used (since vats are used to dye fabrics by other processes as well) but to a dye which has been converted by a reducing agent, such as copperas vat or zinc vat. After the textile has been soaked in a solution of such dye, it is exposed to the air, which reforms the dye and sets it in the fibers. Vat-dyed fabrics are noted for the high degree of permanency of their colors. This process, which was formerly rather time consuming, has now been perfected for high-speed production. Wool and silk as well as cotton can now be vat-dyed.

Textiles are printed in much the same way that paper is printed. Repeat patterns are produced by rollers on rotary presses. Each color requires a separate roller. Therefore, every additional color used in a design ups the cost slightly.

TRADE PRACTICE RULES

A good deal of guesswork will be taken out of textile buying if you will carefully read the fiber content label on most ready-to-wear clothing and fabrics sold by the yard. The silk, rayon, and linen industries have formulated their own trade rules for the truthful labeling of the fiber content of textiles, and the wool industry is similarly regulated by the Wool Products Labeling Act of 1939. All of these trade practices are administered as law by the Federal Trade Commission.

Wool Industry. According to the Wool Products Labeling Act of 1939, which became effective in 1941, all wool products except carpets and upholstery materials, must bear a label indicating the amount of wool, its quality, and the name or registered number of the manufacturer. For example, no textile may be labeled as wool, all wool, 100 per cent wool, or virgin wool unless it contains nothing but pure wool from the fleece of the sheep or lamb or the hair of the Angora or Cashmere goat, or of the camel, alpaca, llama, and vicuna, and has never before been woven, knitted, or manufactured. If the wool has been woven, knitted, or manufactured but never used by a consumer, it must be labeled as reprocessed wool. Wool for reprocessing comes from material left over from cutting by tailors or clothing manufacturers. It is shredded, respun, and rewoven. Wool so treated which has been used or worn by a consumer must be labeled as reused wool.

If the product recontains 5 per cent or more of any other fiber, exclusive of ornamentation, paddings, stiffenings, and so on, it must be identified and the percentage must be indicated.

Rayon Industry. The trade practice rules governing the rayon industry were promulgated in 1937. According to these rules, any rayon product must be labeled as rayon and not as artificial silk or some other product. The process of manufacture, such as viscose or acetate, or the name of the manufacturer or type of weave, such as satin or crepe, may be given if they are accompanied by the word *rayon.* The presence of other fibers must be indicated as well as their percentages.

Silk Industry. In 1938, the silk industry adopted the ruling that no textile could be labeled as silk, pure silk, all silk, or pure dye silk unless it contains nothing but silk, exclusive of dye or finishing material, both of which may not exceed 10 per cent of the finished weight, or 15 per cent if the product is black. If the silk has been weighted with metallic salts, the percentage of weighting must be indicated.

Linen Industry. In 1941, the linen industry ruled that no product could bear the words *linen* or *flax* unless it was made from the fibers of the flax plant. Fibers other than linen in a selvage need not be indicated providing they do not exceed .05 per cent. No terms, such as grass linen, silk linen, lin, and so on, may be used. If the product is part linen, the label must name the other fibers present and indicate their percentages, unless the product is half linen and half some other fiber, in which case it may be called linen and cotton (or whatever the fiber is). If the product bears a lace border or trimming made of some other fiber, that fact must be indicated. No decoration may be labeled as handwork unless it actually is, and no linen product may be labeled as Irish linen unless it was made in Ireland.

FACTS ABOUT FAMILIAR TEXTILES

Airplane Cloth, a plain, closely woven fabric of mercerized, long staple cotton, originally made of linen for airplane wings. Used for shirts, curtains, and so on.

Balloon Cloth, a light weight, closely woven cotton fabric used as a covering for balloons when treated with rubber. It is also bleached, dyed, or printed and used for underclothing or dresses.

Broadcloth, a woolen fabric of twill weave with a heavy nap which is pressed lengthwise, or a cotton fabric of plain weave, usually mercerized. Woolen broadcloth usually comes in a standard width of 54 inches and is used for heavy clothing, such as overcoats. Cotton broadcloth comes in a 36-inch width, and is used for shirts or dresses.

Brocade, a fabric with a woven design produced by yarns of various colors and mate-

rials. The wrong side carries the opposite of the pattern on the right side. Hand-woven brocades may be works of art. Machine-made brocades are woven on a Jacquard loom.

Calico, originally a fine cloth, is a cotton fabric of plain weave, usually printed. Little calico is now made, and that which is found is mostly a low-grade fabric only 27 inches wide. The name comes from Calicut, India, where the material was first made.

Cambric, a fine white cotton cloth of plain weave, similar to longcloth. The standard width is 36 inches, although *lining cambric* is only 25 or 27 inches wide. Cambric has many uses. The name comes from Cambrai, France, where it was originally made of linen. Some linen cambric is still manufactured.

Canvas, a strong, coarse cloth, usually of cotton or linen. The grades of canvas made for household use are usually sold under the name of *duck* (*see below*).

Chiffon, a soft, sheer material of silk or rayon.

Chintz, a printed cotton fabric, either glazed, or unglazed, used chiefly for draperies, slipcovers, and so on. Most chintzes are 50 inches wide, although some are 36 inches.

Corduroy, a ribbed pile fabric of cotton or with a cotton back and a rayon pile. The size of the rib may vary from wide wale to pin wale. Comes in 36-inch and 50-inch widths. Used for sportsclothes, suits, draperies, and so on.

Crepe, one of various kinds of fabrics with a crinkly surface; may be of cotton, wool, silk, or rayon. Woven crepes are made of highly twisted yarns. Crepe finishes may also be produced by chemical or mechanical means, some of which are more or less permanent; others, not at all.

Cretonne, a printed, unglazed fabric, usually of cotton, but sometimes of linen or rayon, used for draperies or slipcovers. Generally heavier and with somewhat bolder designs than chintz.

Damask, a fabric of linen, cotton, rayon, silk or wool with a woven pattern which is in reverse on each side. It differs from brocade in that brocade has a raised pattern, whereas damask patterns are flat. Some damask cloths have warp yarns in one color and weft yarns in another. Fine linen damask has long been used as a covering for dining tables.

Denim, a heavy cotton fabric of twill weave made of yarn dyed before weaving, usually of blue filler yarns and white foundation yarns. Comes in standard widths of 28, 29, and 36 inches, and is used for work clothes. Softer denims are also made which are used for play clothes, draperies, or slipcovers.

Dimity, a sheer cotton fabric of plain weave with corded stripes or bars. May be white, colored, or printed, and is used for curtains or children's clothes.

Duck, a type of light-weight canvas, usually of cotton, and in plain weave. Used for shower curtains, aprons, and uniforms.

Felt, not a woven textile, but a fabric of matted wool or hair in various thicknesses. Has many uses. Felt sold by the yard is 72 inches wide.

Flannel, a napped woolen or worsted fabric in plain or twill weave, either thin or heavy. Comes in widths of from 27 to 54 inches. Used for dresses, suits, and so on. *Outing flannel,* or *flannelette,* usually of cotton or sometimes of cotton and wool, is generally 36 inches wide. Used for baby clothes and other purposes.

Gabardine, a fabric of worsted wool, mercerized cotton, or spun rayon with a twill weave on one side. Wool gabardine is 54 inches wide and is used for suits, coats, and so on. Cotton and rayon gabardine is usually only 36 inches wide, and is used for shirts, dresses, and other clothes, as well as for draperies.

Gingham, a cotton fabric made of predyed yarns in plain weave with typical patterns of stripes, checks, and plaids. *Chambray, shirting madras,* and *cheviot* are all members of the gingham group. Comes in 26-inch to 32-inch widths, as a rule.

Huck, a linen or cotton fabric with a small, woven pattern; used chiefly for towels. Widths vary from 15 to 24 inches.

Jersey, a plain, knitted fabric of rayon, silk, wool, cotton, or mixed yarns, usually in tubular shape. May be smooth or napped. Used for dresses, underwear, and other purposes.

Lawn, a thin, somewhat stiff fabric of cotton or linen in plain weave. Fine linen lawn is called *handkerchief* linen. Used for baby's clothes, lingerie, blouses, and so on.

Madras, two types of fabrics, known as shirting madras and curtain madras. Shirting resembles gingham in weave and texture. Curtain madras is a thin fabric of leno weave with a cutaway design of cotton or rayon yarns. Widths vary from 36 to 50 inches.

Muslin, a firm fabric of bleached or unbleached cotton in plain weave. Comes in many widths and has numerous uses. Wide muslin is often called sheeting.

Percale, a closely woven cotton fabric in plain weave. Printed percales are usually 36 inches wide and are used for shirts, dresses, and other clothes. Wide, plain percales are used for fine sheets.

Poplin, a ribbed fabric of rayon, cotton, wool or silk. Ribs run crosswise. *Bengaline* is a heavy poplin of silk or rayon. *Rep* is a heavy poplin of wool or cotton and is used as an upholstery fabric.

Satin, is a lustrous fabric of silk or rayon. The luster is produced by the *satin weave,* usually made by the warp yarns. In cotton, the satin face is produced by the weft yarns, and the product is called *sateen.* Satin may have a twilled or a crepe back.

Seersucker, a cotton or linen fabric, usually striped, with alternating bands of crepe and plain weave. The crinkly finish is permanent and the fabric requires no ironing. Used for playclothes, dresses, underwear, and so on.

Serge, a worsted wool fabric in twill weave, used for suits, coats, and dresses. Usual width is 54 inches.

Sharkskin, a plain-weave fabric of rayon or cotton woven from strands of fine threads. Used for sportswear, summer suits, playclothes, and children's clothes.

Taffeta, a smooth crisp fabric of silk or rayon in plain weave, usually in widths of 36 or 39 inches. Used for evening gowns and other clothes, and sometimes for draperies, bedspreads, or dressing-table skirts.

Tweed, a durable wool fabric in plain, twill, or herringbone twill weave, usually in yarns of two colors. Used for sportswear, suits, coats, and so on. Genuine Harris tweed is made in the Hebrides Islands by hand and has a characteristic odor which comes from the lichens used for dyeing. This odor never leaves the cloth.

Velvet, a piled fabric of silk, rayon, cotton, or a mixture of these fibers. If the pile is longer than ⅛ of an inch, the fabric is called *plush.* Cotton velvets have a weft pile and are called *velveteen.* Most velvets are 36 or 39 inches wide.

Voile, a sheer fabric in plain weave usually of cotton or rayon, used for curtains, lingerie, and children's clothes. Comes in a 36-inch width. Voile is also made of wool and comes in a 54-inch width. Wool voile is used for dresses.

Slipcover for sofa is constructed in same way as slipcover for chair, except that larger area is covered. Length or width of fabric may be used on sofa back, depending on design of material. If width is used, joining seams should be placed to correspond with cushion edges.

CHAPTER XIII

SLIPCOVERS

SLIPCOVERS once served only as protection for upholstery fabrics which were costly to replace once they had become soiled, worn, or faded. They came out as soon as the rays of the summer sun became strong enough to threaten unprotected colors, or whenever a room or a house had to be closed for a while. Unbleached muslin was the usual choice of fabric for the slipcover, and it hid the lines of the furniture beneath a baggy, lumpy, and drearily plain shape. Nobody liked the slipcover, but it served a purpose and so it was tolerated as an ugly necessity.

When the Depression made a virtue of economy, decorators looked for ways to refurbish rooms at a minimum of expense. If reupholstery cost too much, then why not slipcovers?—but ones which would fit, and perhaps in gay fabrics instead of unbleached muslin. The idea proved such a success that slipcovers soon ceased to be either purely utilitarian or temporary makeshifts dictated by the needs of economy. They became a fashion. The color scheme, the entire personality of a room, can be changed merely by whisking on another set of slipcovers. They can fit as sleekly as upholstery, and they can be made as sedate and formal or as gay and bright as one may wish. The slipcover can transform upholstered odds and ends into one related group of furniture. It can hide unsightly legs and sometimes even mask bad lines by means of a judicious use of pattern. "Then why bother with upholstery material at all?" some women have asked. "Why not buy upholstered pieces in their muslin undercovers, and let them wear slipcovers permanently?" And that's exactly what they do. In that way they also save the cost of the upholstery fabric.

MAKING THE SLIPCOVER

Slipcovers are not hard to make. If you can sew a seam at all, you can make one. Many women hesitate to attempt a slipcover because they feel that it is difficult to achieve the sleek fit which a slipcover must have if it is to be neat. They know that a dress is difficult for all but the most expert to cut and fit without a paper pattern as a guide. Therefore, they want the assurance of a paper pattern for a slipcover, too. They go to endless trouble to cut paper patterns themselves, or they buy "standard size" patterns and try to adjust them to the needs of their own furniture, which somehow never seems to be of a "standard size." All such steps are unnecessary. The easiest way to make a slipcover is to do it as the professional does: cut and fit it on the chair. A chair is stationary. A dress must fit to allow for movement.

Choosing the Fabric. Almost any type of smooth, closely woven fabric can be made into slipcovers. But very heavy fabrics, such as upholstery material, velvets, and plushes are obviously not suitable because of the difficulty of working with them, and also because a smooth fit cannot be achieved with such material by the slipcover method. However, effective slipcovers are sometimes made from cotton corduroy for studio couches. Dress fabrics are sometimes used, particularly gingham, but such materials generally do not give sufficient wear to justify the expense and effort of making slipcovers from them. Dress fabrics such as satins, rayon crepes, taffetas, and moires make poor slipcover materials for the same reason.

The choice of slipcover fabrics will depend partly on the method of cleaning preferred. If the cover is to be washed, it is essential that the fabric be color fast and guaranteed not to shrink more than one per cent. It should be sturdy, but not too heavy to make it difficult to handle while wet. Cottons, of course, wash more easily than most rayons. If the slipcover is to be dry cleaned, shrinkage is of less importance, although it should still be color fast. However, pastel shades tend to look dingy after several trips to the dry cleaner's.

FIG. 1. To estimate amount of material needed for slipcovers, remove cushion and measure chair from A to B, C, D, E, and F. To this total, add measure from I to G to H, and from J to K on cushion, both multiplied by two. Seams, hems, and tuckaways call for approximately 18 inches more. A length of material in standard drapery width equal to total measurement should be sufficient, unless fabric has a difference in weave.

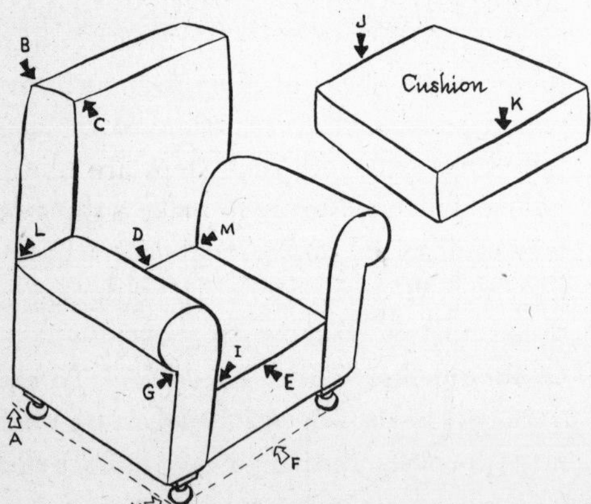

The best slipcover fabrics are those which are made expressly for the purpose. Many of these fabrics are designed to serve more than one decorating job. They are found in the drapery sections of department stores or in special shops handling drapery fabrics. Chintzes, whipcords, cretonnes, and similar materials all make excellent slipcovers.

Estimating Amounts Needed. It pays to determine accurately the amount of material which will be needed to make a slipcover. The usual method is to begin at the floor (point A in Figure 1), stretch the tape measure up and over the top of the chair (points B and C), down the front to D, across the seat to E, and down the front to F. (If the chair has a separate seat cushion, this must be removed before taking measurements.) For an arm chair, then measure from H to G to I, multiply this measurement by two (for the other side) and add this to the first measurement. Increase this total by adding 1½ inches for seam allowance at all joining points or hemlines (in this case, A, B, C, E, F, G, H, I), and in a large upholstered piece, at least 3 inches for the tuckaway between seat and back (at D). The seat cushion is measured separately, from J to K, times two.

This method serves for most plain materials at least as wide as the widest part of the chairs, plus seam allowance, and with no noticeable difference in weave or pattern lengthwise or crosswise. If the material has a large pattern (such as a floral bouquet) which must be centered, extra material will have to be allowed so the motif can be centered on chair back, sides, and seat cushion. Stripes also require extra material to allow for matching.

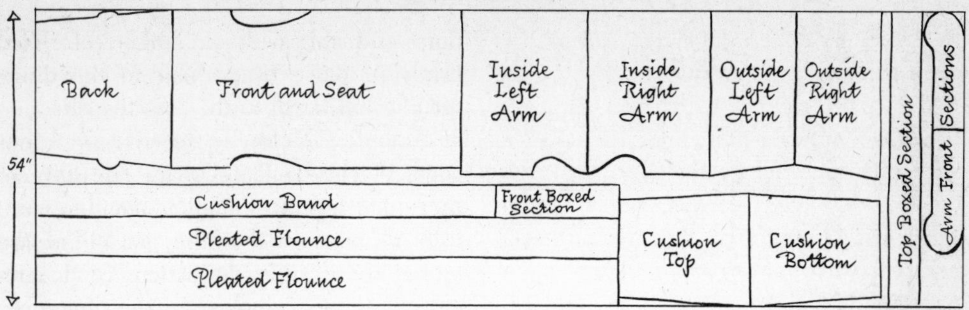

FIG. 2. Choose a fabric in width which can be utilized with most economy. Diagram shows how slipcover was cut from wide material with scarcely any waste. Measure chair and work out diagrams for various widths to find which is best before buying.

The style of the slipcover and the width of the fabric will determine whether additional material must be allowed for a ruffled or pleated flounce, self-welting, and other details. Ordinarily, sufficient material will be left over from a 54-inch wide fabric for a ruffled or pleated flounce. It often pays to work out an exact scale diagram of your measurements to find out what width material could be most economically used for your chair. Figure 2 shows how almost every piece of material was made use of in making the slipcover with a box-pleated flounce for the chair in Figure 1. Of course, the material could have no noticeable difference in weave, lengthwise or crosswise, and it would have to be either plain colored or with a reversible print.

Cutting and Fitting. First, you will need plenty of pins — good, sharp, dressmaker pins — and a sharp pair of scissors. Remove the cushion from the seat, and begin at the back of the chair. If the material has a right or a wrong side, place the *right* side next to the chair. This will save the bother of unpinning and turning seams later, when you are ready to sew. Nearly all chairs are symmetrical enough so that the cover will fit just the same when it is turned.

Place the selvage so that it extends 3/4 of an inch from the side of the back at the widest part, and the end of the material 3/4 of an inch from the top of the chair at its highest point. Pin in place. Now smooth away all fullness from the material, keeping the warp threads in true vertical posi-

FIG. 3. Back of chair showing material pinned into place and trimmed. If fabric has right and wrong side, place right side next to chair to avoid turning of seams when welting is inserted.

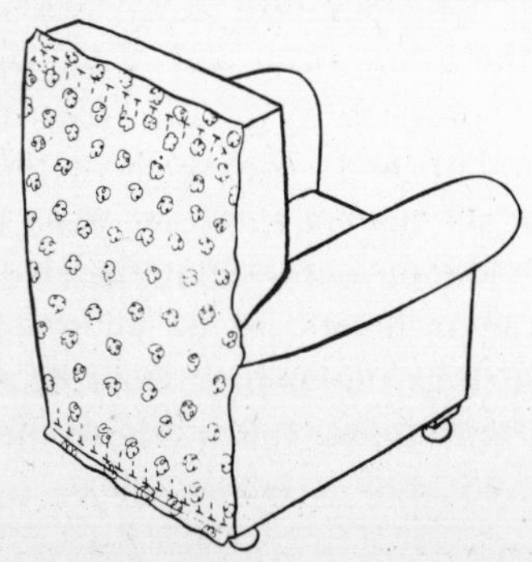

FIG. 4. Fabric is next pinned on front of chair, extending from C to E, and tucked into back about three inches at D. Leave three-inch tuck-away along side at I.

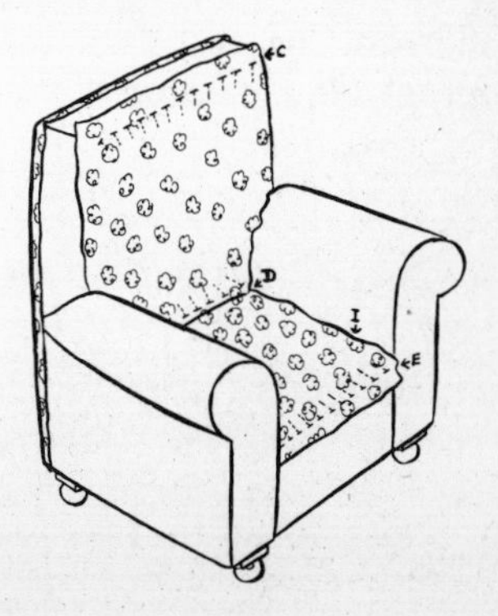

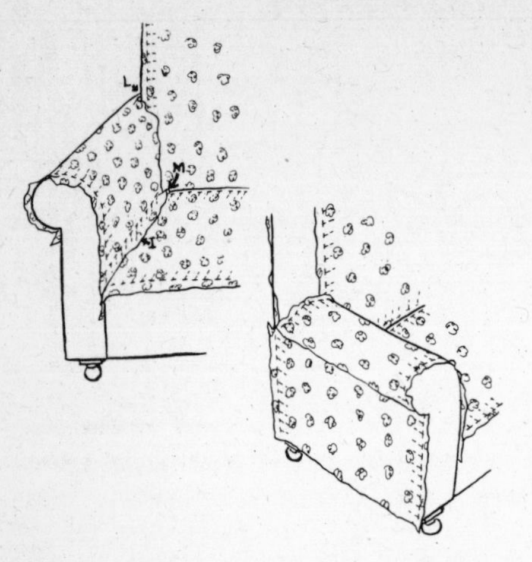

FIG. 5. Inside section of arms is covered. Fit front and arm sections together carefully from L to M, following curve of upholstery seam. Leave three inches on each side at I for tuckaways. If material has distinct pattern, repeat in same position on each side.

FIG. 6. Outside and inside arm sections joined together. If flounce is to be attached, trim fabric off at bottom just below point where flounce will join.

FIG. 7. Boxed section being fitted into place between front and back sections. Join with arm sections at L.

FIG. 8. Shaped section is joined to front of arm. Sometimes paper pattern is made before cutting material.

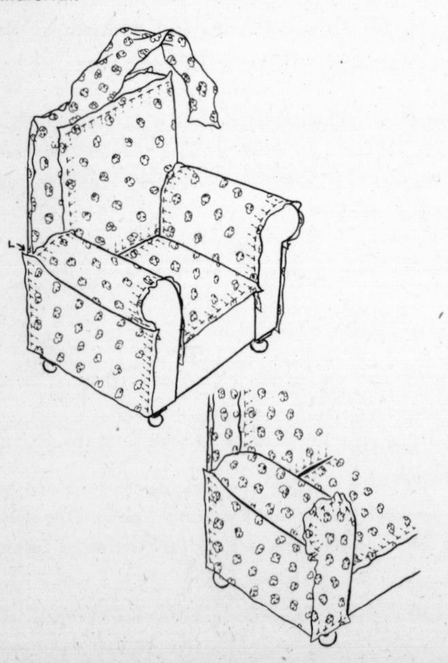

tion, and the weft in horizontal. Hold firmly in place by pinning to the chair, turning pin heads away from the direction of the pull. Pin close to the edge at all four edges of the back, following the lines of the upholstery as a guide. Examine carefully to be sure that the threads of the fabric are straight and true. Then trim, cutting ¾ of an inch from the edge.

Now place the material on the front of the chair as illustrated. Bring it down the front of chair back and across the length of the seat. Pin securely at the top and sides of the back. Trim around the top and sides and part way into the point where the back joins the arm of the chair, leaving ¾ of an inch for seams. Push the material down between the chair back and the seat to make the tuckaway, and cut the material down along the line formed by joining angles of the back and the arms. Be very careful not to cut too much material away at these points. It is better to leave a little extra, and cut it away later, than to cut in too far at first. If this happens, the slipcovers will be strained at these corners instead of fitting smoothly into them.

After the back tuckaway is complete, bring the material to the front of the seat at E, and pin in place. Trim the material at E and I, allowing enough material for the side tuckaway between the chair arms and the seat (about 3 inches).

Place the material crosswise along the top of the chair arm at G, extending it from the front of the arm all the way back to the point where the arm joins the side of the chair at L. Pin along the length of G. Cut the material to correspond roughly to the joining curve of the back and the arm (again being careful not to cut away too much at this point). Smooth material down and across the inside of the chair arm, and trim 3 inches longer than the point where the chair arm joins the seat at I (to allow for side tuckaway). Pin in place around the front edge of the chair arm. Repeat these steps on the other arm of the chair. If the material has a distinct pattern, care should be taken to see that the motifs are in the same position on each arm of the chair.

The width of the material is next placed on the outside of the chair arm at G, with the edge at the front. The straight top edge of the material can now be pinned to the inside chair arm section of the cover along G, allowing 3/4 of an inch on both inside and outside sections for the joining seam. Now pin the material in place along the front edge of the chair arm and at the back edge of the chair, carefully smoothing out all fullness. If the chair is to have a flounce, cut away the bottom of the outside arm section 1 inch below the place where the flounce is to be attached. Repeat these steps on the other side of the chair.

Now cut a straight strip of material the width of the space between B and C (plus 1 1/2 inches more for seams) and long enough to extend all the way across the top and sides of the chair back. Insert this strip between the front and back sections of the slipcover, and into the inside chair-arm section where it joins the back at L. This process of inserting a strip of material between other sections is called *boxing*.

Pin material into place on the curved front section of the arm, being careful to keep the up-and-down threads of the material in a true vertical position. After the material has been fitted to follow carefully the shape of the chair-arm front, trim, again leaving 3/4 of an inch for seam allowance. The bottom edge of the section should extend 1 inch below the point where the flounce is to be attached. Repeat on the other chair-arm front.

FIG. 9. Boxed section is pinned into place across front of chair. Tuckaway of seat section is joined at edge to boxed section. Edges of arm and seat tuckaways are seamed together at sides.

FIG. 10. Pleated flounce is added. Cord welting may be inserted during this operation, or after cover is removed for stitching.

FIG. 11. Cushion cover consists of top and bottom sections joined by straight band. Opening is left at lower seam in back for removal of cushion.

Take a straight strip of material as long as the width of the chair front (plus 1½ inches for seams) and as wide as the depth from E to a point 1 inch below the joining place of the flounce. Fit across the front of the chair and pin to the seat section of the cover along the edge at E. The corner edges will probably have to be rounded off slightly. The side edges of this boxed section are joined to the ends of the side tuckaways of the seat.

The next step is to pin the sections together to form a sleek, tight fit. Be sure that the tuckaways and the bottom edges are well secured with pins so they cannot pull out. Join the sections together at the seams with pins spaced about 2 inches apart, being careful not to allow these pins to catch into the upholstery material of the chair. Stretch the material firmly as you pin until the entire cover fits without a

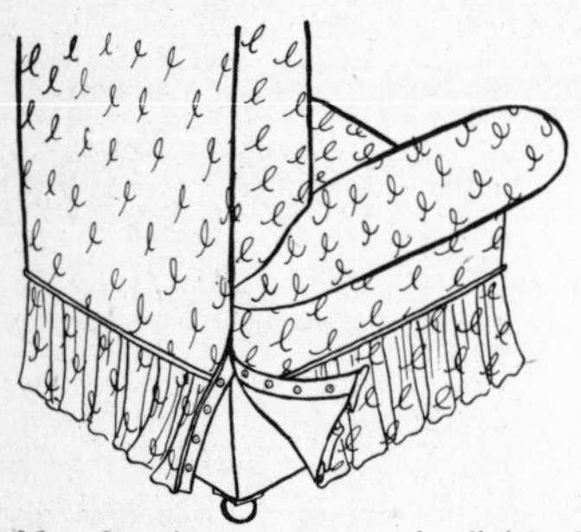

FIG. 12. Opening at corner is finished with snap fastener tape. Length of opening depends on style of chair, but it usually extends several inches above L.

wrinkle. You may find it necessary to cut additional material away now, from L to M, in order to achieve a sleek fit along the corner line going into the seat section. When this is finished, pull out the side tuckaways and pin the edges together. The end of the tuckaway on the seat section is joined to the side edge of the front boxed section. The end of the tuckaway on the arm section is joined to the shaped chair-arm front section.

Reinforce all corners and points where one seam joins another with basting threads. Now remove the pins from the seam joining the chair back section and the left outside arm section to a point slightly above L. Pin down the edges of the material on each section along the line of the seam. Remove all other pins securing the cover to the upholstery. Gently lift the cover from the chair at the back and then at the arms until it can be easily removed.

Sewing and Finishing. Slipcover seams can be plain, French seamed, welted, trimmed with moss edging, or with corded welting. By far the most popular way of finishing, however, is with corded welting, either in contrasting color or in the same material as the slipcover is made of. Contrasting color is often used not only as a decorative accent, but also because a corded welting in a contrasting color can be bought already made up. This saves the time and bother of measuring and cutting material and covering the cord to make such welting from the slipcover fabric.

To make corded welting from the slipcover fabric it is necessary to take the total length of all the seams on the slipcover where the welting is to be used (usually all, except at the tuckaway, and sometimes the corner seams from L to M). Add to this amount the circumference measure around the bottom of the chair, plus some extra for lapovers. You will need at least as much cord as this total measurement, and be sure to buy the cord in one piece. Cord comes in various thicknesses. One about ¼ inch in diameter makes a good size for a slipcover welting.

The material must be cut in bias strips at least 2 inches wide. Find the true bias of the fabric by folding it diagonally so that the selvage lies straight along the weft threads of the material. Mark this diagonal

Screen-printed clipper cloth in "rose festival" pattern makes gay slipcover for loveseat. Seams are finished with large cord welting in contrasting color. Plain clipper cloth for chair slipcover is in harmonizing color. Box pleats in clusters, cording on back and seat, and buttons covered to match add decorative notes.

with a pencil and a yardstick on the wrong side of the fabric. Starting at this diagonal line, measure and mark off 2-inch intervals on each selvage. Rule off more diagonal lines using these points as a guide. Cut the strips along the lines, and seam them together, end to end.

Fold the bias strip, right side out, around the cord. Stitch the strip together, as close to the cord as possible to hold it in place. This can be done more quickly on the sewing machine with the cording foot than by hand. The cording foot is a simple, inexpensive attachment, and is almost indispensable for trimming slipcovers with corded welting.

The finished welting is inserted between the seam, with the covered cord on the right side. This can be done by unpinning the seams of the slipcover, one or two pins at a time, slipping in the cording, and repinning. When the welting is all in place, baste the seams, and turn the slipcover right side out. Now try the slipcover on the chair for a final fitting before sewing the seams on the machine. If any adjustments are necessary, make them at this time. It is easier to sew the seams on the machine before attaching the pleated or ruffled flounce.

All seams are stitched once on the machine with the cording foot, and as close

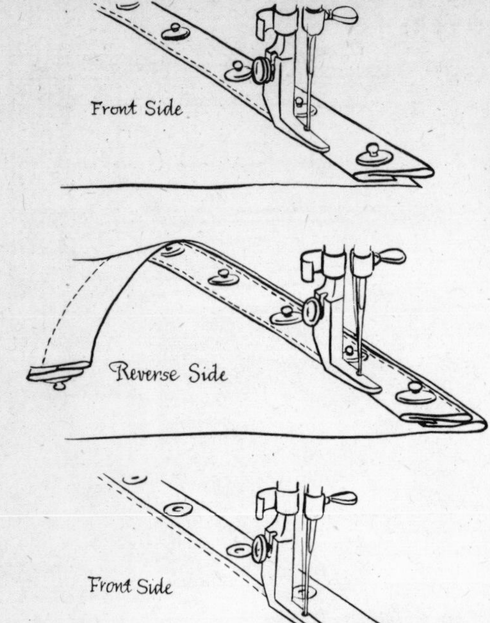

FIG. 13. Stitch stud strip of snap fastener tape to right side of top part of closure, with cording foot of sewing machine. Then turn and stitch to wrong side. Socket strip is stitched to edge of bottom part of closure.

to the corded welting as possible. The seams may be finished if you wish, but it is not necessary. If the stitching is done with good, strong thread, and the machine tension is correct, the seams should last as long as the slipcover fabric. But the slipcover will fit more snugly if you trim the seams to a ½ inch width around all curves. Seams around reverse curves may have to be notched once or twice to ease the strain. Where one end of the corded welting joins another, the ends should be crossed and brought to the wrong side of the seam to form as smooth a juncture as possible. Make these joinings in the least conspicuous places.

After all seams with corded welting are sewed, join the seams of the side tuckaway. You will find that the ends of the back tuckaway will have to be finished off with a dart in order to join smoothly with the side tuckaways.

Flounces. Now return the slipcover to the chair to fit the flounce in place. The flounce may be a straight strip of material gathered along one edge to form a ruffle. Such flounces require a strip one and one-half times as long as the circumference of the chair around the bottom. Box pleated flounces require from twice to three times the circumference, depending on the depth and closeness of the pleats. Box pleats may be either on the outside or inverted.

For most slipcovers, box pleats measured as follows will be satisfactory. Make a mark at the top edge of the flounce at intervals of every five inches. Make another mark at the center of every other interval. Fold the fabric at the marks on each side of the center marks, and bring together at the center mark, as illustrated. However, a more professional job results if care is taken to see that the pleats are spaced at intervals which will permit a pleat to come at each corner. Corner pleats should have extra depth. Such spacing requires taking the measurements of each side of the chair, dividing it into equal spaces, and marking the flounce accordingly.

Hem the bottom edge of the flounce, and fold and pin the pleats. Then baste and press them into place. Turn down the top edge of the flounce ½ inch and baste. Pin the top edge of the flounce to the lower edge of the slipcover, allowing about ½ inch clearance from the floor. The corded welting may be inserted into the

FIG. 14. Box pleats for flounce may be inverted or on face, but should be evenly spaced.

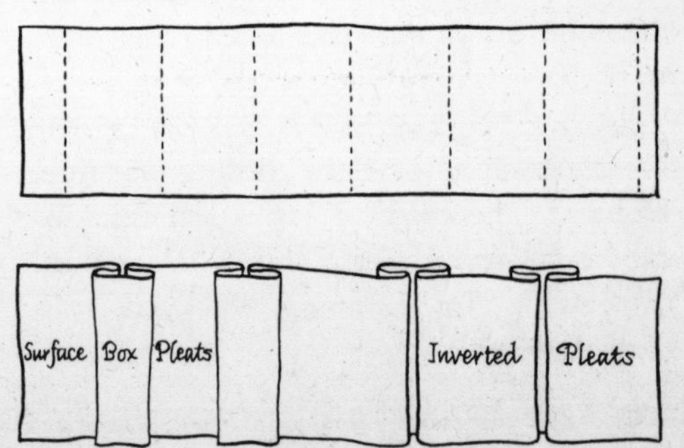

seam during this operation, or it may be put in after the cover is off the chair. Remove the cover, and baste the flounce in place. Machine stitch on the outside.

Slipcover Closings. Slipcovers may be fastened with zippers, string ties, or snap fasteners. Probably the most satisfactory type of closing is made with tape in which the snap fasteners are already sewed. Such tape is bought by the yard and is very simple to apply. The cording foot of the sewing machine is used to sew the tape in place. The stud strip of the tape is first attached to the right side of the top part of the closure, as illustrated. The material is then folded, bringing the tape to the wrong side, and the other edge of the tape

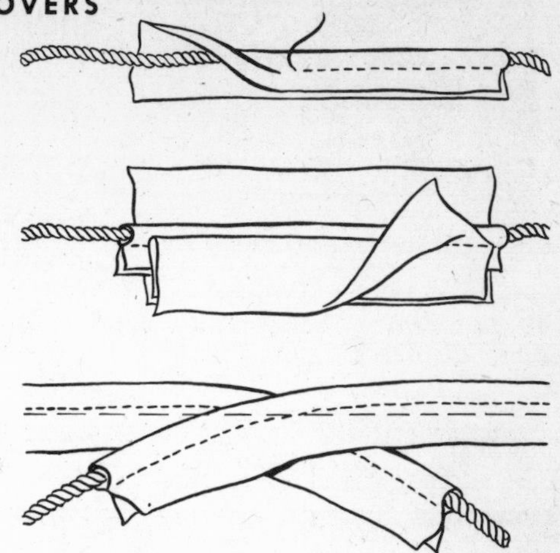

FIG. 15. Fold strips and insert cord. Stitch with cording foot of sewing machine. Join ends of cord welting by overlapping and turning down to wrong side of seam.

Harmony of design and matching colors can blend together three separate prints which might otherwise be a confusing amount of pattern. Armchairs are trimmed in corded welting and moss fringe.

Diamond-texture pattern on plain colored cotton fabric of sofa slipcover serves as foil for brilliant "star magnolia" design of chintz used for cushions and repeated in drapes. Small barrel-back armchair has saucy little box-pleated flounce.

is stitched. The right side of the bottom part of the closure is folded over, and the socket strip of the tape is stitched on top along the edge.

For zipper closings, the corded welting is basted only to the upper part of the closure. Then one side of the zipper tape is laid face down on the edge of the material, just below the cording. Stitch close to the cording. Open the zipper. Turn under the edge of the other part of the closure and lay the zipper, face down, along the wrong side. Be sure the metal part of the zipper is far enough from the edge of the fold so that it is hidden. Stitch in place.

Seat Cushion. The seat-cushion cover consists of two pieces of material cut in the shape of the cushion and joined by one straight band of material as wide as the cushion is deep. A plain rectangular cushion need not be pinned into place before basting. But covers for cushions with corners which project at the sides of the chair seat usually require a pin fitting. Most chair cushions are narrower at the back than at the front. But the closure is always made at the back so as not to show. Therefore, the closure will have to open a few inches around the sides of the cushion as well as across the back to allow the cover to slip over the wide end of the cushion.

Slipcover Styling. Any style of chair can be slipcovered. The lines of the chair often determine the style of the slipcover. But sometimes one does not want to hide the legs of a chair with a beautiful wood frame. In such cases, the slipcover is made without a flounce. The lower edges of the cover are held in place by attaching a piece of plain fabric to one side of the cover, stretching it firmly beneath the seat of the chair, and fastening it to the other side of the cover. The corners are held in place with string ties. The front and back edges of the cover are fastened to the sides of the cross-under panel.

Flounces on straight chairs usually extend from the seat to the floor. They can be trimmed with scalloped borders, swags, fringe, and so forth. The back and the seat of the cover may be of one color, and the flounce of another, or a plain and a patterned fabric may be combined. Plain and patterned fabrics are also often combined successfully in slipcovers for armchairs. Such combinations in armchairs require great skill, however, or the result is apt to look like a crazy quilt.

CHAPTER XIV

DRAPERIES AND CURTAINS

DRAPERIES can be one of the most important accents in a room, especially since they form a frame for the window, which naturally attracts the eye. The style of your draperies should depend to a large extent on the style of your other furnishings. You would not, of course, hang floor-length draperies of heavy satin damask in country cottage rooms. Nor would you put sill-length, cotton homespun curtains in an eighteenth-century style drawing room.

In general, then, the floor-length draperies with draped or shaped valances, belong in the formal period rooms, or in rooms which combine period furniture and modern decoration but retain a formal feeling. However, floor-length draperies are also used in modern rooms, and sometimes valances, too, especially draped valances in wide, dramatic sweeps. Sill-length draperies are for the informal Early American room, the country cottage, and also for modern rooms, depending on how they are used. Draped or shaped valances do not belong with this style of drape, as they tend to look top heavy. But a simple ruffled or pleated straight valance can be used if it is kept in the right proportions. Sheer, ruffled curtains are better in informal rooms or bedrooms.

But the style is by no means the most important point to consider in choosing the right draperies. Equally important, if not more so, is the kind of fabric. Silk or rayon satins, damasks, taffetas, brocades, and velvets are for the formal period room. Glazed chintzes can be used in certain types of formal eighteenth-century English or American rooms as well as in formal or informal modern rooms. Cotton homespuns, chintzes, checked ginghams, cretonnes, crashes, linens, and fabrics of this sort belong in the informal room. The choice of plain or patterned material depends upon the rest of the decorating scheme (*see Chapter on Color Schemes*).

Whatever type of fabric is used, it should, above all, be color fast. Choose fabrics which are guaranteed not to fade from sun or washing. Of course, even such fabrics will lose their brightness in time, but they should be able to retain their colors for years. If the drapes must be cleaned by laundering, make sure that the fabric is washable and either allow for shrinkage or buy fabric that is preshrunk. Draperies which are lined can be washed successfully (if the fabric is washable) when both the drapery and lining fabrics are thoroughly preshrunk. However, drapery headings lose their stiffness when washed, so dry cleaning is preferable.

Glass curtains are curtains of sheer material hung across the window glass to modify or subdue the light and screen the interior of the room from outside view. They may be used alone or combined with overdraperies, and can be sill-length or floor-length. They should be very full in order to be attractive.

Draperies can be used to treat two or more windows as a single unit. This can be done by having a drape at each side and a single valance extending across the entire group. Venetian blinds or glass curtains can be hung above each individual window. Small windows can be made to appear larger by extending the width of the drapes beyond the window frame.

HOW TO MAKE DRAPERIES

It is not difficult to achieve professional-looking drapes which hang in straight, evenly spaced folds if a few simple rules are followed. The secret lies in accurate measurements, cutting, joining with the lining, and laying the pleats at the heading. Drapes must be cut and measured on a flat, level surface large enough to accomodate the entire drape. If you have no table surface as large as this, you can buy a piece of wall board or compo board, which is inexpensive. The material can be held firmly in place while measuring and cutting by sticking the pins directly into the compo board through the fabric. However, if compo board is unobtainable, the floor is a satisfactory, though less convenient, working surface. You will also need plenty of dressmaker's pins, a pair of sharp scissors, a tape measure (a flexible metal tape is more accurate), a yardstick, and a T-square.

Estimating Amount of Material. Generally speaking, each single side drape should be as wide as the entire width of the window. Thus, for drapes at each side of a window 50 inches wide, you would need two lengths of 50-inch wide material. For some windows you may need two widths of material for each side drape, or you may need only a width and a half, which can be gained by splitting one length of material in two and using half on each side. For example, three widths of 36-inch wide material could be used satisfactorily to make drapes for a 50-inch wide window. But if the draperies are to be drawn together, it is better to have them a little too full than a little too skimpy.

To estimate the length of material needed for side drapes, measure the window from the top edge of the frame to the floor for floor-length draperies, or to the bottom of the apron (the frame below the sill) if the draperies are to be short. Multiply this length by the number of widths needed, adding a 3-inch allowance for hem on each width. If the drapes are to have a heading, you must also allow from 3½ to 6½ inches extra on each width. Without heading, this allowance can be 1 inch for a hem. Allow 1 inch for the hem on the inside edge and ⅜ inch for the hem on the outside edge. If the material has a bold pattern, extra material must be allowed for careful matching.

Sometimes draperies are made long enough so that the lower edge lies on the floor, for a lavish effect. However, such draperies interfere with cleaning; they are apt to be stepped on, and they may even present a tripping hazard.

The amount of material needed for a valance will depend on the style of the valance, and whether the length or the width of the material can be used, which is determined by the pattern or the weave. If the valance can be cut from the length, it will usually require enough material to go across the width of the window plus an additional 10 to 12 inches for an extension around the edge of the valance board and for hems. Draped valances will require more and the amount of extra material needed depends on the width of the window. For a window 36 inches wide, a draped valance will require enough material to go across the width of the window, plus one yard extra. Draped valances, or swags as they are often called, usually have side cascades. If the material is very wide, these can often be cut from the same length of material as the swag. Otherwise, additional material should be allowed in the length of the cascade, which is usually about 30 inches, plus at least 1 inch for hems.

Lining. Draperies are nearly always lined. The lining protects the drapery fabric from the sun. It prevents light from showing through the drapes, and it makes the drapes hang better. Sateen is the usual lining material. For white draperies, or printed draperies with a white background, the sateen should always be white. Otherwise it is usually cream colored or light tan. Most drapery materials of closely woven cotton require no other lining. But some rayons and silks need an additional interlining of outing flannel. Use the same method for estimating lining fabric as that used for estimating the drapery fabric, except that allowances need not be made for hems.

Cutting the Drapes. Place the material face down on your cutting surface, so that it lies without a fold or a wrinkle, and in a true straight line. Hold it in place with pins. Measure the exact length needed with the measuring tape and mark it with pins or French chalk. Cut the top of the drape at a true right angle to the length by testing with the T-square. Draw a cutting line with a pencil or French chalk and the yardstick, and cut the fabric along this line.

Lining the Drapes. For lined draperies with headings, a strip of buckram should be placed along the top of the curtain material, about 1 inch from the edge. The buckram should be as deep as you want the heading to be, and the width of the drape minus the 1-inch side seams. Headings vary from about 3 inches for the average-sized window to 5 or 6 inches for very high windows. Fold the 1-inch edge of the drapery material over the buckram and catch-stitch in place. Turn in the side edges of the drapes about 1 inch and catch-stitch in place. Now place the lining fabric, right side up, on the drapery fabric (which is still face down and pinned

FIG. 1. Method of assembling lined drape with stiffened heading. Smooth drapery fabric out, face down, with edges straight. Lay buckram for heading across top edge. Turn in top and side edges of drape and tack in place. Hem bottom edge, sewing metal weights inside at corners. Tack lining first lengthwise (see Fig. 2), and then turn top and side edges and blindstitch to drape. Hem lining separately.

firmly and smoothly in place). Pin the lining in place on top of the drapery material. Cut the lining about ½ inch shorter than the folded edge of the drapery material at the top and sides, and about 1 inch shorter at the bottom. Be very careful, of course, not to cut the drapery material at the same time.

Unpin one side and half of both the top and bottom edges of the lining, and lay the material back along the middle, lengthwise. Tack the center of the lining material to the drapery material with needle and thread to match the drapes. Take loose stitches, keeping them about 6 inches apart, and catch only one or two threads of the drapery fabric, so that the stitches will not show on the outside. Loop the thread and draw the needle through it between stitches to form a knot.

Place two more lengthwise rows of tacking halfway between the center row and the edges, smoothing out the lining and folding it back again before stitching. When the tacking is complete, smooth out the side edges and top of the lining and turn them under about ¼ inch. Pin or baste to the drapery material. Slipstitch the lining in place, being careful not to allow the stitches to show on the outside of the drape. Do not sew the bottom of the lining to the bottom of the drapery fabric. Each is hemmed separately. The drapery fabric is hemmed with blind stitching. The lining may be hemmed by machine; but when hemmed, the lining should be 1 inch shorter than the drape. The drapes will hang better if a small lead weight, about ¾ of an inch or one inch in diameter, is stitched into the hem of the drapery fabric at the inside bottom corner. Such weights are sold at the button or notion counter in department stores. A small brass ring should be tacked to the outside edge of the drape about 6 or 8 inches from the bottom. When the draperies are hung the ring is slipped over a small screwhook placed on the window casing.

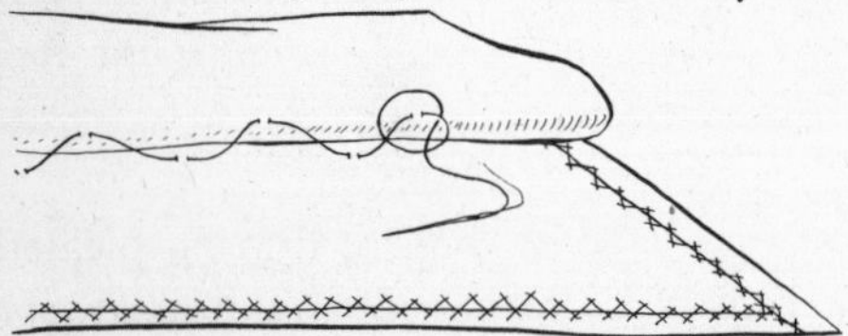

FIG. 2. Tack lining to drapery fabric lengthwise, first through center and then halfway between center and edge on each side. Run needle through only one or two threads of drapery fabric. Space stitches about six inches apart and knot thread between each stitch.

If interlinings are used, they should be cut in the same way that the regular linings are. If the flannel for the interlining is narrower than the drapes, it will have to be pieced. The interlining is laid on the drapery fabric and tacked into place. Then the edges of the drapery fabric are folded over the interlining and tacked. The regular lining is then placed on top of the interlining and tacked. The lining is hemmed and finished in the same way described for draperies without interlining.

Unlined drapes need only be hemmed at sides and bottom. Enough material should be allowed on the top edge of the drape to fold over and entirely cover the strip of buckram. However, most drapery fabrics require lining, and linings always give a more professional appearance to the drapes.

Headings. Headings are usually made with pinch pleats, but sometimes box pleats are used. A heading with pinch pleats is sometimes called a French heading. Each pinch pleat will require about 4 inches of material, and the pleats should be spaced not less than 3 and no more than 6 inches apart, depending on the dimensions of the window and the width of the drape. The first outer pleat should be about 2 inches from the edge. The first inner pleat will

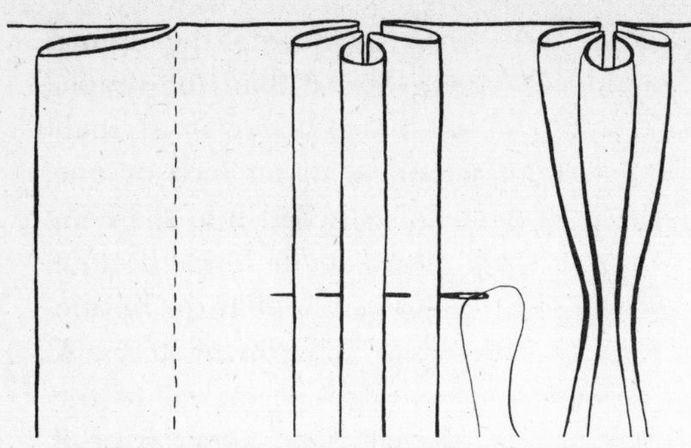

FIG. 3. French pleated heading is made by stitching down through folds of heading at regular intervals. Fold is divided into three small pleats which are stitched into place at bottom edge of heading.

begin close to the inside edge. To determine how many pleats should be used, and how far apart to space them, measure the width of the space you want the finished drape to occupy. Add 2 inches and deduct this sum from the width of the drape. Divide the remaining number of inches by four. The answer will be the number of pleats. Divide the total width (less 2 inches) of the drape by the number of pleats to find how far apart the center of one pleat should be from the center of another. For example, let us suppose we have five pleats to be spaced in a drape 42 inches wide. We deduct 2 inches from the 42, and divide the remaining 40 inches by five, and find that we must place the centers of our pleats 8 inches apart. Since each pleat takes up 4 inches of material, this means that the space between the pleats will be 4 inches. After we have determined the number of pleats to make and the space to allow between them, we space them evenly, fold them into position, and fasten with pins or basting. Then stitch in place on the machine to whatever depth the finished heading is to be (from 3 to 6 inches, depending on height of window). Then divide each pleat into three folds to form three smaller pleats. Sew in place by hand by stitching through all folds of material several times, and placing the stitches at the depth of the heading (*see illustration*).

A patented banding is available which automatically makes French pleats when the curtain rod is drawn through it. The top and bottom edges of the band are simply stitched to the drapery fabric on the wrong side. Its use saves considerable time which otherwise would be spent in measuring and stitching, but it cannot, of course, space the pleats to the exact dimensions which may be required by your windows. Such exact pleats can only be made by individual measuring and sewing.

Box pleats for headings are measured in the same way as French pleats. But after the fold of the pleat is stitched into place, it is *not* gathered into three smaller pleats. Instead, it is flattened out, and the material of the fold is divided evenly on each side of the stitching and pressed down. Tack in place with small, invisible stitches. Sometimes the pleats are not flattened and pressed, but tightly stuffed with cotton to form pipe-organ pleats. These can be very decorative in formal draperies when no valance is used, but the pleats should be fairly close together to be effective.

Simple, cottage type drapes are sometimes merely hemmed at the top. Then rings are stitched on and slipped over the curtain rod. Or such drapes may have a top hem wide enough to serve as a casing through which the rod is slipped. But these treatments are not suitable for formal draperies.

VALANCES

Valances may be shaped, draped, pleated or ruffled. The shaped and draped (or swag) valance must be hung from a valance board. Pleated or ruffled valances may be hung from a double rod (one for drapes, one for valance).

The Valance Board. The valance board is

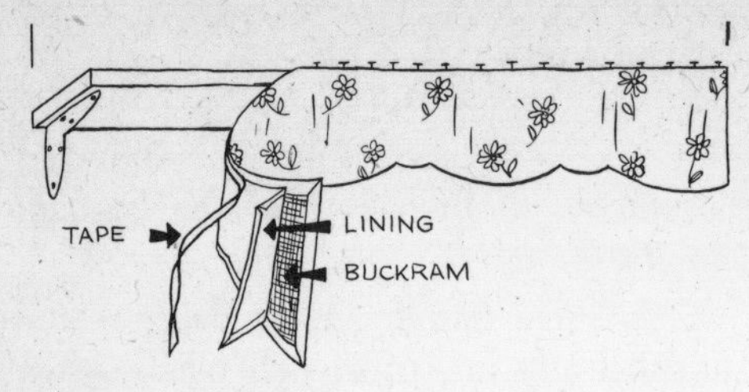

FIG. 4. Board for mounting valances is attached to window frame with angle irons. Tape fastened to valance edge is tacked to board.

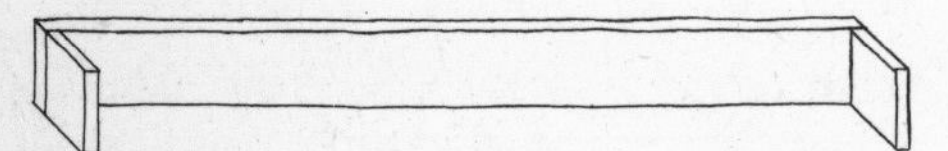

FIG. 5. Cornice board consists of straight front piece and two small side pieces called returns, joined with finishing nails on outside and angle irons inside. Attach cornice to window frame with angle irons. Paint cornice to match woodwork or cover with fabric.

usually about 4 inches wide and as long as the top edge of the window frame. Any 1 x 4 lumber will do, but clear white pine is probably easiest to work with. The board is attached to the window frame with angle irons on the underside at each end, as illustrated. A too-short window can be made to appear higher by placing the valance board on the wall above the window. A too-narrow window can be made to appear wider by extending the valance board beyond the sides of the window frame. The width of the drapes and curtain rods should correspond to the additional width of the valance board, of course. Valances and swags are tacked into place on top of the valance board, as explained further on.

Cornices. A cornice consists of a straight front board and two side boards, called *returns*. The returns are usually attached to the front piece of the cornice with a square joint, reinforced on the inside with angle irons. Nail the joints with finishing nails, which have no heads. They are driven level with the wood by means of a nail set and a hammer. The cornice is attached to the window frame with angle irons. The depth of the cornice depends on the size of the window. But it should be deep enough to hide the heading of the drapes. The returns are usually about 4 inches long. Cornices can be painted to match the woodwork, or they may be covered with cloth. Carved and shaped cornices can be bought at drapery departments, but these are suitable only in very formal rooms.

Shaped Valance. The shaped valance has endless design possibilities, although the beginner may be wise to choose a design that is fairly simple. Symmetrically placed scallops and notched edges are the most popular designs. Sometimes the valance is trimmed with moss fringe or other edgings. Experiment with various designs by cutting them out of wrapping paper. Fold the paper in half and cut through both thicknesses to obtain a symmetrical design. When you find a design you like, use the paper as a pattern to cut by.

Cut the valance foundation from very stiff, heavy buckram, which is sold in drapery departments. The buckram is cut in the exact shape of the finished valance, with no hem allowance. The valance should be wide enough to extend across the valance board and around its sides. The depth of the valance will be determined by the height of the window — very high windows require a deeper valance than windows of average height. Valance depths usually vary from about 12 to 20 inches.

Next, place the cut buckram on the drapery material with which the valance is to be covered. Cut the material in the same design, but allow at least an inch on all sides to be turned over and tacked to the buckram. Cut an interlining of outing flannel in the same way. Place the drapery fabric face down, the interlining on top of it, and the buckram on top of both. Fold the edges of the fabrics over the edge

Draperies, bedspread, slipcover, and dressing table skirt are planned as an ensemble in this feminine bedroom. Washable, glazed cottons in duo prints are combined with plain fabric. Double ruffles on draperies are edged in contrasting color.

FIG. 6. Design suggestions for shaped valances. Buckram interlining is cut in exact shape of valance. Drapery fabric is cut one inch larger around all edges, which are turned over and tacked to buckram. Line back of valance with sateen.

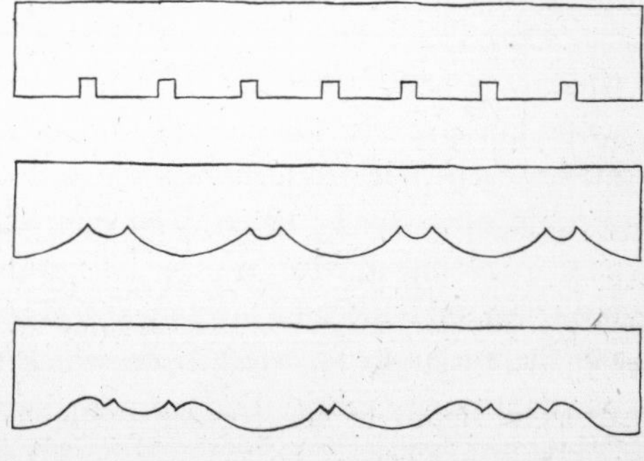

of the buckram and pin in place. Be sure that the fabric fits smoothly and that the folded edges are clean and sharp. The material will have to be notched at the corners of scallops to achieve a smooth fit. Then tack the fabrics to the buckram with long stitches, being careful not to let the stitches show on the right side of the val-

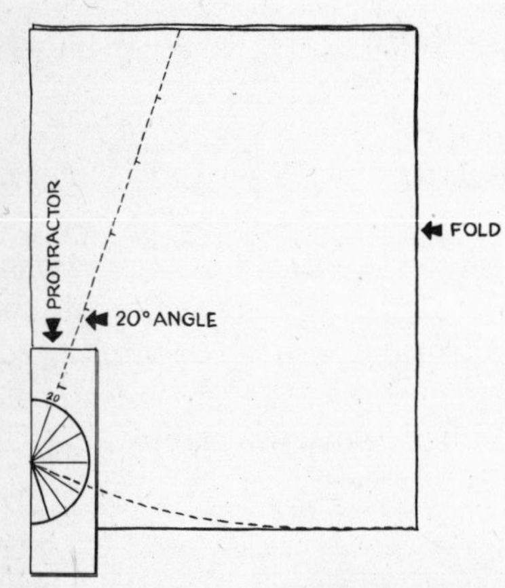

FIG. 7. Fold muslin pattern for swag through center and round off bottom edge. Cut sides at angle of about 20 degrees, using protractor to measure. Mark off pleats at regular intervals along edges.

ance. Cut another lining of sateen to cover the back of the valance. Fold the edges under and blind stitch into place as illustrated. Attach a ½-inch wide tape across the top edge of the valance. The valance it attached to the valance board by tacking through the tape.

Draped, or Swag, Valance. The usual draped valance consists of three pieces: the center swag and the side drapes, or cascades. The center swag for an average window is usually about 15 inches deep when finished and the cascades about 30 inches deep. But proportions vary and no definite rules can be given. The best way is to experiment with a piece of muslin until you find the effect you want. Then use the muslin as a pattern from which to cut the drapery fabric. Furthermore, swag

FIG. 8. Fold edges of swag at marks and bring together to form pleats, all of the same depth. Tack pleats in place on top of valance board.

draperies, to be their most effective and to achieve a truly professional appearance, must be draped with great precision and evenness. Skill in such draping is acquired only through practice, so the amateur who cannot take the time for experimentation would be wiser to make a shaped or ruffled valance.

The muslin should be the length of the valance board plus its sides and the depth of the muslin should be slightly more than one-half this measure, or it may be a little deeper, if you prefer. Fold the muslin in half as illustrated, and cut the bottom edge in a slight curve. The sides are cut at an angle of about 20 degrees (this, too, may vary slightly one way or the other, depending on the effect wanted). To measure an angle, you will need a small device called a protractor, which costs but a few cents at the dime store. It is shaped life a flat half circle and is marked from 0 to 180 at intervals on the edge. Each interval represents a degree. Lay the straight edge of the protractor on the side edge of the material at the point where the bottom curve ends, as illustrated. Place the ruler along a line from the center of the straight edge of the

FIG. 9. Cut cascade as indicated, and bring together in overlapping folds.

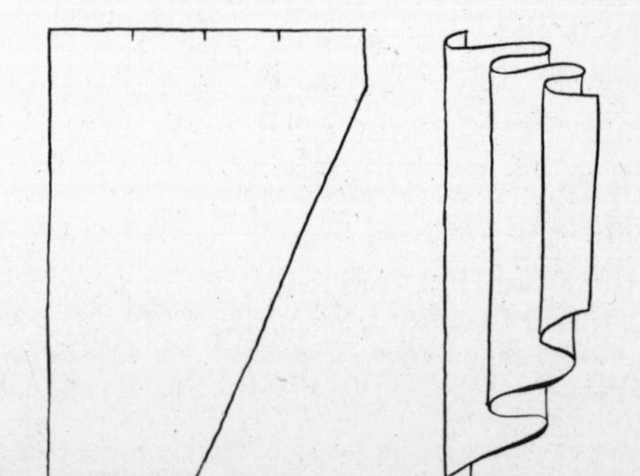

protractor to the 20-degree mark, and draw a line along the edge of the ruler. This will be the direction of your cut.

The number of pleats in the swag will depend on its depth and length. A swag to be 15 inches deep when finished usually requires about four or five pleats. Longer and deeper swags need more pleats. Mark the center of each pleat at regular intervals along the sides of the muslin. Fold the pleats at these marks, making each pleat of the same depth (usually about 2 inches), and pin in place.

Now test the swag on the valance board. The top edge is laid straight along the top of the board, just over the edge, and thumbtacked into place at each end. Bring each pleat up, one by one, and thumbtack in place so that one pleat overlaps the other by one-half or three-quarters. Adjust the folds so that they follow through on the same lines from side to side, and pull each fold slightly downwards at the center. If the effect is satisfactory, cut the swag from the drapery material, following the muslin pattern. Be sure to add 1-inch hem allowance when cutting the drapery material. The swag should be lined in the same manner that drapes are, except that the lining hem is tacked lightly to the drapery hem.

Press the swag before folding in the pleats, so that the hems will lie flat. Lay in the pleats as you have marked them on the muslin pattern. Professional drapers stitch the pleats in place, but the same effect can be achieved by simply thumbtacking the swag to the valance board. Also, it is much easier to have the swag cleaned if the pleats are left unstitched because it can then be readily flattened out.

The cascades are usually placed on top of the swag, but sometimes hang from beneath it. Cut a muslin pattern as shown in Figure 9. The deph should be about 30 inches for the average window, and the top should be about 22 inches. About 4 inches of this will be left unpleated and turned around the side of the valance board so as to bring the edge of the cascade next to the wall. Bring the pleats together, one on top of the other, as illustrated. Test on the valance board, and if satisfactory, cut the cascades from the drapery material and finish in the same manner as the swag.

Quite effective draped valances can be achieved simply by looping a length of material over a curtain pole. Pull into the shape of the swag with folds as even as possible and cut the ends of the material in a diagonal line to form side cascades. Such swags do not give the same precise, formal effect, of course, as the swags and cascades which are cut and draped separately.

The edges of the cascades and swag may be trimmed with any kind of novelty fringe or other trimming that you may choose. Also, the swag may be of a color to contrast with the drapes. Or the cascades may be lined with a contrasting color. If the side draperies are of printed fabric, the swag and cascades may be of a plain color in the dominant tone of the print.

Pleated and Ruffled Valances are usually unlined. They may be hung from a valance

Ruffler attachment of sewing machine can be adjusted to make gathers, and small pleats in a fraction of the time required to sew them by hand.

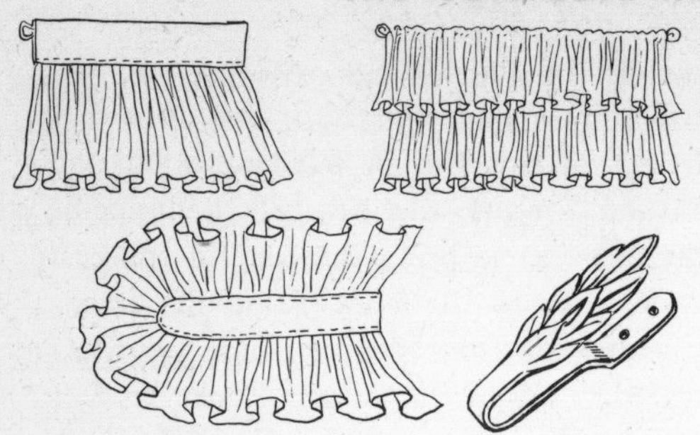

FIG. 10. Ruffled tie-backs are used with ruffled drapes and curtains. Plain tie-backs go with plain drapes, and are interlined with buckram. Sew tiny metal rings to tie-backs and attach to hook screwed into window frame. Fancy metal tie-backs are sometimes used in formal effects, but trend is toward simpler treatments or straight-hanging drapes.

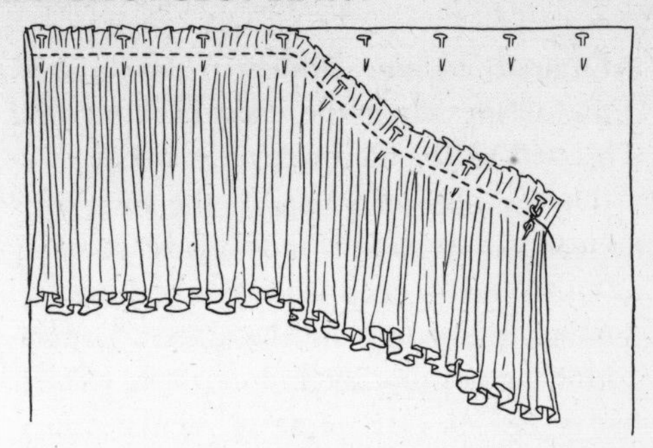

FIG. 11. To gather ruffles evenly by hand, divide both ruffle and curtain edges into equal number of spaces and mark with pins. Match pins together, and gather each space between pins separately.

board, but ordinarily they are simply hung from a curtain rod. Pleated valances will require a strip of material at least double the length of the finished valance. Ruffled valances need about one and one-half to one and three-quarters this length. The depth is a matter of personal taste — 12 inches is a good depth for the average window. If the valance is to be hung from a rod, be sure to allow enough material at the top edge for a casing. The bottom edge is turned up in a hem and slipstitched into place. Pleats can be made by the same method described for the flounce in the chapter on Slipcovers. The fullness for a ruffled valance is adjusted by evening the gathers after the valance is on the rod.

Tie-Backs. Drapes can be drawn to the side and held in place with tie-backs. Probably more shapes and trimmings have been thought of for tie-backs than anything else in the house. Some of these effects are charming, but all too often they are in bad taste. If you are wondering whether to lavish some fancy design or trimming on a tie-back, the best advice is: Don't! Simple tie-backs are always in good taste, but the line between imaginative decoration and over-decoration is not always easy to draw.

Tie-backs of self-fabric to harmonize with the drapes are always good. They should be made over a buckram foundation and lined and interlined in the same way that shaped valances are made. The size of the tie-back depends on the size of the drape. Ruffled tie-backs should be used only if the valance is ruffled, or if the drapes have ruffled edges as trimming.

GLASS CURTAINS

If the house must be decorated on a budget which is too limited to allow for expensive drapery materials, the answer is — glass curtains! Glass curtains may be as elegant and formal or as ruffly and crisp as you please — but do make them full! Measurements for glass curtains are taken in the same way as for drapes, but extra width is needed to achieve a really full effect. Allow about three times the width of the window for glass curtains.

Ready-made glass curtains can be bought in a wide variety of styles, and often the saving in expense between making glass curtains and buying them ready-made is not great enough to justify the labor involved. However, if you want a special effect which cannot be found in ready-mades, you will either have to have them custom made or make them yourself.

Formal glass curtains are made with

French pleated headings in the same way that drapes are made, except that no lining is used. Also, the buckram used to stiffen the heading should match the color of the curtain material. The fabric may be any of the sheer or semi-sheer curtain materials which will drape and hang easily, such as ninon, marquisette, voile, nets, and so on, of rayon or cotton. If the material is not pre-shrunk, allow extra length for shrinkage. This extra length can be taken up in a tuck near the hem or the heading until the curtains are washed. Tightly woven selvages should be trimmed off, or they may draw together after washing and cause the curtain to hang unevenly.

Shaped or swag valances of contrasting drapery fabric may be used with formal glass curtains (as well as informal ones), or you may have a draped swag of the same sheer material used for the curtains. In this case the swag is not lined.

If the glass curtains are hung inside the window frame, they should just clear the window sill. If they are hung on the outside of the frame, they may be either floor length or they may extend as far as the lower edge of the apron. Any in-between length tends to look awkward and should be avoided.

Sheer, ruffled tie-back curtains are not suitable for the formal period or modern room, but they are lovely and fresh-looking almost anywhere else. White, of course, is the favorite choice, but colors are also used. Or the ruffles may be edged in a color which is repeated elsewhere in the room. Suitable materials include organdy, dotted Swiss, net, lawn, muslin, marquisette, and similar fabrics. Organdy which has a permanent finish always retains its crisp appearance.

Ruffled tie-backs may be single or criss-cross, and with or without a valance.

Sheer, ruffled tie-back curtains over straight glass curtains form an appropriate window treatment for this dining room furnished in Early American style.

Sometimes the curtains are stretched between rods slipped through casings at the top and bottom. Such a treatment is often used for kitchen curtains with ruffled tiebacks at the centers. Plain curtains for doors or halls are often mounted in the same way, but without the ruffled tiebacks.

If you intend to make your own ruffled curtains, it will pay you to have a ruffler attachment for your sewing machine. Gathering ruffles evenly by hand for a long curtain is a painstaking and rather difficult task — but it can be done. The material allowance for a straight, gathered ruffle should be from one and three-fourths to twice the length of the finished ruffle. The width is a matter of taste. Fold the strip in half to find the center, and mark it with a pin. Fold each half in half and mark the centers with pins. Very long ruffles will need pin marks between these points as well. Do the same thing with the edge of the curtain. If the ruffle continues around more than one edge of the curtain, each edge will have to be measured separately, as will the corresponding allowance of ruffle for that edge. Make a straight line of even running stitches on the edge of the ruffle from the first pin to the second pin, leaving the thread loose at the end. Do the same between the other pins. Match the pins of the ruffle to the pins of the curtain edge and pull the loose threads until each section of ruffle corresponds in length to the length of the curtain sections. Adjust the gathers to make them as even as possible, and stitch in place.

Ruffles may be attached to the outside or inside edge of the curtain. The curtain edge is turned to the outside when ruffles are attached to the outside. Both edges of the ruffle must then be hemmed. The hemming may be on the same line as the gathering, or above it. Ruffle hems are usually very narrow, and often they are picoted. For picoted hems you will have to take the material to the hemstitcher to be done by machine. The picoted edge is made by cutting through the line of the hemstitching.

If you do not want to make your own ruffles, you can buy ruffling by the yard in many different styles, including fancy embroidered ruffles. Ruffles can also be edged with bias binding, rickrack braid, ball fringe, or some other of the many kinds of novelty trimmings.

Whatever ruffle treatment is used for the curtain should be repeated in the tieback. The ruffle may extend all the way around the tie-back, or just across the bottom edge.

FIXTURES FOR HANGING DRAPES AND CURTAINS

No matter how carefully you have made your curtains, they will not look right unless they are mounted with the proper kind of fixtures. The kind of fixture to use will be determined by the type of drape or curtain.

Curtain rods come in a wide variety of styles. They may be bought as single rods, or in sets of double or triple rods. Drapes or curtains without valances or with valances hung from a valance board need only single rods. Criss-cross curtains or drapes with valances hung from a rod

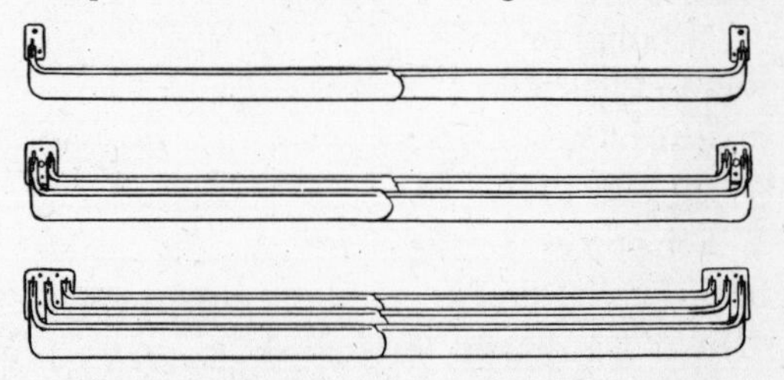

FIG. 12. Extension rods come in double, single, and triple arrangements to accommodate various curtain and drapery treatments. Heavy drapes usually need solid metal poles or wooden rods cut to fit. Curved rods are available for rounded windows.

need double rods. Triple rods are for criss-cross curtains with a valance hung from a rod. If the valance is attached to the curtains, it does not need a separate rod.

Extension rods can be adjusted up to a certain point to fit windows of various widths. Very light-weight extension rods are suitable only for sheer, light-weight curtains. But even heavier extension rods must not have too much strain put on the center. Lined and interlined drapes for big, high windows can be very heavy affairs, and they need sturdy support. Such drapes usually require solid metal rods cut to fit the window. Rods of this type may be bought with fixtures by which they can be made into single, double, or triple rods.

Various types of hooks and rings are available for attaching the drape of curtain to the rod. One of the most practical combinations consists of a metal ring which is slipped over the rod, and a hook, one end of which fits into a small eye on the ring. The other end of the hook is sharp and can be slipped into the center of a pleat in a French heading as easily as a pin and requires no sewing (Figure 13). These hooks also have the advantage of being easily removable when the drapes are to be cleaned. Similar hooks are also available which are made to be stitched to the drape. Be sure that the rings are of the right size to fit the rods.

No rings or hooks are needed for ruffled tie-back curtains. These are made with a casement heading through which the rod is slipped.

Sometimes cottage-type curtains have rings sewn directly to the curtain edge. The rod is slipped through the rings.

Windows treated as a group usually require a separate rod for each window or at least a center support for a single rod. The unit effect is best achieved with a continuous valance.

Casement windows present a special problem. If the casements open out, the rods can be mounted on the frame of the window. But if the casements open in, the rods must be mounted on the casement, and each casement requires a separate rod. If such casements are of metal, then glass curtains cannot be used, but side draperies and a valance can be substituted. If the casements are in a wide group and no valance is used, side draperies can be mounted on bracket fixtures.

Fixtures for Draw Curtains. It is often desirable to have drapes which can be drawn together. Special rods are available with traverse rigging already built in to hang draw curtains from. However, some of these rods are equipped with only a certain number of hooks, and the drape nay have more pleats than the rod has hooks.

A very satisfactory traverse rigging for draw curtains can be made with a single rod, rings, and pulleys. The pulleys are small devices with rotating channels through which the cord is drawn. Fixtures for attaching the rods to the window frame can be bought with the pulleys. Drapery departments and hardware stores also sell cord which is suitable for use with draw curtains. The cord is slipped through the pulleys and rings, as illustrated. Then the curtain is hung from the rings with the same type of hook used for regular draperies.

FIG. 13. Hook for attaching drape to rod. Sharp end is slipped into pleat and needs no sewing.

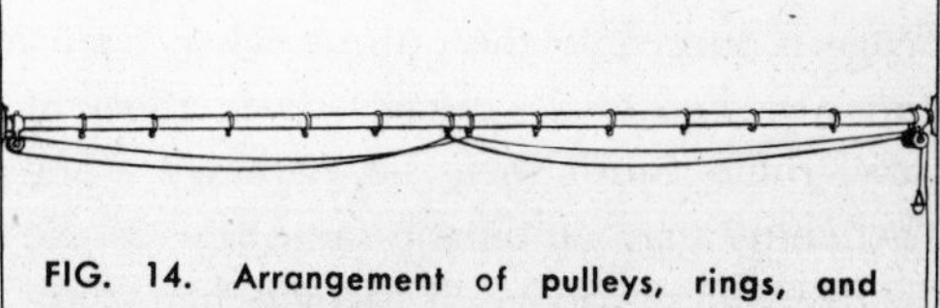

FIG. 14. Arrangement of pulleys, rings, and cords in traverse rigging for draw curtains.

CHAPTER XV

BEDROOM ENSEMBLES

IN BEDROOMS, the drapes, bedspread, dressing table skirt, and slipcovers are often planned as an ensemble by using the same materials for all pieces. Usually two or three fabrics are used — one of plain color, another of print to harmonize with the plain fabric, and possibly a third fabric of plain color in small areas to harmonize with the first plain fabric and to pick up another color from the print. For example, you might have the drapes of printed glazed chintz, with a valance of plain chintz. The top of the spread could be of plain chintz, and the flounces could be of the print. The dressing table skirt might be of the print with a band of plain material around the top over a buckram foundation cut in a design which repeats that of the window valance. The slipcover could be of plain chintz or in the contrasting color. If the plain chintz is used, small cushions in the contrasting color make nice accents. The same color can be picked up in such details as corded weltings on the slipcover, trimming for drapes, bedspreads, dressing table appointments, and in such accessories as lamps, pictures, and so on.

However, you may not want an effect which is too obviously matched. Then an effect of unity can be achieved through color, but fabrics need not be repeated.

BEDSPREADS

A bedspread may consist of a simple rectangular piece of fabric, long enough to cover the pillows and be tucked into a fold underneath them. Or it may be fitted, with a straight piece for the top and a plain, tailored skirt with boxed ends at the foot of the bed. Sometimes skirts are flounced, or pleated, or have set-in godets, or tiers of ruffles. A piece of fabric may be attached in reverse to the top edge of the spread in order that it may be brought back over the pillows and tucked underneath them, as illustrated. Or you can have a separate pillow sham, with ruffles all around the edge. The style of the room should determine whether the bedspread is to be frilly or tailored.

Spreads with long skirts should clear the floor by no more than one or two inches. Any shorter length looks skimpy. However, not all spreads have long skirts. Sometimes they are made to hang only about a foot over the edge of the mattress. Lovely old quilts or crocheted spreads are often used in this way. Sometimes the spread is tucked under the mattress. In either case, the spread is almost always combined with a dust ruffle to give the effect of a long skirt. The dust ruffle may be attached to a separate underspread of muslin if the top spread hangs free. But if the top spread is to be tucked under the mattress, the dust ruffle will have to be attached to the side rails of the bed, and where there is no footboard, to the foot rail as well. Some beds have box-spring foundations to which

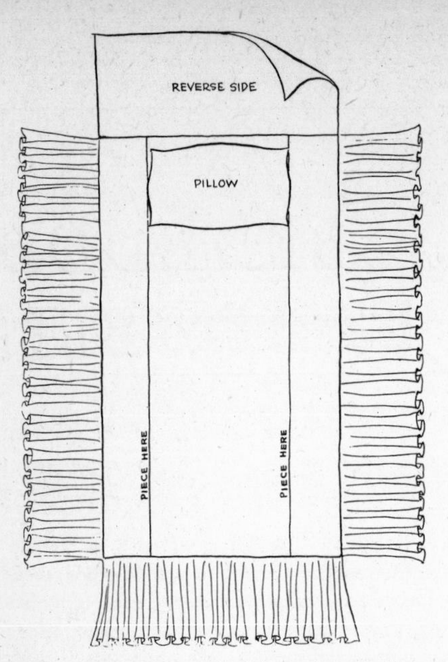

FIG. 1. Bedspread with plain gathered skirt and attached pillow cover. Diagram shows how fabric for pillow cover is reversed so that it can be brought back over pillow and tucked underneath.

dust ruffles cannot be attached. In that case the dust ruffle could be attached to a muslin foundation piece which extends across the bed underneath the mattress.

If the bed has a footboard, the skirt need not extend around the foot of the bed. However the top section of the spread should then be made long enough to extend over the edge of the mattress and to tuck underneath it. If the bed is a four-poster, the skirt sections should be open at the corners.

Very often the headboard is upholstered in the same fabric used for the spread, but usually not when the bed has both a headboard and a footboard. (*To make an upholstered headboard, see the chapter on Reupholstery.*)

Estimating Amount of Material Needed. The amount of material needed for a spread depends on its style, the size of the bed, and the width of the fabric. Fabrics used for decorating purposes are usually wide enough to make the top of a spread for a narrow bed from one width, but require piecing for wider beds. However, the fabric should not be pieced at the center of the bed. Instead, one width of fabric is used so that it is centered on the bed, lengthwise, and another width of fabric is split and pieced to the center section at each side (*see illustration*). Two lengths of material are usually sufficient to make the top of a spread for most beds.

Measure the width and length of the top of the bed, and the distance from the top edge of the mattress to the floor, for spreads which are to extend to the floor. For shorter spreads measure the distance from the top edge of the mattress to the point below the mattress where you want the spread to end. Plain, rectangular spreads are estimated as a single piece. If the spread has a skirt, the top and skirt are estimated separately. A ruffled skirt requires a piece of material wide enough to extend from the top edge of the mattress to the floor and from one and one-half to two times the length of each side of the bed (depending on fullness desired). If the skirt is to extend around the foot of the bed, an additional length of from one and one-half to two times the width of the bed is required. Box-pleated skirts require from twice to three times the length on each side and width.

The style of the spread determines how much material to allow for covering the pillows. For a plain, rectangular spread, the allowance must be sufficient to permit a six-inch tuckaway under the pillows. To this add the height of the pillows and enough material to tuck in at the back. If the spread has a pillow cover made separately and attached in reverse to the spread, this piece must be measured separately (length, width, and height of pillows, plus a six-inch tuckaway under the pillows). Pillow shams are also measured separately in the same way.

Dust ruffles are measured in the same way as the skirt, except that their depth

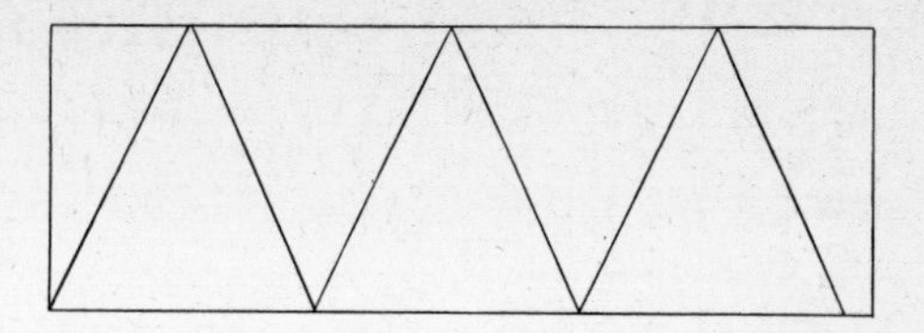

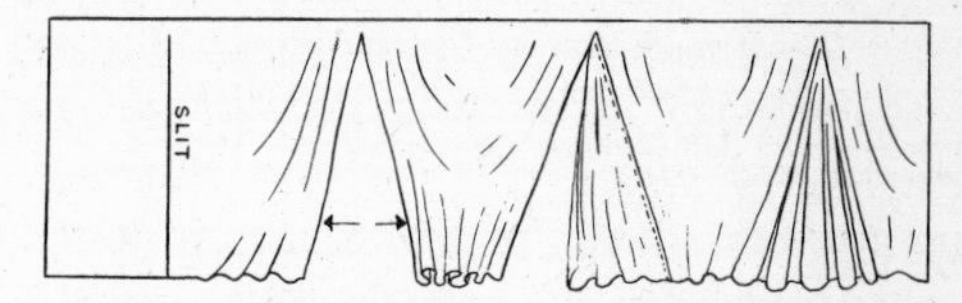

FIG. 2. Godet flounces are made by cutting triangular sections of fabric and inserting them in slits in flounce section. Godet edge is turned under and stitched to edge of slit, or both edges may be seamed together on wrong side.

depends on whether they are to be attached to the rails, to a foundation under the mattress, or to a separate underspread.

To all measurements add seam allowances of 3/4 of an inch at every joining edge, and hem allowances of 1 1/2 inches.

Plain Rectangular Spreads. The side sections may be attached to the center section with plain seams, corded welting (*see chapter on Slipcovers for making corded welting*), or trimmed with moss fringe, applied bands, or other finishing details. Sometimes the spread is lined and sometimes not — professionally made spreads usually are. But a spread made of firmly woven fabric usually needs no lining, and often the spread can be smoothed more neatly without one.

The edges of the spread can be finished simply with a plain hem, either stitched by hand or on the machine. If the bed has no footboard, the spread should be as long at the foot as it is at the sides. In a plain, rectangular spread, this causes the corners to be longer than the sides. To overcome this difficulty, the corners can be rounded off.

If the spread is to tuck under the mattress or hang loose just over the edge of the mattress, a dust ruffle in a contrasting fabric or color is often used. Then the pillow sham or the ruffle on the sham might very well repeat this contrasting color or fabric.

Tailored Spreads with Boxed Corners. A spread of this type has a separate plain skirt attached to the top section. The skirt sections are cut in strips to correspond to the length and width of the top part of the spread, but are brought together at each side of the foot, and seamed to form boxed corners. Such spreads are suitable only for beds without footboards. The pillows should be covered with a piece of fabric attached in reverse to the top of the spread. The seams at the boxed corners may be plain, or if the other seams of the spread are finished with cord welting, the corner seams may be finished in that way, too. Spreads with boxed corners may be either short or long. If short, they are combined with dust ruffles.

Spreads with Ruffled, Pleated, Tiered, or Godet-Flounced Skirts. Plain ruffled skirts can be easily made with the ruffler attachment of the sewing machine. Or ruffles can be gathered by hand by the same method described for making hand-gathered ruffles in the chapter on Drapes and Curtains (Ruffled Tie-Back Curtains). Box-pleated skirts can be measured and made in the same way as a box-pleated ruffle on a slipcover (*see chapter on Slipcovers*).

Tiered ruffles must be attached to a plain underskirt foundation which is attached to the top section of the spread. The edge of one ruffle should overlap the heading of another by at least one inch. The ruffles may all be of the same width, or they may be graduated, with the narrowest ruffle at the top and the widest at the bottom. Sheer and semi-sheer fabrics are especially suited to this style of spread, but other fabrics can be used also. An underspread of muslin or similar material to match the color of the spread is required if the spread is made of sheer or semi-sheer material.

Godet-flounced skirts are made by setting in triangular sections (called *godets*) of fabric into a plain skirt. The godets are cut from the fabric as illustrated. The skirt is slashed vertically along the line of the weave and to a depth which corresponds to the side of the godet. Seam the sides of the godet and the slashed edges together on the inside, or turn under the slashed edges and seam them on top of the godet. The top of the slash will need two small diagonal notches to allow for turning of seams, as illustrated. Graduate the seam so that it is as small as possible toward the top in order to have the godets end in a point.

Pillow Shams and Bolsters. Pillow shams are rectangular pieces of fabric a little larger in size than the length and width of the pillow. They are usually finished with gathered or box-pleated ruffles, depending on the type of skirt used on the spread. For a double bed, each pillow may have a separate sham, or one long sham may cover both pillows. When shams are used, the spread is made only long enough to reach the headboard.

The simplest type of spread is a plain, rectangular piece of material long enough to reach the floor at the foot of the bed and to be tucked under and behind the pillows. If preferred, corners may be rounded off to hang at floor level.

Shaped bolsters are usually hollow cylinders with an opening in the back into which the pillows are fitted. They were once widely used. Their popularity waned for a time, but now they are becoming fashionable again. Such bolsters must be bought ready made, and are usually available in bed or drapery departments. The bolster may be covered separately with fabric to match the spread or its skirt. In this case, the fabric is cut to fit the bolster, stretched firmly around it, and the ends are turned under and stitched to the edges of the back opening in the bolster. The round end pieces are cut to fit and seamed into place before the bolster cover is applied. Finish the seams with corded welting, fringe, or other trimming detail. The spread should be just long enough to reach the headboard when the bolster is covered with the spread. However, sometimes the bolster is covered with the spread. The spread should then be long enough to allow for a tuckaway under the bolster and to completely cover it at the top.

COUCH COVERS

In general, couch covers should be rather tailored in appearance and of fairly sturdy fabric. Sheer materials in frothy ruffles are not suitable. If the couch has a separate mattress, the cover can be made in two pieces so that the mattress can be turned over as one side becomes soiled.

Plain, one-piece boxed covers are made in the same way that boxed spreads are made. Or the cover may consist of a top section, cut to fit the top of the couch, and a ruffled or box-pleated skirt. The skirt may be attached directly to the top section, or it may be attached to a plain band which, in turn, is joined to the top section. The seams may be finished in any of the ways suggested for finishing slipcover seams (*see chapter on Slipcovers*).

Two-piece couch covers consist of a

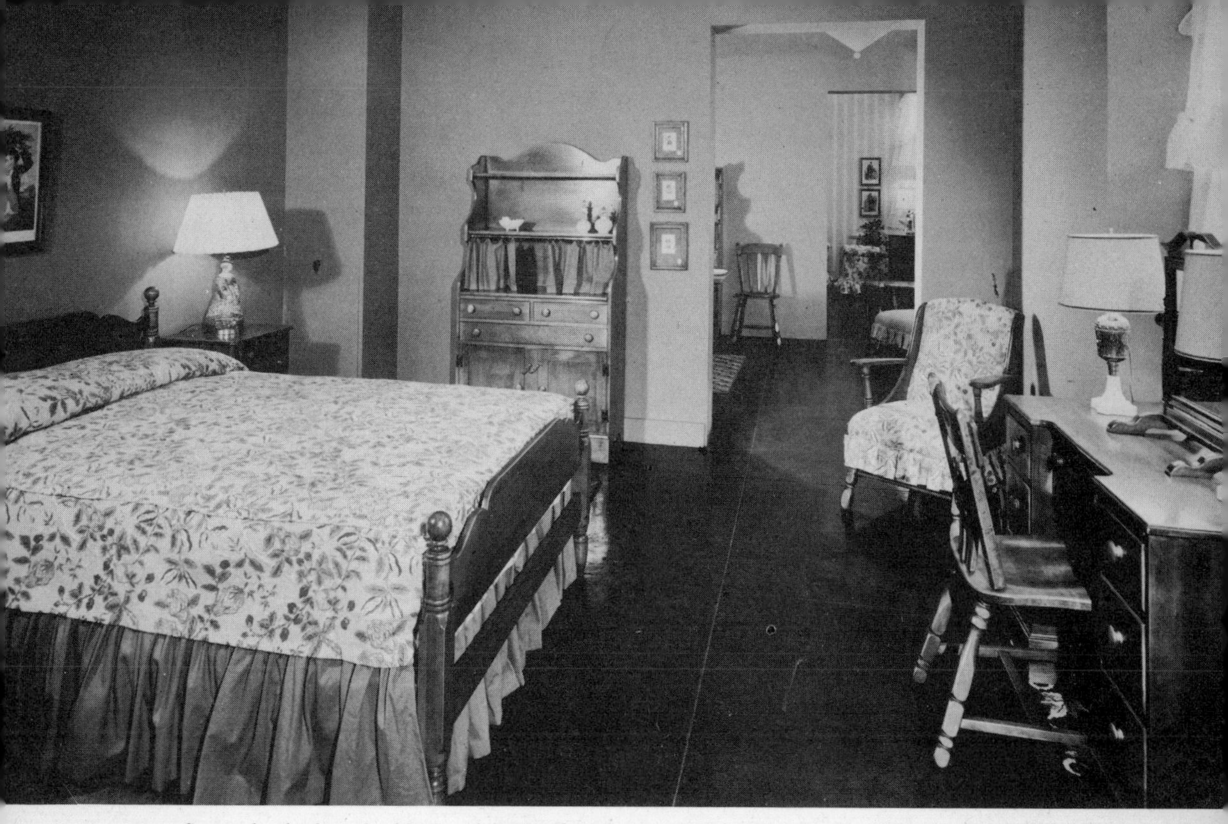

Spread of glazed chintz with short skirt boxed at the corners. Separate under flounce harmonizes in color. Furniture is good interpretation of Early American design.

mattress cover and a cover for the box springs. For the mattress cover, two sections are cut in the exact shape of the top of the mattress. These are joined together with a continuous band as wide as the depth of the mattress. In order to remove the cover, leave an opening which extends across one end and several inches down each side. The edges of the opening can be fastened with snap-fastener tape in the same way that slipcover openings are fastened. The cover for the box springs consists of a ruffled flounce attached to a foundation piece of muslin or similar material which extends across the box spring underneath the mattress.

CUSHIONS AND CUSHION COVERS

Cushions may be bought in their foundation covers, or tickings, in a variety of shapes and sizes and covered at home to match or contrast with the rest of the decorating scheme. The cost depends mainly

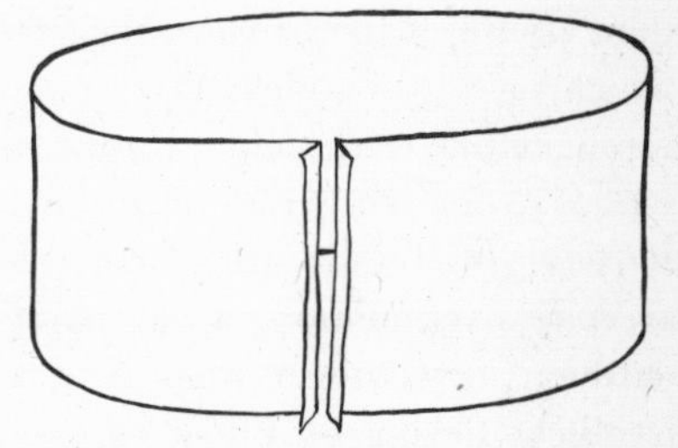

FIG. 3. Round cushion cover can be made by joining ends of straight strip of fabric and gathering one edge tightly together. Ruffle makes harmonious trimming.

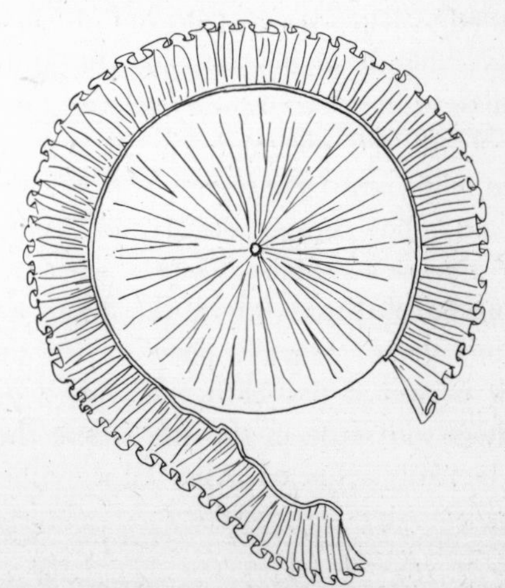

on the type of filling used. Feathers, down, kapok, and cotton are the principal filling materials. Of these, high-grade down is the best and most expensive. Frequently down is combined with feathers. Feathers are graded according to their size and quality. Small, fine feathers make better filling material than coarser feathers. The cheapest feather fillings are those made of chopped chicken feathers. All feathers should be properly cleaned and cured or they tend to have an unpleasant odor. Read the contents label on the cushion carefully before buying.

Kapok is an excellent, inexpensive filling material, but considerably less resilient than down or a good grade of feathers. The cheapest filling material is cotton, but it loses its shape and becomes lumpy with hard use.

Sometimes the filling material from old pillows can be utilized in making new cushions. If the material consists of feathers which need to be cleaned, it is advisable to have this work done professionally. The cost is not high, but only down or feathers of good grade are worth the expense. A new foundation can be made for the cushion in whatever shape you want from pillow ticking or other very firmly woven cotton material. All seams must be tightly stitched. Leave an opening of about twelve inches, more or less, along one seam edge. Rip a seam of the old pillow to make a slightly smaller opening. Place the opening of the new cushion over the opening of the old one and pin securely in place, with pins close together. Now, turn the old pillow upside down and hold it over the new cushion. Gently work the filling material from one to the other, but do not shake. A good place to do this work is over a dry bath tub. Any loose feathers will settle in the tub where they can be easily collected. After all the filling has been transferred, gently unpin the new cushion, being careful to press back the filling. Close and pin the opening as quickly as possible. Do not turn the old pillow inside out and attempt to glean the few remaining feathers which will cling to the inside. Fold it up and dispose of it before the "feathers start to fly."

Turn in the edges of the opening on the new cushion and overcast tightly, with stitches close together. Be sure the old filling is adequate for the new cushion. Pillows must be plump to keep their shape.

Cushion Covers. The cushion cover, of course, must be made in the same shape as the cushion itself. If the cushion has boxed sides, the cover must have boxed sides. However, sometimes there is more than one way of handling the fabric and still have a cover of a certain shape. For example, a round cushion might be covered simply by cutting two round pieces of fabric to fit and seaming the edges together. Or a straight strip of fabric can be tightly gathered along one edge to form the type of cover in Figure 3. To make such a cover, measure the diameter of the cushion (the distance across at its widest point). Divide this figure by two, and you have the radius. The width of the strip of fabric should equal the radius. To find how long the strip should be, multiply the diameter by 3.142, which will give you the circumference, or the distance around the edge of the circle. The length of the strip should be the same as the circumference measure. Add ½ to ¾ of an inch to all edges for the seam allowance. Sew the ends of the strip together, and gather one side with running stitches, drawing the thread up as tightly as possible.

The back section may be made in the same way, or it may consist of a piece of material cut in the shape of a circle to fit. The edges of the front and back sections

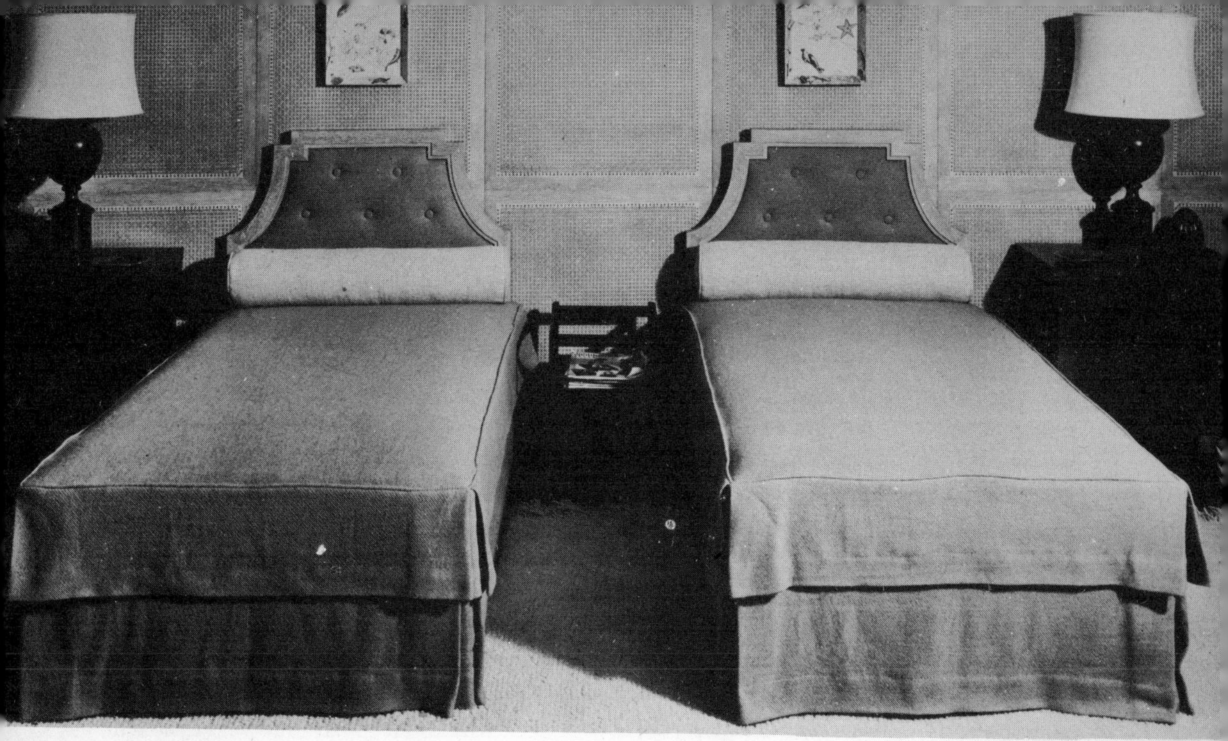

Spreads of tailored elegance in heavy whipcord with short skirts and matching underskirts. Corners are finished with box pleats and seams with neat corded welting. Bolster-shaped day pillows are in contrasting color.

Quilted rayon spreads with plain, gathered flounces are made long enough to cover pillows. Flounces are slit at corners to slip over bed rails. Note the unusual arrangement of miniature paintings above beds.

are sewed together. The most appropriate trimming for this type of cover is a ruffle, the gathered edge of which is inserted into the seam between the two sections. The center of the gathered section of the cushion cover can be finished with a small pompon or a large, flat covered button. Covered buttons are made to order from a piece of your own material by companies specializing in this work.

Covers with boxed sides are made by fitting a continuous band between the top and bottom sections of the cover (*as shown in Figure 11 in the chapter on Slipcovers*). The edges can be finished with cord welting or with moss fringe. Ruffles or wide trimmings are not suitable for boxed covers.

Bolster-shaped cushions are made by sewing a strip of material together at the edges to form a cylinder. The end sections are cut in the shape of a circle and fitted into place. To cut circles of the right size, measure the width of the strip of material and divide this measure by 3.142. Divide the answer by two to find the radius of the circle. Set the arms of the compass so that the distance between equals the radius, and draw a circle. It might be wise to do this on paper first, and then use the paper as a pattern from which to cut the material. Or, if you choose, the end sections may be gathered together at the center in the same way that a round pillow section is made.

FIG. 4. To permit easy removal for cleaning, attach skirt to arms of dressing table with snap fastener tape.

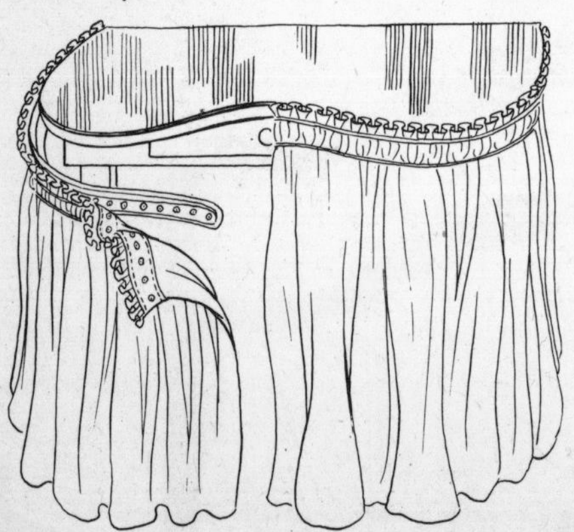

Leave an opening on all cushion covers so they may be removed for washing or dry cleaning. Finish the opening with snap-fastener tape. The opening should be in the least conspicuous place — the under side of the ruffle, cord welting, or other trimming.

DRESSING TABLE SKIRTS

The dressing table can be draped in almost any way that suits the fancy. It should, however, be in harmony with the rest of the furnishings and decorations of the bedroom. Draped dressing tables are especially suitable for feminine rooms.

The dressing table itself can be of whatever shape you prefer. The most popular are the rectangular and kidney-shaped tables. Some dressing tables have straight side sections and a concave center section. Some are made of fine woods to match the rest of the bedroom furniture. However, most women prefer the less expensive unfinished one, which can be either draped as they are, or painted to match the color of the skirt. Ready-made dressing tables have arms in front which swing out to permit access to the drawers. The skirt, which is made in two sections, is attached to the arms and swings with them. However, any small table with one or more drawers can be made to serve as a dressing table which can be draped by nailing a strip of wood, the same length as the table, along the top edge of the drawer, as illustrated. The skirt for such a table is made in three sections. One section is attached to each side, and the third is attached to the strip of wood across the front. When the drawer is closed, the front and side sections of the skirt appear as a unit.

Dressing-table tops should be covered with a material which is impervious to

The cover of this interesting day bed is of pastel plaid cotton. Flounce is separate. Braided rug achieves unusual shape with inserts of separate circular braided sections.

spilled liquids or stains. Glass, mirror, or oilcloth may be used. Ready-made dressing tables can be bought with glass or mirror tops cut to fit.

Making the Skirt. For dressing tables with arms which open at the middle, the measurement is taken from the center front of the tables to the center back. A gathered skirt will require two pieces of material, each with a length of from one and one-half to two times this measure and as wide as the distance from the dressing table top to the floor. Add a 1-inch hem allowance, and from 3 to 4 inches for heading. If the skirt is to be made of tiers of ruffles, they must be attached to a foundation. The foundation requires no fullness, and its measurements should correspond to those of the table.

The skirt is usually finished at the top with a shirred heading or attached to a straight band. Shirred headings can be made on the machine with the ruffler attachment, or by running evenly spaced

FIG. 5. Ordinary small table can be easily converted into skirted dressing table by nailing strip of wood to edge of drawer, so that drawer can be opened without disturbing skirt, which is made in three sections.

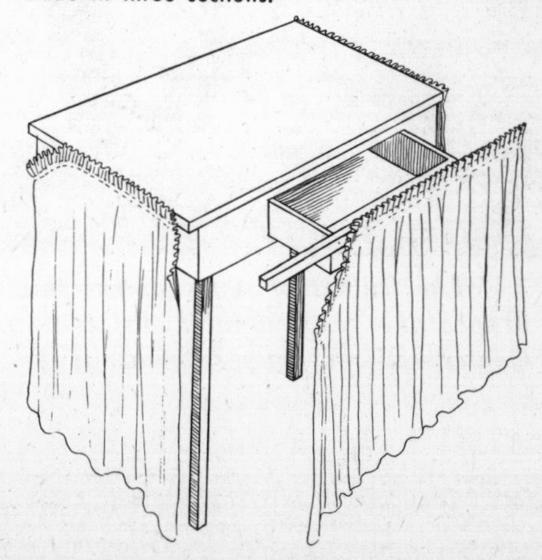

The frilliest of skirts adorns this diminutive dressing table. Side panniers are draped like swag valances. Triple-tiered drapes are set on plain foundation panel. Center section of shaped valance is edged with ruffle to match skirt and glass curtains.

rows of stitches by hand to form gathers. Sometimes the rows of shirring are made over cording. To make the heading, turn the top edge of the material over 1½ to 2 inches. Place the first row of stitches about ½ inch from the turned-over edge (not the folded edge). Continue placing the stitches in rows until the heading is the right depth (usually about 4 inches). Cut two strips of buckram, each 4 inches wide (or the width of the shirring) and the length of the finished skirt section. Face the buckram with muslin, sateen, or the material from which the skirt is made. Stitch one edge of a tape near the top edge of the covered buckram, or stitch the stud strip of a snap-fastener tape flat to the covered buckram. The socket strip is then nailed to the arms and back of the table. This permits the skirt to be easily removed for cleaning or laundering. After the gathers are carefully adjusted to form the shirring, the covered buckram strips are stitched at the top and bottom edges to the back of the shirring. The top edge of the skirt then forms a narrow ruffle which stands up above the edge of the table and conceals it.

If the dressing table is improvised from an ordinary table, the top of the table may extend so far out that the top of the skirt is pushed out. In this case, the best thing to do is to saw the edges off the table and sandpaper them smooth.

The front and back edges of the skirt should be finished with a narrow hem, and the bottom should be finished with a 1-inch hem, or trimmed in whatever way you wish.

To attach a skirt to a plain band, cut two straight strips of material to correspond to the measurements of the table, and twice the width of the band when finished (usually about 4 inches), plus ¾ of an inch for seam allowance. Fold the strip in half lengthwise, and insert a strip of buckram 4 inches wide (or the finished width of the band together along the middle, snap-fastener tape about 1½ or 2 inches from the folded edge. Stitch through the tape, the back of the band, and the buckram, in the same way that th tape was applied to the buckram bana for the shirred heading. Baste the front and back of the band). Attach a plain tape or a stitching through the fabric and the buckram. (An interlining may be required if the buckram shows through the fabric.) Turn the front edge of the fabric over the buckram and lay the gathered edge of the skirt on top. Adjust the edge and baste in place. Stitch on the outside. Corded welting or other trimming may be inserted between the edge of the band and the outside of the skirt before stitching if you desire. Turn under the inside edge of the band so that the folded edge lies just on top of the row of outside stitching. Baste and stitch in place by hand so that the stitches do not show on the outside.

Dressing tables can be trimmed in any number of ways. Shaped bands can be made according to the same methods used for making shaped valances for windows. Such bands can be stitched permanently to the skirt, but it is better to make them separate so that they can be removed when the skirt is cleaned. Attach a tape to the inside of the band and apply the band to the skirt by basting through the tape.

Small draped swags are also used as trimming, and these are made in the same way as swags for windows, except that they are smaller. However, swag trimmings should be used only on fairly large dressing tables, as they tend to make tiny tables look top heavy. Remember, too, that the trimming on the table should correspond to the treatment of the windows and the bed.

Appliqued quilt in "lobster" pattern. The motifs are carried out in dark red and green calico and the white ground is quilted in the feather pattern.

CHAPTER XVI

QUILT MAKING

QUILTING bees were the most wonderful excuses for our great grandmothers to get together for a bit of gossip, a cup of tea, and general social recreation. Of course, they did work on quilts, too. They traded their patterns and scraps of cloth along with their gossip, and a good time was had by all. Some of the quilts they turned out are now in our museums and serve as fine examples of folk art. It is an art which has never died out, although it is practiced far less extensively nowadays. Fine quilting requires thousands and thousands of tiny stitches sewn by hand—work which many women haven't the patience for.

Quilting is the process of stitching together two layers of fabric with padding in between. The lines of stitching follow a design of some kind, or they may be simply in straight, parallel or crisscross rows. In the Italian method of quilting, called *trapunto* work, the layer of padding is omitted. Instead, the two layers of fabric are stitched together and afterwards heavy padding yarn is inserted between the rows of stitching. Trapunto work is occasionally used for bedquilts, but not nearly as often as the first type, which is sometimes called English quilting. The reason, of course, is the purely practical one that a quilt made by the English method is considerably warmer. Warmth, however, is not the primary object in making a quilt. A quilt does serve for warmth, too, and originally that was its principal purpose. But as quilting developed into an art, quilts became more prized for their beauty than for their utilitarian value. Nowadays artistry is the primary aim and justification in quilt making. Warmth in bedding can be obtained more easily with a fleecy, wool-napped blanket which supplies much better insulation than a quilt filled with cotton batting. Of course, purely utilitarian quilting can be made by machine, too, or bought by the yard. While such quilting may be decorative, it naturally is not practiced as an art.

In the traditional methods of quilt making, the quilting design is very often secondary to the design worked into the fabric being quilted. The two methods of working the fabric design are known as *patchwork* and *applique*. Patchwork consists in seaming small pieces of fabric together to form a design. Applique is made by sewing bits of fabric onto another fabric (the foundation) to form a design.

PATCHWORK QUILTS

Just where or when patchwork started is anyone's guess. Thrifty early American housewives practiced it as an economic necessity. Material was precious and every tiny scrap had to be utilized. The bits of material left over after cutting out a dress

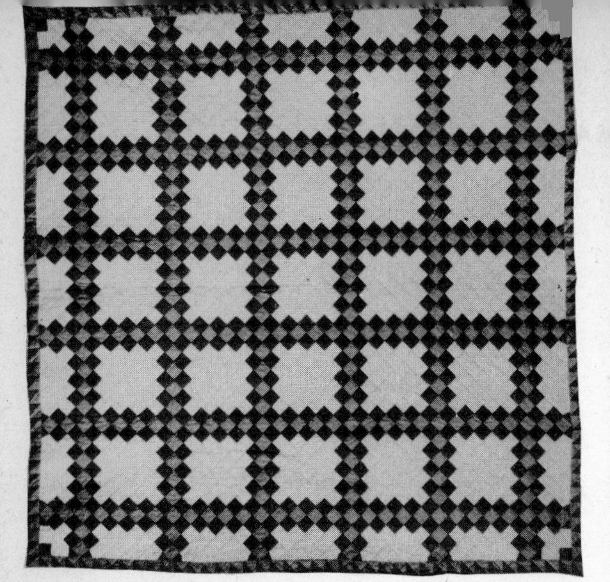

Patchwork quilt composed of pink and white squares of calico worked in the "Irish chain" pattern.

Patchwork quilt worked in the "Star of Bethlehem" or "sunburst" pattern in varying shades of brown. Border is appliquéd.

or other garment could still serve a useful purpose by being sewed together to make a quilt cover. Very often the snippets of cloth were of any size and shape, put together without any effort to achieve a design at all. The result was aptly named a *crazy quilt*. It undoubtedly offered the most thorough opportunity for using every inch of material, but it did not appeal much to the love for pattern in orderly progression. It took more time to cut the bits of cloth into pieces of definite shape and size, but an infinite number of designs could be worked out with such pieces.

Now, as anyone who has ever tried it knows, it is very difficult to seam two curved pieces of cloth together on the wrong side and still keep the line of the curve smooth. Therefore, the technique of patchwork demands straight seams and uncomplicated designs. Nearly all of the traditional patchwork patterns are formed of simple triangles, squares, and oblongs. The pieces are first sewn into blocks,

FIG. 1. Patchwork consists in seaming together small, straight-sided pieces of fabric to form a pattern.

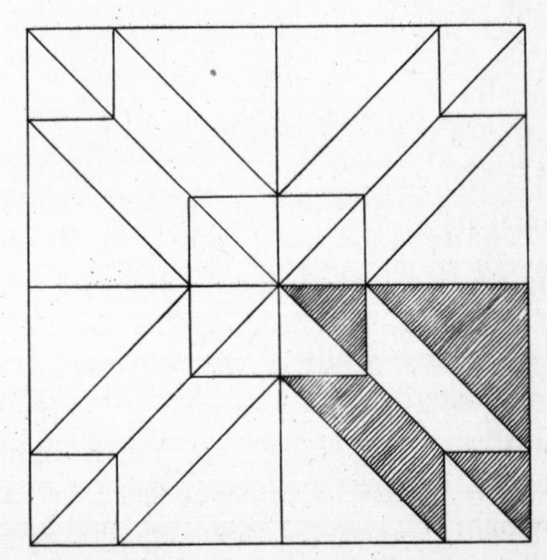

FIG. 2. The patchwork pieces are worked into blocks which are sewn together. Patchwork calls for fine, straight seams.

FIG. 3. A group of traditional patchwork patterns called (top left) bear's paw, (top right) pinwheel, (bottom left) flying geese, and (bottom right) the pine tree.

which, when put together, often make an allover pattern. Many of the traditional quilt patterns are based on two superimposed squares forming an eight-pointed star. But the simple triangle which is one-half of a square probably offered more interesting variations. Some of the traditional patterns made from these triangles have been given names, such as *pinwheel, pine tree,* and *flying geese.*

Piecing the Quilt. After deciding upon your pattern, make a scale drawing of the quilt as it is to appear when finished. To do this, let each inch (or whatever measurement you choose) represent each block. Fill in the dark parts of the design with ink or paint. This may seem like a good deal of work, but it's worth it. A quilt requires so much time to make that the design should not be worked out in hit-or-miss fashion as one proceeds. If the quilt is a disappointment after it is finished, it's too late to rectify mistakes then. Isn't it better to make your changes on paper, first, and have a product you'll be proud of later on?

While the choice of a pattern is more or less limited to one that can be worked out with squares, triangles, and oblongs (because of the technique), one need not be limited to the traditional patterns. More often than not, these may be consulted simply as an inspiration for an entirely new interpretation. Many modern quilters take a single motif and open it up—that is, combine it with plain blocks or other patterns in a new arrangement. Nor are the materials for such quilts necessarily limited to the scraps which come from the sewing bag (although quilting is still a thrifty way to use these bits). Some quilters buy new materials in colors or patterns to match or harmonize with the color scheme of the room.

In order to make blocks which can be matched accurately, the individual pieces must be cut with the greatest of care. Cut a piece of cardboard in the exact dimension of the square, triangle, or oblong, and trace the outline of the piece on the cloth. Align the edges of the right angle sides to correspond exactly with the warp or weft threads of the material. Wrinkled material should be ironed. The individual pieces must be joined together with seams of the exact size. If some seams are wider than others, the blocks will not match accurately. Keep the seams narrow (preferably about ¼ or ⅜ of an inch) to avoid too much bulk. Although hand stitching is traditional for patchwork, there's no reason why the seaming can't be done on the machine as long as it is accurate. Many women find it difficult to stitch so carefully on a machine, however. Be especially careful not to stretch bias seams.

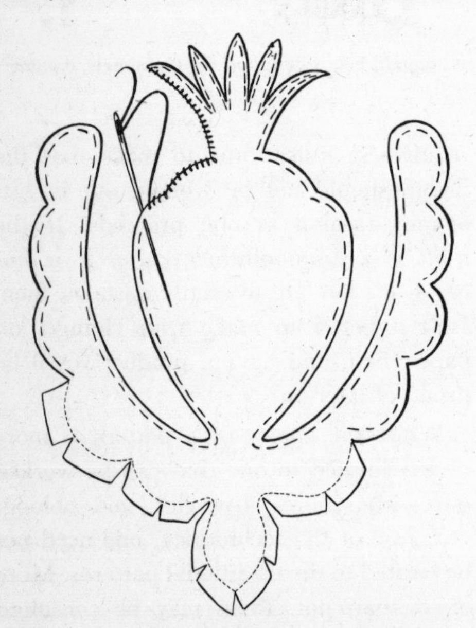

FIG. 4. In applique work, one piece of fabric is cut in a design and stitched to another piece of fabric. The edges of the applique piece are turned under and stitched into place first with basting and then with fine overcasting.

After each block is finished, the seams should be opened and pressed flat. The blocks may either be joined to each other directly or pieced together with bands of fabric (called *sets*). Joining seams are also opened up and pressed flat. The completed quilt top is then ready to be combined with the padding and lining and quilted.

APPLIQUE QUILTS

To great-grandmother, applique was a luxury because it seemed like such a sinful waste of precious material to sew one piece of fabric on top of another when one piece might have been just as useful. But it was such a joy to work the graceful, scrolling designs permitted by the applique technique, that she salved her conscience by proclaiming that a double thickness of material here and there made the quilt a bit warmer. Virtually any design that is not too detailed or delicate can be worked out in applique. The technique of decorating one fabric with designs cut from another is by no means limited to quilts. It has been popular form of embellishing clothing and other articles since ancient times.

Needlewomen with the true creative instinct prefer to make their own designs or adapt them from other sources to suit their needs. No particular drawing skill is needed to do this—the very nature of the work demands simple, straightforward, two-dimensional figures. A design you make yourself usually has more charm because it is fresh and original even if the drawing lacks the preciseness of a stereotyped, ready-made pattern. However, the timid souls who refuse to believe in their creative talents can always buy stamped patterns which are transferred onto the material with a hot iron. Of course, traditional patterns are always in good taste in authentic period rooms.

A cardboard pattern can be cut for the designs which you make yourself. Trace the outline of the cardboard on the fabric. Cut the design from the fabric, leaving a seam allowance of about ¼ of an inch. With a hot iron, press this seam allowance over the cardboard to insure a clean, sharp outline. Of course, the cardboard edge must be smooth and not too thick. The seam allowance will probably have to be notched here and there to eliminate bunching or stretching. Lay the applique piece on the foundation material and baste in place. Join the piece to the foundation with fine overcasting, using thread of the color to match the applique fabric. Applique motifs are often held in place with buttonhole or blanket stitching, but this method is not particularly suitable for quilts, since it is apt to interfere with the quilting stitches. The motifs can be worked on one large piece of foundation material or on separate blocks which are joined

FIG. 6. Traditional applique patterns (from top to bottom): harvest rose, a variation of the English Whig rose; a variation of the Democratic rose; hearts and wreath, a Dutch design; oak leaves with acorn center.

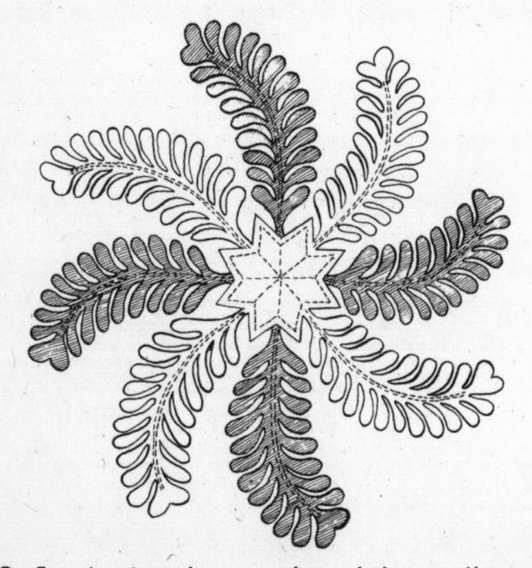

FIG. 5. An American version of the applique design taken from the feathers on the crest of the Prince of Wales. Here the feathers are whorled about the Lemoine star, which eventually was called the "lemon" star.

together. The particular advantage of the blocks is that they can be carried about easily so that one can pick the work up during free moments.

QUILTING

Lining Material. Any firmly woven, not-too-thick material can be used to line the quilt. Sheeting (either muslin or percale) is a good choice because it is obtainable in very wide widths. Other fabrics, white or colored often need to be pieced.

For bound quilts, cut the lining the same size as the quilt top. For unbound quilts, the lining can be cut about 2½ inches larger all around and then brought up over the edge of the quilt top, turned under, and blindstitched into place as a binding.

Padding. The usual padding material used as an interlining in hand-made quilts is cotton batting. Quilt battings of the right size and thickness are sold in most department stores. However, one can also use a worn woolen blanket (single thickness), outing flannel (double or triple thickness), and wool flannel. Avoid piecing the interlining if possible, or the seams will show up badly. Wool batting is more suitable for tufted quilts. Down is too difficult to work with under ordinary conditions.

The Quilting Design. Quilting designs can be as simple or elaborate as you please. In earlier days, women formed their designs from common household equipment. The teacup was one of their chief inspirations. Perhaps they knew little or nothing of geometry, but the teacup helped them to devise many intricate geometrical patterns based on the circle. For that reason, traditional quilting designs based on the circle are often called "teacup" patterns. Zigzag, crisscross, diamond, and parallel rows are other possibilities. The crescent was another figure which offered any number of combinations. An additional motif was the feather, taken from the crest of the Prince of Wales. This motif has a very interesting history which can be traced back to England. English quilters always used the feather in groups of three, as they are carried on the Prince's crest. American quilters, having lost their compunctions about royalty, spread their feathers to suit themselves. It appears in whorls on the applique pieces and again in the quilting pattern itself. In fact, applique patterns are often repeated in the quilting on plain blocks. For some of the beauty of fine quilting is the point and counterpoint of its design. The quilting pattern is an un-

FIG. 7. Simple zigzag quilting designs are effective and easy to stitch without a pattern guide.

FIG. 8. Quilting designs based on the circle are often called "teacup" patterns because the outline was probably traced around the rim of a teacup.

dertone to the dominant overtone of the applique or patchwork patterns.

Your design can be transferred to the cloth by a number of means. One way is to trace the design on paper parchment and prick all around the outline with a pin at intervals of about ¼ of an inch. Then place the paper-parchment pattern in position on the cloth and rub the pricked outline with colored chalk. Or cut a cardboard pattern and trace around it with a pencil. To space motifs accurately, mark off sections on the quilt top with chalked string. Stretch the string across the quilt top. Then, holding the string taut, snap it sharply, so that the chalk leaves a line on the cloth. Allover patterns should first be worked out with scale drawings on paper.

Assembling the Quilt. Lay the lining fabric on the floor or on a table large enough to accommodate the entire quilt. If the fabric has a right side, it should be face down. The fabric must be perfectly smooth and straight. Next, lay the

FIG. 9. Designs based on the crescent motif offer many graceful variations for quilting patterns.

cotton batting or other padding material on top of the lining. On top of the batting or padding, place the quilt top, face up. Next, baste the lining, the interlining, and the quilt top together. Begin the basting stitches at the center and work towards the top, the bottom, each side, and then each corner. Be very careful to keep all three layers in place during the basting. Pin the edges together all around. The assembled quilt is now ready to be set in the quilting frame.

The Quilting Frame. A regulation quilting frame is a device resembling a curtain stretcher. Some women can quilt without a frame. They merely work on a large table top, and manage to keep their work smooth and even. However, the frame makes the work so much easier that it's better to use one if you can. In fact, a perfectly satisfactory frame can be made from two straight strips of lumber for the side stiles and two shorter ones for the top and bottom rails. One-by-two inch white pine is good for this purpose. The pieces can be assembled with square or mitered joints secured with corner braces. Joints must form true right angles and should be carefully tested with the Try-square. Tack 4-inch strips of heavy muslin or duck all around the frames. The edges of the fabric are tacked near the inside edges of the frame. The quilt is pinned to the free edges of the muslin or duck. The frame may be of any size convenient to work on. Only a section of the quilt need be stretched on the frame at a time. Stretch the quilt firmly and evenly while pinning. Regulation frames have clamps which are adjusted to stretch the work. The frame holds the width of the quilt and as much of the length as can be comfortably reached from either side.

Stitching. The quilting is done with tiny, evenly spaced, straight running stitches. The needle is pushed through all three layers of material. A rather short needle will help you to keep the stitches short. Mercerized thread is easier to work with than ordinary cotton thread. As a rule, the color of the thread matches the material being quilted, but it can also contrast.

Hold the left hand under the frame to make sure that the needle penetrates all three layers of material. If the design is complicated, with many curves or changes of direction, the work can be speeded up by keeping several needles in work at once. Then you will not have to shift from one side of the frame to the other quite so often. Simply work one needle along a line until it changes direction so that it must be worked from the other side. Then pick up another needle and do the same with that, and so on.

When you rethread your needles, push the knot through the lining fabric in order to keep the knot from showing.

Finishing the Quilt. The edges of the quilt can be finished in a number of ways. The edges of both the top and lining fabrics may be turned to the inside and the folded edges slipstitched or overcast together. Or the lining fabric may be cut larger than the top, brought back over the top edge, turned under, and stitched in place. Both edges may be bound together with bias binding in a matching or contrasting color. Or they may be finished with cord welting (*see the chapter on Slipcovers for making cord welting*). Sometimes the edges are scalloped or notched.

Machine Quilting. Any design can be quilted on the sewing machine, but complicated or curving ones are quite difficult to do. Machine quilting in parallel rows can be done very quickly and the rows can be evenly spaced if you have a quilting attachment. This resembles a small bar with a foot which can be adjusted to meas-

Appliqued quilt with floral wreaths and feather rosettes in red, green, and lavendar on a white ground. The pattern is sometimes called "Seek No Further" or "Many Mansions."

ure the distance between the rows. The foot is guided along the preceding row, so that the next row being stitched follows in the same direction an even distance away. The tension on the machine must be quite loose for quilting.

TUFTED QUILTS

The process of tufting consists in drawing yarn through the layers of quilting material and tying it to hold the fabrics together. The tufts are usually spaced so as to form some sort of simple design, or they may be merely spaced at regular intervals. Tufting is a good technique to use when one wants a thicker interlining than the ordinary cotton battings used for quilts, although quilts with cotton battings or paddings made of old blankets can be tufted, too. Wool bats, which are usually too thick to be suitable for the quilting process, can easily be tufted. And, of course, wool batting is much warmer than cotton. Or a fabric interlining filled with down or feathers may be used in a tufted quilt. Great care must be taken to keep the down or feathers evenly distributed during the tufting process.

The lining, padding, and cover for a

tufted quilt are assembled in the same way as those for a quilted quilt. Also, the tufting is preferably done in a quilting frame.

For simple rows of tufts, one can tie strings across the frame both vertically and horizontally. Place the strings an even distance apart. The points of intersection can be used to indicate the places where the tufts should be tied. Or begin at the center and mark radiating lines with chalked string for a sunburst effect. Other design possibilities for tufting are stars, spider webs, circles, and diamonds. Designs cannot be complete with tufting, but simple motifs can be worked out. The distance between the tufts depends upon the thickness and kind of material used for the padding. The tufts must be close enough together to hold the interlining in place, yet not so close as to mat it and lessen its insulating properties. If wool batting is used, about 4 or 5 inches is enough space between the tufts.

A four-ply yarn is good for tufting, although yarns of other thicknesses can also be used. Sometimes the tufting is done with very narrow ribbon—a baby's quilt tufted with ribbon is especially charming.

A double strand yarn is threaded through a needle with a large, round eye. A large eye is important because it forces a hole big enough to pull the yarn or ribbon through. If you push a small-eyed needle through several thicknesses of material, the yarn or ribbon will just stick and refuse to budge. Even if you do manage to pull the yarn through by force, you will strain it and cause it to fray or break. After the yarn or ribbon has been pulled through to the wrong side, the needle is pushed through to the right side again not far from the place where it was inserted (about ¼ of an inch or so). The needle should be pointed straight down or straight up when it is pushed through the fabrics. Pull the yarn or ribbon through until it is approximately 2 inches from the end. Clip the other side of the yarn to match in length, and tie the two ends together with a firm, double knot. Clip again so that both ends are of the same length—from ½ to 1 inch, as a rule. Sometimes the yarn is not clipped until it has been tied, although it is easier to tie if it is first clipped. Ribbon tufts might be finished in small bows after the double knot has been tied.

After the tufting is complete, the quilt is finished in any of the ways suggested for a quilted quilt.

VI

YOUR WALLS & FLOORS

CHAPTER XVII

PAINTING, PAPERING, AND SPECIAL TREATMENTS

"We're grateful just to have four walls around us and a roof over our heads." Well, and so we are! Then we take another look and start wishing that the walls were another color, or weren't quite so dirty. And if only that ugly hole in the plaster weren't quite so conspicuous! What to do about it? Oh, many things! The treatment, of course, depends upon the kind of walls you have, the condition they are in, and how much can be spent, both in time and in work.

The foundation surface of the wall commonly consists of plaster. This can be covered with oil paint, casein paint, calcimine, wallpaper, wallboard, plastic materials, wood or plywood panels—or, as far as that goes — almost any covering material that suits your fancy, even cloth or straw matting. But do think twice before attempting anything too novel. There *are* decorators who will advocate almost anything in an effort to achieve gaiety or whimsy. They say something like this: "Let's indulge in hearts-and-flowers nostalgia! Paint the walls with music staffs entwined with posies and fat, puffy little hearts. It's sweetness and light with sly sophistication!" And perhaps it does bring startled gasps of admiration from guests. But could you live with it, day in and day out? And yet whimsical wall decorations can be delightful — in the right place. For example, they are right in keeping with the spirit of a game room.

Occasionally, one covering material can be successfully applied on top of another. But let's begin with the plaster foundation, because it must be in good condition before paints or wallpaper can be applied.

Cracks and Holes in Plaster. Cracks and small holes can be easily mended with one of the commercial crack fillers of plaster mixes prepared for the purpose. These are usually sold in powder form and must be mixed with water according to the manufacturer's directions. Before applying, clean out any broken plaster around the edges of the hole. Undercut the edge slightly so that a more secure joint can be made with the new plaster. Dampen the edges of the hole and fill it with the new plaster mixture. Press it in firmly with a trowel or spatula so that some plaster is forced between the laths, thereby forming a "key" which helps to hold the new plaster in place when it is dry. Smooth the surface with the trowel or spatula to make the patched area level with the rest of the wall. Wipe off any excess plaster. It must be allowed to dry thoroughly and then sized before any paint, paper, or other material is applied. Wall sizing can be mixed at home, but it is much simpler to use one of the commercial preparations.

Revival of wallpaper is mainly due to excellence of modern designs, sometimes executed by recognized artists.

Sometimes a hole occurs between two laths, so that there is no foundation to support the new plaster. In this case, the hole can either be enlarged slightly until a lath is exposed, or strips of dampened newspaper can be stuffed into the hole to form a temporary support until the plaster has dried. Small nail holes can be filled with putty or plaster of Paris. However, plaster of Paris usually takes only three or four minutes to set, and therefore is suitable for patching only very small areas.

Large cracks generally need to be widened before they can be filled with new plaster. Undercut the edge, dampen it, and then follow the same procedure used for filling holes. For hairline cracks, all that is usually necessary is to mix the plaster quite thin and apply it to the crack with a small brush. Cracks in new plaster should not be repaired until the plaster has had time to settle, which may take anywhere from six months to a year.

Any extensive damage to the plaster should be repaired by a skilled plasterer. The amateur will probably find it difficult to achieve satisfactory results if the damaged area is larger than about 8 or 10 inches in diameter.

FIG. 1. To fill small hole in plastered wall, first undercut edges and moisten.

FIG. 2. Cross-section view showing how edges of plaster should be undercut to give firmer grip to new plaster.

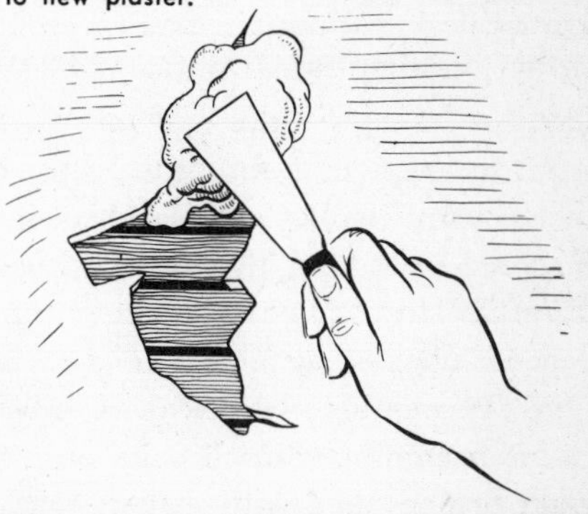

FIG. 3. Plaster mix is pressed between laths with trowel or putty knife. After hole is completely filled, smooth off excess plaster until patched area is level with wall.

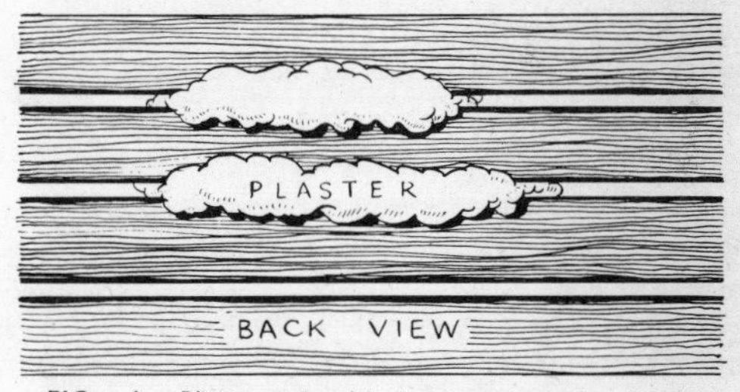

FIG. 4. Plaster should be pressed in firmly enough to squeeze it behind back of laths. When dry, this plaster forms a "key" which holds patched area in place.

PAINTING

Brushes. Good paint jobs require good brushes, and good brushes are expensive. The bristles are firmly set in a rubber or composition base in such a way that it is difficult for them to work loose. Properly cared for, a good brush will last for a long, long time. Cheap brushes shed their bristles easily — and as anyone knows, a trail of bristles does not improve the appearance of a newly painted wall.

The size of the brush should depend upon the job to be done. Naturally, a larger brush can cover more area with fewer strokes than a small one. However, a brush which is so large that its weight causes fatigue in a short space of time may be less of a time and labor saver than a smaller brush. For walls and ceilings, the average person will probably find a 4-inch brush a good choice, although some women prefer a 3½-inch or even a 3-inch brush. Moldings, window sashes, shelf edges or any narrow area can be painted more efficiently with a smaller brush. Of course, it is convenient to have a brush of the right size for every purpose, but if one does not wish to invest too heavily in paint brushes, then perhaps another brush 1½ inches wide will be found adequate for most small areas.

For best results, a brush should always be used for just one purpose, and not dipped into shellac one week, oil paint the next, and so on. It is preferable, too, not to use the same brush to apply both light and dark colors. No matter how carefully a brush is cleaned, some of the pigment may remain in the bristles and mix with the paint the next time the brush is used.

When a paint job has been finished, the brush should be thoroughly cleaned, dried, and carefully stored. The method of cleaning depends upon what the brush has been used in. Turpentine will clean a brush which has been dipped in oil paint or varnish, but brushes used with shellac should be cleaned in alcohol — the kind which is sold in paint or hardware stores for this purpose. After every bit of paint or other material is thoroughly removed, the brush should be washed with soap and warm water and dried. Then wrap the brush in paper and lay it on its side, or hang it up in a cabinet or other place where it will be protected from dust. But never allow the brush to stand on its bristles, or they will become bent. Nor should brushes be exposed to heat or dampness. Never allow paint, varnish, shellac, or other materials to dry out and become hard on any brush. However, if a brush has been mistreated in this way, it can be cleaned with one of the commercial paint solvents sold for this purpose — but it will probably never be quite as good as it was. Brushes used in casein paint can be cleaned with soap and warm water, or according to the manufacturer's directions, but this should be done immediately after using. Calcimine is easily removed with water and a little washing soda, even if it has been allowed to dry on the brush.

Sometimes a paint job cannot be completed at one time, and you may not want to clean and wash a brush which is to be used again the next day on the same job. In that case, a brush used in oil paint or

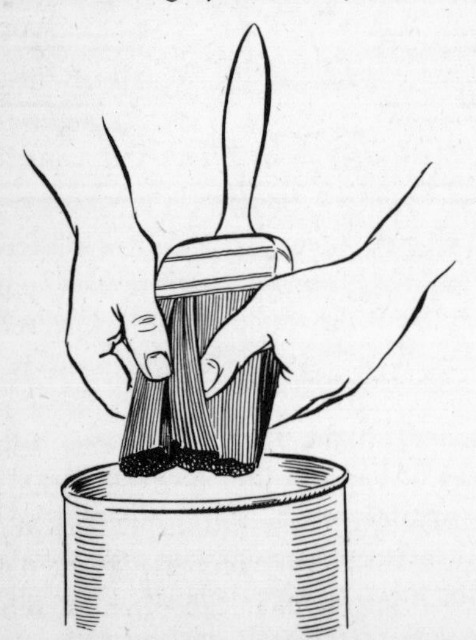

FIG. 5. Clean paint brushes thoroughly after using. Bristles should be worked between fingers to remove pigments.

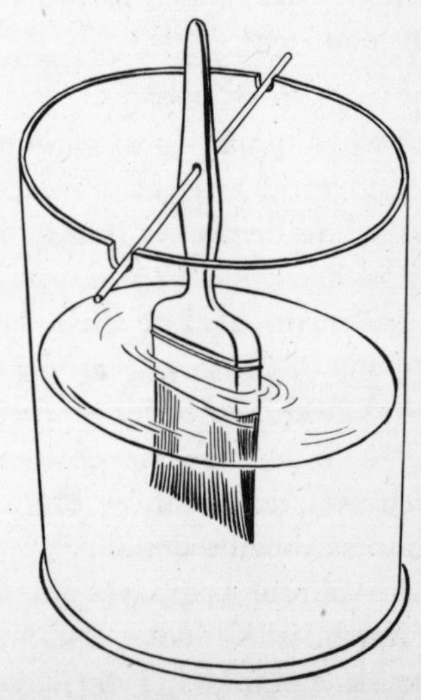

FIG. 6. Store brush for short periods of time by suspending in can filled with enough turpentine to cover bristles.

varnish can be suspended in a can filled with enough turpentine to cover the bristles. But do not rest the brush on its bristles. Instead, drill a small hole through the handle of the brush and hang it on a rod placed across the rim of the can as illustrated. While it is perfectly satisfactory to store brushes in this way for short periods of time, if they are left in turpentine for months, the bristles tend to become too soft. Brushes used in shellac should not be stored in alcohol, but should be cleaned, washed, and dried after every using.

Before using any new brush, twirl it across the palm of the hand to remove any loose bristles. They may be present even in a good brush.

General Hints on Painting. Any type of paint job should be started at the highest part of the area to be covered. If both walls and ceiling are to be decorated, do the ceiling first. This, of course, calls for a good, steady stepladder of the proper height. Protect floors, furniture, and mantels with canvas, old sheets, or newspapers. If window panes, door knobs, and similar exposed surfaces are lightly coated with petroleum jelly before starting to paint, they need only to be wiped afterwards to remove any paint which has been spattered on them accidently. However, if paint has been allowed to harden on unprotected glass or tile, do not attempt to scrape it off with a razor blade without first softening the paint with turpentine or paint remover. Otherwise, the glass or tile may be scratched.

Never overload the brush with paint. It will only run down the handle and probably down your arm as well. In fact, it is better to dip the bristles only an inch or so into the paint, and then give the brush a light tap against the side of the paint container to remove any excess. The proper stroke to use depends upon the type of paint. Casein paints show no brush marks no matter how they are stroked on. Oil paints should be stroked up and down or back and forth to eliminate brush marks.

Protect the hands with cotton gloves or hand creams. And don't forget that paint can spatter on hair if the head is not protected too.

All paints are applied more effectively to clean walls. Washing walls can be every bit as arduous as applying a new coat of paint. But if oil paints are applied to walls which are covered with a film of grease, the paint will not dry thoroughly. Even if no grease is present, dust or dirt mixed with paint will spoil the final effect. But the type of preliminary preparation necessary will depend upon the condition of the wall. Perhaps all that is necessary is a dusting with a piece of cheesecloth or a brush attachment of the vacuum cleaner. But if washing is essential, there are a number of cleaning compounds on the market which are sold under various trade names, and some of them do a most efficient job. Use these according to directions. The active ingredient in many cleaning compounds is trisodium phosphate, which may affect the paint if it is not rinsed off before a new coat is applied.

If old paint has peeled or blistered, it should be removed before new paint is applied. Use one of the paint remover compounds, and after the paint is sufficiently softened, wipe it off, or if necessary, scrape it off with a putty knife or steel wool. Be sure to remove the paint remover with turpentine. Otherwise, new paint will not dry properly. If the damage is not extensive, it can often be repaired by rubbing with sandpaper or steel wool until the peels or blisters have disappeared.

Oil Paints. Such excellent ready-mixed paints are made that it is not worth while to attempt to mix paints at home. However, ready-mixed paints vary in quality. It is wise to buy brands made by reliable manufactruers. Also, ask advice from your paint dealer. Tell him where the paint is to be used, and ask him for a paint which is specifically intended for the purpose. The amount of paint needed depends entirely upon the extent of the surface to be covered and upon the covering qualities of the paint. Again, the best thing to do is to tell your paint dealer the total number of square feet to be covered, and he will be glad to advise you about the amount of paint which is needed to do the job.

Before oil paints are applied to new plaster, it is better to use a primer of some sort. Aluminum paint makes an excellent primer, but glue sizing and shellac are also used. Paint itself serves as the primer on new wood, but the type of paint to be used will depend entirely on what the wood is. Certain woods are more absorbent than others, and no general rule can be given which will apply to all. More turpentine will undoubtedly have to be added to the paint, and sometimes more linseed oil as well. A professional painter can judge the amounts necessary according to the type of wood. But the amateur usually has to experiment a bit until he finds the right proportions. Knots in wood need to be primed with aluminum paint to keep the resin from bleeding through.

It is much simpler to buy paints which are as near to the color wanted as can be obtained than to attempt to mix colors yourself, However, if you are determined to have a color which cannot be found in a ready-mixed paint, then you can ask your paint dealer to give you the necessary pigments and do your own mixing. Color mixing is something that not all professional painters can do really well. Therefore, you had better fortify youself with enough patience to experiment until you find the color you want. You may achieve it without too much difficulty, and then again you may have to work at it for some time. Pigments can be combined in endless ways, and since only you can determine whether the desired color has been attained, no exact mixing recipes can be given. The pigments may be bought dry if you wish, or in tubes mixed with oil (the oil colors used by artists), which are easier to work with. Some of the principal kinds are:

Cadmium (obtainable in various hues from lemon yellow to red orange)
Chrome Yellow (brilliant yellow with slight reddish tinge)
Raw Sienna (brownish yellow)
Burnt Sienna (reddish brown)
Cobalt (deep blue)
Ultramarine (bright blue, usually with purplish tinge)
Emerald or Paris Green (brilliant green)
Chrome Green (yellowish green)
Vermilion (bright red)
Venetian Red (brownish red)
Raw Umber (earthy brown)
Burnt Umber (dark brown, slight reddish tinge)

Perhaps the best way is to select a paint as near in color as possible to the color you wish, but lighter in value. Experiment with a small quantity, making a note of the pigments added, until you find the color you want. Lighter tints are obtained by adding more white; darker values by adding more pigments. Grayed values result when complementary colors are mixed (*see chapter on Color Schemes*). Do not darken the value of a color by adding black, as it gives a dirty look to the tone and is apt to result in streaking when the paint is dry. When mixing paint, stir it very thoroughly and

Painted wall decorations are amusing conceit for bar end of playroom if done with imagination and skill.

continue to stir frequently during application, as the pigments have a tendency to settle to the bottom.

Be sure to mix enough paint for the entire job; otherwise you will undoubtedly have a difficult time trying to match two separate mixes. Remember, too, that some paints are darker and some lighter when dry than when wet. Also, paints appear different on different surfaces. Therefore, test your mix on the actual surface to be covered and let it dry before appraising the results.

Oil paints are made in both glossy and dull, or flat, finishes, as well as in finishes intermediate between glossy and flat. Glossy paints are somewhat easier to wash, and therefore are often preferred for bathroom or kitchen walls. But aside from this, the choice is largely a matter of personal taste. Flat paints are softer in appearance and have no objectionable glare. High quality oil paints give a good, durable wall finish and are widely used, but many people now prefer the less expensive, more easily applied casein paints. For woodwork, however, it is better to use the oil paints or enamel.

Oil paints should not be applied on top of wallpaper, casein paints, or calcimine. Such materials must first be removed.

The number of coats needed for a satisfactory finish may be one, two, or three. If a light color is being applied over a darker one, at least two coats are usually required. But if a light color is being applied on top of the same color, one coat may do the job. New walls or woodwork generally need three coats. A better finish can usually be achieved by applying two coats of fairly thin paint than one thick coat. Any coat must be thoroughly dried before another is applied.

Before using, oil paints should be thoroughly stirred and mixed until they are entirely free from lumps and all the pigment is evenly distributed. Then pour a small quantity of the paint into another container, and refill this as the paint is used, always stirring the paint again first. Leftover paints should be stored in containers to fit the quantity, as empty spaces in cans contain air which forms a crust or skin on the paint. Seal the container tightly so that air cannot enter.

Casein Paints. "Water Paints" once meant calcimine, no matter what it was called. But modern casein paints, although mixed with water, are entirely different from and far superior to calcimine. They are easy to mix and to apply, and they dry without showing brush marks. One coat is usually sufficient to cover. Casein paints can be applied on top of oil paint or wallpaper. But before using it on wallpaper, it is well to remember that it makes the paper considerably more difficult to remove later on.

These paints come either in powder or paste form, both of which must be mixed with water according to directions. Be sure to stir them thoroughly until all lumps have disappeared. The paint may be applied with a large calcimine brush, a 3-inch or 4-inch brush, or with a roller made for the purpose. As the paint dries it tends to streak and mottle in weird effects which may cause alarm. These, however, disappear entirely when the paint is finally dry. Drying usually requires no more than two hours.

The number of colors available in some casein paints is fairly limited. They can, however, be mixed with dry pigments to obtain other colors. But the difficulties of mixing your own colors will be the same as those described under oil paints.

Some casein paints can be washed as well as oil paint. But casein paint is so easy to apply that a new coat can be put on with less effort than it would take to wash the entire wall. If the paint is being applied to new plaster, follow the manufacturer's directions as to the need for a priming coat and what it should consist of.

Calcimine is as easy to mix and apply as casein paint. However, it lacks the same adhesive quality, and in damp places it tends to flake and drop off. Furthermore, it cannot be washed, as washing simply removes it. Its use offers little advantage over casein paint as far as price is concerned. If a new coat of calcimine is to be applied, the old coat must first be removed with water and washing soda (about 2 tablespoonsful of soda to every 3 quarts of water) and a cloth. The best way to apply is to use a large calcimine brush, but since this is rather expensive, any fairly large brush will do.

Varnish is sometimes used to finish woodwork, although it is much less popular for this purpose than it used to be. Decorators now usually paint the woodwork to match the walls, or else combine white painted woodwork with colored walls.

Varnish is not too easy to apply really well. It often tends to dry with a speckled effect, especially if it is cold. Therefore, it should be warmed slightly before applying. Also, stirring creates air bubbles in the varnish which may be locked in as the varnish dries. In fact, in order to achieve a smooth finish, the air should be as free of dust as possible when the varnish is applied.

Enamel, because it dries to a harder finish, is often preferred to paint for woodwork. Generally three coats are required, or four if the wood is new. The first two or three coats must be mixed with an undercoater, usually half and half, but the best procedure is to follow the manufacturer's directions. The final coat should be pure enamel. Flow it on, moving the brush smoothly and slowly. Enamel cannot be brushed on as quickly or easily as paint. Allow each coat to dry for at least two days before applying the next one, unless the instructions on the can specifically state otherwise. A smoother finish is obtained if each coat is lightly sanded before the next is applied.

WALLPAPER

With a little patience, almost anyone can learn to hang paper on walls with satisfactory results. The chief difficulties encountered by the amateur are matching designs and hanging the paper straight. However, one can master the trick of both these steps with practice. Ceilings are another matter. In order to paste a strip of wallpaper on the ceiling in one length, one needs some sort of support or scaffolding to make it possible to reach the ceiling from one end to the other. The unpasted portion of the strip needs support, too, while one is busy smoothing out the rest of it with both hands. Therefore, it is not advisable for the amateur to attempt to paper a ceiling. Instead, it is much better to use a matching or contrasting paint — preferably casein paint, although calcimine is also used, and both are easier to apply than oil paint. This should be done before papering the walls. If the woodwork is to be refinished, that should be done first also.

Choosing the Wallpaper. Design, of course, is the primary consideration in choosing any wallpaper. But quality is important, too. Cheap, thin wallpapers are more apt to tear while wet than papers with more body. On the other hand, some very heavy papers may be quite porous and when wet may be difficult to handle. Cost may not always be an index to the quality of the paper, although good papers are never the cheapest. Some papers are washable. Others are not. When selecting wallpaper, it is always advisable to go to a reliable merchant and ask his advice.

In addition to the regular wallpapers, one can also buy papers which are ready pasted and need only to be dampened according to directions and hung on the wall. They save the bother of mixing and applying paste, but otherwise they are no easier to hang than any other wallpaper.

Estimating Amounts Needed. Wallpapers come in rolls, many of which are 20 feet long and 22 inches wide, or 21 inches after trimming. However, they also come in widths of 18 and 32 inches, and sometimes in other widths and lengths. Some rolls are double and others are single.

To estimate the amount of paper needed, first measure the distance around the walls of the room. Then measure the width of all doors and windows as well as the fireplace, if any, and subtract half this total from the first measurement. Let us say, for example, that the answer amounts to 38 feet, or 456 inches. If we use wallpaper which is 21 inches wide when trimmed, then we must divide 456 inches by 21 inches to find out how many strips are needed. The number, we find, is 22. Let us say that the ceiling is 8 feet high, and that we have selected a paper which comes in single rolls, 20 feet long. That means that we could only cut two whole strips from each roll. Therefore, we would need at least 11 rolls of paper, and it is advisable to allow an extra roll or so for waste or damage in cutting. Since we are cutting only two strips from each roll, we have enough extra to allow for any matching of design in a figured paper. But if you use rolls of another length, be sure to allow for matching. Of course, it is possible to piece a strip in the middle, but the result looks so untidy that the saving is not worth it.

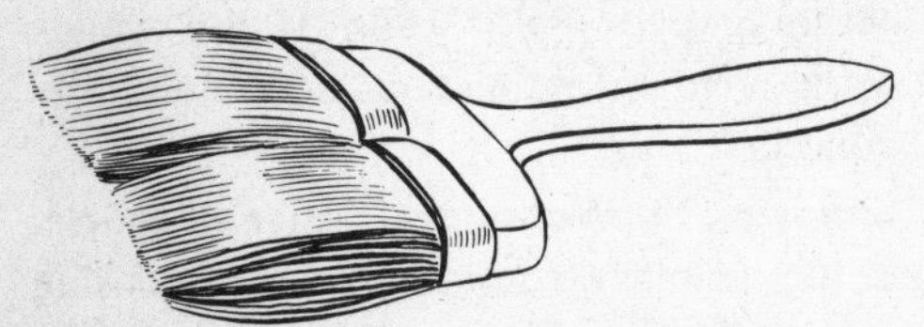

FIG. 7. Paperhanger's brush for pasting wallpaper. If not available, use any large brush.

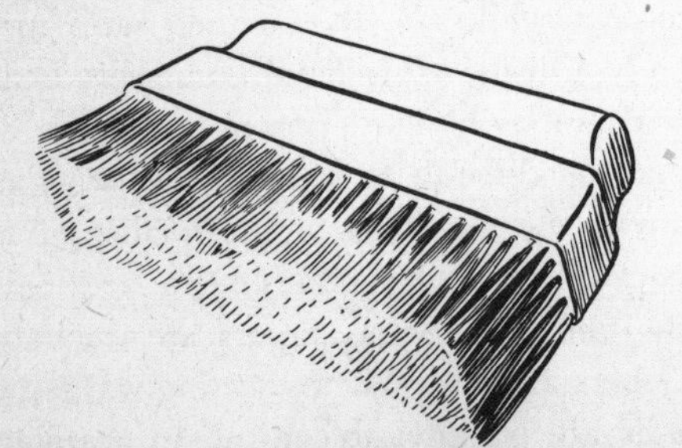

FIG. 8. Paperhanger's brush for smoothing paper on wall.

Tools and Supplies Needed. First, one must have a working surface large enough to lay out the entire strip of paper — or at least most of it. A table, cutting board, a piece of wallboard on a table, or two wide boards supported on trestles will do. Professional paper hangers do not cover the surface with oilcloth — but the average woman will find it a great help because it makes it so easy to wipe any excess paste left from one strip before laying down the next.

Other necessary equipment includes a pair of scissors (large ones cut quicker), a yardstick, and a pencil — all of which you will probably have around the house. In addition, you will need a wallpaper paste brush (although a good sized paint brush will do if necessary), a paperhanger's brush for smoothing out the paper after it is on the wall, a narrow roller for pressing the edges flat, and a plumb line which can be made by tying a weight to a piece of string.

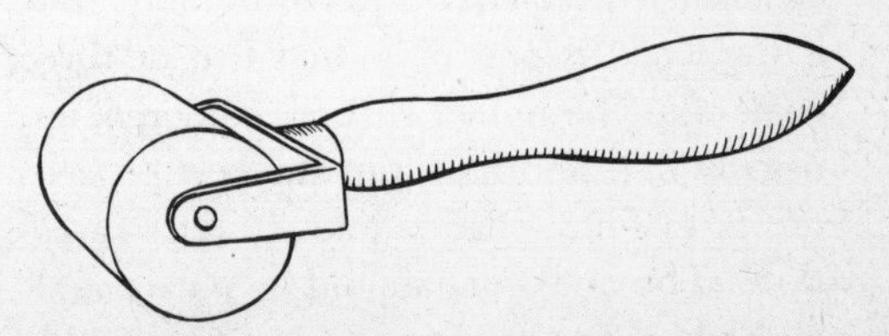

FIG. 9. Small roller for pressing down edges of wallpaper.

Of course, a stepladder is essential, and you also ought to have a supply of clean rags and some kind of a container for the paste.

It's possible to mix your own wallpaper paste, but scarcely worth the trouble because the ready mixed pastes are probably much better than those you would be able to make. Usually, these need only the addition of water, but be sure to follow the manufacturer's directions.

Preparing the Walls. If, in addition to papering the walls, you plan to redecorate the ceiling and the woodwork, the best procedure is first to prepare the walls, if any extensive preparation is necessary. Next, do the ceiling, then the woodwork, and finally hang the paper.

If the walls are covered with calcimine, it will have to be washed off (*see paragraph on Calcimine in this chapter*). After that, a coat of sizing must be applied. Painted walls should be cleaned if they are dirty or greasy, and if the paint is glossy or very smooth, the surface should be roughened with sandpaper. Then apply a coat of sizing. Some casein paints dry hard enough so that they can be treated like oil paints. However, it might be well to ask the advice of your paint dealer if you know which paint was used. If not, wash the wall vigorously with warm water. If the paint tends to dissolve easily, it had better be removed completely before papering.

New plaster sometimes needs at least one coat of size, but usually two are better. If the wall is already covered with paper, it is usually better to remove it instead of putting on another layer. However, this may not be necessary if the wall has only one application of paper and if it adheres firmly and smoothly. The surface need not be sized, but only roughened a bit with sandpaper.

To remove wallpaper, you will need a scraper, a paste brush (or other large brush), and a bucket of hot water. Apply the water to the paper with the brush, beginning at the lower part of the wall and working upward. Be careful not to apply too much water at once. It is better to dampen the paper slowly with several applications. Neither should you dampen all the walls in the room at one time. Instead, soak one section, then another, go back to the first, and so on, until the paper starts to loosen. Then begin near the ceiling and pull the paper off in as large strips as possible. If it sticks at points, use the scraper and more hot water. Some waterproof wallpapers may prove very difficult to remove with hot water. But special preparations are made to penetrate and loosen them.

Removing old paper can be more difficult and take more time than hanging new paper. But the job must be done thoroughly if the new paper is to adhere smoothly. After every bit of paper is off, it is best to apply a new coat of sizing.

Trimming and Cutting the Paper. Most wallpapers have edges left unprinted, and one of these must be cut off. You may have this done by the paper dealer for a small charge, or you may do it yourself. Some papers do not need trimming. Professional paperhangers often trim both edges, and match the strips together without any overlapping. But this is usually rather difficult for the amateur to accomplish. If you decide to trim the paper yourself, simply open the roll, trim one edge with one hand and reroll the paper at the same time with the other. Be sure to trim the same edge on all rolls. After trimming, roll out one strip on your table or other working surface. Measure off a distance to correspond to the height of the wall, from the baseboard to the molding, if there is one,

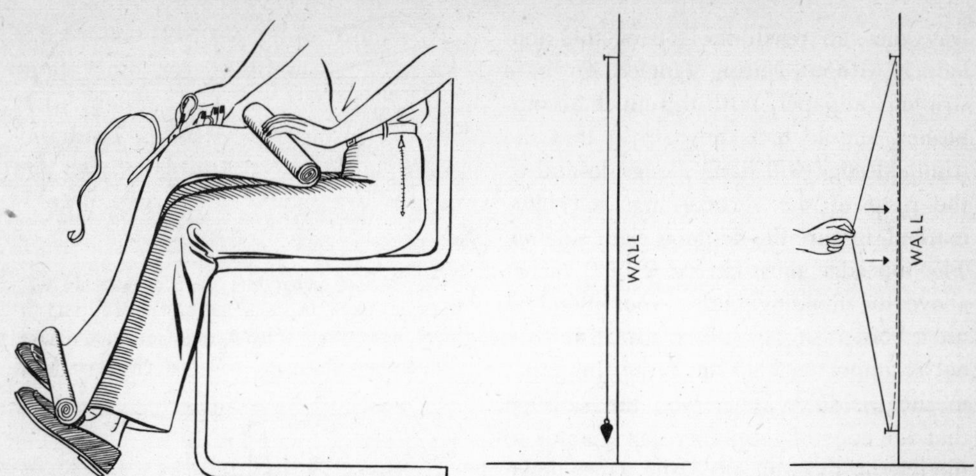

FIG. 10. Trim edge of wallpaper with roll resting on feet. Reroll with other hand.

FIG. 11. Plumb line made of weight tied to string indicates true vertical. Chalk string, fasten it taut, and snap against wall to mark position.

plus an additional 5 or 6 inches. Cut this off at right angles to the edges of the strip. If the paper is patterned, place the strip face up, and then measure off another strip, also face up, but not yet cut from the roll. Place the second strip alongside the first one, and move it up until the pattern matches the first strip. Measure the extra distance which must be allowed for matching. This measurement must be added to all the other strips. For plain papers, no allowance for matching need be made. It is simpler to cut all strips at once before beginning to paste, but not necessary. If you prefer, cut one strip, paste and hang it, and then proceed to the next.

Pasting and Hanging. Before you begin to paste, decide where to hang the first strip. It is better to begin in the least conspicuous place in the room, or next to the edge of a door, because by the time you have gone all around the room you will find that the final strip will not match the pattern of the first one except by accident.

Wherever you decide to begin, place the plumb line so that it hangs along the line where the left edge of the first strip will be placed. Do this even if you begin at the edge of the door, because door frames are not always in a true vertical position, and the wallpaper strips must be. When the plumb line hangs absolutely still, it indicates the true vertical line. Mark this on the wall, either by using the yardstick, or by chalking the cord of the plumb line and snapping it against the wall while holding the weighted end so that the cord is taut. Next, place the stepladder in a position where you can reach the top of the wall at this point.

Now place the first strip of paper face down on the working surface, with one end hanging over the edge of the table if necessary. Apply the paste smoothly so that the paper is evenly dampened. Work from the middle towards the outer edges. If you lift the edges you can apply the paste to them without getting it on the table. Above all, do not allow any paste to get smeared on the surface of the paper.

After pasting more than half the strip, fold the pasted section in half as illustrated, but do not crease the fold. Then move the strip along the table, paste it, and fold the rest of it in half. Very long strips may need to be folded accordion fashion. Place the paper over your left arm so that the folds hang on each side. In this way you can reach the top of the stepladder without getting tangled up in a strip of wallpaper. With this much accomplished, unfold half the strip so that the trimmed edge will hang alongside and to the right of the vertical line you have marked. Be sure the design is right side up. The top edge must extend 2 or 3 inches above the molding, unless you intend to use a border, in which case a neat finish is not so important. Do not paste the paper to the molding. When you are satisfied that the edge of the paper corresponds to the line on the wall, press the paper down along the top. If you find you have not placed it quite accurately, do not worry, because you can remove it with a gentle pull and start over again. Now, with the paperhanger's brush, begin to smooth the paper out and press it down, working downward and away from the edge matching the line on the wall, until you begin to approach the half which is still folded. Next, gently pull this folded section free, and continue brushing the strip in place. If small wrinkles occur, just pull the strip away from the wall to get rid of them, and then brush it back in place again. After the strip is smoothly in place, run the pointed end of a scissors blade across the paper where it meets the baseboard. Pull an inch or so of the paper away from the wall and cut along the mark made by the scissors. Then press the paper back in place again and run the roller along the edge. Do the same thing along the top molding.

The second strip is pasted and folded in the same way as the first. The trimmed edge is placed so that it will overlap the untrimmed edge of the first strip, but while adjusting the strip in place be very careful that no part of the pasted area touches the surface of the first strip. Move the second strip up or down until the pattern matches with that of the first strip. When the second strip is in place, brush it down and trim it as you did the first. Make a firm joint where the edges overlap by pressing them together with the roller. If any paste squeezes out onto the roller, wipe it off before proceeding. Then continue hanging the other strips. Eventually, of course, you will encounter a corner, a door or window frame, or possibly a light switch.

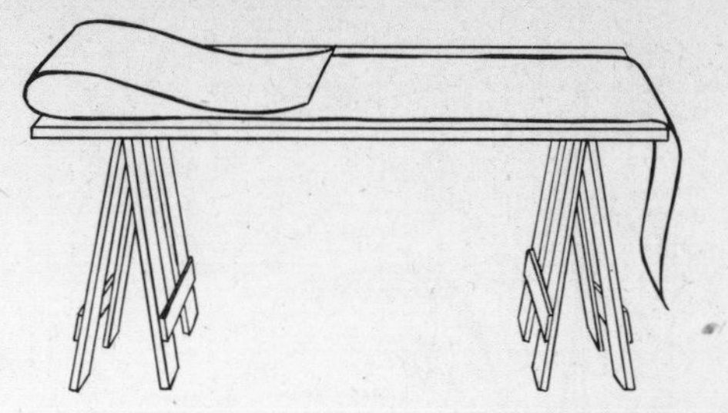

FIG. 12. Lay paper face down on working surface to paste. As one end is pasted, fold it back upon itself without creasing. Slide paper along table and paste and fold the other half.

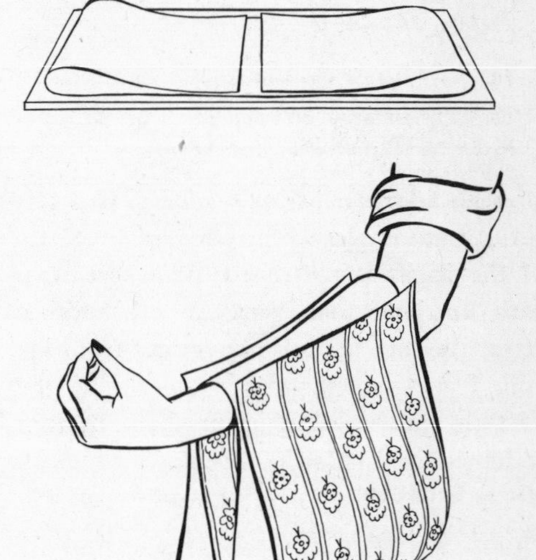

FIG. 13. Place pasted and folded strip over arm while climbing stepladder to reach top of wall.

A strip of wallpaper can be fitted into a corner in one of two ways. The strip may be split into two sections, so that one section fits on one side and the second section

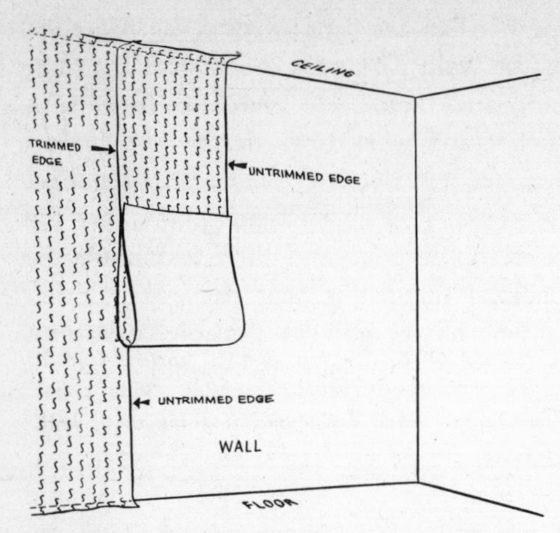

FIG. 14. Unfold top half of strip and place in position. Aline left edge with vertical chalk mark or with right edge of preceding strip. Match design accurately and be careful not to mark preceding strip with paste from following one.

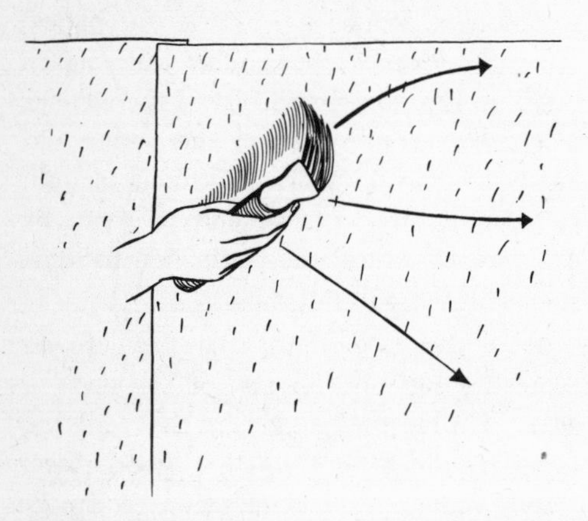

FIG. 15. When strip is correctly placed, brush down smoothly with wallpaper brush, stroking from alined edge outward.

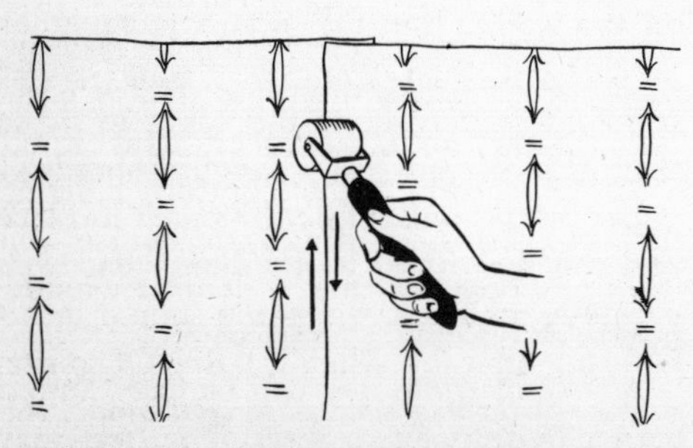

FIG. 16. Overlapping edges of strips must be pressed down firmly with small roller. If paste oozes out, clean roller before continuing.

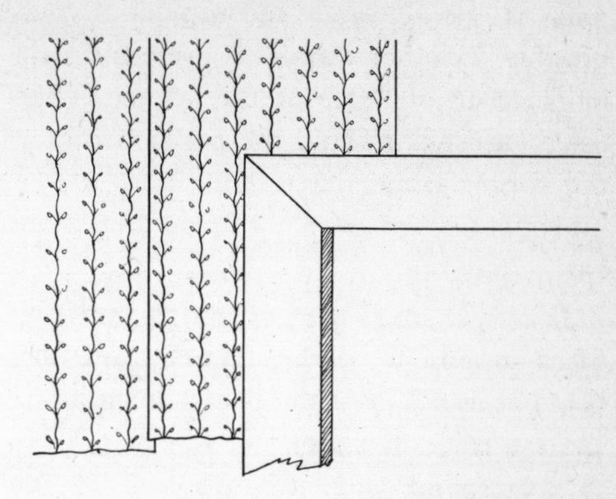

FIG. 17. Wallpaper may be fitted around door or window by cutting strip to correspond to shape of opening or by dividing strip where it meets edge of frame. Two sections are then fitted together carefully without overlapping edges.

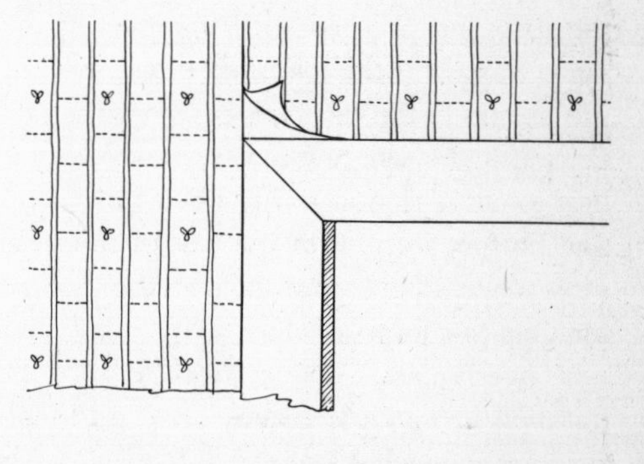

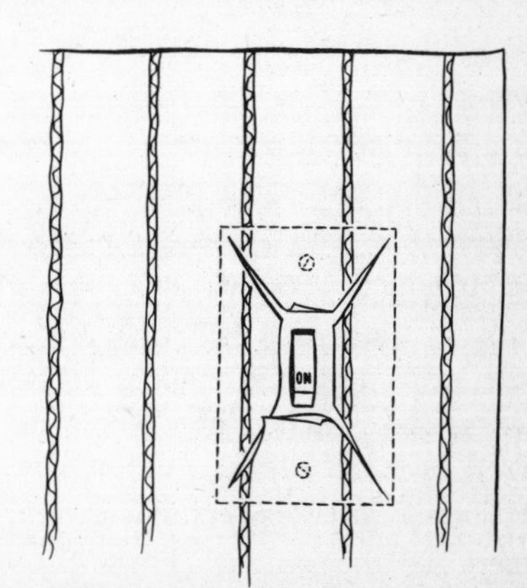

FIG. 18. To paper around light switch, place paper in position, but do not press down. Cut opening directly over switch and slash paper to corners. Press paper into place and trim edges around switch with razor blade.

on the other side, making the two pieces join as closely and inconspicuously as possible. Another way is to press the strip in place on one side of the corner. Then use a yardstick to hold the paper firmly in the corner while the rest of it is pressed into place. Two people can do this more easily than one.

If only a small part of a strip must be fitted around a window frame, you may begin as usual. Press the paper down along the top edge, and then cut the strip away to correspond with the top half of the frame, leaving a margin for trimming. Notch the paper where it meets the corner of the frame. Press the upper half in place. Trim the edge around the top of the frame. Then cut out the lower section of the strip and proceed with this part in the same way. Roll the trimmed edges around the frame. If the distance between the last strip and the window is very narrow, it is best to cut a section to fit. Then fit the top and bottom sections of the rest of the strip into place above and below the frame, making the joint as close as possible, but not overlapping. Door frames can be handled in much the same way, although they are somewhat simpler, since the paper need be fitted only around the top of the frame.

If a light switch is encountered near the edge of the paper, it presents no great problem. The paper is simply notched and then trimmed around the edge of the switch. If the switch comes in the middle of the strip, paste the strip in place as far down as the switch. Then pierce the strip directly over the switch, and cut four diagonal slashes just long enough to reach the corners of the switch. Press the paper down and trim around the edges with a razor blade. For a round switch, cut a series of slashes like pie sections.

Borders. Sometimes decorative or contrasting borders are used around the top edge of the wall. To apply these, trim if necessary, and then paste and fold. Start at a corner and work towards the left (unless you are left handed). If the border must be pieced in a conspicuous place, tear the overlapping edge and then tear away the back of the paper near the edge so that it will be as thin as possible, and thus nearly invisible when it is pasted down.

Cleaning and Patching. Washable wallpapers can be cleaned with lukewarm water and soap, or sometimes with a mild solution of cleaning compound, *if* the instructions on the package state that it is safe for wallpaper. Wallpaper which is not waterproof can sometimes be cleaned with a special composition which is kneaded like dough. Wipe this across the paper, folding it over each time as the surface takes up the dirt. Small bits of the cleaner will crumble and stick to the paper and must be removed with a clean, dry cloth. Certain textures are difficult to clean by this process, so test the paper first in some spot where it will not show.

It is always wise to save any leftover paper for patching in case of any tears or scars. Unless the paper on the wall has faded considerably (which a good paper should not do), the damaged area can be patched so that it does not show too much. Select a section of the new paper from which the design can be matched to that on the wall. From this tear a rectangular patch, and then tear away some paper from the underside of the edges to make them thin. Remove any dangling shreds of paper on the wall. Paste the patch in place and roll the edges. If the design has been carefully matched, the patch should be almost unnoticeable when it is dry. Of course, if the plaster has been damaged too, it will have to be mended and sized before the patch can be put in place.

OTHER FINISHES

Besides the familiar finishes of paint and wallpaper, one can also use any of the numerous other materials available for covering walls. These are so varied, both in kind and in cost, that no detailed description of all could be attempted here. Among them are tile, wallboard, plywood, cork, photomurals, fabric, leather, wall linoleums, metal, thin layers of wood mounted on fabric or metal, glass, mirror, and many different plastic materials. Some are rigid and some are flexible. Some are no more expensive to use than wallpaper and others are strictly in the luxury class. Many materials require installation by skilled workmen, but some can be applied by the average home craftsman without too much difficulty. Certainly, however, if one intends to use anything fairly costly, it would be poor economy to install it oneself without any previous experience.

Wall linoleum is especially suitable for use in a bathroom or kitchen. It is strong and durable, easy to clean, and impervious to water and many stains. It may be fitted around curved surfaces and inset with designs the same as floor linoleums. The proper installation of wall linoleum, however, is a job which had better be left to a skilled workman.

Photomurals offer extremely interesting possibilities for decoration, especially in modern interiors. Those who make a hobby of photography may even have pictures of their own which are suitable for enlargement. Some commercial photographers are equipped to do this work, but the cost is relatively expensive. Most photomurals are too large to do in one piece. Instead, they are enlarged on strips of paper, usually three feet wide, and in a length to correspond to the height of the wall. This work must be done very carefully, so that the strips will match accurately when they are on the wall. They may then be applied like wallpaper, and anyone who can apply that successfully will probably be able to apply photomurals.

Fabric is often used to cover walls, and some interesting decorative effects can be worked out in this way. Sometimes the fabric used for slipcovers or a bedspread is repeated in a panel or on one wall — seldom, however, on all walls. The best fabrics to use in this way are chintz, cretonne, linen, canvas, burlap, or gingham. Fabrics coated with synthetic materials are also used. Most silks and rayons are too difficult to apply directly to the wall and have to be mounted on wood backing. Heavy brocades, however, require no backing, but the use of such materials on walls is suitable only in the most formal period rooms.

The process of applying fabric to walls resembles that of hanging wallpaper, except that a waterproof paste must be used. Some fabrics are mounted on paper backing and may be applied with wallpaper paste.

Wallboard is a rigid composition material which comes in panels 4 feet wide and 8, 10, or 12 feet long and can be cut to order if necessary. There are two principal types. One is a porous, sound absorbing insulating board and the other is a hard surfaced wood composition. Wallboard is often used in unfinished attics, in which case it is simply nailed directly to the wall studs. But it may also be applied over plaster if the nails are driven through the plaster to the studs. In standard wood construction, wall studs are usually located 16 inches apart from center to center, but sometimes they are 12 inches apart. They may be found by examining the baseboard to see where the nails are driven, or by tapping the wall. A tap between the studs reverberates slightly, but one directly over a stud has a dull sound. A 4-foot wallboard,

Plywood panels of oak molded by patented process into striated texture are cut in squares and set with grain running in alternating directions. End wall is of plain oak plywood. Miracle of modern plywood brings beauty of wood-paneled walls within reach of modest budgets.

therefore, must be nailed to every third or fourth stud. Finishing nails are used and a nail set is needed to drive them level with the surface of the wallboard. Wallboard is often used in this way to resurface a poor job of plastering at a cheaper cost than complete replastering. After the wallboard is in place, it can be painted or papered in the usual way. One disadvantage of wallboard is that the joints are frankly visible. However, they are often treated as part of the decorative scheme, instead of being masked, although they can be filled with compositions made for the purpose.

Plywood paneling is available in almost every kind of wood ever used — from the finest hardwoods to common utility woods. Wood-paneled walls have always been greatly admired, yet the cost of solid wood panels was so prohibitive that few people could afford them. But plywood paneling makes it possible to have such walls at moderate cost, and it is not too difficult to install by anyone who can saw evenly and pound a nail in straight. The cost depends upon the type of wood selected. The fine hardwoods, such as oak, mahogany, and walnut, cost more than the utility wood panels, which are usually used for structural work in place of plaster, and may be painted or papered. However, while fine plywood paneling is vastly less expensive than solid wood paneling, it is by no means one of the cheapest wall finishes. Sometimes the panels are used only on one wall, since the wood combines very well with both painted and papered surfaces.

Perhaps the most widely used size of panel is that which is 4 feet wide, 6, 7, or 8 feet in length and from ¼ to ¾ of an inch thick. These panels may be applied directly to the studs in new construction or as a finishing material in an attic, or they

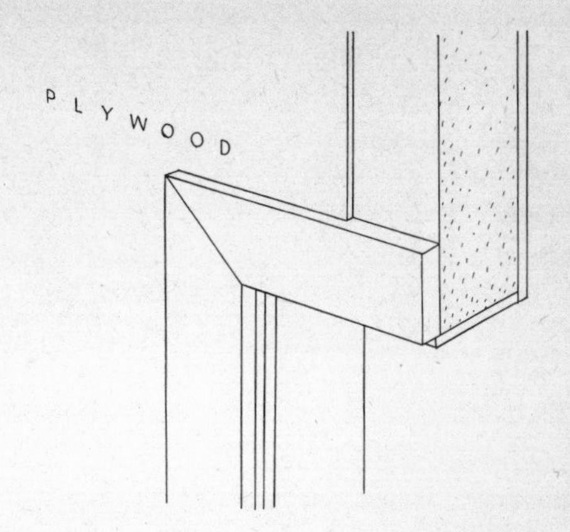

FIG. 20. For installation around door or window, saw plywood paneling to fit shape of frame. Careful measurements are necessary to insure accurate fit.

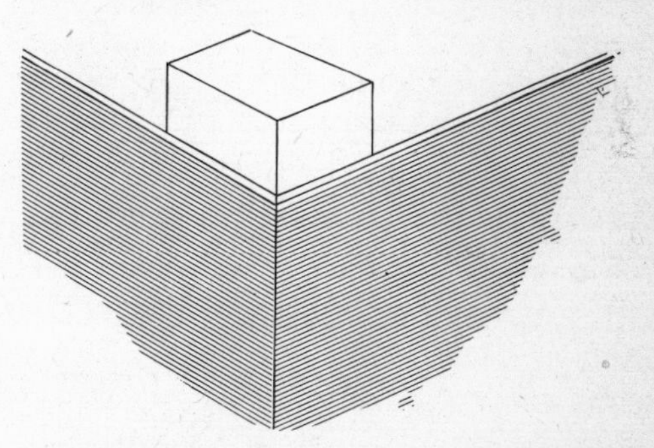

FIG. 21. To fit plywood panels around corners, edges may be planed at an angle for smooth joint or left square for open joint.

FIG. 19. Plywood panels may be installed over old plaster walls if furring strips of plywood are first nailed to wall studs. Panels are then attached to furring strips with finishing nails.

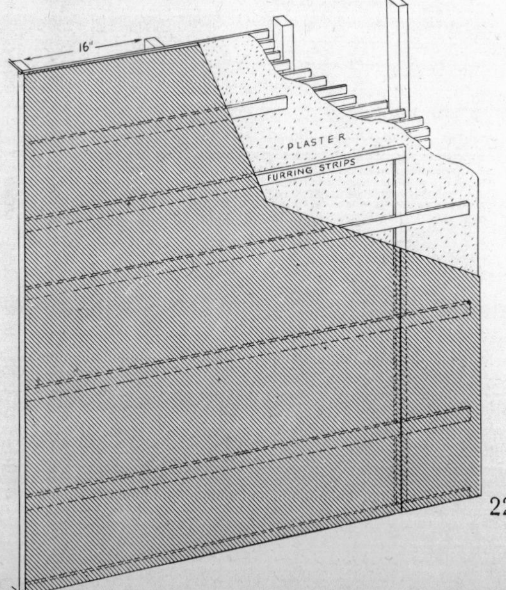

Modern bedroom with walls of mahogany and plywood panels made with grooved edges to give effect of planks.

may be applied on top of plaster walls, in which case the ¼-inch thick panels are usually selected.

Plywood panels can be applied successfully over old walls only if the framing of the house is straight and true, and it should be carefully tested first with a plumb line. To apply plywood over plaster, a framework of furring strips must first be constructed. The best material to use for this purpose is fir plywood strips 2 inches wide and ¼-inch thick, which come in 4-foot lengths. The strips are placed horizontally and nailed to the studs through the plaster with 8d box nails. (*To locate studs, see the paragraph above on Wallboard*). Vertical furring strips are fitted in wherever necessary to provide a nailing surface behind the edges of the plywood panels. A panel 8 feet high requires about four horizontal rows of furring strips placed as illustrated. Then nail the panels to the strip, using a 4d finishing nail for a panel ¼-inch wide, and spacing the nails about 6 inches apart along the outer edges. Force the panels together as tightly as possible. Sink the nail heads with a nail set, and fill the holes with a wood filler or putty. Corners may be fitted together with butt or beveled joints, or with any of several types of corner moldings.

There are several methods of fitting the paneling over or around door and window frames, but perhaps the simplest method is to cut it carefully to correspond to the shape of the frame. The appearance of your present woodwork should be taken into consideration before combining it with wood paneling. Cheap woodwork and fine wood paneling will look out of place together. Perhaps it may be better to have the woodwork removed entirely, and then install the paneling to fit around the windows without trim, which is now done in so many modern interiors. A job of this kind, however, will probably call for professional skill.

After the panels are installed, they should be finished with special finishing lacquer and wax, or they may be bought already finished if you prefer.

Many interesting treatments are possible in plywood paneling. It may be placed horizontally as well as vertically. Or it may be cut in squares which are spaced apart over recessed joints. It also comes in interesting textured effects which can be cut and combined checkerboard fashion, either straight or diagonally. Panels 16 inches wide are also available which have grooved edges. The grooves are slipped into each other and give the effect of planks. These panels are very easy to install over plaster walls because they do not require the use of furring strips. Instead, a special adhesive is used on the back. Nails are applied invisibly through the grooved edges and at top and bottom.

CHAPTER XVIII

REFINISHING FLOORS

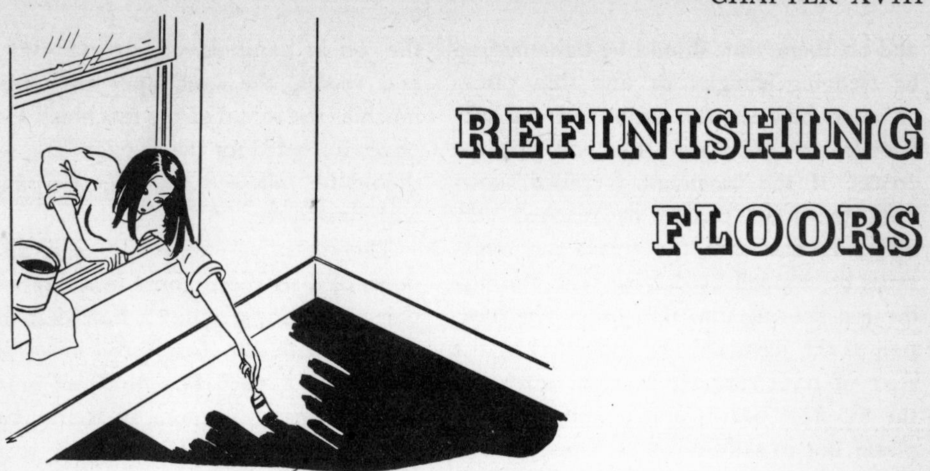

SOME people prefer gleaming, beautifully finished, fine hardwood floors to any type of floor covering, while others feel that they look rather cold and barren. Scatter rugs placed on the areas which receive the heaviest traffic will not only relieve the bare appearance of a wood floor but will also help to protect it. Never lay a scatter rug directly on a polished floor, however, unless you want someone to skid and break his neck. Instead, place scatter rugs on top of rug cushions or anchor them with one of the non-skid devices.

Softwood floors or hardwood floors with no peculiar claim to beauty had better be painted, if more expensive treatments are out of the question. The floors may even be decorated with an allover painted pattern, if that appeals to you. Or perhaps you have a painted floor now, and want to restore its original fine, hardwood finish.

None of these floor refinishing jobs require any great amount of skill, but they do call for much labor—a great deal of it in some cases.

The necessity for removing existing finishes before applying others depends upon what the present one is and what you intend to apply. Paint, shellac, varnish, or stain should never be applied on top of wax. The wax must first be removed. A new wax-removing compound has appeared which has only to be applied with a cloth or mop, left for about three to five minutes, and wiped up. The floor is then rinsed. Paint may be applied on top of paint, varnish, or shellac if they are free of wax. Clear shellac and varnish are also applied sometimes on top of paint as protective coatings. But in order to restore a painted floor to its natural wood finish, it must be completely sanded. Sometimes sanding is also necessary before scuffed shellacked or varnished floors can be refinished.

Loose Boards and Creaking Floors. Good top flooring is usually made of tongue-and-groove floor boards. The "tongue" on the edge of one board fits into a groove on the edge of the next so that it is very difficult for one board to work apart from another. What does sometimes happen is that the boards may become loosened from the subflooring, or the subflooring may not rest firmly on the floor joists. Sometimes first-floor joists are left exposed in the basement, so that someone standing there may observe the subflooring while another person walks around on the first floor. If any of the subfloor boards move up and down a bit as the person above steps on and off them, they should be tightened up by wedging shingles or any thin pieces of wood between the joists and the subfloor boards. As a rule, this will stop the creaks. If the basement is ceiled, however, the joists cannot be reached very easily. In that case, the creaks can sometimes be stopped by driving nails through the top flooring into the joists. The location of the joists may be indicated by the rows of nails running at right angles to the top floor boards and holding them in place. But in skillfully laid floors, no evidence of nailing may be visible. Tapping on the floor with a hammer may reveal the joists. The taps usually reverberate with a hollow sound between the joists and with a dull sound over the joists. The hammer head should be covered with a piece of cloth to avoid damage to the wood. As a rule, joists in standard construction are 16 inches apart from center to center.

After the joists have been located, the nails should be driven in at an angle, one on each side. Use 2-inch finishing nails, and sink them below the surface of the wood with a nail set. Fill the depression with putty. Scrape off the excess and smooth with sandpaper after the putty has hardened. Cracks may be filled in the same way.

Sanding a Wood Floor. The job of sanding a floor is quite simple if you use a pair of electric sanding machines. In many communities, such machines may be hired by the day for a fee which is only a small fraction of what a job of sanding would cost if done by a contractor. The machines should be rented in pairs because a big one is needed for the main area of the floor and a little one for the edges around the baseboards, under the radiators, and so on. When you rent the machines, also buy enough sandpaper to fit them to do the job at hand. If you are sanding several rooms, the sandpaper may cost as much as the rental of the machines. Coarse paper is needed for the first sanding, which should be followed by a second sanding with fine paper.

Theoretically, one could sand all the floors of a six-room house in a day with a pair of sanding machines. But what would you do with the furniture—move it all out of the house? The furniture must be removed from the room, of course, before you begin to sand. However, if you are sanding only the edges of the floor, it is a simple matter to move the furniture to the center of the room.

If the floor has several coats of paint, first slosh on a coat of paint remover. (It will save the cost of extra sandpaper.) Be generous with it, but be very careful not to get it on anything else—especially not on any other painted surface or it will be ruined. After a few minutes, the paint will begin to look bubbly and can be scraped right off in long ribbons. Use a paint scraper for this purpose and be sure to wear old clothes and rubber or canvas gloves.

After you have scraped off as much of the paint as possible, wash the floor with turpentine and wipe it clean. You are now ready to sand. Fit a piece of the coarse paper into the large sanding machine and begin at one end of the room. Move the sander over the floor in the same direction as the grain of the wood. There's no danger of digging holes in the floor as long as you keep the sander moving—which it does practically of its own accord. Replace the paper in the machines as the sand wears off. When the entire floor has been sanded with the coarse paper, resand with fine sandpaper. The next step is to sand around the edges of the floor next to the baseboards and moldings with the little machine, first with coarse and then with fine sandpaper. The wood will now look as new and untouched as the day it came from the lumber mill. Don't walk around on it in your bare shoes—either put socks over the shoes or take them off and walk around on stockinged feet. But step on the floor no more than is absolutely necessary.

A little fine dust has probably sifted from the bag on the machine. Remove as much of this dust as possible with a clean brush or the brush attachment of the vacuum cleaner. If you use the vacuum, wrap soft, clean cloths around the runners of the tank so they cannot mark the floor. The last traces of dust should be removed with a clean cloth slightly dampened with turpentine. The floor is now ready to be shellacked, stained and shellacked, or varnished. Wax is sometimes used, but it is not recommended because a waxed finish on bare wood often looks gummy and dirty and is not very durable.

If sanding machines are unobtainable, it's possible to sand the floor by hand, although you will probably rue the day you ever attempted it. Wrap the paper around a large, smooth block of wood and rub it over the surface of the floor until the bare wood is exposed. Use coarse paper first and finish the work off with fine paper. Rub with the grain of the wood. If the whole family helps, it's not too much of a job.

Shellac. A coat of shellac brings out the grain of the wood and seals the surface against dirt. Either white or orange shellac may be used. White shellac does not darken the wood—just brings out its natural color. Orange shellac darkens the wood slightly. If you want the wood to be a darker color, it will have to be stained first. If not, apply the shellac directly. It dries quite rapidly, so work fast. Brush it on the full length of two boards, then two more, and so on until the entire floor is covered. Of course, we don't have to remind you to work towards a door, and not to get yourself marooned in a corner! The shellac should be completely dry within three or four hours. One or two more coats are recommended for a longer wearing finish. Additional coats should not be applied until the previous coat is thoroughly dry. After the final coat has dried, the floor should be waxed. (*Note: For care and cleaning of brushes, see the chapter on Walls and Woodwork.*)

Varnish. Varnish is a little more difficult to apply than shellac, but it gives satisfactory wear and is preferred by some people. Most varnishes dry with a high gloss, but there are also varnishes that dry with a dull finish, if that is what is wanted. In addition both clear and stain varnishes are obtainable. A clear (or "white") varnish changes the color of the wood only slightly. Stain varnishes combine the properties of both a stain and a varnish and may be had in various colors. Only a varnish intended for use on floors should be applied. Furniture varnishes will not give satisfactory service. Spar varnish is a tough finish with a high resistance to weathering or moisture, and is recommended for porches.

Varnish is difficult to apply when it is cold. If necessary, the can should be placed in a container of warm water until the varnish has reached a temperature of at least 70° F. but no more than 90° F. Stir the varnish as little as possible, to avoid the formation of bubbles. When you are ready to apply it, pour a small amount from the can into another container and dip the brush into this. Apply the varnish to two or three boards at a time, covering their full length before going on to the next. Do not apply the varnish too thick—thin coats are better. The air should be as free of dust as possible while the varnish is being applied. Keep the windows closed to avoid drafts and select a clear day for the work. At least two and preferably three coats are advisable. One coat should be allowed to harden thoroughly before the next is applied. After the final coat is completely dry, the floor may be waxed.

Stain. Both water stains and oil stains are available. Of these, oil stains are recommended for floors, since water stains raise the grain of the wood and make a second sanding operation necessary. Apply the stain with a wide brush and wipe it off with a clean cloth after it has had time enough to sink in until the desired degree of color is obtained. Five to fifteen minutes is long enough as a rule. The less time the stain is left on, the lighter the color will be. If the stain is wiped off before the wood is dark enough, a second coat may be applied. But if the stain is left on until the color is darker than wanted, it can be lightened only by bleaching, which may be quite a bit of extra work. After the stain has been allowed to dry overnight, it must be sealed with two or three coats of shellac. When the shellac is dry, the floor may be waxed.

Paint. Any kind of wood floor may be painted, although most people prefer shellac or varnish for fine hardwood floors so that the beauty of the natural wood grain is not hidden. Softwood floors, however, usually look better painted, if linoleum or some other floor covering is too expensive. Floor paint must be used, as ordinary paint would soon wear off under a little friction. Any previous finish, such as shellac, varnish, or paint need not be removed before painting if the floor is smooth. But all wax must be removed first with turpentine.

Paint is also applied along the length of the floor boards, but it needs to be smoothed out with diagonal strokes followed by lengthwise strokes of the brush. At least two, and preferably three, coats of paint should be applied. Each coat must be completely dry before the next is added. After the final coat is dry, the floor may be waxed.

Decorating with Paint. A very inexpensive way to achieve pattern interest on the floor is to paint it on. It takes quite a bit of work and time, and the wearing qualities of a painted pattern are none too durable. However, it offers unusual decorative possibilities when more expensive treatments are out of the question.

Repeat motifs may be stenciled on the floor, or it may be painted in two colors, checkerboard fashion, splatter dashed, or whatever else suits your fancy. Painted representations of scatter rugs are sometimes amusing, but unless they are done with considerable artistic skill, the results are apt to be anything but amusing.

Stencils are recommended for allover patterned effects, since a precise rendering of the design is essential. Metal stencils are preferred because the paper-parchment ones wear out too quickly. If metal stencils are unavailable, then several paper-parchment ones of the same design should be purchased. After the paint in the background has been applied and allowed to dry thoroughly, the floor must be carefully measured and marked off in equal sections to fit the design. Strong twine stretched across the floor from wall to wall and held taut with nails will serve as guide lines for marking the floor. Mark with chalk, which can be easily removed after the design has been painted on. Walk as little as possible on the chalked floor, and then only in stockinged feet, or the chalked lines will soon become obscured.

Begin in a corner of the room and place

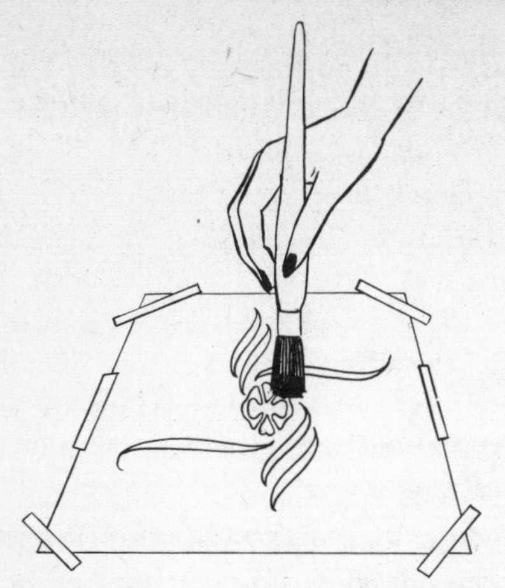

FIG. 1. Stencil brush is held upright and rubbed in a circular motion across the stencil cut-outs.

the stencil in the center of the first section. Attach the stencil with adhesive tape if necessary to prevent slipping, and hold it flat with the palm of the hand. Apply the paint with a round, flat-tipped stencil brush. Dip the brush in the paint and then rub off all excess paint against a piece of glass or an old china plate. Then rub the end of the bristles over the stencil design in a circular motion. More paint may be needed to complete the design, but the excess paint should be rubbed off each time before the brush is applied to the stencil. Don't be tempted to do the work faster by slapping on a brushful of paint. The excess paint will run under the edges of the stencil and spoil the outline of the design. When the design is complete, lift the stencil carefully to avoid smearing, lay it face down on a newspaper, and wipe the back with a clean rag. Then place it in the center of the next section. Repeat this process until the entire floor (or as much of it as you want to cover) is painted. After the designs have dried thoroughly, apply one or two coats of clear white shellac for protection. When the shellac is dry, the floor may be waxed.

A checkerboard design may run parallel with the walls or diagonally to them. The diagonal direction is best because parallel lines of squares produce a static effect. The entire floor is first painted in the color of the light squares. Then the floor is measured and marked off in squares of whatever size you wish. Use string and chalk for marking as for a stenciled design. Tiny squares are too difficult to paint, and very large squares produce a rather startling harlequin effect. Squares with sides of about 6 or 7 inches are better. For sharp, clean outlines, the edges of the squares are protected with masking tape. This tape may be used over and over again, but several rolls of it should be bought to make the work go faster. The tape is laid as illustrated around the *outside* edges of alternating rows of the squares to be painted in the dark color. After the paint is thoroughly dry, the tape

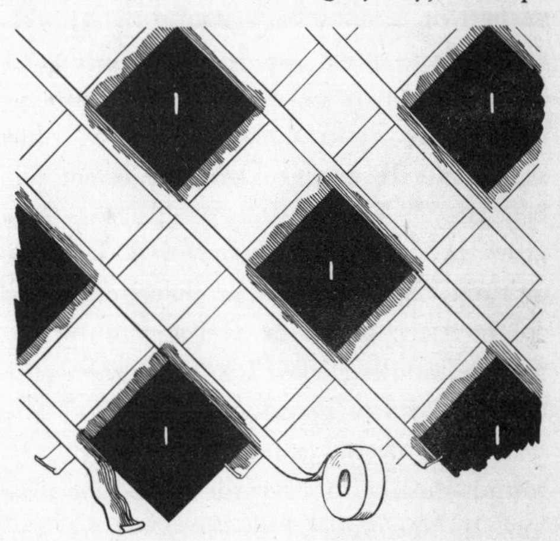

FIG. 2. To paint a floor in checkerboard design, measure squares and outline the edges with masking tape as illustrated. Paint all number 1 squares.

FIG. 3. Remove the tape and replace it to outline the edges of the number 2 squares.

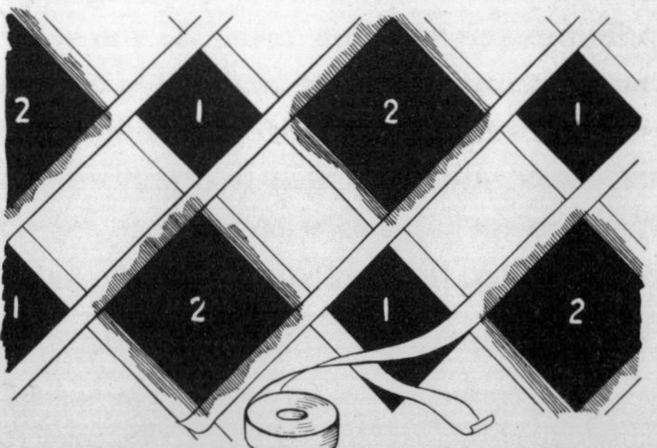

is taken up and relaid along the *outside* edges of the intervening rows, and the squares *diagonal* to the adjoining dark squares are painted. Be very careful to put the paint in the right squares—the very simplicity of a checkerboard pattern leads one to forget which square should be painted.

When all the dark squares have been painted and the floor is completely dry, apply one or two coats of clear white shellac for protection. The floor may be waxed after the shellac is dry. (*Note: An example of a floor painted in checkerboard design may be seen in the photograph reproduced on page 219.*)

Spatter dashing is a very old method of decorating painted floors. Properly done, the effect is not one of pattern, but of texture. Light-colored paint may be spatter dashed on a dark background, or the reverse. Sometimes the spatter dashing is done with two or even three colors of paint. The contrast between the colors should not be too great or the effect will be "busy." The spatter dashing is done after the floor has been covered with two or three coats of paint in the background color. After the floor is thoroughly dry, paint of another color is sprinkled on with a brush. Stand up to do this work, and sprinkle as evenly as possible. An ordinary, round brush with a handle—the type used for cleaning vegetables—is good for this purpose. Too much paint on the brush will produce big blobs on the floor, too little will produce a thinly scattered, speckled effect. Try a few practice sprinkles on newspapers first, in order to judge the right amount of paint to use. If you wish, paint in another color may be sprinkled on after the first is dry. After the final sprinkling, allow the floor to dry thoroughly. Then shellac and wax.

Bleaching. Floors are occasionally bleached. To do this, any existing finishes must be removed completely so that the bare wood is exposed. The process of bleaching a floor is the same as that used on furniture (*see chapter on Refinishing Furniture*). The bleaching solution may raise the grain of the wood enough to require resanding, however. The bleach is not a finish, and after bleaching the floor must be shellacked or finished in some other way.

Waxing. Wax may be applied directly to bare wood, but wood floors finished in this way are not as easy to care for as floors treated in other ways. Wax helps to protect any type of finish, however, as well as to keep it clean and gleaming. Both paste and liquid forms are available. Paste is preferable for use on bare wood. For other surfaces, liquid wax is better because it is so much easier to apply. However, either type may be used. But do not use one type for one application and the other kind for the next.

To wax a bare wood floor, apply only the thinnest coat of the finest paste floor wax. After the wax has dried for h lf an hour, it should be polished. This work can be done by hand, but it's much easier to use an electric polishing machine. Such machines can usually be rented if you don't own one. Sometimes sanding machines can be easily converted into polishing machines. At least three thin coats of wax should be applied and polished. Six or seven coats are even better. A waxed finish must be renewed frequently to be kept in good condition.

Self-polishing liquid waxes are poured from the can and wiped over the surface in a thin film. A long-handled wax applicator makes the work easier. Apply several coats for a better finish, allowing each coat to dry thoroughly before putting on the next. When the wax is thoroughly dry, it can be rubbed briskly for a higher luster.

Concrete Floors. Paint makes a good finish for concrete basement floors, but the floor must be dry before the paint is applied. New concrete floors sometimes take quite a while to dry out thoroughly. To test a concrete floor for dampness, roll out a thick strip of putty about 18 inches long. Form it into a circle on the concrete floor and press the ends together. Within the circle, place a watch crystal, or a small glass container of some kind. Measure a level teaspoonful of granulated anhydrous calcium chloride (obtainable at the drugstore) and place it in the container. Cover the putty with an ordinary piece of glass, pressing it down firmly. Beads of moisture will appear on the glass and the calcium chloride will dissolve wholly or partially within 24 hours if the concrete is damp. The floor should be tested in various parts before it is pronounced dry. If the first test shows dampness, try the floor again in another week or two.

Leaking basement walls and floors are quite a different thing than a mild case of dampness. If water is actually present, you will probably need the services of a contractor to remedy the condition. Very slight cases of dampness can be cured with a rubber-base paint made especially for this purpose. The concrete must be dry at the time of application, however, and for this reason you may have to wait until winter, at which time the basement is usually driest. The paint is applied like ordinary paint and dries within a few hours.

Concrete which tests dry at any time may be painted with regular concrete floor paint. If the floor is rough, there is a product that will smooth the surface. This product is a plastic composition which is smoothed on with a trowel. If you have never tried to smooth such material with a trowel before, you had better practice with some of it on a board first before applying it to the floor. The composition dries in about eight hours. Afterwards it may be painted if it is first sealed with a coat of shellac.

Concrete floors in direct contact with the ground should not be covered with linoleum, but there are composition flooring materials which may be used for this purpose.

CHAPTER XIX

FLOOR COVERINGS

FLOORS, more than any other surface in the house, require finishes and coverings which are *durable,* as well as attractive. And because the floor area is so large and conspicuous, its treatment can make the room seem larger or smaller than it actually is, and it can also add a lively note of decoration. For example, an unbroken expanse of floor space in a solid color makes a room appear larger, while a large allover pattern on the floor helps to unify the big room. Central points of interest can be created by having pattern only in certain areas. One might achieve such an effect with linoleum insets or scatter rugs, for example. Whatever effect is wanted, it can be gained in any one of several different ways of treatment.

Rugs and carpeting not only provide comfort, beauty, and insulation, but they also absorb sound. But one may not wish to hide floors of fine, polished wood beneath allover carpeting. Then smaller scatter rugs may be the answer. Oriental rugs are excellent on such floors. But linoleum floors, painted wood floors, or the wide-plank type of Early American floor, are not appropriate settings for Oriental rugs.

Braided rag rugs and hooked rugs are perfect for the Early American setting, and they are also adaptable to many informal modern rooms. Braided rugs look especially well with the California ranch style of interior. But they do not belong with formal period furniture.

Painted floors are apt to look extremely barren if no rugs are used at all. This appearance can be relieved by a stenciled allover design, but the floor will still act as a sounding board for noise.

Linoleums lack the sound-absorbing quality of thick-pile rugs, but the felt base on which linoleums are laid absorbs considerable sound. Modern inset linoleum designs probably permit more individualized floor treatments than any other type of covering.

LINOLEUM

Linoleum consists of ground cork, oxidized linseed oil and various chemicals, mixed together and pressed onto a backing of jute burlap. It may be plain, inset, printed, or treated in one of the modern permanent textured effects. The quality of the linoleum depends upon thorough seasoning and thickness. The thicker the linoleum, the longer it wears. Printed linoleums are comparatively inexpensive, but the design is only on the surface and will probably wear no longer than floor enamel.

"Battleship" linoleum is simply ordinary linoleum which is thicker than standard grades and of a uniform medium brown color. It is so called because it was originally manufactured to specifications for decks of battleships.

The improved designs, colors, and over-

all effects now available in linoleums have made them very popular for floor coverings throughout the house, whereas once they were limited almost entirely to the kitchen or bathroom. The beautiful linoleum inset designs are achieved by means of precision tools and highly skilled workmen, and should not be attempted by the amateur.

Laying Linoleum. The amateur who has never attempted to lay linoleum is advised that it would probably be better to call in an expert to do the job if he expects really satisfactory results. However, if that is impracticable, it might be a good idea to experiment first on some small floor where mistakes will not show too much before trying it out in some more important room. Plain linoleums are easier to work with than patterned ones.

The first step is to remove all furniture and any old floor coverings from the room and, if possible, to jack up any radiators with a block of wood placed under the projection on the pipe below the valve. The wood flooring under the linoleum should be double, and must be absolutely clean and smooth. Any loose floor boards must be nailed down securely. Rough boards must be planed smooth. All wax, oil, varnish, or paint must be removed, either with paint and varnish remover or with a sanding machine. All cracks should be filled. The quarter-round molding found at the base of most walls should be pried loose with a wide chisel — but very carefully, as it will have to be replaced after the linoleum is laid.

In order to make the linoleum adhere properly, it is almost essential to have a linoleum roller, and if one cannot be borrowed or rented, it would be better not to attempt the work at all. In addition, one needs a sharpened linoleum cutting knife, a notched paste spreader, a 6-foot folding ruler, a 6-foot metal straightedge, a pair of scissors, a putty knife, and a carpenter's square.

Linoleum comes in rolls, usually 2 yards wide. Some linoleums have a special backing which permits them to be pasted directly to the wood flooring. Other linoleums require a preliminary base of lining felt which is made especially for this purpose. This felt usually comes in rolls 3 feet wide, which must be cut into strips to fit the floor. The strips should run in the opposite direction of the floor boards. If the boards run diagonally, lay the felt as illustrated.

Split the first strip in half lengthwise, so that the seams will not come directly beneath those of the linoleum strips. The entire floor should be fitted with the strips before they are pasted into place. Edges must not overlap, and in order to insure a smooth, close fit, each strip should be thumbtacked into place before proceeding to the next. When all strips are fitted, remove the tacks halfway from the first strip and fold it back. Spread linoleum paste on the floor with the notched paste spreader. Replace the strip and roll with the linoleum roller, working from the center towards the wall. Do the same with the rest of the strips, and after the first half of each strip has been pasted in place, repeat the process with the other halves. It is important to have the felt as smooth as the floor beneath it.

Professional installation demands that linoleum must be fitted to conform to every slight deviation in the wall, and to do this every irregularity is transferred onto the linoleum by a method called *scribing*, after which it is cut to fit. This process, however, will probably prove somewhat complicated for the amateur. But if he measures and cuts his linoleum as accurately and carefully as possible, he will probably achieve a fairly close fit.

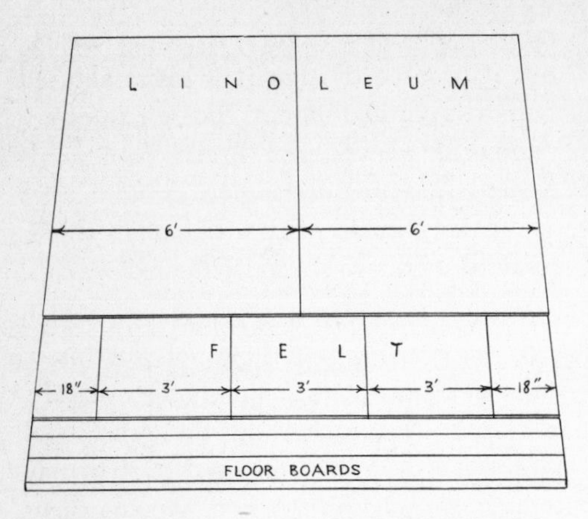

FIG. 1. Linoleum is laid on felt base. First felt strip is split in two so that seams will not coincide with seams of linoleum strips.

Before unrolling or cutting linoleum during cold weather, allow it to stand for at least 48 hours in a warm room. Then measure the strips to correspond to the length of the room and cut them with the linoleum knife, guiding the pointed end with the straightedge. put the strip in place and draw a chalk line along the edge on the felt. Fold back one half the strip.

Eggplant linoleum inset with white linoleum in laurel wreath design sets keynote of classic simplicity for this foyer.

Spread linoleum paste on the felt to within 4 inches of the chalk line. Replace the strip and repeat the process with the other half. Cut the second strip and lay it next to the first, overlapping the edges ¾ of an inch. Lay the straightedge halfway over the overlap, and with the knife cut through the top strip and slightly into the bottom strip. Using the knife mark on the bottom strip as a guide line, trim this strip along the line, being careful not to cut the felt. The edges of the two strips can then be fitted together to form a perfect seam. Fold the second strip back in half. With a putty knife, apply paste under the unpasted edge of the first strip. Then apply paste to the felt under the second strip and replace it. Repeat this process with the other halves of the strips. Roll both strips with the linoleum roller and tap the seam with a hammer covered with a damp cloth. Continue in the same way with additional strips.

If linoleum must be fitted around some permanent object, such as a radiator or a toilet bowl, it will have to be slit and a portion cut out to correspond to the shape of the object. In order to do this as accurately as possible, one should first make a very carefully fitted paper pattern and transfer it with chalk to the linoleum before cutting.

Replace the molding. The nails should be driven into the baseboard at an angle so that they do not pierce the linoleum. Do not nail the molding down too tight, as the linoleum needs a little space in which to expand or contract slightly. After the linoleum has been down for at least 48 hours, wash the floor and then wax it with a self-polishing wax.

Tiles are by no means limited to the ceramic tiles so familiar on bathroom floors. They are also made of rubber, asphalt, cork, plastic composition, and wood. Tiles are easy to apply, long wearing, and decorative. Asphalt and rubber tiles are resilient and tend to absorb sound. The tiles are usually applied by setting them in tile cement. Great care must be taken to match the edges together accurately. Some require a special foundation and some do not, and the manufacturer's specifications should be followed in this matter. Tiled flooring varies widely in cost, depending upon the type of tiling used. If you have a tiled floor in which tiles have come loose, they can be reset with tile cement. Scrape away all old cement from the tile and from the floor before applying the new cement to the back of the tile. After setting in place, remove any excess cement from around the edges. The cement should be allowed to harden at least over night before the tile is walked on or washed.

BUYING RUGS AND CARPETS

Wool Rugs. Good wool rugs and carpets are a major investment. It pays to buy the best grades because a rug of good quality will so far outlast one of poor quality that the higher original cost is more than offset by the extra years of service. If the budget will not permit the purchase of good wool rugs, then buy some other type of floor covering.

A rug is a floor covering made in one piece. Carpeting is a floor covering material, usually with a pile, which is made in various widths and sold from a roll. Such material is usually sold under the name of *broadloom*. Broadloom is not the name of a particular kind of carpet. It merely means that the carpeting has no seams, and is sold in whatever length is needed. It comes in standard widths of 3, 6, 9, 12, 15, and 18 feet in most weaves. If you want to buy a 9 x 12 room-size rug, you can have 12 feet cut from 9-foot wide broadloom.

The principal types of woven pile rugs are Wilton, Axminster, and velvet. Chenille is the most luxurious carpet weave, but it is so costly that it is manufactured only to a limited extent. These names are names of weaves, not brand names, although manufacturers give brand names to their carpets. In addition to these weaves, there are special patented weaves.

Carpets come in various grades, which differ according to the type of yarn used, the density of the pile, the number of tufts to the square inch, and the process of manufacture. The yarns used in rugs may be either woolen or worsted. Woolen yarns are lightly twisted and usually short fibered. Worsted yarns are tightly twisted and long fibered. Generally, worsted yarns give better wear than woolen yarns, but the extent to which this is so will depend upon the quality of the wool itself and upon how the rug is made. The wool pile in rugs is formed by small tufts, or sometimes by loops. The wool may be carried only on the surface of the carpet, or it may extend all the way through to the back, according to the type of weave. The amount of wool used in the rug is the chief factor which determines its price. Cheaper grades have less wool and give correspondingly less wear. Depth of pile alone may not be an indication that a rug contains a great deal of wool. A short-piled rug in which the rows of tufts are packed closely together and are very dense may contain more wool and give better wear than a rug with a long pile but with fewer rows of tufts.

The pile in the rug is held in place by foundation yarns which are usually of jute and cotton or sometimes linen. Jute is a strong fiber that wears well except when it comes in constant contact with moisture. Therefore, in damp climates it tends to disintegrate in a relatively short space of time. To overcome this drawback, some manufacturers substitute plastic-coated yarns for jute. These plastic-coated yarns have proved to be as good as jute, and more durable in damp climates.

Wiltons. The Wilton weave is very complicated. It is made on a Jacquard loom, a complex mechanism which reproduces designs from holes punched in cards. However, the number of colors used in weaving the rug is limited to six, so Wiltons usually have small, conservative patterns. Additional colors can be added by "planting" extra yarns in the carpet, but they are not an integral part of the weave. This process also adds to the cost. The yarns of which the carpet are woven are buried beneath the surface, one above another. As each color is needed, the loom lifts the yarn of that particular color to the surface to form a tuft. The structure of the weave makes the Wilton very durable. Tufts are so securely anchored that they are very difficult to pull loose. The wool which lies buried beneath the surface gives the rug added value.

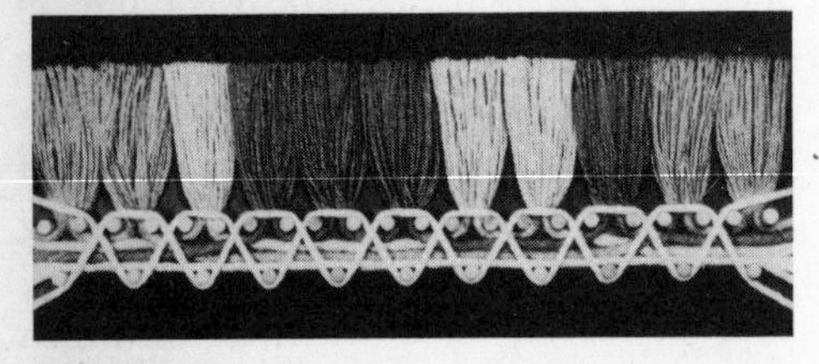

Wilton weave of worsted yarns in three colors (frames). Yarns are "buried" beneath surface until needed to form tufts. "Buried" wool adds to wearing qualities. Two chain warp yarns and three filling shots (end view) hold yarns in place.

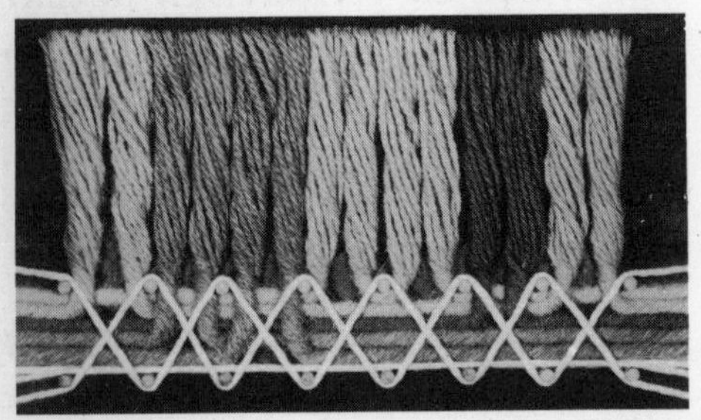

Wilton weave of woolen yarns in five colors. Only two filling shots are generally used with woolen yarn, and fewer "stuffer" warp yarns (on bottom) are needed than in worsted construction.

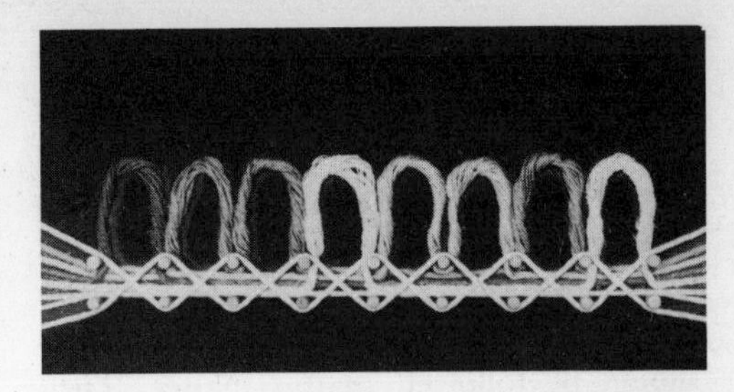

Looped pile Wilton weave (sometimes called Brussels) in four colors. Number of colors may be from one to six, although additional colors are sometimes "planted" into the design.

However, there are grades of Wilton. The better grades are made of worsted yarns, and have a short, dense pile. Wiltons made of woolen yarn have a woolier, thicker pile, but usually do not wear as well. Of course, cheaper grades of Wilton have less yarn than fine grades, and a cheap Wilton will not wear as long as a fine grade of Axminster or velvet. But the best grades of Wilton will probably outwear the best grades of any other kind of woven carpeting, except, perhaps, chenille.

Wiltons are also made with looped tufts. Formerly looped Wilton was called Brussels carpeting and sometimes is still sold under that name.

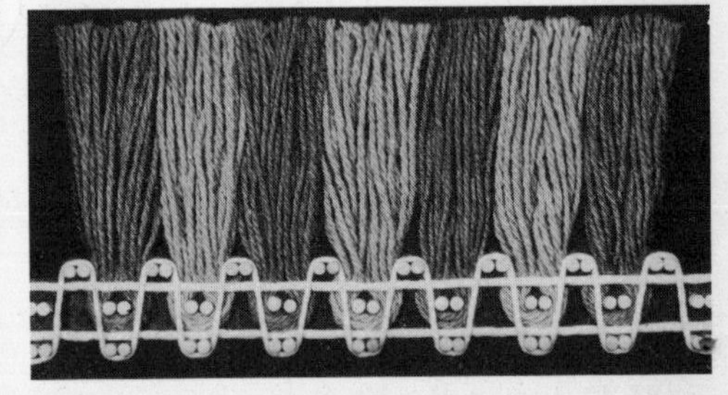

Axminster weave has wool on surface. Any number of colors may be used in pile yarns, resulting in unlimited range of design. Each row of tufts is anchored by three double filling shots.

Axminsters. The structure of this weave is much simpler than that of the Wilton. All the wool is carried on the surface of the rug, and the number of colors which can be used is almost limitless. However, the different colored yarns must be arranged by hand on spools before weaving. Each spool contains enough yarn for one row of tufts, and the various colors must be carefully spaced to follow the design. Naturally, the more colors used, the more work is involved in arranging the yarn on the spools, which means that a plain color Axminster costs less, grade for grade, than a multi-colored one. A good grade of Axminster has a dense, deep pile, which gives it a luxurious feel and makes it a very popular type of carpeting. The more tufts there are to the inch, the more wear and satisfaction the carpet will give. The best grades have nine rows of tufts to the inch, and the cheapest only four. You can find the number of rows of tufts per inch by counting the construction threads on the back. Each row holds one row of tufts. Another characteristic of Axminster is that it can only be rolled lengthwise because of the way in which the jute construction yarns are placed.

Velvets. Velvet weave is the simplest carpet weave of all, and like the Axminster, the wool is all carried on the surface. The most popular velvets are those with textured effects, usually called *frieze velvets.* Solid colors seem to predominate in this weave, but it also comes in patterns. Patterned velvets are made by two entirely different processes. In one process the design is simply printed on the carpet after it is woven. Of course, clear, sharp delineation of colors cannot be obtained all the way through the depth of the pile by this method. As the carpet wears, the pattern will lose its distinctness. The other process is done by dyeing the strands of yarn to conform to the required pattern before the carpet is woven.

Chenilles. Chenille carpeting requires two separate weaving processes. In the first step, the pile is woven into long furry strips resembling a caterpillar — in fact, *chenille* is the French name for caterpillar. These strips are then woven on another loom to make the carpet. This process gives the chenille carpet a very dense, deep pile, and makes it the most luxurious of all domestic carpets. However, it is very costly because it requires a great deal of hand work during the weaving in addition to the two weaving processes. For this reason, some manufacturers do not make chenille at all, or only on special order. Fine chenille wears so well that hotel and theater owners often use it for lobbies, where the hard usage it must withstand probably justifies the expense.

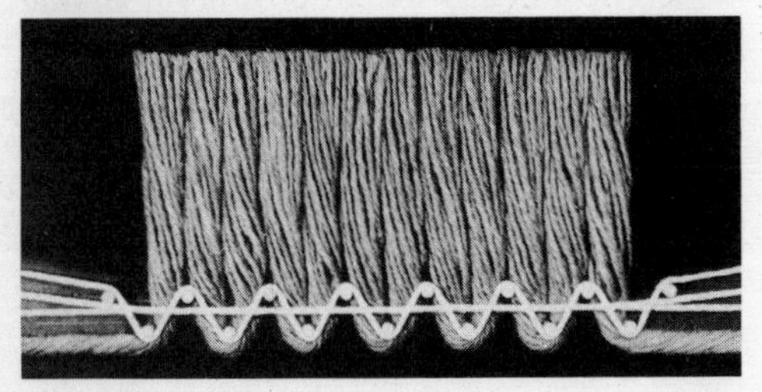

Velvet weave is simplest type of pile construction. Designs may be produced by printing yarn before weaving or by printing carpet after weaving. Tapestry weave is same except loop tufts are uncut.

Patented weave similar to velvet, except that wool extends through to back. After weaving, back is coated with a binding adhesive. Tufts are then said to be "locked," so that carpet may be cut in any direction without raveling.

Miscellaneous Hints. The sculptured and tone-on-tone effects which have become so popular are achieved in various ways. Sometimes the pile is cut or carved away slightly to form a design. For custom-made jobs, this must be done by hand, and can cost a pretty sum. Another effect is achieved by weaving one part of the design with worsted yarn and another part with woolen yarn. Sometimes cut and uncut loops are combined to form a design. Or the loops may be of different heights. It is also possible to have a design cut out of carpeting of one color and inset in a carpet of another color by a patented process. This work is custom made, too, and not cheap at all. But it can be done in such a way that the sections are perfectly joined and will not work loose.

Any rug will wear almost twice as long if it has a rug cushion underneath. Such cushions are usually made of hair which has been treated to repel moths. Rug cushions do not add greatly to the initial investment, and the extra wear they insure, plus the fact that they add softness to the feel of the rug, more than makes them worth the additional cost.

Room-size rugs should be really room size. A margin of floor space no larger than one foot wide should show around the edges of the rug. Less space than this is even better. Skimpy rugs look lost and out of place. If you buy a room-size rug from a broadloom roll, the cost per yard may or may not include binding. Binding is not a costly process, but it is well to find out whether it must be added to the initial cost.

Allover carpeting which covers the entire floor from wall to wall not only makes a room look larger, but it, too, gives a very luxurious effect. It is also more expensive. Allowances must be made for any irregular wall projection, such as a fireplace. Unless it is properly fitted, it may bulge or shrink. Since new allover carpeting represents a major investment, it would be poor economy to attempt to lay and fit it if one has never had experience in such matters. The cost of having this work done by an expert will more than repay itself by the satisfaction it brings, for a poorly laid rug is a waste of money.

However, one may have a carpet which is badly worn only in one section. The unworn section of such a carpet can often be cut down and used in a smaller room. To do this, take up the rug by first removing all the carpet tacks, being very careful not to injure the foundation threads. Cut the rug to its new proportions with a pair of heavy, sharp scissors. The rug will probably have a foundation which will also have to be cut. New binding will have to be applied to some edges, or perhaps all, especially if the new binding differs in color from the original. Rug binding is usually sold at the notions counter of the department store, and it comes in a variety of colors. Some bindings must be sewed on, and this is done with carpet thread in a color to match the rug. Another kind of binding is impregnated with an adhesive substance on the back which makes the tape adhere to the rug when it is pressed with a hot iron. If the rug has remained rolled up for any length of time, it should be left flat for several days before it is finally fitted into place.

The rug may have to be pieced to fit into a projecting niche. This can be done by cutting a section to fit and piecing it. The pieced section is attached to the rug with an overcast seam made with carpet thread on the wrong side. Keep the joining as flat as possible, and take up no more threads of the foundation in the stitches than are necessary to make the seam secure. After the rug lies flat for a few days,

Modern shaggy cotton rugs give excellent service on floors which do not receive hard usage, such as that in a dining room or bedroom.

the joining should not be noticeable.

After the foundation and rug are properly fitted, and all raw edges of the rug are bound, it can be tacked into place with carpet tacks around the edges. Stretch the rug as firmly as possible while tacking.

Stair carpeting will last nearly twice as long if you buy the strip in a length to cover the stairway plus one extra stair tread. This additional length allows the carpet to be shifted from tread to riser as the carpet wears. Stairways require sturdier carpets than any other part of the house.

Second-hand Rugs. Rugs can often be bought second hand for a fraction of what they would cost new. If the rug shows few signs of wear and is of good quality and unfaded, it may be a real bargain. But do not buy a second-hand rug without being thoroughly familiar with qualities and market prices of new rugs. A wise rule to follow might be this: if the second-hand rug is of good quality and in good condition and it can be bought for no more than half of what a similar rug would cost new, then it may be an economy. If the price of a second-hand is even less than half the cost of a new rug, so much the better. Sometimes rug-cleaning establishments in large cities sell unclaimed rugs at auctions, and a careful bidder can occasionally pick up real bargains.

Cotton Rugs. Floors which have no heavy traffic, such as those of most bedrooms, may very well have floor coverings in which length of wear is of less concern than cost. The cotton rug is one of the best answers to this need. Such rugs now come in a large variety of colors and weaves, and many of them give very satisfactory service for what they cost. Tufted cotton rugs can be particularly attractive. The tufts are of cotton string and the rugs are usually constructed by sewing the tufts to a cotton backing. The denser the tufts, the better the rug will wear.

Woven rugs of cotton yarn often have

very interesting "tweedy" textures, and usually are reversible—which adds to their wearing qualities. Commercially manufactured rag rugs sometimes resemble the hand-made kind fairly closely, and are especially suited to Early American interiors.

Other Types of Rugs. Grass rugs are excellent for sun porches or for any room during summer time. They cannot, of course, be expected to give years of service, but they do give adequate wear in return for their very moderate cost.

Oriental rugs are made by hand, and the pile is formed by tying individual knots of wool. Good Orientals are extremely costly, and one should have expert advice on their selection. A good quality domestic rug is always a better selection than an Oriental of poor quality. Machine-manufactured reproductions of Orientals are best avoided — they are still imitations no matter how closely they duplicate the original, and all imitations which pretend to be what they are not are in bad taste.

Sometimes rugs are woven of reprocessed yarn. Such yarn is made by shredding and tearing old wool textiles to loosen the fibers, which are then respun and rewoven, and usually bleached and redyed. The fibers, of course, become shortened during this process and sometimes they are combined with new wool. The technical name for reprocessed wool is *shoddy*. The name implies that it is cheap and unsubstantial. Actually, however, shoddy made from long-fibered wool may outwear textiles made from very short-fibered new wool. But no shoddy will wear as well as textiles or carpets made from long-fibered new wool.

Cleaning and Caring for Rugs. Dirt is the enemy of carpets of all types. Dirt which is allowed to sift into the foundation and remain there will help to grind away the foundation threads and destroy the rug. Sweeping will remove surface dirt, but it cannot remove dirt which is ingrained. Throwing the rug across the line and whacking it with a carpet beater may remove the deeper dirt, but it also weakens the fibers. The best way to keep the rug clean is to vacuum it. However, some dirt will still become ingrained even with regular, thorough vacuuming. If possible, it is advisable to send the rug to a professional rug cleaning establishment once a year. Again, such establishments often send special equipment and trained operators to clean a wall-to-wall rug in your own home at so much per square foot, and this is advisable for fine rugs, or very large ones. But a small rug can be washed fairly successfully by home methods. First make very thick sudsy foam, with a good, mild, soap and tepid water. Do not saturate the rug with water. Use two lintless cloths — one to apply the suds, and one to rinse. Rub the soap foam (or one of the soapless chemical foams made for the purpose) in rotary motions over the rug, working in a small area at a time. Wring the other rag out in clear water as tightly as possible and go over the area again. Repeat until the entire rug is cleaned.

Mending a Rug. An expert professional rug repairer can mend a hole in a rug so that it can scarcely be detected, even on very close examination. Rug repair shops often carry supplies of rug yarns large enough to match almost any color of carpet. The cost for such repair work is estimated on the extent of the damage, and while it is anything but cheap, it is undoubtedly worth it if the rug is otherwise in good condition.

If no such service is available in your community, and the work must be done at home or not at all, a fairly inconspicuous job can sometimes be done with very fine

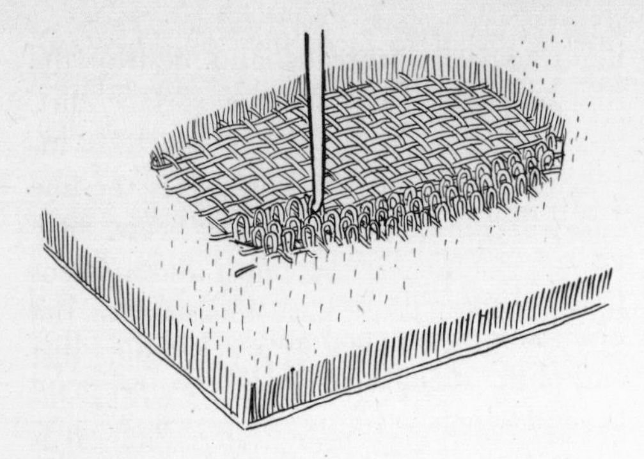

FIG. 8. Hole in carpet can be mended by forming new pile with matching wool. If foundation is destroyed, weave new foundation with stout linen threads. Wool loops can be made with needle or crochet hook. When area is filled, loops are clipped to form new pile.

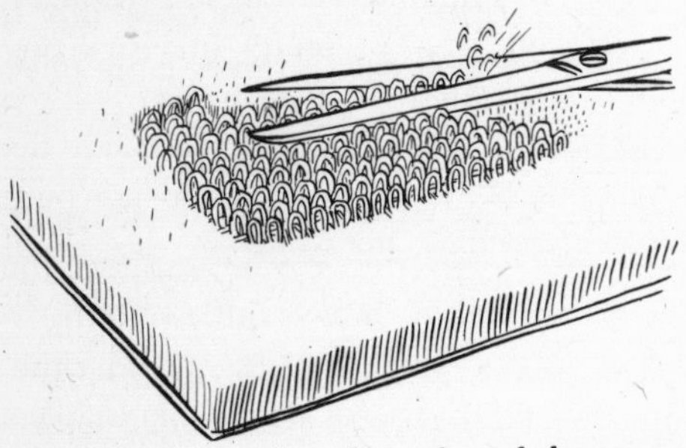

yarn which matches the color of the carpet as closely as possible. If you can obtain the same kind of yarn used in your carpet, of course that is so much to the good. But as a rule, rug manufacturers will not attempt to supply you with yarn to match a rug.

If the foundation threads are gone, as well as the pile, these will have to be replaced too. Use linen or cotton twine of the approximate size of the original foundation threads. Weave this twine back and forth in the same way as you would darn a stocking. Then form new tufts by threading a needle with the matching wool and inserting it between the threads of the rebuilt foundation. Draw the needle up to leave a loop each time, placing the loops as closely together as possible. Or work the loops through from the back with a crochet hook in the same way as a hooked rug is made. When the area is completely filled, trim the loops to a uniform height to correspond with the rest of the pile. A pair of long-bladed manicuring scissors will do this job very well.

HAND-MADE RUGS

Hooked Rugs. Colonial women brought the art of hooking rugs with them when they came to America. Every scrap of material was then so precious that nothing could be wasted. After a garment was too worn for further use as clothing, it could still give valuable service for many years when made into a rug. The women (and the men and children too, for the whole family often worked on the rugs) had to create their own designs. These often showed such real artistic expression that some of these old rugs are museum treasures worth many thousands of dollars.

The modern woman has no such urgent need for making every bit of material count. But thrift is always worth while, and the hooked rug is one of the best ways to make good use of material that might otherwise be thrown out. And you have the opportunity to create something of real beauty that can become an heirloom.

Patterns and Uses. Hooked rugs can be appropriate for almost any setting except the most authentic period rooms. How they are used depends upon their pattern or design. Hooked rugs can even be beautifully effective in modern rooms. For rug hooking is a *technique,* not a style of rug. Some collectors would not agree with this. To them the hooked rug is an antique, and prized as such, and they look upon the modern version with scorn. But so valuable and versatile a craft as rug hooking deserves to be translated into contemporary design for contemporary settings. Yet there is no reason why authentic Colonial patterns should not be reproduced for rooms furnished in the Early American manner.

The woman with artistic abilities can create designs which are truly original. If she can draw at all, she can adapt designs from other sources — not just copy them, but use the motifs in such a way that they form her own expression. Ideas can be borrowed from many places — a tile, a beautifully pottery plate, flower prints, a bookbinding, a textile — in fact, ideas for designs can be found almost anywhere. Nearly all will require rearrangement to be suitable for a rug. Small, fussy details are not suited to this technique. The color areas should be kept fairly broad and simple, and the beginner would do well to start with geometric patterns which require no shading. Designs with shaded color effects should be attempted only by the skilled worker with a sure eye for color.

A simple method of enlarging a small design is to rule vertical and horizontal lines across it to form squares. Then rule the same number of squares on a larger scale, and copy the outline of the design, using the lines as a guide.

An infinite number of geometric designs can be worked out with a compass and a ruler. If no compass is handy, tie one end of a string to a pencil and secure the other end of the string, making it a central point around which to rotate the pencil. A fairly accurate circle will result. Designs can first be worked out on heavy wrapping paper. When you have motifs you like, cut out several repeats of them. Place these on your rug foundation material in various ways until you find an arrangement you like. If you have difficulty in visualizing colors, it might be helpful to buy colored papers at an art goods store, and cut the motifs out of these. It is best to use pure colors in brilliant hues only in very small areas, or else the rug is apt to look garish.

Oval hooked rug with scroll border and floral center. Multi-floral designs make good use of small pieces of wool fabrics in assorted colors if they are blended with care. (American, early 19th century.)

After your design and color scheme for the rug have been worked out, thumbtack the paper patterns in place and trace around them with colored inks and a small brush, or use textile paints. Both paint and ink can be bought at art-goods stores, or in some department stores. Unless you make a small color chart as a guide for working, it might be well, after removing the patterns, to fill in the outlined designs on your rug in solid colors, or at least to place a patch of color on each motif.

If you do not care to work out your own designs, you can buy burlap rug foundations already stamped in a variety of designs at your needlework counter.

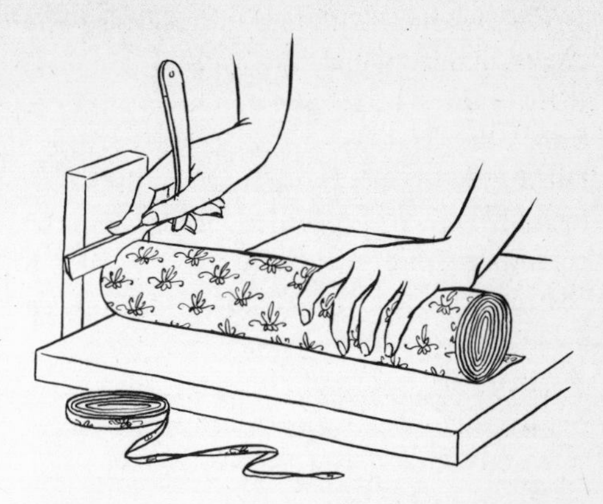

FIG. 2. Easy way of cutting cloth strips for hooked rug is to roll fabric tightly and slice with razor or very sharp knife. Use bread board or similar board with block of wood attached at end to hold roll firmly in place while cutting.

Materials and Their Preparation. Almost any kind of textiles — cotton, linen, silk, rayon, and wool — can be used in hooked rugs. The best material, of course, is wool. It is well worth while to reserve the wools for hooked rugs, because, while they can be very beautiful, they also require much time and labor. The cottons, rayons, and other fabrics can be used in braided or crocheted rugs, which take less time.

Fabrics of approximately the same weight should be selected for use together in one rug. Do not use heavy woolen materials, like those in blankets or men's heavy overcoats. These cannot be cut in fine enough strips. Wool crepes, summer worsteds, light-weight flannels, gabardines, and such are much better. Materials which are soiled should first be washed in mild suds and lukewarm water. Then sort the materials according to their colors. If you have a large assortment of a single neutral or dark color, it might be well to reserve this for the background area of the rug. If you want your rug to have a light background, you will require a large quantity of light-colored wools of a fairly uniform tone. But most women will find that their "rag bags" will yield far fewer light-colored wools than dark ones. But you might exchange wools with your friends to secure the colors you need, or simply persuade them to donate their old garments, if they do not hook rugs themselves.

Dyeing large quantities of fabric to attain a uniform tone in a light color is too tricky to attempt at home as a rule. Darker shades present fewer difficulties. But the dye should be bought in quantity. If no dealer in your community sells dye by the pound, write directly to one of the dye manufacturers. Some fabrics for small areas of colors will probably have to be dyed in limited quantities. This can be done with excellent results by using any of

FIG. 3. Artist's stretchers serve as inexpensive frame for making hooked rug. Special mounted frames can also be bought.

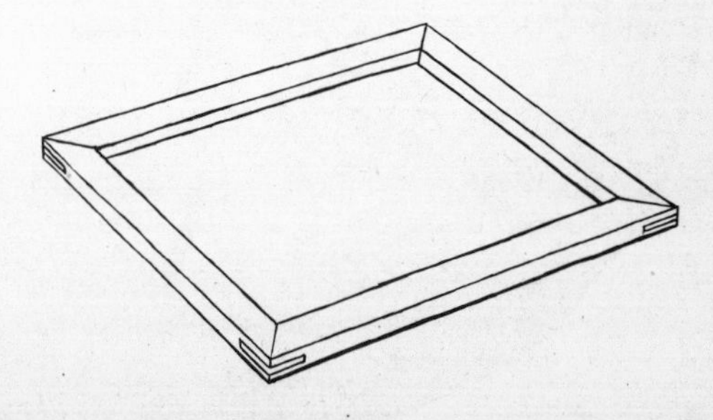

FIG. 4. Burlap foundation for hooked rug is tacked to stretchers. As work progresses, burlap is untacked and moved into new position.

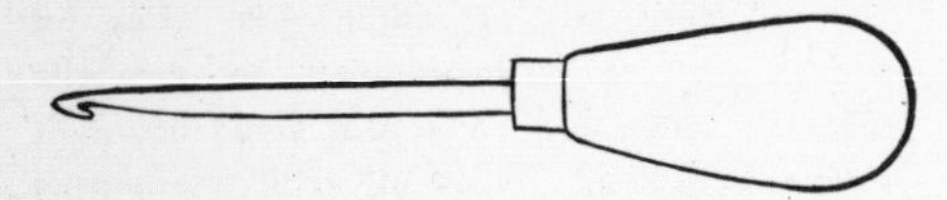

FIG. 5. Typical hook used for making hooked rugs.

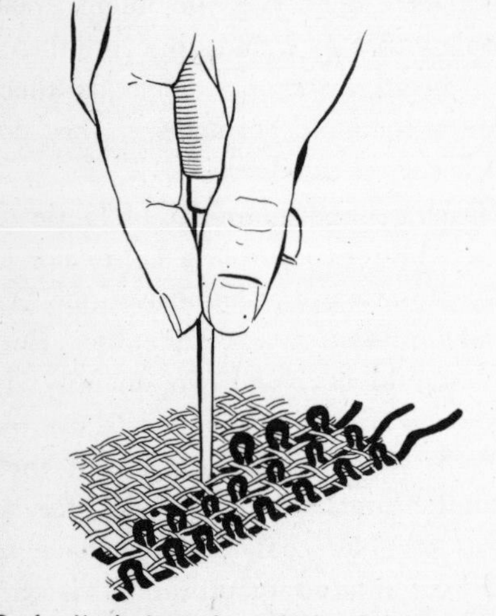

FIG. 6. Hooked rug is made by drawing strips of fabric up through burlap to form loops. Leave two or three threads of burlap between loops.

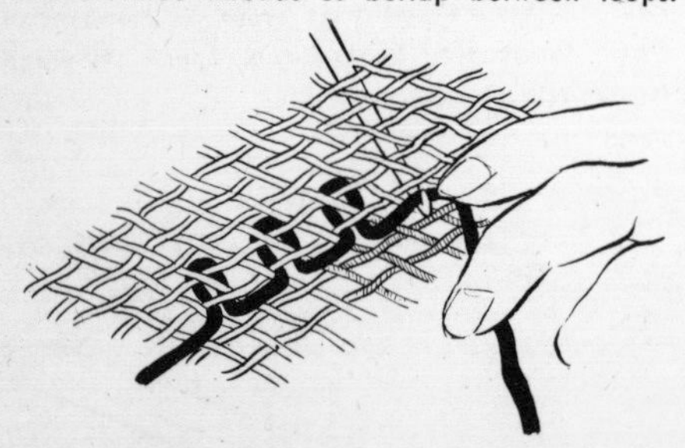

FIG. 7. Strip of fabric is guided with finger on under side of burlap.

the commercial dyes found in any drug, department, or dime store. Simply follow the directions carefully, and rinse so thoroughly after dyeing that the color no longer runs.

Colors need not match exactly to achieve a uniform color effect. If similar tones are skillfully blended together in the work, the effect will be one of solid color.

Badly wrinkled materials will cut better if given a light pressing. Next cut the wools in the largest pieces that the old garments, or whatever the material comes from, will yield. These pieces can then be cut into fine strips along the straight of the goods, preferably lengthwise. The strips can be anywhere from 1/8 inch to 1/2 inch wide, depending on how fine or coarse you want your work to be. Strips 1/4 inch wide or 3/8 inch wide are the usual choice. The strips can be cut one at a time with a sharp pair of scissors, but it will take much less time to roll the material tightly and cut it into strips with a very sharp knife or an old-fashioned razor. To do this, the end of the roll must be kept absolutely even, so that the strips will always be cut along the straight of the goods. You can keep the end even by pressing it against a flat, perpendicular surface before or during each cut. A small board attached at right angles to a bread board will serve nicely for this purpose. As each strip is cut, it need not be uncoiled. Simply mix the strips to be used in one color area together. It is not necessary to sew one strip to another for a hooked rug.

It is impossible to say how much material will be needed to make one rug of any given size, but it will probably take much more than you think. A piece of material will cover approximately one-fifth of its original size, or even less, when it is worked into the rug; and it will be wise to allow more material than this for a large, blended area, in order to avoid any obvious color breaks in conspicuous places.

Foundation. The foundation of the rug into which the strips of material are hooked will probably be burlap, although canvas and linen are sometimes used. Buy the best quality burlap you can find, since cheap burlap will not stand up under hard wear.

It is not essential to stretch the burlap on a frame for working, but it makes the work much easier. Swinging frames made especially for this work, can be bought, but they are comparatively costly. The stretchers on which an artist tacks his canvas to make an oil painting serve as an entirely satisfactory and inexpensive frame for rug making. These can be found at any art-goods store, and are easily assembled. Simply stretch the burlap taut across the frame, and tack it down securely at all sides with thumbtacks. Stretchers come in all sizes, but it is not necessary to buy a set large enough to accommodate the entire rug. Your frame should be only large enough to reach the middle without straining your arms. Simply untack the rug and move it into a new position as the work

Square hooked rug with round floral bouquet center motif in muted colors (American, early 19th century).

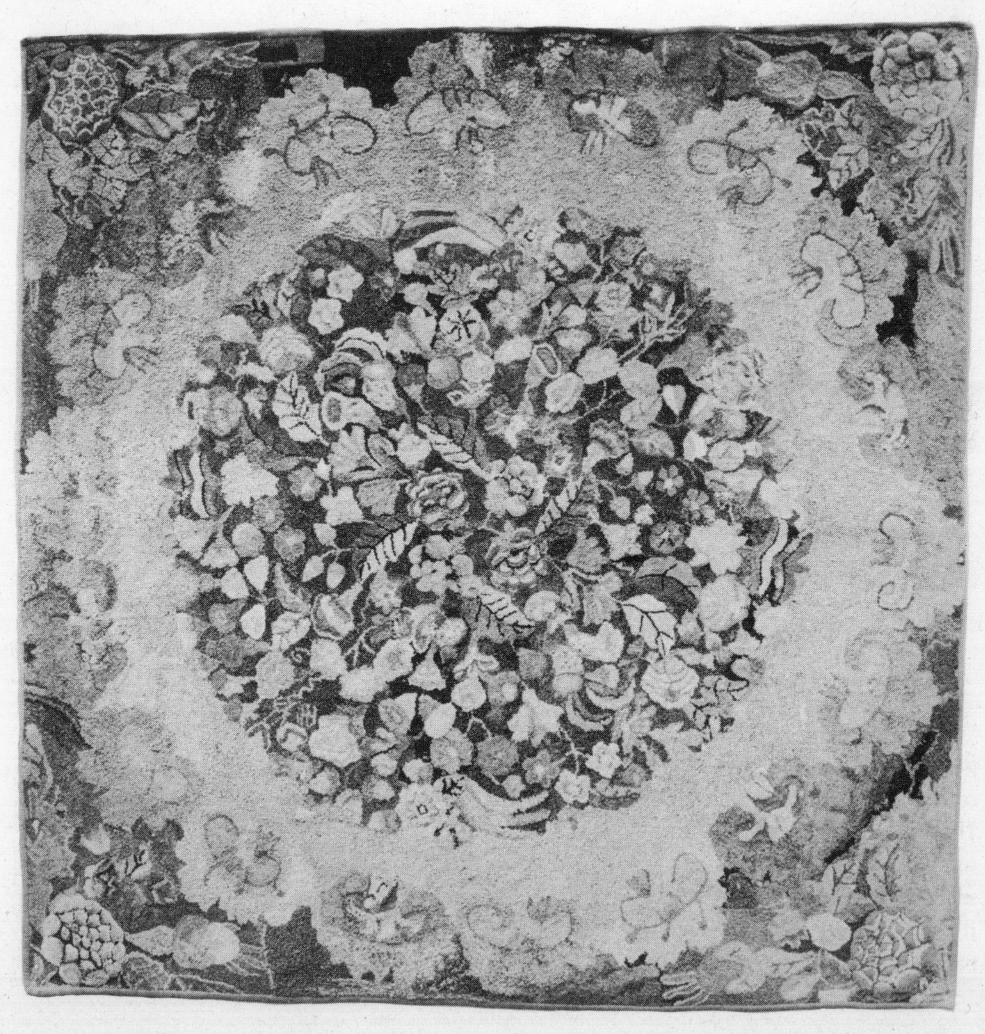

Hooked rug and matching block-printed fabric feature sprightly hunter on horseback and hounds. This charming modern design by Marion Voorhees is a fine example of the artistic effects which can be achieved with the hooked-rug technique. Note the interesting texture created by varying the directions of the rows.

progresses. The rest of the rug can be rolled up and fastened with tapes.

The Hook and How It Is Used. The ordinary rug hook is a simple device which resembles a large steel crochet hook, except that it usually has a wooden handle for easier gripping. It can be purchased at the needlework counter of most department stores. Besides such hook rugs, patented hooking devices are available. These slightly resemble a large sewing machine needle with a handle, and the strips must be threaded through them. They give excellent results when yarn wools are used for hooking, but materials are sometimes apt to snag in them. The patented hooks push the strips of material through the side of the burlap from which you are working, but the ordinary hooks pull them up from underneath.

To work with the ordinary hook, hold the strip of material underneath the frame. Push the hook through the space between the weft and the warp of the burlap, catch the strip in the hook, and pull it up into a loop about ½ inch high. Remove the hook from the strip, move two threads over across the burlap, and repeat the process. Continue pulling loops up in this way until the strip is used up, guiding the material from underneath with the left hand. The end of the strip is simply pulled up to the surface and snipped off level with the other loops. With a very little practice, you will find that it is quite easy to make the loops all fairly uniform in height. A more uniform surface effect is achieved by allowing the line of the loops to follow the warp or weft threads of the burlap over large color areas. But very interesting mosaic effects are sometimes gained by curving the line of loops to follow the outlines of the design, and then continuing the next row of loops along the same line of curve. Sharper color outlines are also obtained in this way.

Finishing. Leave at least an inch or two of burlap around the rug to be turned under the covered with rug tape after the hooking is complete. Stitch one side of the tape close to the loops and the other to the burlap.

Braided Rugs. Braided rugs require strips of material just as hooked rugs do, except that these strips need not be so narrow as for hooked rugs. And if certain cotton or rayon materials are to be used for the braided rug, they can be easily torn into strips instead of cut. Tear the strips anywhere from about 1 inch to 2 inches wide, but be sure that materials of approximately the same weight are all torn into strips of equal width.

The strips must be sewed together to form continuous lengths. This can be done as the work progresses, or a number of strips can be sewn at once and rolled into a ball for easier braiding. Braids of three strands are easiest to make, but five-strand braids can also be used.

The technique of making the rug amounts to nothing more than sewing one braided edge to another. Use a good, stout thread, preferably linen carpet thread, and a sharp needle, strong enough to go through several folds of material without bending or breaking.

The simplest and most popular shapes for braided rugs are the oval and the circle. The oval is first started by doubling the braid back on itself, and then continuing on around in coil formation. The circle is simply a continuous coil. The chief difficulty is to keep the rug flat. It usually tends to hump up in the middle, or to flare into ripples at the edges. This can be avoided by working on a flat surface (and if the rug is very large, the flat surface may have to be the floor), and watching the over-all effect carefully. If strain appears, ease the braids in a little more around the curves. Ripples are less likely to occur, but if they do, you might just as well snip the stitches for a few rows and do them over again.

But the braided rug need not be confined to the usual ovals and circles. Any number of effects can be achieved with braided units of various shapes and colors. These can be combined to form simple patterns. But they can often be difficult to fit together smoothly.

Crocheted Rugs. Only the single crochet stitch is usually used for crocheted rugs.

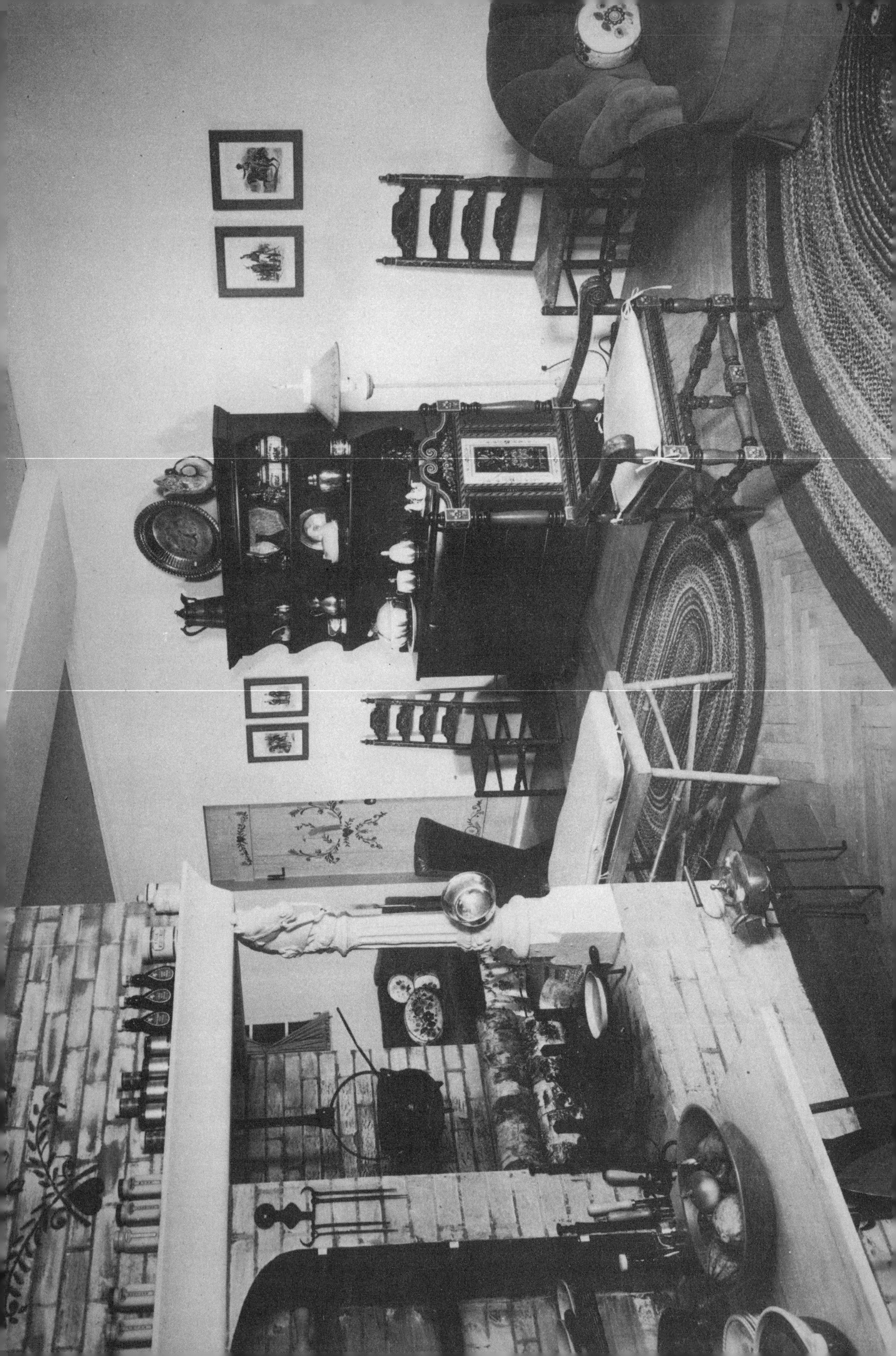

The material should be torn or cut into strips about ½ to ¾ of an inch wide, and the strips should be sewed end to end and rolled into balls before you start to crochet. Large crochet hooks, suitable for use with cloth strips, can be found at the needlework counter. Room-size crocheted rugs are seldom attempted, but some very good effects are achieved with small rugs. The easiest shape to work is a simple rectangle of solid, single crochet. It can be finished with rows of single crochet around the edge in contrasting color. Round or oval shapes can be worked out by following directions for crocheted doilies in solid stitches, but the process on the whole is less satisfactory than hooking or braiding.

Other Kinds of Hand-Made Rugs. Some interesting rugs are made with a sewing machine attachment by which strips of material are sewed in loops to a canvas foundation. And if you want to make rugs without the bother of saving and preparing materials, you may buy yarns in a variety of fibers and colors from your needlecraft counter. These can be worked into hooked rugs, cross-stitched rugs, tufted rugs, or crocheted rugs, and instructions are usually furnished with the materials. The truly enthusiastic craftswoman may even want to weave rugs. But a loom large enough for rug weaving is fairly expensive, and while the craft is not too difficult to learn it is not mastered overnight.

Fabric rug with scrolling vines and stylized flowers made of bits of appliqued felt. Design could be easily adapted for hooked rug. (American, 19th century.)

VII

HOUSEHOLD REPAIRS AND IMPROVEMENT

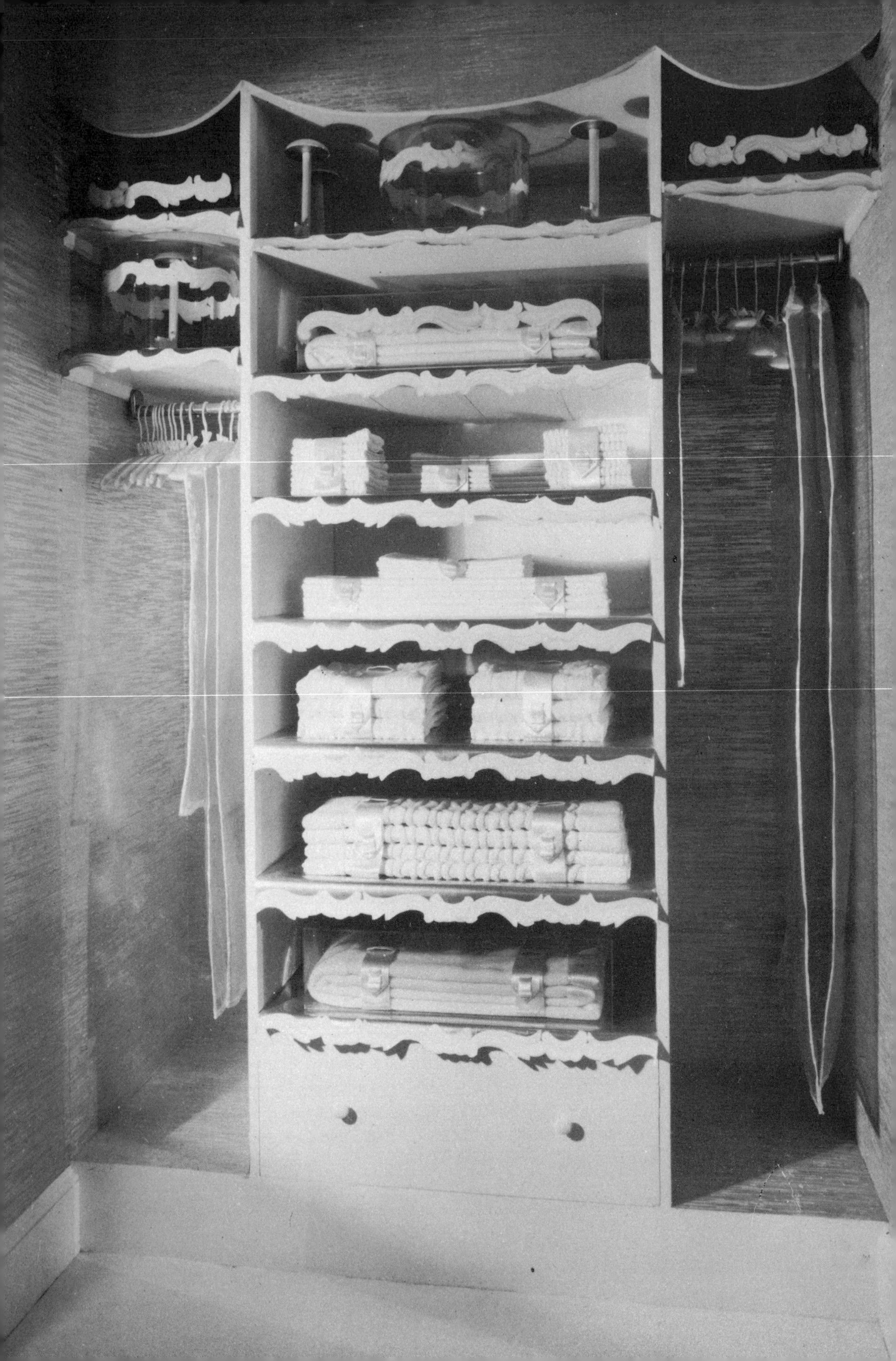

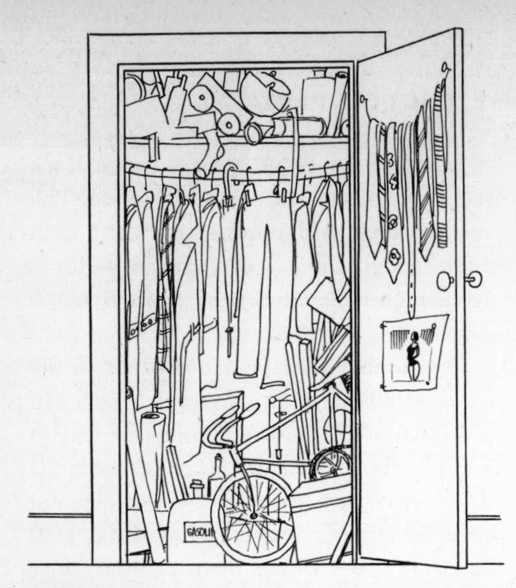

CHAPTER XX

SHELVES AND CLOSETS

"WHEN I build a house, I'm going to eliminate the rooms and just have closets. I've never had enough closets — no, nor shelves either," said a mother of four children as she looked despairingly at the toys all over the floor, the small coats draped limply over the arm of the chair, and the tennis racket resting on the mantel. "What's the use of telling them to pick things up and put them away when there's simply no place to put another thing?" And she showed us, first, the hall closet, ready to burst the hinges off its door. "I could clean it out every morning, and it would look the same by bedtime."

But Johnny and Julia and the two younger children (to say nothing of their father) weren't deliberately careless or untidy. They really didn't know where to put things because nothing had ever been assigned a special storage place of its own. Then their mother decided that something would have to be done about the situation. She removed everything from the closet and took inventory of all the items needing storage space. She found that some could be banished to closets elsewhere. She arranged what was left according to size and purpose, frequency of use, and who used it. She realized then that the reason the younger children seldom hung up their umbrellas or raincoats was because they could not reach the hangers and rod without dragging over a chair to climb on.

New shelves were added inside the closet and shallow shelves were also attached to the closet door. A new partition was installed to accommodate an extra rod at a lower height which the smaller children could easily reach. Each item was assigned a place of its own and that place was given a gaily decorated label as a gentle hint not to lapse into forgetfulness. Miracle of miracles! Everything fitted into place without a bit of clutter. The entire family took such pride in the trim, new appearance — and convenience — of their closet that each member vied with the others to put every article back into place after use.

SHELF INSTALLATION

THE installation of utility shelves involves only the simplest kind of carpentry work, and even the complete novice can learn to do it. All he needs is some lumber, hammer, saw, nails, screws, or other fasteners, and possibly a brace and bits or drill. Then if he takes careful measurements, cuts his wood accurately, and places and fastens it correctly, the results are almost sure to be satisfactory.

Lumber for Shelves. Lumber is sold both by length and by board footage. Lumber is usually sold by board footage when the thickness is more than 1 inch or when a large quantity is involved. Since lumber for shelves is usually 1 inch or less in thickness, its cost can be readily computed by multiplying the length of the lumber by the cost per foot. Costs per foot vary, of course, according to the width, thickness, grade, classification, and the variety of wood.

Lumber is classed as *rough* (lumber as it comes from the sawmill to the lumber yard or factory), *surfaced* (lumber which has been planed smooth), and *worked* (made into moldings, floor boards, and so on). Surfaced lumber dressed on both sides and both edges is the best to buy for shelves.

Hardwoods are not only more difficult to work with than softwoods, but also much more expensive — at least certain kinds. Probably the most satisfactory softwood for shelves is well-seasoned white pine. Like other softwoods, it is graded according to the presence or absence of defects and blemishes (such as knots). *Select* lumber, which is graded as A, B, C, and D, contains few or no blemishes. *Common* lumber, which is graded as 1, 2, 3, 4, and 5, contains anywhere from a few to many blemishes. If the shelves are to be stained, shellacked, or varnished, choose grades A or B select lumber. For painted shelves, grades C and D select or 1 and 2 common are satisfactory. Grades 3, 4, and 5 common usually contain too many blemishes to be used without allowing for considerable waste.

Lumber Sizes. Lumber is sold according to its rough size, but its actual size after dressing is somewhat smaller. For example, a board which is sold as a 1 x 2 (1 inch thick and 2 inches wide) may actually be anywhere from ¾ to ⅞ of an inch thick and from 1⅝ to 1¾ of an inch wide. The average shelf will require lumber 1 inch thick (rough size) and whatever width is needed (usually anywhere from 6 to 10 inches).

The lumber may be ordered cut to the required length or in whatever length can be cut most economically and then cut to the necessary measurements at home. If it is important that the shelves be cut accurately to fit into a given space, it is probably better to cut them yourself, since not all lumber dealers will take the trouble to measure to the fraction of an inch.

Seasoning. Lumber must be thoroughly seasoned or it will warp and shrink. Seasoning is done by drying the lumber in a kiln until the natural moisture in the wood has evaporated. There is no way to look at a piece of lumber and determine whether or not it has been thoroughly seasoned. But no reputable lumber dealer will sell green lumber for seasoned lumber, so the best assurance one has of obtaining well seasoned lumber is to buy from a reliable dealer.

Installing the Shelves. Stationary shelves must be supported by brackets, bearers, or angle irons (movable or adjustable shelves are sometimes fitted into grooves, but their installation usually requires a certain amount of carpentry skill). Shelf

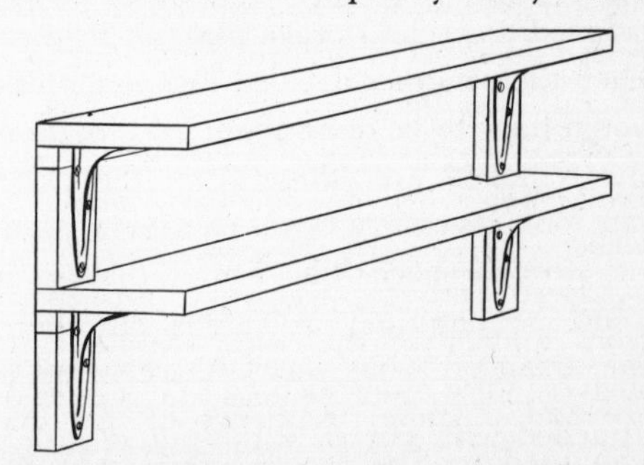

FIG. 1. Open shelves supported by brackets and bearers attached to plaster wall with screws fastened to the wall studs.

brackets can be made from wood, but the metal kinds, which come in various styles and sizes, are much simpler to use. Small shelves which are not expected to carry more than a light weight can usually be attached anywhere to a wall of lath-and-plaster construction by screwing the brackets into the laths and to the underside of the shelf. For larger shelves, the brackets must be screwed to a wall stud or fastened to a lath or a plywood wall with split wing toggle screws (*see the section on Fasteners in the Chapter on Tools and How to Use them for the method of using these screws*). Wall studs, which are usually 16 inches apart, can be located by tapping lightly on the wall with a hammer or your fist. The taps will sound hollow between the studs and dull directly over them. Brackets are generally used for open shelves where end supports cannot be installed. If the shelf is very long, more than two brackets or a back bearer may be needed for adequate support. A bearer is simply a piece of wood or plywood (usually 1 x 1, 1 x 2, or 1 x 3 inch size) that is attached to the wall underneath the shelf to provide support along the back edge. If the shelf must bear considerable weight, the brackets are best screwed to wooden uprights, which, in turn, are screwed to the wall studs.

Brackets are unnecessary and conspicuous for shelves which are fitted into a recessed wall space. Instead, end bearers can be installed on the end walls of the recessed space as supports for the shelves. Long shelves will require back bearers as well.

Closed ends for shelves can be made from lumber of the same width as the shelves. Very often such end pieces can be attached with screws to the side of a door or window frame. Bearers or angle irons are then attached to the inside face of

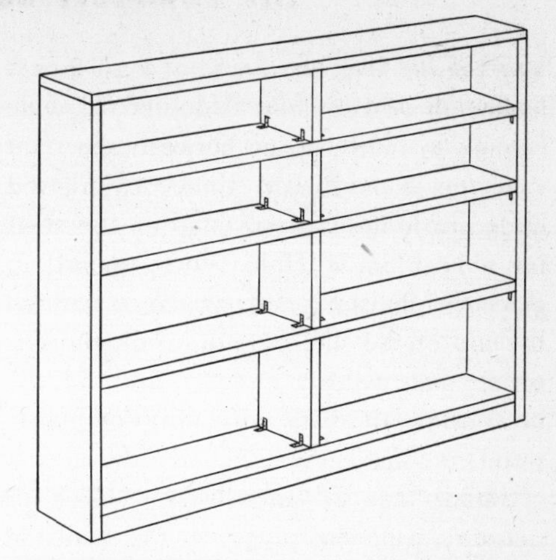

FIG. 2. One way to provide center support for long shelves where back bearers cannot be attached to wall. Angle irons are fastened both above and beneath shelves.

the end piece as shelf supports. Sometimes landlords will not permit tenants to drill holes in walls to attach back bearers for long shelves. One way to provide center support for long shelves in this case is to cut pieces of lumber of the same width as the shelves, so that they fit the spaces between the shelves exactly. These pieces can be attached to both the top and bottom surfaces of the shelves with angle irons. If the pieces are carefully cut to fit the spaces between the shelves and placed directly one above the other, they will act as a solid center support.

Where end pieces cannot be attached to the side of a door or window frame, they can be fastened to 2 x 2 pieces of lumber screwed to the floor. The end piece is then attached to the 2 x 2 piece with screws driven in from the outside of the end piece. The heads of the screws should be countersunk and the holes filled in with putty or plastic wood. The end piece will require temporary support until the shelves are in place.

End pieces especially improve the appearance of shelves which begin near the floor and extend upward any distance.

The bottom shelf should be at least 2 or 3 inches above the floor. A footboard wide enough to fit the space between the shelf and the floor should then be inserted underneath the bottom edge of the shelf for a neat finish. Hold the footboard in place with finishing nails driven in through the top of the shelf. Countersink the finishing nails with a nail set and fill the holes above the nails with putty or plastic wood.

Shelves can be installed on brick or masonry walls by plugging the walls or by fastening the brackets or bearers with a split-wing toggle bolt. To plug a brick or masonry wall, it is necessary to remove the mortar in the joint nearest to the place where the shelf is to be installed. If the wall has been plastered, papered, or painted, so that a joint is not visible, it can be found by driving a long nail into the wall as various points near the place of installation. The nail will not pierce brick or stone, but can be driven into the mortar of a joint rather easily. When one joint has been found in a brick wall, other joints can be located easily, since bricks are usually 9 inches long and 3 inches thick. The joints in a fieldstone wall can be found only by trial. Plug a vertical joint for a horizontal fixture, and a horizontal joint for a vertical fixture. After the joint has been located, dig the mortar out to a depth of 1½ to 2 inches with a seam drill (a tool which resembles a cold chisel). The seam drill is driven into the mortar with a hammer. The hole should be about 2 or 3 inches long.

Next, cut a wooden plug slightly larger than the hole, and taper one end to fit the hole exactly. A hatchet is useful for trimming down the end of the plug, but a plane can also be used. It is essential that the wood be absolutely dry; wood which has swollen from dampness will later shrink as it dries out and become loosened. The slightly tapered end of the plug is then driven into the hole in the wall with a hammer. The plug should be forced in to the depth of the hole or until the plug is so tight it can be driven in no further. The end of the plug should be sawed off flush with the wall. The bracket or bearer is then nailed or screwed to the exposed end of the plug.

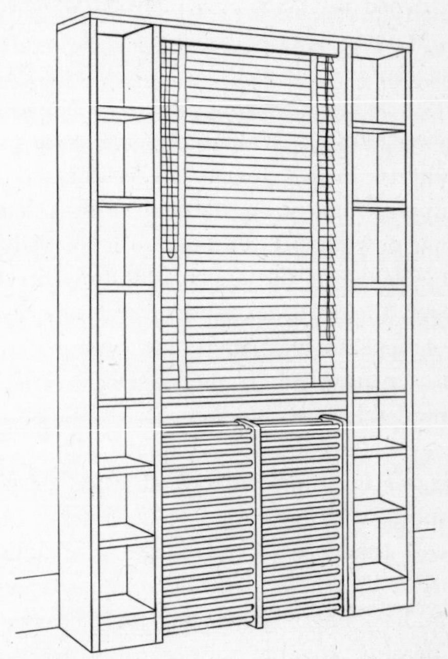

FIG. 3. Radiator beneath a window becomes less prominent with flanking shelves. Dowel rods across the front hide radiator without interfering with heat supply. Wood adjacent to radiator should be flameproofed or lined with asbestos.

Decorative Value of Shelves. Shelves not only offer useful storage space but can also add decorative interest to a room. The horizontal lines of shelves can help to make a too high wall appear lower. If shelves are used on more than one wall, they should all be at the same levels. In that way, the eye is carried in continuous lines from one wall to another. If the space between the shelves varies, the greatest distance should be at the bottom and the least at the top. If the top spaces are greater, the shelves appear to be top-heavy.

An interesting way to disguise an ugly radiator in front of a window is to install shelves on each side of the window. The shelves should project about 1½ or 2 inches beyond the radiator and should be closed with end pieces. Holes are drilled near the exterior edge of the end pieces next to the window frame. Large dowel sticks are fitted into the holes to hide the radiator. If the dowels are spaced about 3 to 6 inches apart, they will not interfere with the heating functions of the radiator. The top of the radiator is hidden with a shelf attached to the end pieces. The shelf can be used to hold plants.

The awkward appearance of the small, high windows which often flank a fireplace can be greatly diminshed by installing shelves on either side of the fireplace. The shelf tops would correspond to the height of the mantel to form an unbroken line, or the shelves may be built up to fit around the windows.

CLOSETS

CLOSETS deserve the same careful planning and decorative treatments that you would give a room, even though a closet door is closed most of the time. The very fact that the closet is not constantly on display makes it possible to use bold or unusual decorative effects that might become tiresome in a room where they had to be looked at all the time. To open the door on a neatly arranged and gaily decorated closet can be as much of a pleasant surprise as unwrapping a pretty present.

Closet Arrangements. Closets usually seem too small and too crowded because we don't make the most efficient use of their space. For example, clothes closets usually contain but one rod for hangers placed high enough to accommodate a long evening gown. Yet the average woman's wardrobe probably contains more skirts and jackets than evening gowns, and a skirt or jacket is only about half the length of an evening gown. Therefore, all the space beneath the skirts and jackets is wasted as a rule. One solution would be to group them all together on the rod and use the space underneath for shelves or storage chests. But we think an even better solution is to partition the closet with plywood panels and to install rods at two different heights on each side of the partition. The space above the lower rod can be fitted with shelves which are much more convenient to reach than shelves nearer the floor level.

In fairly deep closets, the rod for hangers is probably located at the far end, while the side walls have rows of hooks which become catchalls for every sort of garment. Since it does a garment no good to drape it over a hook, why not remove the hooks entirely and install shallow shelves or chests of drawers on the side walls? Sweaters, which might sag out of

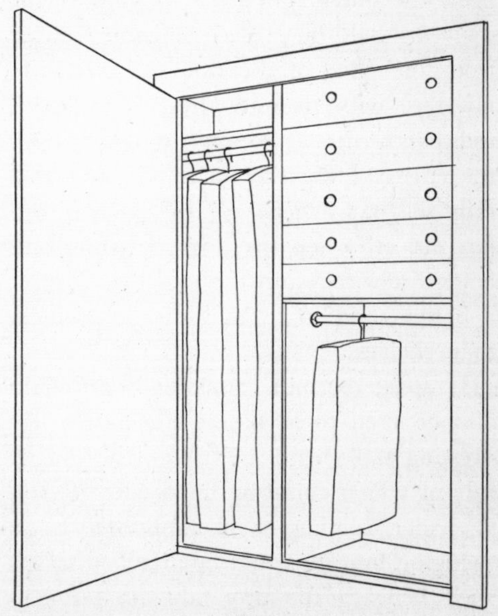

FIG. 4. Hang short garments from low rod and utilize space above for drawers or shelves.

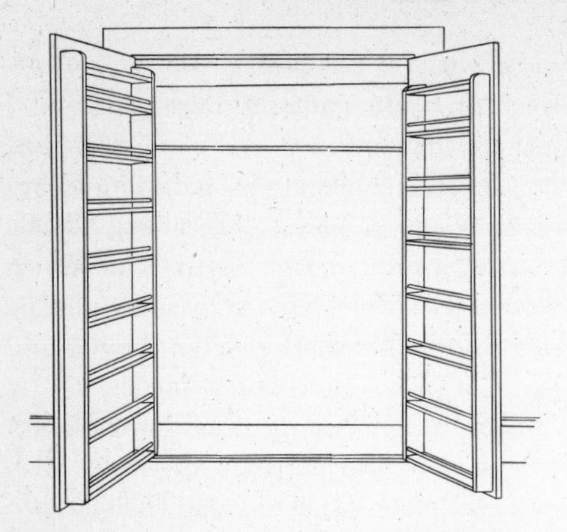

FIG. 5. Shelves attached to closet doors can double the storage space.

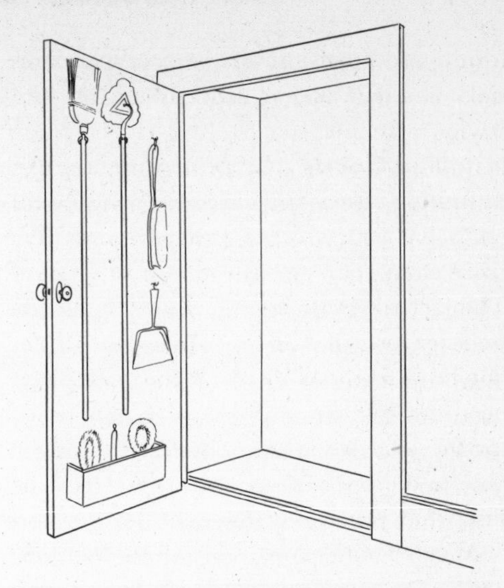

FIG. 6. Cleaning equipment can be kept within easy reach in racks and clips attached to closet door.

shape on a hanger, could be neatly folded and kept in cases on the shelves. Gloves, hose, bags, lingerie, shoes, boxes for costume jewelry, and so on, could all be kept easily accessible on the shelves.

Closet doors can also be utilized for additional storage space. Too often they serve merely as a place to hang a shoe bag or a tie rack. But if shallow shelves are installed on the inside surface of the door, its entire area can be used for storage. The outer end piece to support the shelves should be placed far enough away from the edge of the door so as not to interfere with its outward swing. Dowel rods can be fitted into the end pieces above the edges of the shelves to act as guard rails so that articles on the shelves will not slip off when the door is swung out. Somestimes racks on the closet door offer a better solution to the storage problem than shelves.

If space permits, a closet door could also be used to accommodate a tray-like dressing table with a lift top, the underside of which could be lined with mirror. A wider folding shelf supported by a swinging bracket could be attached to the shelf beneath the tray table to serve as a seat. A closet which is quite roomy can even serve as a dressing room if it is equipped with proper lighting and a dressing table or chest of drawers.

A child's closet should be equipped with a rod for hangers and shelves within easy reach of the youngster. If two children of different ages (and hence, if different heights) share a closet, perhaps it could be partitioned to provide rods at two convenient levels.

Closets for cleaning equipment can be provided with clips attached to the walls or the door for gripping brooms, mops, long-handled brushes and so on. Shelves or racks will provide storage space for smaller brushes, the dustpan, cleaning cloths, and so on.

The storage of hobby equipment must be dealt with on an individual basis, since one family may have a large assortment of golf clubs, tennis rackets, and baseball bats and mitts, while another might collect nothing larger than dominoes, chess pieces, and playing cards. The woman who sews can work more efficiently with a special sewing closet for storing a dress form, yard goods, scraps, and other materials and equipment and sometimes the sewing machine, too.

Installing Closets. If careful planning and utilization of existing closet space still does not solve your storage problems, perhaps more closets can be built in here and there. The actual building of closets calls for some carpentry skill and probably ought not be attempted by the novice, but you need not hire an architect and contractor for the job. Any good carpenter should be able to do it for you if you explain to him just what you want.

A closet can often be tucked into the end of a hall. Twin bedroom closets on either side of a window not only solve storage problems but also make a recessed nook in front of the window which could be a charming frame for a dressing table. Shallow closets along one entire wall need not take up much more room than bookshelves, and yet could serve for storing everything from games to luggage.

If space limitations allow no room for the customary hinged swinging doors for a closet, one could install sliding doors, rollaway doors, or the corrugated folding doors.

Closet Decoration. If you love bright colors, a closet is the place where you can indulge your tastes without any inhibitions. For example, one woman painted the walls and the inside of the door of her closet a brilliant, clear red because she loved that color but hesitated to use it in large quantities in her bedroom. She used brown and white accessories and trimmed the shelves with pleated brown and white shelf edging. A closet in another room boasted vivid emerald green and white striped wallpaper paired with black and green accessories.

For a really luxurious effect, you might

Gaily flowered garment bags, accessory boxes, hat stands, and covered hangers add a feminine touch to her closet.

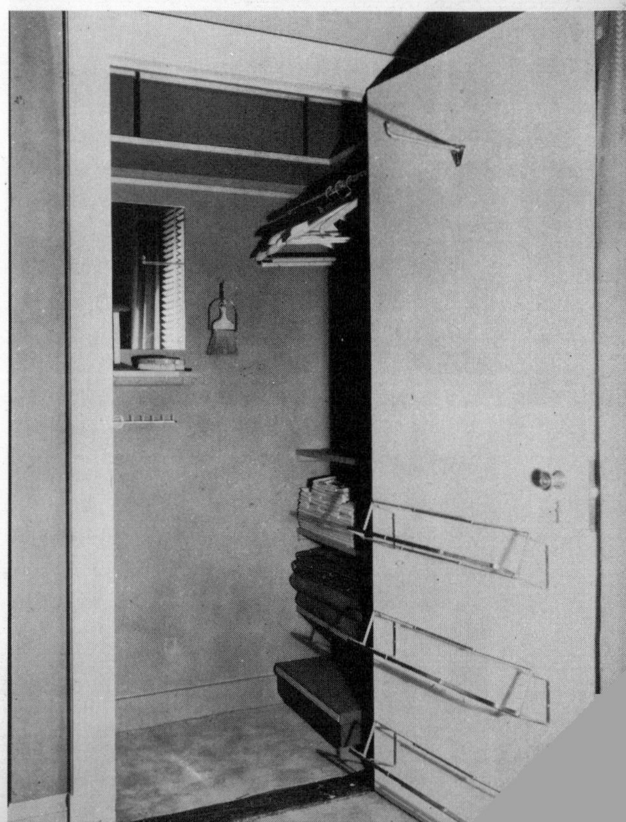

His closet is trimly masculine with metal shoe racks, mirror above tie rack, and clothes brush conveniently placed.

cover the walls, shelves, and even the floor with padded, quilted satin or taffeta. Mattress ticking is more homespun, but it makes a practical fabric for covering closet walls because its close weave repels dust and it is easy to clean with the vacuum cleaner.

The decorative scheme of the closet should be in keeping with its purpose. The closet in a man's bedroom, a hall closet, or a game closet call for a trimly tailored treatment, while mother and daughter may prefer satin bows and red roses in their bedroom closets.

Shelf edgings always add an interesting note of decoration. Such edgings are obtainable in a variety of materials, including fabrics, plastic, paper, and oilcloth and in many prints and plain colors or combinations of both. The shelf edging can be selected to match or contrast with the accessories or the color of the walls.

Baby's own closet is large enough to serve as a dressing room.

Closet Accessories. Garment bags, hat and shoe boxes or racks, and other accessories not only protect the wardrobe but can also help to make a closet look neat and attractive. Matching closet ensembles are made in many colors, but if you don't find exactly what you want, why not make your own? Save all the sturdy cardboard boxes which come your way until you have a collection. Then cover them with wallpaper, crepe paper, or fabric. To make them look really important, pad them with a layer of cotton. Cut the cotton to fit the lid and sides of the box. Then cut strips of crepe paper or fabric long enough to go around the sides and 2 inches wider than the box is deep. Paste one edge of the strip to the bottom of the box and fold the other over the top edge of the box and paste to the inside. If you are working with crepe paper, stretch it taut and smooth as you work. Now tuft the padded and covered sides and lid of the box with yarn or narrow ribbon. or, easier still, with the gold-colored metal shanks sold at stationery stores. Padding should not be used if the box is to be covered with wallpaper. Instead, the wallpaper should be pasted directly to the cardboard. Or use plain-colored paper or one of the brilliant metallic papers as the cover and decorate it with wallpaper cutouts, decalcomanias, gummed stars, braid, or other trimming material. Braid can be attached with "liquid thread."

Plain wooden hangers can be padded with cotton and covered with crepe paper, ribbon, or fabric to match the boxes. To cover with crepe paper, cut it in strips about ¾ of an inch wide. Cut across the grain of the paper. Then paste a small square of crepe paper over the end of the hanger. Place the strip over the square and wrap the strip around and around the hanger, stretching the paper tightly as you wrap. End the strip at the wire hook and use a little paste or scotch tape as a fastener. Begin at the other end and wrap the rest of the hanger. Then wrap the wire hook with a ⅜-of-an-inch strip of crepe paper.

The coat hanger can be wrapped with ribbon in much the same way, or wider ribbon can be made into tubes by seaming the edges together. Wrap the cotton padding with thread so that the padding will not slip when the ribbon tubes are pulled over the ends of the hanger. For a feminine closet, why not sprinkle the cotton padding with sachet?

Piles of sheets, towels, pillow cases, and so on in the linen closet always look neat and secure when they are held with straps, although we doubt whether the straps actually serve any really practical purpose. However, they do look nice, and they are easily made from tape, ribbon, or strips of fabric. Fabric strips can be folded in two, wrong side out, the edges seamed together, and then turned right side out. Make the straps long enough to go around the piles of linen and to allow for a generous lapover. Fold one end of the strap to the wrong side. Slip a metal weight (a dressmaker's weight is good for this purpose) inside the folded end and stitch the edges together. Make a loop of the same material as the strap and sew the ends of the loop to the wrong side of the strap near the other end. This end is then folded back over the ends of the loop and stitched in place for a neat finish. To keep the straps from slipping, tack them in place to the closet shelves. Then lay the piles of linens on top of the straps, loop the straps around the linens, and pull the weighted ends of the straps through the loops.

Closet shops and notion counters offer many kinds of racks and holders for shoes, hats, ties, and so on. Some of these gadgets are very practical, while others take up more space than they deserve.

Coat hanger rods can be bought in any length needed. Both wooden and metal rods are available. Wooden rods can be painted to match the color scheme of the closet, but they are less practical than the metal ones because the rubbing of the coat hanger hooks usually scrapes away the paint. Hangers slide much more easily on an aluminum or chrome finished rod. The rod can be fitted into wood supports with holes drilled to fit the rod — or one can use standard metal brackets.

Lighting the Closet. Groping around in a dark closet can be very annoying, and adequate lighting is just as important in a closet as any other part of the house. However, it is not advisable to light a closet by makeshift methods (*see the Chapter on Wiring and Electrical Repairs*). If properly installed wiring is out of the question, a large flashlight might be placed in some easy-to-reach spot.

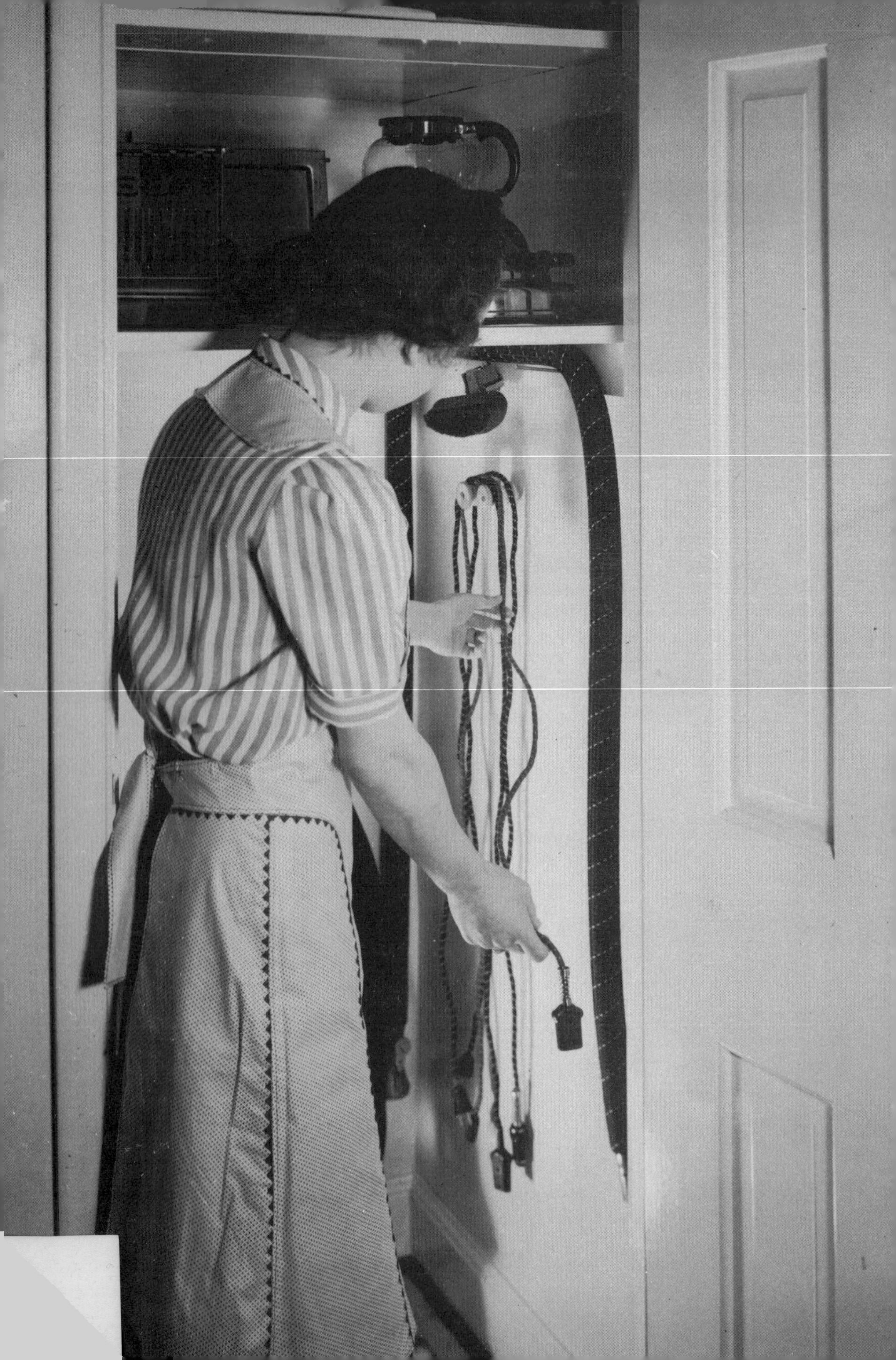

CHAPTER XXI

WIRING AND ELECTRICAL REPAIRS

EVER since man learned to make electricity work for him, new ways of using it have appeared in ever-increasing numbers, until — could we but afford it — most of life's chores could be taken care of by pressing a button or flicking a switch. Electric lights are so commonplace, we wonder how the human race avoided congenital eyestrain after centuries of reading by candlelight. But electricity soon proved it could do many things besides light a bulb. It was put to work on washing machines, sewing machines, vacuum cleaners, ranges, toasters, clocks, radios, fans, irons, refrigerators, mixers, razors, dishwashers, freezers, blankets, and all the other things we'd like to have to make life easier. Most of us look forward to the day when we can have all these wonders brought home and put to work for us without thinking much about where the power will come from to run them. After all, the house is wired for electricity, isn't it? And we made sure that every room had enough outlets. So the electricity is there, as long as we pay for it. But are you sure that adequate power really is there? If your house was built before 1938, there's a fairly good chance that it isn't. And not every house built since then has adequate wiring. So let's investigate the matter before installing more and better electrical equipment.

HOUSE WIRING

AT the very outset, it should be emphasized that no one but a licensed electrician should ever attempt to make any repairs or alterations on the wiring system of the house, Tampering with the house wiring system by anyone else is not only a violation of the building code in most communities, but it may also automatically void any fire insurance policies on the house. Nevertheless, it's a good thing to know how a house wiring system operates.

Amperes, Volts, and Watts. Most of us know that the terms *ampere, volt,* and *watt* have something to do with electricity, but we may not know just what. We probably know that a 100-watt bulb gives more light than a 60-watt bulb, and so we assume that more wattage means more power. And we're right. It does take more electric power to light a 100-watt bulb than a 60-watt one. A watt is simply a unit of electric power. An ampere is the unit whereby the intensity of electric current is measured. A volt is the unit for measuring the force or pressure applied to an ampere. In other words, it takes volts to push amperes over the wire to produce watts. The number of amperes times the number of volts equals the number of watts; thus amperes, volts, and watts are interdependent. The amount of wattage provided by our wiring system will depend upon the volt-ampere capacity of the wire. Electricity does not flow through a pipe like water, but through a copper wire. However, an electric wire might be compared to a water pipe as far as carrying power goes. A water pipe 1-inch in diameter will carry but a fraction of the water which a 12-inch main will carry. In the same way, the available wattage depends upon the "load" the wiring system will carry.

In most of our older houses, two wires bring electricity into the house from the power line on the street. A two-wire system usually allows electricity to enter at a pressure of 105-120 volts. Newer houses have a three-wire system which permits a pressure of 200-240 volts. An electric range or an electric water heater require 230-240 volt service.

Circuits. After the electricity enters the house, it is delivered to the various outlets by separate paths, or *circuits*. Most houses built before 1938 have 15-ampere circuits (No. 14 wires), which are adequate for lights and for a limited number of appliances which do not require too high wattage. But if you expect to use a number of appliances, such as a mixer, a toaster, a grill, a coffee maker, and so on in the kitchen or dining room, you should have 20-ampere circuits (No. 12 wires) for such equipment.

Now, as we said before, the number of amperes times the number of volts equals the number of watts. Therefore, in a two-wire system of 115 volts, each 15-ampere circuit will provide 1,725 watts (15 x 115 = 1,725). Let's say that the two outlets on one wall base in the living room are both on the same 15-ampere circuit in a house with a two-wire system. In one outlet we plug in a reflector floor lamp which uses a 500-watt bulb. The other outlet is the only one convenient to the places where we want two more lamps, each with a 100-watt bulb, and a small radio which uses 30 watts. So we put a three-way outlet-fixture into the wall outlet, and the lamps light and the radio plays. On chilly days we bring in the electric heater, which uses 600 watts, and plug it into the outlet with the lamps and the radio with the aid of a two-way outlet fixture plugged into the three-way one. Now, if we use all this electrical equipment at one time, it consumes 1,330 watts, but since this is still less than the 1,725-watt capacity of the circuit, everything still operates (although not at maximum efficiency).

Then one evening we decide to prepare a little snack in the living room for our guests and we bring in the electric grill. Now the grill always worked very well when we used it in the dining room, but we never realized that the outlets in the dining room were on another circuit and that the grill uses 1,000 watts. When we plug it into the same outlet that the reflector lamp is attached to, we have a total of 2,330 watts on a 1,725 watt circuit. If the wiring system had no safety controls, such an overloaded circuit would burn out the insulation on the wires and probably start a fire. However, that's not what happens. A fuse or circuit breaker simply cuts off the current automatically, and leaves us with no hamburgers sizzling on the grill, no radio playing, no heater warming our toes, and no glowing lamps. If we have an extra fuse handy, it's easy to restore the current, *providing* we first take away the grill. If no one thought to buy fuses, then we just hope we can find some candles somewhere. Next time we will read the information on an appliance telling how much wattage it takes.

A circuit may not be overloaded to the point where the fuse blows, and yet if too many appliances are plugged into one circuit they may not all operate at maximum efficiency. The current is tapped in too many places, and the result is much the same as that of turning on all the cold or hot water faucets in the house at one time. We would not get a full flow of water from any faucet. Current is wasted and our electric bills are higher than they should be. If the lights dim or flicker when the motor in your refrigerator turns on, that is a danger signal that the circuit is handling more work than it can take care of efficiently. Perhaps the circuit covers too large an area. Some of our older homes have only one or two circuits which, when they were installed, were intended to provide current only for electric lights. If the circuit serves a number of rooms and the current is tapped here, there, and the next place for appliances, the system is overworked. If your iron doesn't heat as well as it should, it may not be the fault of the appliance but of the wiring system.

How many circuits should a house have? Of course, that depends on the size of the house. A 15-ampere or general purpose circuit will service up to 500 square feet of floor space. Such a circuit will accommodate lights and such low-wattage appliances as a radio, a vacuum cleaner, a heating pad, a clock, a small fan, or other equipment. A circuit of this size will also handle such appliances as toasters, grills, hand irons, roaster-ovens, coffee percolators, refrigerators, waffle irons, and so on, if the length of the circuit does not exceed approximately 35 feet. As a rule, however, appliances of this kind are better operated on a circuit of at least 20 amperes. High-wattage equipment, such as ranges, water heaters, or automatic washing machines, require separate circuits of their own.

It's easy enough to find out how many circuits you have and (as a rule) the capacity of each, by examining the fuse box or circuit-breaker panel. Each fuse or circuit breaker controls one circuit.

Fuses and Circuit Breakers. The safety valve in the wiring system is the fuse or the circuit breaker. It prevents short circuits or overloading of wires which might cause the wires to become overheated and possibly to set the house afire. Instead, an overheated wire merely melts the soft metal in a fuse and cuts off the current. When that happens, a fuse is said to "blow" or "burn out." It is easy to determine which fuse has blown — it will have a dark smudge or a crack on the mica window over the top. If the circuit is controlled by a circuit breaker, a lever is snapped out of position. All that is necessary to restore the current to the circuit is to replace the blown fuse with a new one or to snap the lever back into position in the circuit breaker panel. However, before doing either, whatever has caused the break in the circuit must be remedied or removed.

A short circuit can be caused when the two conductors in a wire, plug, switch, or socket touch each other. This may happen when the insulation material on a wire has worn or the screws holding the wires in a plug or other fixture have loosened. If the offending wire or fixture can be detached from the circuit, the fuse or lever can safely be replaced. If the trouble has occurred in the circuit wires, an electrician will have to be called. To avoid short circuits, watch for frayed cords or loose wires in plugs, sockets, or other fixtures. If a wire starts to spark, sputter, or smoke, it means that the insulation has worn off and the two conductors are beginning to touch.

When this difficulty occurs on a plug attached to an outlet, unscrew the fuse or pull the lever of the circuit breaker before removing the plug to avoid possible burns or shocks.

Blown fuses or displaced circuit breakers caused by overloading are very simple to remedy. Simply reduce the number of appliances or lights on the circuit to a capacity it can safely handle. Then replace the fuse or the lever in the circuit breaker.

How to Replace a Fuse. After the cause of a blown fuse has been determined and remedied, it should be removed and replaced. If the cause is not remedied, the new fuse will blow, too. Don't be afraid of the fuse—it won't "bite" if you touch only the rim. Unscrew it with your fingers; don't grasp the fuse with a pair of pliers. Then screw the new fuse in place and close the switch. In order not to put too much of a load on the current when it is restored, turn off as many lights or appliances on the circuit as possible before replacing the fuse.

Use only fuses which bear a label stating that they have been approved as meeting the fire prevention standards of the Underwriters' Laboratories. The safety of your house can be endangered by a faulty fuse. Always use the right size of fuse for the size of the circuit. A 15-ampere fuse must be used on a 15-ampere circuit (No. 14 wire). If anyone ever tells you that your appliances will work better if you put a 20-ampere fuse on a 15-ampere circuit, don't listen. It's true that a 20-ampere fuse will permit more current to pass over the circuit, and as a result the appliances may seem to function better. However, the current must work much harder to get over the smaller wire. This is not only wasteful use of current but also a dangerous risk. If the wire carries more current than it should, it will probably become overheated, burn out its insulation, and start a fire.

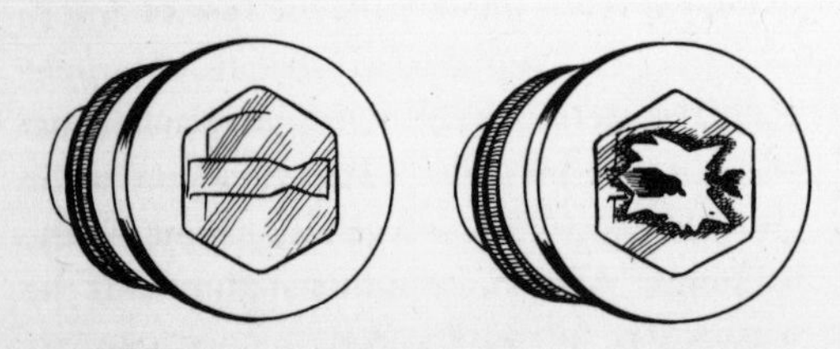

FIG. 1. Fuse (at left) as it appears when new. Blown fuse (right) has blackened smudge on "window."

Current. Electric current flows into a light bulb or appliance on one set of wires in the cord and out again on another set of wires. That is why all cords and cables contain two sets of wires. If the current flows only in one direction, it is called *direct current,* or D.C. for short. If the direction of the flow is alternated at regular intervals, the current is said to be *alternating current,* or A.C. for short. No appliance or fixture of any kind which is made specifically for use with A.C. current should ever be plugged into a D.C. circuit, and vice versa. To do so can burn out a fuse, or, worse yet, ruin the appliance. Radios are especially vulnerable. Some appliances are made for use on either type of current. If such appliances do not seem to operate well, take the plug out, turn it around, and put it back in. If you are not sure of the type of current you have, find out, and then read the information carried on most appliances as to which type of current they are designed for.

CORDS, PLUGS, AND SOCKETS

Cords. As stated before, if the insulation on an electric cord becomes frayed or worn, the two sets of wire strands in the cord may come in contact with each other and cause a short circuit. Before that happens, the cord should be repaired, providing it is worth repairing. If the entire cord is in bad condition, discard it and buy a

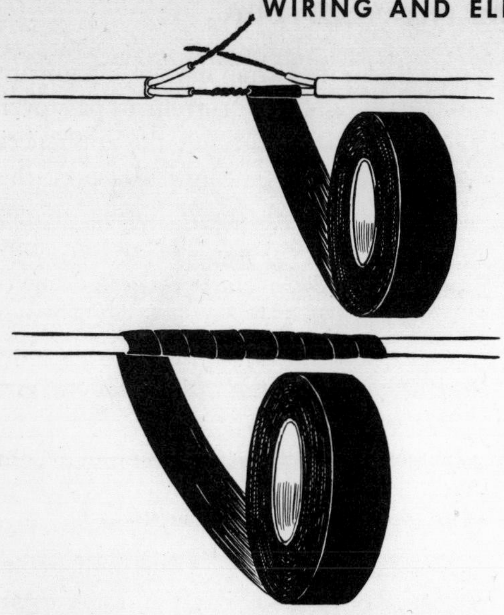

FIG. 2. To splice frayed cord, strip off insulation to expose copper strands. Twist together. Tape each wire separately, and then tape both together.

new cord. But a cord which has merely been damaged in one section can usually be made serviceable again. Before repairing any cord, socket, or plug, first remove the part from any electrical outlet. Cut the cord in two at the point of damage with a pair of pliers or a wire cutter. Strip off the insulation material with a knife or razor blade until about 2 inches of bare wire is exposed on each of the cut ends of the cord. Be careful not to damage the copper strand. Twist one set of strands on one end of the cord together with one set of strands on the other end of the cord. Twist the two ends of the other set of strands together. Wrap each set of strands with electrical insulation tape. Then tape both of the wrapped strands together.

Treat cords with care to prevent damage. All cords will wear out eventually, but their life can be prolonged if they are not abused. Never run a cord under a carpet or along a floor where it can be stepped on or tripped over. Tacked cords can be fire hazards. Above all, *never* drive a tack *through* a cord. If you do not have enough outlets to accommodate your appliances, have more installed by a licensed electrician. An extension cord plugged into an outlet and carried around a wall or over a door or window frame is not a satisfactory substitute for another outlet. Any tacking of cord, even with insulated staples, is not approved by the Underwriters' Laboratories.

Grease rots rubber, so rubber-sheated cords which have become greasy should be wiped off with a soapy cloth. Wipe the soap off the cord with a cloth wrung out of clear water. Never touch a cord with a damp cloth or wet hands while the cord is connected. Always disconnect it first.

Don't knot or twist cords or drape them over any object in such a way that the cord is bent double. Either form the cord into a ring and place it in a drawer or hang it on a wall over a rounded holder. One or two thread spools attached to the wall will make an excellent cord hanger.

Use lamp cord for lamps and small appliances, such as a radio. Higher-wattage appliances require cords made for use on such equipment. All cords should be properly made and thoroughly insulated for the type of service expected of them. To be safe, buy only cords which bear a label stating that the cord meets the fire prevention standards of the Underwriters' Laboratories.

Plugs. If an electric cord has frayed near a plug, the cord should be cut back and the plug rewired. To do this, first release the cord by loosening the two screws inside the plug holding the two strands of copper wire. Some plugs have a cover which must be slipped off the prongs to expose the screws. Slip the cord out through the opening in the bottom of the plug. Cut the frayed section of the cord off with a pair of pliers or wire snippers, but don't cut off any more of the cord than is necessary.

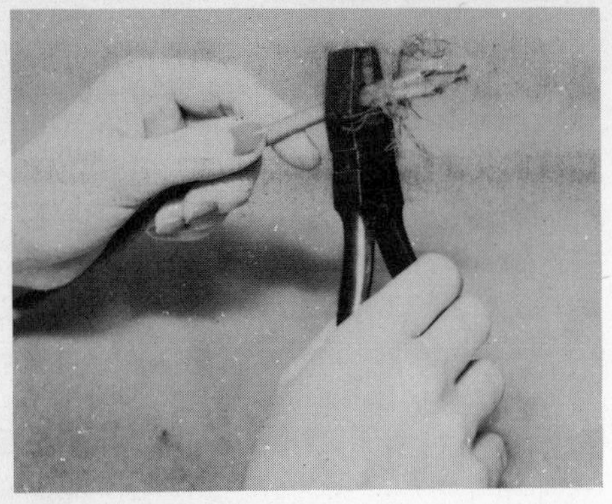

To rewire plug: First *unscrew frayed end and clip off with pliers or wire snippers. Be sure cord is unplugged.*

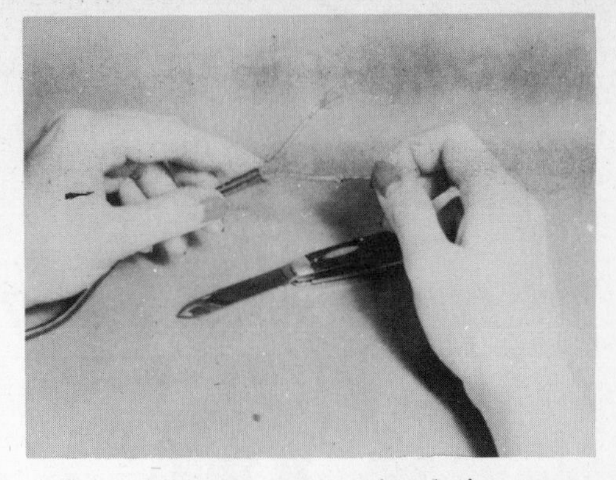

Second, *remove outer insulation to expose the two covered wires. A sharp penknife or a razor blade can be used.*

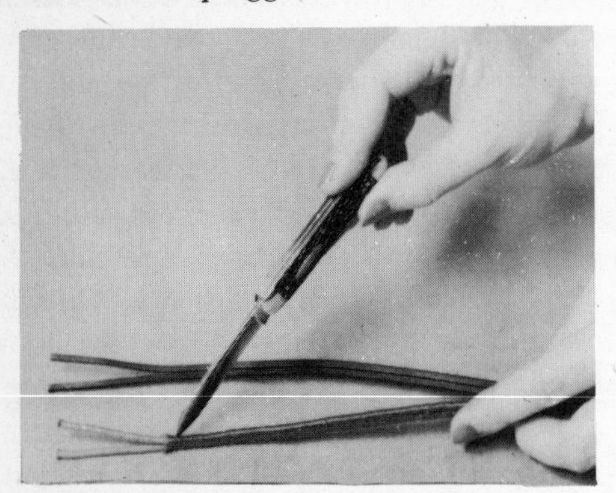

Third, *remove insulation from two inner wires to expose copper strands. Cord in foreground is fabric covered; other cord is insulated with molded rubber. Do not damage copper wires.*

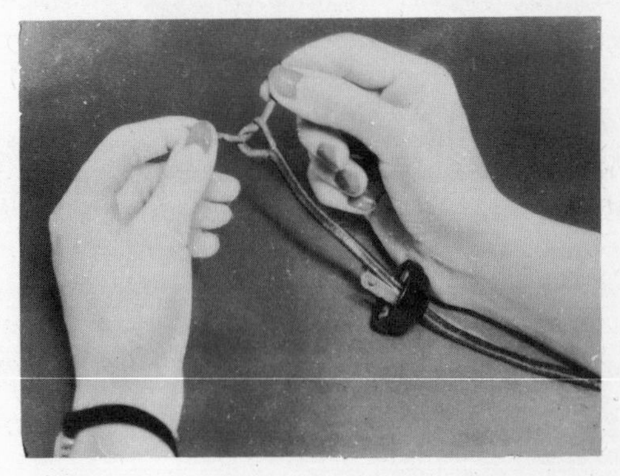

Fourth, *twist each copper strand, insert through end of plug, and tie together in a knot. Be sure to knot insulated part of strands so that exposed copper sections will not touch each other.*

Fifth, *knot is now ready to be pulled down inside plug. Cord ends are then wrapped around prongs of plug to form a letter S.*

Sixth, *loop bare copper ends of strands around screw stems in clockwise direction. Hold in place and tighten screws. Conceal wire under screw head.*

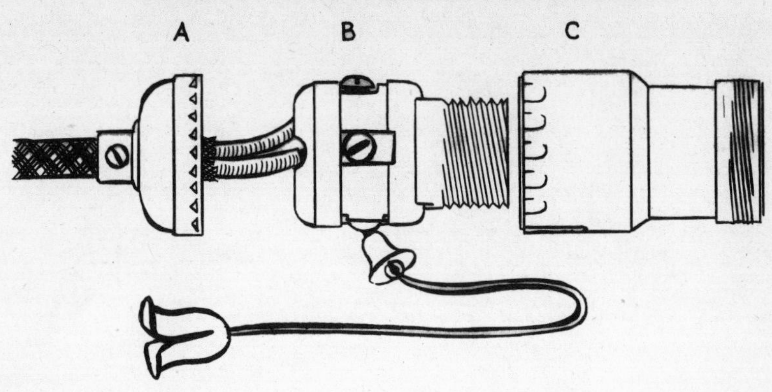

FIG. 3. To rewire lamp socket, press case to loosen part C from A. Loosen screws on B to release old cord. Pull out and replace with new cord.

Strip off 2 inches of the outside insulating material with a knife or a razor blade to expose the two insulated wires inside the cord. Strip off about ¾ of an inch of this insulation until the bare copper strands are exposed. Be careful not to damage the copper strands. Twist the strands on each wire. Slip the cord through the end of the plug and tie the insulated part of the ends in a knot. Pull the knot down inside the plug. Wrap the cord ends around the prongs of the plug in the form of an S. Loop the exposed copper ends around stems of the screws in a clockwise direction. Hold the copper strands in place and tighten the screws firmly. The ends of the copper strands must be concealed beneath the head of the screw and the exposed copper on one set of strands must never come in contact with the exposed copper on the other set of strands.

Sockets. As with any other fixture, be sure that the cord on a lamp has been removed from the outlet before you start to rewire the socket. Remove the bulb from the lamp. Press the socket above the part marked "A" to separate it. Loosen the screws holding the two copper wires on the part marked "B" and pull the cord out through the shaft of the lamp. Pass the new cord through the shaft and through the lower half of the socket. Cut off 2 inches of the outer insulation material from the end of the cord. Then cut about ¾ of an inch of the insulation material on the two wires to expose the copper strands. Tightly twist the strands on each wire. Knot the wires and fasten them to the screws in the manner described for rewiring a plug. If the two wires and the two screws in the socket are of different colors, match up each wire with the screw of the corresponding color. Fit the three parts together again. Attach the other end of the cord to the plug.

THINGS TO REMEMBER ABOUT ELECTRIC APPLIANCES

Elements. The element (the part that heats or lights up) of any electric appliance must be treated with care. Dropping an appliance is one of the chief causes of damage to the element. Even if the wires are not damaged, they may become crossed and thus cause a short circuit which can burn out the element. Never touch a live exposed element to a metal object. For example, a fork should never be used to remove a slice of bread from a toaster — the tines of the fork may touch the element and cause it to burn out. You can also get a serious shock this way. If the element of any electric appliances touches the metal frame, the frame can act as an electrical conductor. It will produce a shock, or it

Dropping is a major cause of damage to irons. If handled with care, a good iron will serve for years.

may even start a fire. Never allow the element of any appliance to come in contact with water. If the element in any appliance has been damaged, take it to an electrician for repair.

Hand Irons. Never keep an iron plugged into an outlet when the iron is not in use. It is not sufficient to turn off the switch — you may think you did when you really didn't. An iron should not be plugged into a lamp socket. Most lamp sockets are not intended to carry enough wattage to heat an iron, and the iron probably won't heat as well as it should. Always be careful not to drop an iron and always repair the cord as soon as the insulation begins to wear.

Vacuum Cleaners. If a vacuum cleaner causes a spark or burns out a fuse when it touches a radiator or water pipe, it is a sign that something is wrong. In any event, the cleaner should be checked by an electrician before it is used again.

Shock Hazards. Water is a very good conductor of electricity. It is dangerous to handle any electric appliance, pull a cord, press a button, or turn on any electric switch with wet hands. Never pull a light cord when you are in the bathtub. Never touch a water faucet and turn on a light or touch an electric appliance at the same time. If there are small children in the family, protect wall outlets with caps made for the purpose so that probing little fingers will not receive a shock.

CHAPTER XXII

HEATING SYSTEMS

GREATER progress has been made in the methods of heating a house during the last half century than in all the thousands of years since man first learned to build a fire in front of his cave. Up until the Middle Ages the universal method of house heating usually consisted in building a fire in the center of a room and letting the smoke find its way out through a hole in the roof—although a few wealthy Romans heated their houses with the hypocaust, a kind of subterranean furnace system with hot air flues under the floor and in the walls. Fireplaces with chimneys built into the wall apparently didn't come into use until some time after A.D. 1300. And the fireplace remained the principal heating device right up until the nineteenth century, although iron and tile stoves had started to gain favor in the late eighteenth century. The radiator appeared about 1860, but central heating for the home was still something of a novelty at the end of the century. Now the radiator is threatened with extinction since the appearance of radiant panel-heating.

HEAT TRANSMISSION

HEAT is transmitted from a warm object to a cooler one in three ways: By conduction, by convection, and by radiation. *Conduction* is the transmission of heat through matter without the aid of motion. In other words, it's the process whereby one end of a poker becomes hot when the other end is placed in the fire. *Convection* is the transmission of heat through circulation (when you swish the water around in the bathtub, you equalize the temperature of the water by convection). *Radiation* is the direct transmission of heat rays to solid objects. That is the way the sun heats, or the way you are warmed when you stand directly in front of a fire or a hot radiator.

In house heating systems, all three processes of heat transmission take place, but the extent to which convection or radiation predominates depends upon the type of heating equipment. A stove, a radiator, a fireplace, or other kind of heater throws off heat by radiation. However, when heat is transmitted from a single source or widely separated sources, the area of radiation is limited. The heat waves are dissipated in the atmosphere. Warm air is lighter than cool air and rises above it. Thus the heating of air causes it to circulate as the cool and warm air shift positions. As the air circulates, the transmission of heat by convection takes place. The heated air passes over the furniture, walls, and other objects in a room, as well as persons, and warms them, but more slowly than direct radiation.

When the temperature outdoors is lower than the temperature indoors, the heat finally penetrates the walls and ceilings of the house and escapes outside by means of conduction. The rate of transmission of the warmer air of the house to the colder air outside depends upon the construction of the walls, ceilings, roof, and so on of a house, and what materials they are made of. Some materials are much better conductors of heat than others. Ordinary window glass transmits heat quite readily, but the transmission of heat through a window is greatly retarded by double panes of glass with "dead" air space in between. Proper insulation of walls and ceilings retards heat loss by conduction. Heat also escapes through the joints in door or window frames or other openings, or when wind forces cold air into the house through any openings.

A house can be kept at a comfortable temperature only by preventing as much heat from escaping as possible or by producing enough heat to make up for that which does escape, especially in houses where heat is distributed primarily by means of convection. Since heat is produced by burning fuel, this means that the more heat escapes, the more fuel must be burned to keep the house warm. Therefore, thorough insulation and weather-stripping of a house can greatly lower the amount of fuel consumed.

FUELS

THE choice of fuel depends upon the type of heating equipment you have or intend to buy and the amount of money that can be invested in it, the relative costs of various types of fuel in your community, and the advantages which one type of fuel may have over another in the way of storage requirements, availability, and so on.

Oil. Fuel oil is graded as light (No. 1, medium (Nos. 2 and 3), and heavy (No. 4). In general, the heavier the oil, the less expensive it is, but a lighter grade usually heats more efficiently. However, the heaviest grade which can be used in any burner depends upon the approval of the National Board of Fire Underwriters. Oil can be stored in an outside tank, thus eliminating the necessity for a basement or else leaving it free for other purposes. Oil is utilized most efficiently with a heater designed to burn oil, but a coal-burning furnace can often be converted to burn oil. Sometimes the operation of converting coal-burning furnaces costs more with oil and sometimes not, and the advice of a reliable heating engineer or contractor should be sought before making the conversion.

Coal. Coal is classified as *hard* coal or *anthracite,* and *soft* coal or *bituminous.* In between these two are *semianthracite* and *semibituminous.* Bituminous coal contains considerable volatile matter which is released as soot and in smoke when the coal is burned. The volatile matter also makes the coal burn comparatively rapidly. Anthracite contains very little volatile matter. It is therefore slow burning and produces little or no soot or smoke.

Anthracite is sorted according to lump size by screening through different sized meshes, as follows:

Name of Size	*Will Pass Through*	*Will Not Pass Through*
Egg	3¼" round mesh	2 7/16" round mesh
Stove	2 7/16" round mesh	1⅝" round mesh
Nut	1⅝" round mesh	1 3/16" round mesh
Pea	1 3/16" round mesh	9/16" round mesh

Bituminous coal is also screened, but sizes are not standardized for all parts of the country. In addition, bituminous is also sold unscreened, or as "run of the mine."

With anthracite coal, stove size is usually ordered, although the less expensive smaller sizes can be used to advantage in furnaces with automatic stokers designed to handle such sizes. In hand-stoked furnaces, the small sizes can also be used by mixing them with a larger size—usually egg. The fire is started with the egg size, and then nut- or pea-size lumps are shoveled on after the fire is burning briskly.

Semianthracite contains a little more volatile matter than anthracite, and semibituminous, a little less than bituminous.

Coke. Coke is coal from which the volatile matter has been removed, leaving a product which is almost pure carbon and which burns with no soot or smoke. Coke often costs less than coal, but it must be handled in such a way that it does not burn too rapidly. Coke sizes, which correspond closely to coal sizes, should be smaller, since the coke is porous and a draft passes through it readily. Dampers on a furnace or stove should be adjusted to prevent too-rapid burning.

Gas. Gas, whether natural or manufactured, is supplied by a utilities company to the home through pipeline and therefore involves no space for storage. The quantity used is measured by a meter and paid for after using, unlike other fuels. A heater designed especially for burning gas usually gives the best results, but coal or oil heaters can sometimes be satisfactorfily converted into gas heaters. A heating engineer or the local gas company can advise whether such a conversion is feasible. Since gas is a fuel which is consumed virtually without residue, it can be used in heaters with special vents instead of regulation chimneys in some communities where gas is the common heating fuel.

Wood. Because wood contains considerable volatile materials, it burns with comparative rapidity. The volume of wood needed to heat a house adequately is much larger than for other fuels, and wood is therefore relatively inefficient as a house-heating fuel. However, it is the preferred fuel for fireplaces, which, in houses with modern heating systems, are valued more for their eye appeal than for their effectiveness as heaters. Hardwoods burn more slowly than softwoods, such as pine or fir. In older houses with chimneys that do not have a lining of fire clay or other corrosion-resitant material, the volatile matter in wood may form a hard condensation of creosote in the chimney shaft, making it highly inflammable. If the condition is serious, the chimney may be unsafe for use.

TYPES OF HEATERS

MANY factors are involved in the choice of a heating plant for a house—the size of the house, its construction, ease of operation of the heater, local costs of various kinds of fuel, the method of distributing the heat, economy of use, and so on. Only a competent heating engineer or heating contractor is qualified to give the best solution to individual heating problems.

OIL BURNERS

OIL BURNERS are examined by the National Board of Fire Underwriters, and no burner which has failed to receive the approval of this Board should ever be selected. Safety requirements are rigid, and approved models which meet the test will all perform satisfactorily, although they may differ slightly in operation. An oil burner is a complex mechanism which should not be cared for, repaired, or adjusted by anyone who does not thoroughly understand its operation. The company which installs the oil burner services it, and the home owner is expected to leave it alone. Therefore, it is important to choose a burner made by a reliable company that can be depended upon to give regular service when it is needed—one that is not likely to go out of business and render spare parts unavailable. You can always make inquiries in a community to find out how well burners in other homes are being serviced. The company which installs the burner usually services it free of charge for the first year. After that, service will have to be arranged for on a contract or other basis.

As stated before, fuel tanks can be buried outside the house, so that an oil heater will occupy only a compartively small space. However, the size of the tank will depend upon how often deliveries of oil can be made. In some small communities, deliveries may be infrequent, so that a large storage tank is necessary. The costs of such a tank and the excavations for it may be quite expensive.

A correctly adjusted oil burner burns without smoke except for a few minutes after starting. If smoking occurs at other times, it may indicate an undersupply of air—and that calls for an adjustment. If the burner turns on and off too frequently, it may be because the tank is nearly empty or because the flow of oil may be clogged. If a previously quiet boiler becomes noisy, some of the parts may be worn and need replacement. The best way to avoid all burner troubles is to have the burner checked at regular and frequent intervals.

When the burner is shut off during the summer or while the house is closed, the ignition should be cut off. To cut off electric ignition, the switch should be opened. For gas ignition, the valve is closed. After the boiler is cool, all metal parts should be given a coat of oil to prevent rust. Then the boiler should be protected from dust with a cover of heavy paper. The tank should be left full to prevent a condensation of moisture from forming and mixing with the oil.

GAS BURNERS

GAS is a clean, smokeless fuel, and where its cost is low enough to use it for house heating, it offers such advantages as the elimination of fuel storage provisions and, in some communities, the absence of a standard chimney. Instead of a chimney, a gas heater may be used with a less expensive flue, designated as type "B". The National Board of Fire Underwriters approves of the use of this flue for gas heaters in communities where gas is the common heating fuel. However, its use may not be permitted except in areas where gas is the principal heating fuel and a general change to some other type of fuel seems unlikely. Gas heaters can also be used with any brick or masonry chimney of standard construction with a fire-clay or other corrosion-resistant lining.

Like oil burners, gas burners are not repaired or adjusted by the home owner but by the utilities company or, sometimes, the plumber. In most cases, the utilities company supplies this service free. Otherwise, the service may be charged for on a contract or a fee basis. If the service is free, it is advisable for the home owner to consult with the local utilities company to find out which make of heater is most popular in the community. By choosing that make of heater, he has a better assurance of the availability of parts and replacements. Only gas heaters which bear the seal of approval of the American Gas Association should be selected. Gas, like other fuels, can be used in connection with steam-, warm-air-, or radiant-heating systems, although its widest use is found in warm-air systems.

One thing to remember is that gas is paid for after use, and that most utilities companies cannot grant credit. If bills are not met on time, delivery of fuel may be suspended, whereas oil or coal, which are bought and paid for in advance of use, will be on hand as long as the supply lasts, regardless of sudden financial difficulties.

COAL-BURNING FURNACES

COAL-BURNING furnaces are of various designs. Some types have pipes which carry heated air to different parts of the house. Others have no pipes, but only a single register opening on the main floor; heat is distributed by circulation. Still others are made as boilers to provide steam or hot water for radiators (or possibly radiant-heating coils). If any make of furnace has special servicing needs, the manufacturer's directions should be followed. The information given here applies to coal-burning furnaces in general.

Hand-Stoked Furnaces. Hand-stoked furnaces usually require regular attention at least twice daily while in operation. In very cold weather, they may require more frequent attention. Small furnaces may also need to be attended to oftener.

Starting the Furnace. To start a fire in the furnace, first cover the grate with a layer of stove- or egg-size coal. Cover the coal with crumpled newspapers, and then add a generous amount of kindling. Set a lighted match to the paper, and when the kindling is thoroughly ablaze, shovel on more coal, but not enough to smother the burning kindling. As soon as this coal is burning steadily, fill the fire chamber.

Adjusting the Dampers. The furnace usually has four dampers: (1) the check damper on the pipe between the furnace and the chimney; (2) the ash-pit damper, which admits air or checks its entry through the opening on the front of the furnace below the grate; (3) the turn damper which should be between the furnace and the check damper, and (4) the slide damper in the fire-chamber door.

Air enters the fire chamber through the opening controlled by the ash-pit damper, passes through the grate, the ashes and burning coal on the grate, on up to the top of the fire chamber, across it, and out

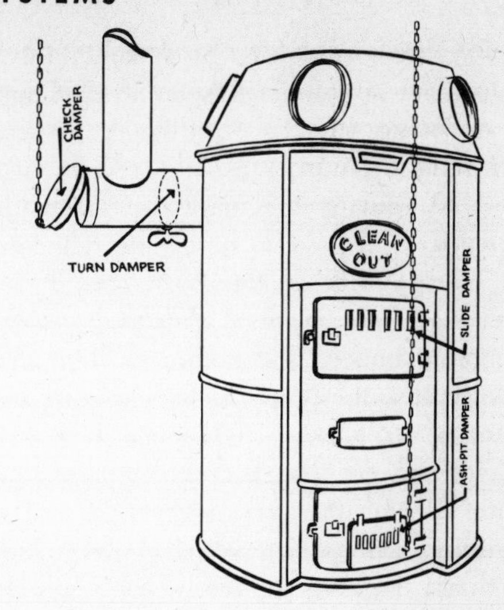

FIG. 1. Typical coal-fired, warm-air furnace, showing location of dampers.

through the smoke pipe to the chimney. The more freely the air flows through the furnace, the brisker the fire will burn. The rate of burning is controlled by adjusting the dampers.

To admit a full flow of air, open the ash-pit damper and the turn damper and close the check damper. The dampers should be adjusted in this way when the fire is started. To check the rate of burning, the ash-pit damper is closed and the check damper is opened. The check damper allows air to enter the smoke pipe without

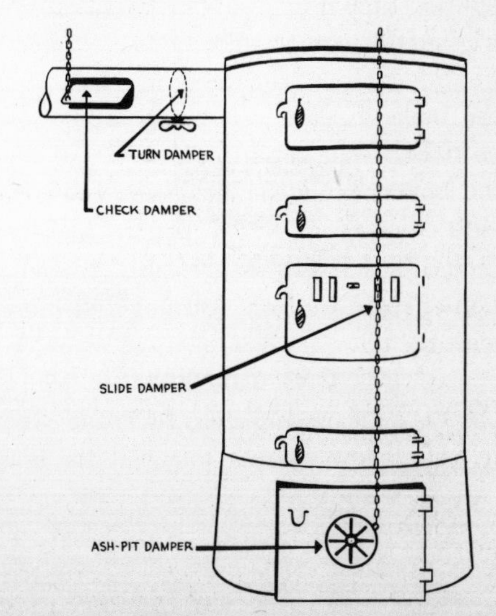

FIG. 2. Typical coal-fired boiler-furnace, showing location of dampers.

going through the fire chamber. Some furnaces have automatic damper control with a chain suspended on pulleys to connect the ash-pit damper and the check damper, so that when one is closed, the other is opened.

The position of the turn damper depends on how much of a draft is created in the chimney. If this damper is opened too widely, the draft through the fire bed may be too strong; if the turn damper is closed too far, the fire may be too sluggish. Testing the turn damper in various positions will indicate which is best to keep the fire burning as freely as it should. However, during stoking, the turn damper should be wide open.

The slide damper admits air to the fire chamber so that gases over the fire bed can be burned off, and therefore should never be closed entirely; but the extent to which this damper should be opened will usually have to be determined by a little experimenting.

Keeping the Fire Going. The door to the fire chamber should be open only during stoking and kept closed at all other times. In order to keep the fire going at a steady rate, the furnace will probably need to be stoked only twice a day if the fire chamber is filled with coal to the level of the door opening each time. A thin fire bed wastes fuel. Before stoking, shake down the ashes, leaving a layer of at least 2 inches. Unless the coal is stove size or larger, the addition of a deep layer of fresh coal would ordinarily smother the fire, because fine coal would pack down too closely to allow air and gas fumes to pass. The gas fumes will not ignite and produce heat, but pass unburned into the chimney and thus be wasted. However, the less expensive smaller sizes of coal can be combined with stove size or larger after a thick bed of live coals has formed. The coals should be raked to one side to form a sloping bank. The smaller coal is then shoveled into the area from which the live coals were raked, leaving the peak of the live coals uncovered. This exposed area of burning coal will ignite the gas formed in the layer of small-size coal. The smaller sizes of coal can be used alone in furnaces with an automatic stoker.

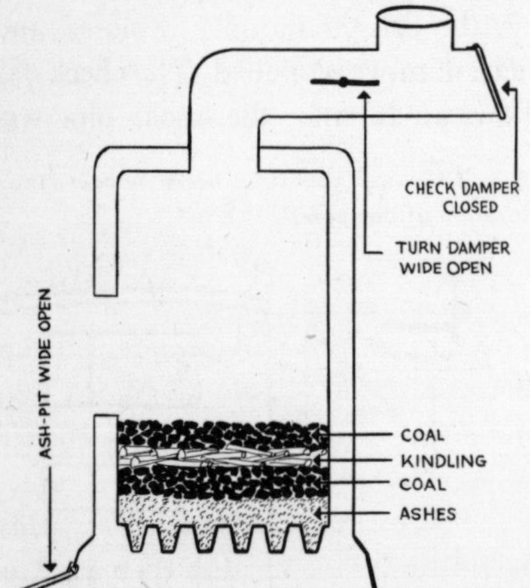

CHECK DAMPER CLOSED
TURN DAMPER WIDE OPEN
ASH-PIT WIDE OPEN
COAL
KINDLING
COAL
ASHES

FIG. 3. Position of dampers when fire is started. Kindling is bedded on either a layer of ashes or a layer of coal.

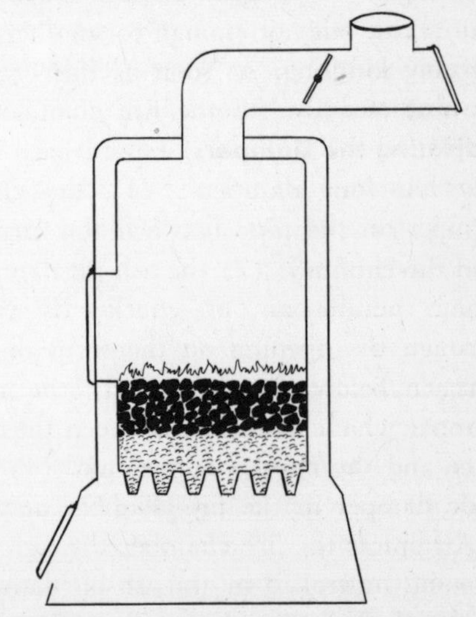

FIG. 4. Method of stoking furnace with large coal. Fire chamber should be filled to level of door opening.

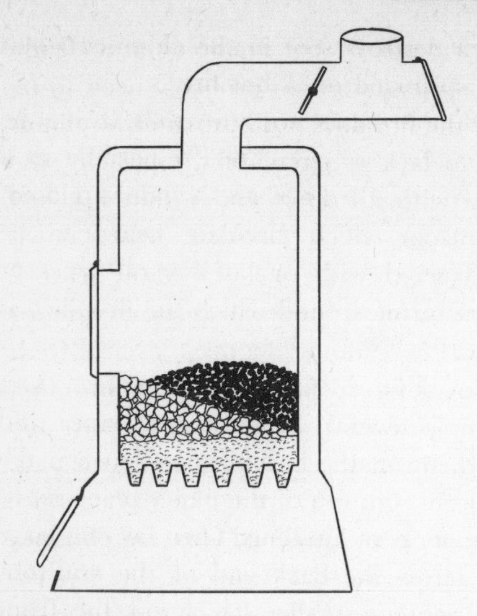

FIG. 5. Method of stoking furnace with small coal. Hot coals are raked to one side to leave a "hot spot" exposed after fresh coal is shoveled in. "Hot spot" keeps small coal from smothering fire.

To bank the fire for the night, open the ash-pit and turn dampers, and close the check damper about twenty minutes before stoking. As soon as the fire is burning briskly, shake the ashes down slightly and add enough fresh fuel to fill the fire chamber to the level of the door opening. Leave the dampers as they are for a few minutes to allow the draft to help ignite the fresh coal. As soon as it is burning, close the ash-pit damper and the turn damper and open the check damper. Do not bank a fire by throwing on a layer of ashes since they will form clinkers if you do.

Ashes. Ashes from the burned coal drop down to the bottom of the grate and must be shaken down into the ash pan underneath. Shake the ashes down by moving the handle of the grate gently—too violent shaking will bring down burning or unburned coal. Never shake down the ashes completely; leave a layer of at least 2 inches on the grate. An even thicker layer should be left if the weather is mild. Ordinarily, the ashes will not need to be shaken down oftener than twice a day.

The ash pan under the grate should be emptied daily; otherwise, piled-up ashes will block the flow of air through the fire bed and the iron grate may become overheated and warp. However, if the ashes are taken out immediately after they are shaken down, and are still hot, ash dust will fly. This can be prevented by leaving them cool. Then, just before the next stoking, they can be removed.

The fire bed should not be poked or disturbed as this causes live or unburned coal to mix with the ashes. When this happens, the ashes may be heated to the melting point and form clinkers. Clinkers can also form when the fire is forced to such an extent that the layer of ashes becomes overheated. Remove clinkers through the clinker door; never pull them up through the fire bed. If the clinker is too large to go through the door, it can be broken up by a few blows with the poker.

Automatic Stokers. An automatic stoker not only eliminates the bothersome chore of stoking the furnace by hand, but also makes it possible to use the less-expensive smaller sizes of coal. Automatic stokers are of various designs, and an ordinary furnace can usually be equipped with one. The method of operation depends upon the make of stoker.

BOILERS

BOILERS are of various types and may be designed to burn coal, oil, or gas. The servicing needs of any boiler depend upon its make, and one should be guided by the manufacturer's directions. Flues and coils must be cleaned and kept free of soot. In the case of oil- or gas-fired boilers, this is probably done by the service man. Coal-fired boilers should also be serviced at whatever intervals the manufacturer recommends. In between servicings, the home owner can usually clean the flues and coils through the clean-out door with a long-handled brush. The soot is simply brushed into the openings in the passages and drops into the fire chamber.

THERMOSTATS

A THERMOSTAT is a device which automatically regulates the operation of the heater according to the temperature of the room. The thermostat can be set for whatever temperature you desire, and the amount of heat is adjusted to maintain that temperature. Any type of heater, burning any kind of fuel, can be thermostatically controlled. Coal-fired heaters must be automatically stoked; or, if hand-stoked, must be of the magazine type.

The position of the thermostat in the room is important. A thermostat which is too close to a hot radiator, a wall register, or a fireplace, will shut off the central heater before other rooms are as warm as they should be. The same thing often happens when a radiator is located on the other side of a wall directly behind a thermostat. The only satisfactory remedy is to have the thermostat moved to another position.

FIREPLACES

A SMOKING fireplace is usually the result of faulty construction, and the trouble can be eliminated only by correcting the design. When a correctly designed fireplace smokes, it may be because the damper is closed or the chimney is clogged with soot. A chimney clogged with soot sometimes has to be cleaned from the roof when the fire is completely out. A bundle of old rags can be made to correspond to the size of the chimney. The rags should be wrapped around bricks for weights and both can be secured with rope. The bundle is lowered down the chimney shaft on a rope long enough to reach the entire length. By raising and lowering the rope, the soot will be brushed off by the rags. There is also a compound on the market which destroys soot in the chimney when it is sprinkled on a hot fire.

If the fire does not burn well, it may be due to lack of circulation, especially in a room with all doors and windows closed. Fireplaces which circulate heat can be constructed with one of several types of metal forms around which the fireplace is built.

To build a fire in a fireplace, first crumple several sheets of newspaper and lay them on the hearth floor between the andirons. On top of the paper place six or eight sticks of kindling. Then lay one large log across the back end of the andirons and another smaller log across the front end. A still smaller log is then laid on top of the first two. Loosely twist a sheet of newspaper into a long roll. Light the crumpled newspaper under the logs and the end of the long roll. Stick the lighted end of the roll up the chimney to start the draft and get the fire blazing without smoking.

SYSTEMS OF HEAT DISTRIBUTION

Radiant Heating. Although not new in principle, modern methods of radiant heating are the newest thing in heat distribution. Heated coils are laid in the floor (a system resembling the hot air flues in the walls and floor in the ancient Roman hypocaust method of heating). Radiant heating differs from older systems in that it heats floors, ceilings, walls, and solid objects in the room much more than the air in the room; while in older systems, the air is heated first and warms the walls and so on through circulation. The air in a radiant-heated room circulates but little. The air in a radiant-heated room can be much cooler than in rooms heated by other methods and yet a person will remain comfortably warm because radiant heat checks the flow of heat from the body. This means that operating costs are usually lower, although such is not always the case. But radiant heating has other advantages. It involves no ugly radiators or wall registers. There are no drafts to start sneezes and no blasts of hot, dry air. The dirty wall areas above radiators are eliminated because there are no hot-air currents to carry dirt. In fact, the entire house stays cleaner. The temperature of the room is practically the same at all levels from floor to ceiling, so that baby can play on the floor without danger of chilly drafts.

The most widely used method of radiant heating is by a network of hot-water pipes. The pipes are buried in concrete floors or in the ceiling. For this reason, radiant heat with hot-water coils must, as a rule, be installed at the time a house is built. The system can be installed in existing houses, but the job involves ripping out the floors and ceilings and replacing them after the coils are installed—a procedure which is too costly in most cases to be worth while. By the same token, any alterations to the coils once they are installed means tearing out the floor or ceiling. Therefore, one should be sure to get expert advice on the design and installation of a radiant-heating system.

In some cases, temperature adjustments of hot-water pipes has lagged behind sudden changes of weather, but improvements in thermostatic control are said to have minimized or eliminated this problem.

The water for the coils is heated in any standard type of boiler using any ordinary fuel, and the water is pumped into the pipes by an ordinary pump.

Another method of radiant heating involves no pipes, no boiler, no pump, and no ordinary heating fuel. Instead, electric cables insulated with a plastic are attached to the laths or to wallboard and covered with plaster. The temperature in each room is controlled independently of other rooms, since each room has its own thermostat. Naturally, the cost of operation depends on local electric rates. In low-rate areas, the cost may be less than that of systems using ordinary fuels. In other places, the cost of operation may be excessive. However, operating costs, even though higher, may be offset by lower installation costs. Only the cable, fuses, thermostats, switches, ceiling insulation and labor are involved. The cables can be installed in existing houses without disturbing floors or ceilings (in most cases, the cables are put in the walls and ceilings, although they can also be put in floors).

Electric radiant heating has not yet been given a blanket approval by the Underwriters' Laboratories on the ground that it becomes a system only after installation.

Adjusting the dampers on a coal-burning furnace.

Modern type of combination oil-burning boiler and water heater.

However, Federal Housing Authority loans have been approved for homes heated by this method.

Radiators. Radiators are used in connection with both steam and hot-water heating systems. In ordinary steam heating systems, water is heated in a boiler until it is turned into steam. The steam rises and is conducted through pipes to radiators where it condenses and returns to the boiler as water. The steam forces air out of the radiator, which is fitted with a valve to allow the air to escape. If the valve does not operate freely, or the pipes have too many sharp turns, the steam may not be able to enter the radiator unless the boiler pressure is raised. Fuel may be wasted by keeping up the boiler pressure. Therefore, when radiators fail to heat as well as they should, it may be advisable to call in a heating contractor to find out where the trouble lies. To test a radiator valve to find out if it is working properly, light a match and hold it over the hole at the end of the valve when the steam is up. If the air is escaping as it should, it will blow out the match.

In vapor-vacuum steam-heating systems, most of the air is driven out of the radiators, which are then sealed, so that a partial vacuum is created inside the radiators. With no resistance of air, the steam rises more quickly than in ordinary steam-heating systems. In order to operate efficiently, radiators, pipes, and boiler must be leak proof so that no air can enter. If leaks do occur, they should be remedied by a repairman.

Hot-water heating systems also involve a boiler, pipes, and radiators. The water is not heated until it turns to steam, but only to a high enough temperature to expand the water and cause it to rise and fill the radiators. Unlike steam radiators, which are hot and cold at intervals, hot-water radiators are warm most of the time. If any of the radiators in a hot-water system fails to heat as it should, it is probably because the system has not been properly installed. Corrections will have to be made by a heating contractor. Hot-water radiators beneath a window should be protected from freezing if the window is opened for any length of time during very cold weather. They can be insulated with a blanket or some other covering.

Warm-Air and Hot-Air Heating Systems. In warm-air heating systems, air is heated by a coal, gas, or sometimes an oil heater, and forced by a blower through ducts connecting with the rooms. The warm air enters the room through a register usually placed at some distance up on the wall. The warm air circulates across the room until it cools, and then sinks to the floor and returns to the heater through another register in the floor or base of the wall; or, in some cases, the cool air finds its way out of the rooms through open doors and stairways and returns to the heater by means of one large register on the ground floor.

The older hot-air heating systems have no blower. Instead, the air must be heated until it is hot enough to expand and rise by its own lightness. In some of the earlier arrangements, the air to be heated is brought in from outdoors. In cold weather, this type of system is very expensive to operate since the heater must be kept going full blast most of the time to bring the air to a comfortable temperature. The air in the house does not need to be changed every time it is heated, as was formerly thought to be the case, because even in well insulated houses enough fresh air is normally admitted to keep it from becoming unhealthful. Hot-air systems can usually be changed into warm-air systems without too much expense.

In small houses, heated air sometimes passes directly from the heater into a room on the lower floor through one large register. No ducts or pipes are involved. Other rooms are warmed by circulation, and the cool air returns to the heater through intakes on the sides of the register. Pipeless heat cannot circulate from room to room if the doors are closed, nor will it circulate well if the ceilings are too high. Sometimes a register in the door or above it will help to distribute the heat.

If coal is the fuel used in connection with a warm- or hot-air heating system and the odor of coal gas is noted in the house, the cause is probably a leakage between the furnace sections. In order to remedy this condition, the furnace usually has to be taken apart and recemented—a job which calls for professional service.

SPACE HEATERS

WHEN a central heating system fails to dispel the chill in all rooms as well as it should, a quick solution is to augment the heat supply with a small, portable space heater. Such heaters are made in a remarkable variety of designs and sizes, and most of them operate with electricity. The radiant-type heaters warm objects in their path without warming the air. In choosing any electric heater, the most important consideration is safety. The best assurance of safety is to select only those heaters which carry a statement to the effect that they have been tested and approved by the Underwriters' Laboratories. Other factors to consider are the size of the heater and the area it will heat and how long it takes to heat up. If you wish to carry it from room to room, be sure it has a handle.

CHAPTER XXIII

PLUMBING

WHEN you cut your finger, you don't call a doctor. You apply first aid, and usually that's all that's necessary. But a broken arm may be something else again. A cut finger and a leaking faucet have little in common except one thing — both usually require little more than first aid treatment. First aid repairs for plumbing are simple, and one doesn't have to be a mechanic to learn how to make them. They are mostly concerned with leaks and stoppages. More serious plumbing troubles must be handled by a professional plumber. But learn how to recognize them, so you will know when to call him and when to fix the job yourself.

LEAKS

Leaks may or may not mean serious trouble, depending on where they occur. If the faucet leaks, it probably needs nothing more than a new washer. But all leaks require attention, and sometimes speedy action. If a pipe bursts, you ought to know what to do in a hurry!

It's probably safe to say that most people have no more knowledge of plumbing fixtures than what their various purposes are for. Perhaps you know that water can be shut off by other means than closing a faucet, but if not, then it might be a good thing to find out where and how before any leaks ever occur. Practically all plumbing installations are equipped with shut-off valves. You may find them underneath the sink or wash basin, one for hot water and one for cold. Or there may be only one main shut-off valve in the basement. In rare cases it is outside of the house. But wherever it is, be sure you know its location. It usually looks very much like the handle of an ordinary faucet and will be attached to a water pipe. After you have found it, test it to be sure it works. It probably will, but it might be very tight and need a little strong-arm persuasion.

Faucets. The chief cause of leaky faucets is a worn out washer. Hot water wears out washers faster than cold, and the hot water faucet in the kitchen is apt to wear out quicker than any other because it is used more often. But washers can usually be replaced quickly and easily. If you don't know what size washer your faucet takes, buy a box of assorted sizes, which costs only a trifle. For tools, you will need a monkey wrench, or a Stillson wrench, a screw driver, and possibly a pair of pliers and a small knife.

Very likely your faucet is of the compression type, which turns on and off by means of screw threads. But before you start to unscrew the faucet cap, be sure that you have closed the shut-off valve

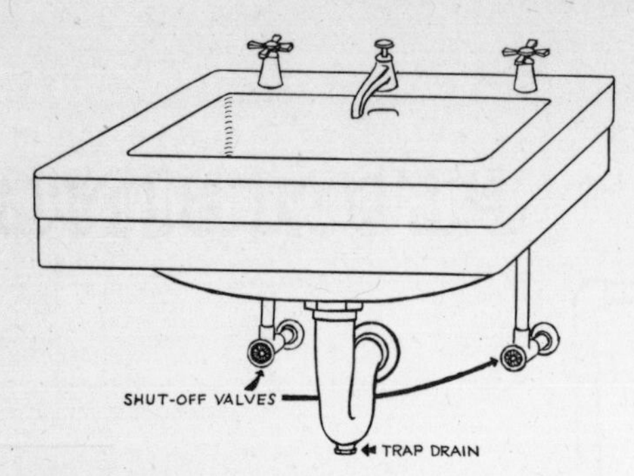

FIG. 1. Local shut-off valves are usually located on pipes underneath plumbing fixtures and must be closed before faucet handles can be removed. Trap drain almost never needs to be opened to clean clogged traps. But it can be opened to recover anything of value that has been lost down drain pipe.

(main or local) tightly. Otherwise, you may be sprayed with a jet of water. Now adjust the wrench to fit around the cap nut, which is a projection below the handle through which the shaft of the faucet passes. A beautifully plated faucet should be protected with a small strip of cloth before the wrench is applied. Next, unscrew the cap nut with the wrench. It may be necessary to turn the handle of the faucet in order to unscrew the valve shaft. The entire inner mechanism, together with the cap nut and the handle, can then be lifted out in one piece. If the mechanism lifts out without turning the handle, you will find a sort of brass tubing, called a *sleeve,* around the shaft. Unscrew this sleeve. At the end of the shaft you will see a screw which holds the washer in place against the ground seat. Remove this screw with the screw driver. Occasionally, this screw is so corroded in an old fixture that it refuses to budge with a screw driver. If you have a metal-working vise, you may be able to turn it in that. File the sides of the screw flat, so that the vise can get a good grip on it. Otherwise, you may have to take the faucet shaft to the plumber. However, the screw will probably turn easily enough. Next, remove the washer, which may be of composition, rubber, or leather, and red, white or black in color. If it sticks, pry it out with the small knife, being very careful not to damage the seat of the shaft. Then replace it with a new washer, which is of the right size and of the correct composition for hot or cold water. Put the screw back on as well as the sleeve, if there is one, and return the shaft to the faucet. If the shaft has no sleeve, screw in the threads by turning the handle. Tighten the cap nut with the monkey wrench, and turn on the shut-off valve. Try the faucet. If it still drips a little, don't worry, as it may take a day or so for the new washer to settle firmly into place.

But if the faucet begins to leak again within a week or two and does so every time the washer is replaced, then the trouble may be that the ground seat which holds the washer has become worn and roughened. In that case, the washer will wear out quickly every time it is replaced. Take the faucet apart again, after closing the shut-off valve, and examine the ground seat. If it appears pitted or rough, it will have to be taken to the plumber. He will probably be able to smooth it down for a small charge. Of course, occasionally a faucet is so old and badly worn

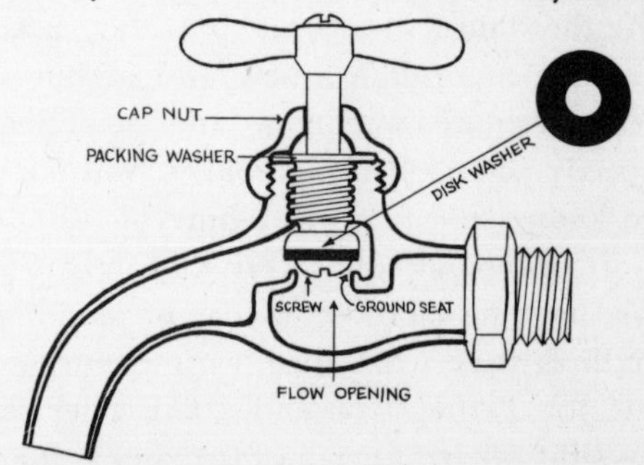

FIG. 2. Cross-section diagram of an ordinary compression faucet. Cap nut is loosened with a wrench to remove shaft of handle, after which disk washer on seat of shaft can be replaced.

that it is beyond repair and has to be replaced by a new one.

If the faucet leaks at the point where the shaft passes through the cap nut, then the packing washer within the nut is probably worn out. You can examine the packing washer by taking the faucet apart and looking underneath the cap nut. You may find one or several washers or perhaps some sort of special packing. Whatever it is, if it is worn, it will have to be replaced by the plumber. The packing washer ordinarily requires replacement far less frequently than the ground seat washer. However, a temporary packing can sometimes be made with greased cotton until the packing washer can be replaced. But this is only a makeshift arrangement, and will not solve the problem permanently.

Perhaps you have one of the older types of faucets that are no longer manufactured. One of these is called a *bibcock,* or sometimes a *Fuller faucet.* The handle of a bibcock points forward when it is shut. It opens by turning either to the right or the left and is wide open when the handle points backward. The washer of a bibcock is a rubber or composition ball located at the end of the inner mechanism near the point where the faucet joins the

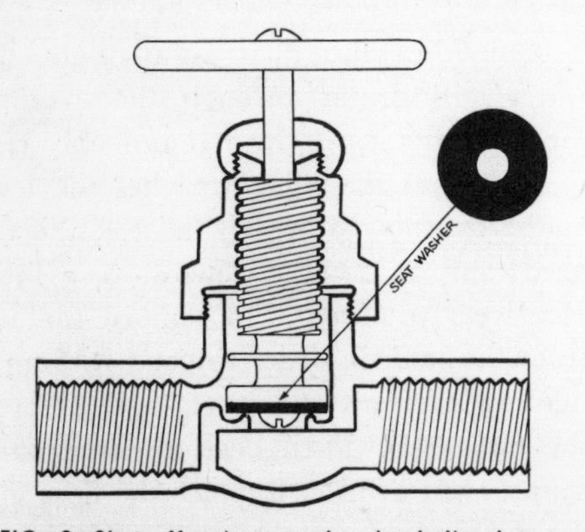

FIG. 3. Shut-off valve on pipe is similar in construction to a faucet. Washers seldom need to be replaced, but procedure for doing so is the same as for faucet.

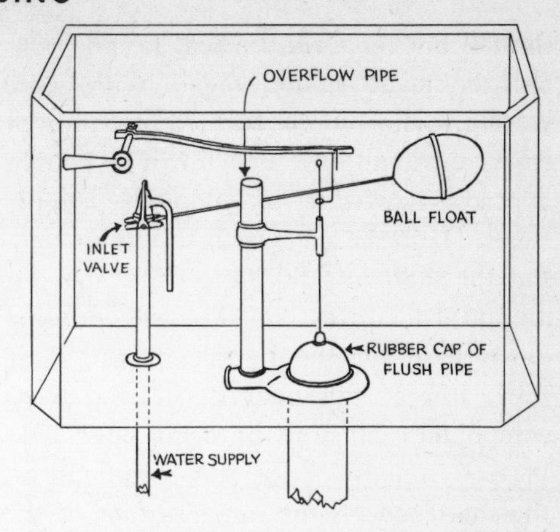

FIG. 4. Inner mechanism of wall tank for ordinary flush toilet. Common causes of trouble are leaky ball float, worn cap on flush pipe, or washer which needs replacing in inlet valve.

pipe. You will probably have to unscrew the faucet from the pipe to get at the washer. It will be held in place by a metal disk or a screw and nut. You may be able to find a new washer to fit a bibcock if you are lucky, but few stores stock them any more. If you cannot, then you had better have the faucet replaced with a modern fixture. It will also have to be replaced if any parts are worn out, because these are no longer made.

An even rarer antique is the *ground cock,* or *ground-key faucet.* If you have one of these, you may fare better than you would with a bibcock, because the ground-key faucet has no washer. Instead, it has a tapered shaft which fits snugly into the faucet. Shaft and handle are usually in one piece. When the handle is turned, the shaft turns with it, and the water flows through a slot in the shaft. When the ground-key faucet leaks, it is usually because the shaft, or the surface of the compartment into which it fits, has become rough or pitted. You can examine the shaft by removing the screw which holds it in place. But first close the shut-off valve. The screw is located beneath the faucet, directly under the handle. If the shaft is not too badly pitted, it can probably be made smooth again with some valve-grinding compound (a mixture of emery dust and oil), which can be bought at most hardware or plumbing supply stores. Daub the shaft with the compound. Put the shaft into the faucet and move it around, backwards and forwards, pressing down hard on the handle at the same time. Repeat this operation, using more compound each time, until the shaft looks perfectly smooth. Wipe the compound off the shaft and off the inner surface of the faucet. Return the shaft to the faucet and replace the screw. Open the shut-off valve and test the faucet. If the shaft is so badly scarred that valve-grinding compound will not smooth it, the faucet will have to be replaced.

The shut-off valve itself may occasionally need a new washer. These valves are usually of the type which has an inner mechanism very similar to that of the compression faucet. Therefore, the valve washer can be replaced in the same way as the washer in a compression faucet.

Toilets. Probably the most common type of flush toilet is the one with a water tank attached to the wall. This tank contains an inner mechanism which controls the inflow and outflow of water. When the handle on the outside of the tank is turned, it lifts an inside lever. The lever, in turn, lifts a wire and the rubber cap at its end. When this cap is raised, it opens the outlet through which the water flows into the toilet bowl. As the water flows out of the tank, a copper ball floating on the surface drops down. This ball is attached to a rod which operates the lever of the intake valve. As the ball drops, it opens the valve, and the water flows into the tank. The ball rises as the tank fills until the proper level is reached to close the inlet valve. The tank is also equipped with an overflow pipe in case the water should rise too high or the inlet valve fail to close. The most common cause of toilet leaks is the improper operation of either the inlet or the outlet valve.

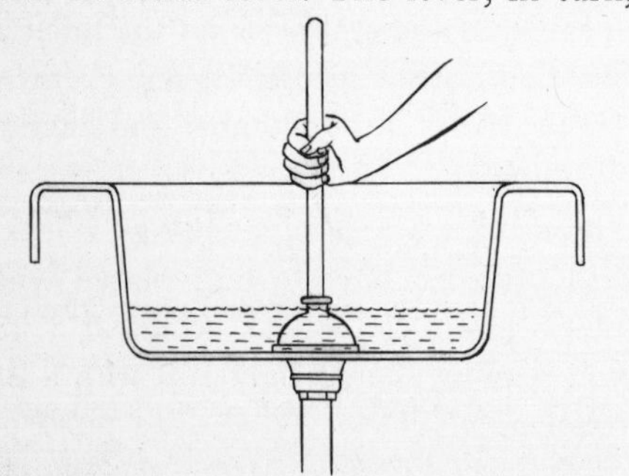

FIG. 5. Clogged drains can usually be opened with suction plunger, often called the "plumber's friend."

The Inlet Valve. Corrosion may eat a hole in the ball float so that it loses its buoyancy and fails to close the inlet valve. When this occurs the water continues to flow into the tank and is drained off through the overflow pipe. This causes a constant gurgling noise in the toilet which can be a source of great annoyance. Lift the lid of the tank and examine the ball float. To do this, you may have to unscrew it from the rod to which it is attached. If the float is damaged, the remedy is simple. Just buy a new float and screw it on the rod in place of the old one.

Sometimes the float is all right but water still drains through the overflow pipe. In that case, the rod probably rises so high that the water reaches the level of the overflow pipe. To fix this, the rod needs only to be bent downwards a little. However, you ought to remove the rod from the tank in order to bend it. Simply unscrew it from the lever, and unscrew the float, too. Then bend the rod carefully — just a little. Replace the float and the rod, and examine its position. It should rest at a point where the inlet valve will close when the water is about an inch or so below the overflow pipe. If, however, the rod rests so low that the valve closes before the tank is sufficiently full, then the rod should be bent upwards slightly.

If the float is all right and the rod is in the proper position, and the water still continues to flow into the tank, then the inlet valve itself probably needs a new washer. In order to examine this valve, first turn off the water by closing the shut-off valve. Then flush the toilet to empty the tank. Find the inlet valve, which may be in the upper or lower part of the tank. Unscrew the levers attached to the lever of the rod. Usually two screws have to be removed, but sometimes only one. If they stick, you may have to use a small pair of pliers. When they are removed, you can lift out the float, the rod, and the levers. Next, lift the valve out and examine the washer at the lower end. If it is worn, remove the screw holding the washer in place, and take or pry out the washer with a small knife. Be careful not to damage the valve seat. Put a new washer of the proper size in place and reassemble the mechanism. If the valve seat has become rough or pitted, it will have to be ground smooth by the plumber, or the washer will soon wear out again. If you cannot take the valve to the plumber, then you will have to call him in.

The Outlet Valve. The flush pipe leading to the toilet bowl is closed by a rubber cap, which is the outlet valve. If this cap fails to seal the opening tightly, a certain amount of water will flow constantly into the bowl and cause the same unpleasant gurgling sound as that of a constantly draining overflow pipe. In order to examine this cap, you will have to drain the tank in the same way described for examining the inlet valve. First, see if the wire or small rod which lifts the cap is adjusted properly. Sometimes the guide through which the wire passes gets out of place so that the cap fails to fall in the right position. If this is the case, the guide can be moved a little so as to bring it into the proper position. Simply loosen the screw which holds the guide in place so that it can be rotated. More likely, the cap itself has become worn. If so, you will have to buy a new one. Almost any plumbing supply store or hardware shop will carry such caps. But you had better take the old one with you to be sure you get one of the right size, as the caps vary somewhat in size and design. The cap will probably come with a new rod attached. The new rod will have to be attached to the lever controlled by the handle on the outside. The wire or rod is usually attached by hooking it into a hole on the lever. The guide wire is generally in two sections, which hook together. The lower section passes through the guide, and then the new rubber cap is screwed on the end.

Sometimes the rubber cap cannot operate properly because it is covered with slime. In that case, all it needs is to be cleaned. Also, it *might* be possible that the inner mechanism fails to work as it should because a mischievous child has dropped some object into the tank.

If water seeps out at the base of the toilet where it joins the floor, it may indicate a crack in the fixture, or it may mean that the seal between the toilet and the floor is not secure. In any event, you had better call the plumber and have him examine it.

Pipes. If a water pipe springs a leak, it will probably have to be replaced with a new section. If the leak occurs at a joint, you may be able to tighten it with a Stillson wrench. However, leaking pipes generally need attention from the plumber, but until he arrives you can apply a few first-aid measures.

If the leak is small and develops in a place which is easily accessible, you may be able to stop it temporarily with some sort of packing. A small section of rubber hose can be slit, wrapped around the pipe, and held in place with a clamp. Perhaps adhesive tape wrapped tightly around the pipe in several layers will do the trick. Even a rag will stop a leak from squirting, and a pan under the pipe will catch the water as it drips. Any such measure will probably be sufficient until the plumber comes. But if the leak is too serious to respond to such temporary treatment, you may have to close the nearest shut-off valve and just do without water from that pipe until it can be repaired.

However, sometimes it is difficult to determine the origin of the leak. It may announce itself only when water begins to seep through the plaster of a wall or ceiling. In that case, the first thing to do is to close the main shut-off valve immediately. If the ceiling is becoming stained and you can find no flooding on any upstairs floor, then the leak has probably occurred in a pipe located in the space between a floor and a ceiling. This space may even have become filled with water which might soak through the plaster and loosen it from the whole ceiling. The best thing to do is to pick a small hole in the damp plaster and drain off the water as quickly as possible. Use any sharp instrument handy — an ice pick or even a nail file if nothing else is available — and collect the water in any assortment of pots, pans, or containers that can be found — but put the whole family to work in a hurry. A small hole in the plaster can be quickly and cheaply mended as soon as the ceiling is dry — but replastering an entire ceiling is another matter, to say nothing of the mess and work of cleaning up the plaster if it falls. The next step, of course, is to keep the water turned off and to call the plumber.

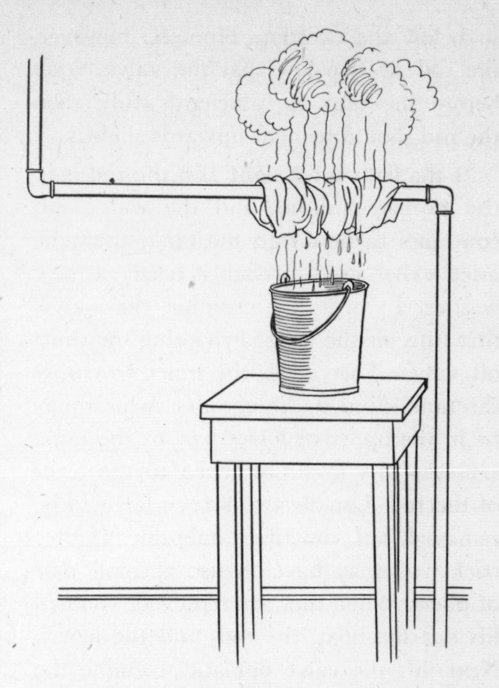

FIG. 7. Frozen pipes can be safely thawed by wrapping with cloths dipped in hot water. Never apply direct flame to a frozen pipe.

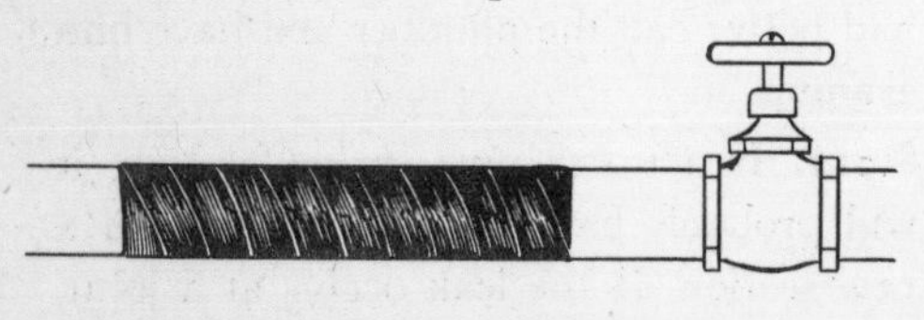

FIG. 6. Leaks in pipes can often be temporarily checked by taping with electrical insulating tape or adhesive tape. Another method is to slit a piece of hose, wrap it around pipe, and hold in place with a C-clamp.

Gas pipes sometimes develop leaks too, although this is less apt to happen than in a water pipe. If you can find the leak, you may be able to stop it temporarily in the same way as you would stop a leak in a water pipe. But above all, don't attempt to test the pipe for a leak by running a lighted match along with it. You may find it that way, but never live to do anything about it. If a gas pipe is leaking, the first thing to do is to close the valve on the pipe, if you know where it is. Gas pipe valves often have no handle and must be turned with a Stillson wrench or sometimes a monkey wrench. The main valve may be near the meter. But such valves vary slightly in design and if you don't know where the valve is or how it operates, then you had better have someone from the gas company give you explicit instructions before you attempt to turn it off. If a leak should develop before you get around to that, then open the doors and windows to keep the house as well ventilated as possible. If the odor of gas is overwhelming, and you cannot locate the leak, or cannot check it, or close the valve, then you had better open the windows and leave the house. Call the gas company, as repairs to gas pipes must usually be made by them, and not by the plumber.

Frozen Pipes. Never attempt to thaw out a frozen pipe with a blow torch, a lighted candle, or any direct flame. Any intense heat may cause the metal to expand so rapidly that it bursts. Instead, wrap the pipes in rags dipped in hot water, changing them as quickly as they cool. This method takes longer, but it's safe. Of course, if the pipes are covered with insulating material, it will have to be removed before you can thaw the pipe out with hot water, because insulation checks both heat and cold. But when pipes freeze in spite of insulation, then there's not enough of it.

CLOGGED DRAINS

Drain pipes are always formed in a U-shaped or S-shaped curve beneath any plumbing fixture. This curve forms a trap which holds the water. The water acts as a seal and prevents entry of foul air, or sewer gas into the house. But, because of its shape, the trap also sometimes becomes clogged by waste materials. If the trap is only partially blocked, the water will not drain as quickly as it should, but when the trap is completely blocked, the water will not drain off at all.

One of the most useful devices for opening up a clogged drain is the rubber suction cup, or force cup, or plunger, which is often called the "plumber's friend." To use this cup in a sink, wash basin, or tub, fill the fixture with just enough water to submerge the cup. Then place the cup over the drain opening, and with a fairly rapid movement force it up and down by pressing and pulling on the handle. Repeat this process until the drain either begins to function or until it becomes evident that it will not respond to this treatment. Very likely it will, and after it does, pour down it one of the chemical drain solvents which are sold commercially under various trade names. Use these according to the manufacturer's directions. In fact, if such a solvent is used regularly, especially in sink drains, which are more apt to become grease filled, clogging will be less likely to occur. But the solvents usually cannot work unless the drain is functioning a little, at least.

If, however, the force cup fails to work, then perhaps a plumbing auger will. This auger consists of a flexible steel coil with a handle on one end. Augers come in various lengths, so get one long enough to reach to the end of the trap. If the drain opening is covered by a screen of some sort, remove it. Then insert the end of the auger and work it down the drain pipe. When it reaches the section that is clogged, you may have some difficulty to force it down any further. In that case, pull it out, and probably some of the stuff that is blocking the pipe will come out, too. If so, remove it from the auger and start over again. Eventually, the drain is almost bound to be cleared so that it functions at least to some extent. In that case, proceed with a chemical drain solvent.

A clogged toilet drain can sometimes be cleared simply by filling the bowl with water. But do not fill it by flushing the toilet, as it may overflow. Just pour the water in until the bowl is nearly full. If the water seeps out slowly, repeat the process several times, and very likely the pressure of the water will remove the obstruction. If not, try the force cup or the auger. But a chemical solvent won't help much to remove any obstruction in the toilet trap. In fact, if the solvent is allowed to remain for any length of time in the stopped-up toilet, it might even cause damage.

If a drain is not used for some time, the water seal in the trap may evaporate and permit sewer gas to escape. Therefore, it is advisable to pour water now and then into any drain that hasn't been in use for awhile. The water is especially apt to evaporate in a little used floor drain in the basement or in a garage.

CARE OF PLUMBING FIXTURES

Modern plumbing fixtures are generally made of porcelain, stainless metals, or iron coated with vitreous enamel which is baked on. All deserve good care. Be especially careful not to scratch them. Scratches are not only unsightly, but also unsanitary. The rim of the tub should not be used as a convenient foot rest on which to shine shoes. Never stand in a tub with shoes on. Don't place flower pots or any other object which may contain sand or grit directly on the bottom of the tub. If the tub must be used as a place to spray plants, protect the surface of the tub with a piece of cloth before putting in the pots. Do not use cleaning powders which are gritty enough to scratch the fixture. Don't allow picture-developing solutions, strong acids, or any corrosive chemicals to come in contact with the fixtures.

Sometimes stubborn stains occur on plumbing fixtures. If you know what caused the stain, the best thing to do is to go to the druggist and have him give you the proper compound to remove that particular stain. Also, there are various commercial compounds on the market which remove many kinds of stains most efficiently, especially the common stains caused by rusting or corroding pipes. Sometimes hydrogen peroxide will work, or a commercial laundry bleach in the right dilution.

If porcelain fixtures become cracked, they cannot be repaired but must be replaced. But if a crack develops in an enameled fixture, it can sometimes be repaired with iron cement. The crack should be completely dry and clean before the cement is applied. The fixture cannot be used until the cement has thoroughly hardened.

The shiny nickel or other plating on faucets often wears off. If this happens, the faucet can be replated at moderate cost. Simply remove the faucet and take it to the plumber or to any shop or plating company that does such work. But the water must be shut off before you remove the faucet, and it must be left off until the faucet is returned, unless you are able to borrow a faucet from the plumber for temporary use. In some sinks or wash basins the faucet must be unscrewed beneath the fixture, and in others, above it. But in any event, you will undoubtedly need either a monkey wrench or a Stillson wrench to get it off. After closing the shut-off valve, drain the water out of the faucet before removing it. Otherwise, the water will flow all over the bathroom floor.

WATER HEATERS

REGARDLESS of how modern and gleaming the fixtures may be, the plumbing system is no better than its water supply. In communities serviced by a public water-supply system, cold water in ample quantities is always available except in times of emergency. Hot water, however, is another matter. The available supply depends upon the size and efficiency of the water-heating equipment. With the installation of such time-saving equipment as electric dishwashers and automatic washing machines, many a home owner finds that his existing water heater is inadequate to meet the increased demands made upon it. Not only do electric dishwashers and automatic washing machines require quantities of hot water, but also water heated to a higher temperature than the hands or body will tolerate.

If the supply of hot water is inadequate for the needs of the household, perhaps the cause is not an inefficient water heater, but one taxed beyond its capacities. It is estimated that a family of four needs a hot-water tank with a capacity of at least 75 gallons if the laundry is done at home. This capacity may need to be increased to a hundred gallons with the installation of an automatic electric dishwasher. The need for a supply of this size is not that any particular piece of equipment will require this much hot water, but that the supply will be large enough to take care of all equipment during those busy hours when many things may be in use at once. Eight o'clock in the morning is the crucial period in most homes. More than 17 per cent of the total daily supply of hot water is ordinarily used at this time.

The kind of water heater and the capacity required depends upon individual needs. Local utility companies should be consulted for their recommendations in this respect. One factor which influences the selection of a tank is the kind of water in any given locality. It is important to have a tank that will be free from corrosion and which will deliver clean water. Among the innovations to overcome corrosion are special glass linings welded to steel and synthetic stone molded inside steel. In some areas, a galvanized iron tank may be satisfactory, depending on the chemicals in the water. Copper tanks have long since proved their serviceability. All the newer models of tanks are automatic and are designed for use with gas, oil, or electricity, or as auxiliaries to coal-fired boilers.

CHAPTER XXIV

HOUSE PAINTING

HOUSE painting is not a job that any but the hardiest housewife would be willing to undertake (or should we say foolhardy?), and she shouldn't prod her husband into doing it unless she's prepared to rub his aching muscles with linament. We asked several husbands who were so prodded and who eventually achieved quite handsome results just how they went about it. To a man, they all were of the opinion that the job had taken them at least three times as long as they had expected, and all except one swore they would never do it again, even though they had saved several hundred dollars by their efforts. So, after this warning, if your husband still feels that his trusty right arm (and left, too), will stay by him through the ordeal, we will pass on a few pointers that we gleaned from our informants.

PAINT

THE reason the painting contractor's fee seems so high is not because paint is such a costly item, but because house painting involves so much labor. Actually paint costs represent only a comparatively small sum, and it doesn't pay to try to economize on the quality of the paint. The very best paint you can buy will in the long run be the least expensive, whereas inferior paint may crack and require a very costly job of removal before new paint can be applied, even though the original cost per gallon was less than for some other paint. Since the home owner cannot be expected to judge the quality of paint by looking at it, the best thing to do is to ask advice from a reliable paint dealer. The best quality paint will cost more (unless it is bought in tremendous quantities), but in the end, it will be more than worth the difference in price.

Even the best paint will wear away in time through exposure to the elements, but it should last for several years—usually four or five, and sometimes longer. Unlike paint of poor quality, good paint will not wear away by cracking or chipping. Instead, the surface very slowly turns to powder, providing the paint was properly applied.

If the present coat of paint has peeled, blistered, or chipped extensively, it usually has to be removed before another coat can be put on. A professional contractor burns the paint off with a blow torch, but this method is too dangerous to be attempted by the amateur. If he is willing to undertake the job, he should use a paint-removing compound, which softens the paint until it can be scraped away. This task will be more laborious than the actual painting, as a rule.

The amount of paint needed depends

upon the type of surface being painted and the square footage involved. It is easy enough to find the square footage of rectangular areas by multiplying the length by the height, but if you want to measure the gables or cornices accurately, you had better dig out your textbooks on trigonometry. A rough estimate can be made by multiplying one half the height of the gable by the width at the base. One gallon of oil paint should be sufficient for one coat on approximately 400 square feet of smooth-surfaced wood which has been previously painted or primed. If the present paint job has weathered down to the wood, the house should have at least two coats of paint.

Different surfaces require different kinds of paint. Regular oil paints can be used on any wood surface, but on concrete, stucco, or brick, it is often better to use paints specially prepared for such surfaces. Paint manufacturers have developed many new paint formulas in recent years. One of these is a two-coat system consisting of a first coat which gives adhesion and a second coat which tends to resist the elements. Always read the manufacturer's directions for using any kind of paint and follow them explicitly.

Colors. It is always advisable to select ready-mixed paint colors. The average home owner just doesn't have the equipment for mixing pigment with enough paint to cover a house. Ready-mixed paints come in a wide enough variety of colors to satisfy almost every need.

When rightly applied, color can help to minimize architectural defects. A chimney which seems out of proportion will become less noticeable if it is painted the same color as the walls of the house. Dormers on mansard roofs look less prominent if they are painted the same color as the roof. A small house appears to gain height when the dormers are painted the same color as the walls. Dark shutters on the upstairs windows painted to match a dark roof and light shutters on the downstairs windows painted to match the walls will help to make the too-high roof seem lower.

Leftover Paint. All leftover paint should be carefully stored. If it is stored in a container large enough to leave an air space at the top, a skin will form on the paint. It is better to have the container completely filled. If a skin does form on the paint, it should be strained into another container through a piece of cheesecloth.

Paint Troubles. When paint blisters or peels, it usually indicates that it was applied to a damp surface, or applied during misty weather. Another cause is oil or grease on the painted surface. Peeling often occurs when too many coats are applied and their combined weight loosens the priming coat.

Sap or resin in wood sometimes bleeds through paint and causes discoloration. To check this, cover the spot with a coat of aluminum paint.

Paint which fails to dry thoroughly can sometimes be hardened by an application of turpentine. If the paint still remains sticky, the only remedy is to remove it.

EQUIPMENT

THE most important piece of equipment for a job of house painting is an extension ladder or two or three ladders of various lengths. A 32-foot extension ladder should be long enough to reach all parts of the walls on an average two-story house with a peaked roof. It is very important that the ladder be sturdy and sound. A broken rung or a wobbling ladder can lead to a bad fall which may result in broken bones. Sometimes certain parts of a house are very difficult to reach without special equipment. For example, a projecting

It took just two coats of paint to transform the apparently nondescript house above into the distinguished-looking one below.

Even a house of no particular architectural distinction takes on an air of freshness when two coats of new paint are applied.

porch can often make the second-story wall above it inaccessible with a ladder resting on the ground. Professional painters rig up a scaffold to reach the difficult places, but the average home owner isn't likely to have such equipment, nor is it advisable that he should attempt to use it unless he knows exactly how to go about it. Sometimes the less accessible places can be reached with a ladder which has a hook on the end of each leg. The hooks can be fastened over the ridgepole of the roof so that the ladder is supported from above instead of below. In other cases, a 1 x 3 board can be securely nailed to the roof as a footing to support the legs of the ladder. However, an arrangement of this kind is not always advisable because the nails may damage the roof. The best plan is to make a careful study of all exterior surfaces of the house and then try to figure out how they can be reached. If the solution seems difficult for a number of places, it may be more practical to have the work done by a professional.

A good paint brush is essential—a 5-inch brush is a good size, but don't try to work on large surfaces with any brush smaller than 4 inches. Smaller brushes are convenient for tight places, but not necessary. It is advisable to get a brush set with real bristles. Such brushes are quite expensive, but they will stand up under considerable usage. You will also need a putty knife, putty, a supply of sandpaper, linseed oil, turpentine, a foot of heavy wire, and a generous amount of old rags to use as drip cloths. Shrubbery, roofs, and cement walks near the area being painted should be covered with the cloths as protection from dripping paint. Of course, the painter should wear overalls or old clothes.

PROCEDURE

FIRST of all, painting must be done only in clear, sunny weather. If rain occurs, the house must be allowed to dry out thoroughly before proceeding with the work. When rains are frequent, the job may easily be prolonged for weeks, but the paint will peel off if it is applied to damp wood.

When you are ready to begin, stir the paint well and pour it from can to can to mix it thoroughly. Then pour enough paint in an empty pail to fill it no more than two-thirds full. Bend the foot of heavy wire into an S shape to hang he pail from the rung of the ladder. Don't attempt to hold the pail in one hand and paint with the other. You will need one hand to hang on to the ladder. When the wire S is placed over the ladder rung, the end should point towards the wall; otherwise the top hook may snag the painter's trousers. Spread the drip cloths and stow the sandpaper and paint brush in handy pockets. Now you are ready to put the ladder in place.

FIG. 1. Method of hanging paint can from ladder. End of top hook should be turned to underside of ladder.

Placing the Ladder. The paint job should be started at the roof line at the highest point, and the ladder should be placed accordingly. The most important thing to remember about placing the ladder is to keep it in its own vertical plane. All four corners must make contact. If the ladder wobbles, it's on an uneven surface that must be leveled off. Never, never climb a wobbly ladder if you want to stay out of the hospital.

If the ladder is vertical and it still wobbles, one of the bottom legs is on uneven ground. Sometimes the ground is soft enough to sink one leg. If not, the ground will have to be evened up. A shingle is often thick enough to do the trick. When the ladder must be placed against the edge of a sloping roof, turn the ladder to one side or the other so that all four corners make contact. In this position, the ladder will look as if it is leaning, but actually it isn't; and if it is properly placed, it should be secure.

The base of the ladder should never be placed farther away from the wall it is leaning against than one-third of the total length of the ladder. In other words, if the ladder is 30 feet long, the base should not be more than 10 feet from the wall. The farther away the base is placed, the more the strain on the ladder increases.

It's no small feat to climb to the top of a high ladder and carry a can of paint at the same time. One man said the height made him so dizzy the first time he tried it, that he backed down, rung by rung, after he was halfway up. Then he made a sling contrivance to hang the paint can around his neck and put the lid back on so the paint wouldn't splash all over him. This contrivance didn't work too well because the can kept bumping against the rungs. It did leave him two free hands to climb with — but after he was up at the top he had to learn to hang on with one hand and paint with the other. After an hour or so, the muscles in his painting arm started to protest so vigorously that he changed the paint brush over to the other hand. But he had never learned to be ambidextrous, and the paint dribbled down his arm and dripped off his elbow. He said his biggest headache, though, was the limited area that could be reached at a time. He tried leaning over farther and farther until he almost lost his balance. After that, he resigned himself to climbing down and moving the ladder over another 3 feet or so.

He thought at first that he could save himself some effort by working through the rungs to paint the surface directly behind

FIG. 2. Distance from base of ladder to the wall should not exceed one-third the height of ladder.

FIG. 3. When base of ladder is too far from the wall, the ladder is strained too much.

the ladder, but the rungs interfered with the sweep of the brush. Once the paint can fell and a stream of paint flowed over the concrete sidewalk. Although the paint was mopped up immediately, and the sidewalk was flushed with turpentine, the spot was still visible since the paint had become imbedded in the rough surface of the concrete. It took the entire contents of a can of paint remover to soften up the paint and a vigorous scrubbing with a wire brush to remove enough paint to make the spot unnoticeable. Some of the shrubbery which was badly spattered later died.

A few other mishaps occurred during the course of the first four days, but our friend kept doggedly at his work. He had learned by this time that he could keep the paint from dribbling quite so much by dipping the brush into the can just deep enough to cover one-third of the bristles. Then he slapped the side of the brush against the sides of the can to remove the excess paint. The paint was easier to apply when the brush wasn't overloaded, and it took less effort to smooth the paint out into a thin film.

The one man who said he would paint his house again tells us that the work is actually relaxing, and that the rhythmic sweep and slap, slap of the brush is a good antidote for raw nerves. We think it only fair to add, however, that his house is but one story high and has no dormers. Dormers, by the way, seem to be the biggest problem of all, and if the dormers are above a second story, about the only way they can be reached is with a ladder hooked over the ridgepole of the roof or by nailing board supports to the roof to rest the base of the ladder on.

Mr. Y. said that no matter how tired he was at the end of the day, he always put everything away in order. It would have

Badly peeled or blistered paint must be removed before new coat is applied.

Surface at left shows wood after old paint was burned off. Base coat of two-coat system has been applied at right.

Second coat makes house look like new.

The two-coat system of painting restored the ante-bellum charm of this Southern home and halted further deterioration.

been easier to leave the ladder leaning against the house, but it presented such a tripping hazard at night that he lowered it and left it resting horizontally against the base of the house. He cleaned his brush in a half cup of turpentine and slipped it over a small rod by means of a hole drilled in the handle. The rod was placed across a can filled with a 50-50 mixture of linseed oil and turpentine so that the bristles were submerged but the ends did not touch the bottom of the can. This treatment kept the bristles straight and pliable. (*For further information on the care of brushes, see the Chapter on Painting, Papering, and Special Treatments.*)

Cracks and Holes. Any cracks or holes in the wood must be filled with putty. This work can be done before the first coat of paint is applied, although some painters claim that the putty holds better if it is put on after the first coat and before the second. If a stucco or cement surface is being painted, cracks or holes should be filled before starting to paint. Special fillers are made for this purpose.

Sandpapering. Although the old paint on the major part of the house may be smooth, a few peeled spots may be found in patches here and there. Perhaps the wood was a little damp in these places when the paint was applied, or maybe that part of the wood contained sap or resin. It's better to sandpaper these spots smooth than to attempt to remove the paint with paint remover. The stuff will probably dribble over the rest of the wall, and the first thing you know you will have to remove the paint from the entire wall.

Fit the sandpaper over a block of wood and tack it at the sides. Make a short handle from a strap of leather and nail it to the back of the wood block. This little gadget will simplify the job of sanding with one hand. A wire-bristled brush and a spatula are also useful for removing peeled or blistered paint.

CANVAS

CHAPTER XXV

MISCELLANEOUS REPAIRS

HOUSES, like people, begin to show their age in little ways. It's the sagging doors, broken sash cords, loose hinges and other signs of wear and tear that make a house begin to look neglected and shabby. To remedy most of the minor ailments around the house seldom requires much skill or, in many cases, even time. But if they are put off from day to day or week to week, they sometimes develop into more serious troubles, or at the very least are constant sources of annoyance or eyesores. Every house needs its handyman, but if he isn't as handy as he should be, don't despair. Just show him how simple it is to be a Mr. Fixit—or better yet, perhaps, just do the job yourself. He will probably want to supervise; then he will become interested, and soon discover his hidden talents as a repair artist.

DOORS

DOORS which have previously functioned well and fitted their frames sometimes become difficult to close. There are several causes for a sticking door. A hinge may be loose. The door may be swollen, or the building may have settled so that the frame is out of line.

Sagging. Sagging doors are sometimes caused by loose hinges. The trouble can often be remedied merely by tightening the screws. To do this, open the door at a right angle to the frame. Wedge a piece of wood or an axe handle underneath the outer edge of the door to prop it up while the screws are being tightened.

If the screw threads will no longer hold in the wood, the hinges will have to be removed and the door taken off. With the chisel, cut new mortises (recessed spaces) in the door frame and on the edge of the door of the same depth as, and just below, the old mortises into which the flaps of the hinge were fitted. Attach one flap of the hinge to the door and fit it into position beside the frame (two people may be needed to do this). Screw the other flaps of both upper and lower hinges into the mortises on the door frame. For a neater finish, the old mortise can be filled with plastic wood. If the paint or varnish was damaged while the new mortises were being cut, the door and frame will need to be refinished. Another method which often works well and eliminates the necessity of chiseling out a new mortise is to plug the screw holes with plastic wood and then rescrew the hinge flaps in place before the plastic wood has completely hardened. If the screw threads are worn, use new screws.

After long usage a door may sag slightly so that the outer end drags on the floor when the door is opened, even though the

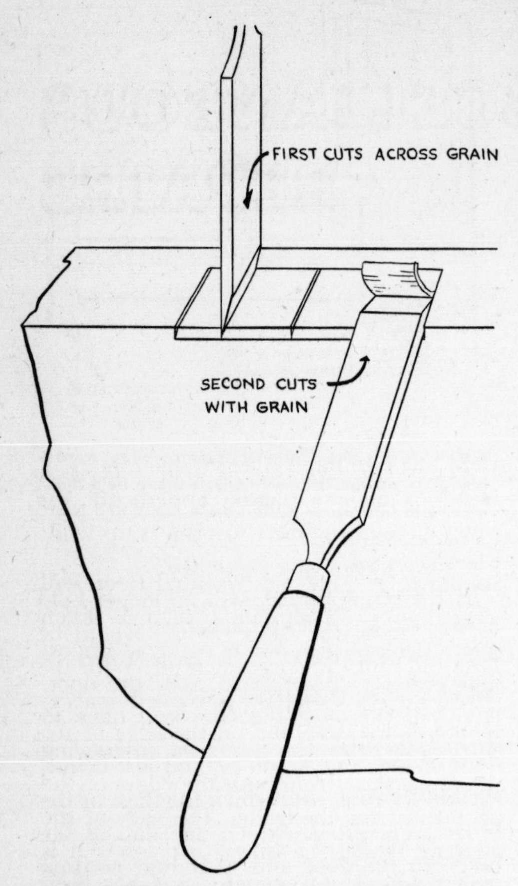

FIG. 1. Chiseling out a mortise on the edge of the door frame.

screws are tight in the hinges. This condition can be remedied by unscrewing the hinges from the frame but not from the door, chiseling off a thin layer of wood from the surface of the top mortise, and packing the bottom mortise with a layer of cardboard. The door is then set back in the frame and the hinges are screwed into place. Letting in the top hinge slightly and packing out the bottom hinge in this way is usually all that is necessary to give the door sufficient clearance.

The edges of a sagging door should never be planed to make the door fit into the frame except as a last resort. It is usually better to remedy the trouble by adjusting the hinges.

Twisting. A door which is made of improperly seasoned lumber, or which is too thin, or which is badly constructed and hung, will often twist or warp. The latch will not fasten as it should and the door will admit drafts because it does not fit snugly against the jamb. If the condition is serious, the best thing to do is to buy a

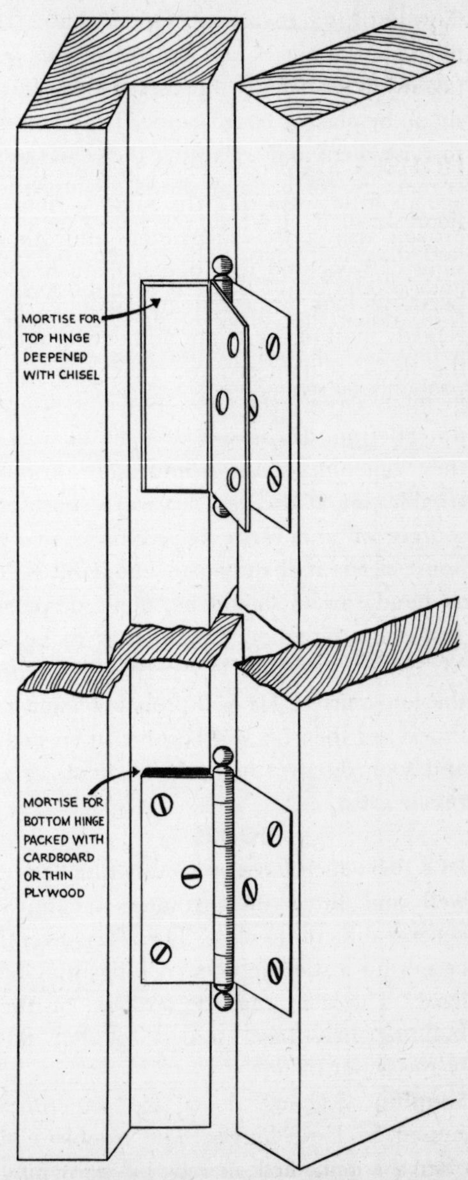

FIG. 2. Method of remedying sagging door by deepening top mortise and packing lower one.

new door. Slight twisting, however, can sometimes be remedied if the door can be left unused for a few days. Insert a short board between the frame and the door either at the top or bottom edge, according to which way the door has twisted. At the other edge, insert a wedge to force the door against the frame (*see Fig.* 3). Leave the door in this position for several days until it recovers its original shape. If the door cannot be left unused, it can be taken off the frame and forced back into shape by placing boards under two corners to raise them and weighting the other two corners to force them down against the floor. Instead of weights, a board can be laid diagonally across the corner and the ends of the board screwed to the floor to force down the corner of the door. After a few days in this position, the door will probably be straight again.

FIG. 3. A twisted door can sometimes be straightened by forcing door in opposite direction of twist.

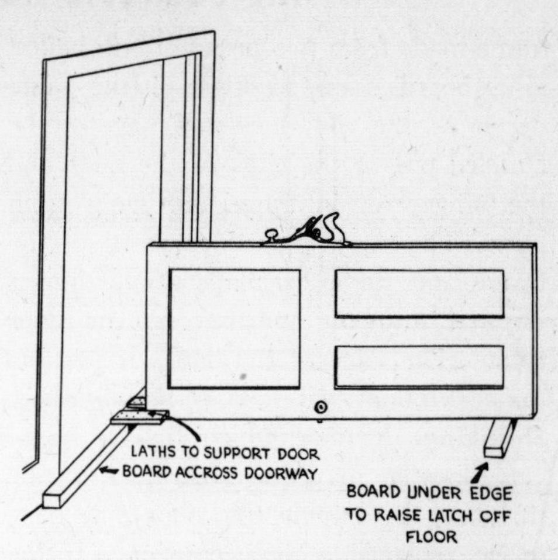

FIG. 4. To support door while planing edge, raise one edge off the floor with a board and hold the other end in a frame made from a board and two pieces of lath.

Swelling. A very tightly fitted door will sometimes swell in damp weather. Even slight swelling can often make it impossible either to open or to close the door. If this is the case, the door will have to be removed from its frame by unscrewing the hinge flaps from both the edges of the door and from the frame. The edge of the door on which the hinges are screwed is then planed until enough wood has been removed to make the door fit the frame. Be careful not to plane away too much of the edge. Approximately 1/16 to 1/8 of an inch is usually enough. Draw a line about 1/16 of an inch from the edge of the door and parallel to it along the face of the stile with the marking gauge. This line will serve as a guide for the amount of wood to be planed away. After planing, check the results. If 1/16 of an inch is not sufficient, plane away another 1/16 of an inch. If an assistant is available to hold the door steady, the work of planing will be much easier. If you must do the job by yourself, the door can be supported by resting the edge of one end on a board, so that the lock or latch clears the floor, and holding the other end in a temporary frame made from two pieces of lath nailed to a board. New mortises of the same depth as the old ones will have to be chiseled out of the edge of the door and the hinges set in them and screwed in place. The door is then returned to the frame and the other flaps of the hinges screwed into the mortises on the door frame. The edge of the door, or possibly the entire door, will have to be refinished.

Shrinking. A door which fits its frame very loosely may have shrunk. If the shrinkage is extreme, the door may have to be replaced with a new one. If the space between the door and the latch is so wide that the latch fails to catch, one remedy is to remove the door and insert several thicknesses of cardboard or thin pieces of plywood underneath the hinge flaps attached to the door frame. The cardboard or plywood pieces should be cut to fit into the mortises. The space between the door and the frame will then be equalized on each side, and the latch should be able to catch.

In some cases, the rails or stiles of the door will shrink in width but not in length. If the shrinkage is considerable, the ends of the tenons on the rails may project beyond the edge of the stile. Such a condition may not interfere with the operation of the door at all unless the hinge pin becomes slack and the door drops a little. Then the tenon ends may rub the door frame. If so, they can be planed off flush with the door edge. It is usually unnecessary to remove the door from the frame to do this. The door can be simply opened as wide as it will go, so that the inner edge can be reached, although it may be a little awkward to reach with the plane.

WINDOWS

Repairing a Broken Sash Cord. The typical double-hung sash window has a top outside sash and a bottom inside sash,

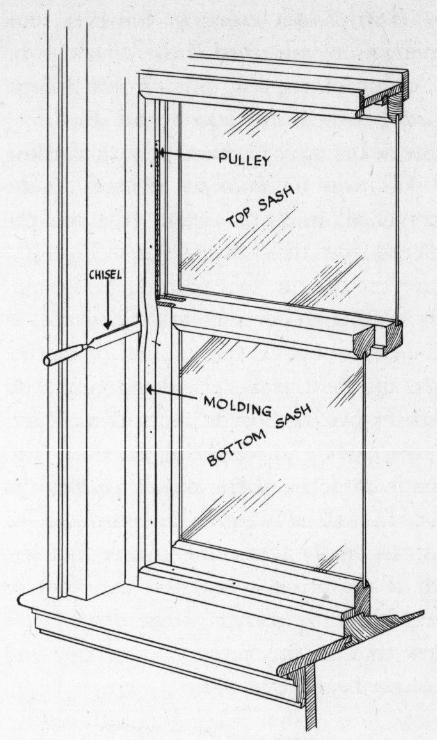

FIG. 5. To repair broken sash cord, first pry off molding.

both of which can be moved up or down to rest in any position because they are counterbalanced by weights inside the frame hung from heavy cords or chains. When the cord on either side breaks, the weight falls down and the sash will slide right down as soon as it is pushed up. In order to remedy this condition, the broken sash cord will have to be replaced with a new one, or, better yet, with a metal sash chain. If chain is not available, buy the special heavy cord made for this purpose. Buy the best obtainable, as it won't be so likely to break and have to be replaced again for a long time.

The first step is to pry off the molding which forms the front part of the groove to hold the frame of the sash in place. Use a chisel to do this, but be careful not to break or splinter the molding. Some window frames are fitted with metal weather strips which must be pried off, too. If the lower sash cord has broken, only the section of molding on the side where the cord is broken has to be pried off.

The next step is to raise the sash slightly and pull it out as far as the unbroken sash cord will allow. Next, remove the broken sash cord from the frame. Near the bottom of the groove on the frame you should find a rectangular section of wood or metal, called a *pocket piece,* fitted into the frame and held in place with a screw or a nail. Remove the screw or nail and lift out the pocket piece. The sash weight, probably attached to the rest of the broken sash cord, will be found in the sash pocket, the small recessed space behind the pocket piece. Remove the weight and the cord.

Fit the two broken sections of cord together to find the correct length of the entire cord, and cut a piece of new cord to size. New sash cord is too difficult to push down into the sash pocket unless it is weighted. Use a large nail or two, a bolt, a heavy screw, a small piece of chain, or something similar as a weight. Attach it to the sash cord with a piece of string.

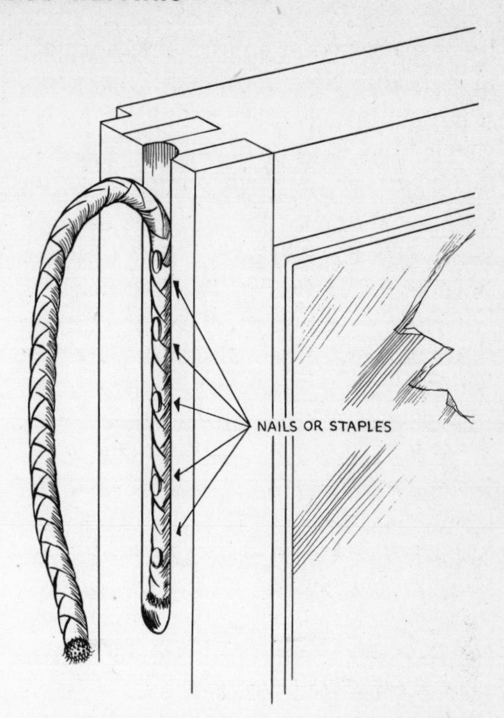

FIG. 7. One end of sash cord is nailed or stapled to window frame.

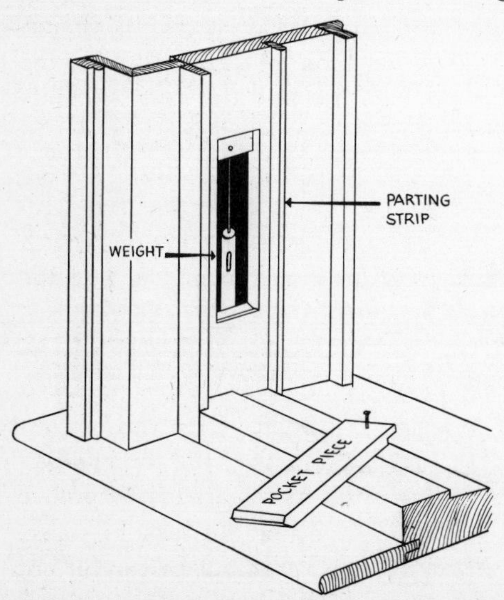

FIG. 6. Sash weight will be found in sash pocket behind pocket piece.

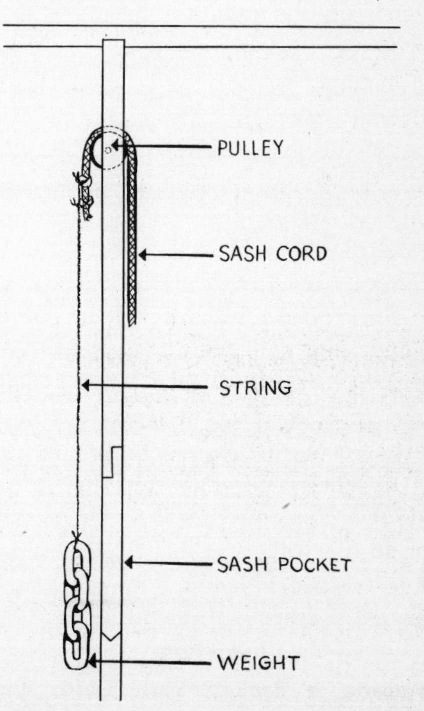

FIG. 8. Tie weight to one end of string and attach other end to sash cord to pull it into pocket.

One end of the string can be tied around the cord and the other end around the weight.

The other end of the cord is nailed to the edge of the window. The weighted end is slipped over the pulley and dropped down into the sash pocket. The cord can then be pulled after it. The sash weight is attached to the cord. Then the pocket piece is screwed or nailed into place, the window sash is returned to its frame, and the molding is nailed into position.

If the upper sash cord has broken, the molding on that side must be pried off as for a lower sash. The lower sash is then pulled out of the frame, and the parting strip between the two sashes is pulled out of the groove into which it is fitted. If the parting strip is difficult to remove because of hardened paint, grasp it with a pair of pliers. Protect the strip with a piece of cloth so the jaws of the pliers will not mar the wood. With the parting strip removed, the upper sash can be pulled out. The pocket piece is unscrewed, the weight is removed, and a new sash cord is installed in the same way as for the lower sash cord. Then replace the top sash, the parting strip, the pocket piece, the bottom sash, and finally, nail the molding on again. If the paint on the frame or molding has been chipped during this work, the frame will probably have to be refinished.

Replacing a Broken Window Pane. Glass is fitted into a window frame in various ways. Some frames have a recessed edge (a *rabbet*) on which the glass is bedded in a layer of putty and held in place with small triangular pieces of metal, called *glazier's points,* or small brads driven parallel with the surface of the pane into the sides of the frame. A wedge-shaped facing of putty is then pressed all around the edge of the frame to further hold it and make the frame leakproof. In other frames, a type of wooden molding, or glass bead, is used instead of putty to hold the pane in place. With this molding, brads or glazier's points are not necessary. In still other frames, the pane of glass is fitted into a groove filled with putty. An examination of the window frame will probably indicate the manner in which the pane has been fitted.

The first step is to remove the broken pane. The frame is easier to work on if it is removed from the window, but this is not essential. If the putty is loose, the broken sections of pane can probably be pulled right out. Protect the hands against injury from the sharp edges of the broken glass by covering it with a piece of cloth. If the broken glass does not come out easily, scrape away the putty facing with an old kitchen knife or a spatula. If the putty is very hard, tap the knife with a hammer. If the glass is fitted with a bead molding, pry it off with a chisel. After the glass is out, every bit of old putty must be cleaned off the frame before the new glass is fitted into place.

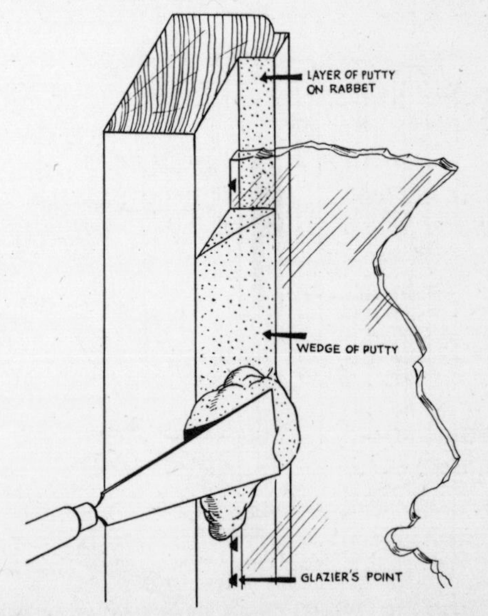

FIG. 9. Window pane fitted into frame with glazier's points and putty.

Measure the frame opening carefully and cut a piece of window glass to fit (*see the section on Picture Framing in the Chapter on Pictures, Lamps, and Ornaments, for the method used to cut glass*). If the frame has a rabbet, cut the glass large enough to rest on the rabbet but 1/16 of an inch shorter and narrower than the actual size of the opening to allow for the expansions and contractions of the glass. Set the glass in the frame. If the original pane was bedded in putty on the rabbet, the new pane can either be set in place in that way or else held in place with a bead molding. (Of course, if bead molding is used on one window frame, the other frames in the room should match in the same way.) When putty is used, press the edge of the pane against the rabbet to force the putty down under the edge of the glass. Drive glazier's points or small brads into the frame on the inside edge of the glass and parallel to its surface. Form a long roll of putty about ½ inch thick between the hands and place it around the edge of the pane. Press the putty against the pane edge and the frame into a wedge shape and smooth the surface with a spatula. After the putty is dry and hard, both putty and frame should be painted.

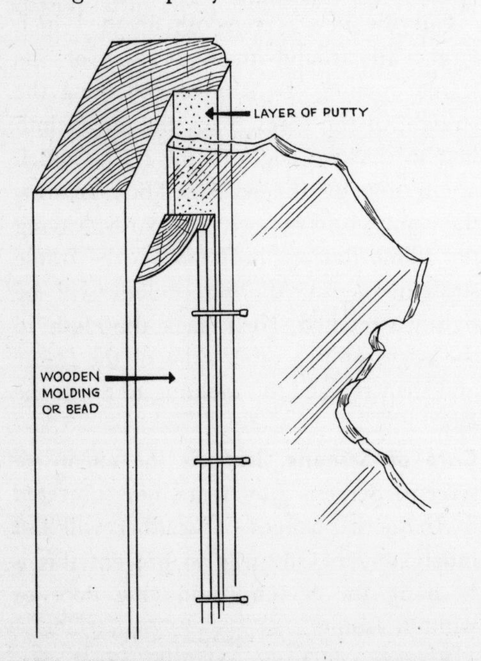

FIG. 10. Window pane fitted into frame with putty, molding, and nails.

If molding is used, a layer of putty is first laid on the rabbet in the same way, but the glass need not be held with glazier's points or brads. Instead, the molding is merely nailed into place on the frame around the edge of the glass. The molding is then painted to match the frame.

If the frame has a grooved edge, it is filled with putty and the pane is fitted into place.

On any type of frame, all excess putty should be removed with a spatula before the putty has had time to dry and harden.

MENDING DOOR AND WINDOW SCREENS

Holes in window or door screens render them as good as useless. Small holes can be easily mended with patches cut from screening or with screen patches sold in assorted sizes by the dime stores. To make a patch, cut a square piece of screening ½ inch larger all around than the size of the hole. Wire snippers or a pair of heavy shears can be used for cutting. Unravel two wires from each edge of the square to expose the ends of the cross-weave wires. Bend the ends of these wires at right angles to form prongs. Press the patch, prong ends down, against the screen over the hole so that the prongs are pushed through to the other side of the screen. Press the prongs flat against the surface of the screen. Lacquer or varnish the patch to prevent rust or stain from the cut ends of the wire. Ready-made patches come with prongs already bent.

Rescreening. If the screencloth is badly rusted, bulging, or too full of holes to be patched, it can be replaced with new screencloth. New screencloth is sold by the foot and comes in aluminum, bronze, copper, galvanized steel, and black-enameled steel. Aluminum is the most expensive and is usually found on screens with metal frames. Such screens cannot be repaired at home but must be sent to the factory. Black-enameled steel screencloth is the cheapest, but it tends to rust as soon as the enamel wears off. When this happens, a coat of screen paint should be applied. Use a small piece of carpeting, pile side out, tacked to a block of wood to apply the paint. If an ordinary paint brush is used, the paint will clog the meshes, but carpeting sinks into the mesh and distributes the paint on the wires in a thin film. Screens do not need to be painted black. For a change, why not try white (especially if the house is painted white). White reflects light, thereby making it difficult to see the interior of the house through the screen. Screens of galvanized steel which have rusted can be painted in the same way.

Bronze and copper screens do not rust, but the metal may become corroded and discolor the frame with a greenish stain. To prevent this, the screen should be wiped with benzine or washed with soap and water, rinsed, and dried, and then given a coat of spar varnish or shellac before the screen is put up for the summer. The same treatment should be repeated before the screens are removed in the fall for winter storage.

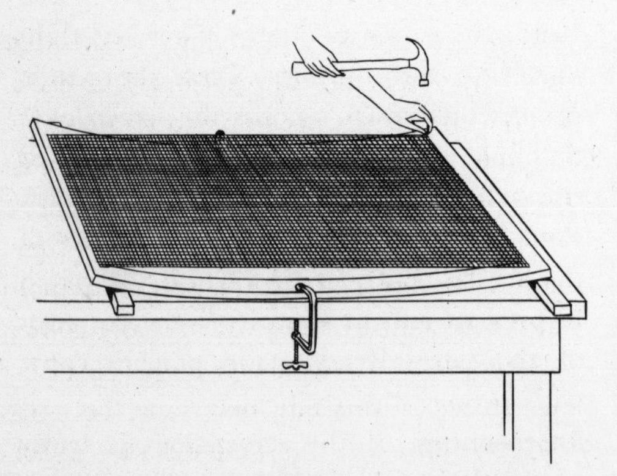

FIG. 11. To tack screencloth to frame, bend it lengthwise and hold in place with clamps.

Bulges in steel or bronze screencloth can sometimes be removed by untacking the cloth, stretching it back into shape, and then retacking. Bulges in copper screen cloth seldom respond to this treatment however, and the screen will probably have to be re-covered.

To re-cover a screen, first lay the screen on a large table and strip off the molding around the edge. Untack the old screen cloth and store it for future patching. Slip a piece of lumber about 1-inch thick and as long as the width of the screen under each end of the frame. Force the sides of the frames against the table and hold them in place with C-clamps. If the wood shows signs of breaking instead of bending, release the tension at once by unscrewing the clamps slightly.

Cut the new screencloth about 1 inch larger all around than the size of the frame opening. Be sure to cut along the straight of the wires. Tack the screencloth first to the two edges of the frame which are resting on the boards. Then unscrew the clamps and remove the boards, leaving the frame flat on the table. As the frame straightens out, the screencloth will be tightly stretched. Next, tack the cloth to the edges of two other sides of the frame and then replace the molding to finish the job.

Care of Screens. Rain is the enemy of screens. Screens which are not subjected to frequent changes of weather will last much longer. One way to prevent this is to hang the screens inside the door or window frame.

Screens which are carefully stored after they are taken down in the fall will ordinarily last for many years. If possible, the screens should be stored in an upright position and should be packed or tied together to keep them standing on end. They can also be stacked flat on the floor if the floor is level, but since most floors are not perfectly level, the screens may become warped.

VENETIAN BLINDS

Cleaning. Venetian blinds are very decorative until they become dirty (which they do quite easily). Then their beauty palls on us a bit if it's up to us to make them spanking clean again. And yet the task can be greatly simplified if we go about it in the right way. Regular dusting helps to keep the blinds clean longer so that they do not need to be washed so often. When they do become grimy, a trip to the tub is usually indicated.

First, find a place near the laundry tubs or any large sink where the blind can be hung. A water pipe or screws driven into a ceiling joist will do. Attach pieces of rope in the form of loops from which the blind can be hung. Next, pull the cord on the blind to draw the slats up to the top of the frame as far as they will go. Lock the cord. Loosen the safety catches or remove the screws which hold the large top slat to the frame. Lift the blind—slats, tapes, cords, and all—off the frame. If the blind has a built-in head, let it be.

Carry the blind to the place you have arranged for it and attach the rope loops to the top slat. Loosen the cord holding the slats together and let the blind down. Tip the slats up and back as far as they will go. With a ripping tool or a screw driver, pull out the tacks holding the ends of the tapes in place on the underside of the bottom slat. Beneath each of the tape ends you will find a small pocket containing the knotted end of the cord. Pull the cord out and unknot it. Then grasp the other end of the cord under the top slat and pull the cord through the holes in the slats until it is free. The slats can now be slipped out of the tapes.

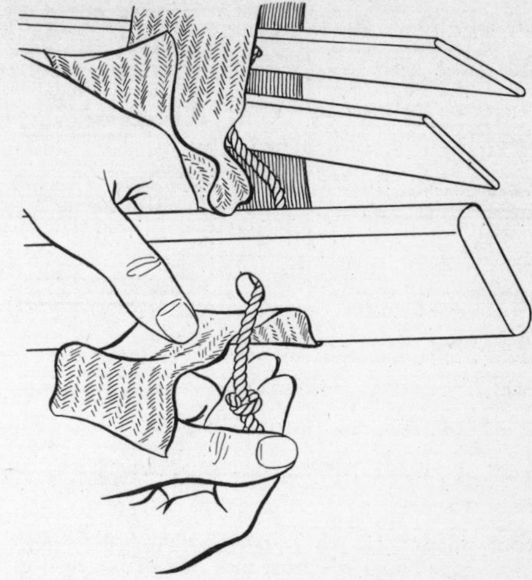

FIG. 12. Bottom slat of Venetian blind. Cord is drawn through and knotted, and tape ends are folded over recessed knot and tacked.

Fill the tub or sink with warm water and add a commercial paint cleaning compound according to the manufacturer's directions. Wash the slats in this solution, a few at a time, and rinse. Twin laundry tubs make this job much easier. The slats can be washed in one tub and rinsed with a rubber hose attached to the faucet in the other tub. After washing and rinsing, stand the slats on end against the wall to drain and dry.

While the slats are dying, wash and rinse the large top and bottom slats with a sponge. It is not necessary to remove the top slat from the tapes unless the blinds are being retaped. Examine the tapes carefully. If they show signs of wear they should be replaced with new tape which can be bought by the yard in many colors at almost any hardware or home-furnishings store. If you buy new tape, be sure the crosstapes are the same distance apart as in the old tape. Worn cords should be replaced, too. If the tapes are merely

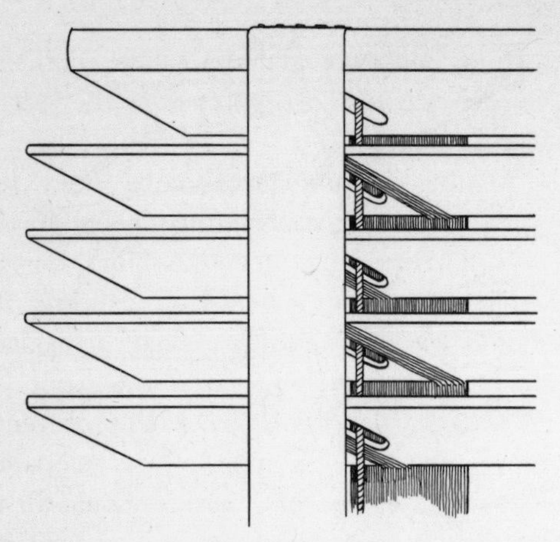

FIG. 13. Cord runs through holes in slats and cross tapes alternate from one side of the cord to the other.

soiled but not worn, they can be dry-cleaned. Do not wash them, as washing shrinks the tapes and the blinds will be much too short to fit the windows. Another remedy for soiled tapes is to cover them with a special gummed tape made for the purpose.

The next step is to return the clean slats to the tapes. Slide the slats in through the cross-tapes so that each one rests in a horizontal position. After the slats are all in place, thread the cords through the holes. The cord runs between the cross tapes so that they alternate from one side to the other of the cord and from slat to slat.

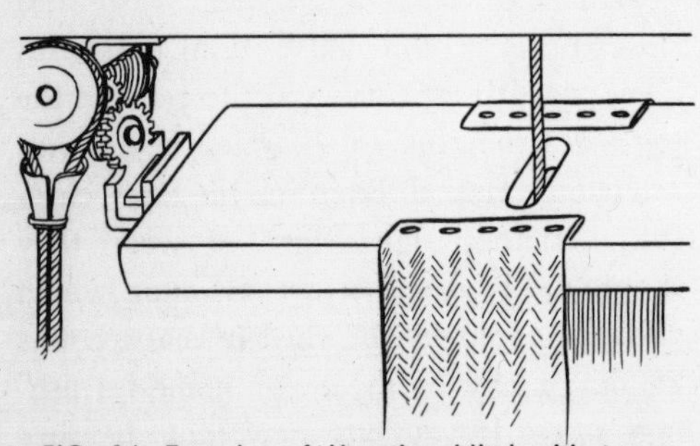

FIG. 14. Top slat of Venetian blind with tapes tacked in place. Cord is run through hole in heading fixture and carried through groove to edge of blind.

When the cord reaches the bottom slat, pull it through the hole and tie a knot in the end of the cord. If the cord is too frayed to get through the hole easily, trim the end a bit. Fold the ends of the tape over and tack in place above the hole. Now test the blind by pulling on the cord to raise and lower it. Pull on the other cord to open and close the slats. If the blind works satisfactorily, pull the slats to the top of the frame and lock the cord. Remove the blind from the rope loops and replace it in the frame on the window. Return the screws or fasten the safety catches, and the job is complete.

AWNINGS

SHABBY, faded awnings can be easily renovated with a coat of paint. Ordinary house or furniture paints should not be used for this purpose as they will crack and stiffen the awning canvas. A special paint made for use on awnings should be applied. Such paint comes in a wide variety of colors and can be bought already mixed with a mildew-prevention compound which serves to protect the canvas from rot in damp weather.

Before the paint is applied, brush the awning well to remove any loose dirt. Any holes in the canvas should be mended also. To do this, first trim the edges of the hole to make it square or oblong, but keep the hole as small as possible. Then cut a canvas patch about 1 inch larger all around than the size of the hole. The canvas patch should match the canvas in the awning, both in color and weave as closely as possible. Fasten the patch to the outside of the awning with rubber cement or a similar compound. By placing the patch on the outside, it is less apt to be loosened by the force of a driving rain.

The awning should be in place at the window for painting. If the awning is very large, release the side arms and lower the awning so that the top can be reached. Apply the paint in long, even strokes, and do the entire job at one time to avoid edge marks. Be careful not to overload the brush. After the paint has been applied, allow the awning to dry in the sun if possible. A second coat can be applied after the awning is dry, although one coat is usually sufficient.

If the awning is striped and you wish to preserve this effect, outline the edges of the stripes with masking tape, laying it first along the edges of the dark stripes. Paint these and after they are dry, remove the tape and apply it along the edges of the light stripes. Then apply the light-colored paint. Other interesting effects can be achieved by painting the outside of the awning one color and the inside another. Garden parasols are painted in the same way as awnings.

Awning paint can also be used to brighten up canvas furniture, fiber, grass, or sisal rugs, and Venetian blind tapes. When it is used on canvas furniture, it should be followed by a coat of sealer made for the purpose, after the paint is thoroughly dry. The sealer will prevent the paint from rubbing off on clothes. Rugs which are very porous should first be given a coat of size before the paint is applied. After the sizing is dry, go over the rug with a dry scrubbing brush to restore its gloss. Then apply the paint, and after it is dry, finish it off with a coat of sealer.

VIII

LAUNDERING

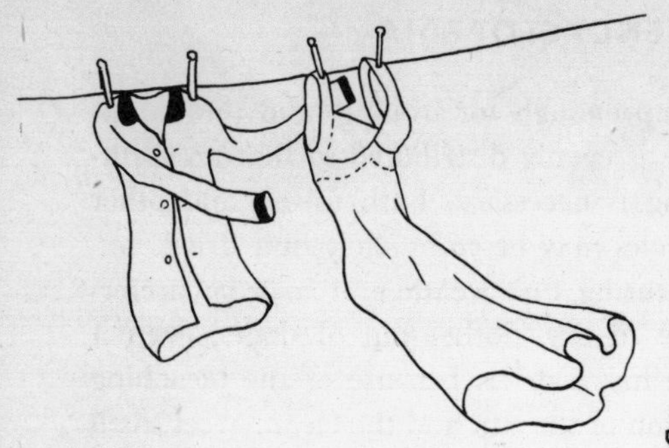

CHAPTER XXVI

LAUNDERING EQUIPMENT AND METHODS

IF cleanliness is a virtue, then it's one, at least, which can now be achieved without most of the toil and ache formerly associated with it. The path towards it may not be strewn with roses exactly, but at least all the thorns and rocks have been removed. Gone are the Monday mornings when the housewife dragged out the wooden or galvanized washtubs (stored away after serving for Saturday night baths), the corrugated washboard and the homemade soap. The soap was not expected to leave her hands soft and white—and it didn't. Next, the reservoir in the coal range and all the large kettles that could be crowded on top were filled with water. After the water was hot, she filled the tubs, put in the clothes, and removed the dirt by soaping and rubbing them, up and down, up and down, on the washboard. If she was lucky, she had a button-smashing hand wringer between the tubs. Otherwise, she wrung them out by hand. All in all, the bending and lifting gave her quite a workout—much more than she needed to keep her figure trim — and at the end of the drudging day, she needed a good night's rest, for, come Tuesday morning, all that washing had to be ironed with sadirons heated on the range top.

The housewife of today who is lucky enough to own the latest home laundry equipment can accomplish her housework, shopping, and weekly washing all in the same day—and still have time enough left over for a good book or a game of bridge. And yet, while the drudgery has gone, so many new fabrics, new washing and cleaning compounds, and new kinds of equipment have appeared, that the modern homemaker may sometimes wonder what should be used for which and how.

LAUNDRY EQUIPMENT

It's still possible to accomplish the family washing with nothing but the laundry tubs and a washboard, of course, but no woman wants to do it that way if she can possibly afford to have a washing machine and other modern labor-saving equipment.

The ideal arrangement is to have a laundry or utility room where all the equipment is installed for the most convenient handling. If that is not possible, the kitchen, the basement, or a porch may have to serve as laundry space. Small families or apartment dwellers may find it more satisfactory to use the services of a commercial laundry rather than to launder at home.

The first-floor laundry with a door leading to the service yard is more convenient than one in the basement because it saves the housewife from having to carry heavy clothes basket up and down stairs. The laundry room should be well lighted and ventilated if possible, and walls and floors should be easy to clean and impervious to moisture. Adequate electric outlets are important.

Tubs. Stationary laundry tubs are useful even if one has a fully automatic washing machine. They may be used for washing fine articles by hand or for washing out a few articles when one doesn't want to bother with the machine. Two tubs are better than one—the second tub can be used for rinsing while the first one is used for washing. The tubs may be of stainless metal, porcelain, or enamel. Soapstone tubs are also made, but they are less easy to clean. A wringer between tubs helps.

The Washing Machine. The choice of a machine is largely a matter of what can be spent and the size needed. It is always advisable to buy a machine made by a recognized manufacturer whose products are known to be reliable. No doubt the fully automatic machines are more convenient because the washing, rinsing, and damp-drying processes are all taken care of without the housewife's having to give them a thought. Semi-automatic models are also available, and there are also less expensive machines which wash the clothes so that all one needs to do is to put them through the wringer and rinse them.

Many women prefer a spin-drier to a wringer on the machine, but the spin-driers cost more. If you choose a machine with a wringer, be sure that it is equipped with a safety release. If the machine does not drain automatically, it should be equipped with a suction pump, if possible.

Drying Equipment. While not an essential piece of equipment, an electric or gas drier is a great convenience, especially during bad weather. The new driers operate automatically with timing devices to turn the heat off when the proper degree of dryness is reached. The clothes may be left just damp enough for ironing, and the dampness is evenly distributed so that no sprinkling is necessary. Bath towels and other articles may be completely fluff dried.

During fine weather, it may be preferable to dry clothes out of doors, even if one has a drier, because of the bleaching action of the sun and the clean, sweet smell which fresh air imparts to the clothes. For this purpose, a good clothesline is necessary, preferably of rope, which may be washed, or of galvanized wire. It should be wiped clean before the clothes are hung. The arrangement of the lines is not of great importance, although some of the lines should be in shade so that colored fabrics will not be exposed to the direct rays of the sun. Plenty of clothespins are also essential, of course. Indoor lines are needed for rainy days, if one has no drier.

Ironing Boards. The regular ironing board with tapered end may be one of the fold-away types which let down from the wall, or a separate unit which can be placed wherever you wish. One of the new models folds away in a trough which, when the board is opened, serves as a shallow tray to keep the clothes off the floor. A smaller sleeve board is a great help for giving a professional ironing touch to a garment. In addition, a wide ironing board greatly speeds up the work of ironing sheets (if they must be ironed and one has no electric ironer), shirts, tablecloths, and so on. Such an ironing board can easily be made from a table.

Ironing boards should be of a height most convenient for the person who has to do the work. In order to conserve energy, learn to iron while sitting.

Firm smooth padding and a clean, white cover are essential for any ironing board. They may be purchased to fit or made at home from old cotton blankets, sheets, mattress covers, duck shower curtains, or

The combination of an automatic washing machine and an automatic drier reduces the work of laundering to a minimum. Clothes need only to be transferred from the one to the other.

similar articles. For safety, the first cover should be an asbestos pad. It makes little difference whether the covers are laced or tacked into place as long as they are firm and smooth. Be sure to cover the ends of the board evenly.

Irons. Contrary to what many women believe, it's not the weight of the iron but the heat that smooths out the fabric. Therefore, a light-weight iron will tire the arm far less than a heavy one. All the good modern irons are equipped with some sort of controls for adjusting the heat. In addition to the regular irons, there are also steam irons which supply moisture to the fabric. A good steam iron may be in stantly adjusted for use as a dry iron. Choice between regular or steam irons is a matter of personal preference.

Electric Ironers. If beautifully iron linens are a "must" in your household, an electric ironer will be a worthwhile investment. Electric ironers are of two types: rotary and flat-plate. The rotary ironer is more common. It smooths the fabric by revolving it between a roller and a shoe. Both one- and two-speed models are available. The flat-plate type is very similar to, but smaller than, the pressing machines used in dry-cleaning establishments. Some ironers have hand controls; others have foot controls. Many have both.

Other Equipment. A two-burner gas or electric plate is convenient for making starch, boiling clothes, or dyeing fabrics. A large table or counters for sorting and stacking are essential. If the surface of a counter is moisture proof, it may serve for sprinkling as well. In addition, you will need clothesbaskets or containers, racks to hold the ironed clothes, a stool, cupboards for supplies, and a clock.

SORTING THE LAUNDRY

Since different fabrics require different washing treatments, we begin by sorting out the weekly wash according to the fiber content of the fabrics, their colors, degree of soiling, weave, and so on. Unless the wash is small, household linens are usually laundered separately from garments. Colored fabrics must be separated from white ones. Linens and cottons should be separated from rayons. Silk or wool must also be washed separately. Draperies, slipcovers, curtains, and blankets ought to be washed by themselves as well. So should the baby's laundry or that of anyone who has been ill. Delicate lingerie, sheer stockings, or any fragile material must be very carefully handled, and thus are preferably washed by hand.

White Cottons and Linens. Some women wash the lightly soiled things, such as sheets and pillow cases, in one washing, and the more soiled white garments, towels, or other things separately. However, if the wash is small, there is no necessity for such separation. Some white clothes or linens may have colored trimmings. Before these pieces can be washed with anything else, the trimming must be tested in an inconspicuous spot for color-fastness. If the color runs, the piece should be washed separately, following the procedure for colored fabrics.

White cottons and linens can be washed more easily and thoroughly in very hot water—between 130° and 140° F. A washing machine must be used for water this hot as the hands cannot tolerate it. Stronger, quicker acting laundry soaps may be safely used on cottons and linens than could be used on wools or silks.

Rayons. Some rayons wash beautifully, and others do not. Many rayon garments now carry labels indicating whether the fabric can be washed, and if so how. If the label recommends dry cleaning, it's safer not to attempt to wash the garment at all. Some of the spun rayons which resemble wool in appearance tend to shrink badly, and unless they are labeled as washable, they had better be dry cleaned. The fine rayons used for lingerie should be washed like silks. Brushed rayons with a fluffy nap can often be washed successfully (unless the label states otherwise) if they are dipped up and down in suds by hand without squeezing. Some rayon taffetas may be washed in the same way. Never twist or wring either one to remove moisture. Roll them up in a turkish towel instead. All rayons are weaker when wet than when dry, some more so than others, and therefore should be handled gently during washing. However, they recover their original strength after thorough drying. Excessive heat is another enemy of rayons. They should not be washed in very hot water, dried under heat, or ironed with a too-warm iron. Acetate rayons will fuse or even melt under a hot iron.

Silks and Nylons. Moisture does not have the same weakening effect on either silk or nylon as it does on rayon. Neveretheless, most of the fabrics made of these fibers should receive gentle handling, not because the fibers are weak, but because the yarns used in many silk and nylon fabrics are very fine and therefore delicate. As a fiber, silk is fairly strong, and nylon, even stronger. Both should be washed and rinsed in lukewarm water and dried away from heat or sun. Nylon is noted for the fact that it dries very rapidly. Use only a mild, neutral soap or one of the soapless detergents. Press with a moderately warm, not hot, iron.

Woolens. Fabrics made of wool may be either woolens or worsteds (*see chapter on Fabrics*). Garments made of worsted fabrics, such as serges, suitings, and gabardines, should not be washed, but dry cleaned. Many woolens may be washed successfully if they are handled with care. Use lukewarm water, a mild, neutral soap or a soapless detergent, and wash as quickly as possible. Strong laundry soaps have an alkaline content which is very harsh on woolens. Hot water is supposed to shrink woolens, and while it is true that it tends to increase shrinkage when combined with rubbing, the principle cause is not the temperature of the water but the rubbing. Wool fibers are covered with microscopically small scales which hook together when the wool is rubbed or pounded. For this reason, wool can easily be made into felt. And that is exactly what happens to woolens, to a lesser extent, when you rub or pound them. Never use bleaching agents on woolens, expose them to excessive heat, or dry them in the sun. Some woolens are now treated with a resin substance which helps them to resist shrinkage.

Colored Fabrics. As said before, the colored fabrics must be washed separately from the white ones. Fabrics of various colors may be washed together if you are sure they are colorfast, so that there is no danger of the color in one fabric running and streaking the other materials.

To test for colorfastness, place a small piece of the colored fabric and another of white fabric together and immerse them in a small pan of warm water. If the fabric is made into a garment, perhaps the end of a belt or a hem can be tested. Wrap a rubber band tightly above the section to be tested to prevent the moisture from spreading. The fabrics must be left in the water not less than seven minutes. Next, remove them, squeeze out the excess moisture, and iron together with a medium warm iron. If the water or the white fabric are stained, the colored fabric either is not colorfast or else it contains excess dye which must be washed out before the garment can be safely washed with other colored clothes. Blacks, browns, and other dark colors may always bleed somewhat, and therefore should never be washed with light pastels. A printed fabric which bleeds or streaks when tested should either be dry cleaned or washed and ironed before the dye has had time to bleed. Since the average time required for moisture to release the dye pigments is seven minutes, a printed fabric can be washed before the colors have time to run if you work very quickly. Everything must be ready before you start—cool suds, rinse water, turkish towel to blot out moisture, ironing board, and heated iron. Of course, if you attempt this method, you must realize that there may always be some danger of not being able to work fast enough to finish the job in time. Such rapid washing is not necessary for solid-colored fabrics which bleed But they should be washed quickly and separately.

If colored fabrics bleed, they should not be soaked. In fact, unless a colored fabric has been soiled by some albuminous substance, it is better not to soak it at all. There is no way to "set" dyes which bleed. Formerly, vinegar and salt solutions were sometimes recommended for this purpose, but they have no effect on modern dyes.

No colored fabric should be washed in water as hot as that used for white linens or cottons. Badly soiled colored cottons, linens, or rayons may have to be washed in a hotter-than-lukewarm temperature to remove the dirt, but the water should not be hoter than 110° F. as a rule, and for colors which bleed, it is safer to have the

The wall cabinet which conceals this ironing board when it is folded away serves as a tray to keep clothes off the floor when the board is in use.

water lukewarm. Light-colored fabrics of the same fiber content can be safely washed together if the colors are fast. So may dark-colored fabrics of the same fiber content, even if the color blends, providing that the colors are solid and of approximately the same shade. All black or dark gray rayon socks may be washed together, for example.

WASHING

Water and Water Softeners. Water is described as "hard" or "soft" according to its mineral content. Hard water contains considerable amounts of magnesium or calcium, which prevent or interfere with the formation of suds. Enough soap will neutralize the effect of these minerals, and then more soap can be added to make suds. But a less wasteful method is to use some counteracting substance, such as washing soda, trisodium phosphate, borax, or ammonia, all of which have an alkaline reaction. The correct amounts to use depend upon the degree of hardness of the water. If you live in a hard-water area, the best thing to do is to ask the advice of the municipal water supply authorities. Even newer and much better are the phosphate compounds, sometimes sold under trade names. The phosphate water softeners combine with the minerals to form soluble salts, leaving the water clear and neutral, whereas the alkaline compounds merely counteract the minerals, leaving a scum to be removed, or giving the water a cloudy appearance.

Best of all are the chemical tanks which soften water as it filters through layers of zeolite. The zeolite absorbs the calcium and magnesium, leaving the water as soft and clear as rain water. Such equipment is rather expensive, but a great boon because it not only softens the water used for washing clothes, but also that used for other purposes, thereby decreasing the amount of soap needed for baths, dishes, and so on, as well as lessening the formation of mineral deposits inside water pipes.

Soaps, Soapless Detergents, and Soap Powders. That common household compound known as soap is produced by the action of an alkali on fat or fat acids, and its cleansing action comes from its power to emulsify grease and dirt. To do this with fabrics, the soap must be combined with water to form suds which penetrate the fibers, loosen the dirt, and hold it in suspension. Soap merely dissolved in water without being whisked into suds has only limited cleansing action on fabrics. The suds must be worked through the fibers by some sort of agitation.

When you buy soaps, select the right one for each job to be done. "All-purpose" soaps cannot be expected to be mild enough for fine silks or woolens and yet strong enough for heavily soiled work clothes. For laundering fine, delicate materials, you need a mild, neutral white soap or a soapless detergent. For cottons, linens, and some rayons, you should use a general purpose laundry soap. Heavily soiled white or colorfast linens and cottons are more easily washed with a strong laundry soap. The stronger soaps and general laundry soaps contain such substances as alkali, naptha, or rosin, which help to remove dirt but which are too harsh for use on silks, wools, or fine rayons, or delicate weaves. The market contains many different brands of soap, and it is not difficult to tell what purpose each is intended for if the label is studied.

Soap may be had in cake, flake, or granulated form. Flakes and granules form suds in a fraction of the time needed with cake soap, and hence are preferable for use in washing machines or whenever quick suds are needed. Flakes are made by pouring thin films of liquid soap to harden on metal sheets, after which it is scraped off and broken into flakes. Granulated soap is made by forcing liquid soap through sprays so that the soap hardens into granules when it comes into contact with the air. The choice between granules and flakes is a matter of preference. One makes suds about as quickly as the other.

As a rule, soap powders are not powdered soap, strictly speaking, although they do contain soap. They are really compounds of alkaline substances mixed with powdered soap. They are suitable for scrubbing, but not for laundering, as they have very little sudsing power.

Soapless detergents are special chemical compounds capable of producing suds. In fact, they produce more suds than soap does, and they have a neutral reaction in water so that no scum forms even in hard water. They are, however, too mild to wash badly soiled clothes or heavy cottons as well as the stronger laundry soaps do. But they give excellent results with silk, wool, and fabrics of delicate texture.

Soaking. All white fabrics and fast-dye cottons will benefit from a preliminary soaking in cool water to loosen any albuminous substance which would otherwise become set if the fabric were plunged directly into hot water. Ten or fifteen minutes is long enough to soak. Nothing is gained by soaking for a longer period. Soap may be added to the water for the preliminary soaking to remove some of the loose dirt, if you prefer.

Washing in the Machine. After filling the machine with the proper amount of hot water (*see section on Sorting the Laundry for correct temperatures*), add a water softener, if necessary, remove the scum, if any, and then add soap flakes or granules and run the machine for a minute to dissolve the soap and form suds. There should be about a two-inch layer of suds. If not, add more soap. Next, wring the clothes from the water in which they are soaking and transfer them to the washing machine. The amount of clothes to be put in at one time depends upon the capacity of the machine, but it should never be overloaded or it cannot operate efficiently. Close the machine after filling, turn on the switch, and let it run for the length of time recommended by the manufacturer, or only as long as certain fabrics should be agitated. If you have an automatic washing machine, just set the dials according to directions. After the machine washing is finished, examine the clothes. If any particularly grimy spots remain, they may have to be rubbed with more soap between the hands or on a board. Then remove the excess soapy water from the clothes either by wringing or with the spin drier, if your machine has one.

Washing without a Machine. Basically, the same procedure is followed for hand washing as for machine washing, except that cooler water must be used for white cottons and linens—since the hands usually cannot tolerate water much hotter than 115° F. Agitation must be supplied either by squeezing, rubbing, or suction. Squeezing is impractical except for washing out small or light-weight articles in a washbasin. Rubbing on a washboard is a thoroughly effective but laborious method of removing dirt. When this is done, less suds may be used and bar soap may be rubbed directly on the garments before each one is rubbed. As stated before, wools must never be washed in this way or they will mat and shrink. It's quite possible to wash large articles in a bathtub, if you have no laundry tubs and feel able to stand the exertion, by making a thick, rich suds and then agitating the article to be washed by plunging up and down with a rubber suction cup on a handle (the kind used for clearing clogged drains).

This arduous labor must be continued for about fifteen or twenty minutes as a rule.

Rinsing. The next step is to put the washed clothes into clear rinse water, unless the machine rinses them automatically. The first rinse water should be quite hot, although not as hot as the wash water. The clothes should be agitated a bit to remove the suds. At least one more rinsing should follow, and two are better. The clothes should be wrung or spin dried between rinsings.

Boiling. It is usually not necessary to boil clothes unless they must be sterilized. For this reason, it is a wise precaution to boil the baby's diapers or any clothing or linens used by a sick person. Fifteen minutes is sufficient boiling time.

Bleaching and Bluing. If white fabrics are thoroughly and frequently washed, well rinsed, and dried in fresh air and sunshine, they should need no bleaching. But household linens which are allowed to remain unused for any length of time may become yellowed. Sometimes dampness may cause mildew to appear on a fabric. Yellowness and light mildew as well as many stains can be removed with one of the bleaching solutions sold under various trade names. If these are used in the exact dilutions recommended on the label, they are entirely safe for all white cottons and linens and some rayons and may even be used on some fast-dye linens and cottons, but never on silks, wools, or other fibers. When using a bleaching agent on a colored fabric, it should be remembered that some degree of fading is likely to occur even with fast-dye fabrics. But if mildew must be removed, a slight loss of color may not be important. Bleaches are generally added to the first rinse water, although they may also be added to the water in which the clothes are soaked. When added to the soaking water, the washing procedure is the same as desired above. But if they are added to the first rinse, it must be followed by two clear rinses. No bleaching solution should remain in the clothes, or it will weaken the fibers.

Bluing is sometimes used to whiten cottons and linens, although it probably does little more than impart the merest trace of a bluish overcast which hides any slight yellow tones. Since yellowing is more effectively removed with one of the modern commercial bleaches, bluing is no longer considered an essential part of the washing routine. However, some housewives still prefer to blue their white things. The bluing may be purchased as a powder, in balls to be put in bags (or sometimes already in bags), or in fluid form. Add the bluing to the last rinse water, but do not use too much, as the clothes should never actually appear to be blue. Stir the water immediately before immersion—the bluing has a tendency to settle. Never allow the clothes to remain in the bluing water or they will streak. Dip the pieces in, one or two at a time, and remove them immediately.

Starching. Many fabrics look better with a stiff finish, but since this is now often added by the manufacturer, home starching is no longer always necessary. A light starching is desirable for some fabrics, not especially to add stiffening, but rather because it helps to keep the material clean longer and counteracts limpness. The degree of stiffness is a matter of personal taste, although garments are seldom starched as stiff now as they once were. Baby clothes should never be starched as starch sometimes irritates tender skin. Nor should permanently stiffened fabrics ever be starched.

If starch is used frequently, it is less trouble to make up a quantity of very thick starch which can be diluted to the right consistency and used as needed. To make this, mix ½ cup of laundry starch with 1 cup of cold water until a smooth paste is formed. Add two quarts of warm water and cook in a double boiler until the starch is clear and thick, stirring constantly. There should be no lumps, but if any have formed during the cooking, the starch should be strained. The mixture is too thick to use as is except for the stiffest type of shirt fronts or collars. For articles which should be of medium stiffness, the starch is diluted with an equal part of hot water. For light starching, dilute with two parts hot water or as much as may be needed for the desired consistency.

Articles to be starched should be damp but not dripping. If the entire article is to be starched it should be immersed in the mixture and moved about so that the starch reaches all parts. If only a part of the garment is to be starched, dip it into the mixture carefully, gathering the material in the hand to keep the starch from spreading beyond the section where it is wanted.

Cold-water starches are available if one does not want to bother to cook starch. They are convenient to use when only one or two articles must be starched. To use, simply follow the directions on the package. Cold starches sometimes leave a slightly chalky-looking finish.

Light stiffenings can be made from gelatin or gum arabic to give a crisp finish to nets, veilings, lace, and similar materials. The stiffening is prepared by softening one tablespoonful of either the gelatin or gum arabic in a little cold water, and then dissolving in one cup of boiling water. Both the gelatin and gum arabic mixtures will have to be diluted with water before using. The amount to use depends upon the degree of stiffness wanted—from eight to ten parts water to one of the mixture is about right. Do not use too much of these stiffenings or the material may have a gummy feeling. After dipping the material in the mixture, blot between turkish towels and iron at once with a warm iron.

Starched clothes should be dried at once. After drying and sprinkling, they should not be allowed to remain unironed too long — especially in warm weather. Mildew forms very quickly in damp, warm, starched fabrics. Therefore, they should be ironed within a few hours after sprinkling if the weather is warm. In cool weather, they may safely be left overnight as a rule, but no longer.

DRYING

Clothes should be dried as soon after washing as possible, preferably out of doors. If the weather is bad or one is in a hurry, it is often more convenient to dry them indoors or in a gas or electric drier, if you have one. Be sure the line is clean—wipe it with a damp cloth first. A badly soiled rope line will have to be washed. Hang the white cottons and linens in the sun, which bleaches them, but keep all colored fabrics, silks, wools, and rayons in the shade. Hang the clothes in groups according to the way they must be ironed (or not ironed) to save time sorting them out later on. For example, put all the shirts together, all the sheets together, and so on. Fold sheets and large tablecloths in two and hang them evenly across the line. Keep them straight and smooth them out. Sheets dried in this way need little or no ironing. Hang shirts by the tails and dresses by the hems. Small articles, such as handkerchiefs and napkins, can be hung together in groups of three. Do not hang them up by one corner or they will be difficult to iron. Shake out all articles before hanging and put them on the line as straight and smoothly as possible. Half the work of ironing can be avoided by hanging the

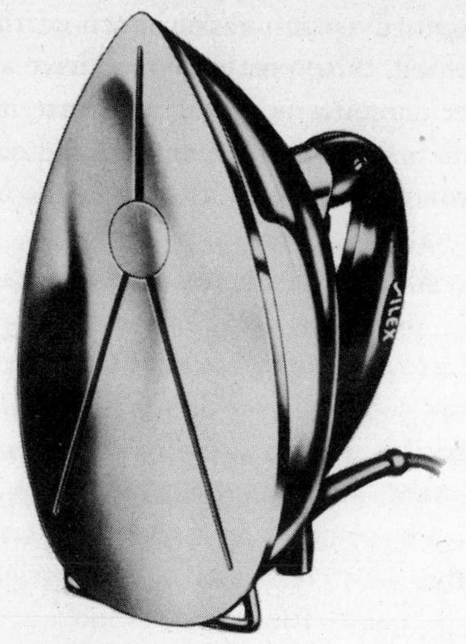

A steam iron eliminates the need for sprinkling or for pressing cloths.

clothes up carefully. Do not allow clothes to remain on the line too long after drying. Nor should they be left on the line in a high wind to rip and tear.

After drying remove the clothes and fold each piece carefully. Sort them out as you take them down, putting those which have to be ironed in one basket, and the things to be left unironed in another. The housewife is often advised to take the clothes off the line when they are just dry enough for ironing to eliminate the necessity for sprinkling them later on. This would be a good procedure if the clothes were to dry evenly all over at the same time. Unfortunately, they don't. Seams and hems usually remain damp long after the rest of a garment is dry. Sheets which are dry near the line will still be wet at the bottom. Therefore, it actually saves time to let things dry out completely and then sprinkle them. The right amount of dampness needed for ironing can be more evenly distributed in this way.

Sweaters and other knitted garments, many fine fabrics, leather gloves, and so on, are not dried on the line (*see following section on Special Handling Problems*).

IRONING

Ironing by hand is hard work when there is a great deal of it to be done, and the busy housewife can save herself many hours by choosing fabrics which require no ironing, such as seersucker and cotton and rayon jersey, or which can be ironed dry, like some rayons. Unless you prefer, sheets which are carefully dried, do not need ironing, nor do kitchen towels, or hand towels. Turkish towels should not be ironed at all. Articles which must be ironed should be evenly dampened first by sprinkling.

Sprinkling. A work surface large enough to lay out an entire garment and covered with a moisture-proof material is needed for sprinkling clothes. The sprinkling may be done with a bottle fitted with a shaker-topped cork and filled with warm water, or one can use a short-handled brush. Simply dip the brush into a pan of warm water and then shake the brush over the clothes. Heavy fabrics need more moisture than thin ones. Linens need more than cottons, and cottons need more than rayon. A little experience will quickly teach you how much water to use. Fabrics which are sprinkled too much take longer to iron.

As soon as each piece is sprinkled, fold or roll it into a smooth bundle, and tuck it away into a basket or container lined with turkish towels or other material. Cover all the sprinkled articles with another turkish towel and set the basket aside for an hour or two to allow the moisture to become evenly distributed. The clothes are then ready to be ironed.

Modern electric irons have temperature controls which can be adjusted to different fabric needs.

Ironing by Hand. Keeping the iron at the right temperature or the fiber content of each fabric is the most important part of ironing. It's a great help to have an iron with a thermostatic control which can be adjusted to proper heat for each fabric. Linens need a fairly hot iron. A little less heat is needed for cottons, and still less for rayons. For acetate rayons, the iron should barely be warm enough to smooth the fabric. Washable woolens are seldom ironed. Always test the iron heat on a scrap of material or in an inconspicuous spot of a garment before applying the iron directly to the fabric. With a little practice, you will soon be able to gauge the temperature accurately. Scorched spots are difficult and sometimes impossible to remove and even a light scorching weakens the fibers. Therefore, it is always better to begin with an iron which is not quite hot enough than one which is too hot.

Flat work can be ironed more quickly on a wide board. Sheets and tablecloths may be folded in two and ironed double, then turned and ironed on the other side. Be sure to have an old clean sheet or clean papers on the floor underneath the board so that the article you are ironing will not become soiled if it touches the floor.

All fabrics should be ironed with the weave up, and down or across. For bias-cut garments, this means that the iron must be moved diagonally across the board. Most rayons and all dark-colored fabrics should be ironed on the wrong side. Ironing usually produces a gloss on the surface of linen. The glossy finish is often preferred for table linens, but if you do not care for it on a linen dress, iron the dress on the wrong side. Cottons may be ironed on the right or wrong side, as preferred. Never iron printed fabrics double unless they are absolutely colorfast.

Shirts and other garments which can be opened up are easier to iron on the wide board. The procedure for ironing a shirt or a blouse is as follows: first, the cuffs, then the sleeves, and next the collar; the yoke follows, and after that, the back, and finally the front.

A dress which does not open up begins in the same way. The sleeves are ironed first, preferably on the sleeveboard. Then the collar, if any, is ironed. Next, slip the bottom of the dress over the end of the board, and pull the dress down until the waist reaches the end of the board. Iron the waist completely. Then move the dress so that a full-length section of the skirt can be ironed at once. If the dress has been ironed on the wrong side, turn it right side out and examine the hem and facings. Sometimes these need to be touched up slightly with the iron on the right side.

If the iron sticks on starched fabrics, rub it with a bit of wax or paraffin. A heavy coating of scorched starch on an iron must be removed before you can continue. The iron must first be allowed to cool completely. The scorched starch can then be washed off with a damp cloth and a little soap or very fine, nonscratching scouring powder. Never dip the iron in water. Never allow it to become overheated, and always be careful not to drop it. If the iron has a removable plug, do not take it out by pulling on the cord, as it will soon become frayed and the wires will break. Grasp the plug, instead. When you are through ironing, put the iron away where it will not become scratched. Special iron covers are available to protect the iron when it is not in use.

Ironing with an Electric Ironer. All the household linens can be put through an electric ironer in a fraction of the time needed to do them by hand. Very little labor is involved as all one needs to do is

Electric ironers save both time and labor.

to guide the piece and operate the controls. Shirts, dresses, and other garments can be ironed on an electric ironer, too, although they take about the same amount of time as ironing by hand. No detailed instructions for operating an electric ironer can be given here because the rotary type operates differently from the flat-plate type, and details vary from model to model. However, any ironer you select will come with complete instructions for ironing every type of article, and these should be carefully followed.

Folding. Sheets are usually folded in half lengthwise and then again in half lengthwise. The long, folded strip is next folded in half and again in half. Sheets folded this way are easy to put on the bed. By varying the placement of the folds from time to time, the sheet will not wear out so quickly along the fold. Towels and pillow cases are usually folded in thirds lengthwise and then again in half. Napkins may be folded in squares or oblongs. However, there are no rules for folding—simply fold things the way you prefer. Shirts may be folded if you like, but a great deal of time is saved just by hanging them on coat hangers.

The ironed and folded articles may be placed on a rack or a table. A rod with coat hangers for dresses, blouses, skirts, and other garments should be within easy reach of the ironing board. As soon as the freshly ironed clothes have had time to dry out thoroughly, put them away.

SPECIAL HANDLING PROBLEMS

Some articles require special handling. For example, many women prefer to wash delicate lingerie and sheer stockings by hand in the washbasin as soon as these garments are taken off. Some special handling needs are given below.

Bedspreads. Be sure the material of the spread is washable. If the spread is heavy, put it in the machine by itself. Chenille spreads can be washed in a cheesecloth sack keep the tufts from working loose. When a chenille spread is nearly dry, brush it to fluf out the tufts.

Blankets can be washed in a machine in lukewarm water and thick, neutral suds if they are not left in too long. Three or four minutes are enough. If the blanket is badly soiled, it may be given another quick washing. Soiled bindings should be rubbed with thick suds and a brush before the blanket is put into the machine. Rinse blanket thoroughly in lukewarm water, handling as little as possible. Hang lengthwise over the line to dry, stretching the blanket into shape evenly. Fluff the nap by brushing towards the bound edges (never crosswise) after blanket is dry. Press the bindings, if you like, but never the blanket. Electric blankets may be washed in the same way.

Diapers. Shake out and rinse in cold water as soon as removed. Diapers should be washed daily and apart from other things. Use very hot water and rich, mild suds (alkaline substances in strong laundry soaps will irritate baby's skin). Boil for ten or fifteen minutes. Rinse thoroughly, and dry in sun whenever possible. Do not iron.

Crepes. Some crepe weaves, especially in rayon fabrics, draw together tightly when they are washed and dried. Very often the original shape is restored by ironing and stretching. If the fabric was stretched by the manufacturer, it will shrink back into its original shape when washed, and no home methods of stretching can lengthen it out again. Crepe textures which are woven are permanent. Those which were pressed into the fabric after weaving are not. Fabrics of this kind cannot be washed or wet, but must be dry cleaned.

Curtains. Sheer, staright glass curtains of cotton net, lace, and similar materials must be dried on stretcher frames in order to hang evenly. Measure the curtain before washing, and adjust the frames accordingly. Several curtains may be dried on one set of frames at once, if the curtains are pinned on one at a time. A light starching improves the appearance of cotton glass curtains. Rayon or silk curtains should not be stretched on frames. Instead, roll in a turkish towel after washing to blot out excess moisture, and iron while damp. Fold curtains in half lengthwise and press on wrong side.

Draperies. Be sure fabric is washable. Shake, brush, or vacuum before washing to remove dust and loose dirt. Remove pins, weights, hooks, and any non-washable trimmings. Wash in thick mild suds in the machine for three or four minutes. If badly soiled, wash a second time. Rinse thoroughly. Remove excess moisture in spin drier or by hand squeezing, but do not wring or twist. Dry by hanging across two parallel lines to prevent creases. Iron while still slightly damp, first on wrong side and then on right.

Embroidery. Iron on wrong side with turkish towel or other thick padding underneath fabric to make the design stand out.

Fringe. Most fringes should be dry cleaned and not washed. To iron linen or cotton napkins or other articles with self-fringed edges, first straighten the fringe by combing with a fine comb.

Girdles and Foundation Garments will wear much longer if they are washed frequently, as perspiration injures the rubber. Wash in lukewarm water and rich, neutral suds. Squeeze the suds through the fabric or dip it up and down, but do not rub or twist the garment. Any badly soiled spots may be rubbed with a soft brush. Rinse thoroughly in lukewarm water, pressing out as much excess moisture as possible without twisting. Roll the wet garment in a turkish towel. Stretch into the shape garment has when dry, and hang up by garters. Open up the top or bottom of the garment so that air can circulate inside and speed drying. Allow to dry thoroughly before putting on again. Never dry near direct heat or in the sun and never iron any rubberized section. Fabric sections may be ironed if you like, but it is not necessary.

Gloves. Never wash leather gloves unless they are labeled as washable. If so, wash them on the hands in lukewarm water and thick, neutral suds. Rinse in lukewarm water. Never soak colored gloves. Blot out excess moisture in turkish towels. Pull gloves into shape and dry on a turkish towel or place gloves on frames to dry. Before leather has dried completely, rub between the hands to soften.

Pleats. First, iron fabric smooth. Then lay pleats in place and pin at top and bottom. Cover with a damp cloth and iron until cloth is dry. If preferred, pleats may be basted into place before washing. Remove bastings before fabric is ironed dry and press again so that thread marks will not show.

Ruffles. Curve the gathered edge of the ruffle so that a section of the ruffle lies flat. Iron, nosing the pointed end of the iron into the gathers. Repeat until entire ruffle is ironed.

Slipcovers. Follow same washing procedure as for draperies. Dry by hanging from two parallel lines, with arms pinned to one line and back pinned to another. The cover may be pressed while still slightly damp, or simply stretched smooth on chair or sofa. Pleats should be pressed.

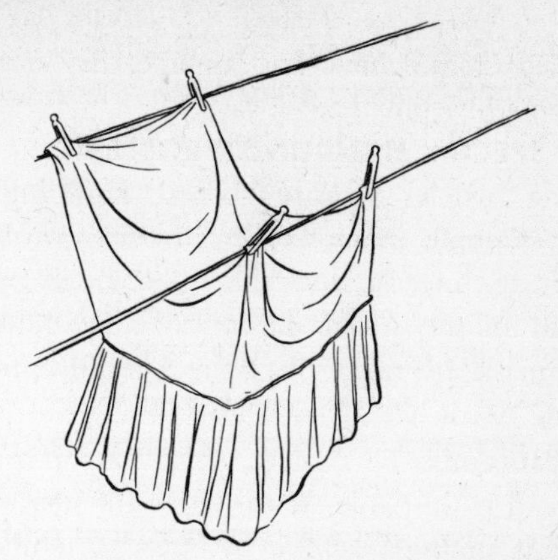

FIG. 11. Slipcovers will dry with few wrinkles when hung from parallel lines.

Sweaters and other knitted garments, if woolen, should be washed according to instructions for washing woolens. Before washing, trace the outline of the garment on a clean sheet of paper. Blot out excess moisture in a turkish towel. Lay garment on paper and pull into shape, using the traced outline as a guide. Pin along edges, sticking pins in upright. Or dry on frame of the correct shape. When garment is nearly dry, it may be pressed lightly under pressing cloth if desired, but this is not essential.

STAIN REMOVAL

THE most important factor in removing stains successfully is: to treat them at once. Removal is normally a simple matter when the stain is fresh, but very difficult when it has been allowed to set. Soap and water may be all that is necessary to remove a fresh stain—providing the fabric is washable.

Most common stains are relatively easy to remove from white linens and cottons, and from some rayons too. Colored fabrics are another matter because so many stain-removal agents are bleaches which sometimes remove color from the fabric as well as from the stain. Therefore, no matter what type of colored fabric you are treating, be sure to test the reaction of any stain removal agent on some inconspicuous part of the garment or article before applying to the stain. The removal of stains from silks, wools, and some rayons may always involve a certain amount of risk, even when these fabrics are washable. If they are not washable, it is probably better to send such fabrics to a reliable dry cleaner and not attempt to treat them at home.

Inflammable cleaning fluids must be used with great caution. Even for so trivial a task as spot removal, work near an open window.

Stain removal agents might be classified as bleaches, solvents, absorbents, softeners, and emulsifiers.

Bleaches. The chlorine laundry bleaches which are sold under various trade names are perfectly safe for all white linens and cottons when they are used according to directions and rinsed well. They should not be used on colored cottons and linens or on any rayons, white or colored, without first testing the fabric to see how it reacts. Chlorine bleaches must never be used on any wool or silk fabric.

The same considerations apply to Javelle water, long used as a laundry bleach, but less popular now than the chlorine bleaches.

Hydrogen peroxide is less effective as a bleach than Javelle water or the chlorine solutions, but can be used with more safety on silks and wools (even so, it may remove dye).

Sodium perborate can be bought in powdered form from the druggist. It is a safe bleach for all types of white fabrics, and for colorfast fabrics if it is used quickly and rinsed out thoroughly. Sodium perborate can be used in powdered form or made into a solution (2 tablespoons to 1 cup of water).

Hydrosulphite is a bleaching agent sold under various trade names, usually through drugstores. Directions must be followed exactly, and the chemical must be rinsed out thoroughly. Always test before using on a colored textile or on rayon.

"Hypo," a shortened version of the term *sodium hyposulphite* (or, more accurately, *sodium thiosulphate*), is a bleach as well as the fixing agent used by photographers. Certain stains respond to "hypo" when nothing else works, but it is a strong chemical and must be used according to directions.

Solvents. Solvents remove spots by dissolving the substance causing the spot. One of the best solvents known is water. Other commonly used solvents for stain removal are carbon tetrachloride, gasoline, naptha, benzine, ether, denatured alcohol, and acetone (nail polish remover). One of the most commonly used of these solvents is carbon tetrachloride. It can be bought under various trade names and has the advantage of being non-inflammable. Gasoline, benzine, ether, naptha, and alcohol are dangerous to use because of their inflammability. Under certain atmospheric conditions, the mere act of rubbing a fabric with gasoline may start a fire. These solvents should never be used near any open flame or fire. Gasoline and benzine especially should be used only with the windows wide open, preferably during rainy or humid weather, and *only* with full appreciation of the risks involved. Never use gasoline from a filling station for cleaning purposes, but only the pure form intended for such use.

Absorbents. Some stains can be removed with substances which have the power to absorb other substances readily. Certain fats, oils, and greases are easily absorbed by such materials as fuller's earth, cornmeal, French chalk, talcum powder (do not use colored talcum), or cornstarch. The quicker they are applied, the better the results.

Softeners and Emulsifiers. Some hardened, sticky or stubborn stains can be removed more easily if they are first softened and then removed with a solvent or other agent. Petroleum jelly, cold cream, lard, turpentine, and glycerine are used to soften stubborn stains caused by such substances as axle grease, paint, cod liver oil, and so on. Albuminous (protein) substances can be softened with powdered pepsin (sold in drugstores), which is harmless to all fabrics. It may be sprinkled on in powder form or used in solution (1 teaspoon to 1 pint of water). Rinse well after using. Soap or alkali on a fabric will destroy the action of the pepsin.

Many fresh or softened stains can be removed merely with water and an emulsifier--the most widely used emulsifier being soap. For delicate fabrics, the emulsifiers known as soapless detergents are also used.

General Procedures. Always, *always* test a fabric before applying any stain remover unless you are sure beyond a doubt that it is safe for that type of fabric. Never use too much of any stain remover—better to proceed with caution. Apply absorbents to both sides of a fabric, if possible. When applying solvents to a stain, place a thick pad of clean cloth, a Turkish towel, or several thicknesses of blotting paper under the stained part of the fabric. As the stain is dissolved and absorbed by the padding material, move it along so the fabric rests on clean padding. Apply solvents with swabs of the same material being cleaned. For example, if you are working on dark-colored rayon, use a swab of the same or similar dark-colored rayon. The solvent should be applied with light, quick brushing strokes, and the strokes should be "feathered" toward the edges to help prevent rings. Do not rub or scrub. Change swab and padding as soon as they are soiled. Shake or air the fabric to dry as quickly as possible. Follow the same procedure for applying bleaching agents, unless the entire garment or article is to be immersed. Apply glycerine, petroleum jelly, and other softeners only to the stained part, not to the surrounding fabric. Use a toothpick wrapped in cotton for this purpose. Rub the stain to make the softener penetrate more easily.

HOW TO REMOVE STAINS FROM WASHABLE FABRICS

Stain	*Type of Fabric*		
	COTTONS AND LINENS	RAYONS	SILKS AND WOOLS
Adhesive Tape Marks	Sponge or swab with carbon tetrachloride or benzine. Wash in hot, soapy water.	Same, except use warm, not hot water.	Same, but wash in lukewarm water.
Argyrol	Must be treated at once. First try washing in hot, soapy water. If stain persists, rinse fabric, sprinkle spot with powdered pepsin. Work pepsin into fabric; sponge off with water in half an hour.	Same as for cotton, but wash in warm suds.	Same as for cotton, but wash in lukewarm suds.
Axle Grease	Rub with petroleum jelly; wash in hot, soapy water.	Same as for cotton, but wash in warm suds.	Same as for rayon.
Blood	Treat at once. Soak in cold water, then wash in warm, soapy water. If trace remains, treat with bleaching fluid.	Same, except bleaching fluid should not be used without first testing on fabric.	Soak in cold water; wash in lukewarm, soapy water. Use no bleaching fluid except hydrogen peroxide.
Candle Wax	Scrape off excess wax. Place blotter under fabric; press with hot iron. Wash in hot, soapy water. If traces of colored wax remain, treat with bleaching fluid.	Scrape off excess. Press fabric between blotters with warm iron. If traces remain, treat with carbon tetrachloride.	Same as for rayon.
Chewing Gum	Wrap fabric around ice cube and pick off as much gum as possible. Then swab with carbon tetrachloride.	Same	Same.
Cod Liver Oil	Easily removed with warm, soapy water if treated at once. If stain has set, removal may be difficult. Try bleaching fluid, or rub with glycerine, rinse, and wash in warm, soapy water.	Wash at once in warm, soapy water. If stain has set, try carbon tetrachloride.	Same as for rayon.
Coffee	Stretch fabric over bowl and pour boiling water on stain. Wash in hot suds. If coffee is mixed with cream, soak fabric in cold water first.	Try warm, soapy water. If stain persists, wipe with warm glycerine; then wash in hot suds. If coffee is mixed with cream, soak fabric in cold water first, then treat with carbon tetrachloride.	Wipe with warm glycerine; wash in lukewarm suds. Soak first in cold water if coffee is mixed with cream.
Cream, Ice Cream, Milk	Soak in cold water; wash in hot suds. If trace remains, use bleaching fluid.	Same, except bleaching fluid must not be used unless first tested on fabric.	Soak in cold water; wash in lukewarm suds. If stain persists, sprinkle with powdered pepsin while fabric is moist. Rinse well in half an hour.

HOW TO REMOVE STAINS FROM WASHABLE FABRICS

Stain	*Type of Fabric*		
	Cottons and Linens	Rayons	Silks and Wools
Chocolate or Cocoa	Wash in hot suds; bleach if necessary.	Wash in warm suds; bleach only if fabric tests safe.	Wash in moderately warm suds. If stain persists, try carbon tetrachloride. Do not bleach except with hydrogen peroxide.
Egg	Scrape off excess. Soak fabric in cold water. If stain persists, sprinkle moist fabric with powdered pepsin. Remove with clear water in half an hour; wash in warm suds.	Same as for cotton.	Soak in cold water; wash in lukewarm suds. Try powdered pepsin if stain persists.
Fruit, Fruit Juice	Stretch fabric over bowl and pour boiling water on stain. Wash in hot suds; bleach if stain persists.	Swab with warm water. If stain persists, sponge with cool water, followed by glycerine. Rinse in half an hour.	Can often be removed if washed immediately in lukewarm suds. If stain persists, stretch fabric over bowl of steaming water; apply hydrogen peroxide to stain by drops at intervals. Or try glycerine.
Grass or Green Vegetable Stains	Wash in hot suds. Use bleaching fluid if stain persists.	Wash in warm suds. Stubborn stains can be bleached if fabric tests safe. If not, test fabric with solution of hydrogen peroxide and sodium perborate.	Wash in lukewarm suds. If stain persists, try hydrogen peroxide.
Gravy	Soak in cold or lukewarm water; then wash in hot suds.	Soak in cold or lukewarm water; wash in warm suds.	Soak in cold water; wash in lukewarm suds. Or try carbon tetrachloride.
Ink: Writing	Soak at once in cool water. Wash in hot suds. Or soak in cold milk for day or so, changing milk as it discolors. Rinse in cold water. Wash in hot suds. Bleach if stain persists. Or try commercial ink removers.	Soak at once in cool water or milk. Wash in warm suds. If stain persists, try hydrogen peroxide or bleaching fluid if fabric tests safe.	Soak at once in cool water or milk. Wash in lukewarm suds. Try hydrogen peroxide for stubborn stains.
Ink: India	Some India inks cannot be removed at all. Try warm suds with few drops of ammonia, or commercial ink remover.	Same as for cottons if fabric is white or colorfast.	Same as for cottons if wool is white. India ink probably cannot be removed successfully from colored wool.
Ink: Red	If fabric is white, soak in solution of sodium perborate. Colorfast fabrics can be dusted with powdered sodium perborate; then rinsed well after a minute or two.	Same as for cotton.	Same as for cotton.

HOW TO REMOVE STAINS FROM WASHABLE FABRICS

Stain	*Type of Fabric*		
	Cottons and Linens	Rayons	Silks and Wools
Iodine	Wash in hot suds; dry in sun if fabric is white. Try bleaching fluid if stain persists. If stain is too set to respond, use hypo solution; rinse well. (Hypo may affect colors.)	Wash in warm suds. If stain persists, try bleaching fluid if fabric tests safe. Or try denatured alcohol, except on acetate rayon.	Wash in warm suds. If stain persists, try denatured alcohol.
Lipstick and Rouge	Rub with petroleum jelly, followed by carbon tetrachloride. Wash in hot suds. If trace of color remains, use bleaching fluid.	Same as for cotton, but wash in warm suds and use bleach only if fabric tests safe.	Same as for cotton, but wash in warm water and use no bleach. Try hydrogen peroxide if stain persists.
Mercurochrome	Unless treated at once, stain may be very difficult to remove. Try denatured alcohol or glycerine, followed by hot suds. If stain persists, try bleaching fluid, or, if white, sodium hydrosulfite; follow directions and rinse well. Stains on colorfast fabrics sometimes respond to sodium perborate powder dusted on and rinsed off in a minute or two.	Try denatured alcohol (not on acetate rayons) or bleaching fluid if fabric tests safe.	Wash in warm suds; Try hydrogen peroxide if stain persists.
Mildew	Light mildew can be removed with hot suds or bleaching fluid. Deep mildew may not respond to any treatment.	Same as for cotton if fabric tests safe for bleaching fluid, but wash in warm suds.	Wash in warm suds or try hydrogen peroxide.
Mud	Allow to dry and brush or scrape off excess. Soak in cool water; wash in hot suds. If trace remains, use bleaching fluid.	Same as for cotton, but wash in warm suds and use bleach only if fabric tests safe.	Same as for cotton, but wash in lukewarm suds and use hydrogen peroxide if trace remains.
Mustard	Wash in hot suds if fresh. If set, rub with glycerine; then wash in hot suds. If stain persists, try bleaching fluid.	Same as for cotton if fabric tests safe for bleach, but wash in warm suds.	Wash in lukewarm suds; try hydrogen peroxide if stain persists.
Nail Polish	Treat with nail-polish remover. Test remover on colored fabrics before applying to stain.	Nail-polish remover will destroy acetate rayons, but can be used on other types. Test for color reaction.	Same as for cotton. Remover may bleach colored wools.
Oils, Fats, Grease	Wash in hot suds if stain is fresh. If set, apply cornstarch, talcum powder, French chalk or other absorbent. Or use carbon tetrachloride.	Wash fresh stains in warm suds. Treat set stains same as for cotton.	Same as for rayon.

HOW TO REMOVE STAINS FROM WASHABLE FABRICS

Stain	*Type of Fabric*		
	Cottons and Linens	Rayons	Silks and Wools
Paint and Varnish	If stain is fresh, swab with turpentine and wash in hot suds. Set stains should be rubbed with lard, followed by turpentine, then soaked in warm water and washed in hot suds. Carbon tetrachloride may also be used.	Same as for cotton, but wash in warm water.	Same as for rayon.
Perspiration	Treat at once. If perspiration changes color badly, nothing will restore it. If stain is fresh, moisten fabric with water and hold over opened ammonia bottle. To remove odor, dampen with vinegar and sprinkle with powdered pepsin. Brush off and rinse after half an hour. Stubborn stains may respond to bleaching.	Same as for cotton, but do not bleach unless fabric tests safe.	Same as for cotton, but do not bleach.
Rust (Iron)	Rub with salt and lemon juice and expose to sun. Or stretch fabric over bowl of boiling water and drip lemon juice on stain.	Same as for cotton.	May respond to salt and lemon juice, but since lemon juice must not be allowed to remain very long, treatment will probably not be satisfactory.
Scorch	If scorch is light, wash in hot suds; bleach in sun. Heavy scorch cannot be removed.	Same as for cotton; or try hydrogen peroxide.	Try hydrogen peroxide.
Shellac	If stain is fresh, it can sometimes be removed with hot suds. Otherwise swab with denatured alcohol.	Same as for cotton, except that alcohol must not be used on acetate rayon.	Same as for cotton, except wash in lukewarm suds.
Tar	Rub with petroleum jelly; wash in hot suds. If trace remains, try carbon tetrachloride.	Same as for cotton, but wash in warm suds.	Rub with petroleum jelly followed by carbon tetrachloride.
Tea (treat same as coffee stains)			
Tobacco	Dampen with cold water; rub with warm glycerine, and then wash in hot suds. If trace remains, use bleaching fluid.	Same as for cotton, but wash in warm suds and bleach only if fabric tests safe.	Same as for cotton, but wash in lukewarm water, and use no bleach, except hydrogen peroxide.
Tomato Juice and Catsup	Soak in cold water, then rub with glycerine. Wash in hot suds after half an hour. If trace remains, use bleaching fluid.	Same as for cotton, but wash in warm suds and bleach only if fabric tests safe.	Same as for cotton, but wash in lukewarm water, and use no bleach, except hydrogen peroxide.
Wine	Cover immediately with plenty of salt. Then treat as for fruit stains.	Same.	Same.

IX

SAFETY IN THE HOME

FRUIT SALAD

CHAPTER XXVII

ACCIDENT PREVENTION

WE think of home as a safe place. We drive out on crowded highways and thread our way through heavy traffic, and after several nerve-wracking hours during which we wonder whether we will return with the fenders on the automobile and our heads on our necks, we come back and say, "At last, safe at home!" Safe, did you say? Well, you're wrong. According to statistics, home must be a very dangerous place indeed because so many accidents occur there. But the most tragic part about these accidents is that most of them need never have happened at all! The great majority of accidents in the home are the result of sheer carelessness or ignorance. If a few simple precautions had been taken, most of them would never have happened.

Don't wait until an accident occurs to remedy the cause. That's like locking the barn after the horse escapes. Begin right now to check up on all the accident hazards in your home and do away with them promptly.

FALLING, SKIDDING, AND SLIPPING HAZARDS

FALLS take first place on the list of home accidents. One of the chief causes of falls is climbing up on a pyramid of boxes, chairs, books, or other objects to reach something. This is risky enough for a man, but a woman in high heels who does it is flirting with broken bones. Don't use makeshift arrangements to climb on. Get a well-constructed step-stool or stepladder.

Scatter rugs on slippery floors cause many falls. Such rugs are especially hazardous at the head or foot of a stairway. Anchor them, or else remove them. There are non-skid devices which can be used under scatter rugs (but test them before you trust them). Use skid-resistant floor wax on linoleum.

From the evidence, stairways seem determined to wage all-out war on the human race. But take another look at the evidence and you will find that the stairway isn't the real villain at all. Instead, it's our own negligence, or in too many cases, just plain laziness. We put things on stairways so we can carry them with us the next time we go up or down the stairs. What happens? Someone else comes along in a hurry, steps on the object, loses his balance — and crash! Down he goes. Horrid things have happened that way. One young housewife stumbled on the stairway leading to the basement and pitched headlong against the concrete wall opposite the bottom of the stairs. There were no doctor or hospital bills involved, though. Her neck was broken instantly. Never leave things on stairs. Teach the

Don't climb on crates or other makeshift arrangements to reach high places. Use a sturdy stepladder instead.

To prevent falling, turn pot handles to the rear of the stove.

children not to leave their toys or game equipment on the stairs. A wagon, toy train, or pair of skates at the head or foot of the stairs or on the stairs can be an admission ticket to heaven.

Do all your stairways have hand rails, and are they secure? If the stairway is open at one side, is it protected with guard rails? If not, call the carpenter in at once.

Do you know how many stairs are in each stairway in your house? Yes? Then did you learn to count them because the stairway was too dark to see all the stairs? But what about others who don't know how many stairs are there! Banish those dark, dangerous corners in your house. Provide adequate light. Paint the stair risers with a luminous paint which will make them glow in the dark, or at least paint them in a light color.

If your stairs are carpeted, check to be sure the carpeting is not loose anywhere. When carpeting slides forward over the edge of the tread, some unwary person will step down, and, instead of finding solid footing, will just have that awful sinking feeling.

More people slip in bathtubs and showers! A stout hand bar next to the tub will help to prevent this from happening. Another precaution is a rubber mat with a honeycombed or corrugated surface in the bottom of the tub or the floor of the shower.

Never sit on the window sill to wash the outside of the window. If there is no other way to reach it, hire a window cleaning company to do the job for you. And did you know that if *you* hire a window cleaner, and he falls and is injured, he may be able to sue for damages? But if the window cleaner is employed by a window-cleaning company and you buy their services, then the company is the employer, and you may not be responsible.

Icy sidewalks and stairs are another major cause of falls. If the walks can't be cleaned immediately, sprinkle them with ashes or sand.

PREVENTING BURNS AND SCALDS

YEAR after year safety counselors warn the public not to let children play with matches, and yet the children do, and they get burned. Until children are old enough to learn that matches can be dangerous, keep them out of reach.

Boiling liquids in pots on the stove have scalded many a curious toddler. Turn the pot handles toward the back out of reach. This precaution protects not only the child but also the busy housewife.

Why do so many women burn and scald themselves when they cook? Because they don't bother to equip their kitchens with the necessary tools to do a job safely. They pull jars of canned food out of the pressure cooker with spoons or forks or with potholders instead of a pair of safety tongs. They drain boiling water from cooked foods and the steam scalds their hands.

ELECTRICAL HAZARDS

FAULTY house wiring and worn cords and equipment are both fire and shock hazards. The Chapter on Wiring and Electrical Repairs explains what you can do about them or what you should have done. A few cautions will be repeated here. Never touch electrical equipment with wet hands. Buy no electrical equipment or cords which do not carry the label of reliability of the Underwriters' Laboratories. Look for safety controls on all electric equipment before buying. Cap unused electrical outlets. Place cords where they can't cause tripping. Don't run cords under carpets or around door or window frames. Don't nail or tack cords — don't even fasten them with "insulated" staples. If you haven't enough outlets, have more installed by a licensed electrician.

Cluttered stairways are one of the major causes of accidents in the home.

Priming a fire with kerosene or gasoline is an invitation to disaster.

FIRE HAZARDS

DO you have fire extinguishers in your home? No? Well, then, you're right there with the majority of other average citizens. We just don't think about fire until it happens, and when it does, all we can think of is to grab the baby, the fur coat, the jewels, and the fire insurance policies (which we intended to put in the safety vault at the bank last year), and dash out of the house.

Yet nearly all fires that originate in the house can be prevented with a little forethought. And if they do occur, they can often be extinguished before they have a chance to spread and do extensive damage.

The careless smoker causes many fires. Be careful where you throw cigarette stubs and matches, and be sure they are out before disposing of them. Don't smoke in bed, especially when you are sleepy. It may be your last smoke for life as well as for the night. Don't hunt for gas leaks with a lighted match or candle. Don't leave piles of oily rags or other combustible materials around. Under certain conditions, they can catch fire all by themselves. Keep oily mop heads in metal containers. Don't use inflammable dry cleaners. Gasoline has been known to explode merely by rubbing a piece of wool in it. Clear out those piles of old newspapers in the attic or the basement.

When lighting a gas oven or broiler with a match, always stand to one side.

Be sure that fireplaces have screens to guard against flying sparks and embers. Be sure your heating equipment is in good working order. Have it checked regularly. Be sure to remove the iron cord from the electric outlet whenever you are called away from your ironing. Hot irons on unprotected ironing boards can burn a hole right through them, drop to the floor, and set the house on fire. For safety's sake, have a metal ironing board, or at least one protected with an asbestos or glass-cloth pad. Use a heat-resistant stand under the iron.

Keep matches in metal containers and out of reach of small children. If the oven or broiler of your gas range does not light automatically, stand to one side when you apply the lighted match to the burner.

When you start a fire in the fireplace, the furnace, or a stove, never pour kerosene or gasoline on the kindling or paper to get the fire going faster — it may, all right, but much faster than you had intended. If you must keep kerosene or gasoline around for some purpose, be sure it is stored outside the house in fireproof containers which are labeled.

Always put or keep hot ashes or coals in metal containers.

Check all ranges for insulation. All walls within 3 feet of the range should be covered with fire-resistant material.

If your home has fire escapes, keep them clear at all times.

WHAT TO DO IN CASE OF FIRE

EVEN though you are watchful of every fire hazard, never take it for granted that a fire cannot occur. Be prepared for it if it does. Don't think that a fire can always be extinguished with a bucket of water. Have fire extinguishers installed in convenient places and learn how to use them. Teach every member of the family how to use them. Excellent fire extinguishers are available which cost much less than most of us spend on moving pictures and other forms of amusement. A very versatile extinguisher for home use is the carbon dioxide type. Carbon dioxide is the harmless gas which makes bread rise or soda water bubble. Yet this gas can also extinguish a blaze by cutting off the supply of oxygen from the fire, and fire cannot burn without oxygen. Carbon dioxide is especially good for smothering flaming grease or oil. Water is useless in such cases—it merely spreads the fire. The fire on a blazing steak in the broiler can be killed with carbon dioxide and the steak can still be eaten in perfect safety.

Don't select fire extinguishers by guesswork. Look for the label of reliability of the Underwriters' Laboratories. Ask your local fire department to advise you about emergency fire equipment for your home. They will be glad to tell you where the most advantageous places are in your home to place fire extinguishers. As a rule, the most likely places are in the kitchen within handy reach of the range, in the heater room, in the hallway, both upstairs and down, in the attic, and in the laundry or utility room. Test all fire extinguishers regularly to be sure they are in good working order at all times.

Every member of the family should know what to do in case of fire before it ever occurs. Schools hold fire drills regularly. Why not hold them at home, too? It isn't courting disaster to take such precautions, nor does the element of fear need to enter into the rehearsals. Children who are taught to act calmly and do the right thing in an emergency will respond automatically if such a situation ever arises. The same thing applies to adults.

Plan your fire drills with these things in mind:

1. Always be calm and act promptly.
2. Call the fire department at once. If you call by telephone, give your name and address to the operator. Find out whether a fire alarm box is near by, and if so, be sure you know its location and how to turn in an alarm in case the telephone cannot be reached or is out of order. Whoever turns in the alarm on an alarm box should be instructed to stay beside it until the fire department arrives.
3. In the meantime, get the nearest fire extinguisher in operation promptly.

Many falls can be prevented by providing adequate lighting for stairways.

Poisonous substances and small children make a bad combination. Keep bottles and boxes out of reach or under lock and key.

4. If clothing catches fire and no fire extinguisher is available, throw rugs or blankets over the victim to smother the flames.

5. Stair wells and air shafts act as chimneys and doors opening onto them will increase the draft. If a fire is blazing in these places, don't open a door or window leading to them. When you are not sure about the fire, test the door to find out if it is warm. Keep transoms closed. Seal the crack under the door with a towel or anything similar. Open an outside window and call for help. Stay calm and wait until

help arrives. Above all, don't get panicky and jump out the window.

After every member of the family has learned these rules, plan what you would do for fires starting in different places. Be sure the children know all exits from the house, and the quickest ways of reaching them.

CUTTING HAZARDS

WHAT does your husband do with his old razor blades? Put them on a shelf in the bathroom closet, we'll bet. What he should do is put them in a safety metal container. No safe can openers around? Too bad, but don't use the butcher knife as a substitute. And speaking of knives, do you keep yours in safety racks or just piled together in a drawer? Cut fingers are such a nuisance, and a cut which becomes infected is much more than a nuisance. Another good way to bring about infection is to step on a rusty nail or an upturned garden rake.

What about those chisels, saws, and axes that are left lying around on the floor for someone to stub his toe against? If father is to blame for those, then mother ought to remember the pins, needles, and scissors she leaves on the chair when she drops her sewing.

Dispose of broken glassware or glass containers where they cannot injure anyone. Never process canned foods in the oven. Glass jars in a hot oven have been known to explode from expanding steam when the oven door was opened.

POISON HAZARDS

KEEP all poisonous compounds out of reach of children. It's even better to keep poisonous substances under lock and key. Poisoning accounts for a large part of the accidents which occur in the home. Don't save medicines prescribed by the doctor after an illness unless he tells you to do so. If he does, label the bottle or box, and never use the contents for any ailment except upon the advice of a doctor. (*If, in spite of all precautions, poisoning does occur, see the Chapter on Antidotes for first aid measures.*)

Many a bad fall has been caused by scatter rugs on slippery floors. Anchor those rugs with non-skid devices.

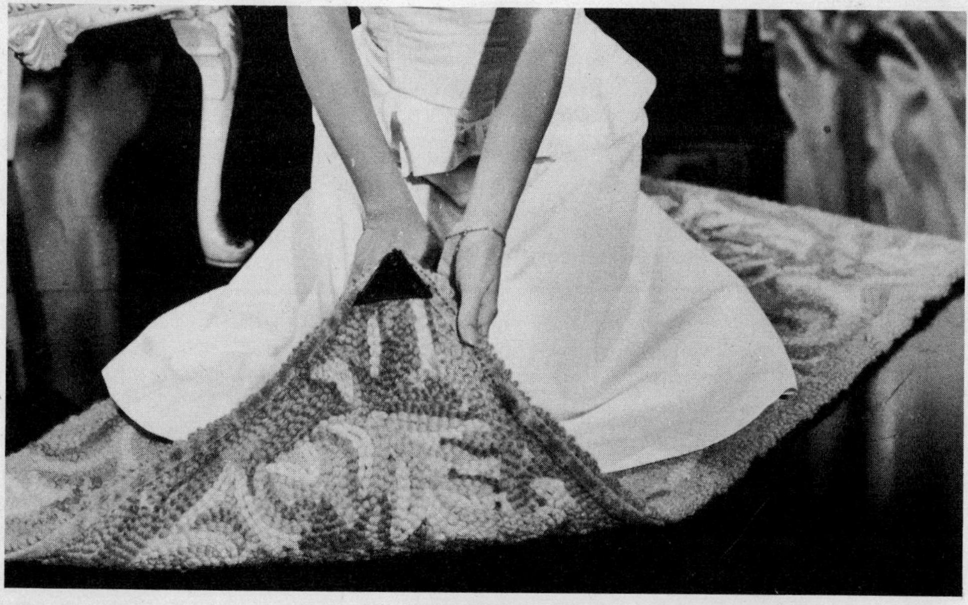

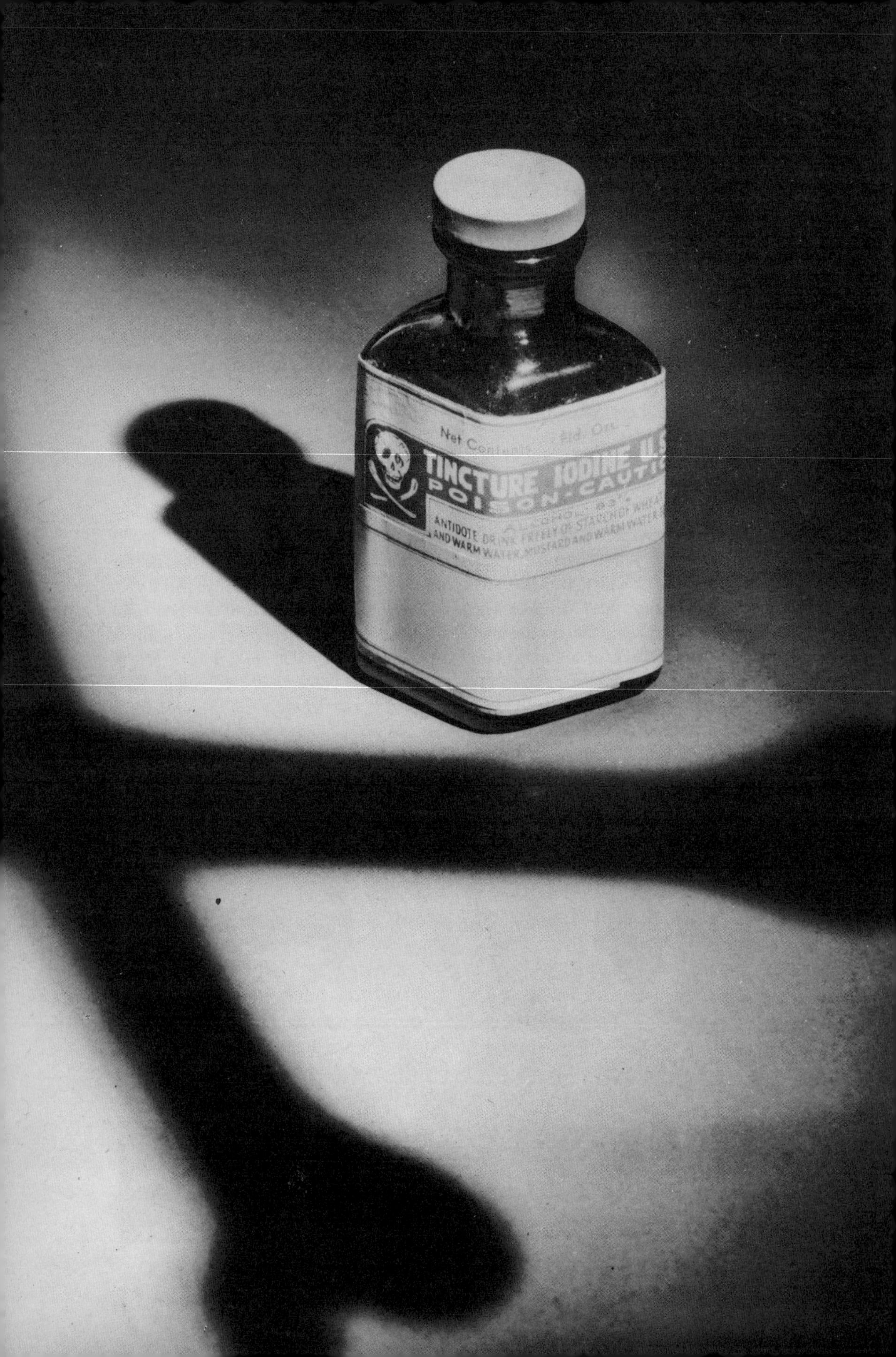
Net Contents
TINCTURE IODINE
POISON
ANTIDOTE
AND WARM

CHAPTER XXVIII

ANTIDOTES

CALL a doctor at once whenever poison has been swallowed. Pending his arrival, the most important measure is usually to get the poison out of the stomach. Vomiting can be induced by making the patient swallow an emetic. Easily prepared emetics are:

1 tablespoonful of common salt in 1 glass of warm water

1 teaspoonful of dry mustard in 1 glass of warm water

1 teaspoonful of soap flakes shaken up in 1 glass of warm water

If further inducement is necessary, tickle the back of the patient's throat. Make the patient continue vomiting until the fluid returning from the stomach is clear.

Do not force the patient to vomit first if a corrosive substance, such as caustic alkali or strong acid, has been swallowed in concentrated form, or if the patient is unconscious.

Poison symptoms vary according to the type of poison swallowed. Among the possible immediate effects are nausea, vomiting, pain, diarrhea, collapse, and convulsions. The patient may even become unconscious. If you do not know what the patient has swallowed, try to find out by questioning him or by examining his surroundings. But do not lose time trying to discover what the poison was. A delay will allow the system to absorb more and more of the poison and the patient may soon be beyond help.

In addition to diluting the poison and washing it out of the stomach by inducing vomiting, an antidote may be given if it is known and is on hand. An antidote is a remedy which counteracts, or works against, the poison. The antidotes for poisons contained in ordinary household preparations are usually given on the label.

After everything possible has been done to remove or counteract the poison, always keep the patient warm and quiet. If he can swallow, give him a soothing drink, such as the raw white of two or three eggs in a little water, a glass or two of milk, or a thin paste of starch or flour and water. Sometimes a stimulating drink, such as hot coffee, helps. If the patient stops breathing, give him artificial respiration at once.

WHAT TO DO WHEN POISON IS SWALLOWED

Acids, Strong (hydrochloric, nitric, sulphuric, oxalic). The patient's lips, mouth, and tongue will be stained and burned. If the poison was swallowed in concentrated form, it is usually better not to force the patient to vomit. To do so may rupture the corroded walls of the stomach and esophagus (gullet). Instead, dilute and counteract the poison by giving 4 tablespoonsful of milk of magnesia in 1 pint of water; or 2 tablespoonsful of baking soda in 1 pint of water (except for oxalic acid); or finely divided chalk in water; or lime in water. (If necessary, lime can be obtained by scraping plaster off the walls; the plaster should be powdered and mixed with water.) After the poison has been diluted and counteracted, give the patient a soothing drink, such as a wineglassful of olive oil, a glass of milk, or a thin paste of starch or flour and water.

Alcohol (*see* WOOD ALCOHOL).

Alkalis, Caustic (ammonia, lye, caustic soda, caustic potash, quicklime). Caustic alkalis will burn and stain the lips, tongue, and mouth. Do not force the patient to vomit if the poison was swallowed in concentrated form. Instead, a caustic alkali should be diluted and counteracted by giving a wineglassful of vinegar or the juice of four lemons in a pint of water. A soothing drink, such as a wineglassful of olive oil, or a glass of milk, or a thin paste of flour or starch and water, should follow.

Ammonia (*see* ALKALIS, CAUSTIC).

Arsenic and Preparations Containing Arsenic (rat poisons, some insect poisons, Paris green, and so on). Induce vomiting at once by giving an emetic of 1 teaspoonful of dry mustard in 1 glass of warm water, or 1 teaspoonful of salt in 1 glass of warm water. Force the patient to vomit repeatedly. In the meantime, ask the druggist to send freshly prepared arsenic antidote (hydrated oxide of iron and magnesia). When it arrives, make the patient swallow a wineglassful and then force him to vomit again. If arsenic antidote is unobtainable, give the patient magnesia or the raw whites of four eggs.

Atropine. Call a doctor immediately. Give an emetic to induce vomiting, followed by an enema or a purge. Then give a stimulant, such as hot black coffee. Keep the patient's body warm. In severe cases, artificial respiration may be necessary.

Barium. Do not induce vomiting in severe cases. Give a soothing drink, such as a glassful of milk, raw white of egg, or a thin paste of flour and water.

Belladonna. Induce vomiting and keep patient warm. If patient stops breathing, give artificial respiration.

Bichloride of Mercury (Corrosive Sublimate). Give the raw whites of from three to five eggs immediately. Then induce vomiting by giving an emetic of warm mustard water or warm salt water. Force the patient to vomit repeatedly.

Bismuth. An overdose of bismuth will probably cause vomiting. If not, give an emetic followed by a purge. Keep the patient warm and give a soothing drink, such as milk, after the stomach has been emptied.

Blue Vitriol (*see* COPPER SULPHATE).

Borax. If swallowed in quantity, induce vomiting by giving an emetic of soapsuds in warm water. Keep the patient warm and give a stimulant, such as strong black coffee.

Bromides. Induce vomiting and then give a soothing drink, such as milk or raw egg whites in a little water. If patient needs a stimulant, give black coffee.

Carbolic Acid (Phenol and preparations containing it). Give soapsuds or 2 tablespoonsful of Epsom salts in a pint of water at once. Follow with enough warm water to induce vomiting. Then give flour and water to soothe the injured tissues. Never give any kind of oil or fat. Skin burns caused by carbolic acid can be checked by washing the affected area with diluted alcohol, whisky, or brandy. But when carbolic acid has been swallowed, alcohol must never be taken internally, as it speeds the absorption of the poison.

Carbon Monoxide. Call a doctor at once. Get patient into fresh air, and, if necessary, give artificial respiration. Keep patient warm. Black coffee can be given as a stimulant.

Chloral (*see* SLEEP-INDUCING DRUGS).

Coal Gas (*see* CARBON MONOXIDE).

Cocaine. Induce vomiting if the patient is conscious. Then give strong black coffee. If necessary, give artificial respiration.

Codeine (*see* SLEEP-INDUCING DRUGS).

Copper Sulphate. Give the whites of three or four eggs at once and then induce vomiting with an emetic. Keep the patient warm.

Corrosive Sublimate (*see* BICHLORIDE OF MERCURY).

Food Poisoning. Call a doctor at once. Food poisoning usually causes vomiting or diarrhea or both. If necessary, induce further vomiting until fluid returning from stomach is clear. Keep patient warm and as quiet as possible until the doctor arrives.

Gas (*see* CARBON MONOXIDE).

Headache Tablets or Powders. If taken in excess, induce vomiting by giving an emetic of warm mustard water. Keep patient warm and lying down, but do not allow him to go to sleep.

Hydrochloric Acid (*see* ACIDS, STRONG).

Iodine. Give several glassfuls of a thin paste of starch or flour in water. Then induce vomiting until fluid returning from stomach no longer has a blue color.

Lead. Give 2 tablespoonsful of Epsom salts in 1 pint of warm water to induce vomiting, followed by enough lukewarm water to force patient to vomit repeatedly. Then give a soothing drink of milk or a thin paste of starch or flour and water.

Lime (Quicklime) (*see* ALKALIS, CAUSTIC).

Lye (*see* ALKALIS, CAUSTIC).

Match Tops (*see* PHOSPHORUS).

Morphine (*see* SLEEP-INDUCING DRUGS).

Muriatic Acid (*see* ACIDS, STRONG).

Nitric Acid (*see* ACIDS, STRONG).

Nux Vomica (*see* STRYCHNINE).

Opium (*see* SLEEP-INDUCING DRUGS).

Paris Green (SEE ARSENIC AND PREPARATIONS CONTAINING ARSENIC).

Phosphorus (match tops or rat poisons containing phosphorus.) Induce vomiting with several glassfuls of warm mustard water. If copper sulphate is available or can be obtained quickly from a drugstore, mix 3 grains (slightly less than can be picked up on the point of a penknife) in a glass of water and give to patient. Repeat this dosage every 15 minutes until vomiting occurs. The copper sulphate forms a coating over the phosphorus so that it cannot be absorbed. Then give warm water and again induce the patient to vomit to remove the coated phosphorus from the stomach. Never give oils or fats.

Ptomaine. Substances in food which cause poisoning were once supposed to be ptomaines, but are now known to be certain poisonous kinds of bacteria. (*see* FOOD POISONING.)

Quicklime (*see* ALKALIS, CAUSTIC).

Rat Poison. Treatment depends upon kind of poison contained in the preparation. Arsenic and phosphorus are commonly used in rat poisons.

Silver Nitrate. Induce vomiting with warm salt water or soapsuds. Then give milk or raw egg white in a little water.

Sleep-inducing Drugs (opium, morphine, codeine, chloral hydrate, and so on). Induce vomiting with several glassfuls of warm mustard water if the patient is conscious. If potassium permanganate crystals are available or can be obtained quickly from the drugstore, mix 4 grains (about as much as can be held on the point of a penknife) in a pint of water. Stir and strain the mixture, and let the patient swallow it a glassful at a time. Then induce vomiting again. Keep the patient awake if possible. Give strong black coffee as a stimulant. If breathing stops, give artificial respiration.

Strychnine (nux vomica, medicines, and vermin-killers containing strychnine). Give 1 tablespoonful of powdered charcoal in water or 1 pint of potassium permanganate solution (to prepare this, see the directions under *Sleep-inducing Drugs, p.* 361). It is important to keep the patient very quiet in a dark room and away from all noises. Do not give a stimulant as it may bring on convulsions.

Toadstools or Poisonous Mushrooms. Severity depends upon variety. Patient will probably vomit, and further vomiting can be induced if necessary. Doctor should be called immediately.

Turpentine. Induce vomiting by giving an emetic. Then give milk or a thin paste of starch or flour in water.

Washing Soda (*see* ALKALIS, CAUSTIC).

White Lead (*see* LEAD).

Wood Alcohol. Induce vomiting by giving an emetic, followed by quantities of warm water. Keep the patient warm. A stimulant of strong, black coffee can be given.

Zinc Oxide. Induce vomiting with an emetic. Then give milk or the whites of raw eggs in a little water.

X

PEST CONTROL

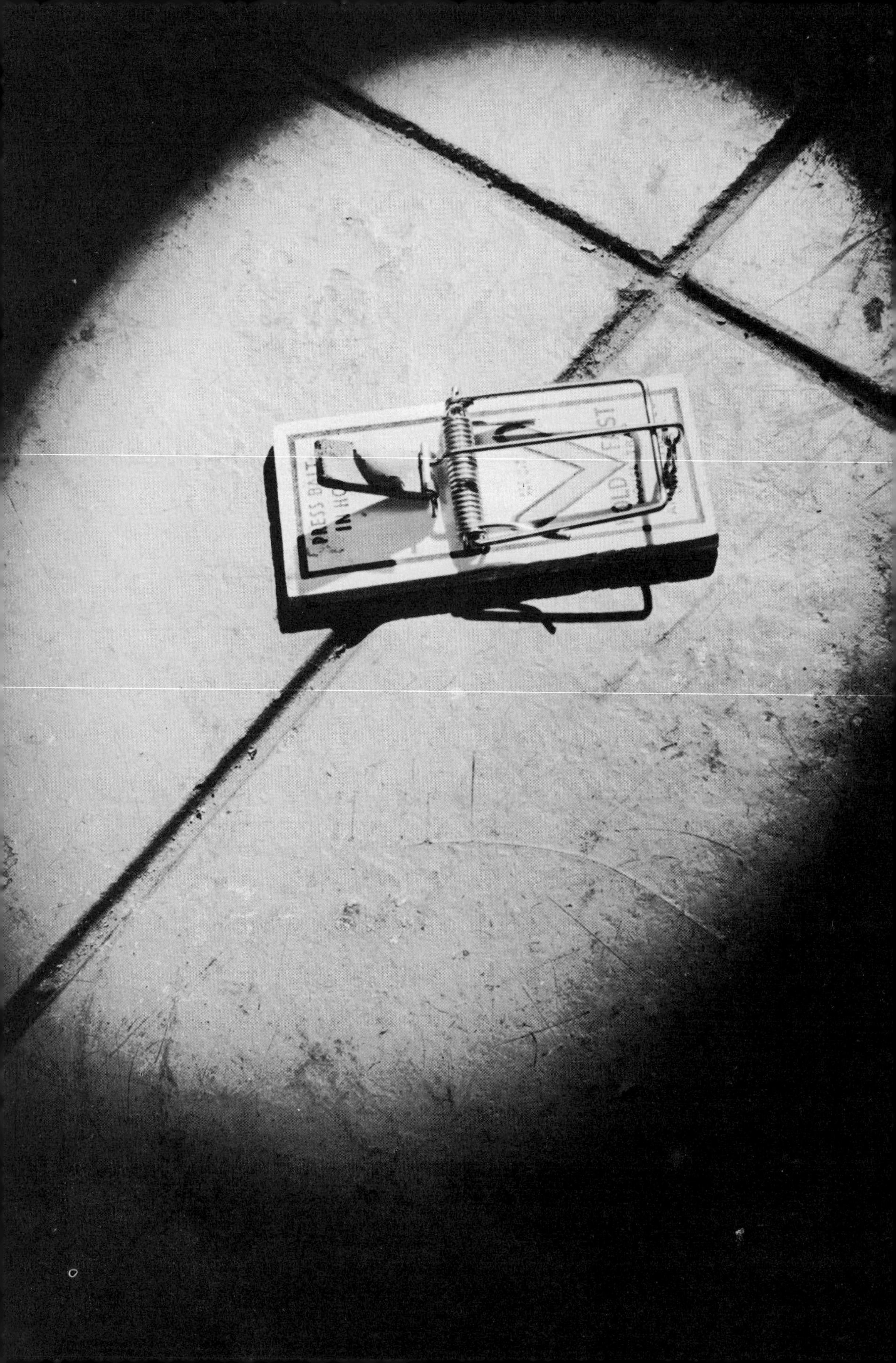
PRESS BAIT

CHAPTER XXIX

INSECTS AND RODENTS

THE most fastidious housewife will sometimes find that pests have invaded her home. The appearance of rats, mice, cockroaches, fleas, bedbugs, and other horrid creatures is not necessarily an indication of laxness on the householder's part, becauses pests can, and sometimes do, infest the very best of homes. Pests find their way into the house of their own accord, or they can be introduced in any number of ways—with grocery deliveries, in clothing after they have been picked up in public places, on pets, and so on. Many insects and rodents can do great damage and some are carriers of disease germs; consequently, their presence is intolerable, quite aside from their loathsomeness. Getting rid of them, however, can often be quite a problem.

INSECTICIDES

DDT (short for dichlorodiphenyl trichloroethane), the insecticide developed during World War II, was widely hailed, after it was released for general use, as the super bug killer that would soon have us living in an insectless world. But enthusiasm began to wane after it was found that DDT often went too far and killed good insects as well as bad and frequently destroyed other forms of wild life, including fish. And there were some bugs on which DDT had little or no effect. DDT's rating took an warranted nose dive because of these rumors and reports that the stuff was far from what it was supposed to be, and that in some cases it wasn't much good at all.

Actually, DDT is a highly effective insecticide when properly used. There are some insects which do not yield to it, but few of these are household pests. The common cockroach is but moderately affected —only slightly more so than by sodium fluoride, the standard cockroach killer of the past. Carpet beetles and some species of ants seem to be completely immune to DDT. But it kills houseflies, mosquitoes, bedbugs, and lice with amazing efficiency. Clothes moths and their larvae cannot withstand its effects, either.

DDT is sold in powder form and in kerosene—and water-base sprays. To be effective, the amount of DDT in a powder should be at least 10 per cent, and in sprays, 5 per cent. DDT, like most insecticides, is poisonous if taken internally, and it is dangerous to breath too much of it as a spray in the air. In powder or water-base sprays, DDT will not irritate the skin, but it might in a kerosene-base spray (kerosense alone will irritate some skins). Irritation can be avoided, however, by promptly washing the skin with soap and water after exposure. DDT powder destroys fleas like magic when it is dusted on the dog, but do not put the powder on his paws, as he may lick it off. Never use DDT on a cat. Any self-respecting cat will promptly lick it all off and, as a result, become very sick. For the same reason, if you keep a cat, never sprinkle DDT powder around baseboards or any place where the cat might walk in it or get it on her fur.

Some manufacturers are making paints, wallpapers, fabrics, and other products already impregnated with DDT. Some of these products are supposed to retain their bug-killing potency for long periods of time.

Newer and even better bug killers than DDT have been announced, and may soon be available commercially. One of these is called *gammexane,* or *666,* which is said to be death to cockroaches as well as many other kinds of insects. Another insecticide is designated simply as *1068,* and according to reports, is about four times as efficient as DDT on some insects.

Among the older types of insecticides, one of the most effective is pyrethrum. Sodium arsenate and sodium fluoride are also used as insecticides.

Any insecticide should be used exactly as the manufacturer directs. *Read the label on the can or package and be guided accordingly.* The U. S. Department of Agriculture very rigidly controls the labeling of insecticides sold in interstate commerce.

INSECTS

INSECTS are destroyed by heat, and sometimes by cold, as well as by insecticides. A temperature of 130° F. or more will kill any household insect, and at 40° F. or below, practically all household insects become inactive. Few can survive exposure to near-zero temperatures, and a house which is closed and left unheated during very cold weather will be rid of insects. Heating a house to a temperature high enough to kill insects is too risky, but heat can be used to kill moth worms in fabrics or furs. A hot iron will destroy moth worms in fabric. Hot sunshine will do the same for either fur or fabric.

Fumigation has long been used to rid badly infected houses of insects and rodents; but with newer insecticides, it would seem to be unnecessary to resort to this method. In any event, it should never be undertaken by anyone other than a licensed exterminator. The fumigant commonly used is hydrocyanic gas, one whiff of which can kill a person. The house must be vacated and sealed during the fumigation period—usually one full day. A less effective fumigant is sulphur, burned as a powder or in candles. Sulphur fumes tarnish metal and bleach fabrics and wallpaper. Since modern insecticides kill more efficiently and without damage to furnishings, sulphur fumigation seems to be outmoded.

House Flies. The common house fly can be easily destroyed with a DDT spray, but if the house is well screened in the first place, he will not have a chance to enter. Fly paper and flyswatters are the time-honored equipment for dealing with these pests, but fly paper is messy and unpleasant, and fly swatting seems like such a useless waste of energy when better methods are available. Open garbage cans are favorite breeding places, and flies will multiply rapidly wherever refuse is left exposed.

Mosquitoes. Mosquitoes, like flies, are easily destroyed by DDT sprays, but when mosquitoes appear in quantities, it usually indicates that they are breeding in standing water near by. A garden pool, a rain barrel, a drip pan under an ice box, clogged gutters, an exposed water tank, floor traps, and any other place where water can collect and be allowed to stand offers a breeding place for mosquitoes. The remedy, of course, is to keep such places or receptacles drained, screened, or covered. A few fish can be placed in a garden pool to eat the wrigglers, or else it can be drained and refilled every few days.

Cockroaches. There are various kinds of cockroaches — winged and wingless, and from ½ to 1 inch or even more in length. One species found in the West Indies is over 3 inches long, and 2-inch flying cockroaches are common in the southern part of the United States. The common cockroach is brown and has a flat body which enables it to hide easily in cracks and crevices. It is very hardy and can be exterminated only by the most persistent efforts. The presence of cockroaches may not be suspected until they become very numerous because they are nocturnal in habit. To check for roaches, turn the light on in the kitchen after several hours of darkness. But look quickly, for they scurry away like lightning, and will even drop from great heights to escape quickly

Roaches won't frequent places where they can't find food or water, so don't leave food around to invite their presence. They seldom have difficulty in finding water, and will even crawl down a drainpipe to reach the water in the trap. A very simple, but slow method of getting rid of roaches is to leave no food around and to make sure that no water is available to them by checking on leaking faucets, closing drains and toilets, wiping sinks dry, and so on. Then mix a solution of 1 teaspoon of powdered borax in a half pint of water and put it in a shallow receptacle placed where the roaches can easily drink from it. Do this every night. Or mix ⅓ borax with ⅔ rancid butter. This method takes more time and effort, but can be used with safety to house pets that might be poisoned by ordinary cockroach powder or DDT.

When used in sufficient quantity, powdered sodium fluoride or a powder containing no less than 10 per cent of DDT will rid the house of cockroaches. The powder must be placed all around baseboards, on shelves, around plumbing pipes, around sinks, behind ranges or refrigerators, and so on, and should be renewed about every ten days until the roaches disappear. Sodium fluoride is very poisonous and the powder is usually colored green to prevent its being mistaken for baking powder. Sprays containing 5 per cent or less of DDT have very little effect on cockroaches.

Moths. There are several varieties of moths which are destructive to wool, fur, feathers, and hair. In common with other

FIG. 1. Common cockroach.

FIG. 2. Case-making clothes moth.

Lepidoptera, they all go through a complete metamorphosis—from egg to wormlike larva, to cocoon, and finally, to the adult, winged moth, but it is only in the larval state that they do their damage. The adults should be killed, however, because they can lay a great many eggs during their short life span. The eggs are white and just large enough to be visible. On smooth-surfaced fabrics, the eggs or larvae, which are only about 1/16 of an inch long when hatched, can be easily brushed off. If left undisturbed, they gorge themselves on fibers until they get to be about 1/2 inch long, when they are ready to spin a sleeping bag. Fabrics which are brushed, aired, or worn frequently are seldom damaged by mothes because, if any eggs are present, they are shaken off before they have a chance to hatch (which takes about a week from the time they are laid). Dry cleaning or pressing also kills the eggs or larvae. It may be more difficult to remove the eggs or larvae from furs or napped fabrics. The best treatment for furs is to have them placed in a cold-storage vault during the summer months. There they are not only protected from moth damage but also from heat which tends to dry out the natural oils.

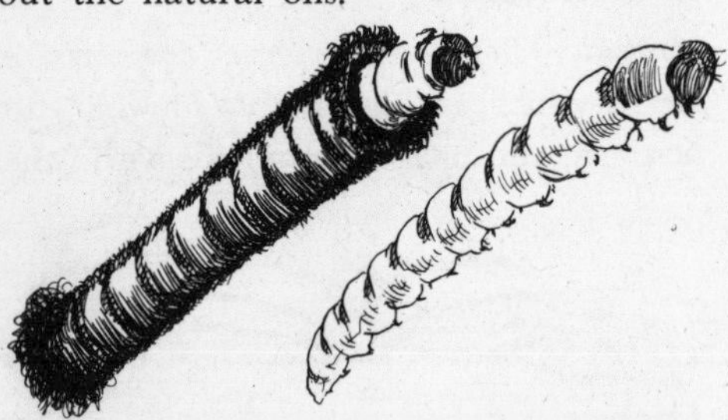

FIG. 3. Cocoon and larva of case-making clothes moth.

Moth killers are sold under a number of trade names, usually in the form of flakes, crystals, or balls. Most of these consist either of naphthalene or paradichlorobenzene. Properly used, both are effective moth killers — much more so than camphor (formerly used for moth prevention). The crystals, flakes, or balls give off a vapor, which, if confined within a limited area, is strong enough to kill the moths in any stage. If the vapor is allowed to escape, however, its effectiveness is lost. It must be enclosed in a tightly sealed chest, bag, or closet. When used in a closet, the crystals, balls, or flakes should be placed on a top shelf as the vapor sinks to the floor. The closet should then be sealed for the season. Weather-stripping can be used to seal the cracks between the door and the frame, and a strip of gummed tape can be placed over the keyhole. Don't overlook the crack between the door and the sill.

Manufacturers have developed new methods of moth-proofing fabrics, and moth-repellent compounds are available for home use. When used according to directions, some of them give satisfactory results, but the treatment should be renewed after every washing or dry cleaning.

The odor given off by cedar is only moderately destructive to moths. Cedar-lined closets seldom prevent moth damage because the lining is usually too thin. A solid cedar chest which shuts tightly will give off enough odor to kill newly hatched larvae, but not those which have started to develop.

The appearance of a moth in the house almost always indicates the presence of others, some of which are probably still in larval form, eating away at your winter woolens. Every effort should be made to find their breeding place before they can do more damage.

Carpet Beetles. There are several varieties of this insect, most of which are only 1/4 of an inch or less in length. Carpet beetles may be black, or black with white or red spots. They are also called *buffalo bugs*

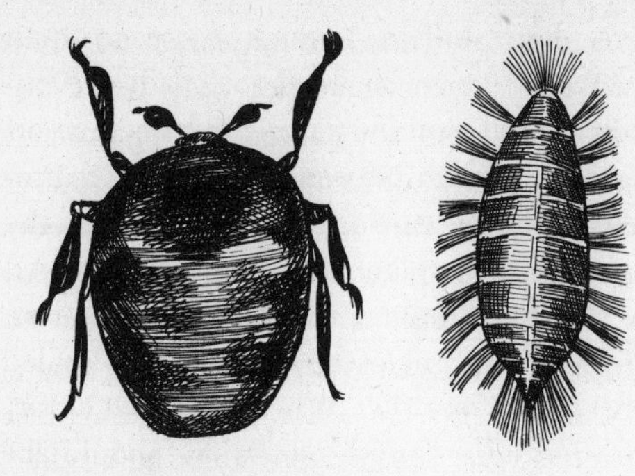

FIG. 4. Carpet beetle and larva.

and *tapestry beetles.* Like moths, they eat animal fibers, such as wool, and while they are not fussy about where it comes from, they usually attack the carpet because they breed in dust which is often present in cracks between the floor boards. Again like moths, it is only in the larval state that they do their damage, but they can present even more of a problem than moths. DDT seems to have no effect on carpet beetles, but they can be killed with moth flakes, crystals, or balls if these are used in sufficient quantity and in a confined space so that the vapor can penetrate the fibers. Since this is seldom practical for a carpet, the best thing to do is to send it to a cleaner if carpet beetles are detected. However, an infestation will seldom occur in a carpet which is frequently and thoroughly vacuumed. The floor beneath the carpet should be vacuumed, too, to remove the dust between the floor boards.

Both moths and carpet beetles enjoy upholstery fabrics of wool, especially mohair, and the hair filling used in fine upholstered furniture. If enough larvae are present, they can actually ruin an upholstered piece. The surest way of getting rid of them is to send the furniture to a licensed exterminator to be fumigated. If this is not practical, move the piece to an unused room, cover the surface with a thick layer of moth flakes or crystals. Wrap the furniture with several thicknesses of heavy brown paper and seal all openings with gummed tape. Leave the wrappings on for at least three days until the vapor from the flakes or crystals has had ample time to penetrate to all parts of the chair. The reason why this treatment should take place in an unused room is that the odor of the flakes or crystals would probably be unbearable elsewhere in the house. It's a good idea to seal off the door to the room to keep the odor from escaping. After the paper and crystals or flakes are removed, the upholstered piece should be left to air for at least another three days.

Cold or heat will also destroy moths or carpet beetles, but cold weather can seldom be taken advantage of, since infestations are more likely to occur during the summer. Exposure to hot sun will usually destroy the eggs or larvae, but the temperature should be at least 120 degrees under direct sunlight, and the upholstered piece should be exposed for at least four or five hours during the middle of the day. This treatment has a drawback, however. Sunlight intense enough to destroy the eggs or larvae can also fade colors and dry out hair, feathers, or wools, so that they lose some of their resiliency.

FIG. 5. Cricket.

Crickets. Crickets dislike the cold, and at the end of summer some species will seek warmth inside the house. They are brown or black in color and not unlike a grasshopper in appearance. The males make a chirping sound by moving their forewings, and while the noise of the "cricket on the hearth" may sound cheerful to some people, these insects should be destroyed because they will eat almost anything — leather, wool, glue in bookbindings, or whatever they can find. Crickets are easy to locate because their presence is betrayed by their chirping, and they can usually be disposed of by direct physical action.

Termites. Termites, also called *white ants,* are social insects that live in colonies, the members of which are divided into distinct castes, each with special duties to perform. It is the wingless worker caste which does the damage. These creatures can eat their way through enough wood to destroy a house, and while they are found throughout the United States, they are most numerous in the South. It is impossible to discover the presence of termites by examining the surface of the wood, and they are usually discovered only after they have tunneled their way through enough wood to weaken it so badly that it collapses. A hole can be drilled in the wood to examine it for termite tunnels. Once a colony has established itself inside the wood, they cannot be destroyed with any kind of surface application. The best defense against termites is termite-proof construction, full information on which can be obtained from the Department of Agriculture for five cents.

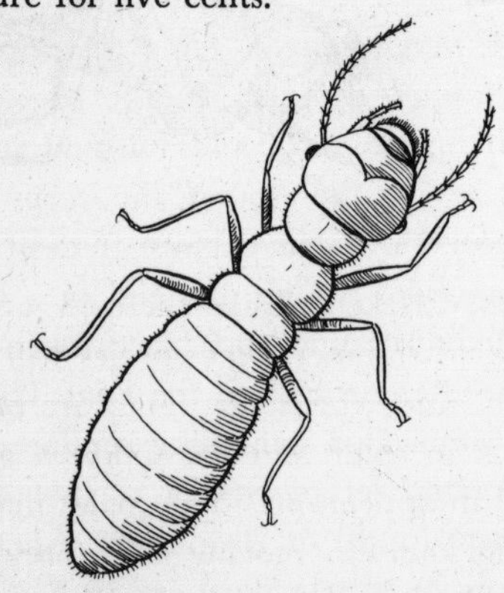

FIG. 6. Termite (worker).

A new product has appeared which is said to protect wood not only from termites but from rot caused by fungus and bacteria. Any untreated wood in direct contact with the ground will rot sooner or later. This new wood preservative can be applied with a brush, spray, or by dipping, and one quart will cover about 200 square feet. In order to protect against termites, the preservative must be applied to the wood before a colony has become established inside. Every single surface must be covered. After the wood has dried, it can be either painted or left in its natural state.

FIG. 7. Bedbug.

Bedbugs. Bedbugs are flat, reddish-brown creatures which breed in cracks in furniture, under the edges of wallpaper, and other places. They used to be very difficult to get rid of except by fumigation, but DDT is sure death to them. The powder should be sprinkled on the mattress and in the springs and joints of the bed. It isn't necessary to apply it elsewhere because all the bugs will be killed when they visit the bed to dine off its occupant.

Fleas. Fleas usually enter a house on pets. If the animal scratches frequently, he should be examined for fleas. His sleeping box or basket should be examined, too, as it may contain eggs (which look like tiny white grains). They can be removed

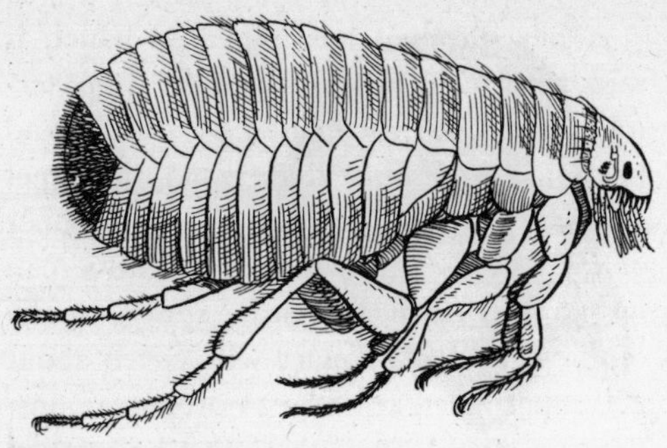

FIG. 8. Common flea.

with a vacuum cleaner. A dog can be dusted with DDT powder to kill the fleas. Cats can be washed with flea soap, but they should be kept in a warm place afterwards until their fur is thoroughly dry.

House Centipedes. House centipedes, many-legged creatures sometimes found in cellars and damp closets, really aren't pests at all. They are perfectly harmless and perform a valuable service by eating flies, roaches, and other insects. They rarely infest a house in numbers and shouldn't be destroyed. But if their presence is objectionable, they can easily be gotten rid of by simply stepping on them.

Praying Mantis. A praying mantis is a large, grotesque insect about 3 inches long, which holds its front legs in an attitude of prayer. This creature rarely enters a house, and then probably by mistake; but if he does, try to shoo him out again without injuring him. He is quite harmless to human beings, and during a summer he will eat his weight in other insects many times over. Moreover, he seems to be especially fond of insects which plague the human race. In some states it is illegal to destroy a praying mantis.

Spiders. Spiders aren't insects, but *arachnids.* Most of them are harmless to human beings, and in this country, only one, the black widow, is dangerous—and it rarely enters a house. Spiders help to destroy flies, but they also spin dirt-catching webs. For this reason, and the fact that many people find them objectionable, no great harm is done by destroying them. The webs can be removed with a vacuum cleaner and the spiders can be killed with an insect spray or by stepping on them.

Ants. Ants are social insects which live in colonies, usually out of doors. They will enter houses to obtain food, and it does little good to destroy the ones that enter because more will arrive from the colony. The thing to do is to get the worker ants to carry poison back to feed the queen. There are ant traps made for this purpose which do the job very well. Or tartar emetic can be mixed with honey (half and half) and placed in a saucer where the ants can reach it easily. Some species like grease better than honey. DDT kills some ants but not others.

Wasps and Hornets. There are various kinds of wasps and hornets, each with different habits. They may build nests under the eaves of a roof or on the ground under a bush. Most are harmless because they will not attack a person unless they are disturbed. They are not night prowlers, and usually go home and go to bed after sundown. Therefore, if the creatures must be destroyed, the time to do so is after dark. If you feel brave enough, you can get rid of them by slipping a paper bag over the nest at night, tying a string securely around the neck of the bag, and then carting it away and burning it. If the nest is near the ground, the wasps can be destroyed with the exhaust fumes from an automobile. Attach one end of a hose to the exhaust pipe and place the other end near the entrance to the nest. Throw an old blanket or something similar over the nest, and let the motor of the automobile run for 15 or 20 minutes. Another method is to turn a hard spray of water from the garden hose on the nest. Insect sprays will also destroy wasps or hornets. As a matter of precaution, it's a good idea to protect the head and neck with netting, and to wear gloves while approaching the nest.

Silverfish. The silverfish, also called the *bristletail,* is a quick-moving, wingless, grayish white, nocturnal creature about ⅜ of an inch long. He eats mostly starch, and can do great damage to bookbindings and wallpaper. An effective remedy is sodium fluoride mixed into a paste with flour (one part sodium fluoride to eight parts flour). Spread this mixture on strips of cardboard and place it on bookshelves behind the books where the silverfish can reach it.

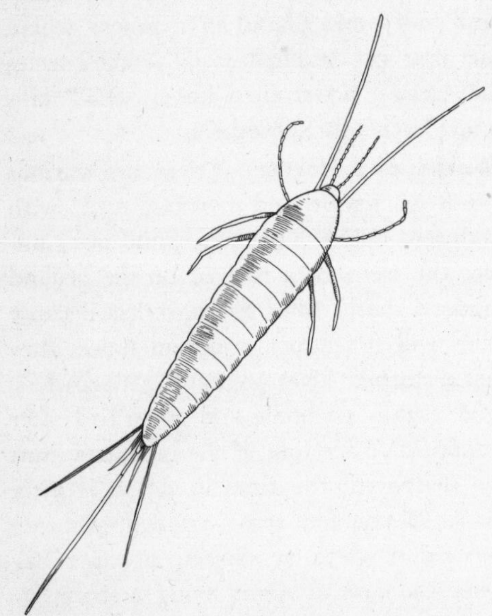

FIG. 9. Silverfish or bristletail.

Weevils. Weevils are of several varieties and are found in dry foods, especially cereals. One species likes ham or bacon. Any food found to be infested with weevils should be burned. The best way to deal with these pests is to keep all foods in tight containers that they cannot enter. They do not live in woodwork or walls, and if they have nothing to eat, they will disappear.

FIG. 10. Rats are destructive — and they carry germs.

RODENTS

Rats. Open garbage pails are an invitation to rats to move into your house. Once there, they may be difficult to get rid of. Rat poisons are often effective, but rats are very wary and sometimes manage to elude both traps and poisons. A good rat terrier can finish off the rats in a house about as quickly as anything except fumigation. Rat poison should not be placed where pets might get hold of it.

Mice. An energetic cat will keep a house free of mice. It is a mistake to think that a cat which is not fed regularly will hunt mice better. Well-fed cats make the best mousers. If you don't like cats or don't want one around, the next best thing is a trap. There are a number of different kinds, but one of the simplest and most efficient is the common spring trap. Place it near a wall and under a table or some other object where it will not be stepped on. Bait the trap with cereal or a small piece of cheese.

Squirrels and Chipmunks. Squirrels and chipmunks sometimes enter a house by means of tree branches. They may establish themselves in the attic, and cause considerable annoyance by scampering back and forth. In many places, it is illegal to harm these little creatures, and most people certainly do not want to do so.

Metal guards around the base of trees will usually cut off their passageway into the house. They can also be driven out with moth balls, the odor of which they dislike very much.

Bats. While not classed as rodents, bats are included here because they will sometimes enter a house, especially when they are attracted by a light. Don't try to kill a bat. In spite of the many superstitions surrounding them, most bats are actually shy, harmless creatures which are beneficial to man because they destroy insects. At least, the majority of species in North America live on insects. The only species of bat which sucks blood is the true vampire, found in South America—and even it isn't dangerous.

If a bat does enter the house, turn out all the lights, open the windows, and lead the bat outside by turning the lights on in first one room and then another.

FIG. 11. A bat is attracted by light.

GLOSSARY AND TABLES OF WEIGHTS AND MEASURES

GLOSSARY

Absorbent — any substance which has the power to absorb another substance readily; common household absorbents used for stain removal are: fuller's earth, cornmeal, French chalk, talcum powder, and cornstarch.

Acetone — an inflammable liquid used as a solvent for fats and resins. Nail-polish removers consist mostly of acetone.

Acid — any sour or biting substance, such as vinegar or lemon juice. Watery solutions of acid will redden vegetable substances such as litmus.

Adam—an eighteenth-century English style of furniture and decoration, named after its designers, the Adam brothers.

Alkali — as generally used, the term *alkali* denotes any substance which can neutralize an acid; more specifically, it refers to a substance which is largely composed of sodium carbonate, potassium carbonate, sodium hydroxide (caustic soda), or potassium hydroxide.

Alternating Current — current which flows first in one direction and then in the other at regular intervals; called *A.C.* for short.

Ammonia — a colorless, pungent gas, or a solution of this gas in water; used for household cleaning purposes.

Ampere — a unit of measure for the intensity of electric current. (*See also* VOLT, WATT.)

Anthracite — a kind of hard coal which contains little or no volatile matter.

Applique — a form of needlework in which one fabric, cut in a design, is hemmed and stitched to the surface of another fabric; used in quilt making and as a decoration for many articles of fabric.

Asphalt — a bituminous composition used for paving, for making floor tiles, and other purposes.

Axminster — a type of carpet weave.

Baseboard — a molding around the base of the walls, sometimes used to finish off the junction of the walls and the floor.

Benzine — a colorless, inflammable liquid derived from petroleum; used as a solvent for fats and oils.

Bibcock — a kind of faucet fitted with a washer consisting of a rubber or composition ball; no longer made.

Bituminous Coal—a kind of soft coal which contains considerable volatile matter.

Bolster — a long pillow, usually round, on a bed or sofa; or a hollow cylinder in the shape of a bolster for holding pillows.

Brad — a small, nearly headless, finishing nail.

Breakfront — in furniture, any piece in which the continuity of the principal surface is broken up into two or more levels; specifically, a secretary having such a front.

Burlap — a coarse fabric woven from jute yarns; used in upholstering, for hooked-rug foundations, and so on.

Broadloom — any kind of carpeting without seams; it is sold by length and in standard widths of 3, 6, 9, 12, 15 and 18 feet.

Carbon Tetrachloride—a non-inflammable solvent used to remove stains of fat or oil and other substances, and sold under various trade names.

Carpeting — in general, any type of woven floor covering; the term is used interchangeably with *rug,* although rug usually refers to a carpet which forms a unit for itself.

Cascade — in drapery, a side piece pleated in loose folds and cut to resemble a cascade.

Casement — a window sash attached by hinges on one side to the window frame and opening inward or outward.

Ceramics — a general term used to designate all forms of pottery.

Chenille — a kind of furry yarn or braid; also a kind of carpeting woven from chenille yarn.

Chippendale—an eighteenth-century English style of furniture, so named after its designer, Thomas Chippendale. A variation is "Chinese" Chippendale, which employs decorative motifs based on Chinese designs.

Circuit — in an electric-wiring system, the path traveled by one set of wires; electricity from a circuit is tapped by outlets.

Circuit Breaker — a device for cutting off the current from an overloaded electric wire.

Clinker — a hard mass sometimes formed in furnaces from ashes which have been heated to the melting point and then become fused.

Coke — the porous, carboniferous residue of bituminous coal after the volatile matter has been burned off.

Comforter — a quilt; usually one with a filling of wool or down.

Compression Faucet—any of various kinds of standard faucets in which the flow of water is controlled by a shaft which turns on screw threads.

Conduction — a process of heat transmission without the aid of motion.

Console — a kind of side table, usually a fixed one supported by two or more console legs, or brackets.

Convection — a process of heat transmission by means of circulation.

Cord Welting — cord covered with a strip of bias fabric; used in seams as a trimming on slipcovers, bedspreads, cushions, and so on.

Cork — the outer bark of the cork tree; used for bottle stoppers and in the manufacture of linoleum, cork tiles, and other products.

Credenza — a kind of sideboard or cupboard for holding books, plates, ornaments, and so on.

Dado — the lower section of a wall when decorated or treated in some manner different from that of the upper part of the wall.

Decalcomania — a printed design, usually in bright colors, on paper attached to cellophane; design can be transferred to furniture, glassware, pottery, or other objects by moistening, pressing into place, and lifting off cellophane backing.

Detergent — a substance with dirt-removing qualities, soap being a common example; detergents other than soap used in laundering are sometimes called *soapless detergents.*

Direct Current — current which flows only in one direction, instead of alternating; also called *D.C.* for short.

Directoire — a late eighteenth-century style of French decoration and furnishings which appeared during the time of the Directory, the governing body of the First Republic; Directoire is a transitional style between Louis Seize and Empire and closely related to the latter.

Dormer — a gable-like structure projecting from a sloping roof and containing a vertical window in the outer end; also, the window itself.

Dovetailing — in woodworking, a method of forming a right-angle joint of two edges cut with notches in the shape of a dove's tail; used especially on the edges of drawers.

Dowel — in woodworking, a peg, stick, or rod, the ends of which are fitted in recessed spaces on the surfaces of two wooden sections to join them together.

Duncan Phyfe — an early-nineteenth-century American style of furniture based on designs of the French Empire; so called after the name of the designer, Duncan Phyfe.

Eaves — that part of a roof which projects beyond the walls.

Element — that part of an electric appliance which gets hot or lights up.

Empire — an early-nineteenth-century French style of furniture and decoration developed during the First French Empire of Napoleon.
Emulsifier — any substance which can hold another substance in suspension in a liquid; soap is the most common household emulsifier.

Fanlight — a window in the shape of a fan, usually above a doorway.
Felt — a fabric of matted wool or hair.
Finishing Nail — a nearly headless nail, which, in woodworking, is sunk below the surface of the wood with a nail set; the space above the head is then filled with putty or plastic wood.
Fire Clay — a corrosion-resistant substance used as a lining in chimneys.
Flashing — strips of sheet metal, such as copper or galvanized iron fitted into the joining angle between a wall and a roof, or between a chimney and a roof, to make a watertight joint.
Flounce — a strip of fabric, the upper edge of which is gathered or pleated and sewed to a bedspread, slipcover, dressing-table skirt, and so on, as a trimming. The lower edge hangs free.
French Provincial — an eighteenth-century French style of furniture and decoration which developed in the provinces of France as a modification of the decorative forms used at the French court.
Fuller's Earth — an earthy substance used in manufacturing as a filter medium or for fulling cloth; for household purposes, it is sometimes used as an absorbent in stain removal.
Furring—strips of wood nailed to wall studs or rafters as a support for wallboard or lath.
Fuse — a device for cutting off the current from an overloaded electric wire.

Gable — the upper part of an end wall, triangular in shape, and extending from the level of the eaves to the ridgepole of the roof.
Gimp — a kind of flat ornamental braid used in upholstery work as a trimming.
Glazier's Point — a small, flat, triangular piece of metal used for holding panes of glass in a window frame.
Godet — a triangular piece of fabric inserted in the edge of another piece of fabric to form a flounce.
Ground-Cock Faucet — an obsolete type of faucet in which the flow of water is controlled by a slotted shaft; also called *ground-key faucet.*
Gum Arabic — a translucent, nearly colorless gum obtained from various species of acacia and used as a stiffening agent for fine fabrics as well as in the manufacture of numerous products.

Hepplewhite— an eighteenth-century English style of furniture, so named after its designer George Hepplewhite.
Hue — any color of full intensity which is not lightened, darkened, or grayed.
Humus — decomposed vegetable matter, such as leaf mold; used in potting house plants to add richness or an acid content to the soil.
Hypo — a fixing agent used in photographic work and as a bleach for the removal of stains (short for *sodium hyposulphite*).

Inlay — any work, such as marquetry, in which one material is inlaid on the surface of another in the form of a design.
Insecticide — any substance with the power to kill insects.

Jamb — an upright piece of the side of a door frame or other opening.
Javelle Water — a bleaching solution used in laundering.
Joist — a horizontal, supporting timber in a floor or ceiling.

Kapok — a silky fabric obtained from the seeds of the silk-cotton tree; used as a filling for pillows, mattresses, and other articles.

Lath — one of the thin strips of wood nailed to the wall studs as a foundation to support plaster.

Lenoweave — a type of weave used in making mesh, net, and so on.
Louver — one of a set of sloping boards or slats, sometimes adjustable, fitted into an opening, as a vent or small window, to provide ventilation.

Malacca Cane — a cane obtained from the rattan palm; used in making summer furniture and other articles.
Marquetry — the art or craft of inlaying a wood surface with small pieces of vari-colored woods, shell, or other material, in the form of a design; also, any example of such work.
Mildew — any of various types of fungus growths, especially the molds which grow on untreated fabrics; dampness and warmth hasten the growth of mildew.
Miter — a corner joint formed by the junction of two pieces at an equally divided angle, usually an angle of 45° to form a square joint; mitered joints are used in picture frames and in many woodworking operations.
Mortise and Tenon — in woodworking, a form of joint made by fitting a projecting piece, the *mortise,* into a recessed space, the *tenon.*
Mullion — a dividing piece of wood or metal to hold and separate individual panes of glass in a window.

Nap — the surface on a fabric formed by soft, short fibers, usually brushed or teazled to lie smoothly in one direction.
Naphtha — an inflammable solvent sometimes used as a stain removal agent.

Oxalic Acid — a powerful chemical used as a bleach, especially on wood.

Parting Strip — the strip which separates the top and bottom sash on a double-hung sash window.
Patchwork — a fabric made of small pieces or patches of cloth sewed together, usually in an arrangement which forms a design of their patterns and colors; used for quilt tops, and so on.
Peat Moss — the moss from which peat is largely formed; also called sphagnum moss; used in potting house plants and in gardening to add lightness and drainage to the soil.
Pepsin — a digestive enzyme used in a powdered form or in a solution to soften albuminous (protein) stains in fabrics or other materials.
Pickled — in wood finishing, an effect achieved by applying white paint to bleached wood and wiping the paint off before it has dried.
Pile — a fur-like surface on a fabric or carpeting. Piles are either cut or uncut (looped). Velvet is a typical piled fabric.
Plain Weave — a kind of basic weave in which warp and weft cross over and under each other without skipping.
Plumber's Friend — a term sometimes applied to a rubber suction cup on the end of a rod; used for opening clogged drains.
Plywood — a wood material made of thin sheets of veneer welded together with the graining in the layers usually at right angles one to another. Top layer is often of fine hardwood.
Pocket Piece — the lid or cover of a sash pocket in a window frame.
Pulley — a wheel, usually small, fitted with a groove which serves as a guide for a cord, chain, or rope passing around the pulley; pulleys are used singly and in combination.
Pumice — powdered volcanic glass used as an abrasive for smoothing and polishing wood and other materials.
Putty — a dough-like substance composed of whiting and linseed oil; used for securing window panes, for filling cracks or holes in wood, and other purposes.

Queen Anne — an English style of furniture which developed during the reign of Queen Anne (1665-1714).
Quilting — the process of stitching together two layers of fabric with a layer of padding in between; the lines of stitching are usually worked in some kind of design; used in quilt making and as a trimming on many articles of fabric.

Rabbet — a recessed edge, such as that on a window or picture frame; also a rectangular groove.
Radiation — in heating, the direct transmission of heat from a source to an object.
Rail — any horizontal member of a frame.
Regency — a modified form of the French Empire style of furniture and decoration; the English interpretation is known as English Regency.
Register — a screened or grilled opening in a wall or floor to discharge or admit warm or cool air.
Ridgepole — a horizontal timber forming the ridge, or peak, of a roof, and serving as the upper support of the rafters.
Riser — the upright part of a step in a stairway.
Rottenstone — the powdered residue of a siliceous limestone; used for fine polishing work on wood or other materials.
Sash — a frame, especially a sliding window frame, which holds the glass.
Sash Cord or Sash Chain—a cord or chain, one end of which is attached to the window frame and the other to a sash weight.
Sash Pocket — a recessed space on the frame of a window for holding a sash weight.
Sash Weight — a weight attached to a sash cord in a window frame to counterbalance the weight of the window frame when it is opened.
Satin Weave — a kind of basic weave.
Scatter Rugs — small rugs placed here or there on the floor — "scattered" about.
Selvage — the woven edge of a textile; a selvage is formed by doubling the weft threads back over the outermost warp threads.
Shade — any color which has been darkened, or grayed and darkened; also a cover for a lamp.
Sham — a loose fabric cover, especially a cover for pillows.
Shoddy — fabric made from woolen cloth which is shredded and rewoven. Because term has become synonymous with poor quality, such fabric is now more often designated as reused wool or reprocessed wool.
Sheraton — an eighteenth-century English style of furniture, so named after its designer, Thomas Sheraton.
Sizing — a glue-like or gelatinous solution used as a glaze, or used to seal the surface of plaster, paper, fabric, and so on.
Sodium Fluoride — a poisonous substance sometimes used as an insecticide.
Sodium Perborate — a chemical substance used for many purposes; in laundering, it is used as a bleach or stain removal agent.
Solvent — any substance capable of dissolving another substance; especially one which dissolves fat or grease.
Sphagnum Moss — peat moss.
Splat — the upright center member of a chair back.
Stile — any vertical member of a frame.
Straightedge — a wood or metal bar with one edge true to a straight line; used for ruling lines on linoleum, wood, and so on.
Stretcher — in furniture, a tie-piece between the bases or legs of a table or other piece to give additional support; also, any kind of frame or device which stretches.
Stud — one of the upright posts in a frame building upon which laths or wallboards are nailed.
Swag — a draped valance with ends drawn up in pleats; also, any similar drapery treatment used as trimming on a dressing table, bedspread, chair, and so on.

Terrarium — a glass case for growing plants; also called Wardian case.
Textile — a fabric formed of interlaced or woven yarns.
Thermostat — a device which automatically controls the operation of a heater according to a rise or fall in the temperature.
Ticking — any firmly woven textile, usually of cotton, from which mattress or pillow coverings, or ticks, are made.
Tint — any color which has been lightened or grayed and lightened.
Tongue-and-groove — in flooring, boards with a projection, or "tongue" on one edge and a groove on the other. With tongues fitted into grooves, boards are held securely in place.

Trap — an S- or U-shaped curve in a drain pipe in which water collects and forms a seal to prevent the entry of sewer gas.

Trapunto — Italian form of quilting in which the stitched design is raised by inserting yarn between two layers of fabric; the layer of padding used in ordinary quilting is omitted.

Tread — the level area of a step in a stairway.

Trisodium Phosphate — a chemical substance, which, when mixed with water to form a solution, is used for various household cleaning purposes.

Twill Weave — a kind of basic weave.

Valance — a vertical piece of drapery carried across the top of the window and usually attached to a valance board. Valances may be flat, ruffled, or pleated. Draped valances are generally called *swags*.

Valve — any of various devices to regulate, start, or stop the flow of water, gas, steam, or similar substances through a pipe or other passageway; in plumbing systems, the flow of water can be stopped by closing the shut-off, or cut-off, valves.

Velvet — a piled fabric of silk or rayon; also a kind of carpet weave.

Veneering — the process of joining a thin sheet of wood, usually a fine hardwood, to a less expensive foundation wood by means of an adhesive substance, heat, and pressure.

Volt — a unit of measure for the force applied to move electric power over a wire. (*See also* AMPERE, WATT.)

Wallboard — flat panels of plywood or composition used in some forms of construction to make finished wall surfaces in place of lath and plaster; or on top of lath and plaster.

Warp — the lengthwise yarns which are woven with the crosswise weft yarns to form a textile; also called the *back* or *foundation*.

Washer — a ring of metal, leather, rubber, or composition material attached by a screw to the base of the shaft inside a faucet or valve case, or under the cap below the handle; sometimes in older types of faucets, a rubber or composition ball.

Watt — a unit of measure for electric power. (*See also* AMPERE, VOLT.)

Weft — the crosswise yarns which are woven with the lengthwise, or warp, yarns to form a textile; also called *woof* or *filling*.

Wilton — a kind of carpet weave.

Woolen — loosely twisted wool yarns, usually of shorter fibers than those used in worsted yarns; also the fabrics made from such yarns.

Worsted — highly twisted wool yarns of long fibers; also the fabrics made of such yarns.

Yard Goods — textiles sold by the yard from bolts.

Zeolite — a chemical substance used in special tanks for filtering out certain minerals in hard water in order to soften it.

WEIGHTS AND MEASURES

Avoirdupois Weight

27-11/32 grains (gr.) — 1 dram (dr.)
16 drams — 1 ounce (oz.)
16 ounces — 1 pound (lb.)
100 pounds — 1 hundredweight (cwt.)
20 hundredweight — 1 ton (tn.)
112 pounds — 1 long hundredweight (l. cwt.)

Troy Weight

24 grains (gr.)	— 1 pennyweight (dwt.)
20 pennyweights	— 1 ounce (oz. t.)
20 ounces	— 1 pound (lb. t.)

Square Measure

144 square inches (sq. in.)	— 1 square foot (sq. ft.)
9 square feet	— 1 square yard (sq. yd.)
30¼ square yards	— 1 square rod (sq. rd.)
160 square rods	— 1 acre (A.)
640 acres	— 1 square mile (sq. mi.)
36 square miles	— 1 township

Cubic Measure

1,728 cubic inches (cu. in.)	— 1 cubic foot (cu. ft.)
27 cubic feet	— 1 cubic yard (cu. yd.)
144 cubic inches	— 1 board foot
128 cubic feet	— 1 cord

Liquid Measure

4 gills (gi.)	— 1 pint (pt.)
2 pints	— 1 quart (qt.)
4 quarts	— 1 gallon (gal.)
31½ gallons	— 1 barrel (bbl.)
2 barrel	— 1 hogshead (hhd.)

Apothecaries' Weight

20 grains (gr.)	— 1 scruple (s. ap.)
3 scruples	— 1 dram (dr. ap.)
8 drams	— 1 ounce (oz. ap.)
12 ounces	— 1 pound (lb. ap.)

Linear Measure

12 inches (in.)	— 1 foot (ft.)
3 feet	— 1 yard (yd.)
5½ yards	— 1 rod (rd.)
40 rods	— 1 furlong (fur.)
8 furlongs	— 1 statute mile (mi.)
3 miles	— 1 league

Dry Measure

2 pints (pt.)	— 1 quart (qt.)
8 quarts	— 1 peck (pk.)
4 pecks	— 1 bushel (bu.)
105 quarts	— 1 barrel (for dry commodities)

Apothecaries' Fluid Measure

60 minims (min. or M)	— 1 fluid dram (fl. dr.)
8 fluid drams	— 1 fluid ounce (fl. oz.)
16 fluid ounces	— 1 pint (O.)
8 pints	— 1 gallon (C.)

Circular Measure

60 seconds (″)	— 1 minute (′)
60 minutes	— 1 degree (°)
90 degrees	— 1 quadrant
4 quadrants	— 1 circle or circumference

Metric Measures of Length

1 myriameter	—	10,000	meters or	6.2137	miles
1 kilometer	—	1,000	meters or	.62137	mile
1 hectometer	—	100	meters or	328	feet 1 inch
1 decameter	—	10	meters or	393.7	inches
1 meter	—	1	meter or	39.37	inches
1 decimeter	—	0.1	meter or	3.937	inches
1 centimeter	—	0.01	meter or	.3937	inch
1 millimeter	—	0.001	meter or	.03937	inch

Metric Surface Measures

1 hectare	— 10,000 square meters	or 2.471	acres
1 are	— 100 square meters	or 119.6	square yards
1 centaire	— 1 square meter	or 1,550	square inches

Metric Capacity Measures

1 kiloliter, or stere	— 1,000	liters	or 1 cu. meter	or 1.308	cu. yd.
1 hectoliter	— 100	liters	or 0.1 cu. meter	or 2.838	bu.
1 decaliter	— 10	liters	or 10 cu. dm.	or 1.135	pk.
1 liter	— 1	liter	or 1 cu. dm.	or .9081	qt.
1 deciliter	— 0.1	liter	or 0.1 cu. dm.	or 6.0125	cu. in.
1 centiliter	— 0.01	liter	or 10 cu. cm.	or .6102	cu. in.
1 milliliter	— 0.001	liter	or 1 cu. cm.	or .061	cu. in.

Metric Measures of Weight

1 metric ton	— 1,000,000	grams	or 1 cu. meter	or 2,204.6	lb.
1 quintal	— 100,000	grams	or 1 hectoliter	or 220.46	lb.
1 myriagram	— 10,000	grams	or 1 decaliter	or 22.046	lb.
1 kilogram, or kilo	— 1,000	grams	or 1 liter	or 2.2046	lb.
1 hectogram	— 100	grams	or 1 deciliter	or 3.5274	oz.
1 decagram	— 10	grams	or 10 cu. cm.	or .3527	oz.
1 gram	— 1	gram	or 1 cu. cm.	or 15.432	gr.
1 decigram	— 0.1	gram	or 0.1 cu. cm.	or 1.5432	gr.
1 centigram	— 0.01	gram	or 10 cu. mllmtrs.	or .1543	gr.
1 milligram	— 0.001	gram	or 1 cu. mllmtr.	or .0154	gr.

WEIGHTS AND MEASURES

Common Measures and Weights
Metric Equivalents for

1 inch	—	2.54	centimeters
1 foot	—	.3048	meter
1 yard	—	.9144	meter
1 rod	—	5.029	meters
1 mile	—	1.6093	kilometers
1 square inch	—	6.452	square centimeters
1 square foot	—	.0929	square meter
1 square yard	—	.8361	square meter
1 square rod	—	25.29	square meters
1 acre	—	.4047	hectare
1 square mile	—	259	hectares
1 cubic inch	—	16.387	cubic centimeters
1 cubic foot	—	.0283	cubic meter
1 cubic yard	—	.7646	cubic meter
1 cord	—	3.625	steres
1 quart (liquid)	—	.9463	liter
1 quart (dry)	—	1.101	liters
1 gallon	—	3.785	liters
1 peck	—	8.809	liters
1 bushel	—	35.24	liters
1 ounce (avoir.)	—	28.35	grams
1 pound (avoir.)	—	.4536	kilogram
1 grain	—	.0648	gram
1 ounce (troy)	—	31.103	grams
1 pound (troy)	—	.3732	kilogram

INDEX

INDEX

INDEX

INDEX

M

S

INDEX

INDEX

COAL
COAL
ASHES
HANDLE
DETACHABLE SIDE
HANDLE
CHUCK
CRANK & HANDLE
JAWS
TOP SASH
MOLDING
BOTTOM SASH
WEDGE OF PUTTY
GLAZIER'S POINT
LAYER